ATLAS OF WARFARE

RICHARD NATKIEL and JOHN PIMLOTT

GALLERY BOOKS
An imprint of W.H. Smith Publishers Inc.
112 Madison Avenue
New York, New York 10016

A Bison Book

Published by Gallery Books
A Division of W H Smith Publishers Inc.
112 Madison Avenue
New York, New York 10016

Produced by
Bison Books Corp.
15 Sherwood Place
Greenwich, CT 06830

ISBN 0-8317-0498-5

Printed in Hong Kong

1 2 3 4 5 6 7 8 9 10

The Authors

Matthew Bennett, MA, is a graduate of King's College, London, and has made a special study of medieval warfare. He has published several articles in historical and literary journals, and is a Senior Lecturer in the Department of Communication Studies at the Royal Military Academy, Sandhurst.

Lieutenant Colonel Michael Chilcott was educated at the Royal Military Academy, Sandhurst, University College, London, and the University of Manchester Institute of Science and Technology. He served for 35 years in the British Army and is Chairman of the Merville Battery Museum Committee.

Adrian Gilbert is a military writer with a special interest in modern warfare. He was Executive Editor of the best-selling magazine *War in Peace*. His previous books include *Vietnam: The History and the Tactics, Modern Fighting Men, World War I in Photographs* and the *Illustrated History of World War I*.

Keith Simpson was educated at Hull University, where he read history, and at the Department of War Studies of King's College, London. He was a Senior Lecturer in War Studies and International Affairs at the Royal Military Academy, Sandhurst, and is now a defense consultant. His previous books include *History of the German Army* and *The Old Contemptibles*.

Paul Szuscikiewicz holds a degree in Hellenic and Roman Studies from Southampton University. He is a member of the Society for the Promotion of Roman Studies and of the Society of Ancients, a group devoted to the study of military history in the ancient world.

Dr John Westwood is a highly experienced historical and military author. Following service in the British Army Intelligence Corps, he taught history at Florida State and Sydney Universities. He has written some 20 books, many of them on aspects of Eastern European history, including *Endurance and Endeavor, Russian History 1812-1980*.

CONTENTS

Page 1: Roman troops put a German village to the torch – a scene from the interminable campaigns along the empire's northern frontier.
Pages 2-3: Napoleon (right foreground) directs his troops at the height of the Battle of Waterloo, June 1815.
Pages 4-5: Marines head for the battered beaches of Kwajalein atoll in the Marshall Islands, early February 1944.

Introduction

War is a fascinating subject, central to any understanding of the world and the way it has developed. Despite the dubious morality of using violence to achieve personal or political aims, the fact remains that it has been used to do just that throughout recorded history. Countries exist because of wars fought against their neighbors or rivals; they retain their independence largely through displaying both an ability and a willingness to fight if threatened, employing armed forces organized, equipped and prepared for such an eventuality.

Any recourse to violence can be dangerous, however, for it implies a release of emotions normally kept in check during times of peace. Once the 'dogs of war' have been unleashed, the results are often chaos, confusion and high cost (in both human and material terms), while there is always the chance that the enemy may prove stronger, leading to defeat and loss of territory, prestige or freedom. War, in short, is an unpredictable business and, because of this, it is hardly surprising that soldiers throughout history have searched for some 'magic solution' to war-fighting – some list of golden rules which, if satisfied, will guarantee victory. Past battles and campaigns have been closely studied and compared, the reasons for defeat or victory examined and a series of 'Principles of War' evolved. These vary from country to country according to historical experience and need, but it is possible to find certain 'common denominators' which apply, not as a check list to be slavishly followed, but as a series of common-sense points to be borne in mind. They also serve as a useful framework for the study of war, lifting it away from mere curiosity about the past into analysis and, hopefully, an appreciation of the lessons of history.

The first, and most important, principle is the selection and maintenance of an aim or objective. It is no good releasing force for the sake of it – the purpose must be clearly stated from the start. At a strategic level, this may be to defend borders, seize territory or impose political ideology; at operational (theater) and tactical (battlefield) levels, it will be to defeat the enemy preparatory to achieving those higher aims. If the aim is muddled, unattainable or suddenly altered in the middle of a campaign, chaos will ensue, seriously reducing the chances of success. Hitler's decision to shift the emphasis of his attack in late summer 1942 from the Caucasus to Stalingrad is a case in point, forcing his armies not only to change direction but also to switch from mobile to urban operations.

Once the aim has been laid down, its satis-

Left: as cavalrymen look on, Roman foot soldiers execute a group of German tribesmen.
Right: the Allied fleet at anchor in Balaklava harbor. The defense of this port in the Crimean War is chiefly remembered for two events – the futile 'Charge of the Light Brigade' and the heroic 'Thin Red Line.'

faction will depend on a number of further principles. In general terms, it is best to take the offensive rather than sit back and wait for the enemy to attack, even if things look desperate. In 1813, for example, Napoleon achieved an enormous amount by constantly attacking his encroaching enemies. Obviously, this can be taken too far – in this particular case, Napoleon was merely delaying his ultimate defeat – and it will only work if the principle of security is satisfied, ensuring that flanks and rear areas are fully protected. As long ago as the third century BC, Alexander recognized this, securing his position along the Mediterranean coast before taking the offensive against Darius in Mesopotamia. In such circumstances, flexibility must be another basic principle, for forces with an ability to shift from attack to defense and to react to the realities of battle as they unfold will stand a far better chance of success. Wellington's army in the Peninsula (1808-14) was particularly good at this flexibility of response.

Similarly, much will be achieved if the principle of surprise is pursued, for if victory is to be gained quickly and at low cost, it is best to catch the enemy unawares, putting him off balance and exploiting his disarray. This may be achieved by appearing suddenly in places he is not expecting – Marlborough's march to the Danube in 1704 is a classic example – or by using new weapons or tactics. The impact of English longbows at Crécy in 1346 and of the tank on the Somme in 1916 illustrate the point, although it is worth bearing in mind that whenever new ideas emerge, it is essential to ensure that they are incorporated into existing skills. Co-operation of forces – whether cavalry and infantry or, in the more modern age, aircraft and ground units – is an important (and sometimes extremely difficult) principle to satisfy. The lack of co-operation between French knights and infantry at Agincourt in 1415 highlights the danger; the close co-ordination of air, ground and naval units at D-Day (6 June 1944) illustrates the advantages.

A further principle is that of concentration, for if an attack is to take place, it would be foolish to use inadequate forces. The concentration of Anglo-Dutch and Prussian armies at Waterloo in 1815 may be cited as an example, although it should be pointed out that the principle of economy of effort may also apply. It is clearly wasteful to take a sledgehammer to crack a nut – something the Americans were accused of doing in Vietnam between 1965 and 1973 – so care must always be taken to match resources to needs. Quite often, the balance between concentration and economy is a fine one, requiring commanders of skill, experience and ability to take the necessary military decisions.

That leads on to the human factor in war – the key to success or failure. Battles are fought by men and, if those men are supplied with weapons, ammunition and food – the principle of administration – they will perform well; if they are neglected, they will often fall apart under enemy pressure, as both Napoleon and Hitler discovered in the vastness of Russia. What is important is the morale or fighting spirit of the soldiers – the final principle – for if they feel motivated to go into battle, they will often perform prodigious feats, even to the extent of snatching victory from the jaws of certain defeat. In the end, it is the soldiers who make the difference – everything else merely contributes to their abilities. It is a point worth remembering throughout the following accounts of the world's major and most decisive battles and campaigns.

Below left: Assurnasirpal (right) was responsible for the early expansion of the Assyrian Empire.
Below: US landing ships unload men and cargo at Inchon during the Korean War.

These pages: the Battle of Salamis, 480 BC.
For the loss of 40 vessels, the Greek states
inflicted a decisive defeat on the 800-strong
Persian fleet.

WARFARE IN THE ANCIENT WORLD

The Egyptian Empire

The Nile valley was the site of one of the world's first civilizations. Around 3100 BC its two natural divisions, Upper and Lower Egypt, were united in one kingdom. For 1300 years afterward the Egyptians conducted their affairs with little reference to the other inhabitants of the Middle East and North Africa. The deserts of the region gave their country a protective wall to shelter behind and restricted their activity to squabbles among themselves. Around 1780 BC this security began to crumble as foreigners from the north moved into the Nile delta in large numbers. Eventually these people, known as the Hyksos, established a kingdom of their own in Lower Egypt. Upper Egypt was reduced to a state of vassalage. The Hyksos' rule was reinforced by two significant military advantages over their Egyptian subjects: they possessed chariots and composite bows.

For around 200 years the alien Hyksos ruled in Egypt. Then, in the 1540s BC, two successive Egyptian rulers, Kamose and Amose, drove the Hyksos out of Egypt in a series of campaigns. The Hyksos capital, Avaris, was sacked, and so began an era in Egyptian history known as the New Kingdom. For the first time Egypt was a major military force in the Middle East. Its armies, based on the combination of chariotry and archery, ranged north into Palestine and Syria in a quest to control the lands from which the Hyksos had come. The desert was no longer considered enough to protect Egypt.

The early rulers of the New Kingdom concentrated their major efforts on Egypt's southern frontier. The state of Kush was conquered, and there were regular campaigns into Nubia. In 1468 BC many of the empire's Syrian and Palestinian vassal princes revolted; however, they were crushed by the Egyptians under Tuthmosis III at the Battle of Megiddo. This was the first stage of 20 years of campaigns that established Egypt as the dominant power in the Middle East. Its closest rivals, the Mitanni of northern Syria, refused to fight the Egyptians. They retired behind a scorched-earth policy when they were invaded.

Egyptian control over Syria eventually brought it into contact with its great enemy: the Hittite Empire. The Hittites inhabited the highlands of Anatolia in Asia Minor. They had steadily supplanted the Mitanni in eastern Asia Minor and northern Syria. By about 1300

BC Egyptian control over Palestine, southern Syria and Lebanon had weakened, and the Pharoah, Seti I, spent the next four years trying to reassert his dominance. In 1298 BC he fought an inconclusive battle with the Hittites near Kadesh. The two powers later signed a treaty recognizing a border between them that ran somewhere south of Kadesh.

Ten years later a second battle was fought in the vicinity of Kadesh. The Egyptians under Ramesses II faced a Hittite army under Mutawallis, and Ramesses was forced to withdraw. The war carried on desultorily for 16 years, and ended in a draw. The peace treaty was effective until the destruction of the Hittite Empire by the barbarian 'Sea Peoples' around 1200 BC. The Sea Peoples became a threat to Egypt around 1190 BC, when they allied with the Libyans.

The Egyptians defeated them in a series of land and naval engagements and avoided the fate of the Hittites. Yet the New Kingdom never properly recovered despite these victories, and around 950 BC a dynasty descended from Libyan settlers took power. The great days of Egypt were at an end.

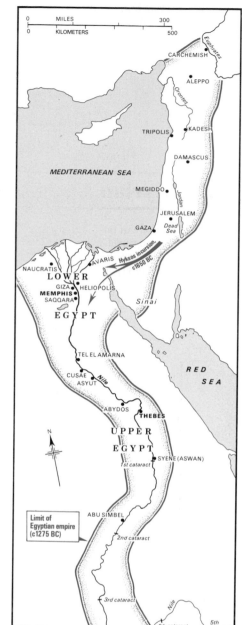

Right: the extent of the Egyptian Empire in 1275 BC and the raids of the Hyksos from the east.
Below: a frieze depicting the victory of Ramesses II over his 'northern enemies.'

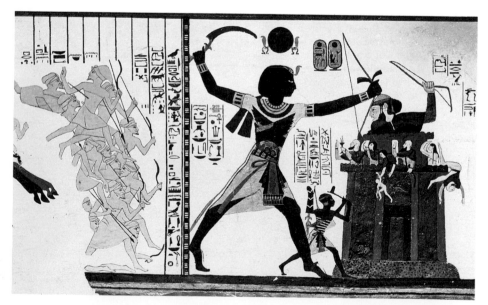

Right: the Assyrian Empire, showing its territorial expansion up to c630 BC.
Below right: Assyrian troops, masters of siege warfare, use battering rams against a formidable city wall.

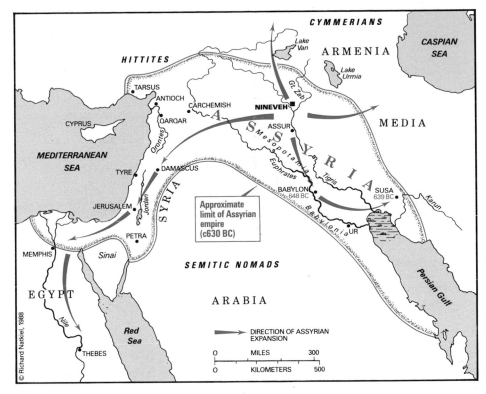

The Assyrian Empire

The Assyrian Empire of the Middle East possessed the most powerful army yet seen in ancient military history. Expansion began in the reign of Assurnasirpal whose campaigns revealed the military skill on which the Assyrians would build an empire: an expertise for siege warfare. In his first three campaigns, Assurnasirpal captured at least five cities in an era when most armies would have regarded the capture of one, or maybe two, a successful conclusion to that number of campaigns. Assurnasirpal's son, Shalamaneser III, continued his father's record of success; furthermore, he pursued a policy of annexations which marked the real beginning of the great Assyrian Empire.

The Assyrians already had control over upper Mesopotamia and under Assurnasirpal they had subjugated Carchemish. Now they pushed farther to the west and south. Shalamaneser defeated a combination of north Syrian states at Lutibu in 858 BC, then pushed his frontier north into Asia Minor and gained control of the important trade routes to Europe. A costly victory at Qarqar in 853 BC, where Israelites, Damascenes and the cities of the Lebanese coast, backed by Egypt, resisted Assyrian expansion southward, briefly blunted Shalamaneser's conquering drive. In the end, Shalamaneser's militarism did not pay off. The last six years of his reign saw a major revolt in the Assyrian heartland, and all of the western conquests were lost – these regions demanded the attention of regular campaigns to reinforce Assyrian supremacy. A 75-year period of wars in the immediate vicinity of Assyria followed.

Assyria's imperial fortunes were restored during the energetic reign of Tiglath-pileser III, who came to the throne in 744 BC. Tiglath-pileser took power in a coup, and immediately he set about restoring the former imperial glories of Assyria. He first spent five years campaigning in the west. Northern Syria once again became part of the Assyrian Empire. Tiglath-pileser also pushed his borders south to incorporate Babylon. By 731 BC, after a second campaign, Palestine, Syria and southeastern Asia Minor were again Assyrian. Tiglath-pileser also defeated the Medes to the east and the Urartian kingdom around Lake Van.

A 100-year era of Assyrian supremacy in the Middle East began after Tiglath-pileser's death. Sennacherib, king from 704 to 681 BC, destroyed once-mighty Babylon and carried Assyrian rule into Egypt. The years of annual campaigns against rebellious vassals and neighboring kings were ended – only eight campaigns took place under Sennacherib's rule. Assyrian decline began around 650 BC, as the Assyrians were once again confronted with renewed rebellions, and – worse – civil war. Ashurbanipal, who defeated his brother to gain the throne, spent three years besieging rebellious Babylon, and annexed Elam and Susa in the following years. One year after his death in 626 BC, the Babylonians again revolted, and this time they maintained their independence. Egypt also fell away from the empire. In 612 BC a coalition of Medes, Babylonians and some Arabs captured the Assyrian capital of Nineveh and brought to an end Assyrian dominance.

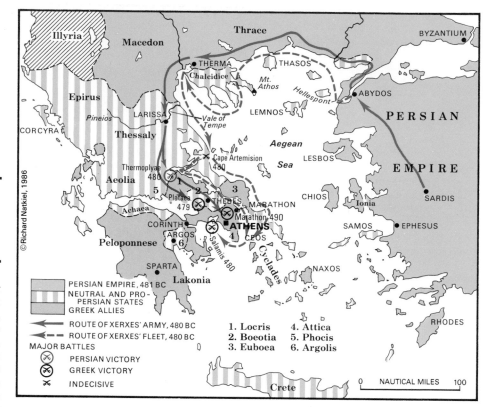

The Persian Wars and The Battle of Salamis

The newly created Persian Empire under Cyrus I soon came into conflict with the Greek colonies on the Ionian coast of Asia Minor, but while Cyrus lived the Ionian Greeks were not badly treated by their Persian overlords. Not until the rule of Cambyses (530-521 BC) and Darius I (521-486 BC) did benevolent rule turn to oppression. A revolt was crushed in spite of the support of Athens, and Darius decided to invade Greece to put an end to Athenian meddling.

The first Persian expedition in 492 failed dismally when the Persian fleet was destroyed in a storm off Mount Athos; unsupported from the sea the large Persian army had no choice but to retire across the Hellespont. A second expedition two years later was decisively beaten by the Athenians and their allies on land at the Battle of Marathon.

From these two humiliating reverses Darius learned that he could never defeat the Greeks without a strong fleet to protect his army's flanks, but his plans to launch a third expedition were delayed by internal troubles in his empire. He died in 486 without seeing his plans come to fruition but his successor Xerxes was equally intent on crushing the Greeks.

The third Persian expedition was on a massive scale, with as many as 180,000 men and 750 galleys. To avoid some of the risk of losing the fleet in a storm on the way Xerxes ordered a canal to be dug through the Athos peninsula, a notoriously stormy area. His intention was to capture as many Greek cities as possible to rob Athens of her allies' support. By the spring of 480 BC the entire force was ready to march against the Greeks.

The state of Athens had not been supine since its reprieve at Marathon. The statesman Themistocles had succeeded in persuading the city's rulers to spend their revenues on building a new fleet of 200 triremes. The other 15 maritime city-states also contributed warships, so that the eventual total of the Greeks' combined fleet was about 385 warships. Because of inter-city rivalry it was necessary to put this fleet under the nominal command of the Spartan Eurybiades but effective control remained in the hands of Themistocles.

The master-plan was to engage the Persian fleet as far to the north as possible, in confined waters where it would be hard for them to deploy their full strength effectively. But the might of the Persians seemed irresistible and threatened to frustrate Themistocles' plans. The Persians were, however, held in an indecisive sea battle at Cape Artemision, but after the failure to stop the Persians on land at Ther-

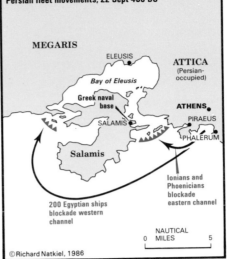

Persian fleet movements, 22 Sept 480 BC

MEGARIS

ELEUSIS

ATTICA
(Persian-occupied)

Bay of Eleusis

Greek naval base

ATHENS

PIRAEUS

SALAMIS

PHALERUM

Salamis

Ionians and Phoenicians blockade eastern channel

200 Egyptian ships blockade western channel

NAUTICAL MILES
0   5

© Richard Natkiel, 1986

The Battle of Salamis, 23 September

Bay of Eleusis

Corinthians 'retreat' to draw Persians into narrow strait

Greek fleet 380 ships
1 Corinthians
2 Athenians
3 Allies
4 Spartans

SALAMIS

PIRAEUS

Cynosura Promontory

Phoenicians

Ionians

Greek fleet inflicts heavy losses on Persians (200 ships) who return to Phalerum. Greeks lose 40 ships

Persian fleet 800 ships

NAUTICAL MILES
0   2

mopylae the northern Greek states made their peace with Xerxes, while the southern states withdrew into the Peloponnese, leaving Athens alone.

Themistocles never lost faith in sea power, even at this point of crisis, and persuaded the Athenians to abandon the city and migrate *en masse* to the island of Salamis, which blocks the entrance to the Bay of Eleusis. He planned to lure the Persians into the narrow strait between Salamis and Athens, in order to offset their numerical advantage.

Xerxes played into the Greeks' hands, sending his Egyptian ships to block the western passage between Salamis and the mainland while the Ionian and Phoenician squadrons blockaded the eastern channel to cover his main force advancing up the strait.

The pre-battle movements were complete by sunset on 22 September and next day battle was joined. The Greeks came out in line ahead, curving to the east to form an arc across the strait while a Corinthian decoy force pretended to retire to the north. The right flank was held by Eurybiades with 16 ships, the center was held by the few remaining allies, and Athenian ships were placed on the left flank. The Persians adopted a clumsy three-line formation which became badly disorganized when it had to reform into columns to pass the island of Psytallia located at the entrance to the strait.

Themistocles had calculated his deploy-

ment to take advantage of the morning breeze, which whipped up a heavy swell in the narrows. This made the job of maneuvering the larger Persian ships harder, and he now launched his own forces in a series of line abreast ramming attacks. With more room to maneuver the Greeks caused havoc among the already disorganized Persians. The Athenian marines were able to overwhelm the Persian archers and the strongly built Greek ships were able to run alongside and shear off the enemy's oars.

The Persians fought bravely, particularly as they were under the personal eye of Xerxes, seated on his golden throne on the mainland shore, but they could do little to stave off defeat. Fighting aboard the crippled Persian ships continued until sunset, by which time 200 Persian ships had been sunk, the Greeks having lost a fifth as many.

The result was decisive: Xerxes ordered an immediate retreat to prevent his army from being trapped. A token army was left in Greece but this force was destroyed the fol-

lowing year at the Battle of Plataea, a defeat which marked the end of Persian attempts to conquer Greece. Without naval supremacy in the Aegean land operations were not feasible, and Hellenic civilization was saved from the grasp of the Persian Empire. Salamis marked the end of westward expansion of the Persians and ushered in a new era of Greek maritime power in the Mediterranean.

Above: the Greek victory at Salamis, September 480 BC.
Below far left: Greek troops advance to complete the rout of the Persian forces at the Battle of Marathon, 490 BC.
Below left: Persian infantry armed with bows and thrusting spears. Lightly armored, they fought the heavier Greek infantry at a disadvantage.
Below: Pheidippides brings news of the Greek victory of Marathon.

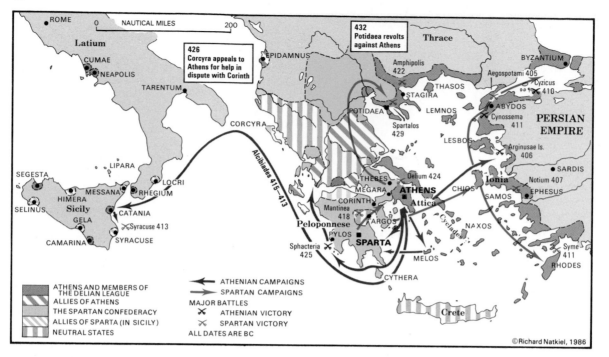

On the map:

432 Potidaea revolts against Athens

426 Corcyra appeals to Athens for help in dispute with Corinth

ATHENS AND MEMBERS OF THE DELIAN LEAGUE
ALLIES OF ATHENS
THE SPARTAN CONFEDERACY
ALLIES OF SPARTA (IN SICILY)
NEUTRAL STATES

ATHENIAN CAMPAIGNS
SPARTAN CAMPAIGNS
MAJOR BATTLES
✗ ATHENIAN VICTORY
✗ SPARTAN VICTORY
ALL DATES ARE BC

©Richard Natkiel, 1986

The Peloponnesian Wars

After the defeat of the Persians the leading Greek city-states were clearly Athens and Sparta. Their interests were soon to come into conflict. Between 460 and 446 BC Athens had won over as allies or subdued many cities in the Peloponnese and central Greece, and although she had been forced to give up these gains under the Thirty Years' Peace of 446, she was regarded as a perpetual threat by the cities in the Peloponnese.

The first move of the war which then began was made by the Spartans and their allies, who invaded Attica in 431 and laid siege to Athens. Pericles, the Athenian leader, countered by sending a hundred ships to ravage the coast of the Peloponnese, and the invaders were forced to withdraw from Attica when their provisions were exhausted.

Under Phormio the Athenian fleet won a surprising victory at Naupactus in the Gulf of Corinth in 430, defeating 47 Corinthian ships with only 20 by superior seamanship. A second action at nearby Rhium in 429 caught Phormio at a disadvantage, with 77 ships ranged against the same 20 which had fought at Naupactus. At first the Spartans prevailed, capturing nine ships but the Athenians rallied and recaptured all but one of their own ships and captured six more.

The defection of Mytilene from the Athenian cause in the early summer of 428 was a serious blow, for it was the only city among Athens' allies which still possessed a large fleet. The Athenians reacted promptly by investing the rebel city, and when its citizens tried to negotiate terms, executed their envoys to crush the rebellion. The effects of the plague, which started in 430, were now being shaken off by the Athenians, and by 425 they were able to take the offensive against the Spartans and their allies.

The first step was to occupy and fortify Pylos. The Spartans were slow to counterattack, and at Sphacteria their attempt to recapture Pylos by land and sea was defeated by Demosthenes. Athens was now in the ascendant, but in the winter of 424 her army suffered a disastrous defeat at Delium. The Spartans then attacked Thessaly and Thrace, and an Athenian naval expedition under Thucydides failed to relieve Amphipolis. Peace was concluded in 421 but neither side was keen to preserve it.

In the winter of 416-15 a larger expedition was planned by the Athenians against the cities in Sicily allied with Corinth and Sparta. It was ultimately to prove a disaster, when in 413 BC the Athenian commander Nicias and the defenders of Syracuse (which Nicias and his army had captured during the previous year) surrendered.

By 411 BC Athens was in desperate straits, and it was clear that her democratic institutions were not suited to the pressures of defeat. Off the harbor of Eretria the Athenians were defeated by a Peloponnesian fleet under Agesandridas, and shortly afterward the province of Euboea broke into open revolt. The Athenian fleet at Samos had mutinied, and Athens now had neither ships nor crews to man them. The result was revolution, and the oligarchs were expelled from the city.

The recall of Alcibiades did much to retrieve some gains from the disaster. In the spring of 410 he destroyed the main Peloponnesian fleet off Cyzicus in the Sea of Marmora after luring them out of harbor by pretending to retreat, freeing the grain route from the Black Sea from interference.

With Persian subsidies the Peloponnesian fleet now re-emerged as a major force, and it was only defeated with great difficulty at the Battle of Arginusae in 406, said to be the bloodiest battle of the war. Persia now determined to help the Spartans bring the war to a close. The Spartan admiral Lysander was given a large subsidy to build up his strength, but in 405 the bulk of the Athenian fleet was destroyed at Aegospotami in the Hellespont by incompetence or treachery.

The result was inevitable: Athens was surrounded by land and sea and starved into submission in 404.

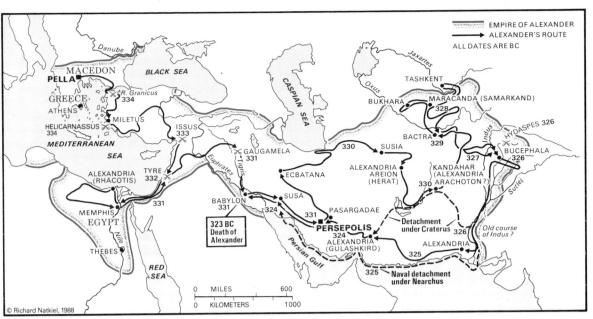

EMPIRE OF ALEXANDER
ALEXANDER'S ROUTE
ALL DATES ARE BC

© Richard Natkiel, 1988

The Campaigns of Alexander

No man in history has caught the imagination of successive generations like Alexander the Great. In the Middle East he became a legendary, godlike figure; in Europe he inspired a host of imitators through the centuries, all of whom cast much smaller shadows across history. His armies carried the classical civilization of the Greek peninsula in their wake and spread it as far as Egypt and India. The immediate impact of Alexander's campaigns was felt by the peoples of the Mediterranean and the Middle East down through the years to the Islamic conquests. Alexander's achievement is without parallel in human history.

He succeeded to the throne of Macedonia in 336 BC at the age of 20, after the assassination of his father, Philip. Macedonia under Philip had imposed a kind of unity on the Greek city-states by his victories over them. At the time there was widespread support among the Greeks for a war of revenge against the Persian Empire. The Persians had invaded Greece twice in the previous century, and had always been ready with funds to promote internecine warfare between the Greek cities. They also controlled the wealthiest part of the Greek world – the cities of Asia Minor along the Aegean coast. Philip had already sent part of his army across into Asia to open the fighting against the Persians at the time of his death. Alexander's first move was to put down, with great severity, a revolt by the Greek city of Thebes. Then, in 334 BC, he crossed the Hellespont into Asia with 40,000 men to begin the conquest of Persia.

Alexander first confronted the army of the Persian governors of Asia Minor at the Battle of the Granicus River in 334 BC. The account of this battle is confused, but Alexander won by charging from his flank across the enemy's front to hit their center. He distinguished himself in the hand-to-hand fighting, as he would do in almost every action. From the Granicus, Alexander and his army marched down the coast. The Greek cities of Asia Minor fell to him after brief sieges. Their possession denied the Persians valuable bases for their powerful fleet and secured Alexander's lines of communication. From Asia Minor he planned to move down the Syrian and Palestinian coasts

Above: a bust of Alexander the Great, without doubt the most able commander of the ancient world.
Right: Alexander's Companion cavalry launch a furious charge at the Battle of the Granicus River, 334 BC.

Below: the backbone of Alexander's forces – the highly disciplined phalanx of well-armed hoplites.
Right: the Battle of Hydaspes, 326 BC.
Below right: the Battle of Gaugamela (Arbela), 331 BC.

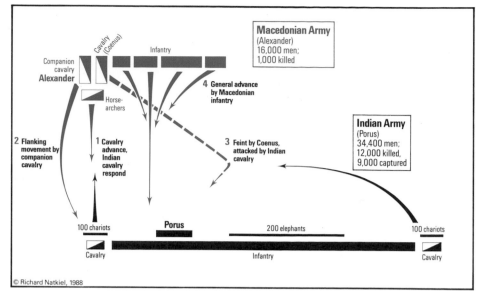

into Egypt. All of the Persian naval bases would then be in his hands.

The Persian Great King, Darius, had assembled a large army in Syria to contest Alexander's advance into that part of his empire. After some strategic maneuvering in which Darius got the better of Alexander, the two armies came to grips at Issus. Alexander's pike phalanxes and his heavy cavalry were the keys to victory, and Darius disgracefully fled the field. The Macedonians were then unopposed by any armies in the field, but were forced to conduct a lengthy siege of Tyre. This island city was only captured after a mole, which still exists, was built from the mainland, so that Alexander's men could assault the settlement directly.

Egypt fell to Alexander in 331 BC and after its capture he moved east. In Mesopotamia Darius had assembled a huge army – largely of poor-quality troops, and in the final battle between the Persians and the Macedonians, at Gaugamela (Arbela) in 331 BC, Alexander out-generalled the Persians to achieve a decisive victory. He occupied Babylon, which was to be his capital afterward. There was now a new Great King.

Alexander spent the next two years occupying the Persian heartlands in central Asia. His generalship in battles against the Scythians along the Jaxartes, where his largely infantry army defeated a cavalry one on open plains, marked him as the most brilliant commander

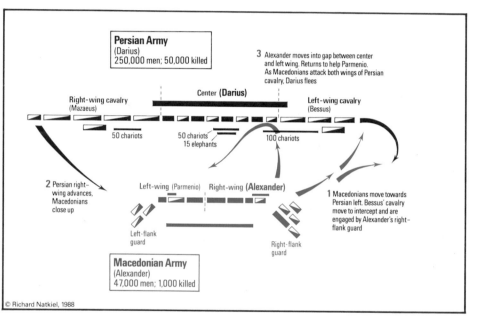

of ancient times. During 329-27 BC he subdued Sogdia and Bactria. From Bactria he kept his troops going and moved into India. In 326 BC, in another battle (Hydaspes) that showed his adaptability in the face of strange, new fighting techniques, he defeated an Indian army, one using elephants in large numbers, with great military skill.

After the battle on the Hydaspes, Alexander led his men farther east, but then faced a mutiny. Alexander was forced to concede to his army's demands to turn back. His army and a newly built fleet then made their way down the Indus, and once they reached the Indian Ocean, they turned west. The army faced a long march through a terrible desert, one of Alexander's most costly mistakes. The fleet also had an adventurous passage, but both fleet and army arrived safely at Babylon. Alexander did not live long after his return to Babylon. Within a few months, after a brief illness, he was dead. His empire did not survive much longer; civil war between his generals tore it apart.

The Punic Wars and the Rise of Rome

As Roman trade expanded in the Western Mediterranean and Roman power grew in southern Italy it was inevitable that she would come into conflict with Carthage. At first the Carthaginians tried to contain the upstart Latin state by treaties recognizing the large Carthaginian trading interests, particularly in Sicily, the first being signed in 508 BC and again in 348 BC. However relations were soured by the presence of Greek colonies in southern Italy, which asked Rome for help in fighting Carthage, and continuing friction eventually led to war in 264 BC.

The first Punic War (the word Punic is derived from Phoenician) lasted 24 years as the Romans and Carthaginians fought for possession of Sicily. The Romans were at first hard put to beat the Carthaginians, being landsmen and good soldiers but not particularly skilled sailors. With typical thoroughness a wrecked Carthaginian quinquereme was copied by the Romans and a fleet of 100 quinqueremes was built, and crews were trained on shore, using dummy rowing benches. When that fleet was wrecked another one was built.

These soldiers turned sailors proved quick learners and inflicted a serious defeat on the Carthaginians at Mylae in 260 BC. Gaius Dui-

lius destroyed the Carthaginian fleet, sinking or capturing more than 40 enemy ships. To commemorate the event a platform for public orators was made in Rome from the bronze rams of captured Carthaginian ships. The Latin word for ram was the word *rostrum*

Above: a Roman trireme. Note the ram; impetus was proved by the ship's galley slaves.

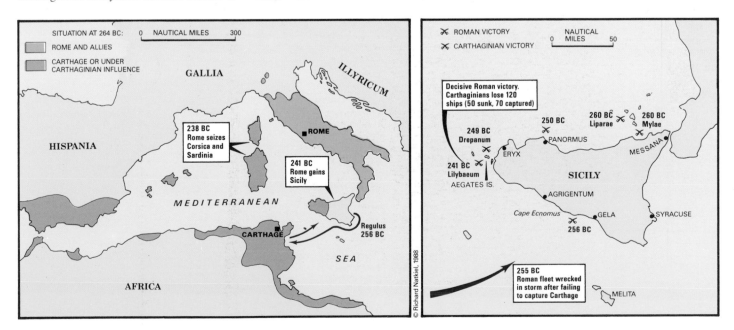

SITUATION AT 264 BC: 0 NAUTICAL MILES 300

ROME AND ALLIES

CARTHAGE OR UNDER CARTHAGINIAN INFLUENCE

GALLIA

ILLYRICUM

HISPANIA

238 BC
Rome seizes
Corsica and
Sardinia

ROME

241 BC
Rome gains
Sicily

MEDITERRANEAN

CARTHAGE

Regulus
256 BC

SEA

AFRICA

© Richard Natkiel, 1988

ROMAN VICTORY

CARTHAGINIAN VICTORY

NAUTICAL
MILES 50

0

Decisive Roman victory.
Carthaginians lose 120
ships (50 sunk, 70 captured)

250 BC

260 BC
Liparae

260 BC
Mylae

249 BC
Drepanum

PANORMUS

ERYX

MESSANA

241 BC
Lilybaeum

AEGATES IS.

SICILY

AGRIGENTUM

Cape Ecnomus

GELA

SYRACUSE

256 BC

255 BC
Roman fleet wrecked
in storm after failing
to capture Carthage

MELITA

Left: a coin decorated with a profile of Hannibal, the greatest Carthaginian general.
Below right: the Battle of Cannae (216 BC), showing Hannibal's encircling attack.
Bottom right: Zama (202 BC), the battle that decided the Second Punic War.

meaning beak, the speakers' platform was known as the *rostra* and gives us the origin of the modern word for such a platform.

An attempt to carry the war to Carthage failed when an expedition under Attilius Regulus was defeated in 256 BC. To add to Rome's humiliation the fleet was wrecked on its way home, but the Romans grimly rebuilt their fleet and returned to the attack. Being soldiers at heart they devised a method of bringing their military strength to bear against Carthaginian seamanship. A drawbridge or gangplank pivoted from the mast of Roman ships, and known from the long 'pecking' spike designed to attach it to enemy vessels as the *corvus* or crow, enabled Roman soldiers to board Carthaginian galleys more easily and proved a war-winning weapon.

In 241 BC the Romans won the final and decisive battle at Lilybaeum (otherwise known as the Battle of Aegates Insulae) which forced the great Hamilcar Barca to surrender Eryx, the last fortress still in Carthaginian hands. Exhausted by the years of attrition Carthage could only sue for peace, and Rome demanded the virtual surrender of Sicily.

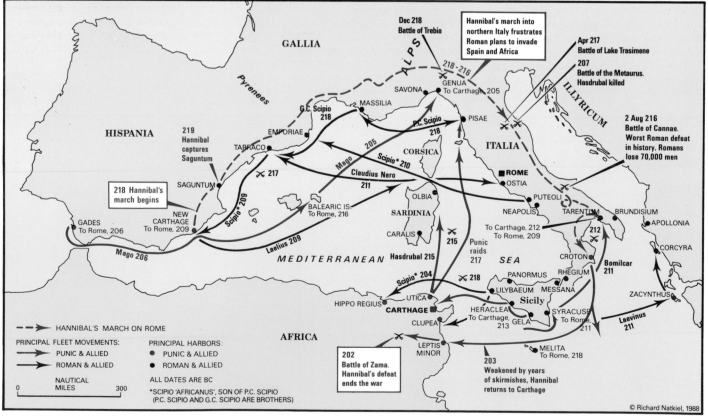

© Richard Natkiel, 1988

Shortly after the peace a mutiny of Carthaginian mercenaries gave the Romans a pretext for renewing hostilities, and as the price of peace, they annexed Sardinia and Corsica. This excluded Carthage from all waters to the west of Italy.

The Second Punic War, which began in 218 BC, was led by Hamilcar's son Hannibal, who longed for revenge on Rome for the humiliating peace signed in 241 BC. His strategy was unorthodox, to catch the Romans off balance but particularly to offset their control of the sea. He transported his army and a 'secret weapon,' war elephants, to Spain, where there already was a large and prosperous Carthaginian colony.

The Carthaginians captured Saguntum in 219 and this led to the outbreak of war. Hannibal set off with his army to march to Italy. The march through southern Gaul took two years, but it accomplished the capture of many important Roman settlements. On 2 August 216 he won a decisive victory at Cannae, slaughtering perhaps as many as 70,000 Roman legionaries, the worst defeat in Roman history. At this point it must have seemed that nothing could stop Hannibal from capturing Rome but the Roman state proved remarkably resilient under stress, and the alliance of Italian cities held firm.

At sea the Carthaginians harassed Roman trade, and the daring naval commander Mago established a forward base at Minorca in the strategic Balearic Islands and succeeded in capturing Genua (Genoa) in 205 BC. But on land the obstinacy of Rome and an adroit use of 'scorched-earth' tactics by Quintus Fabius Maximus wore down Hannibal. Only when that army was subdued and expelled could Publius Cornelius Scipio seize the initiative by attacking Carthaginian possessions in Hispania (Spain).

With her Gallic colonies recaptured and the Carthaginians' base in the Iberian peninsula destroyed it was at length possible to take the offensive directly against Carthage, and in 202 Scipio's forces mustered for the final Battle of Zama. That victory put an end to Carthaginian hopes of dominating the Mediterranean and gave Rome the keys to world-wide power. At the heart of it was Rome's command of the sea. As long as she dominated Mediterranean trade her allies would not desert her, no matter how long Hannibal's army remained at large in Italy. By avoiding disastrous battles with Hannibal after the first defeats, Rome preserved her strength for a counterstroke, and when the time came her naval power enabled her to carry the war to the enemy before he could recover his position.

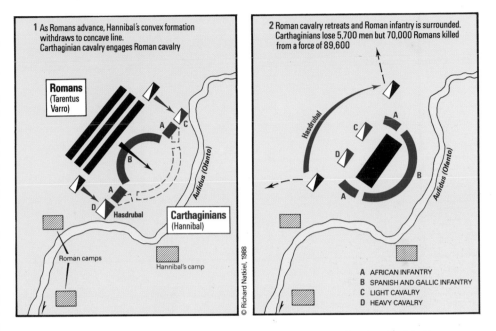

1 As Romans advance, Hannibal's convex formation withdraws to concave line. Carthaginian cavalry engages Roman cavalry

Romans (Tarentus Varro)

Aufidus (Ofanto)

Hasdrubal

Carthaginians (Hannibal)

Roman camps

Hannibal's camp

© Richard Natkiel, 1988

2 Roman cavalry retreats and Roman infantry is surrounded. Carthaginians lose 5,700 men but 70,000 Romans killed from a force of 89,600

Hasdrubal

Aufidus (Ofanto)

A AFRICAN INFANTRY
B SPANISH AND GALLIC INFANTRY
C LIGHT CAVALRY
D HEAVY CAVALRY

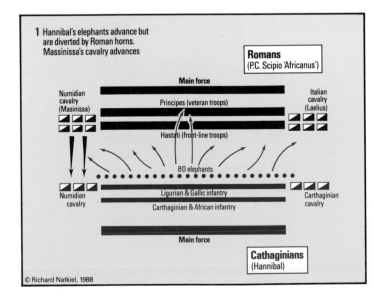

1 Hannibal's elephants advance but are diverted by Roman horns. Massinissa's cavalry advances

Romans (P.C. Scipio 'Africanus')

Main force

Numidian cavalry (Masinissa)

Principes (veteran troops)

Italian cavalry (Laelius)

Hastati (front-line troops)

80 elephants

Numidian cavalry

Ligurian & Gallic infantry

Carthaginian & African infantry

Carthaginian cavalry

Main force

Cathaginians (Hannibal)

© Richard Natkiel, 1988

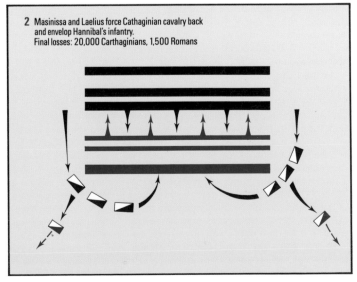

2 Masinissa and Laelius force Cathaginian cavalry back and envelop Hannibal's infantry.
Final losses: 20,000 Carthaginians, 1,500 Romans

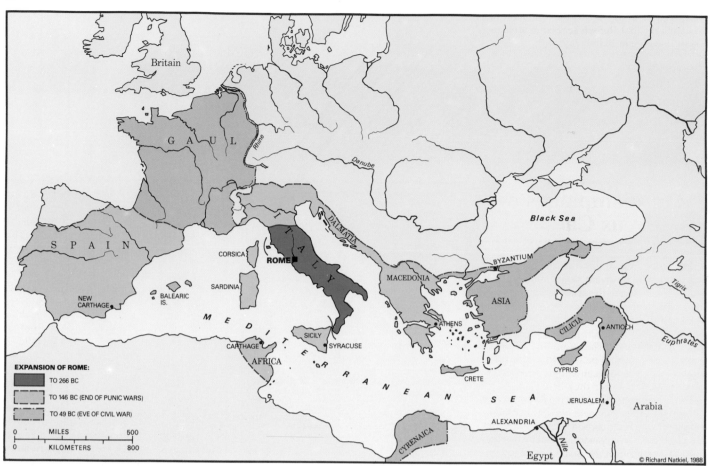

EXPANSION OF ROME:

- TO 266 BC
- TO 146 BC (END OF PUNIC WARS)
- TO 49 BC (EVE OF CIVIL WAR)

© Richard Natkiel, 1988

The Rise of Rome

Rome's rise from a minor Italian city-state to the position of dominant power in the Mediterranean world was a phenomenon that still intrigues classical historians. There was nothing unique about Rome, it had no advantageous natural resources, neither was it located at a strategically vital spot. Its citizens were not unusually brilliant and it suffered a number of catastrophes during its rise that would have halted the progress of would-be imitators elsewhere in the Mediterranean. In the end, the puzzled historians of ancient times concluded that Rome's achievements were due to the adaptability of its institutions and the resilience of its people.

Around the end of the sixth century BC, while the Greek city-states were embarking on a war against the Persians, the Romans deposed their kings. In place of the monarchy they established two consuls, who were to be advised by a council of the state's richest citizens, the Senate. Laws were proposed by the consuls and passed by a popular assembly. There were also tribunes, who protected the interests of the poorer citizens. Until the end of the Republic, this form of government was extremely stable. Rome was free of the class strife that marked the Greek city-states.

Shortly after the monarchy was toppled, Rome was sacked by a marauding band of Gauls. Despite this, the next 200 years was a period of steady expansion down the Italian peninsula. Rome managed to survive another defeat, at the hands of the Samnites in 321 BC. By 280 BC Rome was paramount among the Italian states. That year, a Greek general hired by the city of Tarantum arrived in Italy. Pyrrhus, King of Epirus, defeated the Romans in several battles that were costly victories for him. In the end the Romans beat Pyrrhus – a pattern that was to characterize many of Rome's wars.

A few years after the defeat of Pyrrhus in 265 BC, Rome became embroiled in an epic struggle with Carthage for control of their half of the Mediterranean. Rome emerged victorious and immediately began a series of wars in the western Mediterranean and Spain. Macedonia had followed a policy friendly to Carthage, and the Romans sought revenge. They defeated Macedon twice, in 197 BC and in 168 BC. In between, during 191-189 BC, the Romans defeated the Seleucid Empire of the Middle East. In Spain the Romans had acquired the Carthaginian possessions along the coast and slowly extended their rule inland. By 150 BC Rome was the dominant power in the Mediterranean basin. Four years later two events marked the end of any resistance to this situation – Carthage was totally destroyed and the great Greek city of Corinth was sacked, after both had rebelled against Roman rule.

The next 100 years saw a period of slow growth, as the Roman conquests were absorbed into a republican empire. There

Above: the ruins of Ostia – the port of Rome.

were wars against Mithridates throughout the first half of the first century BC, and a fierce guerrilla war in Africa against the tribes on the fringe of the Sahara. In Rome the stable constitution finally gave way as savage civil wars began. A 30-year period of peace between 80 BC and 50 BC saw the addition of Gaul, Syria and Palestine. When the great civil war between Caesar and Pompey broke out in 49 BC there were only three truly independent states in the Mediterranean: a Berber kingdom in Morocco, Egypt and Rome.

The Campaigns of Julius Caesar

In 59 BC Gaius Julius Caesar was one of
Rome's most important political figures. He
had been elected to the senior of the two consulships, Rome's chief executive positions
designed to replace the long-deposed
monarchs, and was at the pinnacle of a Roman
politician's career. The next step along his
path to power would be to become proconsul
of one of the republican empire's provinces.
Rome's leaders, after they had completed a
term in one of the republic's magistracies, traditionally spent the next year running the
affairs of a province chosen for them randomly
by a lottery. At the conclusion of this year they
returned to serve in the Senate.

Provincial administration was a source of
great power to the senators. In the early stages
of their careers they would exploit the wealth
of the provinces; bribery and extortion would
be used to cream off money from the inhabitants in return for services rendered. This
money would finance campaigns for the next
office on the ladder to the consulships. Consu-
lar governors, known as proconsuls, would
attempt to add to their prestige through
expansion of the empire into new areas. Back
in Rome they would be hailed for their
achievements, and possibly secure another
term as consul and the fortunes that could be
gained from victorious wars.

Caesar's proconsulship was almost unprecedented in Roman political history. He
was granted the administration of three provinces for five years, in place of the usual one
for a single year. His rule encompassed southern France, northern Italy and the east
Adriatic coast; these were the northern limits
of the empire. In March 58 BC he received

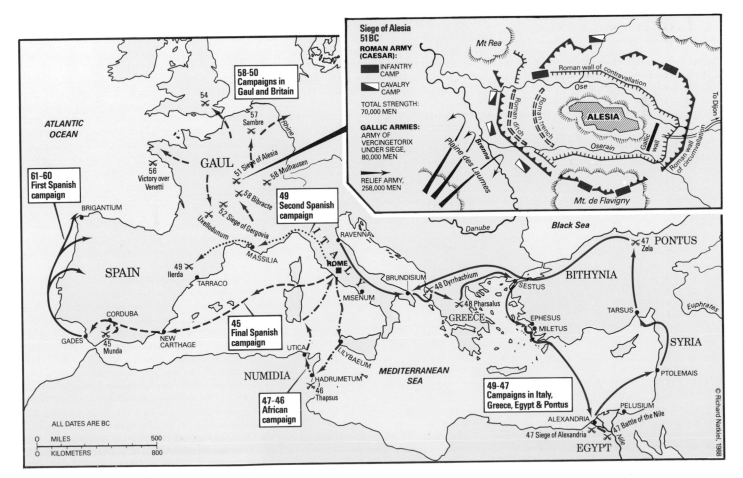

news that a Celtic tribe, the Helvetii, whose lands lay in northwestern Switzerland, was attempting to migrate through Roman territory to southwestern France. Caesar refused to permit them to pass through, so they chose to take a longer route through the territory of the Aedui in eastern France, whose chieftain was willing to grant permission. Caesar now feared that the Helvetii might cause trouble along the border of the Roman province of southern France, known as Gallia Transalpina. Caesar crushed them in two battles, which included Bibracte where many of the Helvetii were killed. The survivors were forced to return to their original homes.

Hot on the heels of this victory, Caesar ordered a tribe of Germans who had settled in Gaul, the Suebi, to cease their attacks on their Celtic neighbors. The Suebi king, Ariovistus, refused to obey so Caesar led his forces against the Germans. After some maneuvering, the two sides fought a battle near Mulhausen. The Suebi were defeated and almost all the Germans then settled in Gaul were forced back

Below: a close-quarters battle between Roman legionaires and Gauls during Julius Caesar's campaign in France.

across the Rhine. Caesar gave some indication of his ambitions by settling his troops in a winter camp nearby. Rome, in the person of Caesar, had plans for the independent parts of Gaul.

The tribes of northern Gaul, known as the Belgae, were alarmed at the arrival of a Roman army so close to their territory. They organized a confederacy and prepared to resist Caesar should he choose to invade their area. Caesar, for his part, feared the power of such a confederacy. The next year he invaded the lands of the Belgae. Some tribes submitted, others did not. Those who resisted the Romans had difficulty, however, feeding the large army they had assembled. The Belgae had to force an action. One day, when Caesar's men were making camp along the Sambre River, the Belgae launched all their forces in a surprise attack. The Romans were victorious, but it had been a near thing. The battle effectively marked the end of Gallic independence. Most of the other tribes were prepared to acknowledge the suzerainty of Rome, and did so as soon as envoys arrived from Caesar.

Caesar faced an uprising by tribes in Brittany and the southwest in 56 BC. He defeated the opposition and scored a particularly spectacular success over the Venetii in a sea battle.

His ships used grappling irons to prevent the Venetii, who were far superior sailors, from maneuvering to gain an advantage over the Romans. The Venetii had been aided by some allies from Britain and in 55 BC, as well as an expedition across the Rhine, Caesar sent a reconnaissance force across to Britain. The next year he led a full-scale invasion of the island, but failed to establish a lasting Roman presence because of damage to his shipping.

Caesar's expedition to Britain did secure a guarantee from the Belgic tribes of its southeastern corner to keep out of involvement in Gallic affairs. Resentment to Roman rule was building up, and one tribe, the Eburones, had surprised a Roman garrison and destroyed it. In 53 BC Caesar's forces totally devastated the land of the Eburones and also crossed the Rhine in another invasion of the Suebi lands. The expedition of the last three years into Germany and across to Britain secured the frontiers of Roman Gaul.

This security came just in time. The tribes of central and southern Gaul now rose in a co-ordinated revolt that marked the most dangerous threat to Roman rule in the province. Poor harvests in recent years had led to a famine, intensified by the need to feed the 40,000 men of the Roman army. The Gallic nobles were appalled at the savagery the Romans used to suppress rebellions, particularly that of the Eburones. Hunger and fear provoked revolt. The Gallic forces were skilfully handled by their leader, Vercingetorix, who refused to fight Caesar's army except at a time and in a place of his own choosing. Caesar was unable to defeat Vercingetorix at Gergovia, and seemed doomed to disaster in the face of the Gallic scorched-earth strategy. Caesar's military brilliance now shone forth. He managed to pin Vercingetorix at Alesia and besieged him there. A huge relieving army was defeated and the Gallic rebellion broken when Vercingetorix and his men surrendered at the end of 51 BC.

Caesar spent the next year subduing the tribes of the southwest and the end of the revolt was secured by victory at Uxellodunum. These victories in Gaul were matched, however, by defeats on the political battlefield of Rome. Caesar's enemies were gaining the upper hand. It had been arranged that Caesar's command in Gaul would expire at the end of 49 BC and that he would take up the consulship in Rome again in 48 BC. The Senate voted against this arrangement at the beginning of 49 BC. Rome was about to be plunged into nearly 20 years of civil war.

The Roman Civil Wars

The last 100 years of the Roman Republic were times of great civil strife. The poorest classes of its citizenry were intensively exploited by the richest, who at the same time impoverished those who were not so poor. Debt and hunger sparked unrest several times in the period and also spawned a new class of politicians, known as *populares* or demagogues, who were ready to alleviate the distress of the poor in return for their votes. At the end of 60 BC the three leading *populares* of the time – Julius Caesar, Pompey and Marcus Crassus – made an agreement to support one another politically, since they would not be able to secure political office if they acted individually. The agreement began to break down after the death of Crassus during a campaign against the Parthians of Mesopotamia and Persia in 53 BC. Pompey feared Caesar's growing influence after the campaigns in Gaul, Germany and Britain. In 49 BC he joined with Caesar's rich opponents in the Senate in a move to bring Caesar to trial for unconstitutional behavior during his consulship in 59 BC. Caesar would certainly have been convicted, and rather than face the ruin of his career, he chose to initiate a civil war, launching his army on a march to Rome from Ravenna.

Pompey fled south at the approach of Caesar, in company with a number of senators. Caesar followed behind but slowly. Whenever Caesar captured opponents of his, he would release them, even if they were raising troops for Pompey. Caesar's stated aim was not vengeance, but reconciliation. He found Pompey holed up in the port of Brundisium and begged him to negotiate, but Pompey refused. After a few days Pompey left Brundisium, crossed the Adriatic and then moved into Greece where he raised an army with the help of the considerable financial resources of Rome's eastern provinces.

At Brundisium Pompey had faced a choice between two strategic and political options. The east was wealthy, but there was a large army loyal to him in Spain. He chose to go where the money was, but Caesar did not follow. Caesar now attacked the army in Spain to defeat what he saw as a threat to his rear. On his way he besieged the city of Massilia, which had declared for the senators. In a series of marches and countermarches which resembled a game of chess, Caesar forced his Pompeian enemies to capitulate at Ilerda. Leaving some troops to mop up the smaller Spanish garrisons, he then turned to fight Pompey in the east.

At the beginning of 48 BC Caesar landed on the coast of Epirus with a large army. He sent a message to Pompey, who was on the march from Thessalonica in Greece, begging for negotiations. Pompey refused and occupied Dyrrhachium where Caesar besieged him. After four months of positional warfare it became apparent that Pompey had gained the upper hand and Caesar withdrew to Thessaly in Greece. Pompey followed and in August offered battle to Caesar at Pharsalus. Despite Pompey's superior numbers Caesar defeated him. He attacked Pompey in the flank with a picked group of about 3000 men, and overcame the enemy's numerical superiority by tactical brilliance.

Pompey fled to Egypt where he was assassinated. Caesar had pursued his enemy to Alexandria where he became embroiled in a civil war between the co-heirs to the Egyptian throne, the notorious Cleopatra and her brother Ptolemy. Caesar and his men were attacked, but fought off the Egyptians and restored order, and Cleopatra became sole ruler. Caesar left Egypt – by then Cleopatra was pregnant with his son – nine months after he had arrived in June 47 BC. He marched

Above: a bust of Pompey.
Below: Caesar's victory at Pharsalus.

north to defeat the King of Pontus, who had supported Pompey.

The remnants of Pompey's forces had fled to the province of Africa, the grain of which land was a vital part of the Roman diet. To

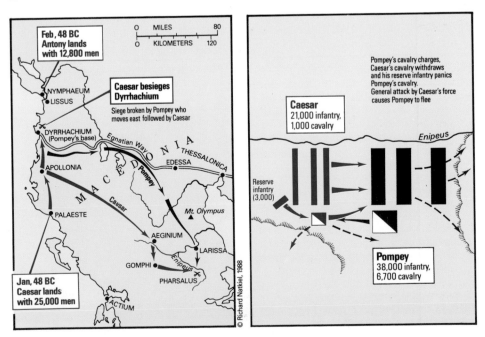

Feb, 48 BC
Antony lands with 12,800 men

0   MILES   80
0   KILOMETERS   120

Caesar besieges Dyrrhachium

Siege broken by Pompey who moves east followed by Caesar

NYMPHAEUM
LISSUS

DYRRHACHIUM (Pompey's base)

Egnatian Way

MACEDONIA

EDESSA

THESSALONICA

APOLLONIA

Caesar

Pompey

PALAESTE

Mt. Olympus

AEGINIUM

LARISSA

GOMPHI

Enipeus

PHARSALUS

Jan, 48 BC
Caesar lands with 25,000 men

ACTIUM

© Richard Natkiel, 1988

Pompey's cavalry charges, Caesar's cavalry withdraws and his reserve infantry panics Pompey's cavalry.
General attack by Caesar's force causes Pompey to flee

Caesar
21,000 infantry, 1,000 cavalry

Enipeus

Reserve infantry (3,000)

Pompey
38,000 infantry, 6,700 cavalry

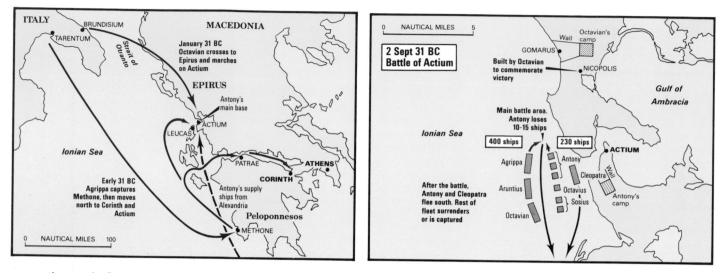

secure the supply Caesar began a new campaign in October 47 BC. Once again he maneuvered the enemy into an unfavorable position and defeated them near Thapsus in February 46 BC. Meanwhile there had been a revolt in Spain and Caesar returned to that province, winning a decisive victory over the rebels at Munda in March 45 BC. He then returned to Rome where he was assassinated by former supporters of Pompey.

Once again the Roman world was divided. The assassins fled to Greece, where they began to raise an army to fight the former supporters of Caesar. Meanwhile in Italy a three-cornered contest broke out between Caesar's political replacement, Mark Antony, the heir to his estate, Octavian, and the Senate. Several battles were fought, but eventually Octavian and Mark Antony reached an understanding and ran the state in their own interests. In the name of the Senate they went to Greece and defeated the army of Caesar's assassins at Philippi in 42 BC. The provinces of the Republic were divided between them, with Octavian receiving the western half and Antony the eastern.

The next ten years saw Octavian mop up the last remaining supporters of Pompey in a naval campaign, while Antony, who had settled in Egypt and become enamored of Cleopatra, fought a campaign against the Parthians that almost ended in disaster. Antony appears to have planned to detach the eastern provinces and rule them from Alexandria as a separate kingdom of the eastern Mediterranean, with Cleopatra as his consort. Octavian saw this scheme as a perfect excuse for a war which would eliminate his last competitor

for supremacy in the Roman world. In 32 BC the two sides went to war.

Once again the Greek peninsula provided the scene for the conflict. The armies and fleets met at Actium on the Ambracian Gulf of the western coast. Octavian refused to fight Antony on land, and eventually forced him to risk a major naval battle on 2 September 31 BC. Antony's inferior numbers were overwhelmed, and he had to flee with the Egyptian squadron. Once in Egypt Antony's army abandoned him, and he and Cleopatra committed suicide in August 30 BC. Octavian was now sole ruler of the Roman world, establishing an imperial monarchy which spelled the end of the republican order.

Above: the Battle of Actium – Octavian's decisive victory over Antony in September 31 BC.
Below: a scene from Actium – one galley settles in the water after being rammed.

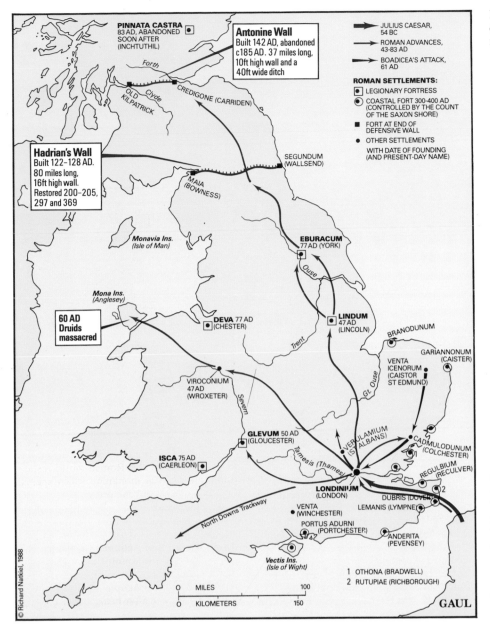

Below: a bust of Hadrian, the Roman emperor responsible for securing the northern border of the province of Britain.

The Roman Conquest of Britain

For almost 100 years after Caesar's invasions of Britain in 55 and 54 BC the Romans largely ignored the island. The civil wars of the last years of the Republic and the need to establish a new imperial order prevented the Romans from resuming any plans they might have had for its conquest. In the meantime the inhabitants of the southeast, where Caesar had landed, had been united under the rule of Cunobelinus, who established a center of power at Cadmulodunum. In the last years of his reign he drove out Verica, the king of the tribes who inhabited what is now southern Surrey and Sussex. Verica went to exile at Rome.

The Emperor Claudius received Verica and heard news of disturbances on the north Gallic coast caused by the successors to Cunobeli-

nus, Togodumnus and Caratacus. Claudius ordered four legions to assemble for the invasion, and they landed at Rutupiae, Dubris and Lemanis in the spring of AD 43, rapidly pushing inland. In a two-day battle at the Medway crossings the Romans defeated the combined forces of Caratacus and Togodumnus, whose army then divided – Togodumnus seems to have been killed. His men retired northward, only to be beaten again by the Romans in a battle along the Thames. Caratacus retreated to the west, to fight another day. A short while after the victory on the Thames, Claudius himself landed in Britain and led the army to another victory, followed by the occupation of Cadmulodunum which became the headquarters of the Roman occupation.

The Celtic tribes of Britain were fully aware of the military power of Rome, and after the largest and most powerful kingdom was defeated, most of the smaller tribes readily submitted to Roman rule. Caratacus alone held out in the west. The future Emperor Vespasian spent a year campaigning in the region,

which was studded with fortresses which had to be captured by assault. By about AD 50 the Romans occupied an area southeast of a line running from the Dorset coast, through Glevum, Viroconium and Lindum, and the surrender of Caratacus in AD 51 seemed to mark the end of serious resistance.

However, a major revolt broke out in AD 61, the result of Roman maladministration. The Iceni, led by their queen Boadicea, combined with other tribes and destroyed the Roman cities of Londinium and Cadmulodunum. This dangerous rebellion was quickly put down with great loss of life. About ten years later the Romans resumed their conquest, and in AD 83, under the governor Julius Agricola, they even advanced into Scotland.

The limits of Roman rule were now being reached. Regular raids by the Picts of Scotland led to the erection of a wall by the Emperor Hadrian, completed in AD 128. Antoninus Pius, the next emperor, advanced the frontier farther north and erected another wall. But it stretched Rome's military in Britain too thinly and only lasted about 40 years. The failed bid by the governor of Britain, Clodius Albinus, for the imperial diadem in AD 196 weakened the province's army further. Saxon raids which began in the middle of the third century led to the construction of a network of sea defenses along the southeast coast which became known as the Saxon Shore. The need to protect the wealthiest part of Britain from barbarian raids marked the beginning of the end of the Roman occupation.

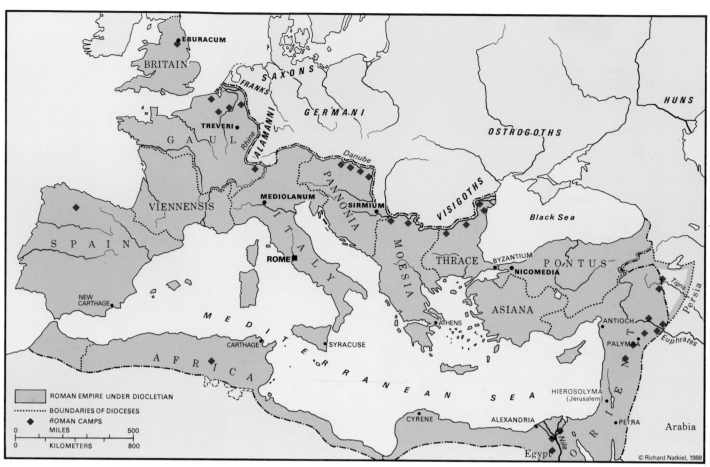

ROMAN EMPIRE UNDER DIOCLETIAN
·········· **BOUNDARIES OF DIOCESES**
◆ **ROMAN CAMPS**

© Richard Natkiel, 1988

The Roman Empire

Five generations of civil strife came to an end with the victory of Octavian over Antony at Actium in 31 BC. Octavian now established an imperial form of government, grafted onto the remains of the old Republic, and also laid the general foundations of future imperial policy. A regular army was now to be maintained, and military actions would only be undertaken to strengthen the empire's borders or in response

Below: Roman soldiers escort barbarians.

to the attacks of others. During his reign, the Danube and the Rhine became the northern border, as Roman legions pushed north from the Balkans and Italy, and east from Gaul. After the death of Augustus, the system he had designed continued to function smoothly. Most of the empire's troubles were due to chronic instability in the imperial house.

In AD 43 Claudius began the annexation of Britain. There were always problems in the east with the Parthians, and Armenia was a constant source of friction between these states as both jockeyed to get their nominee on its throne. The system briefly broke down in AD 67-8. This 'year of the four emperors' was an unwelcome reminder of the last years of the Republic. It also revealed 'the secret of empire': the rule of the emperors was based on military force. Vespasian, the victorious eastern governor, resumed the steady progress of the empire begun by Augustus. Under the next four emperors the main political and military activity was securing the border. In AD 98 Trajan became emperor. His reign was marked by considerable military activity. Dacia, across the Danube from Thrace, was annexed and Mesopotamia was added to the empire in the east. Trajan's successor, Hadrian, abandoned Mesopotamia, but his British wall remains a solid symbol of his policy of border stability. The empire, however, had reached its limits.

The reigns of the next emperors were generally stable, a period characterized by the great historian Gibbon as a 'golden age.' In

AD 193 a new round of civil wars between the various governors of the empire heralded the beginning of a new period of instability. In the German forests beyond the empire's border, overpopulation was making the tribes restive, particularly as they could view the great wealth of the land to the south and west. The Parthians were overthrown and replaced by a Sassanid dynasty with dreams of restoring the old Persian Empire.

In AD 235 these factors, combined with a new outbreak of civil war, produced the events known as 'the third century crisis.' The imperial diadem became a gift the soldiery would grant to the general who promised them the most gold. In the Balkans the Danube border gave way, and Goths and other Germans poured into the rich provinces of Greece, Thrace and Macedonia. The Rhine frontier also broke down and the Sassanids invaded Syria. By AD 260 the empire was on the point of collapse.

It was, however rescued, at least for the moment, by a series of soldier-emperors from Illyria who had risen up through the ranks. They gradually restored order, and the last and greatest of them, Diocletian, reorganized the empire and army. The military basis of imperial rule was fully recognized, and his edicts tried to impose a stern discipline on the army. A new mobile corps of troops was set up in place of the old system of forward defense. These measures were soon to be thoroughly tested, the crises of the third century were only a foretaste of the tribulations to come.

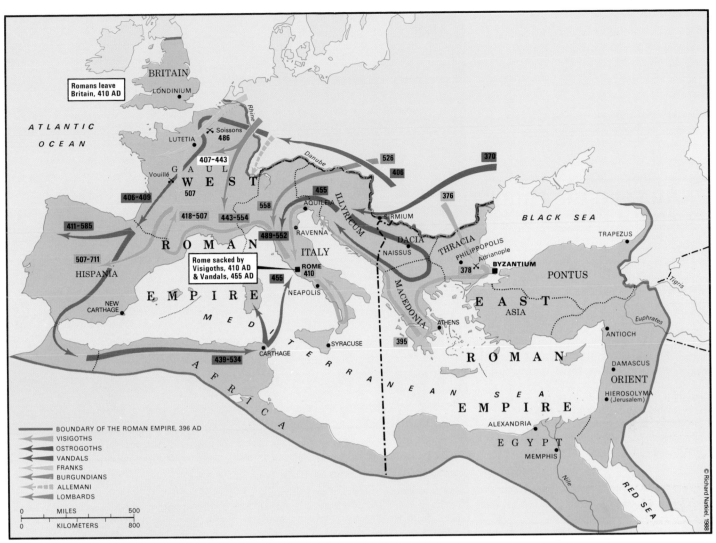

The Barbarian Invasion of Rome

The fall of the Roman Empire is one of history's great tragedies. Many reasons, of varying degrees of plausibility, have been advanced for its decline. The underlying causes were mainly economic – particularly the heavy taxation to finance military expenditures which impoverished the bulk of the population. The surface effects of the underlying discontent were civil war and defeat at the hands of barbarian invaders bent on destroying Rome.

In AD 300 the empire seemed to have recovered from the crisis of the third century. Diocletian had provided firm government and his reorganization of the empire into two halves seemed to give added resilience to a sturdy structure. However, civil war was now endemic to imperial life, and the next 50 years were punctuated by a series of contests between contenders for the purple. Combined with a failed expedition against the Sassanid Persian Empire, these internal squabbles were a costly drain on the trained soldiery of the Roman military at a time when every man would be needed to repel a succession of invaders.

Trouble was brewing north of the Danube frontier. The Huns, a nomadic people that had been moving west from central Asia for a couple of centuries, were pressing toward the Ostrogothic kingdom of southern Russia. As the Ostrogoths shifted westward to avoid the Huns they pushed other Germanic tribes nearer the empire's frontier and over its borders. The Visigoths, a people related to the Ostrogoths, asked permission to cross the Danube and settle in the empire. The Romans agreed (there was a precedent for this: the Franks were settled around the mouth of the Rhine). Unfortunately for the Visigoths, they were mercilessly exploited by the Roman officials of Thrace. The starving barbarians, seemingly hounded on all sides, rebelled against the Romans. They defeated a Roman army and killed the Eastern Emperor at the Battle of Adrianople in AD 378.

Theodosius now became the emperor in the east, and he permitted the Visigoths to settle in the Balkans. Another civil war occurred in 388, and Theodosius, the victor, became the last sole ruler of the Roman Empire. After his death in 395, the Roman Empire was officially divided between his two sons. The Visigoths were soon on the rampage again, and sacked the old capital of Rome (in the west the capital was now Mediolanum but would soon move to Ravenna) in 410. Three years previously the Vandals had broken through the Rhine frontier. They made their way across Gaul, their passage marked by a trail of pillaged farms, villages and towns, and finally settled in Spain in 409.

The Roman Empire was now crumbling. Britain was abandoned in 410. The Huns themselves were soon pressing on the borders, while the Vandals moved to Africa in 429 after the Visigoths, who had settled in southwestern France, had waged a savage war against them. The campaigns of Attila and his Huns during the 440s and 450s were another nail in the imperial coffin. The Ostrogoths were settled in the Balkans in 455, while the Franks expanded their territory into Gaul. In 455 Rome was sacked again, this time by a Vandal raiding force from Africa. Shortly after, the Rhine frontier totally gave way and hordes of Germans crossed into the territory of the former empire. In 476 the Germanic mercenaries of the Western Emperor deposed him. The Ostrogoths moved into Italy with the approval of the Eastern Emperor, marking the end of the old Roman Empire.

Attila and the Huns

The Huns were a Turkic people who originally came from the central Asian steppes. Between the end of the pre-Christian era and the fourth century these nomads moved slowly across the south Russian steppes toward Europe. As they neared the Roman Empire, the Germanic tribes in their path spread terrible tales about the devastation caused by the horse-riding nomads, and to the civilized Christians of the classical world the Huns took on the aspect of satanic demons, servants of the anti-Christ. This frightening picture was based on fact. The Huns were incredibly mobile thanks to their horses, more savage in their pillaging than the Germanic tribesmen and, not being Christians, they showed little respect for churches and monasteries, unlike their Christianized German counterparts. But like the Germans, the Huns were amenable to bribery and could be bought off; also many enlisted as mercenaries in the Roman Army and fought against the Germanic barbarians.

On their arrival in Europe, in the last quarter of the fourth century, the Huns destroyed the Visigothic and Ostrogothic realms of the Balkans and southern Russia. They then moved onto the Hungarian plains, founded a nomadic kingdom, and were parti-

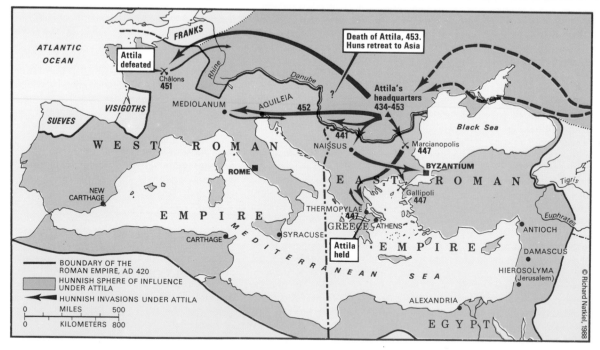

Left: Attila, the supreme ruler of the Huns during their westward migration into Europe during the fifth century AD.
Below: the head of Altheric, one of the victors at Chalons.
Bottom right: Chalons, the battle that forced Attila to retreat from Gaul.

letter. Attila accepted the ring, assuming she was proposing to him, and suggested to Valentinian that Gaul would be a suitable dowry. The Vandals in Africa were also encouraging Attila to partake of the rich pickings in the Western Empire. Valentinian's refusal to abide by his sister's proposal resulted in a Hunnic invasion of his territory.

Attila advanced into Gaul, his immediate objective being the Visigothic kingdom in the southwest. Aetius, as commander of the field army, took his motley array of troops against the Huns, supported by the Visigoths and other allies of Rome. Attila's horde and Aetius' army met at Chalons. The battle lasted all day. The slaughter was considerable, and both sides were exhausted at the end. Attila withdrew to his kingdom along the Danube, and left his bride unclaimed.

The Hun king was not yet finished, however. The next year he led his men south to Italy. He destroyed the ancient town of Aquileia, and 20 years later the site was still almost uninhabited. The other cities of northern Italy were bankrupted by Hunnic extortion and the Po valley was ravaged. But plague wreaked havoc among the Huns and Attila withdrew. In 453, while he was resting after the celebration of his marriage to a new bride, Attila suffered a nosebleed. He drowned in his own blood, a fitting end to a monarch whose reign had been drenched in that of others.

cipants in the barbarian conflicts of the early fifth century. Their king, Rua, died in about 434 and was succeeded by two brothers, Bleda and Attila. They pursued the traditional policy of Hunnic kings and demanded gold from the Romans in return for not attacking the empire. They also continued to permit their warriors to serve in the Roman armies against the Germanic barbarians in Gaul, Spain and Africa. The effective ruler of the western half of the Roman Empire, the general Flavius Aetius, had grown up as a hostage of the Huns and a Hunnic contingent could usually be found in his armies. Under his rule a tacit alliance with the Huns protected the western half of the empire.

In 441, apparently due to Roman violations of a treaty, the Huns invaded the Balkan provinces of the Eastern Empire. They ravaged the provinces along the Danube, and defeated a Roman army several times, once at Gallipoli near the gates of Constantinople. The Eastern Emperor, Theodosius II, chose to buy off Attila and his horde, and agreed to pay a large sum of gold each year. He paid this tribute

once or twice but then refused to pay any more. In the meantime Attila had killed Bleda, his brother and co-ruler, and decided on a policy of national expansion. He refused to supply Aetius with any more Hunnic soldiery, presumably to have more for himself. In 447 the Romans were again breaking their treaty obligations, and Attila led his men south into the Balkans. They defeated the Eastern Empire's army, then ranged south into Greece and west to the gates of Constantinople. Theodosius was forced to sign a new treaty which raised the amount of tribute to be paid and marked a demilitarized zone to the south of the Danube. Theodosius followed these stipulations while the defenses of his empire were strengthened then, as abruptly as before, the treaty was broken.

This time, Attila chose to ignore the provocative actions of the Eastern Emperor. Events in the western half of the empire had attracted his attention. Valentinian III, emperor in the west, had a sister, Honororia, who objected to her brother's choice for her husband. She wrote to Attila, and enclosed a ring with her

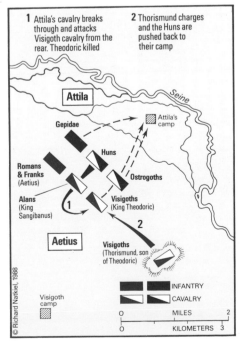

1 Attila's cavalry breaks through and attacks Visigoth cavalry from the rear. Theodoric killed

2 Thorismund charges and the Huns are pushed back to their camp

Attila
Seine
Gepidae
Attila's camp
Huns
Romans & Franks (Aetius)
Ostrogoths
Alans (King Sangibanus)
Visigoths (King Theodoric)
1
2
Aetius
Visigoths (Thorismund, son of Theodoric)

INFANTRY
CAVALRY

Visigoth camp

0   MILES   2
0   KILOMETERS   3

© Richard Natkiel, 1988

The Wars of Justinian

The eastern half of the Roman Empire had tottered under the barbarian onslaught but had not collapsed. It is a historical irony that the Greek east, long deemed effete by westerners, had outlasted the Latin west. Fifty years after the end of the western empire, a new ruler came to the throne in Constantinople. Justinian was inspired by the glories of the Roman past – he liked to boast that Latin was his native tongue – and from the beginning was determined to restore the former Roman Empire in the west.

Justinian was fortunate that he would be well served by his subordinates in his mission, especially at the outset. The empire's frontier with Persia was giving way under the onslaught of Khosroes, the Sassanid leader; and Antioch, the largest city in Syria, was under threat. The desperate situation was restored by the great general Belisarius, who defeated the Sassanid Persians at the Battle of Daras in 531. The next year a peace treaty was signed (known optimistically as the Perpetual Peace) and the Sassanid Persians were bought off for the time being.

Justinian now planned to turn west. Belisarius, after suppressing a brief rebellion in Constantinople, took charge of an army and fleet. He sailed to the former province of Africa (modern Tunisia) which was now an independent kingdom under Vandal rule. He was able to make an unopposed landing in the absence of the Vandal fleet. The Vandal king, Gelimer, mustered a large army and attempted to ambush Belisarius' much smaller force at Ad Decimum; however, the trap was sprung too soon, and Gelimer was defeated and his brother killed. Belisarius entered Carthage and found a feast Gelimer had prepared to celebrate a victory over the Romans. Later in the year Gelimer was defeated again and surrendered. Belisarius returned to Constantinople and was rewarded with the old Roman honor of a triumph.

Africa was to be the scene of more fighting as the Berber tribes of the interior rejected Roman rule; but Justinian's attention now shifted to Italy, where the Ostrogoths had founded a kingdom. Justinian took advantage of a dispute over the succession to send two armies, one under Belisarius, to Italy in 536. Most of the south was soon brought under Roman rule, but Belisarius was unable to win a decisive victory. In 540 he occupied the Ostrogothic capital at Ravenna and signed a peace treaty, but the agreement broke down

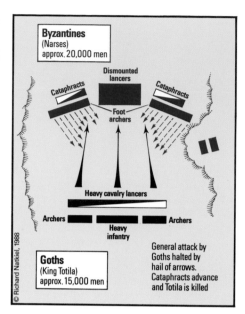

the next year. Belisarius, who complained that Justinian was not providing enough men and money, was unable to bring the Ostrogoths to battle. In 548 he finally left the peninsula for an honorable retirement that Justinian forcibly demanded. Narses, a eunuch, now commanded Justinian's army. He defeated the Goths twice, at Tadinae in 552 and Mons

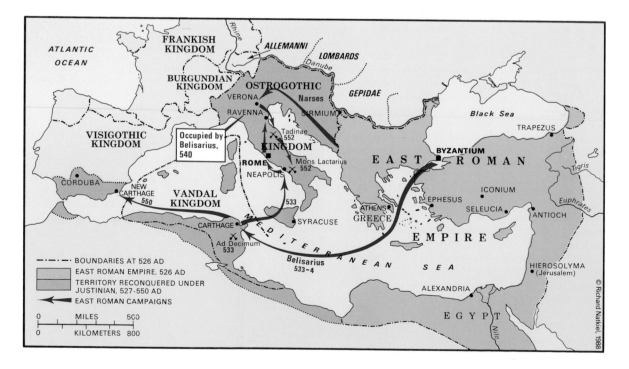

Below left: the Battle of Tadinae, AD 552.
Below: Justinian I, Emperor of Byzantium.
Below right: a medallion struck to
commemorate a victory by Belisarius.
Bottom: a mosaic of Justinian and his court
from Ravenna.

Lactarius in 552, and destroyed their kingdom. Italy once again was a part of the Roman Empire. About the same time Justinian's military intervention in a succession dispute in Spain added a part of that former Roman province to his empire.

When he died in 565, Justinian could consider his reign to have been a great achievement. Although the Perpetual Peace had broken down in 540 and a renewed Persian war had hindered his efforts, he had restored much of the Roman Empire, although it was now in the process of becoming the equally famous Byzantine Empire.

The Rise of Islam

The Middle East, the cradle of many religions, gave birth to a new cult in about 622 when Mohammed, an Arab merchant of Mecca, fled to the neighboring town of Medina to practice his new religion of Islam unhindered. He encouraged his followers to raid the caravans of unbelievers, and after a few attempts they became proficient bandits – their morale aided by the belief that a Moslem who died fighting non-Moslems went straight to Paradise. The merchant oligarchs of Mecca now had commercial as well as theological differences with their erstwhile associate, and they mounted an expedition against him in 626. Mohammed and his men were defeated, but inflicted heavy casualties on the Meccans. A second confrontation in 627 resulted in a Moslem victory, and in 629, after further defeats, the Meccans formally submitted to Mohammed and adopted his religion.

While Mohammed battled with the Meccans, he was also successfully converting the nomad Bedouin tribes of the Arabian peninsula's interior. Thus when he defeated the Meccans, he established a kind of unity which the Arab people had previously lacked. After Mohammed's death in 632, this unity was imperiled. The Moslems close to Mohammed chose his good friend Abu Bekr to lead the religion; he adopted the title Caliph (which means successor). His first task was to defeat the many pretenders that had emerged to claim the mantle of the Prophet. In a year of hard fighting, the rivals of the new Caliph were eliminated and unity was restored.

Right: a scene from the Battle of Tours near Poitiers, AD 732.

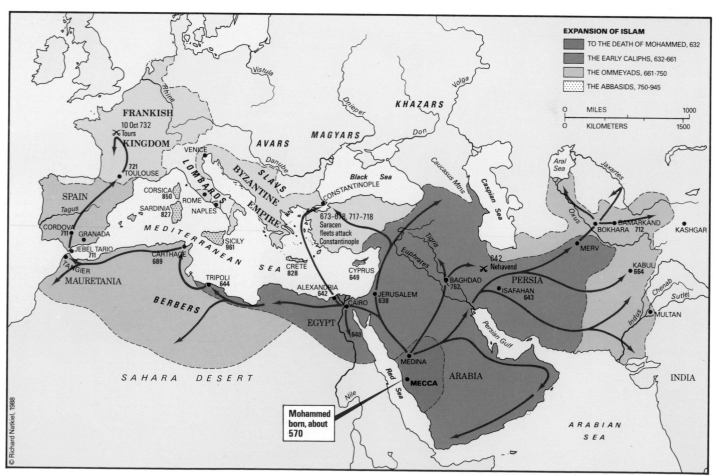

© Richard Natkiel, 1988

The upstart Arab world now came into conflict with the traditional powers of the Middle East: the Byzantine and Sassanid Persian Empires. Petty Arab states along their borders had only recently suffered slights at the hands of these imperial giants; consequently, when these small states converted to Islam, their grievances were taken up by their Arab cousins. In 634 expeditions were sent against both the Sassanids and the Byzantines, and the latter suffered a bad defeat at Deraa.

Abu Bekr died in 634, and was succeeded by Omar. He consciously pursued an expansionist policy and also developed an administrative system to cope with the growing Arab Empire. The war against the Byzantines was pursued vigorously – Damascus fell in September 635. The Byzantines assembled a large army and recovered most of Syria, but they were then defeated on the edge of the Arabian desert by the Moslem Army at the Battle of Yarmuk in 636. Over the next few years the Arabs were able slowly to whittle away the Byzantine occupation of the cities of Syria and Palestine until both regions were fully incorporated into their empire.

The other mighty empire, of the Sassanid Persians, now came under Arab assault. Skirmishes had occurred between Arabs and Sassanids in the recent years, and the combatants finally met in decisive battle in 637 at Qadisiya. The contest raged for three days and the Arabs emerged totally victorious, although at heavy cost. They now had control of Mesopotamia, as well as most of Syria and Palestine. The Arabs barely paused to consolidate their conquests. In 639 they pushed into Egypt and finally drove the Byzantines out in 642. That same year the Arabs crushed the new army organized by the Sassanid Great King at Nehavend and destroyed his military power forever. Over the next ten years Arab columns ranged across the Persian highlands, and brought them under Arab rule.

Omar was assassinated in 644. The new Caliph, Othman, adopted a policy of consolidation. A fleet was built which raided Cyprus in 649, Sicily in 652, Rhodes in 654, and defeated a Byzantine fleet in 655. Othman's policies were not popular and he was murdered in 656. After a five-year civil war Muwaiya became Caliph and the process of expansion was resumed. This time the Arabs were less successful. A war with Byzantium between 668 and 676 ended in an Arab defeat. Some advances were made into India but only a small part of that country was converted. In 680 renewed civil strife began after the death of Muwaiya and it was not resolved until Abdul Malik became Caliph in 691.

With Arab unity once again restored by the sword, their forces were on the march, this time against the west. Byzantine North Africa fell in 698, and after a five-year war against the

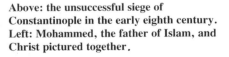

Berber tribesmen, the Arabs reached the Atlantic. The Visigothic kingdom of Spain was smashed in 712, and much of Asia Minor had fallen to the Arabs in 714. The great city of Constantinople was besieged in 717-18, but the Arabs were forced to retire when their fleet was defeated.

Arab power had almost reached its limits. There were raids from Spain into France throughout the next 15 years, and they culminated in 732 with a major incursion far north of the Pyrenees. This was defeated at Poitiers by Charles Martel in a battle which marked the high tide of Moslem power in the west. Defeat in the Caucasus at the hands of the Khazars of southern Russia the previous years halted plans to move north. There were minor actions in succeeding years, but by 750 the great age of Islamic Arab expansion had come to an end.

The map shows:

Sept 717 Moslems begin naval blockade
Spring 718 Moslem reinforcements arrive
June 718 Leo's fleet decisively defeats Suleiman's fleet, then Merdasan's army is repulsed. Maslama lifts siege in August

Defending force (Leo III)

GALATA
Golden Horn
Defensive chain
CONSTANTINOPLE
Moslem armies
Bosporus
Area of two naval battles
Sea of Marmara

Moslem force (Maslama)
Navy: Suleiman
Army: Merdasan

0 MILES 1½
0 KILOMETERS 2

© Richard Natkiel, 1988

Above: the unsuccessful siege of Constantinople in the early eighth century. Left: Mohammed, the father of Islam, and Christ pictured together.

These pages: King Louis journeys from
Damietta by sea and arrives at Acre during
the Eighth Crusade.

THE AGE OF CHIVALRY

KINGDOM OF THE FRANKS, 768
EXTENT OF CHARLEMAGNE'S EMPIRE

© Richard Natkiel, 1988

Far left: a foot soldier of the Carolingian period.
Below: a detail from the shrine of Charlemagne, crowned Holy Roman Emperor in 800.

The Carolingian Empire

The Franks were only one of the many barbarian groups that destroyed the Western Roman Empire in the fifth century. By the early years of the sixth century, however, they had established the most powerful of the new kingdoms then emerging. Under the rule of the Merovingian dynasty they subjugated almost all of the old Roman province of Gaul, and extended Frankish rule east into Germany to lands that had never been Roman.

The Merovingians were generous rulers who made lavish grants of land and possessions to their closest supporters, although in doing this they paved the way for their own downfall. The liberality of the Merovingians increased the power of certain nobles while they impoverished themselves. Merovingian rule came to an end in 751 when the strongest member of the nobility, Pepin the Short, the son of Charles Martel, gained the Pope's support to depose the ruling family. Pepin then took the crown and the Carolingian dynasty was established.

Frankish policy had been traditionally one of expansion, and Pepin continued to add to the kingdom. During his reign he waged campaigns in Aquitaine, Italy, Alamannia and Saxony. His first major war took place in 755-56 when he attacked and defeated the Lombard king of northern Italy who was a rival to Pepin's close ally, the Pope. Lombard power was broken for almost 20 years. Pepin was also forced to wage regular campaigns against the Visigothic nobility of Aquitaine, nominally a part of his kingdom, and against those perennial troublemakers, the Saxons.

Pepin died in 768 and, following the traditional Frankish custom, his kingdom was divided between his sons, Charlemagne and Carloman. They ruled jointly for a little more than three years, until Carloman's death in 771. Charlemagne was now sole ruler, and he pursued an even more energetic policy of expansion than his father. Over the next 30 years several campaigns would be conducted each year along the frontiers of his empire. Charlemagne invaded Italy at the Pope's request in 773. The Lombards were once again attempting to gain control of Rome. The Lombard army was defeated in the shadow of the Alps, and their capital, Pavia, was captured in 774, whereupon Charlemagne annexed their kingdom. Charlemagne's other great victory was over the Avars in a three-year campaign between 791 and 793. They formally submitted to Frankish overlordship in 796 and the boundary of Charlemagne's empire was extended far to the east.

Two regions of Charlemagne's empire were running sores throughout his reign. Saxony was never fully incorporated into the Carolingian realm until 805, and Charlemagne campaigned there annually. The southwest was also a trouble spot, with frequent raids occurring between Moslem Spain and Christian Francia. Among the battles that occurred was Roncesvalles in 778, immortalized in the *Song of Roland*.

Charlemagne was crowned Roman emperor by the Pope in 800, and died in 814. He had planned to divide his kingdom, but was survived by only one son, Louis the Pious. Louis slowed the pace of conquest, and seems to have preferred to Christianize his pagan neighbors. After 830 he faced frequent rebellions by his nobles, and when he died in 840 open warfare broke out between his three sons. In 842 two of them, Charles and Louis, beat the eldest, Lothar, at the Battle of Fontenoy; consequently the Carolingian Empire was divided into three distinct and separate kingdoms in 843.

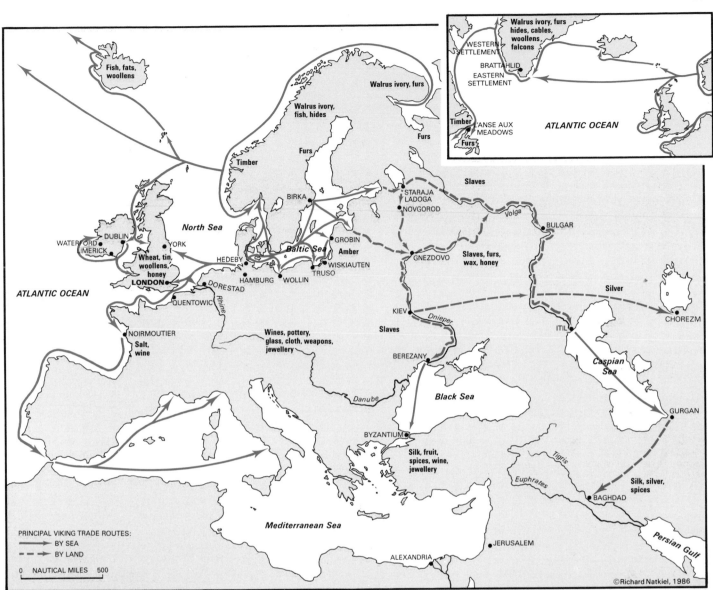

The Viking Explorations

The earliest Viking raid which can be clearly dated was an attack on the monastery at Lindisfarne in Northumbria in 793, and by that date Norse colonies had already been established in the Shetlands and the Orkneys. Settlements were also established later in the Hebrides off western Scotland, and by 841 Vikings had reached Dublin. From these bases it was even easier to raid towns around the coast of Britain and, farther south, even the coast of France.

The Danes followed in the footsteps of the Norwegians about a generation later with an attack on Dorestad in 834. By the middle of that century raids by Danes on coastal towns and abbeys in both Britain and France were commonplace.

France provides one of the best examples of Vikings settling to become part of the local community. The first Viking settlement in what was to become Normandy (the land of the north men) appears to have been established around 843. Soon the Norse raiders were penetrating inland along the rivers and all across northern France. Paris was besieged by a Norse army in 885-86. Many authorities would describe this as the high point of Viking expansion. The powers of the French king were growing, however, and in 911 the Norse leader Rolf (or Rollo) made peace with Charles the Simple who in turn created Rollo the Duke of Normandy.

From about the seventh century onward traders from Sweden had begun to penetrate into Russia, using the great rivers of the country as their highways. These Varangians as they were known established themselves at centers like Novgorod and Kiev while their trading missions made contact with Byzantium and Persia. A Varangian force even attacked Byzantium in 865. Eventually also the Kievan state was to be the forerunner of what was to become modern Russia.

The Vikings also looked west as well as east and skillful and adventurous sailors reached out into the Atlantic. Their settlement of Iceland began about 870 and within 60 years trade was flourishing to the extent that subsequent emigrants from Scandinavia found no room and were forced to sail farther afield to Greenland and beyond.

Bottom left: Frederick Barbarossa at the
Battle of Legnano in 1176. Barbarossa was
defeated by the Milanese and their allies.
Far right: the Battle of Hastings, 1066.
Bottom right: William gives arms and armor
to Harold (foot figures at right) – a scene
from the Bayeux Tapestry.

The Holy Roman Empire

The royal house of the East Frankish kingdom, descendants of Charlemagne, came to
an end in 911. The leading German nobles and
prelates adopted a system of election to select
their next king and chose Conrad, the Duke of
Franconia. He died childless in 918, and the
nobles and prelates elected the man Conrad
had suggested to succeed him, Henry, Duke of
Saxony. Henry was to lay the foundations of
the medieval Holy Roman Empire. He
expanded German rule westward into Lorraine and eastward into Bohemia. He resisted
the depredations of the Magyars, and twice
defeated the pagan Slav tribes east of the
Elbe. His victory at Meresburg over the
Magyars in 933 temporarily halted their raids.

Henry bequeathed a strong kingdom to his
son Otto in 936. Otto was more impressed by
the achievements of Charlemagne than those
of his own father. He actively encouraged
associations to be made linking him to the
illustrious Carolingian emperor. He imposed
a more centralized government on his kingdom, and supported the Church in its expansion eastward. In 955 Otto crushed the
Magyars at the Battle of Lechfeld which finally
put an end to their raids on Germany. He also
established a presence in Italy as protector of
the Papacy. In 962 the Pope rewarded him,
and the title of Holy Roman Emperor, which
had in recent years been the possession of a
series of childless, ineffectual Italian aristocrats, was now handed to the German ruler.

Otto and his ancestors governed their
troublesome realm as best they could. Like
the Carolingians, they were forced to campaign for year after year along the most
threatened of their frontiers, against Slavs,
Magyars or Italians. The German nobles were
often in revolt; the emperors spent much of
their time suppressing rebellions by their
haughty subordinates. In 1046 something of a
high point was reached. Bohemia, Poland and
Magyar Hungary all acknowledged the
emperor as their overlord, while no Pope
could be selected without the express approval
of the emperor.

It did not take long for this supremacy to
crumble. The lengthy minority of Henry IV,
followed by renewed civil war among the Germans and the contest between Pope Gregory
and Henry over who appointed whom, almost
resulted in the collapse of the empire. His son,
Henry V, who had opposed his father in the

civil war, also battled until 1122 with a succession of Popes for control of the Papacy.

A new period of civil strife among the Germans followed, as the nobles twice selected
weak emperors who could not keep their most
powerful and ambitious subjects in line. In
1152 this situation ended with the election of
Frederick Hohenstaufen, known as Barbarossa (Redbeard). He was a ruthless man
imbued with the imperial idea, and he
enforced his rule throughout an empire disrupted by rebellion. However, Frederick's
imperial notions caused his downfall. He
proved faithless in his dealings with the Pope
and was defeated by a Papal army at Legnano
in 1176. This victory marked the end of Charlemagne's concept of an empire and Papacy
linked by common interest. No emperor was
willing to be the Pope's secular instrument,
and no Pope would constrain himself by too
close a relationship with a German emperor.
Barbarossa himself died in ironic circumstances: in 1190 he was drowned while on a
Crusade to Palestine.

THE HOLY ROMAN EMPIRE AT THE ACCESSION
OF FREDERICK BARBAROSSA, 1152

POMERANIA
LUBECK
SAXONY
MAGDEBURG
POLAND
COLOGNE
LOTHARINGIA
Rhine
MAINZ
BOHEMIA
FRANCONIA
MORAVIA
SWABIA
RATISBON
Danube
AUGSBERG
BAVARIA
FRANCE
FRIULI
HUNGARY
BURGUNDY
MILAN
KINGDOM OF ITALY
VENICE
Rhone
CORSICA
ROME
SARDINIA
KINGDOM
OF THE
TWO SICILIES
0 MILES 300
0 KILOMETERS 500
© Richard Natkiel, 1988

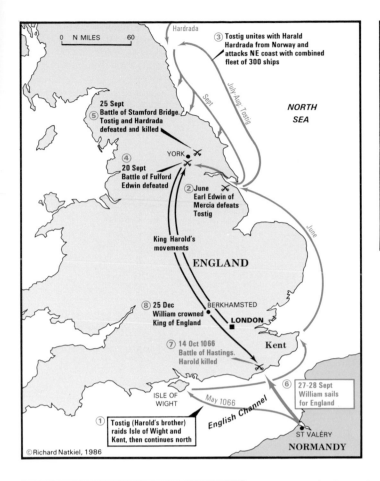

Map 1 (left):
- N MILES 0 — 60
- Hardrada
- ③ Tostig unites with Harald Hardrada from Norway and attacks NE coast with combined fleet of 300 ships
- NORTH SEA
- ⑤ 25 Sept Battle of Stamford Bridge. Tostig and Hardrada defeated and killed
- YORK
- ④ 20 Sept Battle of Fulford Edwin defeated
- ② June Earl Edwin of Mercia defeats Tostig
- July-Aug. Tostig
- Sept
- June
- King Harold's movements
- ENGLAND
- ⑧ 25 Dec William crowned King of England
- BERKHAMSTED
- LONDON
- ⑦ 14 Oct 1066 Battle of Hastings. Harold killed
- Kent
- ISLE OF WIGHT
- May 1066
- English Channel
- ⑥ 27-28 Sept William sails for England
- ① Tostig (Harold's brother) raids Isle of Wight and Kent, then continues north
- ST VALÉRY
- NORMANDY
- ©Richard Natkiel, 1986

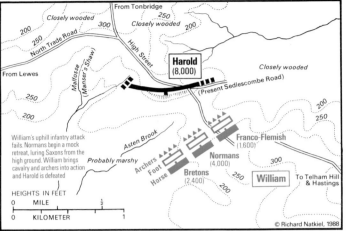

Map 2 (right):
- From Tonbridge
- Closely wooded
- North Trade Road
- High Street
- Harold (8,000)
- Closely wooded
- (Present Sedlescombe Road)
- From Lewes
- Malfosse (Manser's Shaw)
- Asten Brook
- Probably marshy
- Archers
- Foot
- Horse
- Bretons (2,400)
- Normans (4,000)
- Franco-Flemish (1,600)
- William
- To Telham Hill & Hastings
- William's uphill infantry attack fails. Normans begin a mock retreat, luring Saxons from the high ground. William brings cavalry and archers into action and Harold is defeated
- HEIGHTS IN FEET
- 0 MILE ½
- 0 KILOMETER 1
- © Richard Natkiel, 1988

The Norman Conquest of England

The death of Edward the Confessor in 1066 brought an end to the tranquillity established for the English kingdom. The venerated Saxon king had succeeded in holding the balance between Danish and Saxon elements in the realm. Edward was also related to the rulers of Normandy and in the early years of his reign had favored Norman advisers. Edward died childless and the problem of his succession was to prove difficult.

The most powerful English lord, Harold Godwinson, claimed he had been designated as successor by Edward before his death and this claim was supported by the customary election by the noble council or *witan*. Duke William of Normandy was also related to the dead king, however, and claimed that he had been promised the throne by Edward and that Harold had sworn to respect this claim. The Bayeux tapestry, a highly important source of information for the period, naturally casts Harold in the role of perjurer and usurper.

The problems for the new King Harold were complicated by the news that King Harald Hardrada of Norway was about to invade England with a force of 300 ships in alliance with Harold's half-brother Tostig. This forced Harold to act vigorously to defend the north.

Had King Harold won his campaign in 1066 it would be remembered as a masterly fight on two fronts, for he retrieved the defeat of Earl Edwin at Fulford on 20 September by a brilliant victory at Stamford Bridge. In the battle both Harald Hardrada and the rebellious Tostig were killed, leaving Harold free to lead his men on what must have been an exhausting forced march back to the south.

As Harold knew, the Duke of Normandy had been preparing to invade England since the spring, and the Norman fleet had finally sailed three days after the Battle of Stamford Bridge. Although he clearly had considerable powers of leadership and a disciplined army, Harold had insufficient ships to prevent the Norman army from crossing the English Channel, and so his brilliant victory in Yorkshire achieved nothing.

The Battle of Hastings on 14 October 1066 was a hard-fought affair but eventually the Norman superiority in mailed knights prevailed against Saxon infantry tactics, and the death of Harold finally decided the issue.

The long-term significance of the Norman Conquest was the severance of English links with northern Europe. In their place there were to be new links with French and Mediterranean culture. A token of this connection was the care Duke William took to receive the Pope's blessing for his claim. With the new alignment came new laws and a radical reconstruction of society. What might have happened if Harold and his Saxons had defeated the Normans is impossible to say, but the conquest of 1066 was to be the last successful invasion of the British Isles. An adequate navy might not have been able to defeat both the Norwegian and the Norman invasion fleets, but it might at least have prevented one of the landings for long enough to avoid Harold's campaign on two fronts.

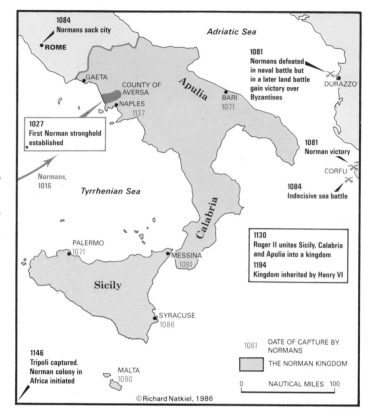

1084
Normans sack city
ROME

Adriatic Sea

1081
Normans defeated
in naval battle but
in a later land battle
gain victory over
Byzantines

DURAZZO

GAETA

COUNTY OF
AVERSA
NAPLES
1137

Apulia

BARI
1071

1027
First Norman stronghold
established

1081
Norman victory

CORFU

Normans,
1016

Tyrrhenian Sea

Calabria

1084
Indecisive sea battle

PALERMO
1071

MESSINA
1061

1130
Roger II unites Sicily, Calabria
and Apulia into a kingdom
1194
Kingdom inherited by Henry VI

Sicily

SYRACUSE
1086

1061   DATE OF CAPTURE BY
        NORMANS

1146
Tripoli captured.
Norman colony in
Africa initiated

MALTA
1090

THE NORMAN KINGDOM

0   NAUTICAL MILES   100

©Richard Natkiel, 1986

The Normans in Italy

The slow recovery of Europe from the anarchy and dislocation of the Dark Ages was helped by the development of feudal authority. Although rulers were in practice weaker than they might claim to be, they made frequent use of Roman law to uphold their claims. The king claimed his rights as 'liege lord' and in theory permitted all his tenants-in-chief to hold land in his name, in return for protection.

Apart from England, the outstanding example of the new theory of government in action was Sicily, which was also conquered by the Normans. Both countries were acquired by conquest, and so the native aristocracy was not too firmly entrenched to impede the imposition of feudal rule but the Normans were also adept at using the existing framework of laws and royal powers in their new territories.

Norman adventurers had established their first foothold north of Naples in 1027, when they carved out the County of Aversa. The most important Norman leaders were Robert Guiscard and his brothers of the remarkable Hauteville family. The fall of Bari and Palermo in 1071 gave them control of much of Apulia and Sicily and by 1081 the Normans were challenging the hitherto supreme power of the Byzantine navy. Like the Romans the Normans' prowess on land was little help to them against a well-trained navy, but their determination went far to redress the balance. Like the Romans they were also prepared to learn by their mistakes.

The campaign of 1061 was marked by an amphibious crossing of the Straits of Messina, with special horse-transports to carry their vital *destriers* or warhorses across the straits. As they learned to use seapower, doubtless with help from Italians and Greeks their gains increased: Palermo in 1071, Trapani in 1077, Taormina in 1079, Syracuse in 1086, Enna in 1087 and Noto in 1091. The fall of Noto marked the final conquest of the island, less then a century after the first appearance of Norman knights in Italy.

Robert Guiscard had earlier laid siege to Durazzo, and survived a defeat at the hands of the Byzantine navy to score a decisive victory over the Emperor Alexius Comnenus on land. With a view to overseas conquest Roger I, brother of Robert Guiscard, went on to take Malta in 1090, leaving his son Roger II to establish a colony on the coast of North Africa between Tunis and Tripoli.

The Norman achievements in Italy were outstanding. Small numbers of knights defeated large numbers of Italians, Greeks and Muslims again and again, by sheer military skill, using the novel shock tactics of charges by armored cavalry armed with the lance. What was equally important was the typically Norman skill in exploiting their military successes by dynastic marriages and sound government.

Above: William the Conqueror grants Richmond to one of his loyal followers, Alan Rufus.

The Decline of Byzantium

The Arabs' unsuccessful siege of Constantinople in 717-18 was a low point in the history of the Byzantine Empire. The once dominant eastern Mediterranean power was now hemmed in to the north by the barbarian Bulgars, and to the south and east by the energetic new Moslem caliphate. Fortunately for Byzantium the new emperor, Leo III, was an able ruler who campaigned against both Bulgars and Arabs. His signal victory over the latter at Akroinion in 739 won back much of Asia Minor. His son, Constantine V, carried the war to Syria in 746 and defeated an Arab fleet in 747 thus providing Byzantium a secure eastern frontier once again. Constantine defeated the Bulgars twice – in 763 and 773 – which gave the empire 30 years of relative peace. However, civil disorder within the empire – which usually revolved around the imperial succession – meant that Byzantium's enemies were always ready to take advantage of its weakness. In 781 and again in 806 there

were major Arab incursions into Asia Minor, and in 811 the Emperor Nikephoros I was killed fighting the Bulgars who went on to besiege Constantinople in 814 (the siege ended when their own king, Krum, died). Arabs gained control of parts of Crete in 827 and parts of Sicily in 831.

This steady erosion of Byzantine power was reversed in 867 when Basil I founded the Macedonian dynasty of emperors. He began by steadily reversing the advances the Arabs had made in Asia Minor. Under the reign of his son, Leo VI, the empire suffered some setbacks, notably a defeat at the hands of the Bulgars at Bulgarophygon in 896; furthermore, his son was a minor and a faction-ridden regency council now controlled the empire's destiny. Fortunately for Byzantium, the power of Bulgaria rested largely in the hands of one man: the Emperor Symeon, whose death in 927 diminished the Bulgarian threat.

The Moslem caliphs of Baghdad had been unable to take advantage of Byzantine weakness, and once the Bulgars ceased to menace them in the west, the Byzantines could resume their expansion to the east. By 944 Byzantine rule had returned to the cities of Upper Mesopotamia, and 20 years later they had regained

some of the cities of northern Syria. The return of Byzantium to the Middle East was capped by the recapture of the great city of Antioch in 969.

With the east strengthened, the Byzantines turned back to the Bulgars. In a series of wars the Bulgarians first lost their independence, and when they showed signs of national revival around 1000, they were crushed by Basil II. Bulgaria was fully incorporated into the empire in 1018. The Byzantine Empire was now supreme from the River Danube to the River Euphrates.

The empire soon tumbled from this peak, however. The army deteriorated as unreliable mercenaries came to be used in place of the steady regulars. In 1055 a buffer state between the empire and the expanding Seljuk Turks was annexed by the Byzantines. Ten years later the Turks took it from the Byzantines and pushed on into Asia Minor. Emperor Romanos IV assembled an army in 1071 to drive back the Turks, but he was totally defeated at Manzikert. This battle marked the end of Byzantine power in the Middle East, and Byzantium was embarked on a slow decline that would last almost 400 years, until the fall of Constantinople.

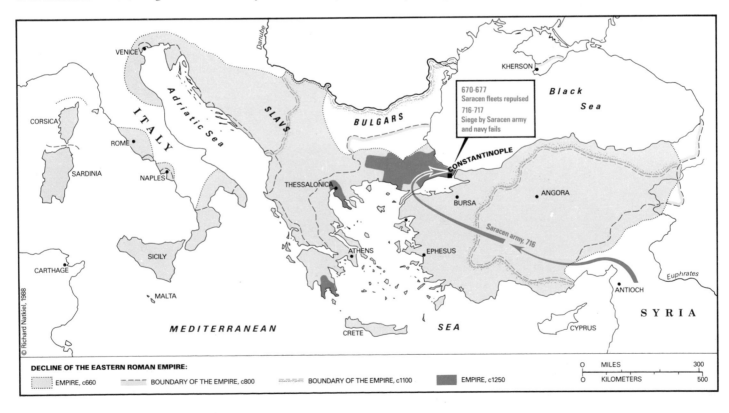

DECLINE OF THE EASTERN ROMAN EMPIRE:

EMPIRE, c660   BOUNDARY OF THE EMPIRE, c800   BOUNDARY OF THE EMPIRE, c1100   EMPIRE, c1250

MILES 300 · KILOMETERS 500

Left: Knights of the Holy Ghost embark for the Holy Land at the beginning of the Third Crusade.
Below right: a fourteenth century manuscript depicting the siege of Acre during the Third Crusade (1189-92).

The Crusades

The underlying causes of the Crusades were complex. Religious enthusiasm certainly played a part but other factors also contributed. Famine in Western Europe had made the populace restless, and this unrest went hand in hand with an acute shortage of land. We know, for example, that many of the keenest Crusaders were landless younger sons of the nobility. The Papacy was under threat from warring factions, and to distract the feud-ing nobles the chance to direct their bellicosity against Islam was understandably appealing.

In such a mixture of secular and religious motives the First Crusade was born. In 1095 at Clermont Pope Urban II preached the need for a Holy War to free the Holy Land from the infidel. Urban had received an appeal for help from the Byzantine Emperor Alexius, and although the schism between the Eastern and Western Churches had created a wide rift, there was considerable sympathy for what were still fellow-Christians.

Byzantium had long been the bulwark of Western civilization against inroads from the east, and while the west struggled to emerge from the Dark Ages the Byzantine Empire preserved much of the best of Greek and Roman civilization. Byzantium's great strength was its professional army and navy, but in 1071 at the Battle of Manzikert the army was totally destroyed by the Seljuk Turks.

The Imperial Army was painstakingly rebuilt but never again would the empire control the vast revenues or the prime recruiting areas lost after Manzikert. By 1096 when the first Crusaders arrived at Constantinople, the empire, although still rich and powerful, was a shadow of its former greatness.

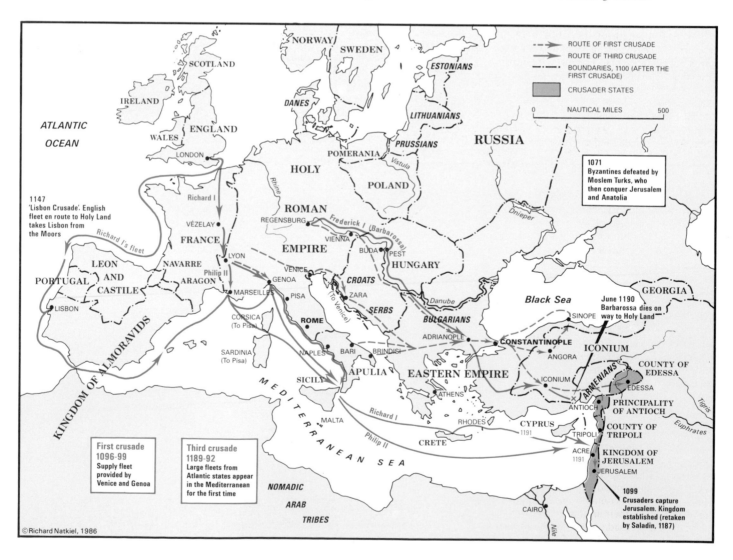

Fourth crusade 1202-04
Crusaders assemble in Venice, where they are promised transport in return for help in recapturing Zara, which is taken in 1202. Venice gains vital strongpoints in the Aegean

©Richard Natkiel, 1986

army landed at Constantinople in 1203 and then proceeded to capture and sack the ancient city in 1204. Quite apart from the treachery and the destruction of irreplaceable treasures, the sack of Constantinople meant the destruction of the inner defenses against the infidel. Nothing else did more to facilitate Turkish incursions into Europe, and the blame for such an act of idiocy by the Crusaders must rest on the shoulders of the cynical Venetians, whose prime concern was to eliminate Byzantium as a trade rival.

The perpetrators of the outrage did not prosper. An attempt to set up a Latin kingdom of Constantinople failed, and in 1261 with the help of the Genoese, enemies of the Venetians, the westerners were finally expelled by the native Greeks.

The great strength of the Crusaders was their armored cavalry, the Frankish and Norman knights whose mail was virtually impervious to Turkish bows. However their *destriers* or warhorses needed to be transported in considerable numbers, and to achieve this *huissiers* or horse transports were used to move them by sea.

The First Crusade (and the far less successful Second Crusade of 1147-49) showed that the land route to Palestine was all but impossible. A huge host of pilgrims and soldiery trekked through Asia Minor, beating off a Turkish attack at Dorylaeum before reaching Antioch. With the aid of Venetian and Pisan fleets it was possible to keep this army supplied, and after capturing Antioch the Crusaders went on to besiege and capture the city of Jerusalem in 1099.

The Crusaders remained in control of the Holy City until 1187, when a united Islamic army under Saladin destroyed the Christian army at Hattin and captured Jerusalem. In response the Third Crusade was launched under the joint leadership of the three most important rulers in Europe, Frederick Barbarossa of Germany, Philip Augustus of France and Richard the Lionheart of England. Frederick died on the way to the Holy Land and Philip and Richard effectively frustrated the aims of the campaign by quarreling but Richard's leadership gained an important land victory at Arsuf. Even more important in the long run was his capture of Cyprus in 1191, which gave the Crusaders a strategic base, without which they could not have supported the operations of their armies in Palestine.

The Fourth Crusade was a hideous fiasco. Backed by Venice, an ill-disciplined western

The struggle between Venice and Genoa

The European economy and society had suffered greatly from 'barbarian' incursions by peoples from the east and the Vikings from the north during the long Dark Ages. The repulse of one such group from the east, the Magyars, at the Battle of the Lech in 955 by the German king and later Holy Roman Emperor Otto I is often taken as a convenient date to mark the beginning of the recovery of Europe from the long period of destruction and economic ruin that had gone before. From then until the early fourteenth century the European economy made a remarkable recovery.

Venice had clearly emerged as an important trade center during the ninth century, though her trade often suffered from piracy in the Adriatic. By 1000 Pisa and Genoa were also recovering from the Moslem attacks of previous times. The involvement of the Italian cities in the Crusades and the related conflicts with the Byzantine Empire have been discussed earlier, but these were only a small part of the increase in more peaceful contacts between the Christian and Moslem worlds.

Venice had become established as the leading seapower in the Adriatic but the competition of the maritime republics of Pisa and Genoa was obviously unwelcome. As things turned out it was only Genoa which Venice had to fear for in 1284 Genoa eliminated her weaker rival Pisa at the Battle of Meloria. In any case Pisa's harbor was becoming silted up and her strength was being sapped by internal squabbles which hastened her decline. Both Venice and Genoa were battling for access to the rich markets of the Levant and what remained of the Byzantine Empire.

The first major war between the two maritime republics broke out in 1253. None of the battles proved decisive but the Genoese lost ground and were forced to surrender the Levantine trade to the Venetians. In compensation, however, they gained the Black Sea trade under a special treaty with the Byzantines. In the second war, which began in 1293 the Genoese gained a handsome revenge. Their admiral Lamba Doria beat the Venetian fleet at the Battle of Curzola Island in 1298. The peace treaty signed the following year gave Genoa a virtual monopoly of the Black Sea trade, while leaving Venice to concentrate on the trade with Alexandria.

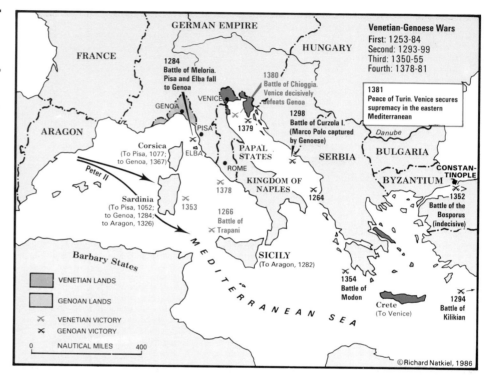

The rivalry continued on a purely commercial level until 1350, when Genoese attempts to secure their grip on the Levant trade led to another outbreak of hostilities. The Venetians suffered a reverse at the Dardanelles but in 1353 they crushed the Genoese at the Battle of La Loiera, off the coast of Sardinia. However, the Battle of Modon, fought off the southwestern coast of Greece in 1354, gave the Genoese a free hand in the Mediterranean. Under Luciano Doria they attacked the Venetians lying at anchor off the island of Sapienza, and 12 Genoese galleys worked their way behind the Venetians to attack them from the rear. But in spite of the sweeping victories of their enemies the Venetians struck a good bargain when the peace was signed in 1355.

The fourth and most decisive war broke out in 1378, when both republics laid claim to the island of Tenedos in the Aegean (modern Bozcaada). Venice had received the island from Byzantium.

The Venetian admiral Vettor Pisani won the first battle in the Tyrrhenian Sea, but the Genoese defeated Pisani the following year at Pola (now Pula in Yugoslavia). In revenge for the death of Luciano Doria the infuriated Genoese butchered many of the 1000 prisoners.

Following up their victory the Genoese under Pietro Doria captured the island of Chioggia south of Venice. With this strategic foothold they were in a position to strangle Venetian sea trade, and when Venice offered peace terms the Genoese countered by demanding unconditional surrender.

Faced with the threat of extinction Venice reacted vigorously. Vettor Pisani was released from prison, and he immediately blocked the channels leading into the lagoon, cutting off Chioggia from reinforcement. The Venetians were still too weak to capture Chioggia until their Levant fleet returned. The safe arrival of this fleet forced a Genoese relief expedition to turn back, and left the garrison isolated. As soon as the Venetians had built up their strength they laid siege to the island and its garrison was forced to surrender in 1380.

Both sides were willing to negotiate now, having been exhausted by the three year war. At the Peace of Turin in 1381 Venice sacrificed some mainland territories but remained strong, whereas Genoa was largely ruined. The defeat at Chioggia marked the start of her decline and by the end of the fourteenth century she had become a vassal of France. Venice was now the leading maritime power in the Mediterranean, a position she did not relinquish until the end of the following century, when confronted by the expansion of the Ottoman Empire.

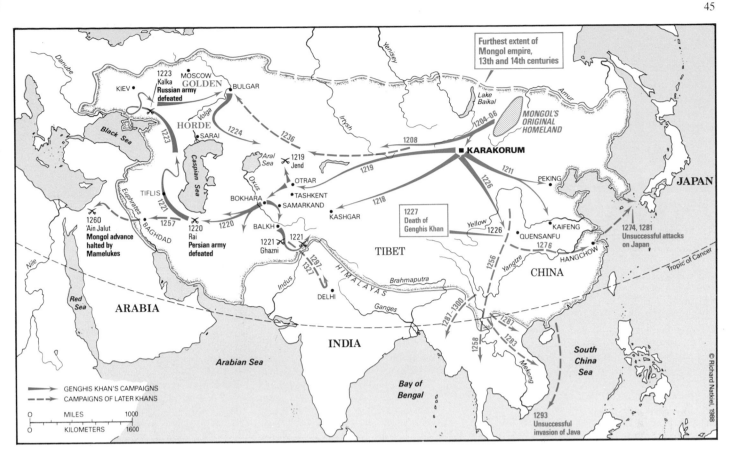

The Mongols in Europe and Asia

At the beginning of the thirteenth century, there arose, quite suddenly, the first major threat to the civilized societies of the Eurasian landmass for 700 years. In 1206 one of the many nomadic tribes which inhabited the Asian steppes to the north of China gained a precarious leadership over their neighbors. They were the Mongols led by Temüchin, who now became Khan with the title Genghis.

Genghis seems to have been determined to end the cutthroat feuding characteristic of his people, which was stimulated by Chinese gold and guile. He began a series of raids against the Chin dynasty of northern China. First he led his hordes of cavalry south against the buffer state of Hsi Hsia which soon submitted. Two years later, in 1208, he began a long-term campaign to subjugate the Chins which culminated in 1215 with the sack of their old capital of Khanbalik near present-day Peking.

Genghis now turned west. He left a part of his army under the command of one of his generals to continue campaigning in China. Genghis himself waged war against the empire of Karakitai, ruled by a Mongol who had earlier fled from Genghis' rule. Karakitai was conquered in 1218, which brought the Mongol realm to the borders of the Moslem state of Khwarezm. The Shah of Khwarezm wanted nothing to do with his new neighbor, and broke a Mongol taboo when he ordered the beards of two ambassadors from Genghis

Khan to be shaved off. After this and other more grave insults, Genghis and his men invaded Khwarezm in 1219. The Shah proved an inept general, despite his reputation and large army. After he was beaten at Jend he never took the field again. In four years the huge expanse of Khwarezm territory was

turned into a new part of the Mongol Empire. Genghis returned to Mongolia through Karakitai, while his army marched through the Caucasus mountains and around the shores of the Caspian Sea.

In 1227 during another successful campaign against Hsi Hsia, Genghis died. His second

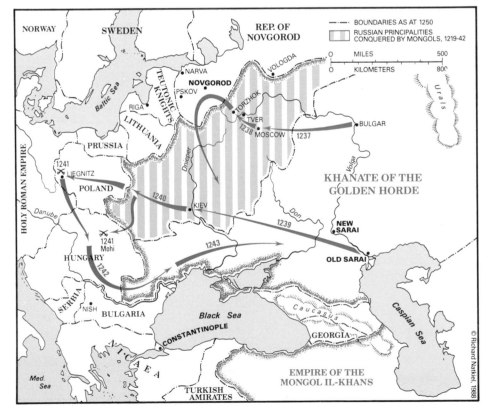

Left: dismounted Mongol horse-archers do battle with an oriental foe. The Mongols were adept at living off the land and, mounted on hardy ponies, were able to outpace most of their enemies when on campaign.

son, Ögödei, was proclaimed Khan in 1229 and a new series of Mongol conquests began. The Chin dynasty was finally destroyed in 1234, and the Mongols once again turned west. Between 1237 and 1240 they terrorized southern and central Russia and forced the Russian princes to pay tribute. In 1241 the Mongols pushed into Europe, where they threatened to absorb much of its eastern part into their empire. The death of Ögödei that year and the defeat at Liegnitz brought a temporary halt to their campaigns, as the scattered Mongol forces returned home to acclaim a new Khan.

For the first time since 1206 there was an unsettled succession, and a new Khan, Güyük, was not chosen until 1246. Güyük died two years later, before he had a chance to launch any new conquering expeditions. There was a brief regency before Möngke became Khan in 1251. He began Mongol attempts to conquer the southern Sung Empire south of the Yangtze in China. He also ordered his brother, Hülegü, to attack the Moslem states of the Middle East. Hülegü was at first very successful – he captured Baghdad and destroyed the 500-year-old 'Abbasid Caliphate in 1257. But he was defeated by the Mameluke forces from Egypt in 1260 at 'Ain

Jalut, an event marking the end of Mongol expansion in Europe and western Asia.

Khan Möngke's death in 1259 sparked off conflict between rival factions in the Mongol Empire, and the direct authority of the Khans remained intact only in the Far East. Kublai Khan finally succeeded in eliminating his rivals, and started on a long and bitter struggle against the Chinese Sung Empire. Kublai Khan finally triumphed in this struggle in 1279.

Japan was an independent country, and from the seventh century had been ruled by a centralized monarchy based on Chinese institutions. By the thirteenth century the Hojo Dynasty was in power, and under their rule cultural institutions as well as military skills flourished. Zen Buddhism was in the ascendant, particularly among the members of the new warrior nobility.

Japanese institutions were to be subjected to the most severe of tests. In November 1274 Kublai Khan launched a huge invasion force against the southern island of Kyushu. Using Korean sailors and auxiliary troops to reinforce his 15,000 Mongol soldiers, the Khan set sail for Kyushu from Korea. The attackers passed southwest of Ikishima and encountered fierce opposition when they tried to land. Bad weather and a lack of arms forced the Mongols to retire at the end of the month, but the Khan was determined to achieve victory.

In 1276 the Japanese started a five-year program to fortify Hakata Bay, building stone ramparts to foil another Mongol attempt to land. Kublai Khan took far greater pains for his next attempt, assembling 50,000 Mongol and Korean troops in Korea, with an even larger force of 100,000 troops in southern China. The two invasion forces sailed in June 1281, and the Korean force landed first, on 23 June. Fierce fighting on the shores of Hakata Bay lasted nearly two months, and under sheer weight of numbers the Japanese began to give ground.

Just when the battle seemed lost a great storm blew up, wrecking the Mongol fleet. The Japanese, convinced that the gods were at last on their side, counterattacked and inflicted great loss on the invaders. The storm was named kamikaze or 'Divine Wind,' and became a major element in Japanese folklore.

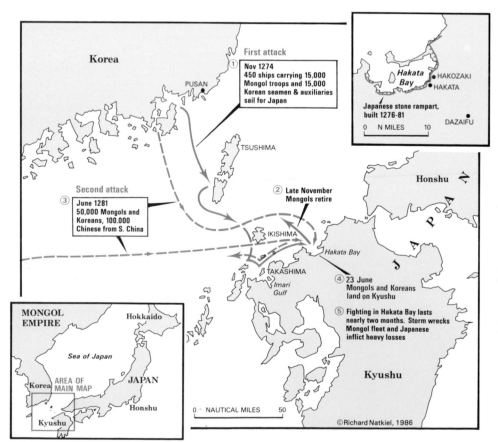

First attack
① Nov 1274
450 ships carrying 15,000 Mongol troops and 15,000 Korean seamen & auxiliaries sail for Japan

Japanese stone rampart, built 1276-81

Second attack
③ June 1281
50,000 Mongols and Koreans, 100,000 Chinese from S. China

② Late November Mongols retire

④ 23 June Mongols and Koreans land on Kyushu

⑤ Fighting in Hakata Bay lasts nearly two months. Storm wrecks Mongol fleet and Japanese inflict heavy losses

©Richard Natkiel, 1986

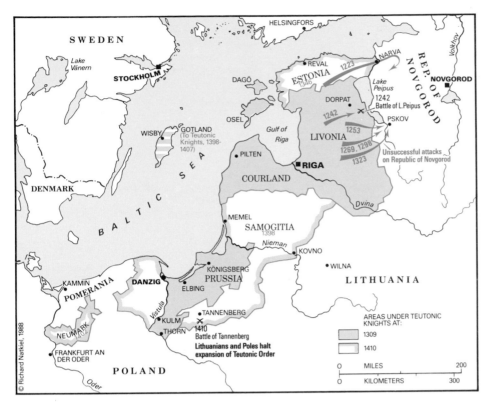

Below: knights of the Teutonic Order battle with Polish and Lithuanian adversaries. Only their defeat at Tannenburg in 1410, ended the knights' ambitions in eastern Europe.

The Teutonic Knights

Although originally founded as a Hospital Order around 1128, the Germanic Teutonic Knights had developed into a military order by the end of the century. The Fifth Crusade (1217-22) and Emperor Frederick II's recovery of Jerusalem in 1228 increased German involvement in the Holy Land. Acre was the seat of the Grand Master and Montfort the Knights' chief castle. But Hermann von Salza (1210-39), a Grand Master, was already convinced that the Christian presence in the Holy Land could not be maintained, and he looked to crusade elsewhere.

The pagan Slav lands which Germans had been colonizing for several centuries presented just such an opportunity. Following an appeal by Christian, the first Bishop of Prussia, and Conrad, Duke of Masovia, in 1226, the Knights established a base at Kulm (1232) in western Prussia; Elbing and Marienwerder followed in 1237. In that year the Knights absorbed the Order of the Sword Brothers founded by the Bishop of Riga in 1200, bringing Livonia and Courland under their control. They also established themselves at Königsberg in 1255.

Meanwhile, as predicted, the Holy Land was lost to the Mamelukes, the city of Acre being the last Christian base to fall in 1291. The Knights accordingly shifted their seat to Marienberg (1309) where they constructed palatial fortifications. Such a process of rapid expansion attracted the enmity of neighboring princes. Alexander Nevsky defined the eastern border of the Ordensland by defeating the Knights at Lake Peipus in 1242, but during the fourteenth century, the Order established some 1400 villages and 93 towns on its ever-expanding lands. Under Winrich von Kniprode (1351-82) the Teutonic Knights reached the zenith of their power.

Poland had been cut off from the Baltic by the Knights' activities, and her rulers sought to win access to the coast and a port. In 1386, Jagiello of Lithuania became King of Poland through a dynastic marriage, and the Order found itself outmatched. Manpower for its expeditions depended heavily upon the annual arrival of visiting Crusaders. The Knights strove to attract such recruits for these reasons. A famous visitor in 1390 was Henry Bolingbroke, Duke of Lancaster (and later King of England). His expedition cost almost £5000 to mount; as much as the Order spent annually on maintaining its island province of Gotland. Such lords were encouraged by the creation of the Table of Honor at which chivalrous deeds were celebrated in memory of King Arthur.

The military resources of the Order were quite formidable in 1400: 426 Brother Knights, almost 6000 sergeants, and a similar number of infantry – half provided by the six main towns and from the abbeys. Despite their strength, the Knights were crushingly defeated by the Poles at Tannenberg in 1410. They were allowed to keep their lands, but were beaten again at Puck in 1462. This time King Casimir demanded Pomerania and access to the Baltic. The Knights were forced to accept the suzerainty of Poland.

England's Welsh and Scottish Wars

Although the Norman Conquest had given new impetus to expansion on England's Welsh border, progress had been piecemeal. This was a result of the policy of leaving any territorial incursions to the great Marcher lords such as the Clares and Mortimers. The thirteenth century saw a revival of native Welsh power, notably through the rulers of Gwynedd. In 1267, Henry III was forced to acknowledge Llywelyn ap Gruffud as 'Prince of Wales.' When Llywelyn refused to pay homage to Henry's more warlike son in 1277, Edward I determined on a campaign to bring Wales to heel.

He deployed a large army of perhaps 1000 knights and 15,000 infantry. While the King's army advanced on a northern route, other forces made thrusts into Cardiganshire and against Llywelyn's main forces in central Wales. These subsidiary attacks reduced the area still resisting to the mountainous heartland of Gwynedd alone. Aware that Llywelyn dare not face him in the field, and wary of a guerrilla campaign, Edward cut the Welsh supply line. While his army advanced along the north coast, a fleet raised from the Cinque Ports attacked Anglesey and captured Llywelyn's entire grain supply. He quickly came to the king's new castle at Rhuddlan to proffer his surrender. The Welsh did not remain quiet for long, however, and stung by widespread pillaging raids, Edward returned in 1282. First, he had to relieve besieged Flint and Rhuddlan. Then Llywelyn refused battle, convincing the king that the struggle would be a long affair. Luckily for Edward, Llywelyn's death in a skirmish in the winter of 1282 brought the revolt to an end.

Edward's castle-building policy was designed to ensure that there should be no repetition. Eight royal castles were constructed: Harlech (1283-95), Beaumaris (during the 1294-95 rebellion and not completed), Builth (in central Wales), Caernarvon (1283-92, completed 1296-1323), Rhuddlan (1277-82), Flint (1277-86), Conway (1283-87) and Aberystwyth – the last five being integrated with fortified towns. The speed and size of the program of fortification was unparalleled. Edward spent £80,000 in 25 years (£27,000 on Caernarvon alone). In addition, his great subjects contributed their own

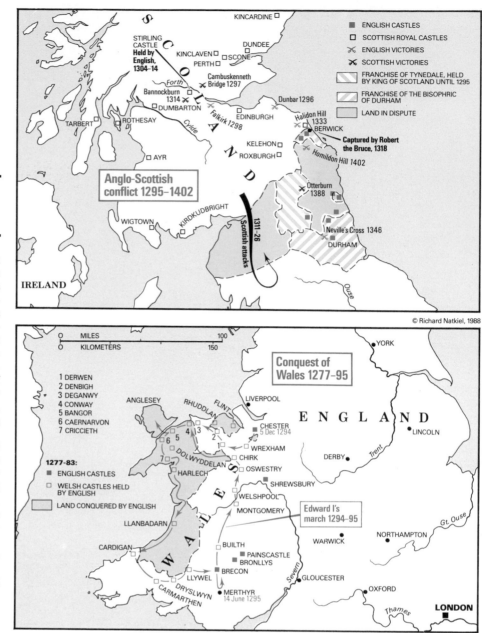

© Richard Natkiel, 1988

private castles, such as Kidwelly or the Clare stronghold of Caerphilly. By these means English rule was riveted on the land.

In 1296, Edward transferred his attention to Scotland. A successional dispute gave him the opportunity to intervene on behalf of John Baliol, his candidate. The English army was now a formidable combination of mounted knights and archers (many of them Welsh). Properly used, this was to prove an invincible weapon in battle.

The important fortress of Berwick fell swiftly to Edward's veterans. When the Scots offered battle at Dunbar, the English archers, under the Earl of Surrey, simply shot their impetuous charge to pieces, capturing many great lords. The issue seemingly decided, Edward returned south; but he had reckoned without William Wallace. Humbly born, he showed great understanding of guerrilla tactics. In the following year his small army inflicted a serious defeat on Surrey at Cam-

buskenneth Bridge near Stirling castle. In fact this was due to John de Warenne's stupidity in allowing part of his force to cross the bridge, whereupon they were cut off and slaughtered. With Scotland now up in arms, Edward's presence was once again required.

He returned with a huge force of 2400 knights and four to five times as many foot. Wallace pursued a scorched-earth policy which was almost successful, but he finally offered battle to the starving English at Falkirk in 1298. Scots armies of the period were largely made up of masses of unarmored spearmen, drawn up in tight-packed 'schiltrons' which were impervious to cavalry charges, as Edward's impetuous knights soon found out. But the king knew how to employ his archers to murderous effect; and they quickly made gaps into which the knights poured to slaughter and rout the tightly packed 'schiltrons' of the Scots.

Despite this victory, the hit-and-run tactics

49

dispute with Henry IV over the payment of a large ransom.

The last act of the Welsh wars was fought out against the background of the usurpation of the throne by Henry Bolingbroke in 1399. Owain Glyndwr's rebellion expressed the resentment felt by the Welsh against English colonization. He had grandiose schemes for a tripartite division of the kingdom with the Earl of Northumberland. But Glyndwr was incapable of launching more than small cross-border raids (1400-05), destructive though these were. In 1403 Northumberland's son, Henry 'Hotspur,' was killed at the Battle of Shrewsbury before Glyndwr could join up with him. In 1405 a French expedition landed at Milford Haven in southern Wales, providing another opportunity to challenge Henry IV, but the combined forces retreated before the king at Worcester. The French soon withdrew and Glyndwr's influence faded away, allowing the English to complete their total conquest of Wales.

employed by the Scottish leaders meant that Edward's later campaigns, although impressive, were largely without result. Wallace was betrayed in 1305, to be replaced by the far greater Robert Bruce. He was crowned in March 1306, and despite suffering defeat in the field later that same year, the harshness of the English repression that followed won him wide support.

Edward I died in 1307 and his son, Edward II, lacked both his determination and military competence. He did not pursue the war with vigor, and Bruce was able to capture many fortresses and raid into England. Finally, with Stirling castle threatened, Edward II took up the challenge and met the Scots in a two-day battle at Bannockburn in June 1314. On the first day the large English army was unable to get at the Scots behind their defenses of streams, marshes and pits. When his forces were able to cross the barriers the next day, Edward failed to deploy his men properly. His knights impaled themselves on the advancing 'schiltrons,' while his archers were struck in the flank by the Scottish cavalry and cut down.

Robert Bruce lived until 1321, and during the period from Bannockburn, the English faced a series of devastating border raids. In 1332, a small force of 'disinherited' nobles, led by Edward Baliol (son of John) invaded Scotland without Edward III's support. His force met the Scots at Duplin Muir and massacred them. The following year King Edward again used the firepower of English archers to rout another Scottish army at Halidon Hill, forcing young King David to flee abroad.

Soon the Scottish wars became just a part of the wider conflict between England and France. In 1346, King David invaded northern England as a French ally. At Neville's Cross, the English archers did their work once more and David was captured, to spend 11 years in the Tower of London. In 1388, another

Franco-Scottish invasion was halted at Otterburn, after a surprise attack by Henry Percy, Duke of Northumberland. As a result Richard II handed over authority in the region to the Marcher lords, an act that was to have repercussions in the following reign. In fact, another Percy victory over a Scottish raiding force at Homildon Hill in 1402 led to a bitter

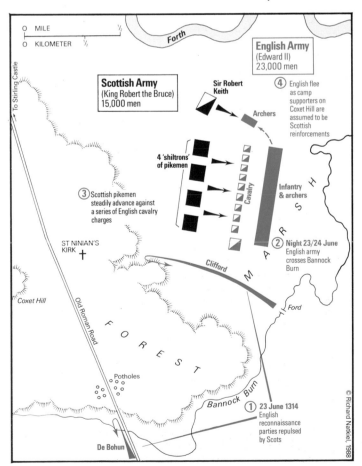

Center right: English longbowmen repulse a
French charge at Poitiers.
Far right: Edward III's great victory at
Crécy in 1346.

The Hundred Years War

The name given to the series of conflicts between England and France from 1337 to 1453 is
rather misleading, and suggests a continuity of
warfare and policy that was often lacking.
While Edward III claimed the French crown
for a while, his wars were essentially designed
to maintain control of valuable Gascony in
southwest France. In contrast, only Henry V's
early death denied him the French throne. Between the two periods of striking English success, 1340-56 and 1415-28, the French regained
much ground, both moral and physical. Similarly, the weak leadership of Henry VI, combined with a French revival, set the English a
hopeless task after the mid-1440s.

The first war was fought over the possession
of Gascony. King John of England had
retained the region while losing Normandy,
and Henry III had only narrowly hung on to it
in 1259. Edward I had been prepared to spend
money on its defense in the 1290s, and by the
time of Edward III the English crown
depended on its revenues from the wine trade.
Edward did homage for Gascony in 1328, but
in 1337 Philip VI declared the territory con-
fiscated. Edward's first response was an inconclusive campaign in Flanders during 1339-40.
The naval victory of Sluys (1340) proved a
pointer to later events, however. Although a
sea battle, it was fought like a land action, and
the English archers and men-at-arms completely overwhelmed the French, capturing
three-quarters of their fleet. One of the best
French strategies – raids on the southern coast
of England – was prevented for two decades.

On land the main English strategy was one
of *chevauchée*, literally a ride through enemy
territory, burning and plundering, to under-
mine the political authority and control of an
opponent. It was on such an expedition in 1346
that Edward III was forced to fight the Battle
of Crécy in August. He had only got his forces
across the river barriers of the Seine and the
Somme with great difficulty, and his small
force was heavily outnumbered. Fortunately
for the English they had their bowmen to
defend a strong position. Unfortunately for
the French, Philip had no plan of attack or
control over his lords and their retinues. In a
score of brave but futile charges, the flower of
French chivalry was mown down. As a result
Edward was able to take Calais after a year-

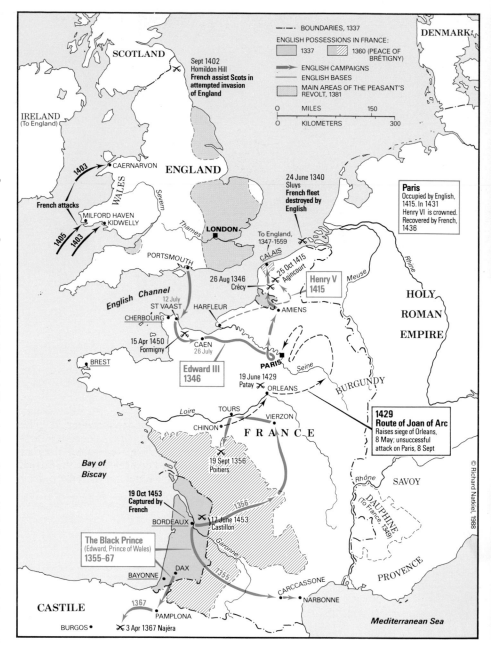

long siege, no relieving force daring to challenge him.

The same strategy led to the Battle of
Poitiers in 1356. The previous year, Edward
the Black Prince had led a *chevauchée* southeast from Bordeaux, burning Carccassone and
Narbonne and reaching the Mediterranean.
He now planned a similar raid north to the
Loire. But the recently crowned King John
was determined to prevent such damaging
incursions. Gathering a large force he pursued
the English on their way back to Bordeaux,
forcing them to turn and fight near Poitiers in
September. The Black Prince, heavily outnumbered, took up a defensive position. The
French came on in three lines. The first
mounted assault was easily shot down. Then
the second division approached dismounted
and engaged in hand-to-hand combat.
Edward was hard pressed but in a lull
launched a counterattack, mounting his men
and delivering a flank charge (led by the Cap-

tal de Buch) simultaneously. Owing to the
defection of the third French division this desperate throw was astoundingly successful. The
king was among 1500 French lords captured in
the ensuing rout.•The Treaty of Brétigny in
1360 confirmed English control of Gascony.

The 1360s saw the appearance of Bertrand
du Guesclin, who rose from poverty to
become Constable of France. A great tactician, he won a battle at Cocherel in 1364 with a
feigned flight and flank attack to negate the
English archers. He was captured attempting
to relieve the siege of Auray later in the year,
when the archers did their work. Ransomed,
he next confronted the English under the
Black Prince in Spain at Nájera (1367). France
and England were supporting rivals for the
throne of Castile in order to win the help of the
kingdom's fleet. Despite du Guesclin's words
of caution, his allies insisted on a headlong
charge which met with inevitable disaster in
the face of English archery. The Cor

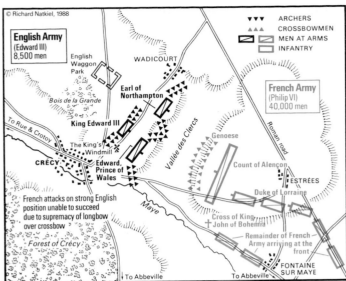

normal strategy was more cautious, however. He believed in a war of harassment since the English held the ace in any pitched battle. This new approach was very successful.

The English persisted with *chevauchée* but with declining effect. Sir John Chandos' raid of 1369 achieved little in the face of well-disciplined opponents who picked off stragglers rather than engaging in battle. Sir Robert Knowles' expedition in the following year ended in utter confusion: his rearguard was overrun as he escaped into Brittany. Also, owing to the eventual success of the French

**Below: a medieval interpretation of Crécy.
Below right: the Battle of Poitiers, 1356.**

candidate in Castile, they won the naval battle of La Rochelle in 1372, causing that port and Poitiers to surrender in the same year.

The English war effort was running out of steam and their great leaders were departing. Sir John Chandos, architect of Crécy, was killed in 1369. Jean de Grailly, Captal de Buch, was captured and refused ransom in 1372. Edward III was in his dotage and the Black Prince mortally ill – both died in 1376. John of Gaunt's ambitious *chevauchée* from Calais to Bordeaux achieved its objective, but with his army in a bedraggled state, the French could count it as a victory. Indeed there was a truce from 1375 to 1383. France's Charles V held the upper hand. He planned an invasion of England in 1386, only to have it blocked by the French naval defeat off Margate the following year. Both sides were exhausted and

England's Richard II, who had provided little leadership, made a 28-year truce in 1396. The deposition of Richard in 1399, and the subsequent troubles of Henry IV's early years, left England the weaker party. Between 1401 and 1405 French expeditions burned ports along the south coast and landed in Wales.

Henry V's invasion of 1415 was the first English attack on France for a generation – but was not well planned. The small town of Harfleur put up such a resistance that Henry's *chevauchée* to Calais was reduced to a dash across country in foul weather. In fact, the French were so well prepared that Henry was only able to cross the Somme by desperate marching. Henry's wet, hungry and sick forces were pinned at Agincourt in October by an army at least four times their number. Once again, however, French overconfidence led to

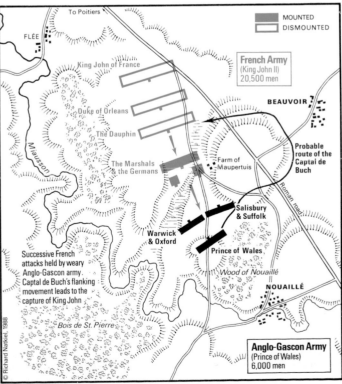

Left: Henry V of England overcomes a French lord at Agincourt. Despite odds of at least four-to-one, the English inflicted a devastating defeat on the French nobility. Below: the Battle of Agincourt in 1415.

their downfall. Their vast superiority in men was turned against them. Attacking on a narrow front, and scarcely able to wield their weapons, they were shot down by the fire of the English archers.

One reason for the French defeat was disputes between their leaders which arose because Charles VI was mentally unstable and incapable of ruling. The situation worsened as the Armagnac faction of those nobles fighting for power murdered their chief opponent, John the Fearless of Burgundy, during a parley in 1419. This gave the English a Burgundian alliance, and Henry gained the regency at the Treaty of Troyes in 1420. He swiftly conquered Normandy (the first time it had been in English hands since 1204) and, after Henry's death in 1422, the French Dauphin, Charles, was restricted to a 'kingdom' south of the River Loire.

Henry's brother, the Duke of Bedford, continued the king's work during the minority of Henry VI. He won battles at Verneuil ('a second Agincourt') in 1424 and near Avranches in 1426. In 1428 he commenced the siege of Orleans, a strongly defended city and the symbol of France's last hope. The tide turned with the emergence of the charismatic Joan of Arc (combined with some shrewd tactics by the French commander), who saved Orleans in July 1429. Within a week the English had been beaten at Patay by a vigorous flank attack and their commanders Talbot and Fastolf captured. Although Joan's star quickly waned (she was captured and burnt as a witch in 1431), she lived to see Charles VII crowned at Rheims. He proved to be a wily operator. With the Peace of Arras in 1435 France resumed the Burgundian alliance to considerable advantage.

After the death of the Duke of Bedford (1435), Sir John Talbot (Earl of Shrewsbury from 1442) fought hardest to preserve England's possessions. But in 1436, de Richemont recovered Paris. Charles reorganized his army with advice from the Bureau brothers, artillery experts. The war was now costing England dear. Henry VI's marriage to Margaret of Anjou, Charles' niece, brought long-term problems and no short-term gains. The French invaded Normandy with three co-ordinated columns in 1449 and were dramatically successful, the duchy falling within a year. De Richemont and Clermont combined to defeat Sir Thomas Kyriell's small force at Formigny in April 1450. The city of Caen fell soon afterward and resistance in Normandy was ended.

Henry VI's weak government did little. Only Talbot hung on in Gascony. In 1453, he attacked one Bureau at Castillon. The old scenario was now reversed. The French now stood on the defensive, well entrenched with artillery, while the English attempted to attack in column. The result was dramatic: an English defeat which was made worse by the death of the Earl of Shrewsbury. Bordeaux itself now fell, ending 300 years of English rule in Gascony. In the northwest only Calais remained of Henry V's wide dominions of a generation earlier.

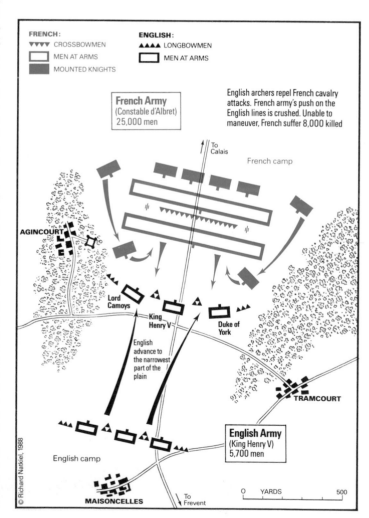

FRENCH:
▼▼▼▼ CROSSBOWMEN
▭ MEN AT ARMS
▬ MOUNTED KNIGHTS

ENGLISH:
▲▲▲▲ LONGBOWMEN
▭ MEN AT ARMS

French Army
(Constable d'Albret)
25,000 men

English archers repel French cavalry attacks. French army's push on the English lines is crushed. Unable to maneuver, French suffer 8,000 killed

To Calais
French camp

AGINCOURT

Lord Camoys

King Henry V

Duke of York

English advance to the narrowest part of the plain

TRAMCOURT

English Army
(King Henry V)
5,700 men

English camp

MAISONCELLES

To Frevent

© Richard Natkiel, 1988

0   YARDS   500

Below right: Swiss infantry (right) in action against dismounted Austrian knights at Sempach. Highly motivated and ruthless, the Swiss set new standards of battlefield efficiency in early Renaissance warfare.

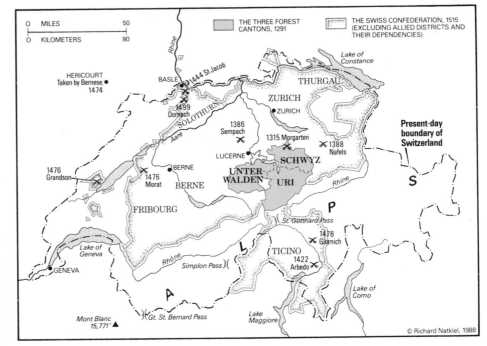

The Rise of Switzerland

In 1291, the Forest Cantons of Uri, Schwyz and Unterwalden formed an 'Everlasting League.' Two centuries later the Swiss Confederation was 13 cantons strong, and its soldiers the most feared in Europe. With armies composed almost entirely of infantry, the Swiss humbled the chivalry of the greatest princes of the age. The Swiss first came to prominence after routing an Austrian invasion force at Morgarten in 1315. Eight thousand men, one-third cavalry, were opposed by only 1500 Swiss. Ambushing the Austrians in a narrow pass and then throwing them into confusion by rolling trees and boulders among them, the Swiss made a vigorous downhill charge and won a remarkable victory. At Laupen in 1339, some 6000 Swiss took on twice their number of Burgundians and allies in an attempt to raise the siege of that city. The Bernese dealt swiftly with the Burgundian foot, but the Forest Cantons suffered under the attacks of enemy knights until the victorious wing of their army came to their aid.

The evident success of this policy of collective self-defense led to greater unification during the fourteenth century when Lucerne (1332), Zurich (1351), Zug and Glarus (1352) and Berne (1352) joined the Confederation. The war against Austria continued – with the Swiss winning independence by 1394. At Sempach in 1386, Austria's Leopold III dismounted his knights when he faced the Swiss. This tactic was almost successful and his armored men drove back the lightly equipped and numerically inferior Swiss. But as the Austrians tired and gaps appeared in their ranks, the Swiss counterattacked and slaughtered them piecemeal.

Swiss strategy was essentially defensive. The Battles of Nafels (1388), Voegelinsegg (1403) and Stoss (1405) were won by the employment of earthworks and palisades to protect the Swiss infantry and as a trap for attackers. The Swiss at this time were chiefly equipped with halberds and other polearms; fire support was mainly provided by crossbowmen. The Swiss did not take up the pike, the weapon for which they are best remembered, until after 1422. This was a result of the Battle of Arbedo in which a small expeditionary force was surrounded by Milanese troops and badly mauled. Even then the proportion of pikes to other arms hardly exceeded one quarter to a third. But the use of swiftly moving, deep columns, flanked by halberdiers and supported by fire from crossbows and handguns, gave the Swiss a decisive tactical advantage over their contemporaries.

In 1476, came the greatest challenge yet. Charles the Bold, Duke of Burgundy, possessed a large, well-equipped army, containing English archers and the most up-to-date field artillery, which he turned against the Swiss. At the Battle of Grandson in March, he was unable to use his cavalry in flank charges and his force was routed, losing all its guns. In June Charles was back, besieging Murten. He had laid out a killing-ground, made up of field-defenses for his archers and artillery, for the enemy infantry columns. But Swiss discipline and tactical flexibility turned the tables with a surprise attack, and Charles lost another army. Finally, in January of the following year he lost his life at Nancy. In a hard-fought encounter his men broke and he was killed in the rout. The Swiss again proved their supremacy by defeating the Emperor Maximilian at Dornach in 1499. In response Maximilian built up his own force of pikemen: the *landsknechts*. The pike was to dominate battlefields for much of the next two centuries – a tribute to the influence of the Swiss.

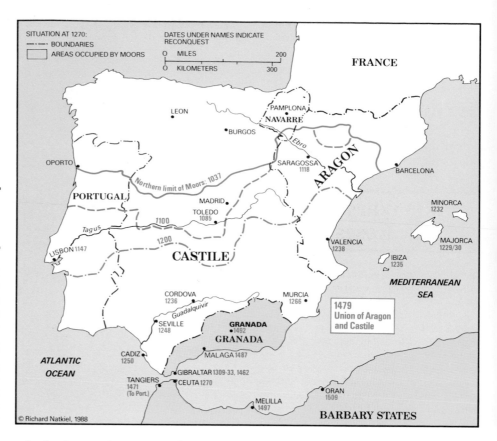

The Spanish Reconquista

The Visigothic kingdom in Spain was swept away within a few years of the Moslem invasion in 711 and the remaining Christian areas were confined to a narrow band in the mountainous north of the country. This territorial balance was maintained for 400 years, although in the tenth century the Berber armies of the Umayyad caliphate pillaged at will without attempting conquest. Under al-Mansur the caliphate was at its height, but it crumbled within a generation of his death in 1002 into a group of often warring successor city-states.

In contrast, King Sancho III of Navarre was able to unite the Christian north. His three sons divided the lands into the kingdoms of Leon and Castile, Navarre and Aragon (1035). Despite fratricidal wars which left Alfonso of Castile dominant, the reconquest of the Moslem south commenced. After forcing many Moslem cities into subjection, Alfonso conquered Toledo in 1085. The Moslem response was swift: the fanatical North African Almoravides poured into Spain and defeated the Christians at Zallacca (1086). Their expansion was only partly checked by El Cid in the 1090s. But the capture of Saragossa by Alfonso I of Aragon indicated that the Reconquista would continue.

The 1140s saw shifts in the balance of power. Portugal became an independent kingdom and captured Lisbon (1147), while Aragon and Barcelona were united and looked across the Mediterranean for other conquests. The Berber Almohads conquered Moslem Spain (1145-50) and pressed on against Castile, defeating Alfonso VIII at Alarcos in 1195. In 1212 he had his revenge at Las Navas de Tolosa, the battle that settled the fate of Moslem Spain. From now on there was to be no recovery or reply.

James I of Aragon, 'The Conqueror,' lived up to his name by capturing the Balearic Islands (1229-35) and the territories of Valencia (1233-45). His Castilian contemporary, Ferdinand III, became the most powerful Iberian ruler after the union with Leon in 1223. His conquests included all of the surviving Moslem city-states save one. Cordova was taken in 1236, Jaén ten years later, and the rich entrepôt of Seville in 1248. Only the Emirate of Granada retained its independence.

In the fourteenth century, Alfonso XI of Castile dealt with the last serious Moslem threat. In alliance with the King of Portugal he defeated a combined Spanish- and Moroccan-Moslem force at Rio Salado (1340). However, the final blow against Granada was not delivered for another 150 years. The executioners were Ferdinand and Isabella. Following a period of civil war which eventually resulted in the union of their two kingdoms of Castile and Aragon in 1479, Ferdinand and Isabella were able to go over to the offensive. In fact, Ferdinand was ambushed and defeated by the Moslems at Loja in 1482, and it took a decade of hard campaigning to capture the city. Reforms in the army, based on the model of the French Ordinances, the creation of a fleet to prevent Moroccan intervention and the systematic conquest of the region around Granada, led to the final siege. After nine grueling months the city eventually fell on 2 January 1492. The Reconquista had been achieved.

Below: the surrender of Granada to the forces of Ferdinand and Isabella – the final act of the Reconquista.

Below right: the bloodiest battle fought on English soil, Towton (1461) saw the utter rout of the Lancastrian forces.

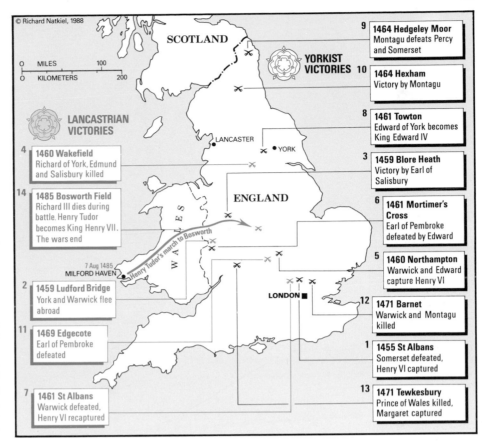

© Richard Natkiel, 1988

SCOTLAND

YORKIST VICTORIES

LANCASTRIAN VICTORIES

LANCASTER
YORK
ENGLAND

7 Aug 1485
MILFORD HAVEN
Henry Tudor's march to Bosworth

W A L E S

LONDON

9 1464 Hedgeley Moor
Montagu defeats Percy and Somerset

10 1464 Hexham
Victory by Montagu

8 1461 Towton
Edward of York becomes King Edward IV

3 1459 Blore Heath
Victory by Earl of Salisbury

6 1461 Mortimer's Cross
Earl of Pembroke defeated by Edward

5 1460 Northampton
Warwick and Edward capture Henry VI

12 1471 Barnet
Warwick and Montagu killed

1 1455 St Albans
Somerset defeated, Henry VI captured

13 1471 Tewkesbury
Prince of Wales killed, Margaret captured

4 1460 Wakefield
Richard of York, Edmund and Salisbury killed

14 1485 Bosworth Field
Richard III dies during battle. Henry Tudor becomes King Henry VII. The wars end

2 1459 Ludford Bridge
York and Warwick flee abroad

11 1469 Edgecote
Earl of Pembroke defeated

7 1461 St Albans
Warwick defeated, Henry VI recaptured

The Wars of the Roses

During 1455, in a battle at St Albans, two ambitious nobles captured England's annointed king. Henry VI had done little to endear himself to his barons. They felt that he had betrayed them by handing over Anjou and Maine to France in 1448, and also resented the influence that his queen, Margaret of Anjou, had over him. The Kentish rebellion of Jack Cade (1450) led to the massacre of his closest advisers, with the king helpless to protect them. In 1452, Richard, Duke of York, botched a coup to take their place. The following year saw the loss of Gascony and the complete mental breakdown of the king. All this, together with the rivalry between the Nevilles and Percies in the north, developed into three decades of often bloody warfare.

The wars were not continuous, however. There were three periods of military activity: 1455-64, 1469-71 and 1483-87 – the middle period being the hardest fought. The victors at St Albans were York and Richard Neville, Earl of Warwick. As yet there was no question of replacing the king and York resumed his role as protector. But this hardly suited the queen, who managed to regain control of her husband and dismiss the Yorkists in 1459. This action led to the Battle of Blore Heath, where the Yorkist Earl of Salisbury destroyed a Lancastrian force. Queen Margaret still pursued her aims, however, and marched with Henry to York's castle at Ludlow. At Ludford Bridge, the duke was outfaced, and both he and Warwick were forced to flee abroad.

In June the following year, Warwick was back accompanied by York's second son Edward, Earl of March, and a small army. Marching to London they won the support of the populace, and with enlarged forces advanced northward. At Northampton, aided by a rainstorm which drenched the opposition's gunpowder and treachery in the royal army, they won a major victory. King Henry, the helpless pawn, fell once more into their hands. Richard, Duke of York, returned from Ireland, this time prepared to claim the throne; but he was ambushed and murdered, together with his eldest son, at the Battle of Wakefield in December 1460.

Increasingly, the war took on the aspect of an aristocratic blood feud. In February 1461 Edward, by now Duke of York, defeated a Lancastrian force at Mortimer's Cross. The battle was followed by the summary execution of captured noblemen. Just two weeks later, Warwick was beaten at the Second Battle of St Albans by the forces of the determined Queen Margaret. But, joining up with the victorious Edward, the Yorkists marched on London, arrived first and declared Edward the monarch. Unsure what to do at this turn of events, the Lancastrians retired northward. Edward pursued them, sweeping aside a delaying force, and on the following day, 29 March 1461, won himself the crown at Towton.

Attacking in a snowstorm, his ability to inspire his men gave him victory in a bloody and very close-fought encounter. The deposed king, queen and Prince Edward fled to Scotland. The new king, Edward IV, had shown himself the best commander of the war: a fine strategist and brave soldier.

In the following three years there was a bitter struggle for the control of several Northumbrian castles. Then, in the matter of a few weeks in 1464, the Yorkists won two decisive victories. First, Lord Montague, Warwick's brother, defeated the main Lancastrian force

Left: the death of Richard III at the Battle of Bosworth.
Below left: Henry Tudor's victory at Bosworth effectively ended the Wars of the Roses.

at Hedgeley Moor (25 April). Meanwhile, King Edward was mustering a huge army in the Midlands. Aware that they had to move swiftly, the Lancastrians attacked again, but were crushed by Montague in a surprise attack at Hexham. The executions that followed destroyed the Lancastrian cause. Queen Margaret and Prince Edward escaped to France; Henry VI went into hiding, before being discovered and put into the Tower of London.

King Edward seemed secure. But Warwick (the 'Kingmaker') now plotted with Edward's younger brother, George, Duke of Clarence, to seize power. The rebellion of Robin of Redesdale in 1469, although Lancastrian inspired, was secretly supported by them. The rebels won a victory at Edgecote, but were defeated in the following year and their leader admitted the involvement of Warwick. The plotters fled to France where, incredibly, Warwick made common cause with Queen Margaret, and returned to overthrow King Edward. Henry VI was released and reinstated.

But this dramatic revolution did not last, King Edward was too good a general for the opposition. He returned with a small expedition in March 1471, landing in the Humber estuary. Marching swiftly south, he evaded blocking forces and raised more troops, including those of the Duke of Clarence, who deserted to his brother. On 14 April he had about 9000 men to challenge Warwick's 12,000 at Barnet. The battle began in thick fog. Richard, Duke of Gloucester, defeated the Lancastrian left wing, while the Yorkist left was driven back by Oxford. Rallying his men, Oxford brought them back to the battlefield, but into the Lancastrian's own rear. This mistake was seen as treachery and a rout followed during which Warwick was killed.

On the same day Queen Margaret landed in England, and made a dash for the security of the Welsh castles. Edward was determined to prevent this, and after a forced march caught up with the Lancastrians at Tewkesbury on 4 May. Once more his tactical skill and personal bravery won the day. It was the end for the Lancastrians: Margaret was captured, Prince Edward killed and their noble supporters massacred. The cause of so much fighting, Henry VI, was murdered in the Tower of London.

The last years of Edward's reign were peaceful, but he died unexpectedly early in 1483. Although he left an heir in his brother, Richard, Duke of Gloucester, seized the throne as Richard III. The Duke of Buckingham led a rebellion which was promptly crushed. The Lancastrian claimant was now Henry Tudor who, landing in Wales in 1485, managed to raise 5000 men to challenge the king. Meeting Richard at Bosworth in August, Henry was outnumbered by the king's army and opposed by a far more experienced general. But the treachery of Lord Stanley betrayed Richard's cause and he was killed.

Henry VII was soon challenged by the rebellion of Lambert Simnel, who claimed to be the son of the Duke of Clarence, in 1487. His mercenary force was massacred near Newark in June. Although there were other alarms for England's first Tudor monarch, this was the last major battle.

The Wars of the Roses had several features which distinguished them from contemporary European campaigns. First, because there were so few fortified towns in England, the issue could be settled – at least temporarily – in open battle, a situation leading to 'decisive' encounters which meant shorter campaigns. It has been calculated that the equivalent of only a single year was spent in active campaigning over the wars' three decades. As a result the wider population was not too badly affected. Also, although the nobility suffered heavily in the early stages of the conflict, by the 1480s there was a general unwillingness to become involved. By then the situation was very different from 30 years earlier when the country was full of veterans of the French Wars. Finally, so much depended on the character of the king: Henry VI was a disaster; Edward IV and Henry VII were both competent rulers.

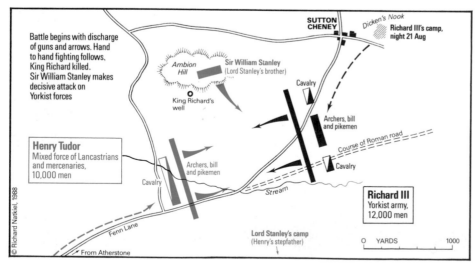

Battle begins with discharge of guns and arrows. Hand to hand fighting follows, King Richard killed. Sir William Stanley makes decisive attack on Yorkist forces

SUTTON CHENEY

Dicken's Nook
Richard III's camp, night 21 Aug

Ambion Hill

Sir William Stanley (Lord Stanley's brother)

King Richard's well

Cavalry

Archers, bill and pikemen

Course of Roman road

Henry Tudor
Mixed force of Lancastrians and mercenaries, 10,000 men

Archers, bill and pikemen

Cavalry

Cavalry

Stream

Richard III
Yorkist army, 12,000 men

Fenn Lane

Lord Stanley's camp
(Henry's stepfather)

0   YARDS   1000

From Atherstone

© Richard Natkiel, 1988

Right: the successful siege of Constantinople by the Turks under Mohammed II in 1453. Below right: Turkish assault troops storm the walls of the Byzantine capital.

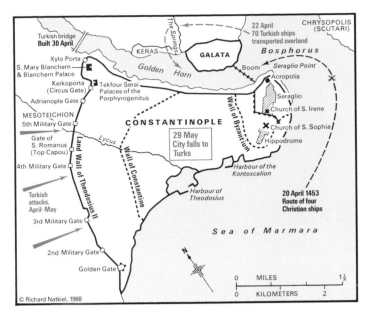

The Fall of Constantinople

In 1261 the Byzantines finally overthrew the shabby regime established by the Fourth Crusade in the wake of its conquest of Constantinople. However, the recovery of the old capital did not unite the empire. The pocket-sized realm left to the heirs of Justinian was pressured from the north by Christian Slavs and from the east by Moslem Turks. The seas around the empire were controlled by the materialist Venetians. The Turks were the greatest danger and in the last half of the fourteenth century the Ottomans spread out from Asia Minor into the Balkans. Only at this late stage did the states of Western Europe realize the value of a strong, Christian empire based on Greece and Asia Minor as a bulwark against threats from the east. Some feeble attempts were made to push the Turks back, but most ended in defeat or sometimes in disaster, as at Varna in 1444.

Seven years later the energetic Mohammed II succeeded his father, the Sultanate. He had but one dream – to capture Constantinople. During 1452 his ambitions became obvious to the last Byzantine emperor, Constantine XI, when a fort was built on the Hellespont to give the Turks control over the approaches to Constantinople. In the spring of 1453 Mohammed led an army of 80,000 men up to the walls of the great city. The siege began on 6 April.

The defenses of Constantinople were formidable: a double wall, fronted by a 100-foot ditch, protected the landward side. The rest of the city was surrounded by the waters of the harbor and the Bosporus. The harbor was sealed off, the defenders blocking it with a huge chain across the mouth. The garrison, 4773 Byzantine soldiers and around 4000 foreign mercenaries (mostly Italians from Genoa), was heavily outnumbered, but early skirmishes proved its fighting men to be far superior to their opponents.

The Turks chose to batter holes in the walls of Constantinople with their siege train of 70 guns led by a Hungarian renegade named Urban. Twelve of these guns were superbombards that fired heavy stone balls, one being a monstrous piece that fired a 1500-pound projectile. The great weight of shot soon breached the walls. These were assaulted vigorously by the Turks, but each time they were driven back and the breaches repaired by a stout palisade. Turkish attempts to mine the walls also failed, mainly due to the stony nature of the ground under the city.

However, a new breach was made in the double wall near the end of May and Mohammed ordered another assault to be made on the 29th. His forces moved into their attack positions in strict silence, the only sounds being made by the rattle of their equipment or their footsteps. At dawn the fighting began and the Turks repeatedly hurled themselves against the walls, only to be driven off at heavy cost. Two hours into the battle, the Sultan sent his elite *janissaries* into action. At about the same time the tactical genius of the defenders, John Giustiniani, the Genoese leader, was badly wounded and withdrew from the fighting. His own men wavered and the *janissaries* pressed their attacks with more vigor. A toehold was gained and widened. The Turkish weight of numbers finally tipped the balance and they broke through the walls. Constantine was in the thickest of the fighting and was slain. His city fell to the Turks shortly afterward and was given over to pillage for three days. The last physical link with the classical world of Greece and Rome had been broken by the sword.

These pages: Gustavus Adolphus, the King of Sweden, prays before the Battle of Lutzen in 1632.

THE DAWN OF PROFESSIONALISM

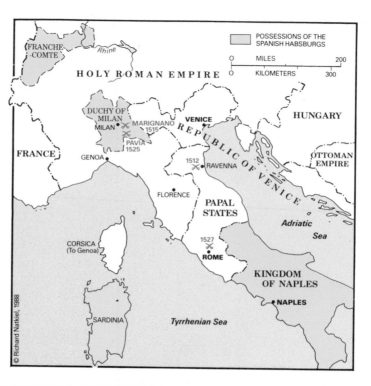

The Italian Wars

In the early sixteenth century Italy was the arena for most of the wars between the Hapsburgs of the Holy Roman Empire and the Valois of France. Still the center of the known world, Italy was the crossroads of the trade routes to and from the Middle East, North Africa and southern Europe, the origin of the New Learning and home of the Papacy. Italy was strategically most important and no ruler of a great nation could afford to ignore events

there. By 1494 France had recovered from the 100 Years War with England, and its kings enjoyed the most efficient military organization and the most efficient tax regime in Europe. As the nobility shared the view of their class that one of a king's functions was to provide them with opportunities for glory, no objections were raised when Charles VIII invaded Italy in pursuit of the Angevin claim to Naples.

For the past 40 years Italy had suffered no serious interference from outside the peninsula and Italians, in their independent city-states, mini-republics and principalities, were astonished at the speed with which the French army moved and defeated the Neapolitans. Such an easy victory encouraged Charles' successor and cousin, Louis XII, to repeat the performance in 1498, with the added dimension of another family claim – via a Visconti marriage – to Milan. In order not to fall foul of Ferdinand of Aragon, whose family also claimed it, Louis agreed to share Naples in 1502. However, subsequent arguments over details led to the Spaniards driving the French out in 1504.

Internal quarrels caused the Italian states to ally with the major powers, against each other; although this strategy was to lead to their ultimate downfall. In 1508 the League of Cambrai brought Louis, the emperor, Spain, the Pope and the Duke of Mantua to attack Venice and divide its lands between them. Success was followed by the inevitable jealousies, and in 1513 a reduced combination of Spain, the emperor and the Pope forced the French out of both the Veneto and the Milanese. During the Battle of Ravenna in 1512 field artillery was used effectively for the first time, driving the French from their entrenchments. When Francis I succeeded his uncle Louis in 1515 he returned to the fray and, defeating the Swiss at the Battle of Marignano, regained Milan. Pope

Below left: Charles V of Spain. Elected to the position of Holy Roman Emperor, he instigated several campaigns against Francis I of France.
Right: the Battle of Pavia in 1525 – a victory of firepower over knightly courage.
Below right: a scene from Pavia with Spanish infantry charging their firearms.

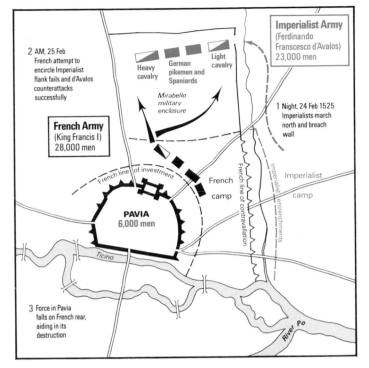

2 AM, 25 Feb
French attempt to encircle Imperialist flank fails and d'Avalos counterattacks successfully

Heavy cavalry | German pikemen and Spaniards | Light cavalry

Mirabello military enclosure

Imperialist Army
(Ferdinando Franscesco d'Avalos)
23,000 men

1 Night, 24 Feb 1525
Imperialists march north and breach wall

French Army
(King Francis I)
28,000 men

French line of investment

French camp

French line of contravallation

Imperialist entrenchments

Imperialist camp

PAVIA
6,000 men

Ticino

3 Force in Pavia falls on French rear, aiding in its destruction

River Po

Leo X concluded a Concordat with Francis and the Treaty of Cambrai in 1517 recognized his pivotal position in Italy.

The truly Hapsburg side of the Italian Wars came to the fore in 1519 with the accession to the Imperial throne of Charles V. The Holy Roman Empire of the House of Hapsburg was the biggest and most important political entity of the early sixteenth century in Europe, and it most nearly approached the medieval ideal of a united Christendom. Under Charles it comprised Spain, Franche-Comte, Naples, Sicily, Sardinia, Austria, the Low Countries and much of southern Germany, as well as over-lordship of Lombardy. Francis I put himself forward as candidate for emperor, partly in hope of exercising some control over Germany and warding off the political and physical encirclement that appeared to threaten France. The electors cared little for a French emperor and Charles' extensive bribes confirmed them in their choice. The Popes, too, feared the possibility of competition in Church affairs from a greatly strengthened empire, inclining them to favor the French against the emperor, even to the detriment of his attempts against the Protestant German princes during the Reformation.

In 1521, the new Imperial Chancellor, Gattinara, planned to remove France from the scene as a rival to the empire. He synchronized an attack by Imperial forces and an invasion by England together with a rebellion, inside France, by the French Constable Charles de Bourbon. All three failed. In 1524, Clement VII formed an alliance with France which brought yet another French army into Italy, this time to be humiliatingly defeated at the siege and Battle of Pavia in 1525, when Francis was himself taken prisoner and sent in captivity to Madrid. But nothing ended there: during negotiations, Francis wrote to the Sultan of Constantinople in an effort to obtain help against the empire (culminating in a formal treaty several years later) and, upon his return to France after the Peace of Madrid in 1526, he repudiated the treaty by which he had renounced his claims to the Duchy of Burgundy and territories in Italy. Despite this, he married Eleanor, the emperor's sister. Francis pleaded that the peace was illegal, being made under duress, and that the basic law of France would allow of no disposal of French territory. Again, he went to war, and this time it was Francis' ally, Pope Clement VII, who suffered. In May 1527 an Imperial army assaulted and sacked Rome. The fact that its pay was in arrears lent an edge to its rapacity. Looting,

rape, cruelty and humiliation were the order of the day, whether by Spaniards or Lutheran German mercenaries.

A more significant achievement for Charles was the attachment to him in 1528 of Andrea Doria, Admiral of the Genoese fleet and dictator of that city. In 1529, Imperial forces beat the French at Landriano and, at the Peace of Cambrai in August, Francis once more renounced his claims on Italy, while Charles gave up his to the Duchy of Burgundy. Francis reneged yet again upon the death of the last Sforza Duke of Milan in 1535, and in a rage Charles challenged him to a medieval trial by combat; an offer instantly disavowed by his ministers. Subsequent events drew the Turks into formal alliance with Francis, and the Poles, Muscovites and Persians into a counter-

alliance with Charles. By this time, however, the seat of war had moved to Flanders as Charles had realized that France was strategically weaker from that direction than from Italy.

Finally, in 1544, Francis agreed, at the Treaty of Crepy, to support Charles against the Turks and the Protestants. Charles was willing to concede other matters to France because his aim was the unity of Christendom, as he saw it; but it was left to other kings and emperors to bring the Valois-Hapsburg duel to a quite unforeseen end in a quite unexpected world; one in which Spain was the political and economic center of the empire and in which states and their rulers were concerned with lofty matters of religion and social order, rather than territorial gain.

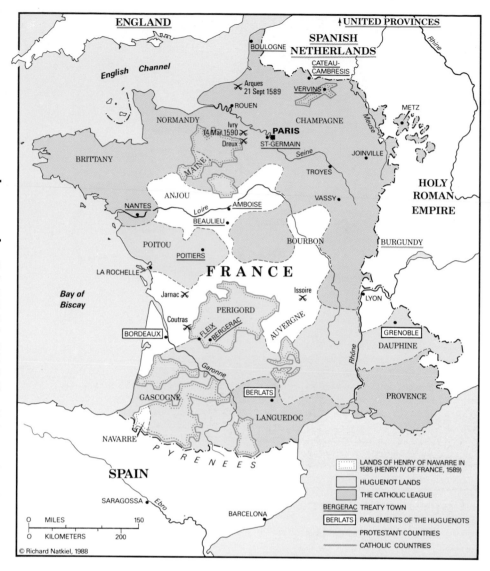

The French Wars of Religion

By 1559 a number of French nobles had taken up a political stance preached by Calvin. They complained of over-centralized government resulting from the Hundred Years War and the Hapsburg-Valois era; they wanted more independent control of their lands. The new urban middle class, who also liked Calvin's view of dynamic self-government, supported the nobles for their own reasons. Nobles wanted freedom from kings; towns, among other things, wanted freedom from nobles. Religion had always dominated society so it was thought that change must affect everything: either all must change or no one; or all non-conformists must leave. These medieval views of Church and State caused emigrations and exiles, persecutions, wars and massacres. The differences might not have mattered had not France suffered from over-powerful subjects and weak kings. From 1559 to 1590 the throne was occupied by three feeble brothers in turn. Rival power groups struggled to control the weak monarchs.

On Henry II's death the Calvinists possessed nearly 2000 churches in France, organized in synods. Their disciplined self-government contained many nobles whose political ideas and attitudes strengthened Huguenot organization. The chief Huguenot protagonists were the Bourbons, King Anthony of Navarre and his brother the Duke of Conde. The Catholic Guise family opposed them (the current duke was regent); they owned great estates and were related to two queens, a cardinal, 15 bishops and other powerful people. A third group, known as the *Politiques*, remained Catholic but disliked the Duke of Guise. The fourth factor was Catherine of Medici who protected her sons and the monarchy by playing the parties off against each other. The persecution of Protestants was underway.

In 1560, Francis II died. Catherine of Medici became regent and issued an edict of religious toleration. An attempt to kill the Duke of Guise in 1562 followed by revenge on Huguenots at Vassy, dissuaded both sides from peace and started the first of seven wars. Mostly fought by mercenaries, each ended quickly either because the combatants ran out of money or because a significant leader was killed and his supporters needed to regroup.

Spain helped the Catholics and England the Huguenots. German Lutherans normally fought for the Catholics, who did well until the Duke of Guise was assassinated outside Orleans. Further Catholic victories were overcome by Coligny who retreated with one army, raised another, attacked Paris and captured the government of France. The Peace of St Germain in 1570 gave the Huguenots four major fortresses and other towns.

Coligny tried to unite France and protect his religion by forming an alliance against Spain in Flanders, signing a defensive treaty with England in 1572. The king's sister married Henry of Navarre (the future Henry IV) but Catholics disapproved and, to stall the Guises, Catherine arranged to murder Coligny. The attempt failed but was repeated on a larger scale on 24 August 1572, St Bartholomew's Day. The bell of the Palace of Justice gave the signal and the Paris mob killed 300 Huguenots, including Coligny, whose head was sent to the Pope; 17,000 died in the provinces.

This act led to the fourth war in which the king's brother and many *Politiques* joined the Huguenots, preferring political to religious unity. A treaty in 1576 formed the Catholic League which completely controlled Henry III. Assassination was his only way out and the Duke of Guise was murdered during Christmas 1588. In 1589, the king was also murdered and Henry of Navarre became Henry IV (and eventually a Catholic). His military talent was well known: he developed the German tactic of cavalry using pistols in the charge and then wheeling away. Perhaps his most important gift as king was a genial nature: he actually liked the common people and they liked him. His Edict of Nantes, which allowed the Huguenots certain political and religious freedoms, brought the French Religious Wars to an end in 1598.

The Dutch Wars of Independence

In 1559, Philip II of Spain appointed the Duchess of Parma Governor-General of the Netherlands. Although the great magnates of the country occupied seats on her Council of State, power was actually exercised by Philip through Cardinal Granvelle. Philip was a centralizing bureaucrat and ran the empire from his desk in Madrid and was often out of touch. He was also a Catholic zealot, a land-owning Spaniard by education and sentiment, a king-emperor and a southern European. The Netherlanders were partly Protestant, divided into a collection of small states jealous of their rights and privileges, holding some republican sympathies; and mercantile Northerners, rich through handling 50 percent of the world's trade. Philip saw it as his duty to stamp out Protestantism and restore the Catholic Church to its former position.

The Netherlands had become the strategic heart of Europe and the country's tax revenue exceeded the value of Mexican silver to Spain by seven times. The people also resented their inferior status and the persecution of Protestants by Spanish troops. In 1564, the Inquisition intensified and Dutch nobles were told to accept the doctrines of the Council of Trent. Calvinist mobs ran riot in Flanders in 1565, destroying religious works of art in dozens of churches and cathedrals despite attempts by their leaders to restrain them. The Duke of Alva was sent with 10,000 Italian and Spanish mercenaries to put down the revolt. Two Dutch leaders were betrayed to Alva and beheaded in 1568. The Prince of Orange fought the Spaniards, although he was no soldier and was unable to beat their superb infantry in the field. However, the task was so expensive that Alva levied a 10 percent sales tax to pay for his troops. This was an attack on Dutch trade and no one, whatever his religion, supported it. In 1572 Dutch pirates, known as 'Sea Beggars,' captured some of the ports of Holland and Zeeland. The Spaniards never recovered these because the Dutch controlled the sluices and dykes. Tens of thousands of Calvinists migrated from the south to the Zuider Zee area, reinforcing its resistance.

In 1576, the Spanish garrison of Antwerp, unpaid for two years, sacked the city, killing about 8000 citizens. Catholic Brabant and Flanders then joined the Calvinists. Philip II replaced Alva with the Duke of Palma, Spain's best general, and 20,000 new troops in 1578. His great victory at Gembloux forced the Southern Provinces into the Catholic Union of Arras. William of Orange formed the Protestant north into the Union of Utrecht and in 1581, the States-General proclaimed an independent Dutch Republic. During the 1580s, Brussels and other Flemish towns fell to Parma; he took Antwerp by building a fortified bridge of boats over the River Schelde that blocked off supplies and any hope of swift reinforcement.

The Dutch also became very skilled at amphibious warfare; in 1590, Maurice of Nassau (who had replaced William) captured Breda by bringing his men into the town center in boats; in 1591, he captured Zutphen and Deventer, north of Nijmegen and at one end of the Spanish fortress-line. His troops then moved quickly by barge to Hulst at the other end of the line, captured it in five days, sailed back to Nijmegen and then captured that city in another six days. Fighting the Spaniards trained Maurice's infantry and cavalry to such effect that at Turnhout (1597) and Nieuport (1600) he twice defeated, first, the Spanish cavalry and, second, in a combined operation, their infantry. Through a combination of the brilliance of Maurice and his field army, English support, the involvement of the Duke of Parma and his troops in other tasks, the stubborn defense of their towns by the Dutch citizenry and their superb fleet which won a great battle against the Spaniards (Gibraltar 1607), the United Provinces were able to force Philip II to accept a 12-year truce at Antwerp in 1609. After another struggle that lasted from 1621 to 1648, the independence of the Dutch was finally recognized in the Peace of The Hague.

Above left: Prince Maurice of Nassau (1567-1625). An outstanding general, he outfought the Spanish occupation forces in the Netherlands.

Below: the high point of Turkish incursions into Europe – the unsuccessful siege of Vienna in 1529.

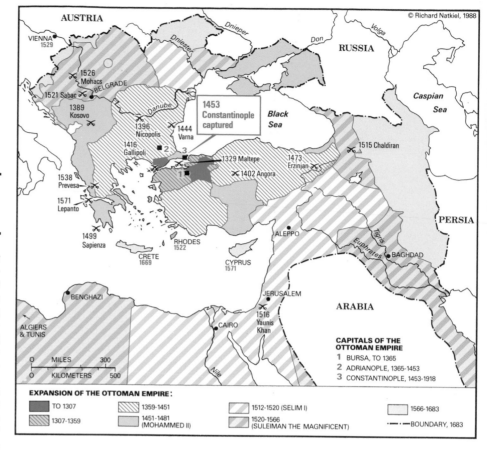

Turkish Incursions into Europe

The thirteenth and fourteenth centuries saw the Ottomans extend their domain by expanding into Byzantium. *Ghazi beys* (Muslim Holy War leaders) won freedom from the Seljuk Empire in captured territories, gaining authority by success. They attracted Turcomans, overtaxed landless peasants fleeing Mongol oppression, outlaws and bandits seeking a strong leader and the rootless who preferred to live at others' expense. By 1301 Osman (hence Ottoman) had won the Turkish leadership, destroying a Byzantine army sent to relieve Iznik which he threatened. His fame spread through Islam, bringing waves of Turkish immigrants to his banner. Ottomans were the 'Sword of God' and believed that their expansion westward was predestined.

Warfare maintained the Ottomans' status. By 1354 they had consolidated around the Sea of Marmora, having captured the Byzantine forts defending Gallipoli. A timely earthquake that destroyed the largest fortress increased, in Moslem eyes, the holiness of *ghaza*. Streams of *ghazi* bands now colonized Rumelia and within seven years Adrianople had fallen. Although they lost Gallipoli in 1366, the Ottomans defeated the Serbian princes at Chirmen in Macedonia in 1371, after

which the Byzantine emperor acknowledged their suzerainty and returned Gallipoli.

Anatolia and Rumelia were the main Turkish bases where they 'protected' princes whose sons were educated at court for tribute. Disloyalty subjected vassals' lands to raids, massacre of their people and seizure of property. Compliance however was beneficial, for the *ghaza* principle employed both carrot and stick to further Islam. The faithful vassal, Moslem or not, shared in the spoils of war and grants of land *(timars)* for life, according to his services. The Sultans fought with a

mass of light cavalry *(sipahis)*, mainly Moslem and the *janissaries* (paid infantry supported by artillery and engineers who were the core of the army). Well disciplined, well trained and completely dependant on the Sultan, they were ex-prisoners of war or young Christian slaves taken as a form of tax; they were almost invincible.

In 1453, the Turks captured Constantinople. Other conquests followed: Serbia (1459), Bosnia (1463), Morea in Greece (1464) and Albania (1478). In 1499, a successful war with Venice gained the Ottomans Lepanto and Modon, while Bosnian forces ravaged the lands between Trieste and Laybach and on to Vicenza. The treaty of 1503 marked the Ottomans as a major sea-power.

After a truce of 18 years, Suleiman the Magnificent captured Belgrade in 1521, Rhodes in 1522, and Budapest in 1526 – all after the *janissaries* rioted through boredom. He destroyed the Hungarian nobility and killed Louis II at Mohacs in 1526. He besieged Vienna late in 1529 but stout resistance by a veteran garrison forced a winter retreat. In 1532, attempts to destroy the Austrian army failed; instead Suleiman scoured Styria and Slavonia. Austria lay at the limit of the Ottomans' range; the climate allowed campaigning from mid-April to October only, and the distance from Constantinople to Vienna was too far for an army to move, conquer and return in that time.

In 1534 the Sultan's corsair leader, Khair ad-Din of Algiers, captured Tunis but lost it again in 1535. The corsairs then raided Valencia and the Balearics and defeated the Venetians in the Gulf of Arta in 1538, forcing them to sur-

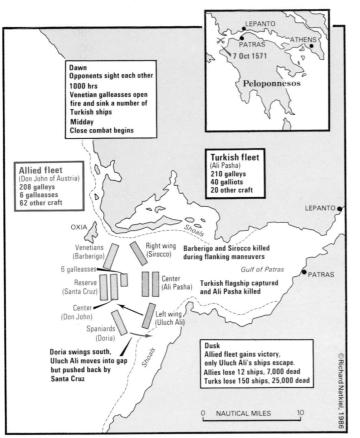

Dawn
Opponents sight each other
1000 hrs
Venetian galleasses open
fire and sink a number of
Turkish ships
Midday
Close combat begins

Turkish fleet
(Ali Pasha)
210 galleys
40 galliots
20 other craft

Allied fleet
(Don John of Austria)
208 galleys
6 galleasses
62 other craft

LEPANTO

OXIA

Venetians
(Barberigo)

Right wing
(Sirocco)

Barberigo and Sirocco killed
during flanking maneuvers

6 galleasses

Gulf of Patras

PATRAS

Reserve
(Santa Cruz)

Center
(Ali Pasha)

Turkish flagship captured
and Ali Pasha killed

Center
(Don John)

Left wing
(Uluch Ali)

Spaniards
(Doria)

Doria swings south,
Uluch Ali moves into gap
but pushed back by
Santa Cruz

Dusk
Allied fleet gains victory,
only Uluch Ali's ships escape.
Allies lose 12 ships, 7,000 dead
Turks lose 150 ships, 25,000 dead

Shoals

©Richard Natkiel, 1986

0   NAUTICAL MILES   10

LEPANTO
PATRAS
ATHENS
7 Oct 1571
Peloponnesos

Left: the Battle of Lepanto (1571).
Below: Turkish galleys attempt to breach the
Christian line at Lepanto.

then took the enemy flagship in tow. On the right, Andrea Doria maneuvered for the Turkish flank and some of his captains, thinking that he was avoiding battle, moved to the center and opened a gap in the division which the Turks exploited. Fortunately, the gap was quickly sealed by Santa Cruz's reserves and Doria himself. The Christians captured some 117 galleys and 274 guns.

The overall strategic balance was not altered, but the west gained in confidence after Lepanto. New ideas, new technology, better training and leadership in the west made the Turkish attacks so costly that, despite being able to recover quickly, the expense gradually weakened their financial structure. They moved farther into Europe, besieging Vienna in 1683. However defeat outside the city lost them Hungary – the start of the long retreat from Europe. An economy weakened by huge military expense; a series of effete Sultans who were pawns of the harem; political intrigues by mutinous household troops; Dutch and English fleets; Sunni Islam's refusal to think outside its own world – all contributed to the long Ottoman decline. Holy War and great efforts by occasional excellent Sultans or Grand Viziers revived the old, terrifying efficiency of the empire from time to time, but the trend was downward. After a mutinous army deposed the Sultan in 1687, Turkey was never again a serious threat to Europe.

render their possessions in Greece and the Aegean. Not until the action at Lepanto in 1571 did the Ottomans lose the advantage at sea.

Suleiman also annexed Bessarabia and forced Ferdinand to pay tribute. Although war broke out again from 1552 until 1562, it did not change the balance of power, but new fortified defenses were developed in depth, manned by professional Christian infantry expert in siege warfare. The cost of attacking these lines discouraged sultans from undertaking long campaigns with little prospect of immediate profit. This phase did see a sea war in which the Turks captured Nice and burned Reggio in 1543, and routed a Spanish fleet off Djerba in 1560. The Knights of St John held Malta in 1565 but in 1571 the Turks took Cyprus, killing some 20,000 in Famagusta, saving the handsome young for slavery.

The Christians avenged this latest horror in the same year when a Hapsburg-Spanish fleet of over 200 galleys, 6 galleasses, 50 lighter rowing craft, several large transports and 80,000 men annihilated an Ottoman fleet of 210 galleys, 40 galliots and 20 smaller craft at Lepanto, sinking or capturing 75 percent of their ships. The conventional method of attack was to ram the enemy ships and grapple them before boarding, but Don John of Austria ordered the rams to be sawn off his ships to give their bow-mounted cannon a clear field of fire. There were few technical differences between the fleets but they were important. Christian galleys mounted five bow cannon to fire ahead. The Turks had three. Only the Christians had galleasses which carried some 30 guns, mounted on a deck above the oarsmen: two in the bow, six aft and 11 cannon per broadside. The rival fleets faced each other in

line, in three divisions of galleys, the Turks slightly overlapping. The Christians placed the galleasses before their divisions so that, as the Turks approached the Christian line, they received broadside after broadside and then were pounded in the rear when the galleasses turned about and followed them toward the Christian galleys. Serious damage was first noticed on the Turkish right where Christian galley-slaves were able to free themselves and join in the fighting. In the center, the battle lasted for an hour and a half until most of the Turks on their flagship were killed and Ali Pasha was decapitated. Don John of Austria

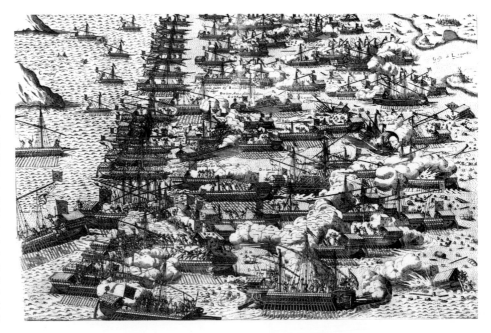

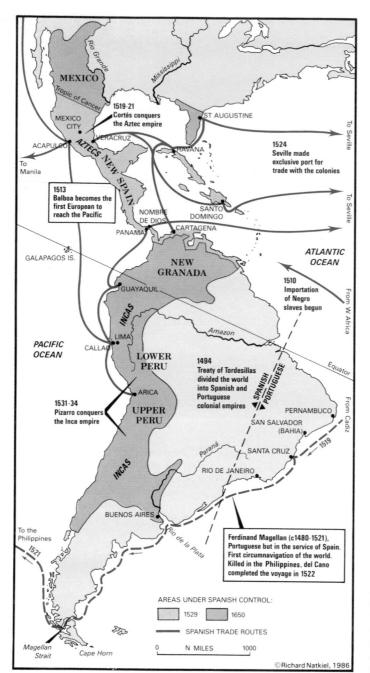

Map labels:

MEXICO
Rio Grande
Mississippi
Tropic of Cancer
MEXICO CITY
VERACRUZ
ST AUGUSTINE
ACAPULCO
AZTECS NEW SPAIN
To Manila

1519-21
Cortés conquers the Aztec empire

1524
Seville made exclusive port for trade with the colonies

To Seville

1513
Balboa becomes the first European to reach the Pacific

NOMBRE DE DIOS
SANTO DOMINGO
HAVANA
PANAMA
CARTAGENA

To Seville

GALAPAGOS IS.

NEW GRANADA

ATLANTIC OCEAN

From W Africa

1510
Importation of Negro slaves begun

GUAYAQUIL
INCAS
LIMA
CALLAO
Amazon

PACIFIC OCEAN

Equator

LOWER PERU

1494
Treaty of Tordesillas divided the world into Spanish and Portuguese colonial empires

SPANISH PORTUGUESE

From Cadiz

1531-34
Pizarro conquers the Inca empire

ARICA
UPPER PERU
PERNAMBUCO
SAN SALVADOR (BAHIA)
SANTA CRUZ
1519

INCAS
Paraná
RIO DE JANEIRO

BUENOS AIRES
Rio de la Plata

To the Philippines
1521

Ferdinand Magellan (c1480-1521),
Portuguese but in the service of Spain.
First circumnavigation of the world.
Killed in the Philippines, del Cano
completed the voyage in 1522

Magellan Strait
Cape Horn

AREAS UNDER SPANISH CONTROL:
1529   1650
SPANISH TRADE ROUTES
0   N MILES   1000
©Richard Natkiel, 1986

Above: a portrait of Francisco Pizarro, the conqueror of the Inca Empire.

Spanish Conquest of the New World

From 1492 to 1517, Spanish explorers reconnoitred the West Indies, Florida and as far south as the Rio de la Plata. Instant, easier trade with Cathay had been expected, but by 1522, it was known that a completely New World had been discovered. Its exploration was made a state enterprise by Spain, to which Pope Alexander VI had awarded, in 1494, all lands discovered west of a north-south line 1000 miles west of the Azores. Two indigenous empires existed: the Aztecs and the Incas. The Aztecs were based in the highlands of Mexico with their capital at Tenochtitlan (now Mexico City) and were known to be rich in gold and

silver, militaristic, unscientific, without literature and philosophically arid. Diego Velazquez, Governor of Cuba, put his former Secretary, Hernan Cortés, in charge of 500 men, 16 horses and a few firearms and sent him to conquer the Aztecs. Cortés burnt his boats immediately on landing in Mexico and arrived in Tenochtitlan on 8 November 1519. The natives thought the Spaniards were the 'white gods' which their religion led them to expect would visit them imminently. This belief robbed them of any aggressive initiative, allowing Cortés to seize Moctezuma II and force him to swear allegiance to the King of Spain. The Spaniards' contempt for Indians led them, in their Christian-missionary zeal, to smash a few idols; reaction was fierce and fighting broke out. Moctezuma tried to stop it and was stoned to death while the Spaniards escaped by night, suffering many casualties.

They turned upon their pursuers at Otumba and although outnumbered by 100:1 they defeated them. Cortés obtained more troops from Cuba and, helped by the Tlascaltecas, an anti-Aztec Indian tribe, attacked the new Aztec king, Cuautemoc, at Tenochtitlan. The coup was intended to be short and sharp, but turned into a long, bloody siege which eventually ended in 1521; after which, the Aztec Empire collapsed.

The Inca Empire, in Peru, was won by a hitherto undistinguished *conquistador*, Francisco Pizarro, who explored the Pacific coast of South America in search of the fabulously rich empire of which men talked. On confirming its existence, he returned to Spain to petition successfully the new Holy Roman Emperor, Charles V, for the governorship of any lands he conquered. The 300-strong expedition left Panama in 1531, and sailed to Peru where they met the Emperor Atahualpa at Cajamarca. Pizarro made his entry under a flag of peace but was met by Atahualpa with 40,000 men. However, Inca passivity proved to be even greater than that of the Aztecs, and encouraged Pizarro to take a dramatic risk. He hid his remaining 180 men and few horses in the buildings surrounding the town square and positioned himself in the center, with his chaplain. When the square had filled with Indians, the chaplain asked Atahualpa to accept the sovereignty of the King of Spain and be instructed in the Catholic faith. The emperor cast the proffered Bible aside and, whether by signal or in their excitement or by mistake, the hidden Spaniards opened fire on the Incas and charged at them with their horses. Panic in the confined space was devastating and decisive and Pizarro captured the emperor. Subsequently, the Spaniards strangled Atahualpa for reasons of state, regardless of the ransom he offered. The capital of Cuzco was later captured with no difficulty and all resistance ended. Twenty years later the Spanish had established a dominant position in South America.

The Spanish Armada

By 1588 the commercial rivalry between Protestant England and Catholic Spain had become open war. Spain was the leading maritime power in the Western world and clearly had the money and resources to match any development by small Northern European countries such as the Netherlands and England but in fact Spanish ideas of naval warfare were old-fashioned and outmoded.

Years of reliance on oared ships went with a version of Roman-type tactics, using soldiers to board and capture the enemy. On the other hand English mythology about the Spanish weakness in ship-guns must be discounted; the Spanish ships were better supplied with heavy 'demi-cannon' and 'periers' (the contemporary names for different calibers) than the English. The real difference lay in tactics and the use of gunpower. Whereas the Spaniards always tried to come alongside and board, the

English tried to attack downwind, using gunfire to cripple the opponent and cause casualties among her crowded boarding parties. Boarding of Spanish ships was expressly forbidden without the admiral's permission.

To humble the truculent Dutch and English King Philip ordered the Duke of Medina Sidonia to assemble a *Felicissima Armada* (translated as the 'Invincible' Armada) to destroy the English fleet and then ferry the Duke of Parma's army in the Low Countries across to complete the task by invading England. The First Line comprised 28 ships, the Second Line had 74 more, and there were in addition 27 supply ships in the Fleet Train.

The Armada left Lisbon in May 1588 and the first contact with the English was made on 29 July, south of the Scilly Isles. This brought on the first action off Plymouth two days later. By the time that the English commander, Lord Howard of Effingham, and his subordinate Drake could work their ships out of Plymouth it was nightfall, but next morning they engaged the Biscayan squadron flagship under

Above: Philip II of Spain, the monarch who created the Spanish Armada.

Vice Admiral Juan Martinez de Recalde. The *San Juan de Portugal* was bombarded for an hour at 'long' range (300 yards) by the *Revenge* (Drake), *Victory* (Hawkins) and *Triumph* (Frobisher). The battered flagship was finally rescued by the ships of her squadron, and the English had to withdraw without having inflicted any serious damage. The Armada's discipline and seamanship

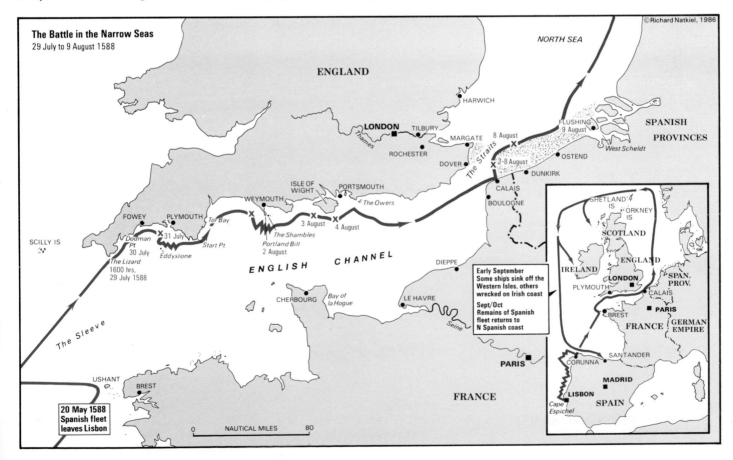

The Battle in the Narrow Seas
29 July to 9 August 1588

©Richard Natkiel, 1986

NORTH SEA

ENGLAND

HARWICH

LONDON TILBURY

MARGATE   8 August   FLUSHING   SPANISH
ROCHESTER   9 August   PROVINCES
                                      West Scheldt
DOVER   The Straits   7-8 August   OSTEND
                      DUNKIRK
ISLE OF   CALAIS
WIGHT   PORTSMOUTH
WEYMOUTH   The Owers   BOULOGNE
                3 August
FOWEY PLYMOUTH   Tor Bay
          31 July   4 August
          Dodman
SCILLY IS   Pt   Start Pt
          30 July
          Eddystone
The Lizard   The Shambles   ENGLISH   CHANNEL
1600 hrs,   Portland Bill
29 July 1588   2 August

SHETLAND
IS   ORKNEY
     IS
SCOTLAND
          ENGLAND
IRELAND   SPAN.
LONDON   PROV.
PLYMOUTH   CALAIS
BREST   PARIS
FRANCE   GERMAN
          EMPIRE
SANTANDER
CORUNNA
MADRID
Cape   LISBON   SPAIN
Espichel

DIEPPE

Early September
Some ships sink off the
Western Isles, others
wrecked on Irish coast

Sept/Oct
Remains of Spanish
fleet returns to
N Spanish coast

CHERBOURG   Bay of
          la Hogue   LE HAVRE

The Sleeve   Seine

USHANT   PARIS
BREST
          FRANCE

20 May 1588
Spanish fleet
leaves Lisbon

0   NAUTICAL MILES   80

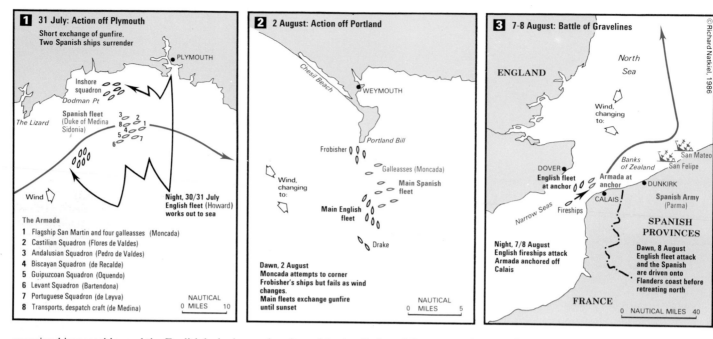

1 31 July: Action off Plymouth
Short exchange of gunfire.
Two Spanish ships surrender

PLYMOUTH

Inshore
squadron
Dodman Pt

Spanish fleet
(Duke of Medina
Sidonia)

The Lizard

Wind

Night, 30/31 July
English fleet (Howard)
works out to sea

The Armada
1 Flagship San Martin and four galleasses (Moncada)
2 Castilian Squadron (Flores de Valdes)
3 Andalusian Squadron (Pedro de Valdes)
4 Biscayan Squadron (de Recalde)
5 Guipuzcoan Squadron (Oquendo)
6 Levant Squadron (Bartendona)
7 Portuguese Squadron (de Leyva)
8 Transports, despatch craft (de Medina)

NAUTICAL MILES 0 — 10

2 2 August: Action off Portland

Chesil Beach
WEYMOUTH
Portland Bill
Frobisher
Galleasses (Moncada)
Main Spanish fleet
Wind, changing to:
Main English fleet
Drake

Dawn, 2 August
Moncada attempts to corner
Frobisher's ships but fails as wind
changes.
Main fleets exchange gunfire
until sunset

NAUTICAL MILES 0 — 5

3 7-8 August: Battle of Gravelines

© Richard Natkiel, 1986

ENGLAND
North Sea
Wind, changing to:
Banks of Zealand
San Mateo
San Felipe
DOVER
English fleet at anchor
Armada at anchor
DUNKIRK
Spanish Army (Parma)
CALAIS
Narrow Seas
Fireships
SPANISH PROVINCES

Night, 7/8 August
English fireships attack
Armada anchored off
Calais

Dawn, 8 August
English fleet attack
and the Spanish
are driven onto
Flanders coast before
retreating north

FRANCE

0 NAUTICAL MILES 40

remained impeccable, and the English lacked sufficient heavy guns capable of penetrating the heavy timbers of the Spanish galleons. It should be remembered that the rate of fire of warship guns was very low. The system of using the gun's recoil force to run it back inside the ship ready for reloading had not yet been devised and instead muzzle-loading cannon had to be reloaded from outside the main structure of the ship. This was obviously a tricky and time-consuming process and in fact ships normally had to break an action off temporarily to accomplish reloading.

On 2 August the running fight flared up again as the Armada crept up the Channel in its ususual crescent formation. Once again the English ships stayed clear and used their guns to good effect, while the Spanish captains tried unsuccessfully to grapple and board. But the Duke of Medina Sidonia was achieving his strategic objective, to get through the Channel and unite with the Duke of Parma, and Howard of Effingham could not stop him. By 4 August the Armada was off the Isle of Wight, having lost the *Nuesta Senora del Rosario*, captured after being disabled in a collision, and the *San Salvador* had been badly damaged by an explosion of gunpowder.

When the Armada reached the haven of Calais on the night of 6 August it seemed almost in sight of victory, but the following night the English sent in eight fireships. Fire being the most dreaded weapon against wooden ships the Spanish ships cut their cables and put to sea in confusion. With their cohesion broken it was now possible for the English to pick off individual Spanish ships, and in the ensuing Battle of Gravelines they drove two more ships ashore.

Even after four hours of fierce fighting the decisive result eluded the English, and during the night of 8-9 August a rising gale forced the two fleets apart. As the gale blew his ships northward the Duke of Medina Sidonia finally gave up any idea of uniting with Parma, and decided to extricate the Armada by making for the northwest coast of Scotland. His crews were being wasted by scurvy and typhus, and with powder and shot nearly exhausted any attempt to get back down the Channel was certain to result in the Armada's destruction.

The return voyage around Scotland turned into a disaster. By 13 August seven First Line ships had been lost, the remainder were badly damaged and a fifth of the men were dead or wounded. Water and food had almost been exhausted, and there were still the hostile shores of Ireland to come.

The first survivors of the Great Enterprise did not get back to the Tagus until the end of September. The full extent of the horror became apparent when only 66 ships limped in, roughly half of the proud fleet which had sailed four months before. The worst losses had been on the west coast of Ireland, where many castaways had been murdered at the behest of English landowners. Storms had achieved what English guns had failed to do.

For England the defeat of the Armada seemed like divine intervention. Freed from the threat of invasion the country could continue to build up her maritime trade at the expense of Spain. Equally important for the future was the establishment of a 'tradition of victory' which was to be of incalculable value to the Royal Navy during the next four centuries. For Spain it was a bitter rebuff, and although by itself the reverse inflicted no deep harm on Spanish naval strength it foreshadowed the economic decline of the next century.

Above: the running fight against the Armada off the southern coast of England.
Left: the *Ark Royal*, pride of the English navy.

The Thirty Years War

The Thirty Years War followed a course that is too complicated to trace in more than broad outline. Although its causes were primarily religious, other factors were involved: any attempt to stabilize the power of the Holy Roman Empire attracted French concern; and any threat to Catholic Europe drew in Spain. For 30 years Europe was torn apart by widespread fighting. When there was a lull in the fighting the countryside was plundered by armies which were frequently too underfed to fight each other and spent their time searching for food. Gustavus Adolphus' Swedish Army was better equipped than any other to cope with a lack of supplies but even his Swedes were eventually reduced to 'foraging,' killing civilians and burning towns and villages in order to stay alive. In 1618, the Holy Roman Empire was composed of hundreds of small states, most of them recognizably German. When the Thirty Years War ended in 1648, large parts of the empire had been laid waste and half of its population was dead; in Bohemia, only some 6000 villages remained out of an original 35,000. A useful way to examine the war is to divide events into three phases: Bohemian 1618-23; Danish 1625-29; and Franco-Swedish 1630-48.

The Religious Peace of Augsburg of 1555 did not finally settle the division of Catholic

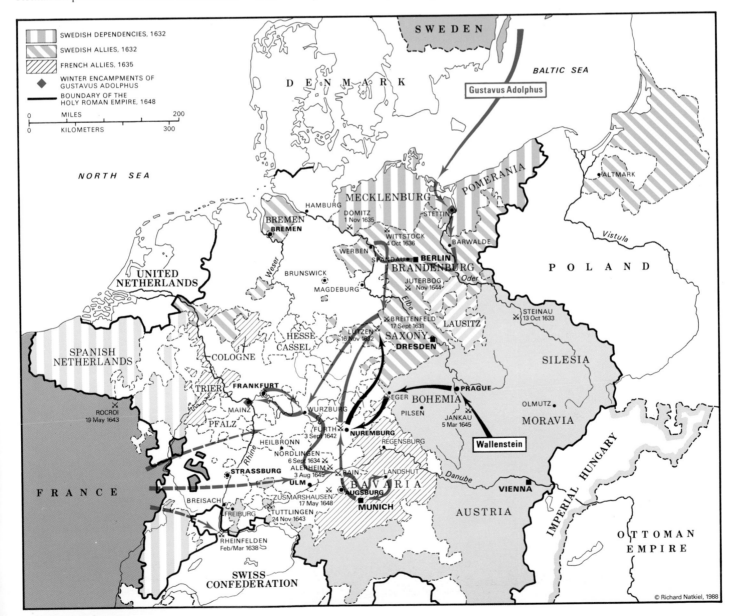

Right: the Battle of Breitenfeld, a victory
won by the tactical genius of Gustavus
Adolphus.

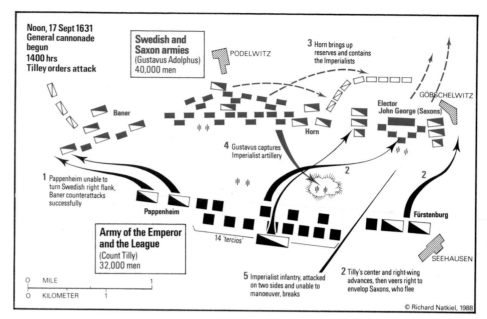

Noon, 17 Sept 1631
General cannonade
begun
1400 hrs
Tilley orders attack

Swedish and
Saxon armies
(Gustavus Adolphus)
40,000 men

PODELWITZ

3 Horn brings up
reserves and contains
the Imperialists

GÖBSCHELWITZ

Baner

Elector
John George (Saxons)

Horn

4 Gustavus captures
Imperialist artillery

2

2

Fürstenburg

1 Pappenheim unable to
turn Swedish right flank,
Baner counterattacks
successfully

Pappenheim

Army of the Emperor
and the League
(Count Tilly)
32,000 men

14 'tercios'

SEEHAUSEN

0   MILE   1

0   KILOMETER   1

5 Imperialist infantry, attacked
on two sides and unable to
manoeuver, breaks

2 Tilly's center and right-wing
advances, then veers right to
envelop Saxons, who flee

© Richard Natkiel, 1988

and Protestant in European states as had been
hoped. Central Europe was still medieval in its
thinking and, as it transpired, it required only
a few powerful and reactionary men to open
the religious issue again. The pious, honest
and well-intentioned Ferdinand of Styria, the
first ruler to have been educated by the
Jesuits, believed along with many others at
that time that all Christendom should be
united and that there should be no heretics in
his lands. In 1598 he began 'liquidating' heretics in Styria. In 1608 persecutions and other
signs of religious intolerance obliged some of
the Protestant princes and city-states to form
an Evangelical Union in self-defense. In 1609,
many Catholic princes responded with the
creation of the Catholic League. Tensions between religions and states increased and in
1617, the centenary of the Reformation, when
pamphlets, broadsheets and books were excit-
ing everyone with contesting accounts of
events and their theology, Ferdinand was
elected emperor.

To the Protestants of Bohemia the news was
grim. A previous emperor had granted them a
Charter of Toleration which was imperfectly
applied. Under the new emperor, a known
persecutor and protagonist of the Counter-
Reformation, they stood no chance of being
able to worship freely. Led by a Calvinist

noble, Henry Matthias of Thurn, they planned
to rebel at the first convenient opportunity. It
came soon. A Bohemian Royal Decree ban-
ning Protestant assemblies, discussed between
some nobles and two Catholic ministers, Mar-
tinitz and Slawata, led to the ban being
enforced and their secretary being thrown out
of a window of the Hradshin Palace in Prague.
A government of the Estates was set up with
help from Count von Mansfeldt, a mercenary
leader of the Duke of Savoy. Unable to stand
up to the emperor by themselves, the Bohe-
mians immediately sought allies and, deposing
Ferdinand as king, they elected in his stead the
Elector Palatine, Frederick V. The elector
was a Calvinist, the grandson of William the
Silent and the son-in-law of James I of
England. He combined many attributes of the
ideal Protestant leader but he was not a

soldier. He lost the Battle of the White
Mountain near Prague in 1620 to the League
army of Catholics and Lutheran Saxons led by
Tilly. Bohemian hopes were dashed. Ferdinand then turned the country into a colonial
state and reduced its peasantry to serfdom.
Tilly went on to capture Heidelberg and won
other Catholic victories in Lower Saxony.

In 1625, supported by Dutch, English and
French subsidies, Christian IV of Denmark
entered the war on the Protestant side. A
strong motive for his entering the fray was the
hope of providing money for his sons from the
proceeds of any Catholic bishoprics that might
be acquired. The year before, Ferdinand II
changed commanders: he removed Maximilian of Bavaria, replacing him with Wallenstein, a military adventurer and a good land-
lord who could make a profit out of war – or
anything. He was extremely rich and had
fought well against the Turks. Offering to
raise an army of 50,000 at his own expense, he
only asked that he might keep the booty for
himself and his troops; captured guns and
ammunition were for the emperor. By 1626 he
had beaten von Mansfeldt at the Bridge of
Dessau and chased him into Hungary. In the
same year, Tilly defeated Christian of Denmark at Lutter in Thuringia, causing that
prince to recast his sons' fortunes. He and
Wallenstein then pursued Christian to Jutland, the latter being appointed Generalis-
simo of the Baltic and the Northern Seas.

An Edict of Restitution was issued by the
Catholic Electors in 1629, returning all ex-
Catholic property in Protestant North Ger-
many to its previous owners. Wallenstein
enforced it and caused many, Protestant and
Catholic alike, to suspect him of excessive
ambition, either for himself or the emperor.
At the Diet of Ratisbon in 1630 Maximilian of
Bavaria obtained his removal from the com-
mand. Protestant fortunes looked bleak and

Left: heavy fighting during the Battle of
Leipzig in 1631.

Above: the opposed crossing of the River Lech by the Swedes in 1632.

needed a new injection of men and money. Cardinal Richelieu of France saw Germany share his dismay at the dominance of Austria and used the occasion to persuade Gustavus Adolphus of Sweden, a devout Protestant and the greatest soldier of the age, to restore the balance and put heart back into the Protestant cause. The Swedish king obliged, invading North Germany in 1630 to acquire the coast of Mecklenburg and Pomerania, thus protecting his position in the Baltic. The first year was spent consolidating his coastal base; fortunately, the army most able to harass him at this time had been disbanded and Adolphus Gustavus was able to recruit some of Wallenstein's ex-soldiers.

In May 1631 Tilly the Imperial general and his Catholic army, which had fought at Lutter and into Jutland, was not far away looking for supplies and besieging Magdeburg. It was known to be a Protestant depot, full of food. Gustavus marched to its relief but Tilly captured it first with little difficulty. The Imperial mercenaries were by now out of control and vented their frustration and suffering on the inhabitants. Thirty thousand people died in the fire which destroyed the town – along with all the supplies that Tilly wanted. The Saxon princes allied themselves to Gustavus who pursued Tilly to Breitenfeld and destroyed his army. In particular, he was able to demonstrate the flexibility of his forces in battle based on the balanced power of maneuver that their novel organization gave. The standard Imperial army was organized along Spanish lines, using large blocks of men about 50 deep, with the obvious rigidity that such numbers imply, especially against infantry firearms or mobile field artillery.

Gustavus was the first great commander in history to apply to the business of war a mind educated by the renaissance in technology, science, tactics, languages, administration, organization and history. His army was quite unlike any other because he had considered every detail and implication of its aims, use and stucture. Organized into small and more maneuverable units, it was a mutually supporting 'all-arms' army of great flexibility, both in the weapons it used and how it employed them. Gustavus' most significant military qualities were his grasp of fire and movement and his understanding of administration and organization. His soldiers were drilled to produce instant reaction and their NCOs were encouraged to use and develop initiative and responsibility. All ranks were trained in the appropriate skills. Senior officers, for instance, besides having a knowledge of diplomacy, learned practical science and geography. Recruiting, uniforms, punishments, medical services, engineers, supply and artillery, were all organized systematically and provided in a form that the modern soldier can instantly appreciate.

Other armies engaged in the same conflict stayed together as long as they were paid. Wallenstein's army was tied neither to Catholic nor Protestant and, although discipline was good in camp, the men plundered freely. The prevailing doctrine assumed that towns and villages in the seat of a campaign should maintain the contending armies. While money and supplies existed, people could benefit, but when armies moved slowly or ran out of cash, or stocks of food and fodder ran low, then local inhabitants suffered severely.

The populations of villages around Ulm in Bavaria retreated to that city for protection more than 20 times during the course of a few years. Most of their villages were burned to the ground; large numbers of the inhabitants were brutally, cruelly and wantonly killed, or died from famine or the plague acquired in the overcrowded city. Most of their horses and stock met the same fate; tools, money, furniture, books – property of any kind or value was taken to sell for survival or destroyed to deny it to others.

Gustavus defeated and killed Tilly in 1632 at Rain on the Lech and then marched on Munich and Nuremberg; he was about to march on Vienna when Wallenstein was recalled as commander in chief with special powers. He drove the Saxons out of Bohemia, forcing the Elector to attach himself to the emperor, and then moved north to attack Gustavus' line of communication. They met at Nuremberg but Wallenstein dug in and would not fight, knowing that shortage of supplies would make the Swedish king attack him on ground of his own choosing. Gustavus did attack and was repulsed. He then made for the Danube once again, but Wallenstein continued north and the Swedes had to follow him. Finally, Gustavus unexpectedly attacked Wallenstein at Lutzen in 1632 and beat him. However, the king was also killed. Wallenstein soon recovered and beat the Swedish army at Steinau in 1633. For these remarkable services and fearing either his subordinate's ambition, that his own reputation suffered by comparison, or that Wallenstein might exert a liberal influence at any peace discussions, Ferdinand called him south, dismissed him in 1634, and allowed the Jesuits to employ Irish soldiers to assassinate him in the same year.

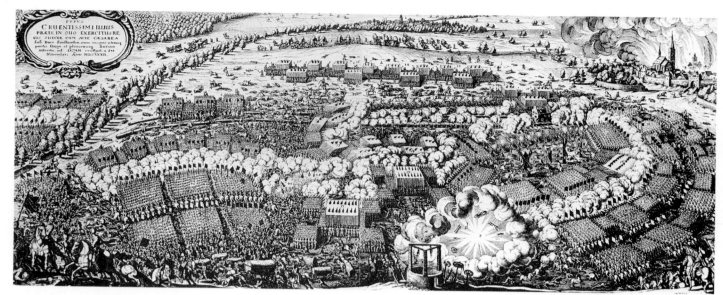

Above: pike blocks and musketeers, supported by cavalry on the flanks, at Lutzen in 1632.
Below right: the Battle of Rocroi in 1643.

Imperial forces again defeated the Swedes under Bernard of Saxe-Weimar and General Horn, at Nordlingen (September 1634) and in 1635 the Elector of Saxony sued for peace on behalf of the Lutherans. The subsequent Peace of Prague was accepted by the important princes and free city-states as being a sensible arrangement. It also committed everyone to removal of the Swedes from Germany.

Now that Gustavus was dead and the emperor and the majority of the princes were reconciled, the war took on a wholly selfish flavor of Great Power politics. Cardinal Richelieu of France allied himself to Sweden and the Protestant Dutch Republic against Protestant Germany, Catholic Austria and Spain. Sweden wanted Pomerania; France, Alsace and any other territory up to the bank of the Rhine. These last 13 years of war in which Germany had no interest were also the most destructive. France and Sweden desired to keep the empire off balance and their armies lived in Germany, though not in Imperial lands. France had not been at war since Henry IV and needed time to become effective. Le Tellier, Minister for War, undertook the necessary modernization from 1643, with good results. In 1643 the Duke d'Enghien defeated the Spanish at Rocroi, and in the western Ardennes, demolishing what military capacity remained to Spain. From that date Spain was unable either to recruit or pay troops of a similar quality, for neither the men nor the money were available in the homeland. In 1645 Torstensson, now commanding the Swedes, defeated the Imperialists at Jankau as did Turenne at Alerheim. From now on, serious peace talks took place in the separate towns of Osnabruck and Munster. By 1648, after more battles, more plunder, more suffering and more talks, the definitive Peace of Westphalia was finally signed.

The countries that gained the most territory from the war were France and Sweden. The former acquired Alsace and Lorraine and a border on the Rhine, with bridgeheads at Breisach and Philippsburg. Sweden gained Bremen, part of Pomerania with Stettin, and Wismar and Verden with control of the mouths of the Weser, Elbe and Oder. Bavaria and other states also acquired territory, though the most important results of the treaty were not measured in acres but in the quality and extent of political autonomy. Switzerland and the United Provinces left the empire, which disintegrated into a confederation of politically and militarily powerless states. Imperial privileges regarding legislation and treaties could be exercised only with the approval of the Diet. The Estates also acquired the right to make treaties as long as they were directed neither against the empire nor the emperor; they enjoyed a greater measure of freedom but the same laws applied and very similar taxes were imposed. Once religion had come again under the rules of the Peace of Augsburg and the Hapsburgs had been reduced in size, it seems almost as though the German states were prepared to carry on where they had left off. The Hapsburgs were no longer in charge and Austria confined its interest more and more to the east, where very important matters demanded attention and from which the continuation of the Thirty Years War had been a worrying distraction. The Ottomans had still to be driven back to Asia. The professional soldiers who had lived on other people's misery for so long either went home or were able to join the forces which continued to fight the Turks.

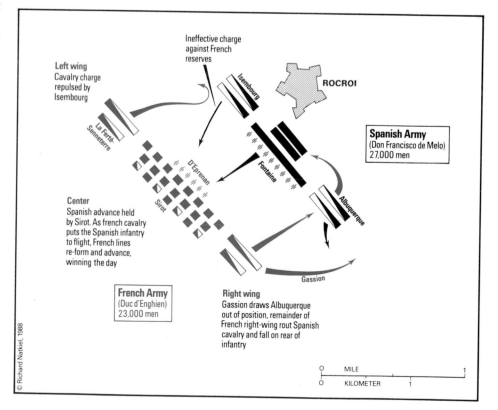

Ineffective charge against French reserves

Left wing
Cavalry charge repulsed by Isembourg

ROCROI

Spanish Army
(Don Francisco de Melo)
27,000 men

La Ferté-Senneterre

Isembourg

D'Eprenan

Fontaine

Sirot

Albuquerque

Center
Spanish advance held by Sirot. As french cavalry puts the Spanish infantry to flight, French lines re-form and advance, winning the day

French Army
(Duc d'Enghien)
23,000 men

Right wing
Gassion draws Albuquerque out of position, remainder of French right-wing rout Spanish cavalry and fall on rear of infantry

Gassion

© Richard Natkiel, 1988

0   MILE   1

0   KILOMETER   1

Below: Charles I of England. His attempt to impose his will on the English parliament sparked the outbreak of civil war.

The English Civil War

In 1603 James I came to rule three kingdoms, each with a different religion, an opposing religious minority and its own views on the duties and responsibilities of government. Progress toward unity over the following years was hindered by several factors, the most important of which were: the doctrine of the Divine Right of Kings to rule without Parliament; the Scottish Church's wish to impose its religious views on England; the wish of many MPs to govern the realm; the inability of the king to live off his own money as the cost of government rose with inflation and new warship construction technology; and the character of King Charles I. Matters came to a head in 1641 when an Irish Catholic massacre of Ulster Protestants provoked a debate in Parliament over the army. Charles attempted to arrest five MPs who opposed his will in the affair but, on entering Westminster to apprehend them, he found that 'the birds had flown.' The London mob forced Charles himself to flee a few days later and he raised his standard at Nottingham in 1642.

To the astonishment of Parliament the first months of the war favored Charles. The Parliamentary side had obvious advantages: interior lines; London and the clothing towns; the wealth of the City; the industrial base in London was capable of equipping almost any force; the fleet would not support the king and could therefore ensure the safety of London by sea. However, the rebellious MPs had not understood that many people might quarrel with the king but would never take up arms against him; also, many didn't like Puritans. No clear-cut class divisions split the country; the allegiance of the lords and gentry could not be easily predicted; merchants and lawyers tended to Parliament because of their business interests. Laborers generally supported the king, unless in London or the southeast.

The first battle of consequence was fought at Edgehill in 1642 and the king held the Parliamentary forces to a draw. Royal armies included officers who had fought in European wars, whether for Protestant or Catholic; though the former did not hold very senior posts. Both sides enlisted experienced volunteers easily at first, but it was some while before they were used properly. Gentlemen on both sides raised and paid for their own units, not taking kindly to advice from professionals as competence came after social rank. No regular or mercenary troops existed; the nearest thing to a professional force was the trained band of the county. Few of them were trained, however, except for the 18,000 apprentices of London who proved to be steady, well-disciplined soldiers, saving London more than once. Discipline, noted largely by its absence, depended too much on goodwill and loot. Worse in the Parliamentary armies, its irregularity prevented generals from winning battles and it protracted the war.

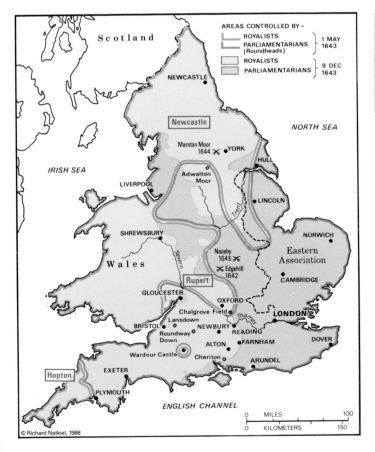

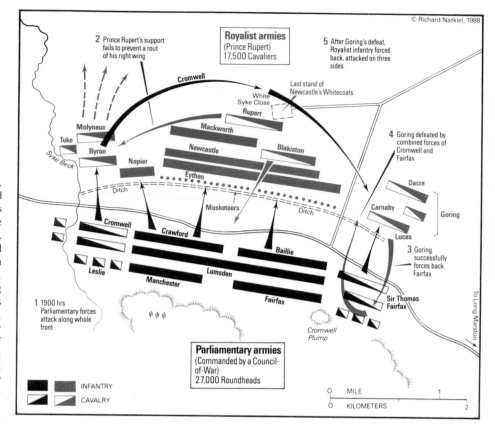

© Richard Natkiel, 1988

2 Prince Rupert's support fails to prevent a rout of his right wing

Royalist armies
(Prince Rupert)
17,500 Cavaliers

5 After Goring's defeat, Royalist infantry forced back, attacked on three sides

Cromwell

Last stand of Newcastle's Whitecoats

White Syke Close

Rupert

Molyneux

Mackworth

4 Goring defeated by combined forces of Cromwell and Fairfax

Tuke

Newcastle

Blakiston

Dacre

Byron

Syke Beck

Napier

Eythen

Carnaby

Goring

Ditch

Musketeers

Ditch

Lucas

Cromwell

Crawford

3 Goring successfully forces back Fairfax

Baillie

Leslie

Lumsden

Manchester

Sir Thomas Fairfax

1 1900 hrs Parliamentary forces attack along whole front

Fairfax

Cromwell Plump

Parliamentary armies
(Commanded by a Council-of-War)
27,000 Roundheads

To Long Marston

INFANTRY

CAVALRY

MILE   1
0
0   KILOMETERS   2

Strategy varied according to circumstances. Both sides found it important, at first, to hold territory rather than concentrate their forces for offensive action as it enabled them to raise recruits, taxes and supplies. Here and there, great lords raised their own forces and did battle, with more or less effect, depending on luck, competence and the size of their force. The main armies roamed the country, seeking or avoiding each other, laying or raising sieges to towns and cities as required. Here again, the Royalists enjoyed an early advantage for the king's nephew, Prince Rupert, a soldier of the German wars, knew cavalry tactics, the movement of armies and siegecraft. He showed to advantage in raising the siege of York in July 1644, when his army completely out-maneuvred the forces of Fairfax and Manchester, and a Scottish army under Alexander Leslie that had crossed the border in January in response to a Parliamentary request for help. No swearing, no women, death for plundering, rape or drunkenness; they were led by the Earl of Leven who learned his trade under Gustavus Adolphus. After York was relieved, the bloodiest battle of the civil war took place on Marston Moor.

Rupert started early, expecting to attack the Parliamentarians with infantry from York. Unfortunately his allies were reluctant to fight; the Marquis of Newcastle was unused to obeying orders so briskly, and anyway many of his infantry were still out plundering the enemy siege-lines; Lord Eythin disliked Rupert and criticized his plans. They arrived about four o'clock, 12 hours late. By then Rupert deployed some 18,000 troops; Leven nearer 30,000. Both armies faced each other till about seven o'clock when Rupert, thinking that the enemy would behave like his allies, went off to dinner. At 1930 there occurred a hailstorm and, as if at a signal, Leven's army charged. Prince Rupert's cavalry on the royal right were quickly dispersed by Cromwell's Ironsides;

Cromwell then held his horse in check, a tactic unusual for that time. The Parliamentary right also collapsed and Leven retired smartly. Cromwell's Ironsides then came across the field and took the Royalist cavalry in rear. In the center, Newcastle's infantry broke Fairfax's infantry only to be slaughtered later by Cromwell's and Leslie's cavalry. Only 30 were captured, the remainder dying where they stood. In two hours, finishing in moonlight, the Royalists lost 4150 dead to the Parliamentarians' 300. Leven's men captured 1500 prisoners, 100 colors and some 6000 arms. York fell on 16 July, on generous, Christian terms. This unnecessary defeat was matched in August by the Earl of Essex, who led a Parliamentarian army to surrender at Lostwithiel; he escaped by sea.

Parliament was given several chances of defeating the king because, with time, its advantages began to tell. An attack at Newbury in October let the king's army escape due to Manchester's failure to follow the plan. Though they did well in the north, Parliament's generals quarreled over freedom of conscience and the Presbyterian religion which the Scots wanted to establish in England. Cromwell was a leader of the War Party, but only because he thought that the war would end more quickly if efficiently fought. During this time Fairfax raised, organized and trained his New Model Army in the teeth of opposition from the Peace Party in Parliament. Established at a strength of 22,000 men, it took many months to achieve that figure. Little effort was needed to recruit 7600 troopers for the horse; most of them were men of some means and their pay of two shill-

Left: the Battle of Marston Moor, 1644.
Below left: Prince Rupert leads at charge at Marston Moor.
Right: the decisive battle of the war, Naseby also saw the debut of the New Model Army.
Below right: Cromwell reads the king's abandoned correspondence after Naseby.

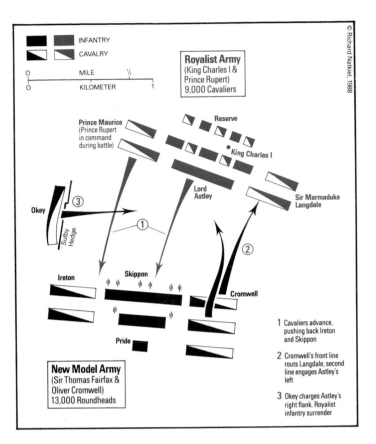

INFANTRY

CAVALRY

MILE

KILOMETER

Royalist Army
(King Charles I & Prince Rupert) 9,000 Cavaliers

© Richard Natkiel, 1988

Prince Maurice (Prince Rupert in command during battle)

Reserve

King Charles I

Lord Astley

Sir Marmaduke Langdale

Okey

Sulby Hedge

Ireton

Skippon

Cromwell

Pride

New Model Army
(Sir Thomas Fairfax & Oliver Cromwell) 13,000 Roundheads

1 Cavaliers advance, pushing back Ireton and Skippon

2 Cromwell's front line routs Langdale, second line engages Astley's left

3 Okey charges Astley's right flank. Royalist infantry surrender

ings a day gave them a good living. They were also hand-picked, godly men who fought a zealous war. Tactics, developed from the Dutch, were shared with Rupert. Charging the enemy with drawn sword was accompanied by a discharge of pistols at close range. The trooper carried two pistols and a straight sword; he wore an expensive leather jacket under his simple armor.

The infantry was paid 1s 6d per day, subject to deductions. Twelve regiments were raised and most of their recruits were mutinous, impressed, underfed and likely to desert. Even at Naseby they were understrength. The first 'redcoats,' they wore boots, breeches and knee-length stockings and were armed with musket and pike; that is, two musketeers to every pikeman in the companies. The pikes resisted enemy charges and were about 16 feet long, needing strength to wield them. Musketeers used the Swedish system whereby three ranks fired at once, kneeling, bending, and standing. Apart from a few gunners there were no technical troops.

The New Model Army changed everything, but not at first. More quarrels and indecision in the Parliamentary ranks left the initiative with the Royalists. In the confusion of the time, Leicester was a prize worth some royal risk, and its capture shook Parliament, many blaming the Scots for desertion. Prince Rupert then started out to raise the siege of Oxford and found himself being tracked by the New Model Army before he could obtain reinforcements. Ireton's troops captured some Royalists at Naseby and Charles and Rupert were surprised to discover the enemy was so close. Rupert wanted to retreat to gather reinforcements but the courtiers would hear none of it. Both sides then moved early to look for good ground on which to fight, evetually facing each other across Broad Moor Farm, nearly two miles north of Naseby. Rupert was the Royal Commander in Chief but he decided to lead his own cavalry into battle. On the right, he intended to attack quickly, while the enemy was off-balance, to help make up for his much lower numbers. Rupert charged uphill, fired on by some dragoons in ambush behind a hedge, went straight through the New Model ranks and on to the baggage train, some distance to the rear. On the other flank, Cromwell did much the same but with more discipline, thoroughly dispersing the Royalist cavalry. The infantry battle in the center went well for the king, despite being outnumbered 3:2. But Cromwell's horse, about 3000-strong at this stage, were able to charge the Royalist

center in the flank. Other New Model horse, not properly dispersed by Rupert's charge, mustered and attacked Charles' other flank. Rupert eventually got his cavalry to halt and remuster and brought them back to the battle in time to rescue the king from futile gestures and capture. Four-and-a-half thousand royal infantry were captured with all Charles' guns, baggage and nearly all his army's stores. But worst of all was the loss of his confidential correspondence. When published in London, it revealed that Charles had been prepared to rescind the anti-Catholic laws, hire foreign mercenaries and raise an Irish army to fight in England. Charles never led an army again.

Charles gave himself up to the Scottish army in April 1645 rather than be captured by Par-

liament or surrender on their terms. In 1647, after the Scottish Parliament refused him as King of Scotland, Charles was delivered to the English and imprisoned at Holmby House in Northamptonshire. In November he escaped to the Isle of Wight from where he continued to plot with the Scots. this led to the 'second' Civil War, the Battle of Preston, which Cromwell won handsomely against a much larger Scottish army, and various attempts at insurrection of behalf of the king. The revolutionaries in the New Model Army who used to preach to their fellow soldiers abolished the monarchy and the House of Lords and killed the king. But in 1660 both England and Scotland welcomed his son back to his reconstituted throne.

These pages: relenting to pressure from the revolutionary forces, Lord Howe evacuates Boston during the American War of Independence.

THE STRUGGLE FOR EUROPE

The First Anglo-Dutch War

Although once united in the common fight against Spain in the sixteenth century, the English and Dutch found themselves increasingly in competition as they helped themselves to portions of Spain's sprawling empire. In the years leading up the English Civil War (1642-51) it is fair to say that only the weakness of successive Stuart governments in Britain prevented war from breaking out. After the Civil War Parliament enacted legislation aimed at excluding the Dutch from domestic trade, and by May 1652 both sides were spoiling for a fight.

The pretext was the appearance of Marten Tromp's squadron in a sheltered anchorage in the English Channel near Dover, on 28 May 1652. English Admiral Blake arrived the next day, demanded a salute from the Dutch and when it was refused, fired a warning shot. This was answered by a broadside from Tromp's flagship the *Brederode*. After five hours of

hard fighting the Dutch withdrew, having inflicted severe damage on the *James*, Blake's flagship. Although war had still not been declared, Blake was ordered to attack the important Dutch herring fleet and this finally precipitated full hostilities in July.

Blake met Tromp's successor, Witte de With on 8 October off the sandbank known as the Kentish Knock as the Dutch were returning from a cruise in the Channel. This time Blake won convincingly, capturing two Dutch ships, damaging many more and forcing Witte de With to take shelter behind the sandbanks off the Dutch coast. The victory was so convincing that the English Parliament ordered all the major warships to be laid up 'in Ordinary' (reserve) for the winter, but the Dutch, furious at their defeat, kept their entire fleet in commission. As a direct result Blake had only 40 ships against Tromp's 100 when the two fleets next met off Dungeness on 10 December 1652. With Marten Tromp reinstated as commander in chief the Dutch had little difficulty in beating the English.

On 28 February 1653 Blake intercepted Tromp as he tried to shepherd a convoy through the Channel, and in a running fight

lasting three days the Dutch ran out of ammunition and lost 19 warships and 57 merchantmen before Tromp could extricate his ships.

The new English Fighting Instructions and the revised code of discipline were tested by the Battle of the Gabbard Bank on 12 June 1653. The new 'General at Sea' George Monk and his subordinate Richard Deane engaged Tromp and the next day Blake arrived with reinforcements. By using their superior gunpower the English ships prevented the Dutch from coming to close quarters, and the Dutch lost some 20 ships and 1300 prisoners, while the English lost no ships and only 126 men.

After the Gabbard victory (also known as the Battle of North Foreland) the Dutch coast was blockaded, forcing the Dutch to sue for peace, but the English terms were so harsh that the Dutch resolved to make one supreme effort to stave off defeat. On 10 August Tromp met Monk in the Battle of Scheveningen, a bloody clash of two doughty admirals.

Both sides were now feeling the strain of the war and when the English Parliament moderated its demands the United Provinces accepted them. The war was brought to an end by the Treaty of Westminster, on 5 April 1654.

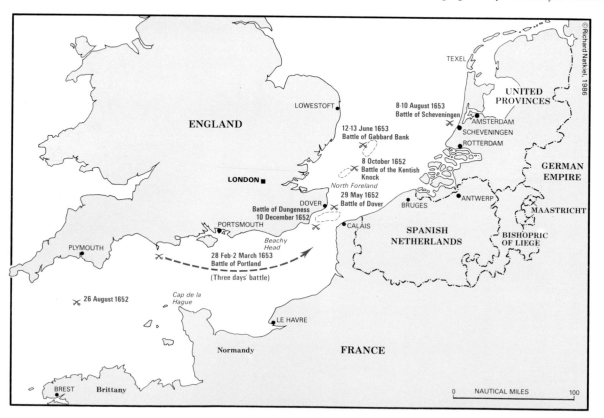

The Second Anglo-Dutch War

At his restoration to the English throne in 1660 King Charles II inherited all the financial and commercial muddle of the last days of the Commonwealth, but he was also bequeathed a powerful navy. It was, therefore, tempting to continue Cromwell's policy of enhancing the country's wealth and prestige, chiefly at the expense of the Dutch. 'Make wars with Dutchmen, Peace with Spain, Then we shall have money and trade again' ran the popular jingle.

With the Dutch equally determined to safeguard their trading interests conflict was inevitable and as was often the case in those days it began 'beyond the line,' far from European waters. Fighting broke out early in 1664 when Captain Robert Holmes recaptured several trading posts in West Africa which had been occupied by the Dutch and then went on to occupy some of the Dutch-owned settlements. In August of the same year a force ejected the Dutch from New Amsterdam, renaming it New York in honor of James, Duke of York. At the end of the year there was a further attack on a Dutch convoy in the Straits of Gibraltar, and it is only surprising that formal hostilities did not break out until the middle of March the following year. Nonetheless, de Ruyter had already led a Dutch squadron from the Mediterranean to recover the recently lost trading posts in Africa.

Although energetically led the newly christened Royal Navy was soon to show the effect of government parsimony when war formally began. In April 1665 a successful cruise off the Dutch coast by the Duke of York had to be cut short because of the shortage of supplies. While trying to follow up this withdrawal the Dutch were drawn into the Battle of Lowestoft on 13 June. Although belittled in England as an indecisive action it achieved the destruction or capture of 31 Dutch ships.

An English attempt to attack a Dutch convoy homeward-bound from the East Indies forced it to take shelter in Bergen in July-August 1665, but a spirited defense by the Dutch and their Danish allies (Norway was under Danish rule at the time) drove off the English attackers.

The outbreak of plague in London, coupled with the government's chronic shortage of money, affected the Royal Navy's ability to control the waters around the English coast.

In October the new Dutch commander in chief, de Ruyter, was able to operate in the Thames estuary unmolested before returning to Holland to lay his ships up for the winter. France declared war on England the following January, but keeping her fleet out of action proved comparatively easy. It did, however, mean that when the Dutch Fleet put to sea at the end of May 1666 the Duke of Albemarle (formerly General George Monk) was badly outnumbered nearly two-to-one by de Ruyter.

The resulting Four Days' Fight, which lasted from 11 to 14 June, was a bloody slogging match. Twenty of Albemarle's ships were sunk to de Ruyter's six, and the English suffered nearly 4000 casualties.

Repairs to Monk's fleet were delayed by shortages of essential stores, and once again de Ruyter's squadron was seen in the Thames. Not until the end of June did Monk get to sea once more, but he was able to inflict a defeat on de Ruyter at the St James's Day Fight on 4-5 August. Further retribution followed, when Robert Holmes (now Sir Robert) destroyed a newly arrived East Indies convoy in the anchorage known as the Vlie. This action, known as 'Holmes's Bonfire,' resulted in the destruction of 150 merchant ships, a severe blow to Dutch trade.

Despite the victories at sea, by early 1667 the English were heartily tired of the war and 'peace feelers' were put out. When the Dutch seemed willing to come to the conference table the king's ministers decided to economize by not recommissioning the warships which had been laid up 'in Ordinary' during the winter. The Dutch kept talking at Breda but all the while prepared the fleet for a devastating blow against the English.

On 21 June 1667 de Ruyter entered the Medway with his light forces, attacking shipping in the river and landing troops to occupy Sheerness and Chatham. Chatham Dockyard suffered severely, with three ships of the line burned at their moorings and the 90-gun *Royal Charles* towed back to Holland as a prize.

The negotiations at Breda terminated rapidly and on terms much more favorable to the Dutch, exactly as de Ruyter had intended they should be.

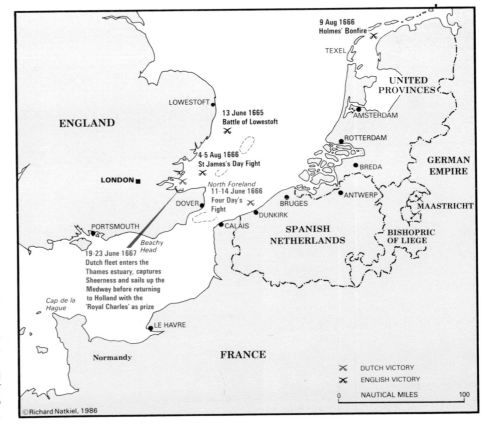

The Third Anglo-Dutch War

Following the two Battles of Schooneveldt in June 1673 the next major engagement of the Anglo-Dutch Wars was the Battle of the Texel on 21 August. As before de Ruyter fought shrewdly, choosing his moment to retire. Once again England's new-found allies, the French, were present under Comte d'Estrées.

As at Sole Bay de Ruyter had no difficulty in distracting the attention of the French, leaving him free to concentrate on the English center under Prince Rupert and the rear squadron commanded by Admiral Sir Edward Spragge.

On the allies' side there was a particularly disgraceful moment when 12 Dutch ships

under Bankert ran through 20 French ships without a shot being fired at them. The conduct of the French squadron throughout suggests that d'Estrées may have had secret orders from King Louis XIV to avoid action with the Dutch. Less easily explained is an extraordinary lapse of fleet discipline on the part of Sir Edward Spragge. To make good a boast to King Charles that he would bring back Cornelius Tromp alive or dead he made the whole of the rearguard squadron stop to enable him to engage Tromp.

The private war was fought as bitterly as the main battle. Spragge was forced to shift his flag twice, and on the second occasion while moving in a boat to his new flagship he was cut in two by a roundshot. His folly, combined with the timidity or treachery of the French, left Rupert isolated in the center, but de Ruyter lacked sufficient ships to defeat the

Above left: a naval engagement during the Third Anglo-Dutch War.
Above: the seal of the Duke of York.
Below: the Battle of Texel, August 1673.

English, and he finally withdrew at the end of the day.

Nine days after the battle Holland was offered a tempting alliance by Spain, Lorraine and Germany, an offer which was immediately matched by King Louis. In England the king's alliance with France was immensely unpopular, and the following February he bowed to popular clamor and signed a separate peace. But in spite of de Ruyter's heroic endeavors the Dutch had suffered a strategic defeat. No longer could they dominate the English Channel or the southern half of the North Sea, their main objective throughout the long conflict.

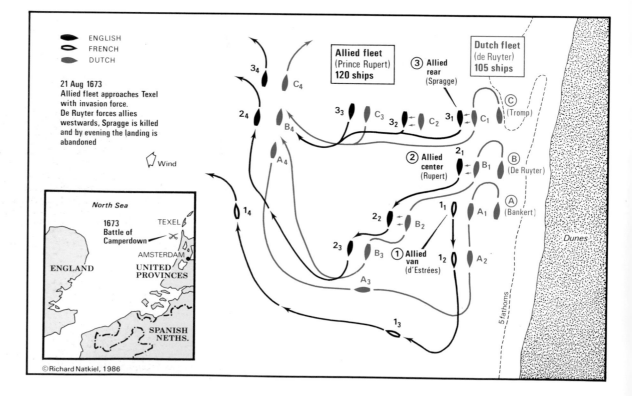

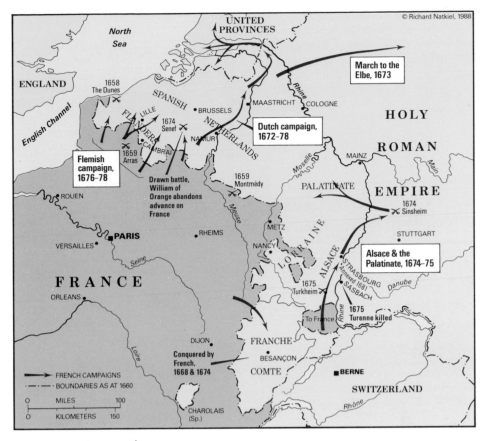

The Wars of Louis XIV and Turenne

In France, the end of the Thirty Years War was followed by the Fronde, a confused rebellion against the Court. This gave Turenne, who had been one of the most outstanding French generals of the preceding war, a chance to distinguish himself further. Spain assisted the anti-Court faction, and in 1651 Turenne led a Spanish army into southern France against the French Court, but was promptly bribed and changed sides. A few years later, after the Court had secured the alliance of England, Turenne commanded an English army which defeated the Spanish near Dunkirk at the Battle of the Dunes (1658). The Peace of the Pyrenees which followed gave France possession of several Spanish territories in Flanders and Luxembourg.

The young King Louis XIV, bent on military glory and an expansion of his realm, was given an opportunity for even greater expansion during the succession dispute that followed the death of the Spanish king in 1665. Louis claimed the Spanish Netherlands and, not receiving satisfaction, invaded that territory in 1667. Turenne's campaign captured a number of Flemish towns, including Lille, which henceforth would be regarded as part of France. However, France's aggression alarmed her neighbors. The English and Dutch promptly stopped fighting each other, and so did the Spanish and Portuguese. Moreover the Dutch, Swedes and English formed a Triple Alliance against France.

This did not last long. After making peace with Spain at the Treaty of Aix-la-Chapelle (1668) Louis persuaded Charles II of England to join with him in a potentially profitable war against the Dutch, and also bribed the Swedes to give what they hoped was merely moral support. But this war was not the short victorious conflict that had been anticipated. The Dutch defeated the British at sea, and opened their dykes to prevent Turenne capturing Amsterdam; they rebelled against their own republic and appointed William of Orange, an implacable foe of the French, as their leader. The British fears of growing French power, forced Charles II to withdraw from the war in 1674. Meanwhile, alarmed by the French success, Brandenburg, Austria and Spain joined in the war. The Swedes were obliged to fight Brandenburg in northern Germany and were

defeated at the Battle of Fehrbellin in 1675. This battle damaged Sweden's military reputation and was an early manifestation of Prussian prowess on the battlefield.

The French generals did well against the loose and ill-organized coalition, but in 1675 Turenne was killed at the Battle of Sasbach in southern Germany. The war dragged on until the Treaty of Nijmegan was completed in 1679. This treaty allocated to France much of the Spanish Netherlands, as well as Franche-Comte and German-speaking Alsace and Lorraine. The latter two acquisitions, although strengthening the eastern frontier, condemned France to German resentment for two centuries. England acquired Dutch territory in North America, and her early departure from the war enabled her to take over Dutch seaborne trade; this was a crucial first step toward Britain's dominance of the seas.

Right: the Sedgemoor campaign of 1685.
Below: infantry loyal to James II defeat the
peasant forces of the Duke of Monmouth at
Sedgemoor.

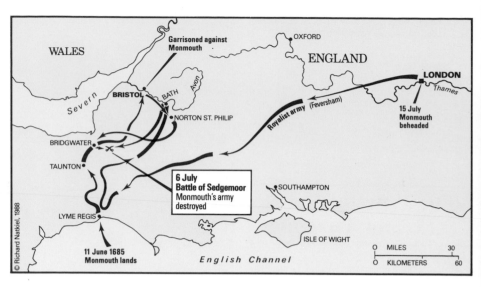

The Wars of the English Succession

The end of Cromwell's republic and the more-or-less triumphant reign of King Charles II by no means stabilized the line of succession to the English throne. Charles was succeeded by his brother James II in 1685 but the latter, whose open Roman Catholicism was resented and feared by many powerful subjects, was unpopular. The Duke of Monmouth, Charles II's illegitimate son and Protestant claimant to the throne, raised his flag in the west of England in 1685. In this part of the country he gained encouraging support, and the county militias, England's nearest approach to a standing army, proved unreliable, with many of their leaders defecting to the rebels. King James despatched troops under the nominal command of a French Roman Catholic but actually commanded by John Churchill, the future Duke of Marlborough. This army met the rebels at Sedgemoor in Somerset and, helped by the possession of some of the new flintlock muskets, won a crushing victory against men who were brave but virtually untrained. James used this revolt as an excuse for establishing a true standing army, an idea repugnant to most English parliamentarians.

The two English political parties then separately appealed to William of Orange, the ruler of the Dutch United Provinces. Some vague promises were made and William, not quite sure what the expedition would bring but hoping at least to create an English alliance for his struggle against France, set sail with 15,000 men, landing at Torbay in November 1688. Once he was landed his Whig and Tory sponsors began to disagree about what to do with him, and since James had an army double the size of William's, the expedition was in danger of collapse. James sent his army to the road junction of Salisbury. As it marched the desertion rate grew, which so unnerved James that he rejected Churchill's advice to fight and then ordered a withdrawal. Churchill thereupon mounted his horse and joined William. Other key figures soon abandoned the royal cause and James ordered the disbandment of his army before fleeing to France, leaving William to accept the British throne as King William III, his legitimacy deriving from his wife Mary who was James's Protestant daughter.

James II's standing army had proved ineffective so far as repelling an invasion was concerned but it might have still caused problems at home – once James was gone steps were taken to disband it. However, at that point Europe was beginning a general war, and James landed in Ireland. Instead of being dissolved, the British Army had to be enlarged.

Meanwhile James called on friendly Scottish forces to rally to his banner. The Presbyterian Lowlanders were generally hostile to him, and they offered the Scottish crown to William and Mary. But the Highlanders rallied to support James. Led by James Graham, they managed to rout a government force at the Battle of Killiekrankie in August 1689. But Graham was killed and, bereft of good leadership, the Highlanders stood little chance the next time they took on government troops. This happened a few weeks later, when they fell victim to a regiment of Cameronians at Dunkeld. The following year, the Highland chiefs swore allegiance to William, although this did not prevent them rising again in 1715, and finally in 1745.

James landed in Ireland in March 1689, and brought with him 8000 French troops. The Catholics of Ireland rallied enthusiastically to his cause; these included, notably, the Anglo-Catholics who, having settled in Ireland over the previous centuries, wished to retain the supremacy of the English crown so long as that crown was favorably disposed toward their interests. The Protestant forces by the late spring of 1689 were pressed into a small area of northern Ireland, holding only Londonderry and Enniskellen. William, not wishing to dissipate his small forces, sent only a few troops commanded by a colonel to Ireland. After a good deal of waiting and watching, this force managed to raise the siege of Londonderry in late July. Meanwhile, one of William's officers reached Enniskellen and organized the Protestants who were holding out there: the latter won a small but psychologically important victory in July by marching out to destroy a Catholic detachment at Newton Butler.

By the end of the summer William had managed to collect an army of 10,000 men, most of whom were untrained. Commanded by

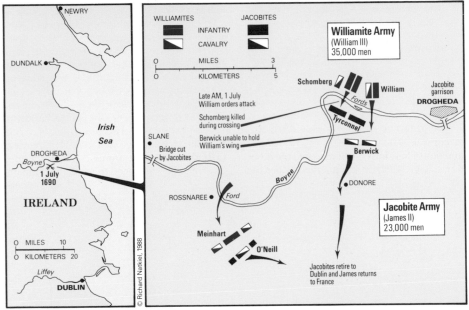

Above left: James II (1633-1701).
Above: the victory of the Dutch and English forces at the Boyne.
Left: the Battle of the Boyne, June 1690.
Below: the flight of James II from Ireland.

with the surrender of Limerick, the Irish war drew to a close.

In the long run, this Irish war not only failed to solve Irish difficulties but was destined to become a foundation of the Irish problem. In the short run, only the Irish Protestants and Louis XIV of France benefited from it. For Louis, it was a lesson in the value of sea power, for the failure of the English and Dutch navies to prevent the landing of a small French force in 1689 meant that England had been forced to station thousands of scarce troops in Ireland for two years.

General Schomberg, a French Protestant exile, they settled down for the winter in Dundalk where they were joined by 4000 Irish Protestant volunteers. Badly supplied, badly sheltered, and facing an early, cold, wet winter, these troops steadily died, the bodies on one occasion being used to build a windbreak. In November Schomberg decided he had to leave or perish, and ordered his surviving 7000 men to retreat to Belfast.

At the beginning of 1690, therefore, the Jacobite Catholic cause seemed triumphant in Ireland, a success which threatened William and Mary's hold on Britain. William, realizing that this campaign must take precedence over his continental conflict, decided to lead a 35,000-man army to Ireland. In July, at the Battle of the Boyne, not far from Dublin, James's army was decisively defeated, and a couple of months later William decided it was safe to return to England, leaving his Dutch general, Ginkel, in command. The Catholic forces were pushed toward the southwest into Galway and Limerick, and in October 1691,

The Wars of the League of Augsburg

Often known as the Nine Years War, the Wars of the League of Augsburg lasted from 1688 to 1697. France under Louis XIV had emerged as the greatest military power in Europe and, although she was technically at peace, had for a decade been acquiring by purchase, alliances or threats (supported by flimsy legalistic arguments) strongpoints outside the frontiers fixed by the Nijmegan Treaty. In these ways, French forces had occupied Strasbourg, commanding the Rhine; Dinant, leading to Namur; Luxemburg, a good base for another attack on the Spanish Netherlands; and several other key points. Fortresses had been built or rebuilt by Vauban, universally regarded as a genius in siege and defensive warfare.

Vauban introduced many novelties into fortress warfare, including ricochet gunfire, and the defense or capture of fortified points had become the principal objective of warring armies. This slow-moving strategy was further developed by the careful siting of huge supply points for the use of the French Army in wartime. These magazines enabled armies to move with fewer delays for provisioning, but also made them reluctant to move too far away from their supply bases.

The decade of peaceful French gains ended in 1688 when Louis XIV, thwarted in his hope of placing a French nominee as Elector of Cologne, despatched troops to occupy Bonn and other territory around Cologne, and also into the German states further south where his forces occupied Mainz, Heidelburg and Mannheim as well as threatening Frankfurt and Coblenz. But the French advance into Germany made it easier for William of Orange to gain the support of his Dutch people and to hire troops from German princes for his successful landing in England and assumption of the British crown as William III. This was, in effect, the most important event of the Nine Years War, even though it occurred before that war had officially started, because William, France's enemy, thereby added the strength of England to his own Dutch forces.

Of the principal states united, more or less, in the new defensive war against France, Austria was hampered by her struggle against Turkey and also by the antiquated organization of her army. At the peak of her endeavor she provided about 50,000 troops for the coalition. The Dutch raised about 72,000 men, including some English and Scottish units as well as troops hired from German states and from Sweden. Toward the end of the war,

Below left: the Battle of Neerwinden, 12 March 1693.
Below right: ships of the Anglo-Dutch fleet under the Earl of Oxford attack the French at La Hougue.

Britain was providing more than 90,000 soldiers, some of whom were foreign, as well as a navy of about 45,000 men. France with its large population could match these numbers and, in addition, possessed outstanding generals. The reforms of Louis's minister Louvois, who had ensured that the army made an early change from the matchlock to the flintlock and from the plug bayonet to the ring bayonet, also made the French forces a formidable foe. Administrative reforms meant that the French Army was better disciplined than those of its enemies.

After the 1688 French invasion of the Rhineland territories, four of the biggest German states (Brandenburg, Saxony, Brunswick-Luneburg and Hesse-Cassel) agreed to unite in defense of the middle and lower Rhine. Their troops, strengthened by Bavarian and Austrian units transferred by the emperor from the Turkish front, forced the French to abandon the siege of Koblenz, although they failed to recapture Philippsburg.

Spain was in no position to fight a war but, promised Dutch troops to defend the Spanish Netherlands, allowed itself to be dragged in. This meant that the main contest would be in the Netherlands, and France began to transfer troops there from the Rhineland. To discourage German forces from reoccupying the territory vacated by these French troops, the surrounding countryside and towns like Heidelburg and Trier were ravaged by fire – a policy which led to such devastation that the Allies, especially the Germans, were strengthened in their resolve.

William III was unable to persuade the Austrian emperor to make peace with the Turks and thereby free more troops, but he did in the spring of 1689 succeed in formulating war aims acceptable to the British, Dutch and the emperor. Briefly, these aims were the restoration of the situation left by the treaties of Westphalia and the Pyrenees; that is, to push back the French to their frontiers of 1659.

In 1689, the first year of general war, the French were on the defensive in the Spanish Netherlands but they embarrassed Spain by crossing into Catalonia, one of the most restless parts of Spain proper. They also embarrassed the English by landing ex-King James II in Ireland, forcing William to allocate 10,000 of his troops for Irish service. In Germany, three Imperial armies held the French, and on the middle Rhine recaptured Mainz. On the lower Rhine, Brandenburgian and Hanoverian troops recaptured Kaiserlautern, thereby securing Cologne, but then lost impetus by

besieging strategically insignificant Bonn. By the end of the year the French still held Philippsburg, but elsewhere the Allies controlled most of the Rhine.

1690 did not go well for the Allies. The French landed troops in Ireland and the Anglo-Dutch fleet, due to lack of coordination, was defeated off Beachy Head in June. But the French nevertheless failed to cut the British supply route to Ireland, where their protégé James II was defeated at the Boyne. In the Netherlands two French armies succeeded in joining forces and at the Battle of Fleurus forced the Dutch-Spanish army to withdraw, both sides suffering heavy casualties. Savoy was bribed to join the Allies, but was defeated at the Battle of Staffarda. Meanwhile, the Turks took the offensive, and the German states had to send troops to help the Austrian emperor on that front.

1691 was another year of great activity but little result. The French landed more troops in Ireland but despite this were driven to surrender their last stronghold, Limerick, in the fall. Meanwhile William III took personal command in the Netherlands, but failed to defeat the French who, beginning their campaign early, captured the Mons fortress and almost captured Liège. In Italy an Allied army of Spaniards, Savoyards, Bavarians and Austrians outnumbered the French, but its generals proved uncooperative. This campaign ended amid Allied recriminations and

with the French capture of the towns of Nice and Villafranca.

The French assembled troops for an invasion of England in 1692 but, their fleet having been defeated at Barfleur (May) and La Hougue (June), expedition was called off and

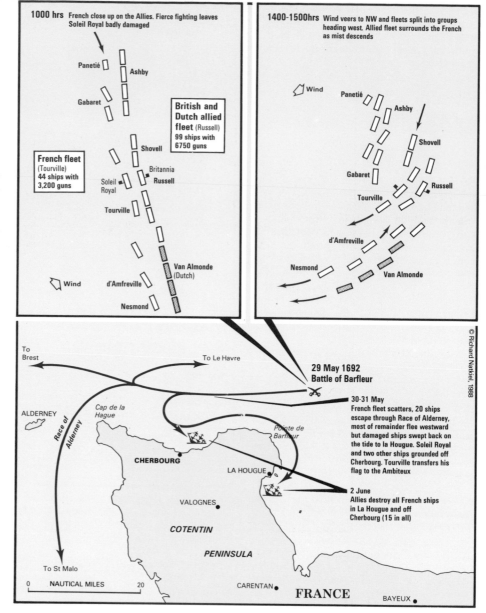

1000 hrs French close up on the Allies. Fierce fighting leaves Soleil Royal badly damaged

Panetié   Ashby

Gabaret

British and Dutch allied fleet (Russell) 99 ships with 6750 guns

French fleet (Tourville) 44 ships with 3,200 guns

Shovell

Britannia

Soleil Royal   Russell

Tourville

Wind   d'Amfreville   Van Almonde (Dutch)

Nesmond

1400-1500hrs Wind veers to NW and fleets split into groups heading west. Allied fleet surrounds the French as mist descends

Wind   Panetié   Ashby

Shovell

Gabaret   Russell

Tourville

d'Amfreville

Nesmond   Van Almonde

© Richard Natkiel, 1988

To Brest   To Le Havre

29 May 1692 Battle of Barfleur

ALDERNEY   Cap de la Hague

Race of Alderney

Pointe de Barfleur

CHERBOURG

LA HOUGUE

30-31 May French fleet scatters, 20 ships escape through Race of Alderney, most of remainder flee westward but damaged ships swept back on the tide to la Hougue. Soleil Royal and two other ships grounded off Cherbourg. Tourville transfers his flag to the Ambiteux

VALOGNES

2 June Allies destroy all French ships in La Hougue and off Cherbourg (15 in all)

COTENTIN

PENINSULA

0   NAUTICAL MILES   20

To St Malo

CARENTAN

FRANCE

BAYEUX

henceforth French naval activity concentrated on highly destructive raids on British and Dutch shipping. In the Netherlands that year, the outnumbered French managed to capture Namur, and having succeeded in bringing them to battle at Steinkirk William narrowly missed a victory there; both sides suffered heavy losses but it was William who finally withdrew. Fighting continued on the Rhine, with the French holding off the superior forces of the emperor. From Savoy, the Allies launched an attack through the Alps into southern France, where they won a few towns but then disagreed about what to do next and finally withdrew.

By this time financial and economic exhaustion was compelling the belligerents to consider a compromise peace. These thoughts loosened the cohesion of the Allies, who began to suspect that one or other member of the alliance was planning to make a separate peace. In the Netherlands William failed to hold the French and was forced to withdraw to Brussels while the French captured Charleroi. In Italy, the French general Catinat won a victory at Marsaglia after the Allies had failed to capture Pinerolo; not for the first time the Allies suffered from lack of close co-operation between the generals of the different national armies. But despite all this, the following year went quite well for the Allies, mainly because France was suffering from economic and financial difficulties. Except in the minor Catalonian campaign, the French were on the defensive that year, but yielding little.

1695 was marked by a major French defeat

Above: the Battle of Barfleur.
Below: the fighting at La Hougue.

in the Netherlands with the loss of Namur. In the following year there was so much talk of ending the war that campaigns were only half-fought. Savoy changed sides as a means of recovering lost territory. Britain was unable to pay its troops properly and mutinies seemed likely to break out. In the end the Treaty of Rijswick was drawn up. The French were required to hand back some of their recent acquisitions but they kept what was most precious to them, Strasbourg. They abandoned other Rhine fortresses, and handed back to Spain most of their gains in the Netherlands, including Luxembourg, Mons and Charleroi, and also their final conquest of the war, Barcelona. The British and Dutch gained nothing, but Britain in fact emerged stronger. Her commercial position had been reinforced at the expense of France and her navy had been reorganized under the pressure of war. Her experience in financing the war not by taxing the poor as in France, but by fair taxation and by creating a debt, gave her the confidence to face future wars.

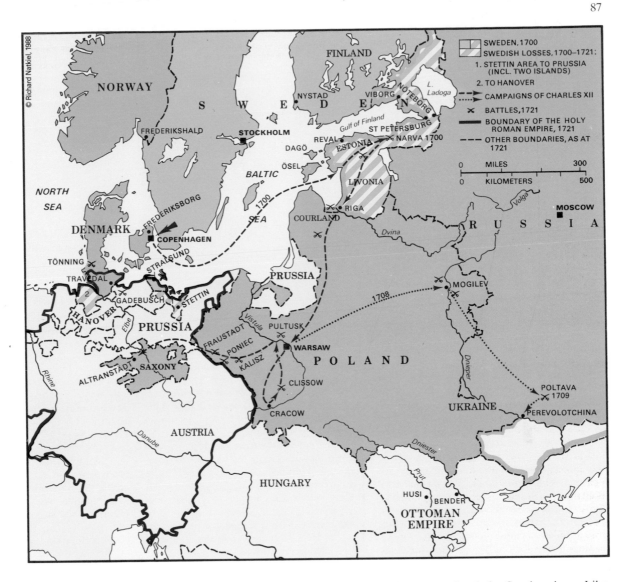

SWEDEN, 1700
SWEDISH LOSSES, 1700–1721:
1. STETTIN AREA TO PRUSSIA (INCL. TWO ISLANDS)
2. TO HANOVER
→ → CAMPAIGNS OF CHARLES XII
✕ BATTLES, 1721
▬ BOUNDARY OF THE HOLY ROMAN EMPIRE, 1721
- - - OTHER BOUNDARIES, AS AT 1721

The Great Northern War

In 1698 Augustus, ruler of Saxony and also King of Poland, joined with Russia and Denmark to make war on Sweden with the aim of sharing out the Swedish Empire. But the 16-year-old Charles XII of Sweden was unexpectedly revealed as one of the most gifted generals of the age, actually loving adversity and also endowed with a fast-moving tactical brain.

When Czar Peter I (the future Peter the Great) advanced to besiege the Swedish-held town of Narva (1700), he expected Sweden to be fully committed to beating back a Danish invasion. Charles XII unexpectedly defeated the Danes and forced them to make peace. The Swedish Army then hurried to tackle a surprised Peter at Narva. The czar abandoned his troops, who were put to flight next day, a snowstorm having concealed the Swedes' five-to-one numerical inferiority. Charles spent the winter at Dorpat and the following summer set out to attack the Saxons, whom he routed at Dunamunde before occupying

Courland. He captured Warsaw in May 1702, beat the Saxon-Polish Army at Klissow and went on to take Krakow in July. In spring 1703 he again beat the Saxons, at Pultusk, and later appointed his own nominee as King of Poland in place of Augustus II.

Peter launched his own counterattack while Charles XII was engaged in the west. In Sweden's Baltic territories he won victories at Errestfer and Hummelsdorf in 1702, and in the following year he captured enough of Swedish Ingria to enable him to found his city of St Petersburg on the Baltic. Then his troops, commanded by the Scottish general Ogilvie, took Dorpat and Narva before continuing to pursue a Swedish army into Riga in 1705.

In early 1706 Charles XII turned east but the Russians, entrenched at Grodno, would not emerge to fight. Meanwhile Augustus and his Saxons advanced against another Swedish army. The intention was to defeat this and then take Charles XII and his army in the rear while the Russians attacked his front. But at Fraustadt the Saxons were routed by the first Swedish army, after which the Russians withdrew so fast that they abandoned their heavy guns. The Swedes then moved west again and forced Augustus to abandon his Russian alliance and his claim to the Polish crown.

Peter now faced the Swedes alone. Like several of his successors, he withdrew into Russia, drawing his enemy into a campaign where time, space, cold and hunger would do his work for him. In September 1707 the Swedes turned once more toward Russia, this time with an army of 24,000 cavalry and 20,000 infantry. Unable to get to grips with Peter's army, Charles turned south after wintering near Minsk. He forced a crossing of the Berezina at Borisov and in July 1708 defeated the Russians at Holowczyn before moving on to capture Mogilev. He then made an agreement with Mazeppa, leader of the Ukrainians, guaranteeing to take the Ukraine, which nominally belonged to Poland and Russia, under his protection in exchange for the use of 30,000 Ukrainian Cossacks.

In August Charles crossed the Dnieper and after defeating Peter's Army at Dobry entered Russia, only to discover the meaning of a scorched-earth policy. Disregarding advice to await the arrival of a supply column commanded by General Lewenhaupt, he moved south to join Mazeppa. This was expected to force Peter to fight in unpromising circumstances; in addition, the Poles were to enter Russia and march in two columns against Smolensk and Kiev, while a smaller Swedish

army was to be sent from Finland to recapture the province of Ingria.

From about this time Charles began to be defeated by his own genius. On the battlefield, flitting from one critical point to another, making snap decisions that always turned out to be exactly right, he had enabled numerically inferior Swedish forces to win great victories. But by this stage he was so confident that he was prepared to flaunt all the rules of strategy and tactics. The decision to move off without waiting for Lewenhaupt's much-needed supplies was foolish; Lewenhaupt was eventually attacked by stronger Russian forces at Lesna, near Polotsk, and was forced to bury his artillery and burn his supplies in

order to break through and catch up with Charles. Meanwhile the attack on Ingria had been repulsed with heavy losses. These Swedish defeats weakened Mazeppa's position and he was deposed. The Swedes were now alone in Russia without supplies and facing an exceptionally cold winter.

Charles did capture Romny, which was well stocked, but Peter tempted him out by occupying the nearby town of Gadiatz. Charles went to capture Gadiatz, and as soon as he left Romny Peter's army moved in. Gadiatz was meanwhile burned, so Charles was forced to wander around from township to township, losing at least 3000 men from the combined effects of hunger and cold.

In the spring of 1709 Charles, although advised by his generals to leave Russia, decided to besiege Poltava. He had only about 17,000 men left, and the approaching Russian army had 80,000. Nevertheless, he might have won the battle had he not been shot in the foot the day before. Without battlefield mobility, he could no longer command effectively. He depended on spontaneity and audacity to throw opponents off balance, and this was no longer possible.

After the Poltava defeat Charles fled south to Turkey. Here he helped the Sultan plan his own campaign against southern Russia. He was incensed when the Turks made peace with Russia after an inconclusive battle on the River Prut in 1711, and was soon expelled. On his way home he defended Stralsund against combined British, Prussian, Russian, Saxon and Danish forces, and abandoned it only when it was in ruins. Later, in 1718, he led another army against Norway, but was killed in the fighting. The Great Northern War finally ended when Sweden and Russia made peace in 1721 at Nystad. The terms, granting Russia Livonia, Estonia, Ingria, and part of Finland, implied the end of the Swedish Empire.

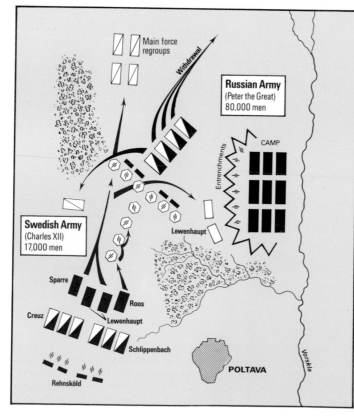

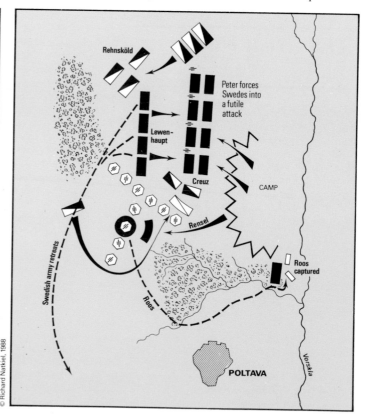

The War of the Spanish Succession

When the childless Spanish king Charles II died in 1700 he left all his possessions to Philip of Anjou, the grandson of King Louis XIV, but stipulated that if Philip refused, the entire Spanish Empire should go to the Austrian emperor. After some hesitation, Louis accepted on behalf of his grandson. Although aware that his decision must have alarmed other rulers, he began to indulge in sundry acts of aggression that could only harden their attitude. He sent troops into the Spanish Netherlands, occupied several Dutch frontier towns and forced Spain to grant him slave-trading rights in its empire. A Grand Alliance against France was an immediate result, founded at a meeting between the English Duke of Marlborough and the Grand Pensionary of the Dutch United Provinces.

This alliance had clear aims which were maintained throughout the ensuing war and finally secured by the Treaty of Utrecht which ended the conflict after 12 years. King William III did not want the French to have the Spanish Netherlands, Spanish Italy and the Spanish Mediterranean islands, and was content that these should go to Austria, which was not a naval or commercial competitor of the British or Dutch. There was no objection to the French Philip ruling in Spain and the Spanish Indies, so long as the crowns of Spain and France were not united. William's successor, Queen Anne, maintained this policy which was fully supported by most Englishmen. The French proclamation of the Pretender as King James III of England, and the French threat to British commerce and security were enough to persuade property owners to accept a high land tax to help finance the war. The Dutch likewise regarded war as unavoidable, knowing that the French seizure of their fortified frontier towns threatened the continued existence of their independent state.

The Grand Alliance of 1701 was between Austria, Britain and the Dutch United Provinces. Austria, claiming the entire Spanish inheritance but not supported in this demand by the British and Dutch, had already sent an army into Italy to capture Milan. Subsequently various German states joined the alliance. These included Hanover, Baden and Brandenburg. The Austrian emperor, as head of the loose confederation of German states acknowledging allegiance to the Holy Roman Empire, had bribed Brandenburg's ruler by granting him permission to style himself King of Prussia. But apart from Brandenburg, these states assisted only by hiring out troops. Moreover, Bavaria and Cologne chose to support France.

Thanks to William III's reforms, the Dutch Army was excellent, and eventually grew to nearly 140,000 men. Britain's expeditionary force amounted to 70,000 men at its peak, but relied on the Dutch for siege engineers and heavy artillery. Both the British and Dutch armies were partly composed of hired German

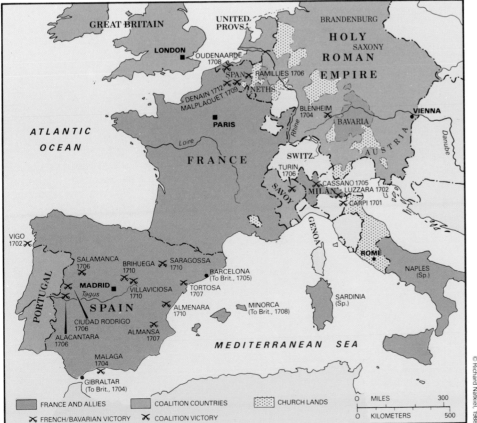

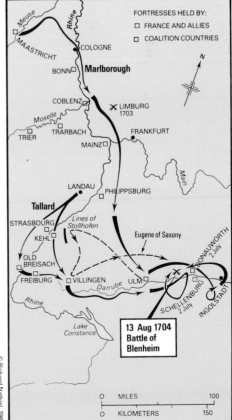

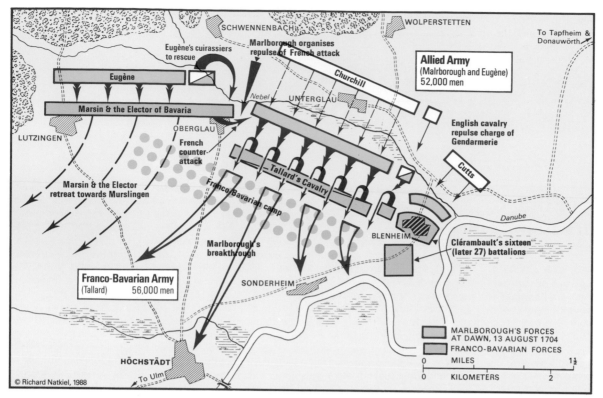

Map labels:

SCHWENNENBACH
WOLPERSTETTEN
To Tapfheim & Donauwörth

Eugène's cuirassiers to rescue
Marlborough organises repulse of French attack

Allied Army (Marlborough and Eugène) 52,000 men

Eugène
Churchill
Nebel
UNTERGLAU
Marsin & the Elector of Bavaria

English cavalry repulse charge of Gendarmerie

OBERGLAU
LUTZINGEN
French counter-attack

Cutts

Marsin & the Elector retreat towards Murslingen
Tallard's Cavalry
Franco-Bavarian camp

Danube

Marlborough's breakthrough
BLENHEIM

Clérambault's sixteen (later 27) battalions

Franco-Bavarian Army (Tallard) 56,000 men

SONDERHEIM

MARLBOROUGH'S FORCES AT DAWN, 13 AUGUST 1704
FRANCO-BAVARIAN FORCES

0   MILES   1½
0   KILOMETERS   2

HÖCHSTÄDT
To Ulm

© Richard Natkiel, 1988

and Danish troops. In the naval war the British made the greatest effort, for whereas Britain was able to finance the war largely by taxation, the Dutch had to borrow money at high interest rates and were unable to finance both a strong army and a strong navy. As for the emperor's Austrian forces, these amounted to about 130,000 men, but they were not well administered. On the other

Left: the Battle of Blenheim.
Below left: three scenes from Blenheim – the
attack on Blenheim village; an attack on the
French center; and Eugène orders the attack
on the French left.
Right: the Battle of Ramillies.
Below right: Marlborough at Ramillies.

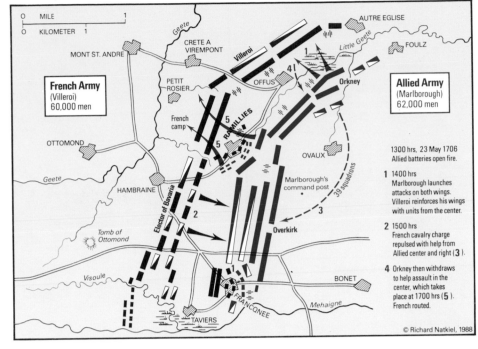

French Army
(Villeroi)
60,000 men

Allied Army
(Marlborough)
62,000 men

1300 hrs, 23 May 1706
Allied batteries open fire.

1 1400 hrs
Marlborough launches
attacks on both wings.
Villeroi reinforces his wings
with units from the center.

2 1500 hrs
French cavalry charge
repulsed with help from
Allied center and right (3).

4 Orkney then withdraws
to help assault in the
center, which takes
place at 1700 hrs (5).
French routed.

© Richard Natkiel, 1988

hand, the Austrian general Eugène was an
outstanding commander and this more than
offset the mediocrity of the troops. Luckily,
hostilities against Turkey had ceased, but
some troops were required to discourage
rebellion in Hungary.

Against these forces the French could raise
a quarter of a million troops by 1705, and had
the advantages of interior lines of communication, single command without inter-Allied
bickering and an army that was well equipped
and well disciplined. With Philip on the
Spanish throne, Louis could also count on co-
operation in the Spanish Netherlands even
though Spain itself had little military strength.
French troops were allowed to take over the
Spanish fortresses in the Netherlands, and a
line of rivers and fortresses curving almost the
whole way from Antwerp to Namur – the
Lines of Brabant – blocked the advance of all
but the strongest Allied formations.

The Dutch accepted Marlborough as commander in chief, having control over their
armies so long as they were acting with British
forces. However, he was to be accompanied
by Dutch political commissars, called field
deputies, who could veto his orders and on
several occasions did employ this power to
hold Marlborough back. The emperor did not
subscribe to unity of command, and retained
complete control of his army's operations, but
his general Eugène co-operated loyally and
generously with Marlborough in their joint
campaigns.

Marlborough, a masterful diplomat and
great general, was also a remarkable leader,
who took as much trouble over details of
administration as over grand questions of strategy. He overturned the accepted form of military campaigns, based on sieges and depen-
dence on supply dumps. He returned to
offensive strategies which military technology
had made more practical. The introduction of
the faster-firing flintlock and the replacement
of pikes by bayonets meant that infantry could
now move faster and hit harder in battle.
Marlborough's favorite battle tactic was to pin
down the enemy with continuous infantry
attacks and only then release his cavalry to
make a decisive breakthrough.

War was declared in May 1702, and Marlborough's immediate concern were to prevent
a French occupation of the United Provinces,
and to avoid the defeat of Austria by the
French and Spanish, the former advancing
through friendly Savoy and the latter from
their territories in Italy. His plan was to dislodge the French from their strongholds along

the Meuse and lower Rhine. An Anglo-Dutch
fleet was to capture Cadiz in Spain, establish a
base and, from there, command the western
Mediterranean, thereby threatening southern
France and disrupting Spanish communications with Italy. The Cadiz expedition failed
but the crestfallen fleet had the good fortune
to take by surprise the Spanish treasure fleet
and some French warships at Vigo. This great
victory was small strategic compensation for
the Cadiz failure, but on land Marlborough
did well, despite the timorous interference of
his Dutch field deputies. He not only won control of the Meuse and lower Rhine, but also
invaded Cologne and later captured Bonn.
The Dutch and German princes meanwhile
captured Kaiserwerth. Marlborough then
attempted to take Antwerp, but was thwarted
by an insubordinate Dutch general.

But in southern Germany the best of the
French generals, Villars, defeated the Baden
Army at Friedlingen and proceeded through

the Black Forest to join the Bavarians. The
latter, however, refused to march against
Vienna. In September Villars won a victory
against the Austrians at Hochstadt, and again
urged the Bavarians to join in a quick advance
on Vienna. This time the argument turned
into a quarrel, and Louis XIV recalled Villars,
replacing him with a less effective general,
Marsin. Nevertheless, that winter the
Austrian situation was perilous and Austrian
troops were withdrawn from Italy to help
defend Vienna.

At the end of 1703 the only bright spots for
the alliance were the defections of Portugal
and Savoy from the French side. Portugal's
adherence to the alliance, acceleratd by the
impression made by the Vigo victory,
promised to provide the southern naval base
that the alliance so badly needed. However,
the French intended to knock Austria out of
the war in the 1704 campaigning season, and
the Allies seemed powerless to prevent this.

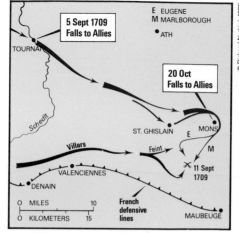

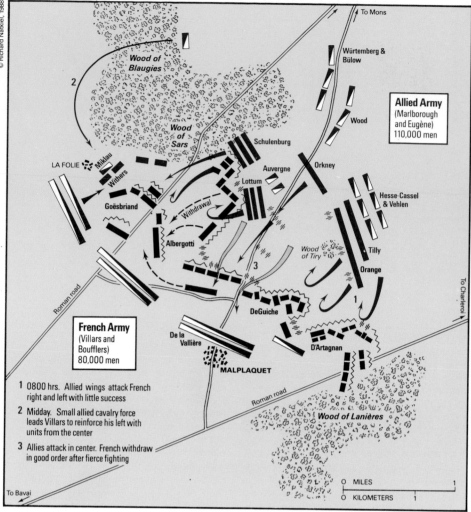

Allied Army
(Marlborough
and Eugène)
110,000 men

French Army
(Villars and
Boufflers)
80,000 men

1 0800 hrs. Allied wings attack French right and left with little success

2 Midday. Small allied cavalry force leads Villars to reinforce his left with units from the center

3 Allies attack in center. French withdraw in good order after fierce fighting

Marlborough decided to move his British troops south to the Danube. This was a risky maneuver for his forces in that their passage south would expose their flanks to successive French armies. Organization and administration would be all-important if his troops were to arrive intact and in good heart, but this organization would have to be highly secret. The Dutch were also to be deceived – for they would want to prevent the diversion of British troops from the Dutch theater.

Marlborough let it be known that he intended to fight the 1704 campaign on the Moselle. The Dutch made their expected objections, but Marlborough took his army south and reached Koblenz at the end of May. Here, instead of turning to advance along the Moselle, he surprised his friends and enemies by continuing south to Mainz instead. This element of surprise prevented the French attacking him at Koblenz and, now believing he was intent on capturing Philippsburg, they prepared to meet him at Landau, across the Rhine from Philippsburg. But instead of turning to the west he continued south, once more evading the French. He then linked up with the Baden Army and with Eugène's Austrian troops that had been sent to support him. Early in July he had reached Donauwörth, a strongpoint commanding the Danube and several vital roads. As a siege would have given the main French forces time to catch up with him. Marlborough decided on a shock assault against the French garrison. He attacked its fortified high ground, the Schellenberg, first with a strong force of infantry and then, when the enemy was fully engaged, with a second column approaching under cover of the hillside.

The capture of Donauwörth was an important success, but Marlborough had still not won the decisive battle that was needed to relieve Vienna. Near Blenheim, joined with Eugène's army, he took up positions to await the French and Bavarians. The latter were expecting their appearance to induce the outnumbered Allies to withdraw, but in fact Marlborough attacked, with infantry assaults sucking in the French reserves at Blenheim village, followed by an Austrian assault on the other flank, until the time came for the main force to break through the denuded center.

Blenheim, the British Army's greatest victory on foreign soil since Agincourt, destroyed Louis XIV's hopes and his army's reputation for invincibility. But the war dragged on for another eight years. The main reason for this was that Britain, in order to obtain the alliance with Portugal, had promised that the Austrian Archduke Charles would become King of Spain. Anxious to keep their valuable docking facilities at Lisbon, the British tried to keep this bargain with Portugal and it was not until an unrewarding campaign had been fought in the Iberian Peninsula, with Madrid captured and then lost, that Britain finally decided that the Frenchman Philip would after all have to remain on the Spanish throne. A second hindrance to peace negotiations was that the Dutch demanded a guarantee for their frontier towns, the so-called barrier towns.

Louis XIV made his first secret peace offers in 1705 but with little success, and in the following year the Allies had a run of successes. Using tactics similar to those of Blenheim, Marlborough defeated a French army at Ramillies near Namur (May 1706), after which the inhabitants of the Spanish Netherlands revolted against the Spaniards and their French allies. In Italy, Eugène and his Austrians routed the French who had been besieging Turin and thereby confirmed Austrian domination of northern Italy.

It was not long before the French recovered in the Netherlands. The confused infantry Battle of Oudenarde in 1708 was indecisive, and the Dutch generals vetoed Marlborough's project to march on Paris without first taking Lille. This fortress did not surrender until December 1708, and the French forces then withdrew into France. Louis refused to sign a treaty which did not guarantee the Spanish crown to his grandson, and in 1709 prepared for a renewal of the war. Marlborough captured some fortress towns in Flanders and on the way to take Mons fought at Malplaquet, where the Dutch infantry was shattered but the French were driven into retreat.

Because there were so many combatants and so many conflicting claims, the Treaty of Utrecht was not ready for signing until 1713. By it, Spain was retained by Philip, although the crowns of France and Spain were permanently separated. The Dutch won back most of their barrier fortresses, and Austria received much of Italy, including Lombardy and Naples as well as Sardinia. Britain, whose sound financing had supported the alliance, benefited enormously from the decline of Dutch seapower, and also held on to newly conquered Gibraltar as well as Newfoundland and Nova Scotia. As in previous wars, Britain did not appear to make gains, but the future would show that she was the real winner.

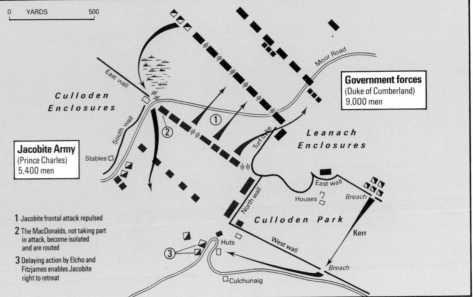

ROUTE OF PRINCE
CHARLES EDWARD
STUART, 1745-46

Returns to France

16 Apr 1746
Culloden

ERISKAY

From France

GLASGOW

21 Sept 1745
Prestonpans

17 Jan 1746 Falkirk

CARLISLE

GREAT BRITAIN

DERBY

© Richard Natkiel, 1988

YARDS 500

Moor Road

East wall

Culloden
Enclosures

South wall

Government forces
(Duke of Cumberland)
9,000 men

Jacobite Army
(Prince Charles)
5,400 men

Leanach
Enclosures

Stables

Turfdyke

North wall

Houses

Breach

East wall

Culloden Park

Kerr

1 Jacobite frontal attack repulsed

2 The MacDonalds, not taking part
in attack, become isolated
and are routed

3 Delaying action by Elcho and
Fitzjames enables Jacobite
right to retreat

West wall

Breach

Huts

Culchunaig

The 1745 Jacobite Rebellion

The return of James II and his descendants to the English throne had long been an aim of the French and they drew comfort from the fact that many of the chieftains of the Scottish Highlands also favored the old House of Stuart. In 1715 5000 Highlanders marched from Perth but were checked by the Duke of Argyle's army outside Stirling. Other Jacobite rebels from Northumberland and the Scottish lowlands marched south, rather than join the Highlanders. The rebellion collapsed when the divided Highland rebels were defeated at Sheriffmuir and at Preston. James Stuart, James II's heir, only landed when the war was practically lost and returned to France a few weeks later.

Another chance came in 1745, when France was at war with Britain; James Stuart was proclaimed James III of England and a French frigate landed his son, Prince Charles, with a few companions, some weapons and a stock of gold in the Hebrides. The Highlanders rallied to Prince Charles and within three weeks he had raised his standard at Glenfinnan. In September his new army captured Edinburgh, where he proclaimed his father King James VIII of Scotland. Local government forces were then defeated at the Battle of Prestonpans. Prince Charles then wanted to invade England, hoping this would persuade the French to launch their own cross-Channel invasion in support, for they had assembled 15,000 men at Dunkirk for that purpose. However, Prince Charles overestimated the depth of his support: many of his men preferred to stay in Scotland and he only crossed into England in October.

About a quarter of his 6000 men deserted before he reached Manchester. Meanwhile the government recalled the Duke of Cumber-

land and his English and Hanoverian troops from the Netherlands. When part of the Prince's force turned into north Wales, Cumberland made the mistake of pursuing it, giving Charles's main force a clear road to the south. Charles reached Derby, but eventually turned back when it became evident that the English navy was successfully blocking the French invasion fleet.

Back in Scotland after a sorry retreat, Charles easily raised more men and defeated the English again at Falkirk. But Cumberland, after a brief recall to the south when the French invasion seemed imminent, was sent north again and entered Edinburgh in late January 1746, while Charles retreated to Inverness. When Cumberland moved north from Aberdeen with an army double the size of Charles's, the latter's Irish advisers recommended a surprise night attack on Cumberland's men at Nairn. But after a difficult night's march the Jacobites were still some distance from Nairn, so had to fall back on their old position at Culloden, near Inverness. Here

the army spent the morning, waiting in wind and rain, before it was ordered to charge Cumberland's advancing army. Having 18 field guns at his disposal, Cumberland could hardly lose, and within an hour the Highlanders were shattered. A few prepared to make a stand at Ruthven, but were ordered by Prince Charles to disband. Culloden marked the end of Jacobite hopes, and heralded the destruction of traditional Highland society, which was callously remolded by fire and sword.

Above far left: the campaign and Battle of Malplaquet.
Above: the 1745 Jacobite rebellion and the Battle of Culloden.
Below: the clans reach the Duke of Cumberland's line at Culloden.

The War of the Austrian Succession

This war was ostensibly about the succession to the Austrian throne but, in reality, it was about the place of Prussia in the modern European world. From this and the following Seven Years War, Prussia emerged as a great military power and, as events turned out, the wars also enabled Britain finally and incontestably to become the world's dominant naval and colonial power. The conduct of war changed rapidly in the mid-eighteenth century, and nowhere so rapidly as in Prussia. After having for years been marched over by foreign armies, Prussia became a militarized state in the period, raising an army half as large as the French, even though the population was only one-tenth that of France. Conscription, a willingness to devote almost the entire state budget to the army and the acceptance of a barrackroom society were the essential ingredients of this militarization, which was to affect the course of European history for the next 200 years.

Although the Prussians placed great importance on artillery, the greatest technical changes were to be seen in the infantry, whose role was enhanced by emphasis on fast and accurate musketry. Wooden ramrods, which had a habit of breaking in action, were replaced by iron ones, and intensive rifle drill enabled Prussian infantrymen to fire up to four shots per minute. Drill for all arms was well thought out, enabling Prussian armies to deploy rather faster than their opponents.

The reputation of the French Army was maintained largely because its generals were skilled in arranging battles where its weaknesses would be undiscovered. Unlike the Prussian Army, it was officered by men who had bought their commissions and were often unable to handle their men even in peacetime barracks. Promotion by favoritism rather than merit compounded this weakness. In addition, the army was no longer kept properly supplied due to the state's financial incompetence and lived by foraging and pillage. The British were adversely affected by the country's general mistrust of standing armies which meant that it took time to raise a wartime army. As in other armies, the British infantry had begun to play an enhanced role and its brisk, steady musketry turned the tide of several battles.

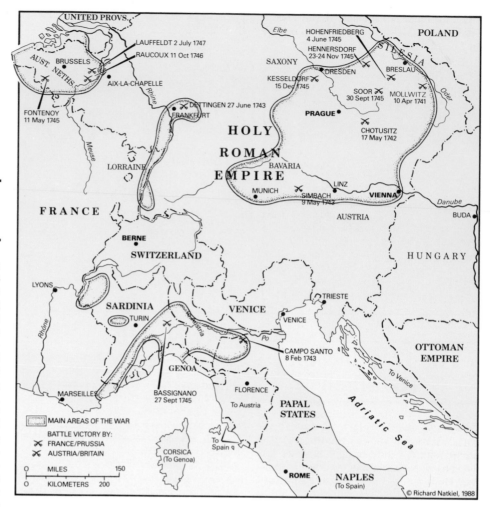

The Austrian emperor died in 1740. His daughter Maria Theresa's right to succeed him had been recognized by all the important European rulers apart from that of Bavaria, but her political inexperience, financial and military weakness and, above all, her sex were an irresistible temptation to Frederick II of Prussia. Apart from being a militarist and a misogynist, Frederick was ambitious both on his own behalf and on that of Prussia as a state. He had a fine army, he was a fine general, and he was not troubled by scruples.

His first move was a surprise, quite unprovoked, invasion of Austria's Silesian territory. Not averse to winter warfare, he sent his army into Silesia to advance on Breslau in mid-December 1740, and at the Battle of Mollwitz in the following spring his well-trained infantry defeated the Austrian Army. This victory and that at Chotusitz a year later made clear to other rulers how weak Austria really was. It was not long before an anti-Austrian coalition was hastily formed. France was a member because it wanted the Austrian (formerly Spanish) Netherlands for which it had fought several previous wars. Bavaria joined because its ruler wanted to become Holy Roman Emperor, while Saxony joined in the hope of extending its territories in Poland.

The Bavarians advanced toward Vienna along the Danube, while the French, still not officially at war with Austria, crossed the Rhine to reach Bohemia. Linz, only three days from Vienna, was occupied by the French and Bavarians, and Prague was captured in November. By summer 1741 Austria seemed on the verge of collapse: Bavarian troops were threatening Vienna; one French army had captured Prague and another was in the Austrian Netherlands. But, quite unexpectedly, Maria Theresa recovered. She was an appealing figure, and her Hungarian aristocrats in an outburst of chivalry rallied round her. The French were expelled from Prague and the Bavarians lost Munich. Sardinia, too, had joined in to support Austria. Britain had been fighting a naval war against Spain in the West Indies since 1739, and in 1741 implicitly decided to join in the European struggle on the side of Austria. This was largely because French dominance in the Netherlands was feared, and beyond that there was the possibility of a French threat to Hanover which was closely linked to the British crown.

Britain began to raise an army in 1741, although war was not actually declared until 1744. A 62,000-man force was financed, and most was sent to the Low Countries from where it moved to Germany for a junction with Austrian and Hanoverian forces. The combined army was then outmaneuvered. At Dettingen on the River Main it was penned into a small area surrounded by water, wooded hills, and the French. But a premature French advance into the fire of the well-trained British infantry, followed by a British

**Right: the Battle of Fontenoy, 11 May 1745.
Below right: a view of Fontenoy from behind
the French lines.**

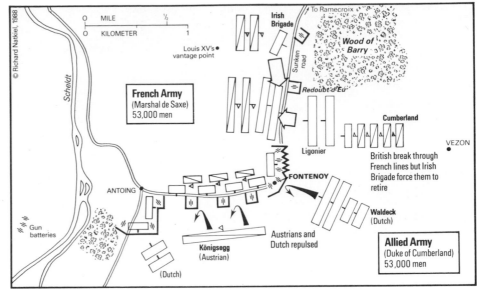

cavalry charge, resulted in a French rout. This
victory, which King George II led in person,
was not at all conclusive, but did suggest that
an invasion of France was becoming feasible.

Frederick, having lost 4000 of his Prussian
troops in a vain attempt to drive the Austrians
out of Prague, was willing to listen to British
attempts at mediation. He soon withdrew
Prussia from the war by making a peace with
Austria and he secured Silesia which was what
he really wanted – he was not especially interested in the Austrian succession itself.
Saxony also abandoned the war, leaving
Maria Theresa so triumphant, so avid for the
destruction of France, that she rejected any
suggestions of peace.

In 1743 Britain, Sardinia, and Austria
formed an alliance to continue the war against
France. Sardinia deserted France because the
latter's fleet had landed Spanish troops in
northern Italy, a hostile act as it was linked to
the entry of Naples into the war against Austria. However, the British fleet bombarded
the city of Naples, persuading that state to
make a rapid return to neutrality. The Spanish
forces nevertheless campaigned in Italy, meeting a combined Austro-Sardinian force and
failing to beat it at Campo Santo in early 1743.
Britain's naval intervention meanwhile cut
Spain's communications with its Italian troops
which meant that Maria Theresa's Italian territories were saved. But Frederick, deciding
that Austria was becoming far too strong, re-
entered the war and launched his Prussians
into Bohemia to capture Prague. Austria was
once more on the defensive and the French
king, in his turn, saw great opportunities and
abandoned any thoughts of making peace.

Louis sent his army, under de Saxe, back
into the Austrian Netherlands. Here there was
a combined Austrian, British, Dutch and
Hanoverian army that attacked the French at
Fontenoy in May 1745, even though the
French position was extremely strong with its
center and one flank protected by fortified villages and its other flank by earthworks and
hills. The 25-year-old Duke of Cumberland,
commanding the Allied army, soon lost control of his formations and, although the British
and Hanoverian infantry displayed great stea-
diness, the French won.

In 1746 de Saxe, taking advantage of the
despatch of most of the British to deal with the
Young Pretender in Scotland, went on the
offensive again, winning decisively at the
Battle of Raucoux. By 1747 Cumberland and
the British were back, but were then beaten at
the Battle of Lauffeldt. This was followed by

96

Below: the Battle of Hohenfriedburg, 4 June 1745.

the French capture of Bergen-op-Zoom which meant that the French had not only held on to the Austrian Netherlands but had also made inroads in Dutch Brabant.

In 1745 the French were doing so well that Louis could envisage not only the acquisition of the Netherlands but also the placing of a friendly Stuart monarch on the British throne. But Prince Charles was defeated at Culloden, and a French invasion fleet aimed at Britain

was frustrated by storms. In Bohemia, meanwhile, Frederick was forced to make some withdrawals, even though he won battles against his Austrian and Saxon opponents at Hohenfriedburg and Kesselsdorf in 1745. The Austrians became convinced that peace was worth negotiating. The Dresden Peace guaranteed Silesia and Glatz to Frederick and left Austria, as Frederick wished, strong enough to fight the French, with Maria Theresa still on

her throne and her husband confirmed as Holy Roman Emperor. In Italy, the Austrians and their Savoy allies, hard pressed by French and Spanish armies, were glad to sign the Peace of Aix-la-Chapelle in 1748 which allocated Parma to Spain and brought the war to an end. France had decided to abandon her gains in the Netherlands, having heard that the apparently defeated but well-financed British were about to hire a Russian army.

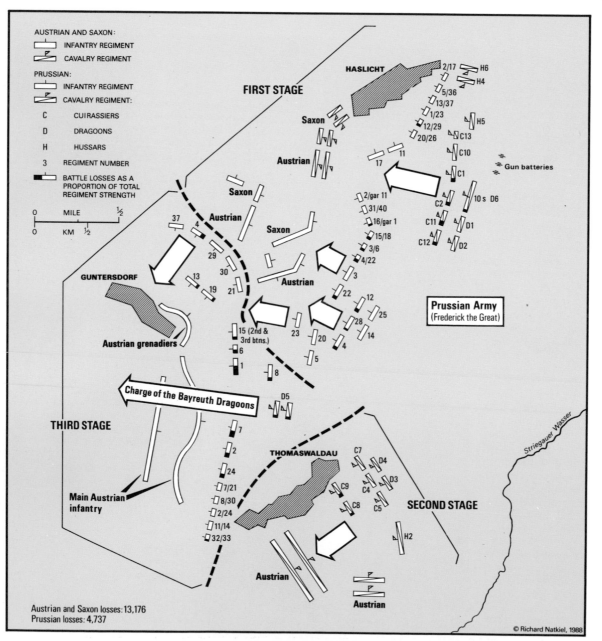

Austrian and Saxon losses: 13,176
Prussian losses: 4,737

© Richard Natkiel, 1988

The French and Indian Wars

'The French and Indian Wars' is the general name given to a series of four wars fought between English and French colonists in North America between 1689 and 1763. Insofar as the colonials were concerned, the concept of individual 'wars' was to some extent notional, since local armed hostilities tended to persist even during the intervals of 'peace' recognized by the mother countries. Geographically, there were two main theaters of conflict: the border between New England and New France, an ill-defined zone that ran, a little to the south of the St Lawrence River, northeast from Lake Erie to the Atlantic; and the disputed interior of the continent that lay west of the Appalachians. French strategy consisted

in attempting to discourage English expansion north and west by means of incessant harassing raids conducted by French troops and their Indian allies along the peripheries of the English colonies. The English counter-strategy was to try to neutralize the key French bases: Montreal and Quebec on the St Lawrence, various port settlements in Nova Scotia and on Ile Royale (Cape Breton Island) and the chains of forts the French had built in the interior.

The final phase of this protracted struggle began in 1755 (one of the periods of formal 'peace') when British Major General Edward Braddock led a body of about 2000 regulars and Virginia militia in an assault on France's Fort Duquesne, situated at the confluence of the Allegheny and Monongahela Rivers. Braddock unwisely let his troops become strung out during his advance, and on 9 July his forward force of 1200 was ambushed by 900 French regulars, Canadian militia and

Above: General Edward Braddock, killed at the Battle of Monongahela (1755) during the French and Indian Wars.

Indians. The result was a resounding British defeat: 914 English soldiers killed, including 63 officers, of whom Braddock was one. (Among the survivors was Braddock's aide-de-camp, Colonel George Washington.) Braddock's tactics in this battle – the attenuated force, the lack of forward scouting, the close-order formations used by the regular infantry – came to be regarded as virtually a textbook example of how *not* to conduct wilderness warfare.

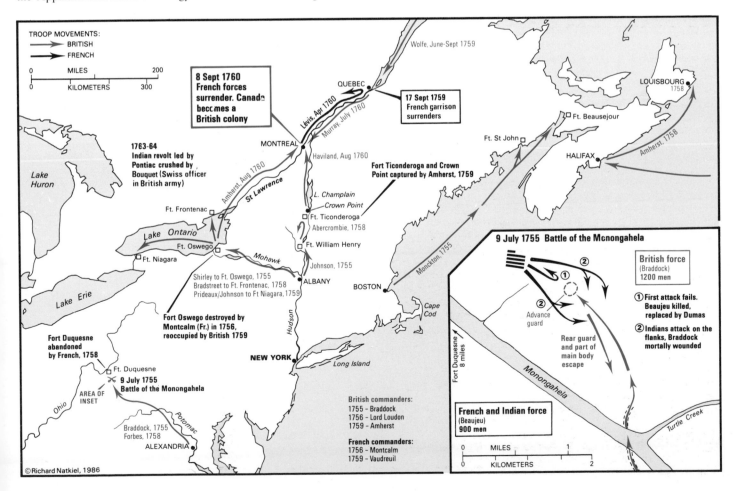

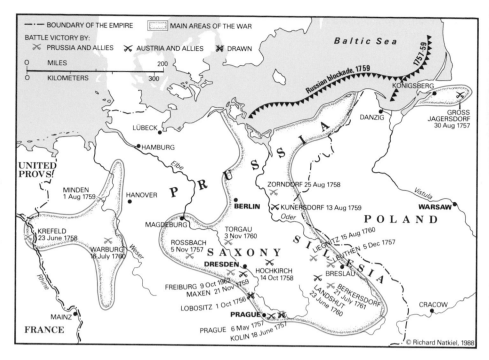

The Seven Years War

After the Treaty of Aix-la-Chapelle in 1748 there was a realignment, the first sign of which was an alliance between France and Austria. This was a defensive treaty, but it was not long before the French government, alarmed at the success of Frederick II, unwisely joined Austria in preparing for a war against Prussia, a war which would have some degree of support from Russia, Sweden and Saxony.

Frederick, aware that the Russian czarina was urging Austria to speed up war preparations, decided on a pre-emptive blow. He would be outnumbered by at least three-to-one in a war against the new anti-Prussian alliance and, although Prussia would enjoy the freedom of strategy offered by interior lines of communication, the lack of any defensible frontiers made her very vulnerable. The Austrians, once they had entered the territory of their ally Saxony, would be only about 40 miles from Berlin. In the east the Russians would have to cross the Oder, but they would then be only 50 miles from Berlin. The Swedes, who could concentrate at Stralsund on the Baltic coast, would be 130 miles away, but they were a serious threat in conjunction

with their allies. The French would enter Prussian territory at Halle which was only about 100 miles from Frederick's capital. Prussia was virtually surrounded and its best hope for victory lay in striking fast, while its enemies were still in different stages of preparation for war and therefore might be tackled individually.

Even after the deduction of 11,000 men to watch the Swedes, 26,000 to watch the Russians and 37,000 to hold Silesia, Frederick still had 70,000 left for the first blow. This was against Saxony which was invaded suddenly and without any declaration of war. Dresden was captured in September 1756, a couple of weeks after the frontier had been crossed, and in the following month the Prussians defeated an Austrian army that had been sent to hold them at Lobositz. With the capital, Dresden,

in his hands, Frederick had the Saxon treasury at his disposal, and he also began to incorporate Saxon units into his own army. In May 1757, after the snows had melted in the passes, he pushed on into Bohemia toward Prague. There he won another battle against the Austrians but then, confronted at Kolin by an Austrian army about double the size of his own, he followed his usual tactic of attacking at once, but was thrown back and lost more than a third of his men. He at once withdrew into Saxony to await fresh onslaughts.

His apparently unprovoked attack on Saxony had drawn upon him the hostility of the other German states, who were now willing to support his French and Russian foes. Having limited population, Frederick could not continually replenish his army and there-

Below far left: a romanticized portrait of
Frederick the Great.
Below left: attacked from front and rear, a
highly disciplined Prussian line regiment
holds enemy cavalry at bay.
Below right: the Prussian victory at Leuthen,
December 1757.

fore could not hope to win alone. But William
Pitt (the Elder), leading the British, persuaded himself that Frederick, thus beleaguered, must be a symbolic champion of
basic liberties as well as of the Protestant faith.
Although the British did not send any troops
specifically to help Frederick, they maintained
an army on the continent, sent money, helped
Frederick's ally Brunswick, and raided the
French coast.

The British-supported army, called the
'Army of Observation,' consisted of Hessian,
Prussian and Hanoverian troops commanded
by the Duke of Cumberland. It was stationed
in western Germany and was instructed to
fight the French only if they should invade.
When the French did cross the frontier they
soon defeated the Army of Observation at
Hastenbeck. This force was pushed northward
until it was trapped by the sea. Cumberland
then agreed, in September 1757, to disband his
troops in exchange for a guarantee of Hanover's neutrality, but London repudiated this
agreement and the Army of Observation,
renamed the 'Army of Execution,' was placed
under a new commander, Ferdinand of Brunswick, and went on to win some important and
decisive victories.

But English support, although valuable,
was not the key reason for Frederick's survival. That reason was Frederick himself who
somehow, in defeat as much as in victory,
seemed able to inspire his Prussians to feats of
exceptional self-sacrifice and exertion. The
Prussian Army lost a third of its strength in the
first year, but what remained was battle-
hardened and resolute. Defeat of the army, it
was felt, would mean the end of Prussia as a
nation, so even when Cossacks reached Berlin
there was no thought of abandoning the king.

In the spring of 1757 Prussia's enemies could
put almost 400,000 men in the field. The
French under Richelieu accounted for about
100,000 of these but after defeating Cumberland they wasted precious weeks plundering
the German countryside. Meanwhile, a
smaller French force under Soubise
approached Magdeburg and threatened
Berlin. At the same time the Russians were
approaching from the east and defeated an
outnumbered Prussian army at Gross-Jagers-
dorf in August. However, after this exertion
the Russian troops lost their will to fight and
instead of continuing to Berlin, which they
could easily have captured, they concentrated
on solving their supply problems.

Frederick, who realized that his position
was desperate and was therefore even more

willing than usual to take risks, decided to
attack the French. He allocated some troops
to hold the other advancing armies and then
marched to Erfurt. Richelieu's strong army
was rendered temporarily incapacitated by a
well-timed and considerable bribe paid to its
commander. Frederick pushed on in search of
Soubise. While he was thus engaged, an
Austrian force entered Berlin from the south,
but left after receiving a sum of money. Soubise continued to evade Frederick, but was
finally persuaded by his officers to attack the
latter's considerably smaller army when it was
encamped at Rossbach. The French
attempted an attack on the left flank of the
Prussians and when the latter, whose speed of
action and maneuver was unusually fast,
began to take up their positions, the French
mistook the moves for a hurried withdrawal.
Then the Prussians attacked. The French were
taken by surprise and were soon in flight,
having lost several thousand men. This defeat
damaged France's inflated military reputation
and persuaded the enthusiastic British parliament to increase Frederick's subsidy to over a
million pounds sterling.

The victory at Rossbach came in November
1757 and instead of going into winter quarters
as his enemies expected, Frederick marched
to Leipzig and then to Parchwitz and Neu-

markt. Surprised by his rapid advance, the
Austrians left their heavy guns at Breslau and
hurried to meet him. The Battle of Leuthen
took place on 5 December. Frederick, outnumbered, employed his favorite tactic of
holding his main force inactive while sending a
proportion of his men to attack one flank of
the enemy army and thereby draw in its
reserves. When he finally brought his main
force to bear, the Austrians were routed and
suffered about 10,000 casualties with more
than 20,000 men taken prisoner. This campaign, in which the depleted and weary Prussian Army managed to defeat two great
powers in quick succession and regain Saxony
and Silesia, would later be regarded as a military classic, confirming Frederick as one of the
greatest generals of all time.

Meanwhile the British-sponsored Army of
Execution pushed the French back across the
Rhine in spring 1758, and won a decisive victory at Krefeld in June. But the following year
the French returned, and drove the Army of
Execution back, threatening Hanover. Ten
thousand British troops were sent as reinforcements and, thanks to the bravery of the
British infantry, the French were thoroughly
defeated at the Battle of Minden in August,
although the failure of the British cavalry to
charge when ordered to do so allowed the

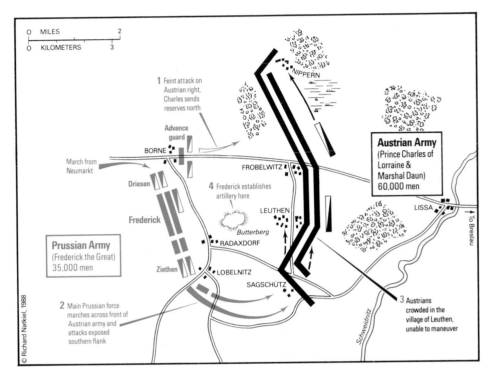

MILES 0 — 2
KILOMETERS 0 — 3

1 Feint attack on
Austrian right,
Charles sends
reserves north

Advance
guard

March from
Neumarkt

BORNE

Driesen

Frederick

Prussian Army
(Frederick the Great)
35,000 men

Ziethen

2 Main Prussian force
marches across front of
Austrian army and
attacks exposed
southern flank

NIPPERN

FROBELWITZ

4 Frederick establishes
artillery here

LEUTHEN

Butterberg

RADAXDORF

LOBELNITZ

SAGSCHÜTZ

Schweidnitz

Austrian Army
(Prince Charles of
Lorraine &
Marshal Daun)
60,000 men

LISSA

To Breslau

3 Austrians
crowded in the
village of Leuthen,
unable to maneuver

© Richard Natkiel, 1988

Right: the Allied triumph over the French at Minden in August 1759.
Below: the rout of the French cavalry at Minden.

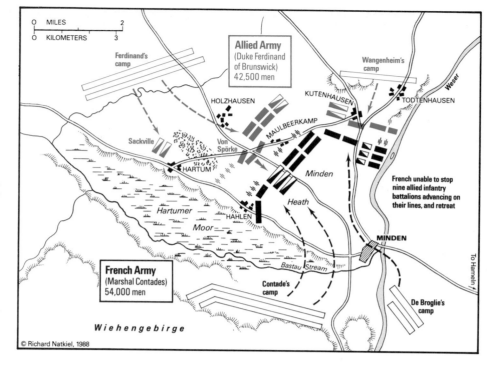

French to make an orderly retreat. 1759 was a year of victories for Britain, especially because France, occupied with the continental war, failed to protect its Indian and Canadian possessions from British conquest.

Prussia was still in peril, however. But Frederick's two most powerful enemies, Austria and Russia, were wary of each other and rarely co-ordinated their efforts. His generalship snatched victory from expected defeat on several occasions, and notably at the battles of Liegnitz and Torgau in 1760 and Schweidnitz in 1762. When the Prussians were on the edge of collapse, luck seemed to favor them. At the Battle of Zorndorf in 1758, where the Prussians avoided defeat only at heavy cost, the opposing army turned away when it needed to deliver only one more blow to destroy Prussian power. When the Russians beat Frederick at Kunersdorf in 1759 the Russian commander chose an alcoholic celebration in preference to

pursuing his beaten enemy.

Luck, finally, saved Frederick when Czarina Elizabeth of Russia died in 1762. Her troops were in possession of Colmar, of much of Pomerania, and already showing themselves at Frankfurt-on-Oder and Berlin. Eliza-

beth had hated Frederick, but her successor Czar Peter III was an admirer, and promptly withdrew Russia from the war. Loss of the Russian ally, and renewed Turkish attacks in the east, persuaded Maria Theresa to sign the Treaty of Hubertsburg in 1763.

The Capture of Quebec

One of British Prime Minister William Pitt's main objectives in the Seven Years' War was to attack French possessions in North America, so while a series of 'pinprick' raids on the French coast distracted French attention General Amherst and 12,000 troops were dispatched across the Atlantic in 1758 to attack Louisbourg on Cape Breton Island.

After the fall of Louisbourg a second expedition was sent a year later to attack Canada. This was a much more hazardous enterprise because the upper reaches of the St Lawrence river were commanded by the guns of Quebec.

At first sight the British commanders were an ill-assorted pair. Major General James Wolfe was talented and imaginative but erratic and mercurial in temperament, whereas his opposite number, Admiral Saunders, was phlegmatic and prudent.

The French commander, the Marquis de Montcalm, had about 5000 men against some 3000 under Wolfe and although Quebec's fortifications were considered to be impregnable the French were short of supplies. Montcalm's only hope was for autumn storms and fog in the St Lawrence to drive the British away but the Royal Navy's experience on blockade duty stood it in good stead. On 9 June 1759 Saunders' fleet entered the St Lawrence and just

over two weeks later the troops were ashore well upstream.

On the night of 12-13 September Wolfe launched his surprise attack, with his troops in flat-bottomed boats. With oars muffled, the force made its way up the river, creeping past the guardboats and sentries on shore. They landed well upriver of Quebec at a point

where a little-known path led to the top of the cliffs. After a long and difficult scramble Wolfe's troops reached the level ground in

Above: British troops land at the foot of the Heights of Abraham.
Below: the death of Wolfe at Quebec.

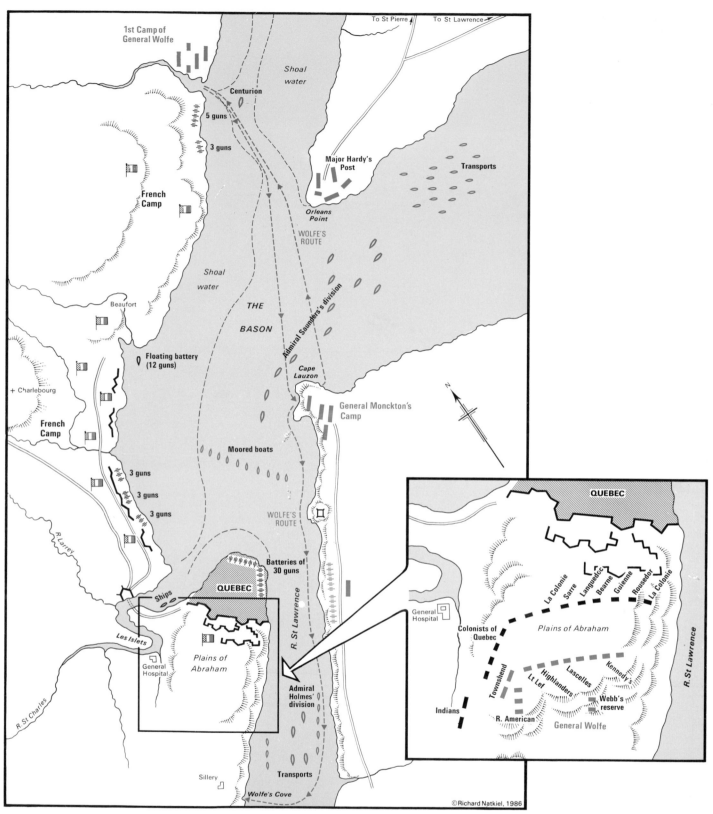

To St Pierre   To St Lawrence

1st Camp of
General Wolfe

*Shoal
water*

Centurion

5 guns

3 guns

Major Hardy's
Post

Transports

**French
Camp**

*Orleans
Point*

WOLFE'S
ROUTE

*Shoal
water*

Beaufort

THE

BASON

Admiral Saunders's division

Floating battery
(12 guns)

*Cape
Lauzon*

+ Charlebourg

General Monckton's
Camp

**French
Camp**

Moored boats

3 guns

3 guns

WOLFE'S
ROUTE

3 guns

R Larrey

Batteries of
30 guns

QUEBEC

Ships

Les Islets

Admiral
Holmes'
division

R. St Charles

*Plains of
Abraham*

General
Hospital

Sillery

Transports

Wolfe's Cove

©Richard Natkiel, 1986

QUEBEC

General
Hospital

La Colonie   Sarre   Languedoc   Bearne   Guienne   Rousedor   La Colonie

**Colonists of
Quebec**

Plains of Abraham

R. St Lawrence

Townshend   Lt Lef   Highlanders   Lascelles   Kennedy's   Webb's
reserve

Indians   R. American   General Wolfe

front of Quebec's landward defenses, known as the Plains of Abraham, and began their march on Quebec.

In the battle which followed Montcalm's troops fought bravely but they were no match for Wolfe's disciplined redcoats. After a first tremendous volley at only 100 yards' range the French never recovered, and the battle ended after little more than 15 minutes with the French in full retreat. Both Wolfe and Mont-

calm were fatally wounded in the deadly exchanges of musketry but few British victories had been so easily won.

With Quebec in British hands it was only a matter of time before Montreal fell, and with it went French dominion over Canada. With only 82,000 French colonists against some 1,300,000 in British North America the French position in Canada was untenable, a fact which was recognized at the end of the war in

1763 with the cession of French possessions in Canada to Great Britain.

The conquest of Canada was to have far-reaching consequences. It afforded a useful base during the War of the American Revolution in 1776-83 but its real worth was only realized during the Napoleonic Wars. When Napoleon tried to exclude the British from the Baltic to deny them timber supplies it was the forests of America which filled the gap.

Left: the Battle of Quebec.
Below right: the Battle of Chesma.

The Battle of Chesma

Although the armies of the Russian Empress Catherine the Great had scored great successes against Turkey in the Russo-Ottoman War, she was determined to use her naval power to drive the Turks out of Europe altogether. In the autumn of 1769 she sent three squadrons, a total of 12 ships of the line, under Admiral Orlov from the Baltic to the Mediterranean. The squadron made a landfall at Navarino in the Morea (Peloponnese), where the Russians were soon able to foment a Greek revolt against the Turks.

Great Britain was sympathetic to the Russian aims and several officers including the Scottish Vice Admiral John Elphinston, were serving in the Russian Mediterranean fleet. Elphinston's aim was to take his squadron of four ships of the line and supporting frigates through the Dardanelles to attack the Turkish fleet in the Black Sea. While approaching the straits his superior Orlov encountered the Turks on 6 July at Chesma (also rendered Chesme, Cesme, Tchesme or Tsheshme), a harbor on the Anatolian coast opposite Chios. The main Russian fleet included 9 ships of the line and 11 other vessels, while the Turks under Hassan Pasha had 14 ships of the line and several frigates, as well as some 200 transports and storeships lying outside the harbor.

The firing was desultory at first, but after four hours the two flagships *Sviatoy Yevstafy* and *Real Mustapha* caught fire and blew up. The explosion was so enormous that the Turks retired in confusion and withdrew into Chesma. Most of the flagships' crews had been killed, but had the Turks known it, the Russian loss was greater than theirs.

Next morning Elphinston's squadron arrived, and under his energetic direction Lieutenants Dugdale and Mackenzie sailed fireships into Chesma harbor. At first the Turks welcomed them, thinking that they were deserters, but the strangers promptly ran alongside the nearest row of ships lying at their moorings, and lashed themselves alongside with grappling-hooks. Within minutes rockets and inflammable materials were being fired into the packed Turkish ships. An immense blaze soon engulfed the Turkish Fleet, and out of the holocaust only one 64-gun ship and a few galleys escaped.

With the Dardanelles undefended it was the moment to force the straits and even try to capture Constantinople, as Elphinston hoped,

but Alexei Orlov was too cautious. While he wasted time besieging Lemnos, Turkey's French allies fortified the straits. Within a few days Baron de Tott had improvised apparently impregnable defenses with 30,000 soldiers to

defend them.

For Russia it was to transpire to be the last chance of attacking Constantinople directly, but the victory was an important check to the military power of the Turks.

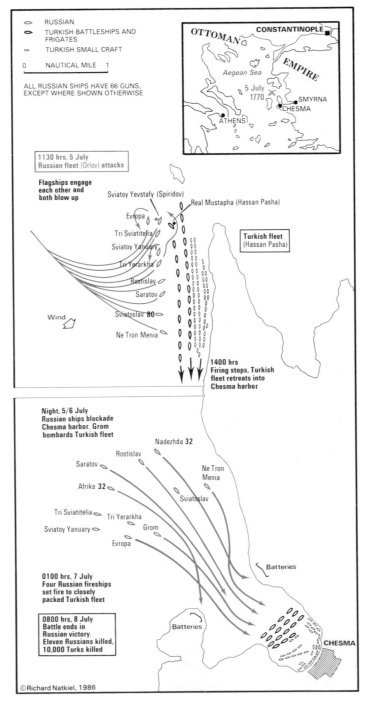

© Richard Natkiel, 1986

The American War of Independence

Even before the end of the French and Indian Wars relations between the English colonies in America and the mother country had begun to erode. Within a decade of the signing of the Treaty of Paris in 1763 American resentment over British policies toward local self-rule, taxation, trade, territorial expansion and a host of other issues had so fulminated that the colonies were on the brink of rebellion. Hostilities began in earnest on 18 April 1775 when a band of Massachusetts militiamen clashed with British regulars at Lexington, 20 miles outside Boston. In the ensuing 48-hour skirmish 95 militiamen and nearly 275 British soldiers were killed. Thereafter the spread of fighting could not be contained. While a large force of Colonial militiamen surrounded Boston, placing the British garrison there under loose siege, other militias seized British forts

at Ticonderoga, Crown Point and St Johns. On 15 June the American Second Continental Congress created a Continental Army and named General George Washington as its commander. Two days later, on the outskirts of Boston, a force of 2200 British regulars, under the command of Major General William Howe, assailed an American fortified position atop Breed's Hill on the Charlestown peninsula. Only after two sanguinary failures did the British close-order frontal assault finally succeed in overrunning the hill, and then perhaps only because the militiamen had run short of ammunition. In this so-called Battle

of Bunker Hill (named for a neighboring hill), the British had accomplished virtually nothing, at a cost of 1054 casualties. Most of the defenders had escaped, simply to take up new positions nearby, and the siege of Boston remained unbroken. It continued into the spring of the following year, the size and fire-power of the investing forces, now under Washington's personal direction, growing the while. At last, on 13 April 1776, the British garrison began its evacuation of the city.

Above: the Battle of Bunker Hill.
Below: the defense of Breed's Hill.

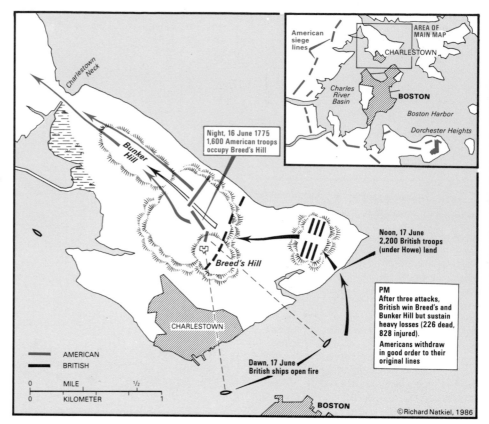

Night, 16 June 1775
1,600 American troops occupy Breed's Hill

Noon, 17 June
2,200 British troops (under Howe) land

PM
After three attacks, British win Breed's and Bunker Hill but sustain heavy losses (226 dead, 828 injured).

Americans withdraw in good order to their original lines

Dawn, 17 June
British ships open fire

AMERICAN
BRITISH

©Richard Natkiel, 1986

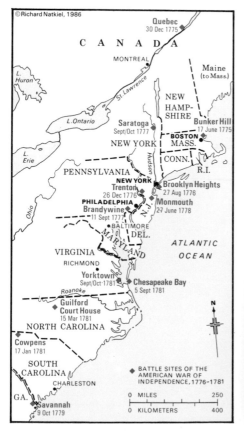

©Richard Natkiel, 1986

BATTLE SITES OF THE AMERICAN WAR OF INDEPENDENCE, 1776-1781

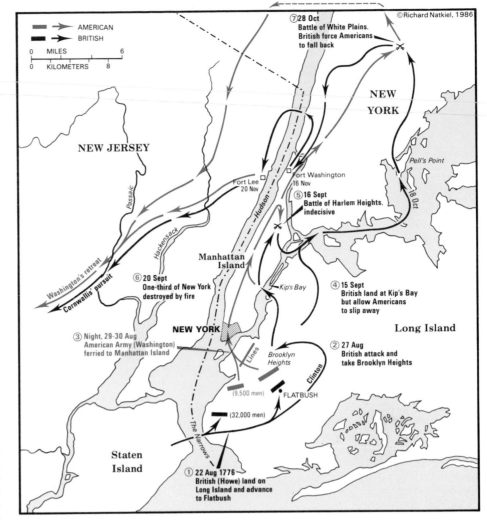

The New York Campaign and Trenton

Washington, correctly anticipating that the next British move would be a thrust at New York City, quickly moved south with about 19,000 men – a nucleus of Continentals and a large preponderance of militia. The bulk of this force he positioned on Brooklyn Heights on Long Island, hoping thereby to dominate the southern tip of Manhattan. Sir William Howe's seaborne British invasion force, 32,000 strong, duly arrived at New York on 4 July 1776. On 22 August Howe landed troops behind Washington's Brooklyn Heights position, forcing the out-flanked Americans to retire across the East River to Manhattan. Howe pursued them, inexorably driving them north up the narrow island. When the Americans attempted to make a stand at Harlem Heights, Howe again out-flanked them (on 18 October) by landing four brigades at Pell's Point, behind the American lines. Once again Washington narrowly escaped encirclement, but he was now obliged to split his retreating army, sending half his troops to the comparative safety of New Jersey while the remainder fought on to try to slow the momentum of Howe's northward advance. In the event, Howe concluded that this remnant was not worth pursuing beyond White Plains, 20 miles north of Manhattan, where a battle was fought on the 28th. The campaign was now drawing to a close.

Below: Washington crosses the Delaware before the Battle of Trenton, December 1776.

While Howe's main force retired to winter quarters in New York City, a large detachment, under General Charles, Lord Cornwallis, was despatched southwest into New Jersey to mop up what was left of the American army there. Though Washington now had barely 3000 effective Continentals and militiamen left under his command, he was not content to leave the initiative to the British. Under cover of darkness on 25 December he ferried his ragged troops across the Delaware River, marched down the east bank and at dawn on the 26th made a surprise attack on the three Hessian regiments stationed at Trenton. This was a brilliant success, netting over 900 prisoners at the cost of only eight American

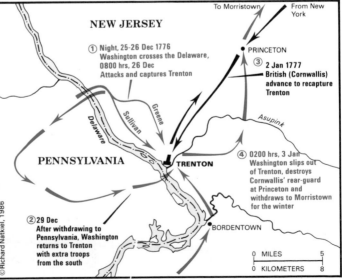

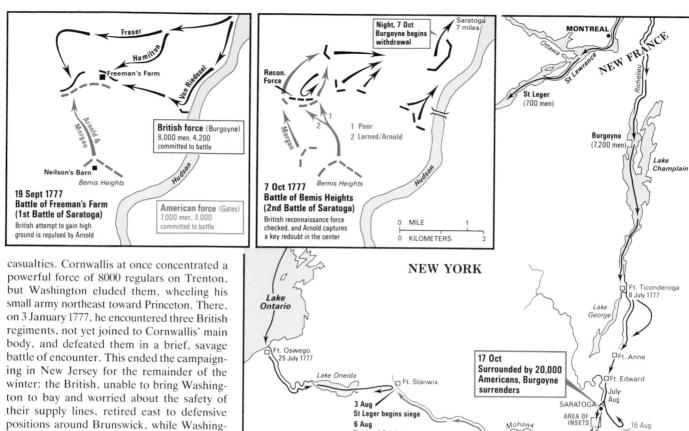

19 Sept 1777
Battle of Freeman's Farm
(1st Battle of Saratoga)
British attempt to gain high ground is repulsed by Arnold

British force (Burgoyne)
6,000 men, 4,200 committed to battle

American force (Gates)
7,000 men, 3,000 committed to battle

7 Oct 1777
Battle of Bemis Heights
(2nd Battle of Saratoga)
British reconnaissance force checked, and Arnold captures a key redoubt in the center

Night, 7 Oct Burgoyne begins withdrawal

1 Poor
2 Lerned/Arnold

NEW YORK

St Leger (700 men)

Burgoyne (7,200 men)

Ft. Ticonderoga 6 July 1777

Ft. Oswego 25 July 1777

Ft. Stanwix

3 Aug
St Leger begins siege
6 Aug
Battle of Oriskany
22 Aug
Retreats to Fort Oswego

17 Oct
Surrounded by 20,000 Americans, Burgoyne surrenders

Ft. Anne
Ft. Edward
July-Aug
SARATOGA
AREA OF INSETS
16 Aug
BENNINGTON
Stark
ALBANY

©Richard Natkiel, 1986

casualties. Cornwallis at once concentrated a powerful force of 8000 regulars on Trenton, but Washington eluded them, wheeling his small army northeast toward Princeton. There, on 3 January 1777, he encountered three British regiments, not yet joined to Cornwallis' main body, and defeated them in a brief, savage battle of encounter. This ended the campaigning in New Jersey for the remainder of the winter: the British, unable to bring Washington to bay and worried about the safety of their supply lines, retired east to defensive positions around Brunswick, while Washington led his army north to winter quarters.

Below: an attack on a redoubt during the Saratoga battles.

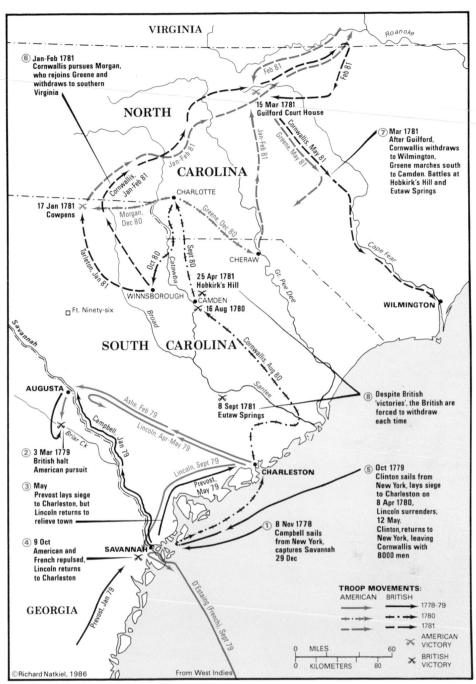

The Philadelphia and Saratoga Campaigns

When active campaigning resumed in the spring of 1777 the British mounted two independent large-scale offensives. One, directed by Howe, was aimed at taking the American capital of Philadelphia. The second, under the overall command of General Sir John Burgoyne, was intended as an ambitious pincer movement that would originate from the vicinity of Montreal and would ultimately close its jaws on the key New York city of Albany. With Albany secured, it was planned that Howe would move north from New York to join forces with Burgoyne, thus establishing a line that would effectively cut off all of New England from the other colonies.

Howe's somewhat ponderous seaborne campaign against Philadelphia was successful, but of secondary strategic importance. Washington failed to halt Howe's advance on the city when the Americans were defeated at Brandywine Creek in September, and Washington's subsequent efforts to dislodge Howe from Philadelphia were equally unsuccessful. By December, the American general was obliged to withdraw his battered army to winter quarters at Valley Forge. Yet, contrary to Howe's hopes, the fall of the capital did not in itself significantly blunt the American war effort.

Burgoyne's much more dangerous campaign began in June 1777, his main force moving due south along Lake Champlain, while a smaller right wing, under Lieutenant Colonel Barry St Leger, swung southwest down the St Lawrence to Lake Ontario, thence to re-curve southeast through the Mohawk valley toward the common objective of Albany. By early July Burgoyne had taken Fort Ticonderoga, roughly halfway to Albany, but St Leger's advance in the Mohawk valley had been decisively stopped by American militia at the Battle of Oriskany, fought near Fort Stanwix. Burgoyne nevertheless pressed on against stiffening American resistance. On 19 September American troops under General Daniel Morgan (the principal lieutenant of the American theater commander, General Horatio Gates) checked Burgoyne's southward advance at the savage battle of Freeman's Farm. For the next 18 days, while American local forces swelled to an unprecedented 22,000, the two armies skirmished in place. Then, on 7 October, Burgoyne tried to break the impasse with an assault on the American positions on Bemis Heights. In this battle Gates and Morgan so routed the attackers that the British were forced to beat a hasty retreat eight miles north

to Saratoga. There, on 17 October 1777, Burgoyne formally surrendered his remaining 5700 men to Gates. This victory was in some ways the most decisive of the war, for in addition to lifting American morale at a critical time and proving that major British forces could be defeated in open battle, it at last persuaded hesitating France to enter the war on the American side.

The Invasion of the South

In the following year, 1778, British strategy took a completely new turn. General Sir Henry Clinton, Howe's successor, evacuated Philadelphia and concentrated his troops in New York, thereafter fighting only small holding actions against Washington's forces in the north. Meantime, the British launched a major land/sea campaign against the southern

colonies. In December Savannah was captured, and by the following spring Augusta and most of the rest of Georgia was under British control. By April 1780 the British had captured the port of Charleston, South Carolina, and were preparing to subdue that colony, as well. Washington attempted to prevent this by sending 4000 men under Gates into South Carolina, but on 16 August this force was roundly defeated at Camden by General Cornwallis' disciplined regulars, and it now seemed that both of the Carolinas and Virginia must shortly share the fate of Georgia.

That this did not happen was due to the skillful resistance put up both by local independent militias and by the two small Continental armies (one under Daniel Morgan and another under General Nathaniel Greene) still operating in the Carolinas. Though by the

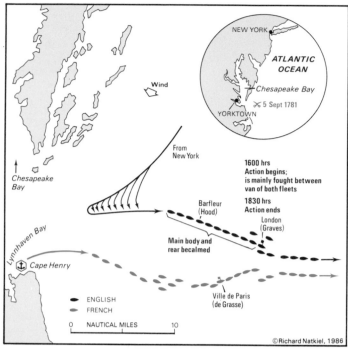

Above right: the Battle of Chesapeake Bay. Above: the British garrison of Yorktown marches into captivity with full military honors.

Below: Washington receives Lord Cornwallis' sword at Yorktown.

spring of 1781 Cornwallis had advanced as far north as Virginia, virtually none of the areas through which he had passed since leaving Charleston had been truly pacified, and now he faced two fresh Continental armies, led respectively by General Friedrich Wilhelm, Baron von Steuben, and by General Marie-Joseph du Motier, le Marquis de Lafayette. Rather than try to deal with these armies (which he could still probably have defeated in open battle) Cornwallis withdrew to the Virginia port of Yorktown.

Yorktown

Quick to seize the opportunity presented by Cornwallis' withdrawal to Yorktown, Washington rushed reinforcements to the Yorktown area – his own forces from New York and those of General Jean-Baptiste de Vimeur, le Comte de Rochambeau, from

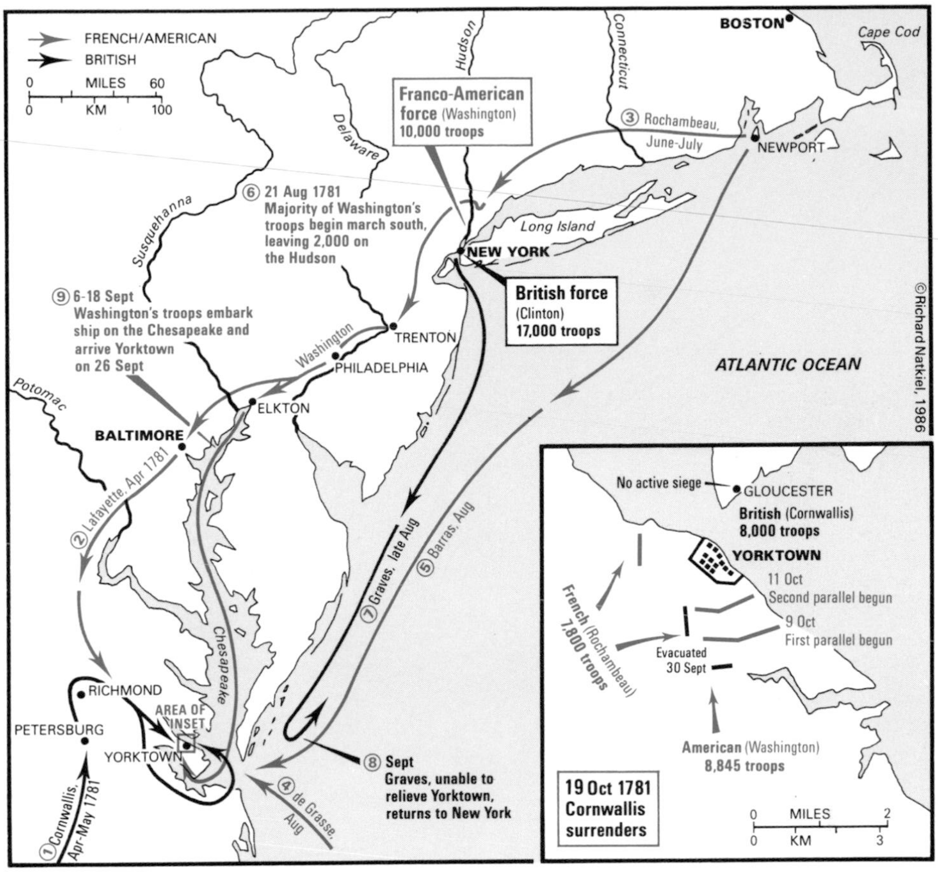

FRENCH/AMERICAN
BRITISH
0 MILES 60
0 KM 100
Hudson
Connecticut
BOSTON
Cape Cod
Delaware
Franco-American force (Washington) 10,000 troops
③ Rochambeau, June-July
NEWPORT
⑥ 21 Aug 1781 Majority of Washington's troops begin march south, leaving 2,000 on the Hudson
Susquehanna
Long Island
NEW YORK
British force (Clinton) 17,000 troops
⑨ 6-18 Sept Washington's troops embark ship on the Chesapeake and arrive Yorktown on 26 Sept
TRENTON
Washington
PHILADELPHIA
ATLANTIC OCEAN
©Richard Natkiel, 1986
Potomac
ELKTON
BALTIMORE
② Lafayette, Apr 1781
⑤ Barras, Aug
⑦ Graves, late Aug
Chesapeake
RICHMOND
AREA OF INSET
PETERSBURG
YORKTOWN
⑧ Sept Graves, unable to relieve Yorktown, returns to New York
④ de Grasse, Aug
① Cornwallis, Apr-May 1781
No active siege
GLOUCESTER
British (Cornwallis) 8,000 troops
YORKTOWN
11 Oct Second parallel begun
9 Oct First parallel begun
French (Rochambeau) 7,800 troops
Evacuated 30 Sept
American (Washington) 8,845 troops
19 Oct 1781 Cornwallis surrenders
0 MILES 2
0 KM 3

Rhode Island. In short order, Cornwallis was well and truly besieged in Yorktown, and the timely intercession of the British fleet had become for him not a convenience but a necessity. Now the full value of the Franco-American alliance became fully manifest. When, on 5 September, Admiral Thomas Graves' relieving fleet approached the entrance to Chesapeake Bay, it found its way blocked by a slightly larger French squadron under the command of Admiral François-Joseph, le Comte de Grasse. In strictly naval terms the desultory battle that followed was decisive only in that Graves could not force his way past the French, but that was quite enough to decide the outcome of the war on land. Denied hope either of reinforcement or of evacuation by sea, surrounded by 9000 American and 8000 French troops, Cornwallis had no choice but to surrender.

The American victory at Yorktown marked the end of all serious British military activity in North America. Although a formal state of war persisted for another two years, it was clear that American independence had been won and that only the details of a peace treaty remained to be worked out. A draft of this treaty was negotiated in November 1782; it was ratified by the Continental Congress the following April; and on 3 September 1783, with the formal signing of the Treaty of Paris, the war ended.

The Battle of the Saintes

The surrender of Yorktown in October 1781 marked the nadir of the Royal Navy's fortunes in the War of American Independence. Fighting the French in the Indian Ocean as well as the Atlantic, and its supplies of cordage, tar and timber threatened by the League of Armed Neutrality in the Baltic, the whole organization was under severe strain. Yet in spite of all its tribulations the Royal Navy rose to the challenge and brought off a brilliant counterstroke.

On 5 April 1782 Admiral Rodney learned that the French Admiral Count de Grasse and a combined Franco-Spanish squadron had sailed from Martinique. Rodney guessed correctly that de Grasse intended to attack Jamaica and determined to intercept the attack. Off the small group of islands known as the Saintes he finally managed to bring de Grasse to action, the French being impeded by the need to tow the damaged *Zélé* (she had been in collision three days earlier). At first Rodney was content to engage in succession but a sudden shift of wind enabled him to pierce the French line, and the orderly cannonade soon degenerated into a general action. Rodney had 36 ships to 30 French, and by breaking the French line he was able to concentrate overwhelming force against portions of the enemy fleet.

Although Rodney was in poor health his fleet was in first-class fighting condition. Not only were his men comparatively free of scurvy because of the use of anti-scorbutics but Rodney had also begun to adopt the radical reforms of the gunnery expert Captain Charles Douglas, captain of his flagship HMS *Formidable.* Douglas had the satisfaction of seeing the *Formidable's* broadsides dismast a French ship as she passed through the line. Douglas had stepped up gunnery practice and had changed the guns' equipment to allow a more rapid rate of fire and a wider field of fire. These changes had been widely imitated in the fleet and French accounts of the battle were to stress the superior British gunnery.

The formation of de Grasse's fleet was totally destroyed, and in the confusion five ships of the line and the French admiral were captured. The flagship, the 100-gun *Ville de Paris* was the last to submit, at 1830. She fought with great gallantry, and sustained fire from seven British ships in succession. It is said that toward the end of the day her gun crews ran out of powder cartridges but continued loading the guns with handfuls of gunpowder scooped out of kegs in the magazine.

Rodney's energetic second-in-command, Sir Samuel Hood pleaded with him to allow a vigorous pursuit but the old admiral was content to round up the prizes, saying 'Come, we have done very handsomely.' He was right in a way, for the battle had put an end to French ambitions in the Caribbean. The tentative peace negotiations between Great Britain and the United States had already begun, and in the months after Yorktown it had looked to the British as if they might be forced to relinquish Canada. The news from the West Indies stiffened their resolve, and although peace did not come finally until 1783, the British were in a much stronger position.

Hood need not have fretted about his failure to capture more ships, for a week later his squadron made four captures, the 64-gun ships *Caton* and *Jason,* as well as a frigate and a corvette.

Although the War of the American Revolution had been a harrowing experience for the Royal Navy it served to eradicate many weaknesses in tactics and training. Political neglect and a tendency to bask in the glory of the Seven Years War had reduced the Royal Navy's effectiveness but the frustrations and failures of 1776-82 generated reforms at all levels. Two important innovations were introduced, the carronade and coppering. The former, a short-barreled but light gun of heavy caliber gave Royal Navy ships an important advantage in short-range fighting, while the technique of covering the bottom planking of ships with copper sheets preventing fouling by marine growths and protected the timber from wood-boring worms. A 'coppered' ship could remain at sea for up to six months without an appreciable loss of speed, and for the Royal Navy this meant an important freedom of action on the far side of the Atlantic.

These pages: the Old Guard protects Napoleon during the final stages of the Battle of Waterloo, June 1815.

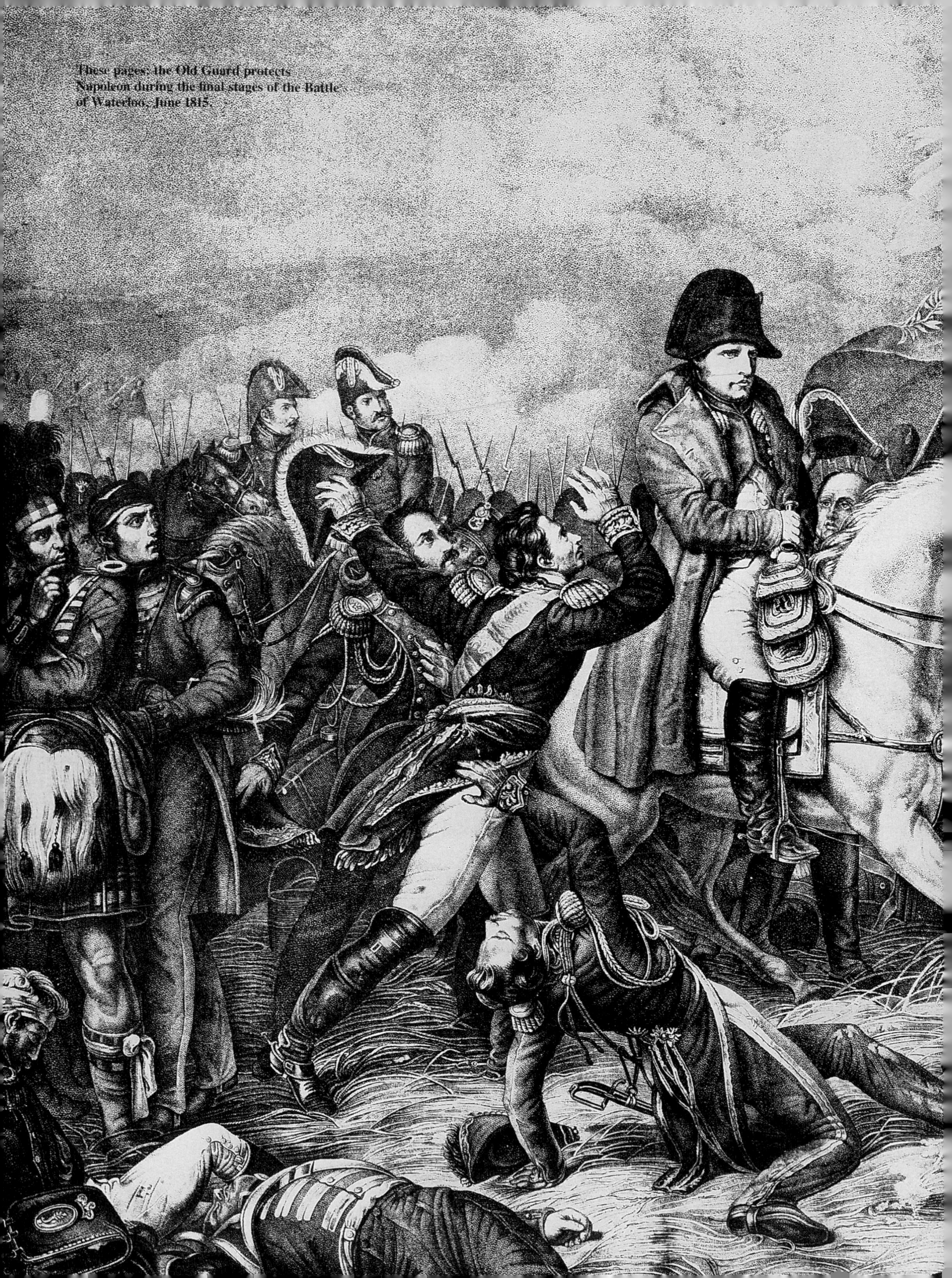

THE CAMPAIGNS OF NAPOLEON

The French Revolution

By the late 1780s the political corruption, economic inefficiency and deep social divisions of France were building up to a crisis which threatened the stability not just of France itself but of Europe as a whole. In May 1789 King Louis XVI, desperate for new taxes, convened the States General, a legislative parliament containing representatives of the three 'Estates' – aristocracy, Church and people. It was the Third Estate, reflecting the grievances of the broad mass of French society, which spearheaded the Revolution, demanding reforms which the king was unwilling to make. On 14 July 1789 the Paris mob stormed the prison of the Bastille, triggering a process whereby more moderate elements of the Third Estate would be swept aside.

Alarmed by these developments, the 'ancient monarchies' of continental Europe, including Austria, Prussia and Russia, adopted the Declaration of Pillnitz in April 1791, threatening the French with concerted military action if the discernible trend toward republicanism continued. Far from calming the situation, however, this merely fueled the

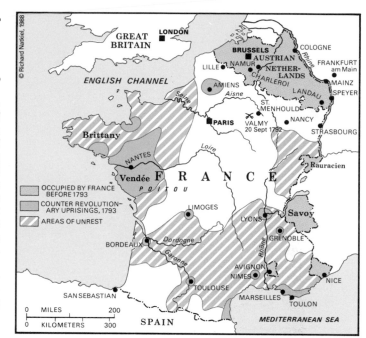

Revolution, providing just the excuse needed for more extreme action. In June the king, attempting to flee to the safety of the Austrian Netherlands, was arrested and forced to return to Paris.

Incidents such as this made hostilities in Europe inevitable, although it was the French who set the pace. On 20 April 1792 the Brissotin government in Paris, worried about the activities of *emigré* royalists in the Rhineland – part of the Austrian (Holy Roman) Empire – declared war on Austria. It was a foolish move, made at a time when the French Army, split down the middle by the Revolution and riddled with subversive elements, was weak. The Legislative Assembly hastily called for volunteers (*fédérés*) but, although many responded, they were incapable of defending France. An attempted invasion of the Austrian Netherlands ended in disaster, with units fleeing and officers being killed by their own men. This, in turn, caused the war to spread as other powers in Europe, convinced that the time was ripe for the destruction of the Revolution, gathered for the kill. A Prussian army under the Duke of Brunswick appeared in the Moselle valley, openly threatening intervention if the French Royal Family was harmed. The Legislative Assembly responded by abolishing the monarchy and declaring a republic, preparatory to putting the king on trial.

But the allies were poorly co-ordinated, and although they achieved some success as they

moved into France, capturing the border fortresses at Longwy and Verdun, their advance did not pick up the momentum needed for outright victory. Nevertheless, their appearance on the borders did trigger panic on the streets of Paris and, as Jacobin extremists took over, this was manifested in the 'Terror,' with mass executions of reactionary elements.

It looked as if France was doomed, but on 20 September 1792 French troops under General Dumouriez – a mixture of regulars and poorly trained *fédérés* – stood firm at Valmy, to the northwest of Verdun, blunting the Prussian advance. As the Duke of Brunswick's assault materialized, Dumouriez placed his scratch force across the Prussian line of advance near Sainte Ménéhould. Joined by General Kellermann (the Elder), the French force rose to approximately 52,000 men and, as the Prussians pushed forward with an army of 34,000, the French occupied a semicircular defensive location, with General Stengel on the right, Kellermann in the center and Chabot on the left. Early on 20 September, the Prussians advanced through the mist to occupy La Lune, drawing up a battle line from there to Somme-Bionne in the north. Kellermann, occupying high ground around a distinctive windmill, came under artillery attack but, surprisingly, his soldiers did not panic. At 1300 hours, as the Prussians marched forward, they were met by a hail of musket fire and temporarily halted, failing to take advantage of a

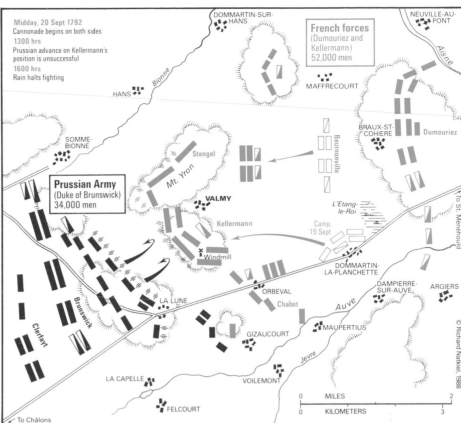

lucky cannon shot which detonated French ammunition wagons close to the windmill. By the end of the day, as artillery fire continued to be exchanged, the French had suffered 300 casualties to the Prussian 180, but Brunswick, hesitant and bemused, had already decided to pull back to the Rhine.

Dumouriez immediately marched north to defeat an Austrian army at Jemappes (6 November) and these two victories put new heart into the French. By the beginning of 1793, they had advanced to seize Brussels, Frankfurt, Nice and Savoy and were gearing up for a more prolonged war, using conscription (the *levée en masse*) to raise an army of more than one-and-a-half million men. This was just as well for, in the aftermath of Louis XVI's execution in January 1793, other European powers, including Britain, went to war, forming the First Coalition, dedicated to the overthrow of the Revolutionary government. An Austrian army entered Belgium, while the Duke of York landed in Flanders at the head of a British force. At the same time, serious uprisings occurred in La Vendée and Provence, with an allied naval force occupying Toulon.

But the French soon recovered. On 6 September 1793 the British were defeated at Hondschoote, near Dunkirk and, five weeks later, the Austrians were turned back at Wattignies. In addition, an army was put together to quell the revolt in La Vendée and the allies were forced to abandon Toulon, partly through the actions of a hitherto obscure artillery captain, Napoleon Bonaparte. The First Coalition began to fall apart as first Russia and then Britain withdrew its army, leaving the Prussians and Austrians to face the French alone. On 26 June 1794, the Austrians were defeated at Fleurus, enabling the French to occupy Holland, while similar advances farther south opened up the western Alps and threatened northern Italy. A month later, in the *coup d'état de Thermidor*, the Jacobin extremists under Robespierre were ousted and a new government – the 'Directory of Seven' – installed. It was they who decided that, in 1796, a concerted attack against the Austrians in Germany and northern Italy would be carried out, with Vienna as the goal. Their choice as commander of the 'Army of Italy' was Napoleon Bonaparte.

**Left: the storming of the Bastille.
Above right: the Battle of Valmy, 20 September 1792.
Right: French casualties at Valmy.**

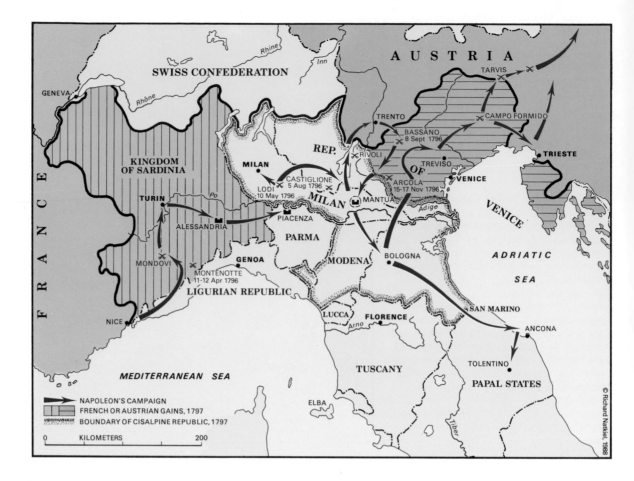

Legend:
- NAPOLEON'S CAMPAIGN
- FRENCH OR AUSTRIAN GAINS, 1797
- BOUNDARY OF CISALPINE REPUBLIC, 1797

0   KILOMETERS   200

The Campaign in Italy, 1796-97

Napoleon Bonaparte, not yet 27 years old, took command of the French forces at Nice on 27 March 1796, under orders to advance into northwest Italy. His army was small (less than 38,000 men), poorly equipped and low on morale; it faced 31,000 Austrians under General Beaulieu to the north and 20,000 Piedmontese under General Colli to the northwest.

Napoleon's only chance was to drive a wedge between the allied armies, isolating and defeating Colli before the Austrians could come to his aid, and then switching north to take on Beaulieu. On 11 April the French attack began, catching the Austrians at Montonette 24 hours later and forcing them to withdraw to the north. This left Colli unsupported and, as Napoleon's troops pushed through Carcare to Ceva and Mondovi, the Piedmontese hastily sued for peace. By 23 April the campaign was over.

But Napoleon could not afford to rest, for although Beaulieu had withdrawn across the River Po at Valenza, his forces were intact, posing an obvious threat. Feint attacks against Valenza and Pavia – the natural crossing points on the Po – kept the Austrians occupied, while an elite force of grenadiers rushed some 50 miles east to seize Piacenza. Crossings were made on 7 May, leaving Beaulieu,

still around Valenza, in danger of being outflanked; he quickly withdrew to the River Adda at Lodi. The French followed close on his heels, seizing the bridge at Lodi on 10 May in an epic frontal assault. Beaulieu pulled back to the River Mincio, leaving Napoleon to capture Milan without firing a shot.

The new Austrian line, protected by Lake Garda to the north and the fortress of Mantua to the south, looked unassailable, but the French wasted no time in assaulting it. On 30

May they captured a bridge across the Mincio at Borghetto, forcing the Austrians even farther east, to the River Adige, as well as toward Trento in the north. Verona fell, although a French attempt to storm Mantua failed, presaging a lengthy siege.

Mantua soon became a 'running sore,' absorbing French manpower and resources while the Austrians recovered. On 31 July Count Würmser, replacing the discredited Beaulieu, initiated a three-pronged attack,

Below left: Napoleon directs his troops at Rivoli.
Right: the Battle of Rivoli, fought in January 1797, saw Napoleon inflict a crushing defeat on the Austrians under D'Alvinci.

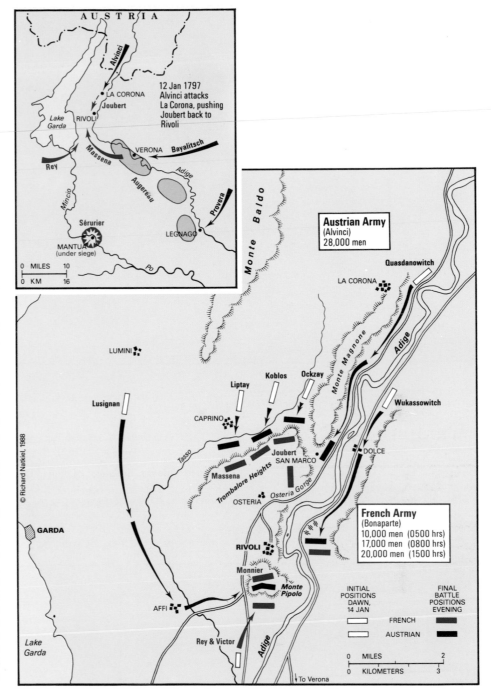

sending columns down the Brenta valley as well as along both shores of Lake Garda. Napoleon hastily abandoned the siege of Mantua (losing 179 guns) and pulled back to the Mincio, aiming to prevent a link-up of the Lake Garda columns. He did so by defeating each in turn – that on the west bank under General Quasdanovitch at Lonato on 3 August, and that on the east bank under Würmser himself at Castiglione 48 hours later. Once again, the Austrians retreated, although the danger was by no means over. Instead of going onto the defensive, Würmser merely reinforced his column in the Brenta valley, threatening a move from the east.

Napoleon followed him into the valley from the north after seizing Trent. On 8 September the two armies clashed at Bassano; despite another Austrian defeat, Würmser continued toward Mantua, entering the city on the 12th to increase its garrison to a formidable 23,000 men. Two months later, when a new Austrian army of 46,000 men under Baron d'Alvinci crossed the River Adige, Napoleon's position began to look precarious.

His reaction was typical. Mustering all available forces he moved east, aiming to take the village of Villa Nova in d'Alvinci's rear and force the Austrians to fight in marshy ground between the Alpone and Adige rivers. On 15 November, the French crossed the Adige at Ronco, seized the village of Porcile and advanced toward Villa Nova. Their route was blocked at Arcola, however, where Austrian forces held a vital bridge, and for three days a bitter fight ensued. By the time Arcola was taken by exhausted French troops late on the 17th, d'Alvinci had escaped from the trap, pulling back to the east.

The French now went onto the defensive, determined to concentrate on the siege of Mantua, but the lull in the fighting was short lived. On 12 January 1797, a new Austrian attack came in from the north, forcing the French to abandon La Corona and fall back on prepared positions at Rivoli, to the east of Lake Garda. Napoleon rushed reinforcements north, despite diversionary Austrian attacks along the River Adige, realizing that Rivoli was the key. If d'Alvinci could be defeated in a set-piece battle, the other attacks would wither away.

French positions at Rivoli were strong, occupying dominating ground on the Tromba-lore Heights between the Tasso and Adige rivers. The only roads past the Heights hugged the banks of the Adige, channeling the Austrians into a potential killing zone just to the north of Rivoli, where the west-bank road passed through the Osteria Gorge. Napoleon deployed his men to cover both the Heights and the Gorge, tempting the enemy into his trap. D'Alvinci obliged, sending his main column along both banks of the Adige early on 14 January. However, his decision to attack the Trombalore Heights from the north, using forces under Generals Liptay, Koblos and Ockzay, while sending a column under Lusignan in an outflanking move to the west, was worrying.

In the event, the battle went Napoleon's way, with the attacks on the Heights contained and the main Austrian column destroyed in the Osteria Gorge. By the morning of the 15th, the Austrians were in retreat, having lost some 14,000 men. Napoleon then moved south to protect Mantua, and although he was too late to prevent General Provera from reinforcing the garrison, the Austrian position was hopeless. On 2 February, Mantua surrendered.

Napoleon immediately organized a pursuit, pushing the enemy northeastward toward Vienna. By late February his troops had crossed the Brenta; by 16 March they had seized crossings on the Tagliamento, advancing to take Tarvis, Laybach and Trieste by the end of the month. On 29 March, Napoleon entered Klagenfurt and, when he demanded surrender, the Austrians agreed, signing the Preliminaries of Leoben on 18 April (ratified in October as the Peace of Campo Formio). It was the end of a remarkable campaign and the beginning of a yet more remarkable military career. Napoleon had made his mark.

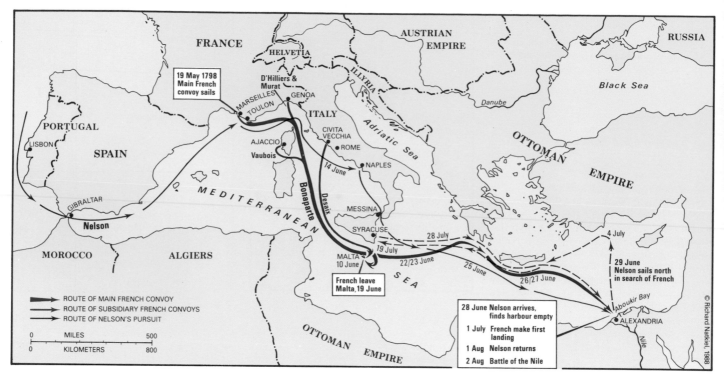

The Egyptian Campaign, 1798-99

On 19 May 1798, a French expeditionary force under Napoleon Bonaparte set sail from Toulon. Joined by smaller fleets from Marseilles, Genoa, Ajaccio and Civita Vecchia, the combined force of 38,000 men was under orders to seize Malta before proceeding to Egypt, a region under nominal Turkish control, vital to British trade.

Malta fell on 10 June and Napoleon led his men ashore at Marabout, on the Egyptian coast, on 1 July, having narrowly escaped interception by British warships under Rear Admiral Nelson. Early the next morning the French advanced to seize Alexandria before striking southeast, across the desert, toward the Nile and Cairo. The march was a nightmare for soldiers unused to the heat, but on 10 July they reached the river. By then, the re-

presentatives of the Turks in Egypt, Murad and Ibrahim Bey, had massed two armies to protect Cairo, one on each bank of the Nile. Such a split gave Napoleon the opportunity he needed: advancing down the west bank against Murad, his force of 25,000 men approached the village of Embabeh on 21 July. Murad released his Marmeluke cavalry, only to see it swept aside by disciplined French fire; by late afternoon the Egyptians were in full retreat and the 'Battle of the Pyramids' was over, having cost the French less than 30 dead.

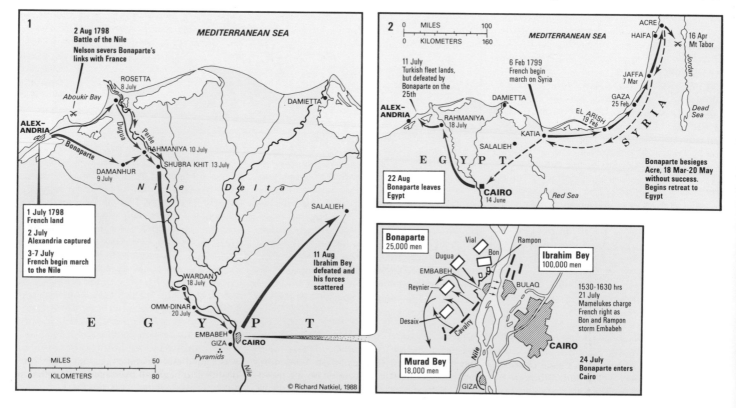

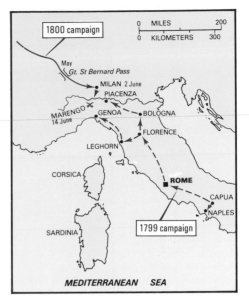

Ibrahim withdrew, allowing Napoleon to enter Cairo unopposed on the 24th, but elsewhere problems were emerging. On 2 August, the French fleet was destroyed in Aboukir Bay by Nelson, cutting the army off from its homeland; a month later Turkey declared war on France, putting together two armies, in Syria (the 'Army of Damascus') and the eastern Mediterranean (the 'Army of Rhodes') respectively. Their appearance would undoubtedly take time – allowing Napoleon to complete his conquest of Upper Egypt, from Cairo to the Red Sea – but renewed fighting was clearly inevitable.

Napoleon decided to pre-empt the Turks by marching into Palestine, aiming to defeat the Army of Damascus before the Army of Rhodes landed in Egypt. He began the advance on 6 February 1799, only to encounter unexpected opposition at El Arish which imposed a delay of 11 days. This enabled the British naval officer Sir William Sidney Smith to reinforce the garrison at Acre, farther north, so that when Napoleon eventually arrived before the port on 18 March, he faced the prospect of a lengthy siege. Meanwhile, the Army of Damascus had begun to advance toward Acre from the north; despite a French victory at Mount Tabor on 16 April, as a result of which the Turks withdrew in disarray, Napoleon had no choice but to abandon the siege and pull back to the Nile.

The Army of Rhodes landed at Aboukir on 11 July, only to be defeated two weeks later. As the Turks retreated, French rule in Egypt seemed secure, but by this time the politically ambitious Napoleon had decided to return to Paris. Accompanied by only a handful of advisers and generals, he abandoned his army on 22 August: 30,000 high-grade soldiers were not to see their homeland again until 1802.

Campaigns in Europe, 1798-1802

Napoleon reached Paris in October 1799, to find French politics in crisis. French leaders had meddled in the affairs of Germany, alienating both the Austrians and the Russians, had seized parts of Switzerland and attacked Rome. One result had been the creation of the Second Coalition, with Austro-Russian forces wiping out most of Napoleon's gains in northern Italy by early 1799, and although by October the situation had been stabilized, it

was obvious that the days of the Directory were numbered. Napoleon, quick to seize the opportunity, allied himself to Director Sieyès and on 9/10 November 1799, in the *coup d'état de Brumaire*, effectively took power. By December, he was First Consul of France.

With the danger of two threatening Austrian armies under General Kray in the Black Forest and General Melas in Italy, Napoleon's initial intention, outlined in late 1799, was to concentrate on operations in Germany before turning south toward the Po valley, but Moreau refused to co-operate. Instead, the First Consul had to shift the emphasis to Italy first, using Moreau to push Kray back toward Ulm while the Army of the Reserve moved south through the Alpine passes of Switzerland to reinforce Massena.

The campaign began badly, for on 5 April 1800, before the French were fully prepared, Melas attacked Massena, forcing him to seek shelter in Genoa. A siege began, putting pressure on Napoleon to carry out his plan as quickly as possible. Fortunately, preliminary orders had already gone out, directing elements of the Army of the Reserve to march to Geneva and open routes to the Great St Bernard, Simplon and St Gothard passes. The aim was to concentrate the army at Stradella, between Piacenza and Alessandria on the Po.

Moreau crossed the Rhine at Schaffhausen on 20 April, pushing Kray toward Ulm, and this enabled the Army of the Reserve to approach the Alps from the north. Using the Great St Bernard pass, Lannes' corps led the way on 15 May, reaching Aosta 24 hours later. As he pushed forward, however, he was halted at Fort Bard, where a small Austrian force blocked the narrow road; although infantry by-passed the fortress, artillery could not proceed. By 24 May, Napoleon had reached the Po valley with 40,000 men, but he was accompanied by only six guns.

Despite this weakness, the French pushed on to take Milan on 2 June and, as units radiated out from the city, Murat and Lannes fought through to the Po, seizing crossing at Belgiosi and Piacenza by the 7th. In response, the Austrians – having forced the surrender of Genoa on 4 June – concentrated around Alessandria, to the west of Stradella, intent on battle. As Napoleon advanced toward them, he seemed to be unaware of their intention, diverting corps to north and south until his reserve was dangerously reduced. Thus when the Austrians left their camp at Alessandria and crossed the River Bormida on the morning of 14 June, the French, occupying positions

around the village of Marengo, were caught by surprise. Three Austrian columns, under Generals Ott, Melas and O'Reilly, spread out on the Marengo plain; as Melas attacked the French center, the other commanders probed left and right in search of an exposed flank. Ott almost succeeded, suddenly appearing in the north in front of Castel Ceriolo, protected by less than 4000 Frenchmen under Monnier.

Napoleon's lack of a strong reserve led to problems and, as the fighting intensified, the French in the south fell back from Marengo towards St Guiliano Vecchio. An Austrian victory seemed assured. Fortunately, in the afternoon, detached corps under Desaix and Boudet, having heard the sound of battle, arrived on the scene. Backed by Marmont's artillery (a total of only 18 guns) and Kellermann (the Younger's) cuirassiers, they mounted an immediate counterattack to the west of St Guiliano. As they set off, Desaix was killed, but when a lucky artillery shot hit an Austrian ammunition wagon, Kellermann seized the opportunity to charge. The enemy faltered and ran. By nightfall, the Austrians had lost 14,000 men (to the French 7000) and Melas had no choice but to seek an armistice.

Negotiations for a more lasting peace began, but the Austrians were not finished. In November 1800 a new Austrian army, under Archduke John, crossed the River Inn to threaten Munich, advancing toward Moreau's army in the forest of Hohenlinden. In appalling winter weather on 3 December, the French center held firm against an Austrian attack while flank forces encircled Archduke John, inflicting over 18,000 casualties. Further operations in northern Italy led to similar French victories and, by February 1801, the Austrians were ready to accept the Peace of Luneville. The Second Coalition had collapsed, leaving Britain isolated and alone. Despite a successful campaign in Egypt later in 1801, the British government negotiated terms: on 25 March 1802 the Peace of Amiens was signed and hostilities ceased. They were destined to begin all over again in less than a year.

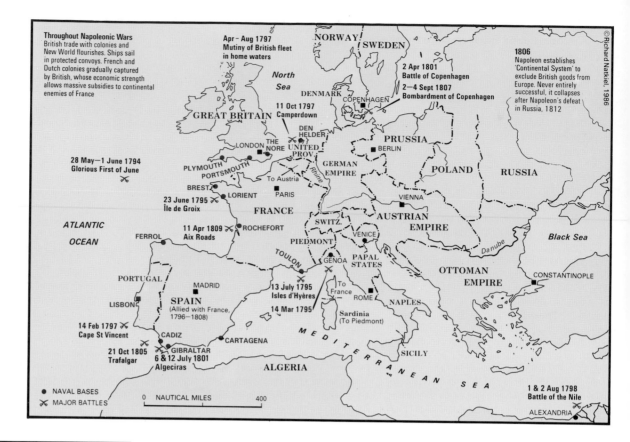

Throughout Napoleonic Wars British trade with colonies and New World flourishes. Ships sail in protected convoys. French and Dutch colonies gradually captured by British, whose economic strength allows massive subsidies to continental enemies of France

Apr – Aug 1797 Mutiny of British fleet in home waters

2 Apr 1801 Battle of Copenhagen
2–4 Sept 1807 Bombardment of Copenhagen

1806 Napoleon establishes 'Continental System' to exclude British goods from Europe. Never entirely successful, it collapses after Napoleon's defeat in Russia, 1812

11 Oct 1797 Camperdown

28 May–1 June 1794 Glorious First of June

23 June 1795 Île de Groix

11 Apr 1809 Aix Roads

13 July 1795 Isles d'Hyères

14 Mar 1795

14 Feb 1797 Cape St Vincent

21 Oct 1805 Trafalgar

6 & 12 July 1801 Algeciras

1 & 2 Aug 1798 Battle of the Nile

● NAVAL BASES
✕ MAJOR BATTLES

0   NAUTICAL MILES   400

Sea Power versus Land Power

Although the land campaigns against the French Revolution proved largely ineffective the Royal Navy rapidly shook off its peacetime lethargy and established a dominance which was at times shaken but never lost. The French Navy, with many of its aristocratic officers either in exile or guillotined, was in no shape to meet the highly professional Royal Navy on equal terms, and a blockade, applied even more rigorously than in previous wars, kept the French fleet penned in its harbors except for rare forays which achieved little. Not even the mutinies on British ships at the main home bases at the Nore and Spithead in 1797 could be exploited by the French and their Dutch allies, and that chance never recurred. Shortly after the Nore mutiny was put down Admiral Duncan inflicted a terrible defeat on the Dutch at Camperdown, virtually destroying them as a naval power. Earlier that year France's Spanish allies had been severely defeated at Cape St Vincent, leaving the Royal Navy with no serious challengers to its control of the oceans.

Hemmed in by British sea power, Napoleon sought to project French military power with little success. In 1798 his occupation of Egypt was checkmated by Nelson's brilliant victory at Aboukir Bay. When he turned his attention to Northern Europe Denmark was swiftly knocked out and the Danish fleet was captured by Nelson.

Napoleon reigned supreme over Europe but the incessant blockade could not be offset by internal trade, and all France's nominal allies and vassals became increasingly uneasy.

To enable resources to be replenished the emperor negotiated the Peace of Amiens in 1802 but this was never more than a temporary truce and when hostilities reopened he soon put into effect his plan for a Continental System. Under this grandiose scheme British trade would be excluded from the continent of Europe, and heavy punishments would be inflicted on any nation caught trading with Perfidious Albion. It went wrong for two reasons: first, most European nations became increasingly restive under the harsh regulations needed to make the Continental System watertight; and second, the British were opening up new markets in North America, so did not rely exclusively on European trade.

Attempts to coerce his allies to keep to the system led Napoleon to put his brother on the throne of Spain in 1808, which immediately precipitated a Spanish popular uprising. The British were quick to profit by this blunder, and went to the aid of a nation that had once been France's most loyal ally. Britain's trade benefited greatly by contacts with Spain and Spanish colonies in South America. Tiring of the long guerrilla war in Spain, Napoleon turned his attention to his Russian allies, and in 1812 began the fatal march on Moscow in a futile attempt to coerce the czar to adhere fully to the Continental System.

The war at sea lasted for nearly ten years after the destruction of the French fleet at Trafalgar in 1805, but control of the seas was never again in dispute. Despite the distraction of the 1812 war with the United States the Royal Navy slowly but surely tightened its grip on France. By 1814 the Duke of Wellington's army could cross the Pyrenees and invade France itself without any French naval threat to its supply lines.

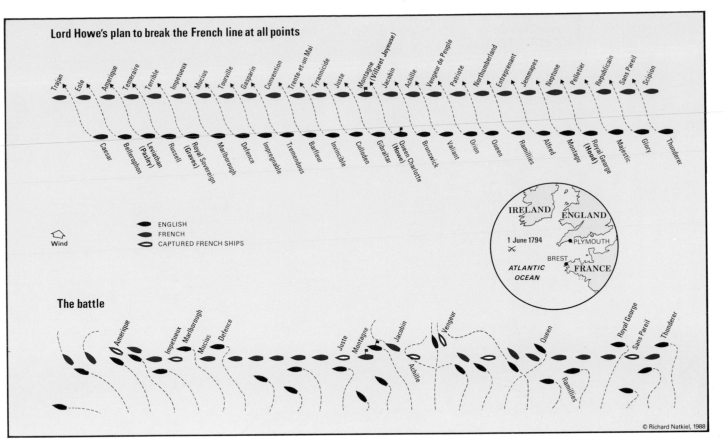

Lord Howe's plan to break the French line at all points

Trajan · Eole · Apperique · Temeraire · Terrible · Impetueux · Mucius · Tourville · Gasparin · Convention · Trente-et-un Mai · Tyrannicide · Juste · Montagne (Villaret Joyeuse) · Jacobin · Achille · Vengeur de Peuple · Patriote · Northumberland · Entreprenant · Jemmapes · Neptune · Pelletier · Republicain · Sans Pareil · Scipion

Caesar · Bellerophon · Leviathan (Pasley) · Russell · Royal Sovereign (Graves) · Marlborough · Defence · Impregnable · Tremendous · Barfleur · Invincible · Culloden · Gibraltar · Queen Charlotte (Howe) · Brunswick · Valiant · Orion · Queen · Ramilies · Alfred · Montagu · Royal George (Hood) · Majestic · Glory · Thunderer

Wind

- ENGLISH
- FRENCH
- CAPTURED FRENCH SHIPS

IRELAND ENGLAND
1 June 1794
PLYMOUTH
BREST
ATLANTIC OCEAN
FRANCE

The battle

Amerique · Impetueux · Marlborough · Mucius · Defence · Juste · Montagne · Jacobin · Achille · Vengeur · Queen · Ramilies · Royal George · Sans Pareil · Thunderer

© Richard Natkiel, 1988

Above: the Glorious First of June.
Below: a scene from the Battle of
Camperdown, 11 October 1797.

The Glorious First of June

Although the outbreak of the French Revolution in 1789 worried the British it was not until January 1793 when King Louis XVI went to the guillotine that the British government felt impelled to go to war. But the French National Convention pre-empted any decision by declaring war itself on 1 February.

The Royal Navy was outwardly weak in 1793, having dropped to a strength of only 20,000 sailors and marines since the end of the American War. With most of the 100 or more ships of the line laid up in reserve or in home squadrons it took time to recruit or impress enough seamen to send a squadron to the Mediterranean and to bring the Channel Fleet up to full strength. In fact the Channel Fleet Commander, Lord Howe, did not get his fleet to sea until July, when a blockade of the French Atlantic coast was instituted.

The economy of revolutionary France was in a parlous state, and the arrival of a large grain convoy was expected in the spring of 1794. Howe was cruising off Ushant when he learned that Admiral Villaret Joyeuse had taken the Brest Squadron to sea on 16 May, and immediately set off to find the French ships. After an indecisive action between the 74-gun ship HMS *Audacious* and the 110-gun *Revolutionnaire* on 28 May the two fleets remained close, but fog kept them apart for another two days. Not until 1 June did Howe finally sight the enemy fleet, and when the fog

lifted the French were only six miles to the leeward of the British.

Howe's fleet formed line ahead and action was joined at 0900. Howe in his flagship *Queen Charlotte* made a determined effort to break the French line but as she passed under the stern of the French flagship, the 120-gun *Montagne*, she lost her foremast and was forced to remain on her opponent's quarter. From there, however, the *Queen Charlotte* directed such a hot fire on the *Montagne* that she was forced to bear away from the French line, and with that movement the French line began to lose cohesion. The rest of Howe's fleet was also hotly engaged. *L'Amerique* was battered to a hulk by the *Leviathan* and the *Marlborough* reduced *L'Impetueux* to sinking condition. The *Brunswick* and *Vengeur* battered each other for nearly three hours, and at the end the French ship sank. Her consort *Achille* had tried to come to her rescue but had been dismasted by a broadside from the *Brunswick* and was forced to strike her colors before the fleets drew apart.

There was considerable criticism of 'Black Dick' Howe when it was learned that the grain convoy had got through, although modern historians tend to be skeptical about the chances of strangling the Revolution at birth.

Even without the grain convoy the victory was impressive: the 80-gun ships *Juste* and *Sans Pareil*, and the 74s *Achille*, *Amerique*, *Impetueux*, *Vengeur* and *Northumberland* were either captured or sunk. It should have served as a warning to the hotheads in Paris that, in sea warfare, patriotism and revolutionary fervor were no substitute for basic seafaring skill and experience.

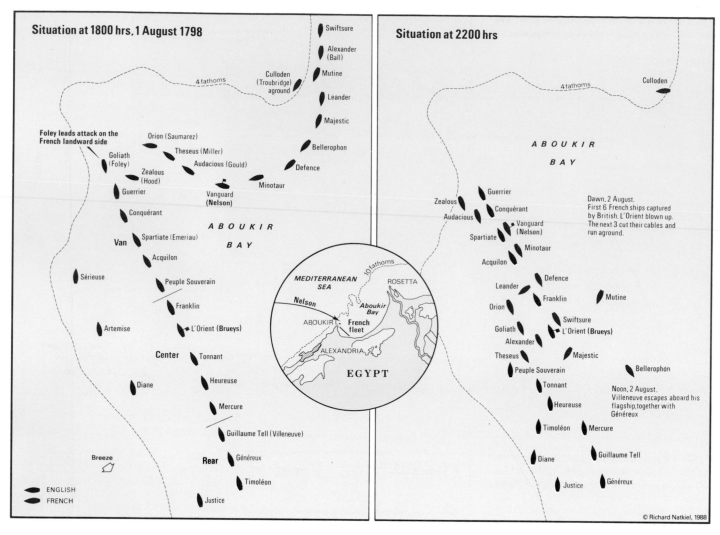

Situation at 1800 hrs, 1 August 1798

Swiftsure
Alexander (Ball)
Mutine
Culloden (Troubridge) aground
4 fathoms
Leander
Majestic

Foley leads attack on the French landward side
Orion (Saumarez)
Goliath (Foley)
Theseus (Miller)
Audacious (Gould)
Bellerophon
Zealous (Hood)
Defence
Guerrier
Vanguard (Nelson)
Minotaur
Conquérant
ABOUKIR
Van
Spartiate (Emeriau)
BAY
Acquilon
Sérieuse
Peuple Souverain
Franklin
Artemise
L'Orient (Brueys)
Center
Tonnant
Diane
Heureuse
Mercure
Guillaume Tell (Villeneuve)
Breeze
Rear
Généreux
Timoléon
Justice

ENGLISH
FRENCH

MEDITERRANEAN SEA
10 fathoms
ROSETTA
Nelson
Aboukir Bay
ABOUKIR I.
French fleet
ALEXANDRIA
EGYPT

Situation at 2200 hrs

Culloden
4 fathoms

ABOUKIR BAY

Guerrier
Zealous
Conquérant
Audacious
Vanguard (Nelson)
Spartiate
Minotaur
Acquilon
Leander
Defence
Orion
Franklin
Mutine
Goliath
Swiftsure
Alexander
L'Orient (Brueys)
Theseus
Majestic
Peuple Souverain
Bellerophon
Tonnant
Heureuse
Timoléon
Mercure
Diane
Guillaume Tell
Justice
Généreux

Dawn, 2 August. First 6 French ships captured by British. L'Orient blown up. The next 3 cut their cables and run aground.

Noon, 2 August. Villeneuve escapes aboard his flagship, together with Généreux

© Richard Natkiel, 1988

The Battle of the Nile

The first of Nelson's great victories was in many ways the most interesting. Its strategic impact was more profound than Copenhagen or Trafalgar, for it shattered Napoleon's dreams of an eastern empire. In the tactical sense it was most unorthodox, using double envelopment against an enemy at anchor, under cover of darkness.

Sir John Jervis, commanding the British fleet blockading the Spanish port of Cadiz, knew that the French were preparing to dispatch a fleet and landing force from Toulon under Napoleon's command. The task of finding out the destination of Napoleon's expedition was entrusted to Nelson, then a young and comparatively inexperienced rear admiral. His first landfall in Egypt found no French ships, but after a short search he found the fleet of Admiral François Brueys sheltering in Aboukir Bay, in what was clearly thought to be a safe anchorage. The French fleet consisted of the 120-gun flagship *L'Orient;* three 80-gun ships, *Franklin, Guillaume Tell* and *Tonnant;* nine 74-gun ships and four frigates.

The British, all 74-gun ships except the 50-gun *Leander* and the smaller *Mutine,* crept up both sides of the French line pouring broadside after broadside into the helpless French ships. During the night the French flagship *L'Orient* caught fire, and when the flames reached her magazine she was destroyed in a huge explosion.

When dawn broke the French fleet was in fearful disarray. Only the *Généreux* and *Guillaume Tell* and two frigates had made their escape; all the remaining ships were aground or lay dismasted and helpless.

This was the most decisive victory won by the Royal Navy to date, the sort of 'battle of annihilation' that Nelson dreamed of. Bonaparte abandoned his garrison in Egypt, leaving them to be mopped up later by the British.

The Battle of Trafalgar

Following the brief Peace of Amiens in 1802-03 Napoleon returned to his grand design for the conquest of Europe. After his attempt to revive the Armed Neutrality was thwarted by Nelson's victory over the Danes at Copenhagen in 1801 he had to try other means to outflank British sea power.

Napoleon's new method was to be more sophisticated. An 'Army of England' was assembled in northern France, with a flotilla of flat-bottomed boats to transport it across the Channel. While the army was preparing to cross the Channel it was planned that small detachments of French and Spanish warships would slip out of their harbors and evade the British blockading squadrons. Once clear of the blockade they would head for a secret rendezvous and then swoop back on the Channel while the main strength of the Royal Navy was dispersed to hunt for them.

It was a preposterously complicated scheme, which took no account of weather and tides, or of what the British might do. In fact the Admiralty ordered what had always been done in times of difficulty since the days

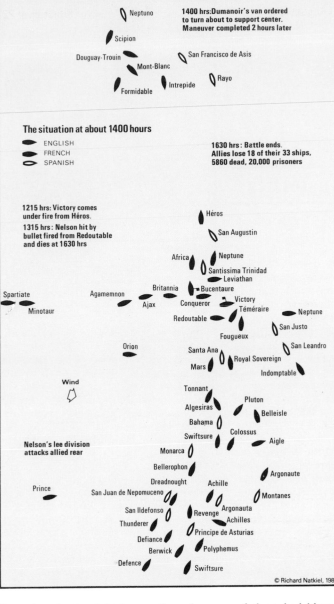

The situation at about 1400 hours

ENGLISH
FRENCH
SPANISH

1400 hrs: Dumanoir's van ordered to turn about to support center. Maneuver completed 2 hours later

1630 hrs: Battle ends. Allies lose 18 of their 33 ships, 5860 dead, 20,000 prisoners

1215 hrs: Victory comes under fire from Héros.
1315 hrs: Nelson hit by bullet fired from Redoutable and dies at 1630 hrs

Nelson's lee division attacks allied rear

© Richard Natkiel, 1988

of the Armada; its squadrons were ordered to fall back on the Channel, rather than be dispersed. There they were well placed to deny the French Army the clear fortnight it would need to get its 150,000 men across the Channel and could still maintain the blockade of Brest.

Nelson had been put in command of the Mediterranean Fleet, with strict orders to prevent the French Toulon Fleet under Admiral Villeneuve from uniting with any other force. The French left Toulon in January 1805 and after a wild goose chase through the Mediterranean Nelson learned that Villeneuve had returned to port briefly but had left Toulon a second time, headed this time for the West Indies. In fact Martinique was the secret rendezvous, and Nelson pursued the French right across the Atlantic, so hot on Villeneuve's heels that the French admiral was forced to hurry back across the Atlantic.

After a brief action off Cape Finisterre with a British force commanded by Sir Robert Calder, Villeneuve abandoned the idea of putting into Ferrol and slipped into Vigo instead. Armed with that priceless information the First Lord of the Admiralty, Lord Barham, was able to act vigorously to bring about the ruin of Napoleon's master plan.

What Barham did was to reduce the blockading force at Brest in order to concentrate a large force off the coast of Spain, where it was most likely to bring Villeneuve to action. The main strategic aim was to prevent the French from slipping back into the Mediterranean, and the British fleet was therefore divided between Ferrol and Brest.

Napoleon knew that his hopes of invading England were over, but to avoid the public humiliation of admitting defeat he continued to bombard the luckless Villeneuve with instructions to unite with Admiral Ganteaume's fleet at Brest. On 13 August 1805 Villeneuve got to sea but was forced to put into Cadiz, where a small Spanish squadron was being watched by a British force commanded by Collingwood. With the main Franco-Spanish fleet now concentrated in one harbor all that remained for Barham to do was to appoint Nelson to command the fleet off the port of Cadiz.

Villeneuve finally got his Combined Fleet to sea again in October, 18 French and 15 Spanish ships of the line against 27 British, and was sighted on the morning of the 21st. The British formed themselves in two columns as Nelson had planned, the port or Weather Division led by Nelson in the *Victory* and the starboard or Lee Division led by Collingwood in the *Royal*

Sovereign. In the light breeze the columns moved slowly downwind, while the enemy line lay apparently mesmerized. In theory Nelson's ships should have been annihilated by the enemy gunfire but Nelson knew that the French always fired high at the masts and rigging of enemy ships, and would be unable to destroy his two columns before they had closed the range.

The British columns were punished heavily, but they held their fire until within a few hundred yards. The effect of their broadsides was all the more shattering at such close range, and it is said that a double-shotted broadside from the *Victory* killed 400 men aboard Villeneuve's flagship the *Bucentaure*. The Franco-Spanish line was broken in several places, and even though Nelson was mortally wounded by a sharpshooter firing from the rigging of the *Redoutable* at the height of the battle, the issue was beyond doubt. All around the French and Spanish ships were being devastated by disciplined gunfire.

By 1630 when the battle ended 18 French and Spanish ships had struck their colors (one

of these had blown up), 11 had escaped to Cadiz and four more made off to the south. Several of the prizes were so badly damaged that they were scuttled, and other prizes were later able to make their escape after the small British prize-crews were overpowered. Although only four of the captured ships were brought into a British port, Trafalgar was a clear-cut victory which wiped out the French invasion plans.

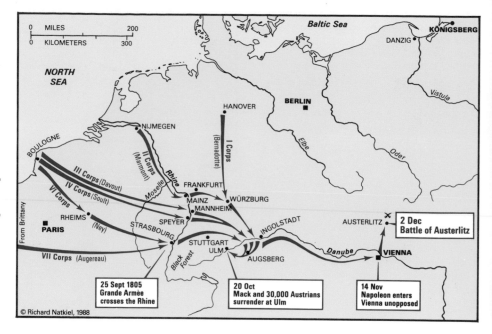

Ulm and Austerlitz

On 11 April 1805 representatives of Britain, Austria, Russia and Sweden signed the Convention of St Petersburg to create the Third Coalition, dedicated to the defeat of France. Napoleon, by now emperor, reacted in typical fashion, postponing his intended invasion of England and ordering his newly formed *Grande Armée* to march with all speed to the east. His intention was to cross the Rhine, catch the Austrians on the Danube and destroy them before the Russians could intervene. He would then be able to concentrate all his forces against the Russian advance.

The campaign against Austria was a masterpiece of maneuver. As 40,000 men under Murat pushed across the Rhine at Strasbourg, General Mack's main Austrian army of 70,000 advanced to meet them in the defiles of the Black Forest, leaving the line of communication back to Vienna exposed. Napoleon then led the bulk of the *Grande Armée* (some 210,000 men) across the Rhine farther north, aiming to swing south in an encircling move.

It worked like a charm. Despite deteriorating weather, the *Grande Armée* made good progress, crossing the Rhine on the night of 24/25 September and wheeling south toward the Danube on 2 October. Forward units under Soult reached Donauwörth five days later, preparing the way for the rest of the army to cross the Danube and capture Augsburg. Meanwhile, Mack had pushed forward from Ulm in response to Murat's probing advance, leaving Napoleon free to concentrate on sending units out in all directions from Augsburg to sever Austrian lines of supply and communication. Clashes inevitably occurred – at Wertingen (8 October), Albeck (11 October) and Elchingen (14 October) – but they merely reinforced the desperate nature of Mack's position. On 20 October, caught between the anvil of Murat's force and the approaching hammer of the *Grande Armée*, the Austrian commander surrendered at Ulm at the head of 30,000 men. The campaign had lasted 26 days.

Napoleon shifted his attention to the Russians, approaching from the east under Field Marshals Kutuzov and Buxhöwden, for it was imperative that they be defeated before the Austrians recovered. If any delays occurred, the Allies could conceivably gather 400,000 men to overwhelm the French, tired after their recent exertions. With this in mind,

Napoleon pushed on toward Vienna, clashing with Kutuzov at Amstetten (5 November) and Maria Zell (8 November) before taking the Austrian capital. Kutuzov refused to offer battle, however, preferring to withdraw to the northeast, hoping to overextend the French, whose soldiers were beginning to suffer from the poor winter conditions. On 23 November, having taken Hollabrünn and Brünn, Napoleon was forced to call a halt for rest and reorganization.

He now faced a problem, for the longer he remained static the more likely it was that the Austro-Russian army of 90,000 men concentrated at Olmutz to his north would attack, cutting him off from the Danube. He decided to play one of the oldest tricks in the book, feigning weakness and indecision to tempt the enemy into a full-scale assault on ground of his choosing. The site, to the west of the village of Austerlitz, had already been reconnoitred and a battle plan worked out. As part of the decep-

tion, Napoleon decided to abandon what appeared to be the key topographical feature of the area – the Pratzen Heights – and concentrate his forces instead along the Goldbach stream to the west. In addition, he presented a weak defense along the stream, where Soult's corps held nearly five miles of frontage, hoping that this would tempt the Allies to mount their main assault in that area. Meanwhile, the main French positions were constructed in the north, on and around the Zurlan Hill: as soon as the enemy attack toward the stream began, Napoleon intended to lead his more powerful force back on to the Pratzen Heights, splitting the Austro-Russian army in two and destroying those units engaging Soult. By 2 December – the anniversary of Napoleon's coronation as emperor – all was ready: Kutuzov had occupied the Pratzen Heights and was about to fall into the trap.

The rival armies began to prepare for battle at 0400 hours, protected by a dense morning

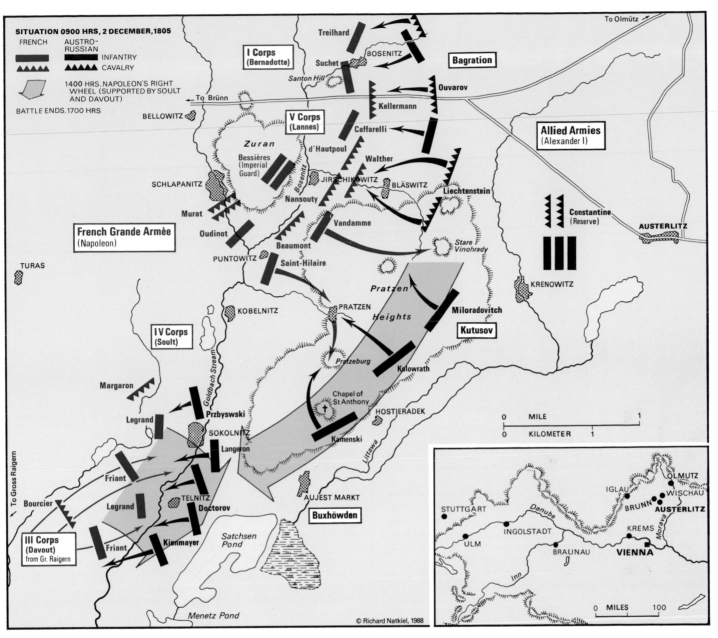

SITUATION 0900 HRS, 2 DECEMBER, 1805

FRENCH · AUSTRO-RUSSIAN · INFANTRY

FRENCH · AUSTRO-RUSSIAN · CAVALRY

1400 HRS, NAPOLEON'S RIGHT WHEEL (SUPPORTED BY SOULT AND DAVOUT)

BATTLE ENDS, 1700 HRS

To Olmütz

Treilhard

BOSENITZ

Suchet

I Corps (Bernadotte)

Santon Hill

Bagration

To Brünn

Ouvarov

Kellermann

BELLOWITZ

V Corps (Lannes)

Caffarelli

Allied Armies (Alexander I)

Zuran

Bessières (Imperial Guard)

d'Hautpoul

Walther

SCHLAPANITZ

Bosenitz

JIRSCHIKOWITZ

BLÄSWITZ

Liechtenstein

Constantine (Reserve)

AUSTERLITZ

Nansouty

Vandamme

Murat

French Grande Armèe (Napoleon)

Oudinot

Beaumont

Stare Vinohrady

TURAS

PUNTOWITZ

Saint-Hilaire

KRENOWITZ

KOBELNITZ

Pratzen

PRATZEN

Heights

Miloradovitch

IV Corps (Soult)

Kutusov

Goldbach Stream

Pratzeburg

Kolowrath

Margaron

Chapel of St Anthony

HOSTIERADEK

Legrand

Przbyswski

SOKOLNITZ

Littawa

Langeron

Kamenski

To Gross Raigern

Friant

AUJEST MARKT

Bourcier

Legrand

TELNITZ

Doctorov

Buxhöwden

III Corps (Davout) from Gr. Raigern

Friant

Kienmayer

Satchsen Pond

Menetz Pond

© Richard Natkiel, 1988

0   MILE   1

0   KILOMETER   1

STUTTGART

ULM

INGOLSTADT

Danube

IGLAU

OLMUTZ

WISCHAU

BRUNN

AUSTERLITZ

KREMS

Morava

BRAUNAU

VIENNA

Inn

0   MILES   100

mist which left the Allies even less clear about French dispositions. Nevertheless, it was the Allies who started the action, concentrating against Napoleon's extended right wing along the Goldbach stream and attacking the villages of Sokolnitz and Telnitz. Heavy fighting ensued, during which Soult's men were forced to relinquish the villages, but the sudden intervention of 6600 fresh troops under Davout, marching up from the southwest, stabilized the line. This persuaded the Allies to commit the bulk of their forces from the Pratzen Heights at 0830 hours and, as soon as this move became obvious, Napoleon played his masterstroke. At 0900 hours, units under St Hilaire (part of Soult's corps) advanced out of

Above: the Battle of Austerlitz, December 1805.
Left: Russian prisoners look on as Napoleon directs his forces at Austerlitz.

the mist to attack the village of Pratzen, catching the Allies completely by surprise. At the same time, forces under Lannes and Murat emerged from the Zurlan Hill to prevent Russian reinforcements under General Bagration from joining the main Allied army.

But the Allies were not defeated yet. At 1030 hours Kutuzov launched a vicious counterattack which almost breached the French line at Pratzen, repeating the move at 1300 hours with elements of the Russian Imperial Guard, brought forward from Austerlitz. The French held on despite heavy casualties and, an hour later, Napoleon committed his Imperial Guard to complete the capture of the Pratzen Heights. The Allied forces under Buxhöwden were now trapped in a series of frozen lakes (or meres) between the Heights and the Goldbach stream. Some soldiers tried to escape across the ice but their weight, plus French artillery fire, sent them crashing through to a frozen death. As Kutuzov and Bagration pulled back in the center and north,

Allied units in the south had no choice but to surrender. By mid-afternoon, the Allies had lost some 27,000 casualties (a third of their effective strength), compared to Napoleon's 8300. Within 24 hours, the Austrians were requesting an armistice and, as the Russians retreated to their homeland, the Third Coalition collapsed.

123

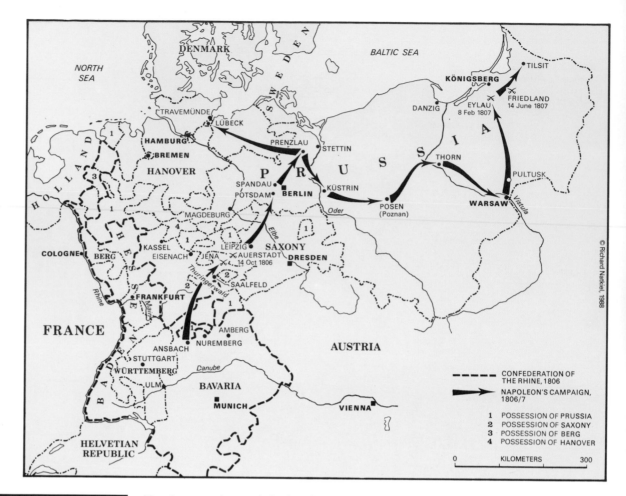

The Battles of Jena and Auerstädt

Napoleon's victory at Austerlitz in December 1805 shattered the Third Coalition, leaving the Austrians defeated and the Russians in disarray. It also placed the French in possession of key areas east of the Rhine, a situation of deep concern to the Prussians. Although they congratulated the emperor on his great triumph, they secretly prepared for war. By September 1806 King Frederick William III had over 170,000 men under arms.

But the Prussian commanders were indecisive, arguing endlessly about the best strategy to adopt. This allowed Napoleon to prepare his own offensive, calling up reservists and concentrating a *Grande Armée* of 180,000 men around Ansbach and Nuremberg. His aim was to defeat the Prussians before the Russians arrived on the scene; his intention was to drive north, through the Thuringerwald toward Leipzig, thence to Berlin. The advance began on 8 October, before the Prussians had completed their laborious preparations.

The *Grande Armée* pressed north in three main columns, giving Napoleon maximum opportunity to locate the enemy and then concentrate against him at speed. Thus, when the left-hand column under Lannes reported considerable Prussian forces to the west of the River Saale near Jena on 13 October,

Napoleon raced toward the location, calling for other formations to follow without delay. He arrived at Lannes' headquarters at 1600 hours and, from what he could see before him, he imagined that he had found the main Prussian force. What he did not know was that Frederick William, with at least 60,000 men, was moving north toward Auerstädt, leaving only 38,000 men under Hohenlohe to face the French.

Throughout the night and into the next morning (14 October), various French corps marched to join the emperor, until over 90,000 men were preparing for battle. Napoleon's plan was a familiar one – while two corps, under Davout and Bernadotte, moved in a wide sweep toward Auerstädt, the main French force would pin the Prussians at Jena. Not realizing that Auerstädt was well defended, Napoleon expected Davout and Bernadotte to have a relatively easy passage, appearing astride the Prussian lines of retreat, ready to destroy any formation pulling back from Jena. It did not quite work out like that.

The action at Jena began as early as 0600 hours on the 14th, when French units advanced to occupy more open ground, and by 1000 hours, as the morning fog slowly lifted, most of the *Grande Armée* was at its battle stations. Hohenlohe, realizing that he was greatly outnumbered, sent out urgent requests for reinforcement, but to no avail. Even so, when the battle began in earnest, the French seemed close to disaster: the impetuous Ney, tired of inactivity, launched an unauthorized

attack in the center. Prussian cavalry charged the flank of the exposed French corps, virtually cutting it off, and it was only when other French units reinforced Ney that his men were saved. This had the effect of escalating the fighting until, by 1300 hours, nearly all forces on both sides were hotly engaged. It was an unequal struggle, characterized for the Prussians by a seemingly endless stream of French units appearing on the battlefield. By 1500 hours, the Prussians were in full retreat. It looked like a decisive victory for Napoleon.

But this was not quite the case, for the main battle of the day had been taking place at Auerstädt where Davout, with only 27,000 men (Bernadotte had disobeyed orders and turned south, along the east bank of the Saale) defeated at least 60,000 Prussians. As Davout had tried to carry out Napoleon's orders, he had suddenly found himself in the midst of the main Prussian force and in grave danger of being overwhelmed. He had fought a dogged battle during the morning of 14 October, placing his infantry in a series of mutually supporting squares and seeing off attack after attack. At 1100 hours he had suddenly ordered his men to advance and the Prussians had broken. The road to Berlin lay open.

The Prussian capital was taken by Napoleon on 25 October, but the campaign was by no means over. Although Stettin fell on 29 October, followed by Lübeck and Magdeburg a week later, the Prussians refused to sue for peace, looking to the Russians to provide reinforcements. Aware of this threat, Napoleon

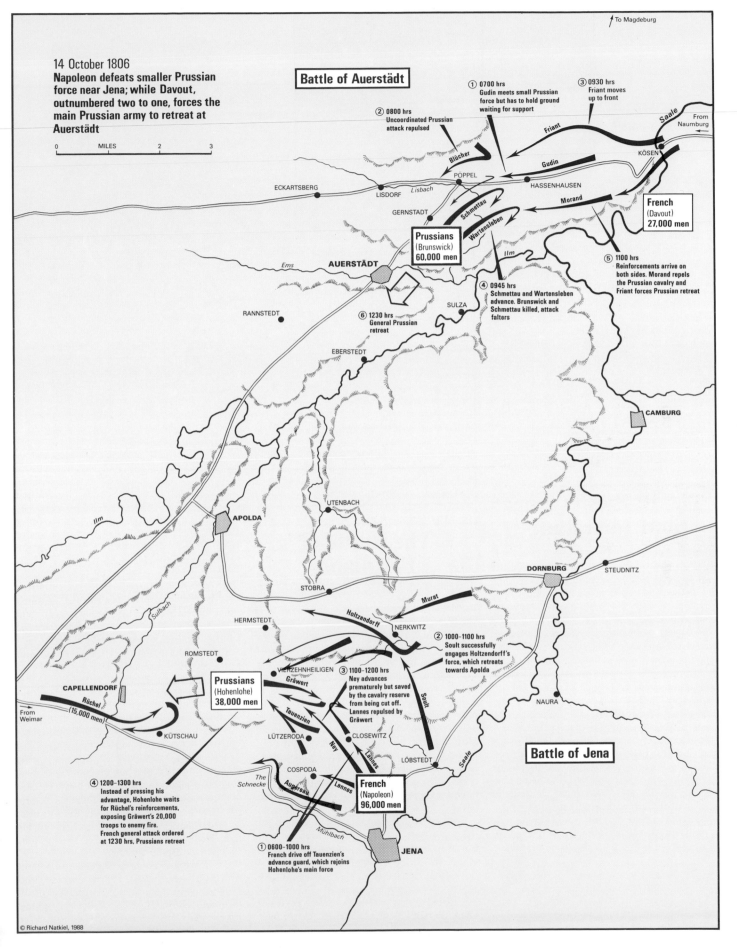

To Magdeburg

14 October 1806
Napoleon defeats smaller Prussian
force near Jena; while Davout,
outnumbered two to one, forces the
main Prussian army to retreat at
Auerstädt

0   MILES   2   3

Battle of Auerstädt

① 0700 hrs
Gudin meets small Prussian
force but has to hold ground
waiting for support

③ 0930 hrs
Friant moves
up to front

② 0800 hrs
Uncoordinated Prussian
attack repulsed

Saale

From
Naumburg

Friant

Blücher

Gudin

KÖSEN

PÖPPEL

HASSENHAUSEN

ECKARTSBERG

LISDORF

Lisbach

Schmettau

Morand

GERNSTADT

Wartensleben

French
(Davout)
27,000 men

Ems

AUERSTÄDT

Ilm

Prussians
(Brunswick)
60,000 men

⑤ 1100 hrs
Reinforcements arrive on
both sides. Morand repels
the Prussian cavalry and
Friant forces Prussian retreat

RANNSTEDT

④ 0945 hrs
Schmettau and Wartensleben
advance. Brunswick and
Schmettau killed, attack
falters

SULZA

⑥ 1230 hrs
General Prussian
retreat

EBERSTEDT

CAMBURG

UTENBACH

APOLDA

Ilm

DORNBURG

STEUDNITZ

STOBRA

Sulbach

HERMSTEDT

Holtzendorff

Murat

NERKWITZ

② 1000-1100 hrs
Soult successfully
engages Holtzendorff's
force, which retreats
towards Apolda

ROMSTEDT

VIERZEHNHEILIGEN

Prussians
(Hohenlohe)
38,000 men

Gräwert

③ 1100-1200 hrs
Ney advances
prematurely but saved
by the cavalry reserve
from being cut off.
Lannes repulsed by Gräwert

Soult

NAURA

CAPELLENDORF

Rüchel
(15,000 men)

Tauenzien

Ney

CLOSEWITZ

Lannes

From
Weimar

KÜTSCHAU

LÜTZERODA

LÖBSTEDT

Saale

Battle of Jena

④ 1200-1300 hrs
Instead of pressing his
advantage, Hohenlohe waits
for Rüchel's reinforcements,
exposing Gräwert's 20,000
troops to enemy fire.
French general attack ordered
at 1230 hrs, Prussians retreat

COSPODA

The
Schnecke

Augereau

Lannes

French
(Napoleon)
96,000 men

Mühlbach

① 0600-1000 hrs
French drive off Tauenzien's
advance guard, which rejoins
Hohenlohe's main force

JENA

ordered Davout to conduct a wide-ranging reconnaissance of eastern Prussia and, when he reported no contacts as far east as Posnan, Napoleon decided to 'fill the vacuum,' occupying Thorn and Warsaw in late November. By 1 December, Russian forces under General Levin Bennigsen, having probed forward toward the Vistula, had begun to pull back to the comparative safety of the fortress at Königsberg. As both armies sought winter quarters, it seemed as if the campaign was over, at least until the spring.

In January 1807, however, Bennigsen renewed his advance. Napoleon, with his customary eye for strategy, tried to lure the enemy into a trap around Danzig, but the Russian commander refused to comply, withdrawing toward the town of Eylau. The French pursued, despite appalling winter conditions and, as Bennigsen turned to face them at Eylau, a battle became inevitable. Forward elements of the *Grande Armée*, although outnumbered – Napoleon had 45,000 men to Bennigsen's 67,000 – took Eylau itself on 7 February, seeking shelter from the snow and freezing conditions.

On 8 February – another bitterly cold day – the two armies faced each other across a snow-filled landscape. Napoleon decided to pin the Russian center down while sending more mobile forces under Ney and Davout around the flanks, but when neither of these commanders arrived, the battle quickly degenerated into a slogging match. As the French flanks came under attack, Napoleon tried to relieve the pressure by advancing against the Russian center, only to see his men cut down by enemy artillery. The Russians then counterattacked, retaking Eylau and almost capturing Napoleon's headquarters: the emperor, in desperation, committed his last reserve, Murat's cavalry corps. At 1130 hours, Murat led an epic charge through the Russian center, and as Davout at last arrived to put in a flank attack from the south, a vital breathing space was gained. By nightfall, the battle had become a stalemate. That night, Bennigsen decided to withdraw, leaving Napoleon in possession of the field. But it was not a major victory: having lost 10,000 men, the emperor was in no condition to pursue the Russian force.

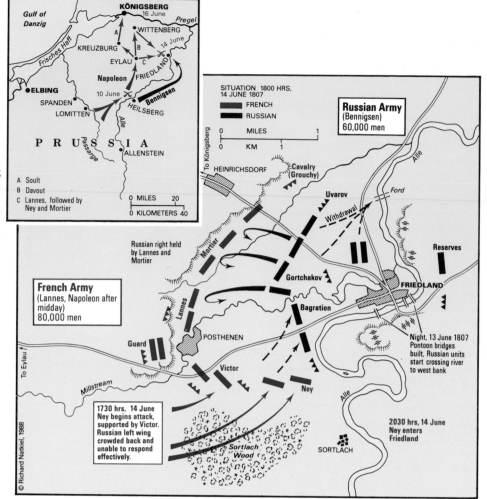

The Battle of Friedland

In the immediate aftermath of the 'drawn' battle at Eylau in February 1807, both the French and Russian armies returned to winter quarters. Napoleon concentrated the bulk of his force at Spanden and Lamitten, sending Lefebvre to lay siege to Danzig. On 5 June, the Russians under Bennigsen advanced toward Napoleon: their intention was to relieve the pressure on Danzig but, when news reached them that the port had fallen on 27 May, they hesitated. Napoleon immediately advanced to meet Bennigsen at Heilsberg (10 June), and although this was by no means a decisive action, it persuaded the Russians to fall back toward their base at Friedland on the River Alle.

Convinced that Bennigsen was aiming for the security of Königsberg, Napoleon sent fast-moving corps to cut him off, and it was one of these, under Lannes, that reported a substantial Russian force at Friedland late on 13 June. Skirmishes took place, but neither side was present in strength: by 0900 hours on the 14th, Lannes had less than 20,000 men opposing 45,000 Russians.

Three hours later, Napoleon arrived with reinforcements. Ignoring the advice of his staff, he decided to mount an immediate attack, recognizing that Bennigsen, with his back to the Alle, was in a potentially dangerous situation. By 1600 hours, the French could muster 80,000 men, while Bennigsen had only 60,000, the bulk of whom were badly deployed astride a millstream which bisected the battle area. Russian infantry, moreover, were concentrated in the center, with only Cossacks and light troops on the flanks. Ordering Ney to attack in the south, crushing the Russians against the river, Napoleon directed Grouchy in the north and the main body of the infantry under Mortier and Lannes in the center to wait until the Russians began to crack before advancing for the kill.

The attack began at 1730 hours, catching Bennigsen by surprise (he had presumed that the day was too far gone for a major battle). Nevertheless, when Ney advanced through the Sortlach Wood, he encountered stiff resistance from Cossacks and artillery, and it was not until Victor, with part of his corps, joined him that the enemy began to wilt. The Russian infantry units in the center, assailed by artillery which did fearful damage at very close range, seemed set to panic, so Bennigsen, in desperation, ordered them to advance toward Mortier and Lannes. They made little headway and, by adding to the chaos, allowed Ney to resume his drive northward. Despite a sud-

Left: the Battle of Friedland, June 1807. For the loss of 9000 men, Napoleon dealt a decisive blow against the Russians.
Below right: Napoleon as the Emperor of the French.

den counterattack on the outskirts of Friedland by the Russian Imperial Guard, Ney was in possession of the town by 2030 hours.

Bennigsen now concentrated on saving as much of his army as possible, ordering it to pull back to east of the Alle. The Russians were aided by Grouchy's reluctance to release his cavalry and by the discovery of a ford, but by 2300 hours they were in full retreat, having lost over 20,000 men. The French, by comparison, had lost only 9000 and had gained an undisputed victory, opening the way to a peace treaty which would leave Napoleon the master of Europe.

The French Empire

By 1812, the First French Empire was at its height. In territorial terms, French rule had been extended – by treaty, usurpation of political power or force of arms – to include the United Provinces (Holland), Westphalia, the Confederation of the Rhine, the Grand Duchy of Warsaw (Poland), Helvetia (Switzerland), Italy, Illyria (the Dalmatian coast) and Spain. French armies had been triumphant in most corners of the continent, from Madrid in the west to Friedland in the east, the great powers of Austria and Prussia had been humiliated, Russia was about to be invaded and Britain lay isolated.

Such a remarkable achievement owed its success almost entirely to Napoleon, whose rise to power in France in 1799 had ended the chaos of the post-Revolution period. Not only did he restore stability to France but, more significantly, he reformed the French Army, creating an instrument with which he could dominate Europe. Napoleon's ability to destroy successive coalitions of his opponents was based on a speed of concentration which allowed him to bring enemy armies to decisive battle in the shortest possible time. The destruction of the Austrians at Ulm and, together with the Russians, at Austerlitz in 1805 set the pattern, and it was one which was to be repeated – albeit never quite so dramatically – on a number of subsequent occasions.

Nor was this all, for of equal importance was Napoleon's almost uncanny ability to win battles once they had been joined. His success in this respect owed much to his adoption of the *corps d'armée* system, whereby self-contained formations under trusted commanders could fight against seemingly overwhelming odds until other, similar formations rushed to

their aid. In most cases, the aim was to pin the enemy center while other forces secretly moved around the flanks; as soon as the moment was right (usually when the enemy, convinced that the forces facing him were close to exhaustion, committed his reserve), the flank formations would emerge to push in the enemy wings or sever his lines of communication. The enemy would invariably react by rushing forces to protect his flanks, thus weakening the center; Napoleon would then release his own reserve and crash through the enemy line, spreading panic and achieving victory. By 1812, these tactics were well established and battle proven.

But there were chinks in the armor. Despite successive campaigns and peace treaties, Napoleon had yet to decisively defeat either Russia or Britain. Indeed, his strategy against the latter – the closing of Europe to British trade through the 'Continental System' of rules imposed on the countries he controlled – had already drawn him into Spain and Portugal, giving Britain an opportunity to commit an army to the continent, and was about to lure him deep into Russia with disastrous consequences. At the same time, other armies by 1812 were beginning to analyse the reasons for French success on the battlefield and to put forward effective responses, concealing forces behind natural obstacles to tempt the enemy

into premature moves, protecting their flanks and training their soldiers to absorb the impact of the main assault. Within two years, such ploys were to leave the French Empire in ruins.

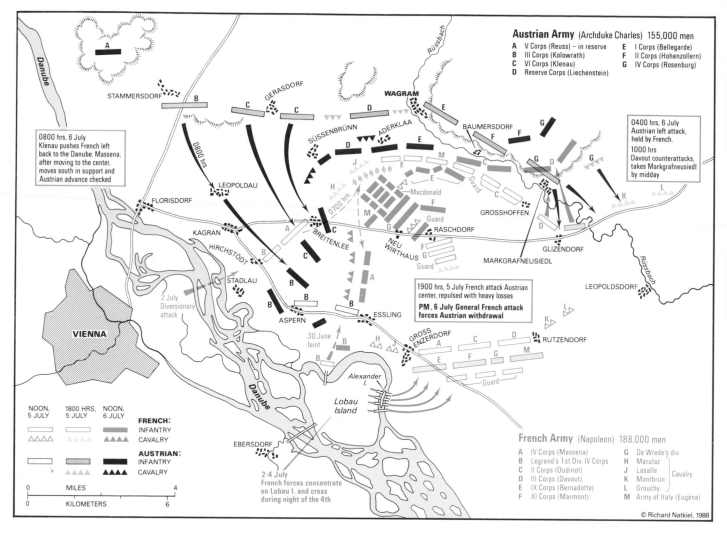

The map contains the following labels and annotations:

Austrian Army (Archduke Charles) 155,000 men
A V Corps (Reuss) – in reserve   E I Corps (Bellegarde)
B III Corps (Kolowrath)   F II Corps (Hohenzollern)
C VI Corps (Klenau)   G IV Corps (Rosenburg)
D Reserve Corps (Liechenstein)

0800 hrs, 6 July
Klenau pushes French left
back to the Danube. Massena,
after moving to the center,
moves south in support and
Austrian advance checked

0400 hrs, 6 July
Austrian left attack,
held by French.
1000 hrs
Davout counterattacks,
takes Markgrafneusiedl
by midday

1900 hrs, 5 July French attack Austrian
center, repulsed with heavy losses
PM, 6 July General French attack
forces Austrian withdrawal

Place names: STAMMERSDORF, GERASDORF, WAGRAM, SÜSSENBRÜNN, ADERKLAA, BAUMERSDORF, LEOPOLDAU, FLORISDORF, GROSSHOFFEN, Macdonald, KAGRAN, BREITENLEE, RASCHDORF, GLIZENDORF, HIRCHSTÖDT, NEU WIRTHAUS, MARKGRAFNEUSIEDL, STADLAU, Guard, LEOPOLDSDORF, VIENNA, ASPERN, ESSLING, GROSS ENZERDORF, RUTZENDORF, Alexander I., Lobau Island, EBERSDORF, Danube, Russbach

2 July Diversionary attack
30 June feint
2–4 July French forces concentrate on Lobau I. and cross during night of the 4th

NOON, 5 July   1800 HRS, 5 July   NOON, 6 July
FRENCH:
INFANTRY
CAVALRY
AUSTRIAN:
INFANTRY
CAVALRY

MILES 0 — 4
KILOMETERS 0 — 6

French Army (Napoleon) 188,000 men
A IV Corps (Massena)   G De Wrede's div
B Legrand's 1st Div, IV Corps H Marulaz
C II Corps (Oudinot)   J Lasalle   Cavalry
D III Corps (Davout)   K Montbrun
E IX Corps (Bernadotte)   L Grouchy
F XI Corps (Marmont)   M Army of Italy (Eugène)

© Richard Natkiel, 1988

The Battle of Wagram

On 9 April 1809 Austrian forces under Archduke Charles, intent on exploiting Napoleon's apparent preoccupation with Spain, attacked Bavaria, catching the French by surprise. Napoleon rushed to the scene, launching an immediate counterattack at Abensberg (20 April) to regain the initiative. Charles, his army split, pulled back beyond the barrier of the Danube, allowing Napoleon to occupy Vienna on 13 May without a fight.

The Austrians soon recovered, posing a threat to French positions and forcing Napoleon to seek a battle across the river. He occupied Lobau Island, to the southeast of Vienna, and ordered bridges to be constructed to allow his army to cross; his aim was to occupy a number of villages just beyond the river, using them as a line from which further attacks could be made. But Charles was ready and, on 21 and 22 May, he organized attacks against the villages of Aspern and Essling. Amid bitter fighting, the French withdrew to the safety of Lobau, which now became a fortified base. With reinforcements joining both armies, by early July Napoleon had 188,000

men and 500 guns facing an Austrian force of 155,000 men and 450 guns.

French units renewed their offensive during the night of 4-5 July, crossing the river on secretly constructed pontoons to achieve maximum surprise. On 5 July they advanced to create a huge salient, stretching from Aspern in the south, almost to Wagram in the north and to Glizendorf in the east. Charles, who had predicted a major assault on Aspern, tried to rectify the situation by personally leading a counterattack in that direction, but to no avail. At the same time, French forces attempted a large-scale assault against the Austrian center, only to be repulsed with heavy losses. As night fell, both armies sank into an exhausted quiet as their commanders pondered the next move.

Charles attacked first, early on 6 July, pressing into French positions at Aderklaa and forcing Bernadotte's corps to retreat (much to Napoleon's displeasure). A French attack against the Austrian left at Markgrafneusiedl seemed more successful, only to face problems when Charles put in his main assault from Gerasdorf at 0800 hours, on the opposite flank. French links with Lobau Island were threatened; only Napoleon's decision to shift forces south from the Aderklaa action saved the day. Even then, the Austrian assault had to be finally broken up by massed French artil-

lery on the island.

Meanwhile Davout had begun to make progress against the enemy left, taking Markgrafneusiedl by 1200 hours, and this diverted Austrian attention sufficiently to allow Napoleon to organize an assault against Gerasdorf using Macdonald's corps. In the process, a dangerous gap opened up in the French center, but this was quickly plugged by artillery and the Imperial Guard. Macdonald's advance drove a wedge deep into the Austrian line and, by 1600 hours, Charles had been forced to withdraw. Despite fairly equal losses – 39,500 French to 40,000 Austrians – Napoleon was master of the field. On 12 July, the Austrians agreed to an armistice.

Above: the Battle of Wagram, July 1809.
Above right: an episode from the advance on Moscow in 1812 – the Battle of Smolensk.

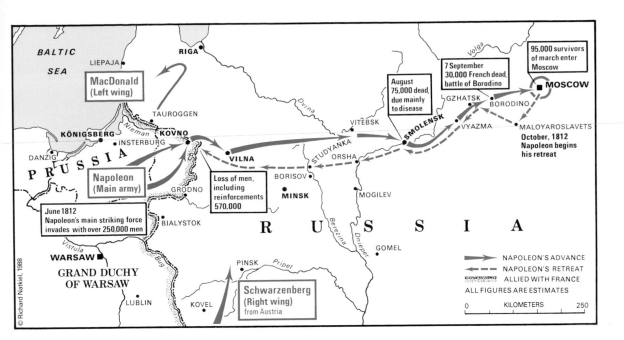

The Russian Campaign

On 24 June 1812, Napoleon's *Grande Armée de Russie*, comprising a central army group of 450,000 men, 250,000 horses and over 1000 guns, protected by Prussian and Austrian flank forces of 32,000 and 34,000 men respectively, crossed the River Niemen into Russian Poland. Relations between Napoleon and Czar Alexander I had been poor since 1809, when the latter had done little to prevent an Austrian attack on Bavaria while Napoleon was preoccupied with Spain, and had worsened as the czar refused to play his part in imposing the Continental System of trade embargoes against the British. As the Russian Army concentrated along the Dvina River and began a process of modernization, Napoleon feared the worst – an attack from the east. Convinced that a short, sharp campaign would force the Russians into battles they could not win, he decided to attack first.

His central army group marched to the north of the Pripet marshes, threatening St Petersburg and Moscow simultaneously, hoping to destroy the Russian First Army under Prince Barclay de Tolly before it could link up with the Second Army under Prince Bagration farther south. The plan did not work. Almost immediately, the Russians adopted a policy of strategic withdrawal and 'scorched earth,' pulling Napoleon deeper into western Russia and making him dependent on tenuous supply lines, made worse by the blazing summer heat and poor roads. Despite actions at Vilna and Vitebsk, Napoleon could not come to grips with the enemy and could do nothing to prevent a link-up between Barclay and Bagration to the west of Smolensk in late July.

The French continued to advance, searching for the decisive battle. A chance occurred in mid-August, when a sudden crossing of the Dnieper caught the Russians by surprise, but despite heavy fighting in the suburbs of Smolensk (17-19 August), the outcome was indecisive. It was at this point that Napoleon made the fateful decision to advance on Moscow, 280 miles farther east.

By this time, the czar had reorganized his command, placing the main Russian force under the 67-year-old Field Marshal Kutuzov. Ordered to protect the approaches to Moscow, he reached the army on 29 August some 70 miles to the west of the city, near the town of Borodino. Here the Russians prepared to fight, manning a series of redoubts and *flèches* running south from the Koloch River. They were only just in time: on 5 September, after an epic march of 200 miles, the first French troops arrived. They gradually built up their forces on the 6th, probing the Russian defenses, constructing bridges across the Koloch and generally gaining a picture of the enemy positions. The bridges seemed to imply an attack on the Russian right, beyond Borodino, so Kutuzov concentrated the bulk of his force in that area; in reality, Napoleon planned to put in feint attacks on both flanks – around Borodino on his left and Utitsa on his right – while massing his main force of 133,000 men in the center.

The battle began at 0600 hours on 7 September with the French flanking moves. Borodino fell quickly, but Prince Poniatowski on the right soon got caught up in woods to the north of Utitsa. Even so, the Russians were initially caught by surprise in the center when, under a massive artillery bombardment, the main French force advanced against the defensive works. The fighting was hard and for a time, in mid-morning, it looked as if Kutuzov might achieve victory. Aware that the attack on

Right and below right: the bloody Battle of
Borodino. Heavy losses did not prevent the
Grand Armée from pushing on to Moscow.
Below far right: French cavalry put down a
popular rising in Madrid.

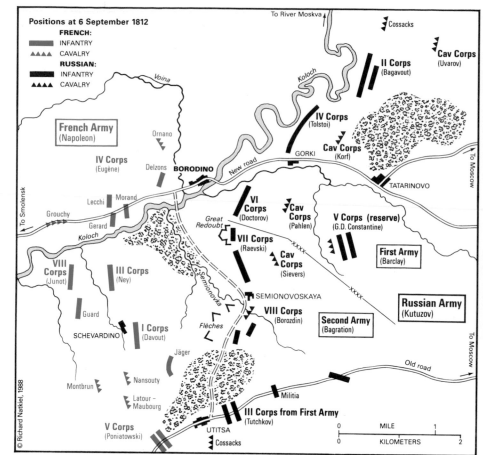

Borodino was a feint, he transferred his right
wing farther south, releasing nearly 5000
cavalry and Cossacks against Ney. But the
French continued their main assault, capturing the Great Redoubt in bitter hand-to-hand
fighting. Kutuzov decided to pull back to a
ridge in his rear – a maneuver he was able to
carry out when Napoleon (who was strangely
inactive throughout the day) refused to commit his last reserve, the 20,000 strong Imperial
Guard. By nightfall, as the Russians turned
defiantly to face the French from their new
positions, both sides fell into a torpor of
mutual exhaustion. Over 30,000 French and
more than 40,000 Russian casualties lay on the
field of battle.

In the event, Kutuzov decided to withdraw
to the southeast, leaving the road to Moscow
open. Napoleon took the deserted city on 14
September, but it was a Pyrrhic victory, made
worse by a great fire which swept through the
streets 24 hours later. By then, Napoleon had
fewer than 100,000 operational troops left; as
Kutuzov was being reinforced and other
Russian armies were closing in from north and
south, the continued occupation of Moscow
was dangerous. On 23 October, in near-freez-
ing temperatures, the French began to withdraw, intending to fall back on supply dumps
at Smolensk and to prepare for a renewed
campaign in 1813.

It was a disastrous move, exposing the
Grande Armée to the ravages of a Russian
winter and endless harassing attacks by parti-
sans and Cossacks. The French column, more
than 50 miles long, rapidly lost cohesion – on 9
November lead elements went on a rampage
of looting in Smolensk which destroyed most
of the vital supplies – while the Russians
closed in, aiming to reach the Berezina River
before Napoleon, trapping him in a final
battle. By 22 November, Russian forces had
won the race and it took all Napoleon's tactical
skill to avoid complete disaster. A feint attack
allowed the French to exploit a gap in the
Russian defenses, throwing trestle bridges
across the raging torrent of the Berezina.
Some 40,000 French troops escaped to the
west by 29 November, but nearly 50,000 were
killed or captured. The *Grande Armée* had virtually ceased to exist. On 5 December
Napoleon abandoned his shattered forces for
Paris, leaving Murat to lead them on into the
comparative safety of Poland. By then, only
25,000 of the original 450,000 had survived,
together with 18,000 horses and only 120 guns.
It was a major defeat and the beginning of the
end of Napoleon's empire.

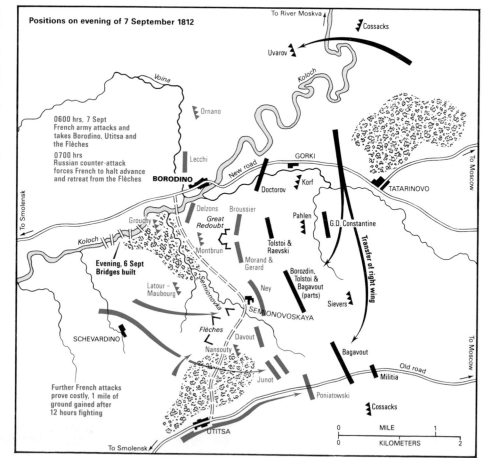

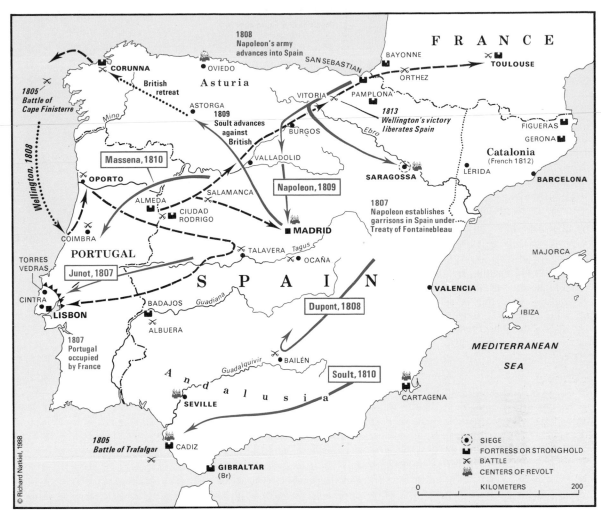

The map labels, reading across:

1808 Napoleon's army advances into Spain

FRANCE

BAYONNE · SAN SEBASTIAN · TOULOUSE

CORUNNA · OVIEDO · ORTHEZ

Asturia · VITORIA · PAMPLONA

1805 Battle of Cape Finisterre

British retreat

ASTORGA

1809 Soult advances against British

Mino

Massena, 1810

1813 Wellington's victory liberates Spain

FIGUERAS

GERONA

Wellington, 1808

OPORTO · VALLADOLID · BURGOS · Ebro · SARAGOSSA

Catalonia (French 1812) · LÉRIDA · BARCELONA

Napoleon, 1809

ALMEDA · SALAMANCA

CIUDAD RODRIGO

1807 Napoleon establishes garrisons in Spain under Treaty of Fontainebleau

COIMBRA · MADRID

PORTUGAL · TALAVERA · Tagus · OCAÑA

TORRES VEDRAS

Junot, 1807

MAJORCA

CINTRA · LISBON · BADAJOS · Guadiana

S P A I N · VALENCIA

ALBUERA · Dupont, 1808 · IBIZA

1807 Portugal occupied by France

A n d a l u s i a · Guadalquivir · BAILÉN · Soult, 1810 · MEDITERRANEAN SEA

SEVILLE · CARTAGENA

1805 Battle of Trafalgar · CADIZ

SIEGE
FORTRESS OR STRONGHOLD
BATTLE
CENTERS OF REVOLT

GIBRALTAR (Br)

0 · KILOMETERS · 200

© Richard Natkiel, 1988

The Peninsular War

The French first became involved in the Iberian Peninsula in October 1807, when an army of 24,000 men under Junot invaded Portugal in an attempt to deny ports to the Royal Navy. On this occasion, they were supported by Spain, which helped to rule the occupied state once Lisbon had been taken in November, but Franco-Spanish relations were not good. Shocked by the corruption and inefficiency of Spanish government and convinced that the country, dominated by Prince Godoy, was about to switch allegiance to Britain, Napoleon decided to intervene. On 16 February 1808 he sent units to secure the Pyrenean passes and on 24 March French forces marched into Madrid. Within a week, Napoleon had 'persuaded' the ineffectual Spanish Royal Family to relinquish the throne to his brother Joseph.

French rule was not popular, forcing Napoleon to send strong columns of troops into Valencia and toward Seville to quieten unrest. They encountered partisan ('guerrilla') opposition and, on 1 August 1808, this was boosted with news that the British had landed a force under Lieutenant General Sir Arthur Wellesley in Portugal. French detachments were defeated at Obidos and Rolica (16

and 17 August); on 21 August the main French force under Junot was mauled at Vimeiro, north of Lisbon, forcing him to sign the Convention of Cintra and evacuate Portugal entirely.

Napoleon was furious; after hurried talks with Czar Alexander of Russia at Erfurt (to secure his rear against Austrian or Prussian

attack), the emperor rushed to Spain to take personal command. On 6 November he led a strong force toward Madrid, taking Burgos on the 9th and marching into the capital, temporarily abandoned to the Spanish, on 4 December. Meanwhile, a 30,000 strong British army under General Sir John Moore had arrived in

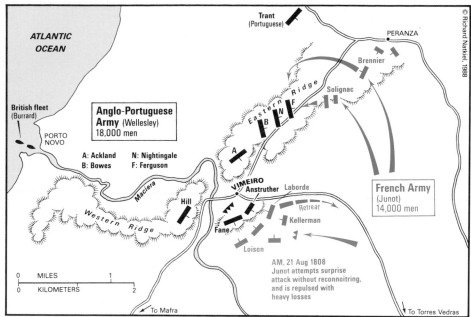

Lisbon and was marching toward Salamanca, posing a threat to Napoleon's line of communication back to France. French actions against Spanish forces elsewhere soon left Moore isolated, and he began to pull back, in difficult winter conditions, toward Corunna. Napoleon left Soult to finish the British off but they survived, avoiding a major battle until Corunna had been reached on 16 January 1809. Although Moore was killed in the subsequent action, the bulk of the British force escaped by sea. The French reoccupied most of Portugal.

An exception was the area around Lisbon and it was here, on 22 April, that Wellesley returned at the head of 40,000 fresh British troops. He faced a daunting task, for although Portuguese and Spanish forces remained active, they were scattered, ill-led and uncoordinated. He began by securing his own base, advancing to defeat Soult at Oporto (12 May) and then pushing into Spain to link up with his allies. Despite a British victory at Talavera (27-28 July), however, French forces began to converge on Wellesley and he was forced to pull back toward prepared defenses in Portu-

Above left: Sir John Moore, the British commander at Corunna.

Above: the Battle of Vimeiro.

133

**Right: the Battle of Talavera in July 1809.
Below right: the Duke of Wellington's victory
at Salamanca in 1812.**

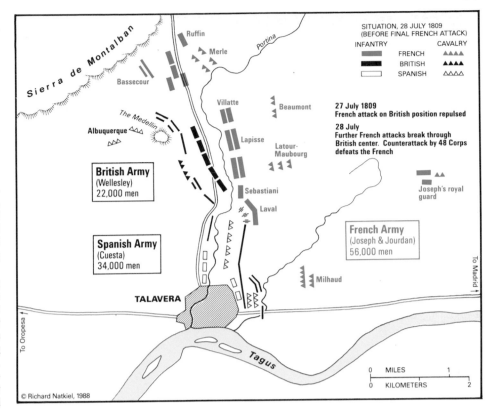

gal – the Lines of the Torres Vedras.
Napoleon, fresh from his victory at Wagram,
sent reinforcements to the Peninsula and
tasked Massena to secure the area once and
for all. At the same time, Soult's renamed
Army of the South was to deal with remaining
Spanish forces in Andalusia.

Massena advanced on 28 May 1810, securing
the key border fortresses of Ciudad Rodrigo
and Almeida before moving on to Lisbon. But
Wellington (as Wellesley had become after
Talavera) was ready: the Torres Vedras
defenses were secure and the surrounding
countryside was stripped of all provisions.
Thus, although Massena made steady progress, his army was denied its customary
ability to live off the land and, as winter closed
in, he had little choice but to withdraw. He
began to pull back in early March 1811, pursued by Wellington. On 5 May the two armies
clashed at Fuentes de Onoro: as the British
gained victory, Napoleon replaced Massena
with Marmont, ordering him to co-operate
with Soult to mount a two-pronged attack on
Portugal. However, the latter's defeat at
Albuera (16 May) gave Wellington a respite.

The year 1812 saw a change of emphasis, as
Napoleon concentrated his forces for the invasion of Russia. Wellington, by now in command of battle-hardened troops, assumed the
offensive, capturing Ciudad Rodrigo (19
January) and Badajoz (6 April) before marching into Spain. Facing Marmont in the center
and Soult in the south, he chose to concentrate
against the former, advancing toward Burgos
while Spanish guerrillas diverted Soult's attention. It was a gamble which seemed to pay off,
for after weeks of marching and countermarching, Wellington caught the French at
Salamanca (22 July), exploiting a sudden
weakness as they advanced in pursuit, so they
thought, of a retreating British force. Marmont was wounded by cannon fire, leaving the
French army without overall leadership at a
key moment: by the end of the day, over
14,000 Frenchmen had been killed or
wounded and Wellington was in a position to
dominate both central and northern Spain. He
occupied Madrid on 12 August although, as
French reinforcements began to arrive in
Spain, he was forced to withdraw to Ciudad
Rodrigo for the winter.

**Center left: British forces defeat the French
at Fuentes de Onoro in 1811.
Left: Wellington in the thick of the action at
Salamanca.**

Once again, the new year saw a shift of
emphasis, for once the French had been
defeated in Russia, Napoleon had to devote
most of his forces to fighting the Sixth Coalition in Germany. This meant that when Wellington resumed operations, aiming to exert
frontal pressure on the French while other
forces moved around their northern flank, his
chances of success were high. The French
withdrew from river line to river line: on 21
June 1813 their main force under Joseph was
defeated at Vitoria and this marked the beginning of the end of Napoleon's adventure in
Spain. Soult, threatened with isolation, with-

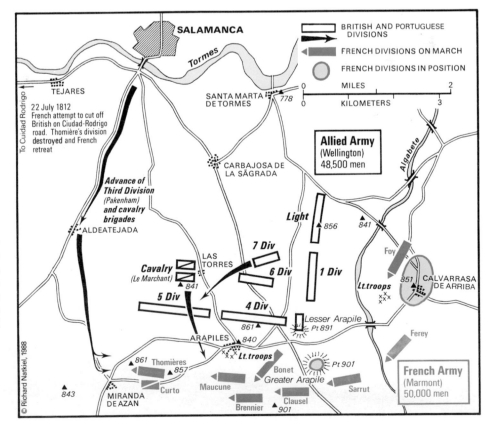

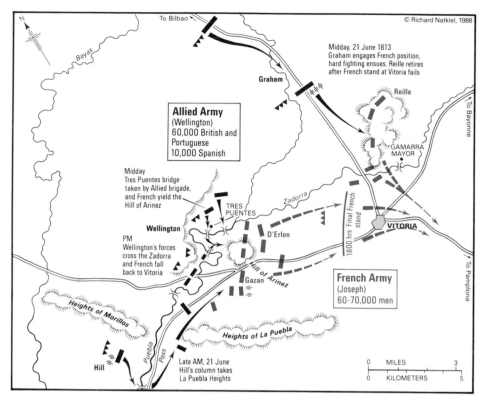

drew from the south and assumed overall command, mounting a sudden counteroffensive in July to raise the sieges of Pamplona and San Sebastian, but Wellington was now strong enough to absorb the shock. By early August, Soult had been forced back over the border into France.

Both Pamplona and San Sebastian were captured by the British in late October, by which time Wellington had crossed onto French soil toward Bayonne. In early November he defeated Soult on the Nivelle and again, a month later, on the Nive, but the French continued to fight. In 1814, as Napoleon fought for survival around Paris, Wellington pushed farther into France, winning battles at Orthez (27 February) and Toulouse (11 April) – the latter after Napoleon had abdicated but before the news had spread. By then, the 'running sore' of the Peninsula –

essentially a peripheral theater once Napoleon had invaded Russia – had cost the French over half a million casualties.

Above: the Battle of Vitoria in 1813.
Below: French and British troops clash at Vitoria.

The 1813 Campaign

Napoleon's defeat in Russia in 1812 led to renewed efforts by the Allied powers to liberate Germany from French rule. In March 1813 Prussia and Russia joined forces, advancing as far as Dresden with a combined army of 100,000 men. Their aim was to conduct a major campaign west of the Elbe, but Napoleon, in typical fashion, decided to strike before they were fully prepared. Hastily gathering a force of 120,000 men – a prodigious effort in the aftermath of the Russian campaign – he crossed the River Saale on 30 April and occupied Leipzig.

The Allies responded by advancing toward Lützen, threatening the French right flank. On 2 May, as Ney pushed forces south of Lützen to occupy a series of small villages, the first clashes occurred. Field Marshal Wittgenstein, the Allied commander, concentrated on the village of Kaja, believing it to be inadequately defended, but he encountered French divisions in Gross-Gorschen and Starsiedel, barring his way. Ney rushed to the area, closely followed by Napoleon at the head of two corps under Macdonald and Marmont. His plan was to pin the Allied center while sending troops to left and right in a familiar encircling move. At 1730 hours on 2 May, the Imperial Guard carried out the first of these maneuvers, while Macdonald and Marmont pushed round the flanks. By 1900 hours the Allies, having suffered 20,000 casualties, were in retreat.

As Allied units converged on the Saxon town of Bautzen, their commanders ordered them to make a stand. Napoleon, hampered in his pursuit after Lützen by lack of cavalry, caught up on 16 May with a force of 115,000 men and 150 guns. Once again, he went for an encircling move, aiming to pin down the Allied center while Ney advanced from the north to appear behind the enemy army and cut off its line of retreat. Simultaneously, Oudinot was to come from the south to link up. Three corps, under Marmont, Macdonald and Bertrand, were responsible for the center.

The Battle of Bautzen opened at noon on 20 May with French artillery fire followed, in mid-afternoon, by a frontal attack across the River Spree by Napoleon's central corps. By 1800 hours, French troops had captured most of the Allied frontline positions, including Bautzen itself, while Oudinot in the south had made steady progress and Ney in the north had advanced close to the battle area. On the 21st, the fighting continued all along the line, with Marmont and Macdonald increasing their foothold on the east bank of the Spree. Meanwhile, Napoleon kept Bertrand back, hoping to launch his corps against the northern sector of the Allied line when it turned to face Ney. In general terms, the plan worked, for although Ney was delayed (it appears that he misunderstood his orders and allowed his men to become committed to village fighting when they should have been pushing ruthlessly southward) and the Allied line of retreat could not be cut, Bertrand's attack at 1330 hours hit the 'hinge' of the Allied right flank and sent it reeling back. As at Lützen, Napoleon lacked the cavalry to conduct a close pursuit, but the Allies were sufficiently demoralized to seek an armistice, signed on 4 June. Both sides, having suffered an estimated 20,000 casualties apiece, took the opportunity to recuperate.

Fighting broke out again in August when the Allies (joined now by Austria) advanced on Dresden. Initially, Napoleon was caught

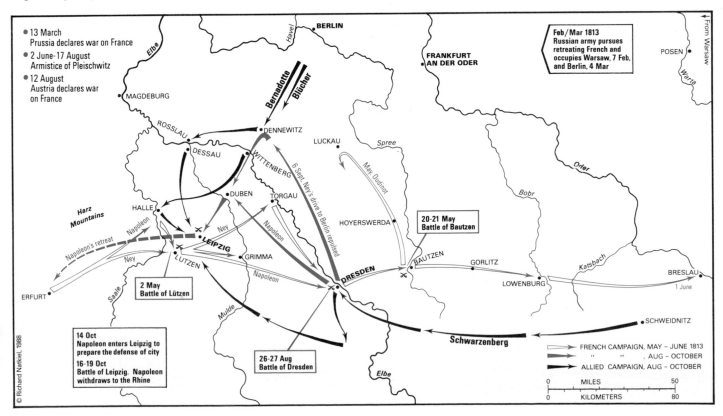

136

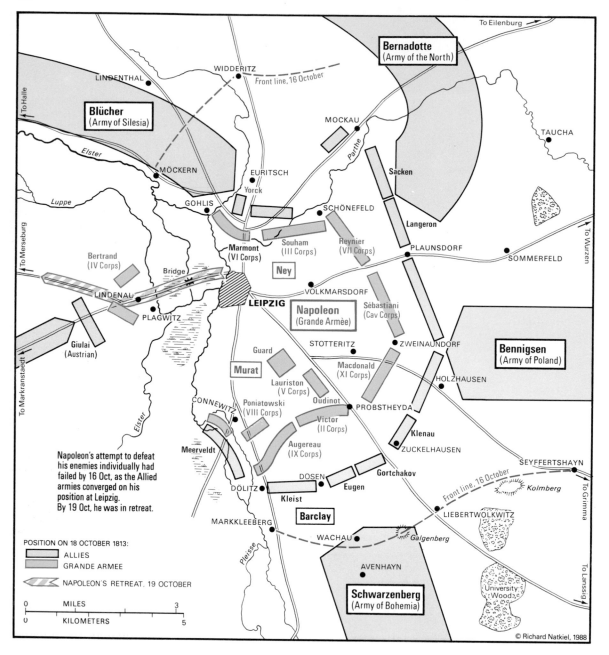

Napoleon's attempt to defeat
his enemies individually had
failed by 16 Oct, as the Allied
armies converged on his
position at Leipzig.
By 19 Oct, he was in retreat.

POSITION ON 18 OCTOBER 1813:

ALLIES

GRANDE ARMEE

NAPOLEON'S RETREAT, 19 OCTOBER

© Richard Natkiel, 1988

unawares – the bulk of his army was farther east, preparing to attack the Prussians on the River Bobr – and Dresden seemed doomed. He quickly gathered all available units and rushed to the beleaguered city, leaving a single corps under Vandamme to guard against outflanking moves from the north.

Napoleon reached Dresden on 26 August, just as the Allies were conducting a major assault. Amid heavy fighting, the French survived the onslaught and, at 1730 hours, put in a counterattack which recovered lost ground. On the 27th, the Allies massed 138,000 troops for a final knock-out blow, while Napoleon prepared for his traditional encircling maneuver. At 0600 hours, the emperor seized the initiative, attacking the Allied right wing and making threatening moves on the left. The main Allied force, concentrated in the center, was in danger of being outflanked, forcing the Austrian commander of the Allied army, Field Marshal Schwarzenberg, to pull

back. Napoleon followed, hoping to occupy Berlin, but was thwarted as new Allied armies converged on his line of advance. Field Marshal Blücher of Prussia and Bernadotte, King of Sweden, crossed the Elbe in early October, threatening the French from the north, while Schwarzenberg moved up from the south. By 15 October, Napoleon had pulled back to Leipzig with 123,000 men: the scene was set for the 'Battle of the Nations,' the largest single engagement of the Napoleonic Wars.

The battle began on 16 October, when Schwarzenberg attacked the outer defenses of Leipzig, although without success. At the same time, Blücher clashed with Marmont in the northwest near Möckern; the fighting was hard, but the French held on. A pause on the 17th allowed Napoleon to reorganize his defenses, but it also enabled additional Allied armies, under Bernadotte and Bennigsen, to reach the battle area from the north and east respectively, increasing the Allied force to

365,000 men. On the 18th, this enormous mass of military power was used to mount a series of concentric attacks on all parts of the French position. There was little even Napoleon could do to prevent defeat; after nine hours of exceptionally heavy fighting, he ordered a phased withdrawal through Leipzig and across the River Elster, still in French hands.

Allied commanders ordered an immediate pursuit, but Napoleon was not finished. Maintaining close control of his soldiers, he fought an effective action at Hanau on 30 October to prevent enthusiastic pursuit, although by then he had suffered considerable losses in terms of both manpower and equipment. As the winter weather closed in, he was forced to pull back almost to the French frontier, abandoning his German territories. The 1813 campaign, characterized by set-piece battles of increasing intensity, had cost Napoleon half a million men he could ill afford. The outlook for the French in 1814 was bleak.

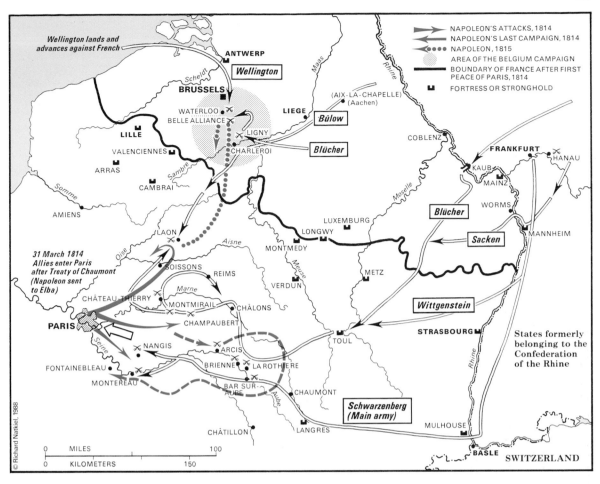

The 1814 Campaign

By November 1813, France was effectively under siege, with Allied armies closing in along the Rhine as well as in the Pyrenees and northern Italy. The greatest threat was from the east, where Blücher's Army of Silesia was poised to cross the Rhine between Coblenz and Mannheim, and Schwarzenberg's Army of Bohemia was marching to the west of Basle. Both armies were converging on Paris; Napoleon's overriding priority was to prevent their conjunction by defeating each in turn.

It was a daunting task, made worse by a shortage of troops and an Allied decision to continue operations during the winter months. By early January 1814, Blücher had reached the River Marne and Schwarzenberg, although cautious, had occupied the Langres plateau. An Allied victory seemed assured.

Napoleon decided to concentrate against Blücher first, chiefly because he was closer to Paris. Leaving Marmont to contain Schwarzenberg, the emperor rushed north at the head of 34,000 men. On 29 January he attacked Blücher's spearhead at Brienne, capturing the town and forcing the Army of Silesia to retreat. But it was only a temporary respite: on 1 February, before the French had consolidated their defenses, Blücher counterattacked at La Rothière. Amid heavy snow, the French held on until nightfall, when they had to pull back. Blücher celebrated victory.

But the Allies also had problems, particularly in terms of poor co-ordination between Blücher and Schwarzenberg. Thus, when the advance continued, Napoleon was able to mask the more cautious Schwarzenberg and maintain the pressure on Blücher, whose army was becoming dangerously strung out. On 10 February, Russian outposts at Champaubert were destroyed, followed 24 hours later by similar action against Blücher's main force at Montmirail. A third French success at Vauchamps on 14 February forced the Army of Silesia into retreat, leaving Napoleon free to march south to inflict a series of local defeats on the Army of Bohemia. The strategy seemed to be working.

Blücher took the opportunity to resume his advance up to the Marne. Napoleon rushed north again, attacking the enemy at Craonne on 7 March and forcing Blücher to pull back, this time to Laon. Marmont was ordered to carry out an outflanking march but failed to do so with sufficient skill, giving Blücher time to recover: on 9 March his units caught Marmont by surprise and virtually destroyed his corps. At the same time, Schwarzenberg pushed toward Arcis-sur-Aube, mounting a determined attack on 21 March. Napoleon arrived at the town at 1300 hours, in time to witness a successful French cavalry charge, but there was little that 28,000 French troops could do against 80,000 Austrians. Schwarzenberg missed a golden opportunity to finish the campaign when he allowed the bulk of the French army to escape, but the withdrawal allowed

him to link up the Blücher on the 25th. Together, the Allies pushed on toward Paris, inflicting defeat after defeat on hard-pressed French forces. The city fell on 31 March; six days later, Napoleon agreed to abdicate the thrones of France and Italy in exchange for sovereignty over the island of Elba. The First French Empire was at an end.

Above left: the Battle of Leipzig.
Below: the exiled Napoleon.

The Waterloo Campaign

On 1 March 1815, Napoleon landed in France at the head of only 1000 men, having escaped from Elba. As he marched toward Paris, soldiers sent to oppose him by the Royalists changed sides and local communities rallied to his support. On 19 March the Royal Court abandoned Paris, but Napoleon soon faced opposition – Britain, Prussia, Austria and Russia formed the Seventh Coalition.

Napoleon's only hope was to concentrate against the more threatening Allied armies first – a plan which drew him toward Wellington and Blücher – aiming to defeat them before the others could intervene.

French troops began to cross the River Sambre into Belgium on 15 June. Early on 16 June, convinced that Blücher was already withdrawing, Napoleon ordered Ney to secure Quatre Bras as a matter of priority, leaving Grouchy to maintain the pressure on the right at his own pace. This plan did not last long: as reports from Grouchy came in, indicating that the Prussians were preparing to make a stand along the Ligny stream, the emperor altered the emphasis of his advance. Grouchy was given priority and Ney ordered to divert d'Erlon's corps for a march against the Prussian flank.

The attack on Ligny began at 1430 hours and heavy fighting quickly developed. By nightfall, the Prussians were withdrawing, but north rather than northeast as Napoleon expected: as Blücher's men staggered into Wavre, the two Allied armies were still close enough to effect a link if required.

Meanwhile, also on the 16th, Ney had continued his advance on Quatre Bras, fielding 20,000 men against an Allied force which was initially no more than 8000 strong. But he moved cautiously and, by 1600 hours, Wellington had effectively blocked further French progress. He then pulled back to Mont St Jean, near the village of Waterloo.

The rival armies spent a miserable night in the rain and mud. As they stirred awake early on 18 June, Napoleon had 72,000 men and 241 guns to pit against an Anglo-Dutch force of 68,000 men and 156 guns. Grouchy, with a further 33,000 Frenchmen, was tied down in the east, but the two Prussian corps promised by Blücher (a further 72,000 men) were already marching toward Mont St Jean.

Wellington deployed the bulk of his army along the ridge, with a distinct emphasis on his right and center, leaving his left to be filled by the Prussians when they arrived. Outposts were established at Hougoumont, La Haye Sainte and La Haye. Napoleon's plan was to open the battle with an artillery bombardment, followed closely by a diversionary attack toward Hougoumont, forcing Wellington to commit forces to its defense. This would weaken the Allied center, allowing d'Erlon to spearhead a major assault.

It did not work out that way. Napoleon delayed the artillery bombardment until 1130 hours to give the ground time to dry out, and this gave Wellington some of the respite he so desperately needed. Moreover, neither the bombardment nor the attack on Hougoumont achieved the desired effects. By 1330 Wellington's position had not been weakened whereas Napoleon, aware that Prussian forces were moving toward him from the east, had been forced to divert elements of his reserve to create a defensive flank around Plancenoit.

D'Erlon's main assault on Wellington's center took place while this redeployment was in progress. Horrendous casualties were inflicted by the British guns and then by Picton's infantry, well protected in hedgerow positions. As the French waivered, Uxbridge completed their destruction by ordering a massed cavalry charge.

But the battle was far from over for, as Prussian troops came nearer, Ney led a furious cavalry counter-charge, aimed at Wellington's right center. By 1730 hours the Allied line was looking thin; the only bright spot was that the Prussians had at last begun to engage the French at Plancenoit.

Half an hour later, the defenders of La Haye Sainte ran out of ammunition, allowing the French to exploit a gap in the Allied center. Napoleon, sensing victory, committed his Imperial Guard. As they advanced steadily toward La Haye Sainte, the French veered too far to their left, marching straight toward British troops hitherto spared the worst of the fighting. Under Wellington's personal command, the British infantry poured volley after volley into the enemy ranks. At the same time, more Prussian forces arrived on the ridgeline. Seizing the moment, Wellington ordered a general advance.

By nightfall, it was all over. For the loss of 22,000 men, Wellington had inflicted 49,000 casualties on the French, shattering Napoleon's new empire. He surrendered in early July. The Napoleonic Wars were over.

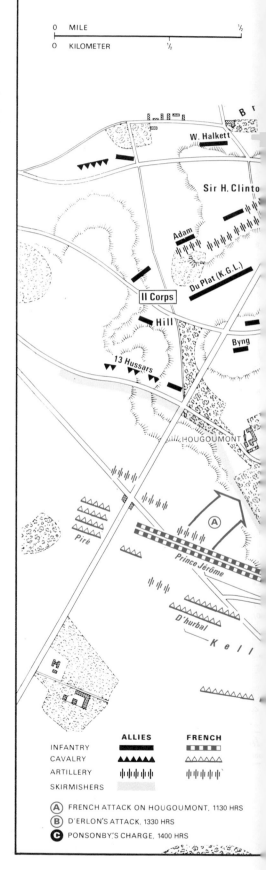

The battle of Waterloo from 11am to 3pm, 18 June

0 MILE ½
0 KILOMETER ½

	ALLIES	FRENCH
INFANTRY		
CAVALRY		
ARTILLERY		
SKIRMISHERS		

Ⓐ FRENCH ATTACK ON HOUGOUMONT, 1130 HRS
Ⓑ D'ERLON'S ATTACK, 1330 HRS
Ⓒ PONSONBY'S CHARGE, 1400 HRS

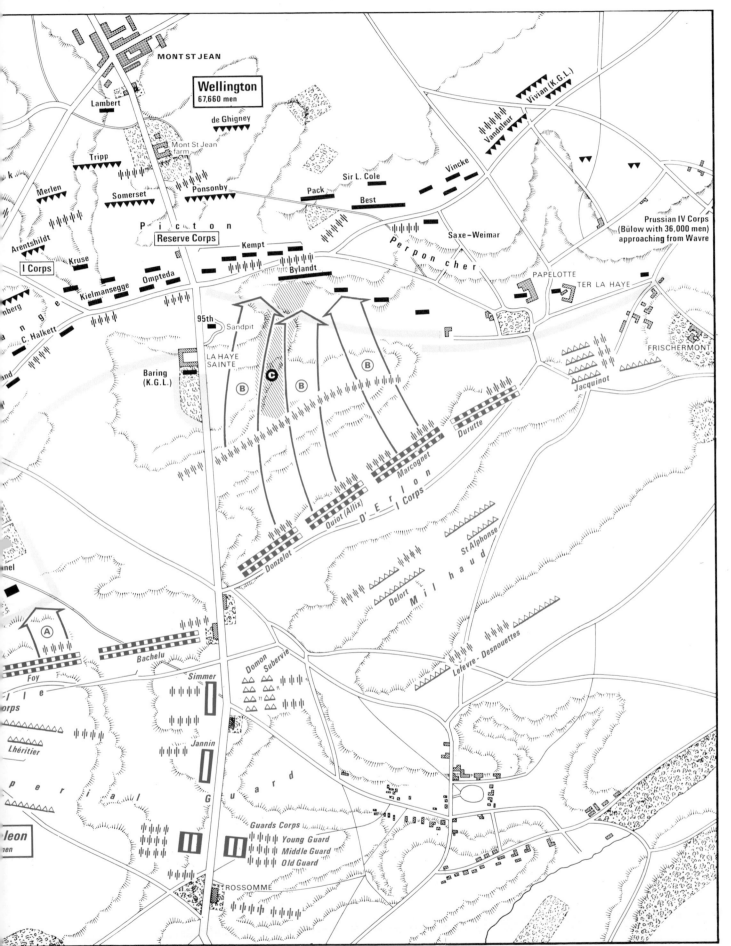

MONT ST JEAN

Wellington
67,660 men

Lambert

de Ghigney

Mont St Jean farm

Tripp

Ponsonby

Sir L. Cole

Vincke

Vivian (K.G.L.)

Vandeleur

Merlen

Somerset

Pack

Best

P i c t o n

Saxe-Weimar

Reserve Corps

Arentshildt

Kruse

Kempt

P e r p o n c h e r

Prussian IV Corps
(Bülow with 36,000 men)
approaching from Wavre

I Corps

Ompteda

Bylandt

PAPELOTTE

TER LA HAYE

Kielmansegge

nberg

C. Halkett

95th

Sandpit

FRISCHERMONT

LA HAYE
SAINTE

Ⓒ

Baring
(K.G.L.)

Ⓑ

Ⓑ

Ⓑ

Jacquinot

Durutte

Marcognet

D' E r l o n

Quiot (Allix)

I Corps

St Alphonse

Donzelot

M i l h a u d

Delort

nel

Ⓐ

Bachelu

Simmer

Domon

Subervie

Lefèvre - Desnouettes

Foy

l l e

Jannin

o r p s

Lhéritier

Guards Corps

Young Guard

leon

G u a r d

Middle Guard

Old Guard

ROSSOMME

These pages: Union forces cross Burnside bridge during the Battle of Antietam, an action in the American Civil War.

THE ADVENT
OF TOTAL WAR

Right: the Battle of Lake Erie. Perry's victory secured the Great Lakes for the US forces in the war of 1812.
Below right: the aftermath of a fight between frigates off Sandy Hook, 15 January 1815.

The War of 1812

The reasons that prompted the United States to go to war with Great Britain in 1812 were less substantive than emotional. The British policy of interdicting all neutral maritime trade with France had occasioned the seizure of numerous American merchant ships, causing some genuine financial distress to American shipowners and tempting many other Americans to blame – not always accurately – various domestic economic difficulties on the loss of foreign markets. Even more offensive to American pride was the Royal Navy's practice of routinely impressing into British naval service American merchant crewmen who could not prove they were not British subjects. When the British tried to extend their insatiable hunt for 'deserters' to the crews of American warships, a succession of inflammatory naval incidents inevitably followed. Diplomatic efforts to defuse this dangerous situation came too late. Amid rumors that the British were fomenting Indian attacks on American frontier settlements the US Congress at last succumbed to the national war fever and declared war on 18 June 1812.

The small, ill-prepared US Army immediately took the offensive in an ambitious three-pronged attack on Canada. By mid-August the westernmost of these attacks had been utterly defeated, with the losses of Fort Mackinac, Fort Dearborn and Detroit leaving most of the Northwest Territory under British control. The central attack, across the Niagara Frontier, foundered in October, when nearly 1000 American troops were surrounded and forced to surrender at Queenston, Canada. The easternmost attack, on Montreal, petered out by the end of November. However, the war was far from over.

The Naval War

For the Americans the effects of these initial disasters on land were somewhat mitigated by the simultaneous successes of the little US Navy. On 19 August the frigate USS *Constitution*, 44 guns, Captain Isaac Hull, destroyed HMS *Guerrière*, 38, off Nova Scotia. In short order thereafter USS *Essex*, 32, took HMS *Alert*, 20; and in October *Constitution's* sister ship, USS *United States*, Captain Stephen Decatur, took HMS *Macedonian*, 38. The climax of this dazzling season came in December, when *Constitution*, now under Captain

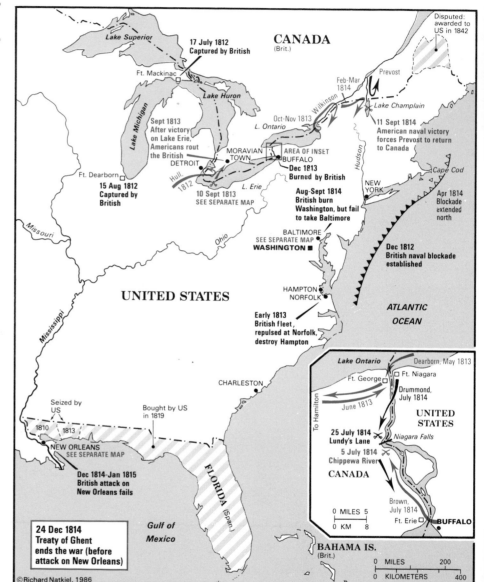

Thomas Bainbridge, took HMS *Java*, 38, off the coast of Brazil. Though these single-ship actions amounted to the greatest humiliation the Royal Navy had endured for a generation, they were not of great strategic importance. By early 1813 the overwhelmingly powerful British fleet held America's Atlantic seaboard under such tight blockade that American warships had the greatest difficulty in making sorties from their ports.

On land, throughout 1813 the Americans continued to try to press their attacks on Canada. From the Niagara Frontier east,

these efforts again came to nothing. (Indeed, so sharp were the British ripostes that the town of Buffalo was burned and the key American base at Sackett's Harbor was nearly lost to siege.) But to the west, on Lake Erie and in the Michigan peninsula, progress was made. On Lake Erie Commander Oliver Hazard Perry, USN, had assembled a small squadron of two gun brigs and seven schooners. On 10 September this flotilla decisively defeated a British squadron of two ships, two brigs and two schooners, commanded by Commodore R H Barclay. Perry's victory

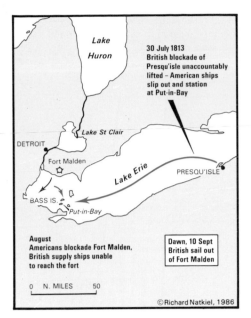

30 July 1813
British blockade of
Presqu'isle unaccountably
lifted – American ships
slip out and station
at Put-in-Bay

Lake Huron

Lake St Clair

DETROIT

Fort Malden

Lake Erie

PRESQU'ISLE

BASS IS.

Put-in-Bay

August
Americans blockade Fort Malden,
British supply ships unable
to reach the fort

Dawn, 10 Sept
British sail out
of Fort Malden

0   N. MILES   50

© Richard Natkiel, 1986

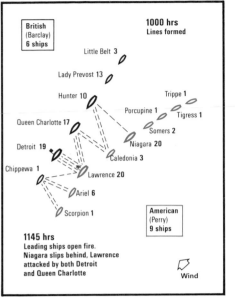

British
(Barclay)
6 ships

1000 hrs
Lines formed

Little Belt 3

Lady Prevost 13

Hunter 10

Trippe 1

Porcupine 1

Tigress 1

Queen Charlotte 17

Somers 2

Detroit 19

Niagara 20

Caledonia 3

Chippewa 1

Lawrence 20

Ariel 6

Scorpion 1

American
(Perry)
9 ships

1145 hrs
Leading ships open fire.
Niagara slips behind, Lawrence
attacked by both Detroit
and Queen Charlotte

Wind

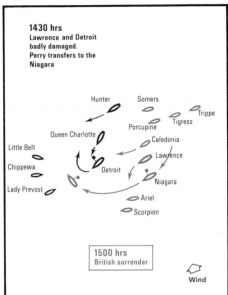

1430 hrs
Lawrence and Detroit
badly damaged.
Perry transfers to the
Niagara

Hunter

Somers

Trippe

Queen Charlotte

Porcupine

Tigress

Little Belt

Caledonia

Detroit

Lawrence

Chippewa

Niagara

Lady Prevost

Ariel

Scorpion

1500 hrs
British surrender

Wind

made the key British positions on the western end of the lake – Detroit and Fort Malden – suddenly vulnerable. Under pressure from advancing American troops, led by Brigadier General William Henry Harrison, the British abandoned both these bases and fell back into the interior of Upper Canada. On 5 October Harrison caught up with and destroyed this retreating British army on the Thames River.

As a result, most of the Northwest Territory, including Lake Erie and the proximate part of Upper Canada, passed under direct American military control.

The British naval blockade had effectively drawn the fangs of America's 16-ship seagoing navy, and in May 1813 the British broke the string of American frigate victories when HMS *Shannon*, 38, Captain Philip Broke, defeated USS *Chesapeake*, 38, Captain James Lawrence, off Boston. But of far greater consequence was the fulmination of American privateering. By early 1813 some 600 American privateers were scourging British commerce in the North and South Atlantic, the Caribbean, the North Sea and even the English Channel. By the war's end they had taken over 1300 British merchantmen (and

Far right: the Battle of New Orleans, the last major land action between British and US troops in the 1812-15 war.
Below: General Winfield Scott, the commander of the US Army.
Below far right: Andrew Jackson encourages his men at New Orleans.

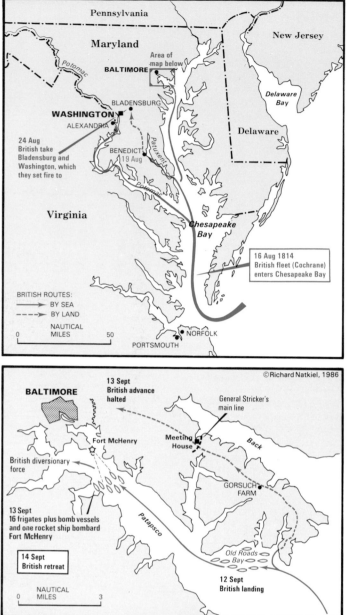

some naval vessels), had driven maritime insurance rates to ruinous heights and had prompted merchants' associations in such cities as Bristol, Glasgow and Liverpool to petition the government to end the war before England's merchant marine was destroyed.

Campaigns of 1814

In 1814 the Americans renewed their attack on the Niagara Frontier. A well-trained 3500-man American force, under Brigadier Generals Jacob Brown and Winfield Scott, began well enough by capturing Fort Erie, at the mouth of the Niagara River, and then, on 5 July, by besting the regular troops of Sir Gordon Drummond and General Phineas Riall at the Battle of the Chippewa River. But on 25 July the two armies clashed again at Lundy's Lane, a bloody encounter which, though indecisive in itself, so weakened the Americans that they could not continue. In the following months the British were reinforced and the Americans were not, and by November the

Americans had been forced out of the Niagara peninsula entirely.

To the east, along the Montreal-Lake Champlain-Albany axis, the situation was reversed, for here the British launched an invasion of their own. A 12,000-man army, under the command of General Sir George Prevost, and a naval squadron of one frigate, one brig, two sloops and 12 galley-gunboats, under the command of Commodore George Downie, moved rapidly down Lake Champlain to Plattsburg. At this point Downie's squadron was intercepted by Commodore Thomas Macdonough's US Navy lake squadron, composed of a corvette, a brig, a schooner, a sloop and 10 galley-gunboats. Although outnumbered and considerably outgunned, Macdonough sank or captured every one of the British vessels. Deprived of naval support, Prevost concluded that his invasion could not succeed and returned to Canada.

In the meantime, far to the south, a British amphibious raiding force had sailed into Che-

sapeake Bay, marched on virtually undefended Washington and burnt the Capitol, the White House and several other government buildings. This force then re-embarked and sailed on to Baltimore. Here, on 13 September, they were met with a spirited defense. Their land attack, led by Major General Robert Ross, failed to get past the earthwork redoubts that Major General Samuel Smith's Maryland militia had set up east of the city; and Vice-Admiral Alexander Cochrane's powerful naval squadron could not force its way past Fort McHenry, guardian of the entrance to Baltimore's harbor. Frustrated at Baltimore, the British force returned to the West Indies, there to plan another operation: an attack on New Orleans.

The Battle of New Orleans

For the New Orleans assault the British assembled 8000 veteran troops, under the command of Major General Sir Edward Pakenham, and some 50 supporting warships

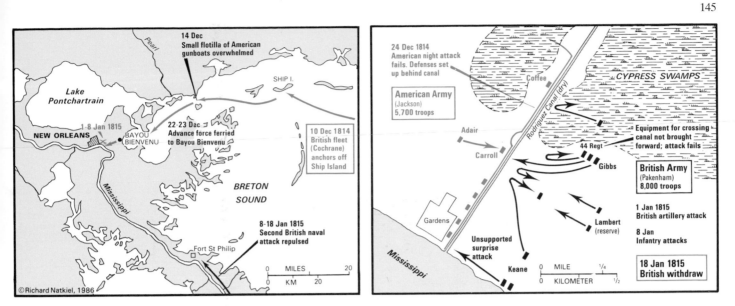

The maps detail the British approach to New Orleans and the battle dispositions.

Left map:

14 Dec
Small flotilla of American gunboats overwhelmed

Pearl

Lake Pontchartrain

SHIP I.

1-8 Jan 1815

NEW ORLEANS

BAYOU BIENVENU

22-23 Dec
Advance force ferried to Bayou Bienvenu

10 Dec 1814
British fleet (Cochrane) anchors off Ship Island

BRETON SOUND

Mississippi

8-18 Jan 1815
Second British naval attack repulsed

Fort St Philip

© Richard Natkiel, 1986

0 MILES 20
0 KM 20

Right map:

24 Dec 1814
American night attack fails. Defenses set up behind canal

Coffee

CYPRESS SWAMPS

Rodriguez Canal (dry)

American Army (Jackson) 5,700 troops

Adair

Carroll

44 Regt

Gibbs

Equipment for crossing canal not brought forward; attack fails

British Army (Pakenham) 8,000 troops

1 Jan 1815
British artillery attack

8 Jan
Infantry attacks

Lambert (reserve)

Gardens

Unsupported surprise attack

Mississippi

Keane

18 Jan 1815
British withdraw

0 MILE ¼
0 KILOMETER ½

and transports. Defending the city were 5700 troops, mostly irregular, under the command of Major General Andrew Jackson. The British came on shore at Bayou Bienvenu on 23 December and made their way west toward the city. Their approach route left little room for maneuver, since the Mississippi River lay on their left, and a nearly impenetrable cypress swamp lay on their right. Between these obstacles the Americans had erected a high earthwork fortification, well defended by artillery and supported by additional artillery sited on the Mississippi's opposite bank. When the British attempted a frontal assault, on 8 January 1815, the inevitable result was carnage – 2000 British dead, among them Pakenham. The shattered British expeditionary force then withdrew to the coast, made a half-hearted attack on Fort Bowyer, at the entrance to Mobile harbor and finally, upon learning that peace negotiations had been concluded in Ghent two weeks before the Battle of New Orleans had been fought, sailed back to the West Indies.

The news that the war was over took even longer to reach ships at sea. Thus the famous *Constitution*, now under the command of Captain Charles Stewart, fought her last, and in some ways most brilliant fight on 20 February 1815, when she took HMS *Cyane,* 32, and HMS *Levant,* 20, in a single engagement. The fact that this victory occurred nearly two months after the formal cessation of hostilities was on a par with the confused manner in which this largely pointless war had been fought from the outset.

The Battle of Navarino

The first nationalist uprisings in 1821 by the Greeks against their Turkish rulers touched off a wave of pro-Greek sympathy in Britain and France, whose cultural traditions enshrined respect for Hellenic values, and in Russia, through sympathy for fellow-members of the Orthodox Church. For six years a desultory war went on between badly led Turkish forces and daring but ill-disciplined Greek irregular forces, who were helped by funds and volunteers from Western Europe but not overtly supported by any of the Great Powers.

Only when the Sultan of Turkey called for help from his vassal the ruler of Egypt, Mehemet Ali, did Western and Russian intervention become likely. Mehemet Ali and his stepson Ibrahim Pasha commanded an efficient army and navy, and were likely to crush Greek resistance without difficulty. Although Russia was clearly eager to intervene, the British and French governments were reluctant to initiate any action which could weaken Turkey, which was the traditional buffer keeping Russia out of the Mediterranean.

Against this uncertain background, in the autumn of 1827 three allied squadrons, one British comprising four ships of the line, three frigates and four smaller warships under Admiral Sir Edward Codrington; one French, comprising four ships of the line, a frigate and two smaller ships under Contre-Amiral Comte de Rigny; and a Russian force of four ships of the line and four frigates under Rear Admiral Count de Heyden, were sent to the eastern Mediterranean. Their mission was the almost impossible task of forcing an armistice on the Greeks and Turks without any fighting.

The Egyptian and Turkish fleets lay in Navarino Bay on the west coast of the Morea, ready to support a land attack on the Greeks at Patras. The combined fleet of seven ships of the line, 15 frigates, 26 corvettes and 17 smaller vessels was moored in a semi-circle in the bay, and after a warning to Ibrahim to stop his army from devastating the Morea, on 20 October Codrington ordered the allied ships into position to prevent the Egyptian and Turkish ships from getting to sea. The fleet was to enter the bay in two columns, the British leading the French in one, and the Russians forming the second, but the Russians finally formed up astern of the French. In an ominous hush the

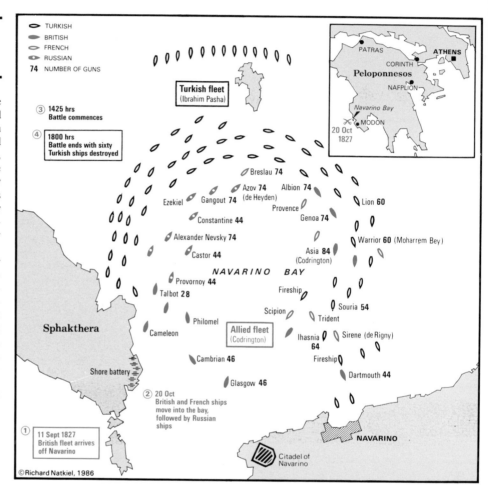

British 44-gun frigate *Dartmouth* sent a boat to insist that a Turkish fireship should keep its distance. Suddenly a shot was fired at the boat, and then a French boat from the French flagship, the frigate *Sirène,* trying to explain that the allied ships had orders not to fire first, was fired on, killing the messenger.

The waiting British and French gun crews immediately replied with a heavy fire, blanketing the scene with heavy smoke. Although numerically superior, the Egyptians and Turks were no match for well-trained gunners and seamen, and after some two-and-a-half hours of heavy firing all that remained of Ibrahim Pasha's fleet was a handful of transports and small ships, all of which were destroyed the next day. Apart from a Turkish frigate which struck her colors to the *Armide,* the majority of Egyptian and Turkish ships fought until they were sunk or set on fire by their own officers to avoid capture.

The Russians took a long time to come into

action, partly because of the thick smoke obscuring visibility, but also because of their lack of practice in sailing in formation. The British ships bore the brunt of the action and so suffered the most casualties, whereas the French and Russians suffered rather less. Several ships were damaged but not severely.

Navarino was the last of the traditional battles under sail, a slogging match fought at close range with virtually no tactical maneuvering once action was joined. Although embarrassing to the British and French governments, Codrington's victory was so popular that an attempt to censure him for disobeying orders could only be pressed half-heartedly. However far-sighted the statesmen might be in propping up Turkey, the public recognized that the threat to Greek independence had been destroyed, and welcomed it as a decisive victory. Four years later Codrington was appointed to command the Channel Squadron in recognition of his achievement.

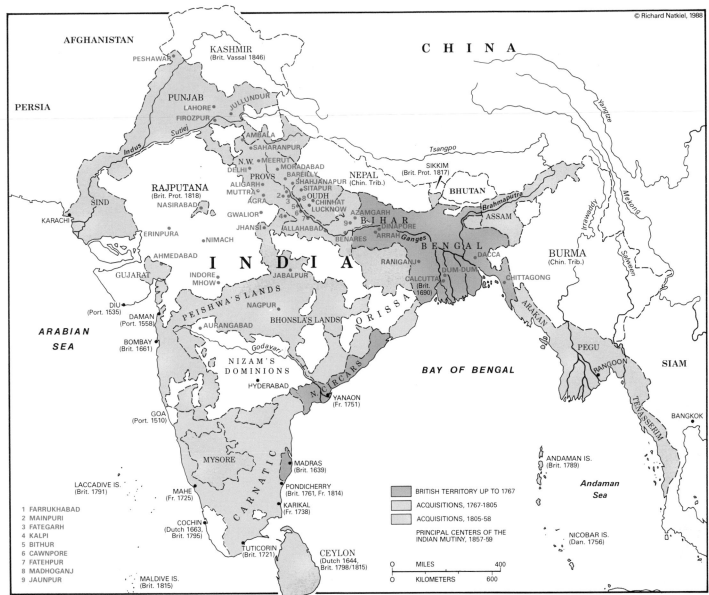

Map labels:

AFGHANISTAN
PERSIA
CHINA
KASHMIR (Brit. Vassal 1846)
PESHAWAR
PUNJAB
LAHORE
FIROZPUR
JULLUNDUR
Sutlej
AMBALA
SAHARANPUR
Indus
N.W. MEERUT
DELHI MORADABAD
PROVS BAREILLY
ALIGARH SHAHJANPUR
MUTTRA SITAPUR
OUDH CHINHAT
LUCKNOW
Tsangpo
SIKKIM (Brit. Prot. 1817)
NEPAL (Chin. Trib.)
BHUTAN
Brahmaputra
ASSAM
RAJPUTANA (Brit. Prot. 1818)
NASIRABAD
AGRA
GWALIOR
JHANSI
ALLAHABAD
BIHAR
DINAPORE
AZAMGARH
BENARES ARRAH Ganges
BENGAL
DACCA
BURMA (Chin. Trib.)
SIND
KARACHI
ERINPURA
NIMACH
AHMEDABAD
INDORE
MHOW
JABALPUR
RANIGANJ
CALCUTTA (Brit. 1690)
DUM-DUM
CHITTAGONG
I N D I A
GUJARAT
DIU (Port. 1535)
DAMAN (Port. 1558)
ARABIAN SEA
PEISHWA'S LANDS
NAGPUR
BHONSLA'S LANDS
ORISSA
Godavari
BOMBAY (Brit. 1661)
AURANGABAD
NIZAM'S DOMINIONS
HYDERABAD
ARAKAN
PEGU
RANGOON
SIAM
Irrawaddy
Mekong
Salween
Yangtze
BAY OF BENGAL
N. CIRCARS
YANAON (Fr. 1751)
GOA (Port. 1510)
BANGKOK
MYSORE
MADRAS (Brit. 1639)
CARNATIC
PONDICHERRY (Brit. 1761, Fr. 1814)
KARIKAL (Fr. 1738)
MAHE (Fr. 1725)
LACCADIVE IS. (Brit. 1791)
COCHIN (Dutch 1663, Brit. 1795)
TUTICORIN (Brit. 1721)
CEYLON (Dutch 1644, Brit. 1798/1815)
MALDIVE IS. (Brit. 1815)
ANDAMAN IS. (Brit. 1789)
Andaman Sea
NICOBAR IS. (Dan. 1756)
TENASSERIM

1 FARRUKHABAD
2 MAINPURI
3 FATEGARH
4 KALPI
5 BITHUR
6 CAWNPORE
7 FATEHPUR
8 MADHOGANJ
9 JAUNPUR

Legend:
BRITISH TERRITORY UP TO 1767
ACQUISITIONS, 1767-1805
ACQUISITIONS, 1805-58
PRINCIPAL CENTERS OF THE INDIAN MUTINY, 1857-59

0 MILES 400
0 KILOMETERS 600

The Indian Mutiny

The 1857 mutiny of native troops in India was the greatest threat to British rule on the sub-continent during the nineteenth century. It was the last gamble of the old India of princes and maharajahs to restore the fortunes of the native dynasties and the first stirrings of modern Indian nationalism which would finally force the British out of India in the twentieth century. The mutiny grew out of the determination of successive British governors-general to modernize Indian society. From about 1820 onward a number of steps were taken to eliminate long-established Indian practices and traditions that the British thought either hindered economic development or were morally wrong. Most worrying to India's wealthy classes was the imposition of a western legal system: landlords whose families had held their estates for centuries by the right of the sword were dispossessed when the British demanded to see written deeds.

During the 1850s the British began to take away the domains of rulers whom they deemed corrupt and incompetent, and also refused to recognize the Indian tradition of succession by adoption. This led to a series of annexations that struck hard at the privileges enjoyed by the Indian Army's sepoys (native soldiers) who came from territories previously not under direct British rule. Signs of the violent unrest to come were increasingly apparent during 1856.

The outbreak came at Meerut where the native sepoys were being issued with new Enfield rifled muskets in place of their old smoothbores. To load the new weapon it was necessary to bite open a paper cartridge that was greased to keep its contents dry. A rumor spread through the sepoys' ranks that the grease was made from the fat of cows and pigs, animals whose meat was forbidden to the followers of the Hindu and Moslem faiths. Although the rumor was true, the British officers did not know this and attempted to force their men to accept the Enfields. The conflict began on 10 May 1857 and was

heralded by the slaughter of the officers and their families. The mutineers then marched to Delhi, the capital of the old Moghul Empire and a focal point of Indian nationalism. They arrived the next day. Once again the mutineers butchered any Europeans they found and any Christianized Indians.

The British administration was slow to respond to the mutiny. Further outbreaks occurred across India but the most serious took place in the most populous part of India, the Ganges plain. Calcutta, the center of British rule, was secure, however. From here the governor-general, Lord Canning, began to marshal his armies. The Punjab provided the Delhi Field Force, while a Central India Field Force was ordered to suppress the rebellion in the region south of the Ganges. A third army, eventually named the Army of Oudh, was to operate along the Grand Trunk Road heading west from Calcutta. In particular, it would strive to rescue the beleaguered garrisons at Cawnpore and Lucknow.

At Cawnpore the situation was grim. About 500 men, women and children had taken

refuge in two buildings surrounded by an earthwork beside the Ganges. They were besieged by thousands of mutineers and rebels who kept them under constant musket and artillery fire. An assault on 23 June was beaten off, but the British predicament was hopeless. They accepted their besiegers' terms on 26 June and prepared to sail down the river to safety the next day. Instead, many were massacred as they sat in their boats. It was an event that inspired the harsh treatment meted out by the British to the rebels and mutineers that fell into their hands.

In the west Delhi was now under siege from a force that had advanced along the Grand Trunk Road from Peshawar; in the east General Henry Havelock occupied the ruins of Cawnpore on 17 July. Here he waited six weeks for reinforcements before pressing on to relieve Lucknow. In central India, the Rani of Jhansi defeated an invasion of her state by the armies of two neighbors trying to use the confused situation to add to their territories. Unfortunately for the Rani, they were allied to the British, while she was helped by some mutineers; henceforth she was regarded as an enemy by the British.

Delhi was recaptured after seven days of hard fighting against stout opposition. General Havelock's attempt to relieve Lucknow was not as successful as the operations before Delhi. On 25 September the British forces smashed their way through the rebel lines and broke into Lucknow. The rebels in the area were numerous, however, and the relieving force found itself besieged.

By the beginning of October the momentum of the mutiny had died out and Delhi, an important symbol of the mutineers' cause, had been lost. The incidences of open rebellion had also sharply decreased. Although large forces of ex-sepoys and the levies of rebellious princes had assembled, they were confined to an area between Cawnpore and Delhi, Nepal and Jhansi. The British meanwhile had reinforced their armies to the east and south.

General Sir Colin Campbell led a sizable force to relieve Lucknow for a second time on 17 November. The Residency was now evacuated and the British withdrew to Cawnpore. A considerable number of rebels pursued Campbell and his men, but they were routed at the Battle of Cawnpore on 6 December.

At about the same time General Hugh Rose led the Central India Field Force into action. He spent three months fighting a series of sharp actions to secure his supply lines, then moved against Jhansi. The city was protected by a seemingly impregnable fortress sited on top of a rocky hill; Rose's forces began a bombardment. However, their attacks were interrupted by the arrival of a rebel army that was defeated at the Battle of Betwa on 1 April and Jhansi was captured after a three-day assault on 6 April. The Rani fled to the rebel army and Rose pursued. After their defeat at the Betwa the rebels regrouped around Kalpi, only to be defeated twice more by Rose at the Battles of Kunch (7 May) and Kalpi (23 May). Campbell had defeated the northern rebels at Bareilly and Mohamdi in the same month. The rebellion seemed over.

A few thousand rebels, with the Rani of Jhansi, then appeared outside the loyal city of Gwalior and took it. Rose and his men advanced there from Kalpi. In a three-day period (16-19 June) the rebels were repeatedly beaten. They scattered and Gwalior was recovered. The surviving rebels and mutineers kept up a guerrilla war in the jungles and hills of central and northern India for almost a year, but by the end of April 1859 all organized resistance had ended.

Above left: mutineers attack the Redan battery at Lucknow.
Below: the remains of the rebels slaughtered by the British during the relief of Lucknow.

Below right: British forces occupy the remains of one of the Taku forts, August 1860.

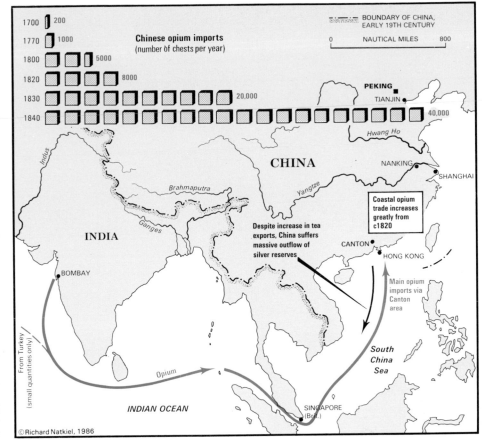

Chinese opium imports
(number of chests per year)

Year	Chests
1700	200
1770	1000
1800	5000
1820	8000
1830	20,000
1840	40,000

BOUNDARY OF CHINA, EARLY 19TH CENTURY

0 NAUTICAL MILES 800

PEKING
TIANJIN
Hwang Ho
CHINA
NANKING
SHANGHAI
Yangtze

Coastal opium trade increases greatly from c1820

Despite increase in tea exports, China suffers massive outflow of silver reserves

CANTON
HONG KONG

Main opium imports via Canton area

Indus
Brahmaputra
Ganges
INDIA
BOMBAY

From Turkey (small quantities only)

Opium

South China Sea

INDIAN OCEAN

SINGAPORE (Brit.)

© Richard Natkiel, 1986

The Opium Wars and the China Trade

By the beginning of the nineteenth century China was approaching a crisis. Until the seventeenth century she had been in many ways more advanced than the West, and during the next 100 years the new Manchu dynasty's armies achieved even higher levels of prosperity by adding vast tracts of new territory in central Asia. By 1800, however, this prosperity was fading.

What was not changing was the usual Chinese perception of the outer world. The ruling class was nurtured in an unquestioning belief in Chinese supremacy, and an increasingly inward-looking society remained unaware of technological developments in Europe. Thus when European traders appeared in increasing numbers they were belittled as barbarians, and were not recognized as the harbingers of irreversible change they were. Chinese diplomats were unable to comprehend the nature of the challenge from the West and the nation's institutions were therefore not modernized to meet it.

Local friction over opium trafficking led to open warfare at Canton in 1839, and in a desultory campaign lasting three years the British defeated the Chinese decisively. Under the Treaty of Nanking, signed in August 1842, China was forced to cede the island of Hong Kong and to grant trading concessions at five ports, in addition to paying a heavy indemnity.

The defeat weakened imperial prestige, contributing to the general unrest and dissatisfaction with the weak imperial government, and in the 1850s the first of a series of major rebellions broke out. The worst of these was the Tai'ping T'ien-kuo, or Heavenly Kingdom of Great Peace. Despite its name it caused widespread suffering, and an estimated 12 million Chinese died during a decade of fighting. Although the Court in Peking preferred to devote its energies to restoring traditional values, a few far-sighted officials took steps to hire foreign mercenaries capable of training soldiers to put down the rebellions. The most famous of these, a British officer Major Charles Gordon, achieved remarkable results in the 1860s, and with only a handful of European officers succeeded in defeating the Tai'ping rebels.

Trade relations were still a major problem, and in 1856 another local dispute at Canton led to warfare. This time the British and French conducted joint military operations, and after a reverse at the Peh-Ho River in June 1859, succeeded in forcing their way upriver to Peking the following year. Once again large Chinese armies were dispersed with contemptuous ease by small Anglo-French forces, but when the Manchu leaders proved unwilling to negotiate and tortured some British prisoners the order was given to inflict reprisals. Knowing how much the ruling class revered its glorious past, the British and French leaders ordered the beautiful Summer Palace to be looted and destroyed. This act of gross vandalism so shocked the Chinese that they signed the Treaty of Peking (18 October 1860), which in turn ratified the Treaty of Tientsin, signed over two years earlier.

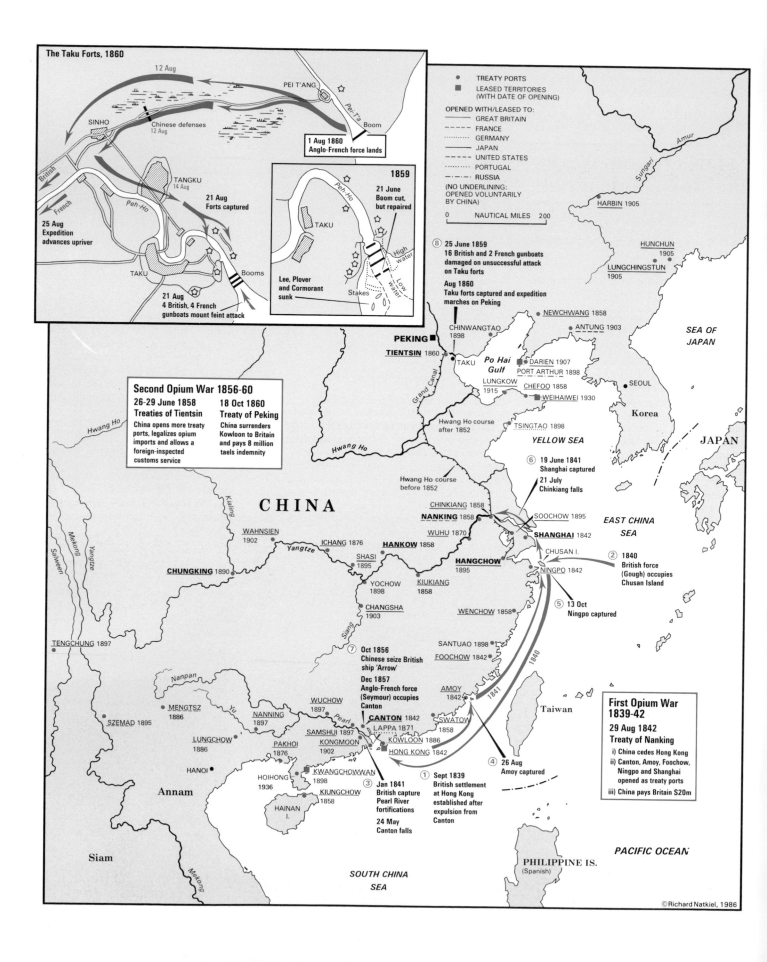

The Taku Forts, 1860

12 Aug

PEI T'ANG

Pei T'a

SINHO
Chinese defenses
12 Aug

Boom

1 Aug 1860
Anglo-French force lands

British

TANGKU
14 Aug

Peh-Ho

21 Aug
Forts captured

French

25 Aug
Expedition
advances upriver

TAKU

Booms

21 Aug
4 British, 4 French
gunboats mount feint attack

1859

Peh-Ho

21 June
Boom cut,
but repaired

TAKU

High water

Lee, Plover
and Cormorant
sunk

Low water

Stakes

● TREATY PORTS
■ LEASED TERRITORIES
(WITH DATE OF OPENING)

OPENED WITH/LEASED TO:
———— GREAT BRITAIN
- - - - FRANCE
········· GERMANY
——— JAPAN
– – – UNITED STATES
·-·-· PORTUGAL
—·—· RUSSIA
(NO UNDERLINING:
OPENED VOLUNTARILY
BY CHINA)

0   NAUTICAL MILES   200

⑧ **25 June 1859**
16 British and 2 French gunboats
damaged on unsuccessful attack
on Taku forts

Aug 1860
Taku forts captured and expedition
marches on Peking

Amur

Sungari

HARBIN 1905

HUNCHUN
1905

LUNGCHINGSTUN
1905

CHINWANGTAO
1898

NEWCHWANG 1858

ANTUNG 1903

PEKING ■

TIENTSIN 1860

TAKU

Po Hai
Gulf

DARIEN 1907
PORT ARTHUR 1898

LUNGKOW
1915

CHEFOO 1858

WEIHAIWEI 1930

SEOUL

**SEA OF
JAPAN**

Korea

JAPAN

Hwang Ho course
after 1852

Grand Canal

TSINGTAO 1898

YELLOW SEA

Second Opium War 1856-60

26-29 June 1858
Treaties of Tientsin
China opens more treaty
ports, legalizes opium
imports and allows a
foreign-inspected
customs service

18 Oct 1860
Treaty of Peking
China surrenders
Kowloon to Britain
and pays 8 million
taels indemnity

Hwang Ho

Hwang Ho course
before 1852

CHINA

Kialing

⑥ **19 June 1841**
Shanghai captured

21 July
Chinkiang falls

CHINKIANG 1858

SOOCHOW 1895

**EAST CHINA
SEA**

WAHNSIEN
1902

Yangtze

ICHANG 1876

HANKOW 1858

WUHU 1870

NANKING 1858

SHANGHAI 1842

SHASI
1895

HANGCHOW
1895

CHUSAN I.

② **1840**
British force
(Gough) occupies
Chusan Island

CHUNGKING 1890

YOCHOW
1898

KIUKIANG
1858

NINGPO 1842

Siang

CHANGSHA
1903

WENCHOW 1858

⑤ **13 Oct**
Ningpo captured

TENGCHUNG 1897

Mekong

Salween

Nanpan

SANTUAO 1898

FOOCHOW 1842

⑦ **Oct 1856**
Chinese seize British
ship 'Arrow'

Dec 1857
Anglo-French force
(Seymour) occupies
Canton

WUCHOW
1897

AMOY
1842

Taiwan

**First Opium War
1839-42**

29 Aug 1842
Treaty of Nanking

i) China cedes Hong Kong

ii) Canton, Amoy, Foochow,
Ningpo and Shanghai
opened as treaty ports

iii) China pays Britain $20m

MENGTSZ
1886

NANNING
1897

Pearl

CANTON 1842

LAPPA 1871

SWATOW
1858

SZEMAD 1895

Yu

SAMSHUI 1897

KONGMOON
1902

KOWLOON 1886

LUNGCHOW
1886

PAKHOI
1876

HONG KONG 1842

④ **26 Aug**
Amoy captured

HANOI ●

HOIHONG
1936

KWANGCHOWWAN
1898

KIUNGCHOW
1858

③ **Jan 1841**
British capture
Pearl River
fortifications

24 May
Canton falls

① **Sept 1839**
British settlement
at Hong Kong
established after
expulsion from
Canton

Annam

HAINAN
I.

Siam

Mekong

**SOUTH CHINA
SEA**

PHILIPPINE IS.
(Spanish)

PACIFIC OCEAN

©Richard Natkiel, 1986

The Fight for Texan Independence

Between 1820 and 1830 about 20,000 Americans had settled in the northern Mexican province of Texas. At first the Mexican government encouraged this immigration, thinking the settlers would help to cultivate the barren land and to subdue the local Indians, but the newcomers soon proved to be troublesome. They ignored both the government's injunctions that they convert to Catholicism and its proscriptions against slave-owning. Worse, they set up an insistent clamor for ever more extensive rights of self-government. In 1830 Mexico forbade further immigration into Texas; and in 1835 the government, now under the control of strongman General Antonio López de Santa Ana, attempted to bring the Texans to heel by garrisoning the province with Federal troops. Several violent clashes occurred between settlers and these troops, and the Texans now threatened secession. Determined to quash this attempt at self-determination, Santa Ana led a punitive expedition of 6000 regulars into the fractious province.

His first target was the Alamo in San Antonio, an abandoned mission that the Texans had fortified. The Alamo garrison, under the command of Lieutenant Colonel William Travis, consisted of only 183 men – among them the famous frontiersmen Davy Crockett and Jim Bowie – too few to man effectively the quarter-mile of perimeter wall that enclosed the mission compound. Yet the Texans managed to withstand Santa Ana's siege for 10 days, until, on 6 March 1836, they were overwhelmed by a massive 3000-man assault. In all, the Mexicans lost 1500 men at the Alamo; the few Texans who survived the fight were summarily executed. Three weeks later 300 Texans who had surrendered to Santa Ana's lieutenant, General José Urrea, at Goliad were similarly executed. 'Remember the Alamo; remember Goliad' became the rallying cry of the Texas revolt, now in full spate.

The only significant Texan force left in the field consisted of about 600 men led by Sam Houston, who had been chosen to command the army of Texas after the province declared its independence on 2 March. Santa Ana relentlessly pursued this small force westward, but in the process he permitted his army to become divided. Thus when he caught up with Houston in April his effective local command numbered only about 1250. Sensing an opportunity, Houston quickly turned and attacked, catching Santa Ana by surprise. The engagement, which took place on a grassy plain between San Jacinto Creek and Buffalo Bayou on 21 April, was a fairly straightforward linear confrontation, a cavalry duel occupying the western flank while Texan infantry assailed the center and attempted to turn the Mexican right on the east. In the center and on both flanks the Texans prevailed. The Mexicans lost about 600 men, against only 9 Texans, and Santa Ana was taken prisoner.

The victory at the Battle of San Jacinto confirmed Texas' *de facto* independence. But because Mexico continued to lay claim to the territory and because the Texans were now actively petitioning to become one of the United States, the seeds of a new international conflict were rapidly being sown.

Below: Sam Houston receives the surrender of Santa Ana after the Battle of San Jacinto.

152

Right: Stephen Austin (1793-1836), one of the men behind the creation of Texas.

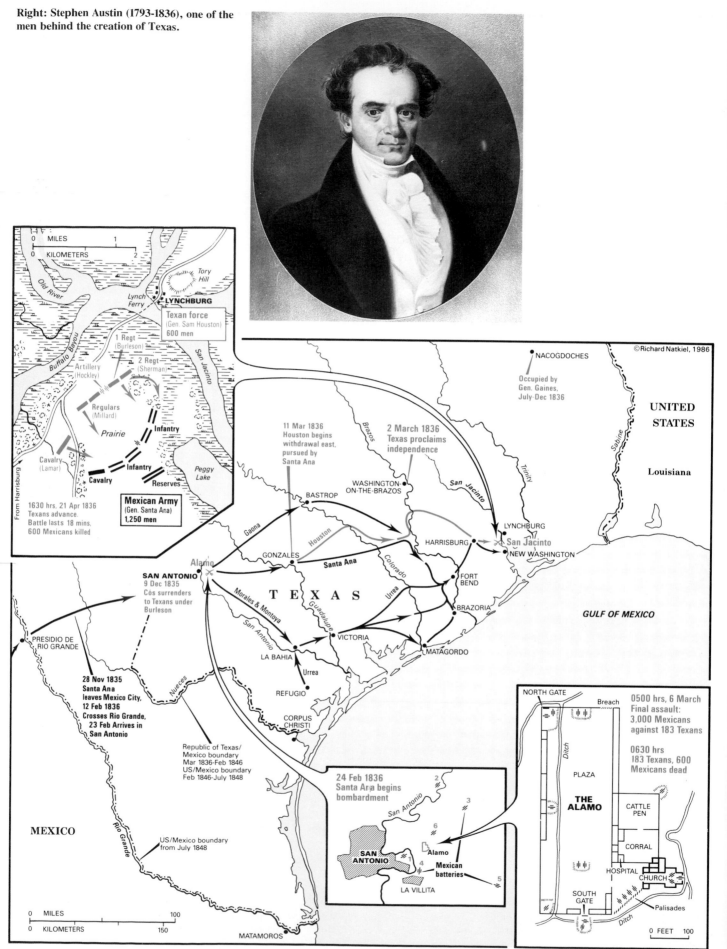

MILES
0   1
KILOMETERS
0   2

Old River

Tory Hill

Buffalo Bayou

Lynch Ferry

LYNCHBURG

San Jacinto

Texan force
(Gen. Sam Houston)
600 men

1 Regt (Burleson)

2 Regt (Sherman)

Artillery (Hockley)

Regulars (Millard)

Prairie

Infantry

Peggy Lake

Cavalry (Lamar)

From Harrisburg

Cavalry

Infantry

Reserves

1630 hrs, 21 Apr 1836
Texans advance.
Battle lasts 18 mins.
600 Mexicans killed

Mexican Army
(Gen. Santa Ana)
1,250 men

NACOGDOCHES

Occupied by
Gen. Gaines,
July-Dec 1836

UNITED STATES

11 Mar 1836
Houston begins
withdrawal east,
pursued by
Santa Ana

2 March 1836
Texas proclaims
independence

Brazos

WASHINGTON-
ON-THE-BRAZOS

San Jacinto

Trinity

Sabine

Louisiana

BASTROP

Gaona

Houston

GONZALES

Santa Ana

Colorado

LYNCHBURG

San Jacinto

NEW WASHINGTON

HARRISBURG

Alamo

SAN ANTONIO
9 Dec 1835
Cós surrenders
to Texans under
Burleson

T E X A S

Morales & Montoya

San Antonio

Guadalupe

Urrea

FORT BEND

BRAZORIA

GULF OF MEXICO

VICTORIA

LA BAHIA

Urrea

MATAGORDO

PRESIDIO DE
RIO GRANDE

28 Nov 1835
Santa Ana
leaves Mexico City,
12 Feb 1836
Crosses Rio Grande,
23 Feb Arrives in
San Antonio

Nueces

REFUGIO

CORPUS CHRISTI

Republic of Texas/
Mexico boundary
Mar 1836-Feb 1846
US/Mexico boundary
Feb 1846-July 1848

MEXICO

Rio Grande

US/Mexico boundary
from July 1848

24 Feb 1836
Santa Ana begins
bombardment

San Antonio

2

3

6

SAN ANTONIO

Alamo

1

4

Mexican batteries

5

LA VILLITA

NORTH GATE

Breach

Ditch

PLAZA

THE ALAMO

CATTLE PEN

CORRAL

HOSPITAL

CHURCH

SOUTH GATE

Palisades

Ditch

0500 hrs, 6 March
Final assault:
3,000 Mexicans
against 183 Texans

0630 hrs
183 Texans, 600
Mexicans dead

MILES
0   100
KILOMETERS
0   150

MATAMOROS

0   FEET   100

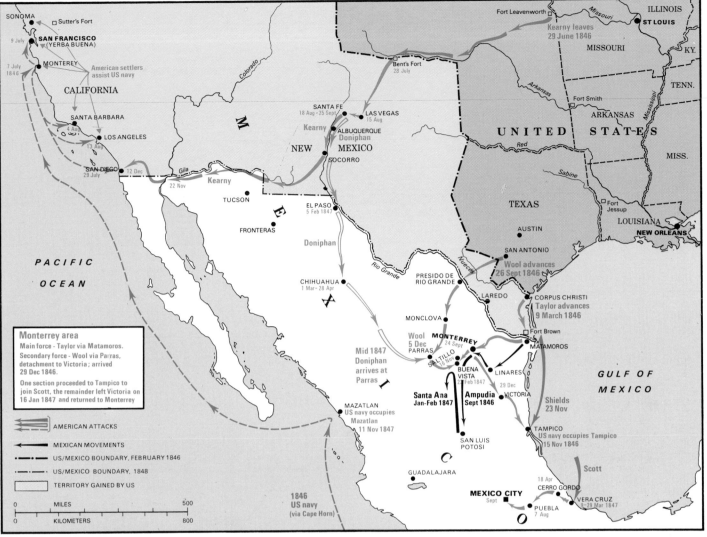

Map labels include:

SONOMA, Sutter's Fort, SAN FRANCISCO (YERBA BUENA), 9 July, 7 July 1846, MONTEREY, American settlers assist US navy, CALIFORNIA, SANTA BARBARA, 4 Aug, LOS ANGELES, 13 Aug, SAN DIEGO 12 Dec, 29 July, Gila, Kearny 22 Nov, TUCSON, FRONTERAS, PACIFIC OCEAN, Colorado, SANTA FE 18 Aug-25 Sept, LAS VEGAS 15 Aug, Kearny, ALBUQUERQUE, Doniphan, NEW MEXICO, SOCORRO, EL PASO 5 Feb 1847, Doniphan, CHIHUAHUA 1 Mar-28 Apr, MONCLOVA, Fort Leavenworth, Kearny leaves 29 June 1846, Missouri, ILLINOIS, ST LOUIS, MISSOURI, KY., Bent's Fort 28 July, Arkansas, Fort Smith, ARKANSAS, TENN., UNITED STATES, Red, TEXAS, AUSTIN, MISS., Sabine, Fort Jessup, LOUISIANA, NEW ORLEANS, SAN ANTONIO, Wool advances 26 Sept 1846, Nueces, PRESIDO DE RIO GRANDE, Rio Grande, LAREDO, CORPUS CHRISTI, Taylor advances 9 March 1846, Fort Brown, MATAMOROS, Fort Brown, Wool 5 Dec PARRAS, MONTERREY 24 Sept, SALTILLO 16 Nov, BUENA VISTA 22 Feb 1847, LINARES, 29 Dec, VICTORIA, Shields 23 Nov, GULF OF MEXICO, Mid 1847 Doniphan arrives at Parras, Santa Ana Jan-Feb 1847, Ampudia Sept 1846, SAN LUIS POTOSI, TAMPICO, US navy occupies Tampico 15 Nov 1846, MAZATLAN, US navy occupies Mazatlan 11 Nov 1847, GUADALAJARA, Scott, 18 Apr, CERRO GORDO, VERA CRUZ 9-29 Mar 1847, MEXICO CITY Sept, PUEBLA 7 Aug, 1846 US navy (via Cape Horn)

Monterrey area
Main force - Taylor via Matamoros.
Secondary force - Wool via Parras, detachment to Victoria; arrived 29 Dec 1846.
One section proceeded to Tampico to join Scott, the remainder left Victoria on 16 Jan 1847 and returned to Monterrey

AMERICAN ATTACKS
MEXICAN MOVEMENTS
US/MEXICO BOUNDARY, FEBRUARY 1846
US/MEXICO BOUNDARY, 1848
TERRITORY GAINED BY US

| MILES | 0 | 500 |
| KILOMETERS | 0 | 800 |

The Mexican War

The self-proclaimed Republic of Texas began asking to be admitted into the United States almost immediately after Sam Houston's victory over the Mexicans at San Jacinto in 1836. But American domestic political considerations (would Texas be admitted as a slave or a free state?) and fear of offending Mexico, which still claimed Texas, prevented the United States from acting on the Texans' request for nearly ten years. In March 1845, however, an expansion-minded president and Congress were finally able to set aside such inhibitions and invited Texas to join the Union. Mexico at once broke off diplomatic relations. Anticipating war, newly elected President James Polk ordered Brevet Brigadier General Zachary Taylor to move US troops into the Texas territory.

By the time Mexico formally declared war, on 25 April 1846, Taylor had assembled about 4000 men in southeastern Texas. On 7 May an approximately equal Mexican force set upon Taylor at Palo Alto, a little north of the mouth of the Rio Grande, and was bloodily defeated, mainly by superior American artillery. Taylor

pursued the retreating Mexicans westward, inflicting further casualties on them at Resaca de la Palma, but lost touch with them when they fled south across the Rio Grande. After being reinforced, Taylor also crossed the river, taking Monterrey on 24 September and Saltillo on 16 November. Subsequently, and much to Taylor's disgust, Polk ordered him to detach the bulk of his army and send it off to reinforce another army that Major General Winfield Scott was assembling at Tampico in preparation for an attack on Vera Cruz. Thus Taylor had less than 5000 men left in his command when, on 23 February 1847, 15,000 Mexican regulars, under the command of General Antonio López de Santa Ana, attacked him near the hacienda Buena Vista, south of Saltillo. Although the issue of the Battle of Buena Vista was several times in doubt, Taylor's accurate artillery fire and the success of his dragoons in breaking up Mexican infantry charges finally tilted the decision in the Americans' favor. This victory, combined with another won by a force of Missouri volunteers farther north, at Chihuahua, effectively put northern Mexico in American hands. Even before that time US Army, Navy and militia forces had succeeded in removing all Mexican military presence from New Mexico

and California. Thus the Americans' sole remaining objective was the conquest of central Mexico.

General Scott's 13,000-man army at Tampico mounted an amphibious attack on Vera Cruz in March and, after a two-week siege, took the city on the 27th. Scott then made his way slowly west toward Mexico City, defeating Santa Ana's 12,000-man opposing army at Cerro Gordo on 18 April and finally arriving in the vicinity of the capital in August. For more than a month Scott was obliged to fight a succession of fierce (and, on his part, brilliantly conducted) battles around the city's periphery – at El Pedregal, Contraras, Churubusco, El Molino de Rey, Chapultepec and several other points – and it was not until 14 September that Santa Ana at last surrendered the city itself. On 2 February 1848 the war was formally ended and the present southern boundary of the United States was fixed by the signing of the Treaty of Guadelupe Hidalgo.

In strict military terms, American prosecution of the war had been exemplary, for the opposing Mexican armies were usually more numerous and were at all times well equipped and led. Whether America's motives for fighting the war in the first place were equally praiseworthy is less clear.

The Crimean War

In 1853 there was a disagreement between Russia and France over jurisdiction within the Holy Places of Turkish-ruled Jerusalem. Czar Nicholas I saw this as an opportunity to dominate Turkey and secure an entrance into the Mediterranean through the Turkish Straits, and in July a Russian army occupied Turkey's Rumanian provinces. The French were determined not to let Russia get away with this blatant attempt to coerce Turkey, and Britain was opposed to any change in the region's balance of power. So British and French fleets were sent to Constantinople to support the Turks. On 4 October Turkey declared war on Russia and on 4 November defeated the Russians in southern Rumania, but the Russians were able to destroy a Turkish naval force at Sinope on the 30th. As a result of this an Anglo-French fleet entered the Black Sea to protect the Turkish coast. On 20 March 1854 the Russians invaded Bulgaria, and the British and French declared war on Russia on the 28th.

An Anglo-French expeditionary force moved to Varna to assist in repelling the Russian invasion. After the British frigate *Furious* had been fired on while under a flag of truce at Odessa, an Anglo-French naval squadron bombarded the shore batteries. In April the Austrians concentrated an army of 50,000 men in Galicia and Transylvania and, with Turkish permission, moved into Turkey's Danube territories. In the face of this threat the Russians withdrew most of their troops from Bulgaria, but they rejected the joint peace conditions of Austria, Britain, France and Prussia in August. Although the Russian withdrawal from Bulgaria had achieved the objective of the allied expeditionary force, the allies were determined to break Russian power in the Black Sea by destroying the naval base at Sevastopol. No real thought or planning went into the preparation of this expedition, which was jointly commanded by the British Lord Raglan and the French Marshal Saint-Arnaud.

On 7 September the allied force was transported from Varna by sea to the Crimea in a great convoy. It was not until the Crimean shore was reached that any thought was given to a point of debarkation. Between the 13th and 18th, in bad weather, the troops were landed on an open beach some 30 miles north of Sevastopol. However, no attempt was

made by the Russian commander, Prince Menshikov, to oppose the landing. On the 19th the allies moved south on Sevastopol with the fleet keeping pace along the coast. The expeditionary force consisted of 51,000 British, French and Turkish infantry and 1000 British cavalry.

Prince Menshikov with a force of 36,400 men had decided to defend the approaches to Sevastopol on the bank of the Alma River, his left flank out of range of the allied fleet and his right secure on a ridge. The Battle of Alma was a fairly straightforward affair: the allies attacked across the river without much difficulty, but the British then found themselves faced by a steep slope which was carried only after a hard fight, Menshikov then withdrew without molestation, having lost 5700 casualties. The allies lost some 3000, the majority of whom were British.

After the Battle of Alma the allies were in sight of Sevastopol by 25 September but, without a secure base, a siege of the port was impossible. The allies made a flank march of 15 miles round the south side of Sevastopol to establish bases and regain contact with the fleet. The British established their base at Balaklava and the French at Kamish. While the allies were undertaking their flanking

march, Menshikov left a garrison at Sevastopol and marched the remainder of his army north to Bakhchisari to join reinforcements being sent there.

An immediate assault of Sevastopol by the allies might have been successful, but instead they decided to extemporize a siege corps and begin a formal investment. On 29 September Marshal Saint-Arnaud died of cholera and was succeeded by General Canrobert. The delay in beginning the formal investment of Sevastopol allowed the Russian chief engineer, Colonel Todleben, to strengthen the fortifications. The first bombardment began on 17 October and the ensuing counterbattery fire caused serious losses on both sides, but no permanent damage to the defense works. Meanwhile the allied fleet blockaded the port.

On 25 October Menshikov's field army attempted to drive a wedge between the siege lines and the British base at Balaklava. The

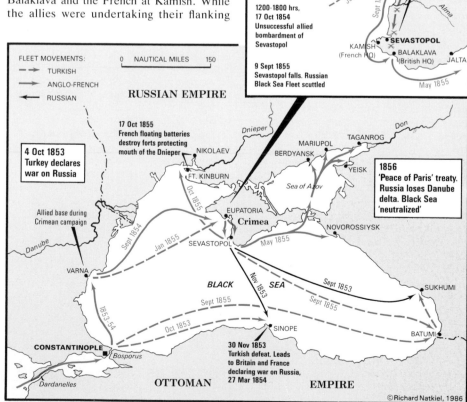

©Richard Natkiel, 1986

155

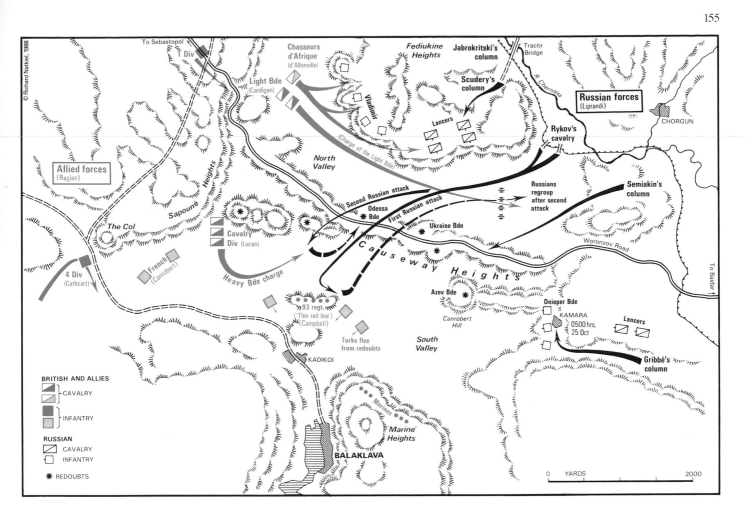

Russians succeeded in penetrating the position, capturing some Turkish guns, but the British fought a dogged battle and the stand of the 93rd Highlanders, the famous 'thin red line,' enabled reinforcements to be rushed up. Russian cavalry attempting to exploit the breakthrough were repelled by the British Heavy Cavalry Brigade. Due to a misinterpretation of orders, the British Light Cavalry Brigade under the command of Lord Cardigan charged the Russian field batteries to their front and on either flank up a mile-long valley. Although the charge reached the guns and the Russian cavalry behind, 270 men out of 673 were lost. As a result of the Battle of Balaklava, the Russians controlled the Vorontosov ridge commanding the Balaklava-Sevastopol road, but they failed to take Balaklava.

On 5 November Menshikov again tried to break through between the besieging troops and their field support at Inkerman. The brunt of the all-day action fell on the British, during which all command and control on both sides was lost. It was a true infantry battle, and the British refused to give ground despite heavy losses. The arrival of General Bosquet's French division to reinforce the British finally tipped the balance, and Menshikov withdrew, having lost some 12,000 men against an allied loss, mainly British, of 3300 men.

The allies with their sea communications unhindered should have had few problems in bringing the siege to a speedy conclusion. But on the 14th a heavy storm destroyed 30 transports and most of the existing rations, forage and clothing. With the Russians sitting astride the only road between Balaklava and the siege lines it was almost impossible to bring supplies forward. The British troops, without shelter or adequate winter clothing, virtually starved and there was little that could be done to prevent cholera. By February 1855 the effective British strength was reduced to 12,000 men,

and the French had to take over part of the British sector. The Russians' incessant activity and engineering skills meant that, despite the allied bombardment, their defenses grew stronger every day.

On 17 February the Russian field army commanded by Prince Gorchakov, who had replaced Menshikov, made a sortie to attempt to interfere with the siege but this was

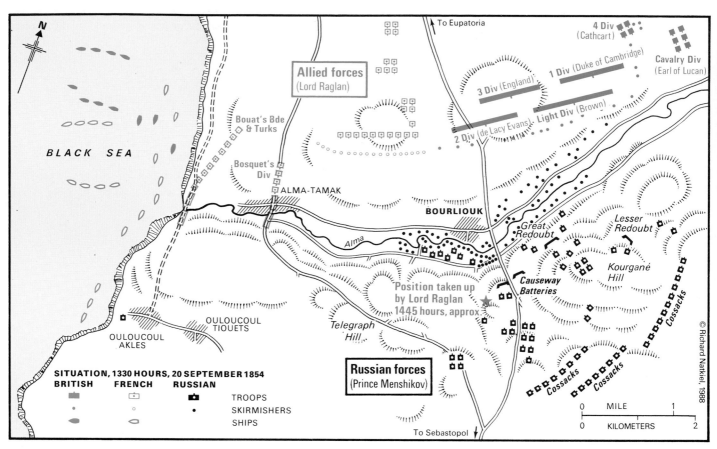

Above: The Battle of Alma.

SITUATION, 1330 HOURS, 20 SEPTEMBER 1854

BRITISH	FRENCH	RUSSIAN	
			TROOPS
			SKIRMISHERS
			SHIPS

Above: The Battle of Alma.
Below right: a Victorian representation of the British cavalry charge at Balaklava.

repulsed by the Turks near Eupatoria. Between 8 and 18 April a major part of the Russian defenses were destroyed but the allies, instead of making an immediate assault, were hamstrung by a bitter squabble with their home governments. On 24 May an allied naval expedition cleared the Sea of Azov of Russian ships and on 7 June the allies seized part of the outer defenses of Sevastopol, inflicting 8500 Russian casualties for a loss of 6900 men.

A renewed allied assault on 17 June failed to capture two of Sevastopol's strongpoints, the Malakoff and the Redan. The attackers lost 4000 men in the effort. During July and August the allied bombardment slowly drained the strength of Sevastopol's garrison, and Gorchakov decided to make one final breakthrough attempt on 16 August. At the Battle of Tractir two Russian corps failed in a five-hour battle to push French and Sardinian troops off the commanding heights above the Chernaya River.

On 8 September the allies finally launched the one carefully planned and executed operation of the war. After an intense bombardment the French attacked the Malakoff, which was in their hands by nightfall. The British assault on the Redan was repulsed, but the French turned their fire on that strongpoint and drove the Russians out with heavy losses. That night Gorchakov evacuated Sevastopol after blowing up the remainder of the fortifications, and the allies then occupied the city.

Apart from operations in the Crimea, there was intense but indecisive fighting between the Turks and the Russians in the Caucasus, and allied naval operations in the Baltic. By the time peace was signed at the Congress of Paris in March 1856 the Russians had lost 256,000 men, of whom 120,000 died of disease, while the allies lost 252,000 men, 180,000 through disease.

Below: Louis Napoleon of France confers the rank of marshal on General MacMahon after the Battle of Magenta.

The Struggle for Italy

On 9 March 1859, Piedmont mobilized its armed forces. King Victor Emmanuel II and his prime minister, Count Cavour, saw an opportunity to renew the struggle for Italian independence: they had been assured of French support in a war to expel Austria from northern Italy by secret treaty. On 9 April Austria mobilized, and the Austrian government presented an ultimatum demanding immediate Piedmontese demobilization on the 23rd. This provided France with an excuse to intervene after Piedmont had rejected the Austrian demands. Six days later the Austrians invaded Piedmont.

General Gyulai commanded the Austrian Army in Lombardy which numbered over 100,000 men and outnumbered the Piedmontese by at least two to one. Gyulai should have immediately attacked the Piedmontese before French help arrived. Instead of which, for some incomprehensible reason, he did nothing for several weeks. After pointless marching and countermarching up and down the east bank of the River Ticino, he finally crossed on 8 May, but had not made up his mind as to his objective. After some desultory marching, Gyulai amazed his men by withdrawing back into Lombardy. Meanwhile the French had been sending troops by land and sea, and there were 107,000 French soldiers in Italy by the 18th. Napoleon III and Victor Emmanuel agreed that the first major objective should be Milan and that the main line of advance should be along the road which ran from Novara via the small town of Magenta on the east bank of the Ticino.

On 20 May an Austrian corps of 20,000 troops clashed with a much smaller French and Piedmontese force at Montebello, and were outfought and forced to retreat. Ten days later a Franco-Piedmontese force crossed the River Sesia and captured the village of Palesto, a victory that enabled the bulk of the two armies to close on the small town of Magenta.

The Battle of Magenta was won by the French more by good luck than by judgment. Coherent command was hindered by the fact that the terrain made it difficult to control movement. At dawn on 4 June the French blundered into the Austrian positions, and what followed was a series of disconnected engagements. Neither Marshal Canrobert nor

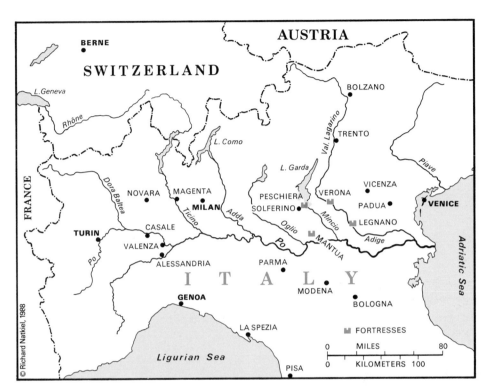

General MacMahon showed much tactical skill in deploying their troops. The Austrians fought a bitter street battle for Magenta, displaying their admirable fighting qualities, and the French were forced to clear the town house by house. Only a proportion of both armies were actually engaged but the battle cost the French 4000 killed and wounded and 600 missing. The Austrians lost 5100 killed and wounded and 4500 prisoners. With the uncommitted troops under his command Gyulai could well have stood his ground. However, he chose to interpret this minor tactical reverse as a major strategic disaster and

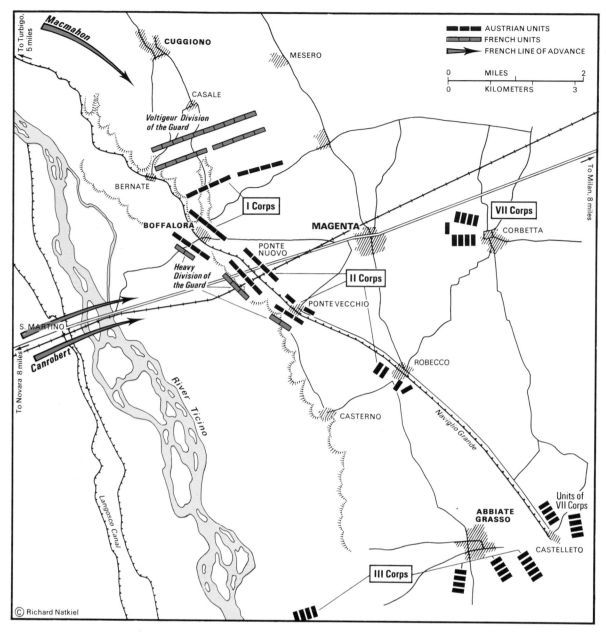

The map shows the Battle of Magenta with labels:

To Turbigo, 5 miles
Macmahon
CUGGIONO
MESERO
CASALE
Voltigeur Division of the Guard
BERNATE
I Corps
BOFFALORA
MAGENTA
VII Corps
CORBETTA
PONTE NUOVO
Heavy Division of the Guard
II Corps
PONTE VECCHIO
S. MARTINO
Canrobert
To Novara 8 miles
River Ticino
ROBECCO
CASTERNO
Naviglio Grande
Langosco Canal
To Milan, 8 miles
Units of VII Corps
ABBIATE GRASSO
CASTELLETO
III Corps

AUSTRIAN UNITS
FRENCH UNITS
FRENCH LINE OF ADVANCE

MILES 0 — 2
KILOMETERS 0 — 3

© Richard Natkiel

ordered the immediate evacuation of Lombardy, including Milan. His forces retreated to the 'Quadrilateral' of fortresses 100 miles to the east. On 8 June Napoleon III and Victor Emmanuel entered Milan in triumph.

On the 17th Emperor Franz Josef of Austria dismissed Gyulai and took over command himself. After lengthy consultations with his senior officers, Franz Josef decided that his forces should recross the Mincio, resume the offensive and catch the enemy off balance. The Franco-Piedmontese forces had also resumed their advance and on the 21st crossed the River Chiese, where a halt was called before crossing the Mincio.

Both Napoleon III and Victor Emmanuel were convinced that the campaign's deciding battle would be fought on its eastern bank. It was around the village of Solferino, a position equidistant between the Chiese and Mincio Rivers and the southern tip of Lake Garda, that the two opposing armies blundered into each other. The Piedmontese Army was 55,000 strong, the French Army 173,000, and the Austrian 146,000. Of these three the French was the most professional and experienced.

Because of the shocking blunders perpetrated by senior commanders on all sides prior to and during the battle, Solferino was a fight between 'lions led by donkeys.' There were a series of bloody encounter engagements along the Mincio River in which the respective high commands lost all control of their forces. The spirit of the French soldiers, the vigor of their individual corps commanders and French generals such as MacMahon, Canrobert, Niel and d'Hilliers, decided the issue after a sanguinary all-day battle. The Austrian Army was saved from total rout by the dogged rearguard action of General von Benedek. Allied losses totaled 17,000, Austrian 22,000. On 11 July at the Conference of Villafranca, Franz Josef agreed that most of Lombardy should go to Piedmont, but Austria was able to keep the region of Venetia.

Above: the Battle of Magenta, May 1859. Below: French troops storm the town of Magenta.

The US Civil War

Disputes over a variety of moral and economic issues related to the institution of slavery – and especially to the question of whether it should be allowed to spread into new states and the western territories – had progressively soured relations between the Northern and Southern United States since the early years of the nineteenth century. By the mid-1850s the government's capacity to paper over these irreconcilable sectional differences with legislative compromise was exhausted. When, in 1860, Abraham Lincoln, candidate of the antislavery Republican party, was elected president, many in the Deep South concluded that they could no longer go on working within the constitutional framework of the Union. By the time of Lincoln's inauguration on 4 March 1861 seven Southern states had seceded, formed a Confederate States of America (CSA) and elected Jefferson Davis as its president. Lincoln's efforts to undo this crisis through conciliation collapsed when, on 12 April, South Carolinian troops attacked the Federal garrison at Fort Sumter in Charleston harbor. Three days later Lincoln declared the secessionist states to be in rebellion. With war now plainly inevitable, and as four more border states hastened to join the CSA, both sides began to assemble their armies around a core of professional officers and men.

The war about to be fought was the bloodiest in American history. War-related deaths would total nearly 500,000, about 90,000 more than the total for World War II. (In relation to contemporary populations, the Civil War death rate was more than five times that of World War II.) Technological innovations that vastly increased battlefield firepower

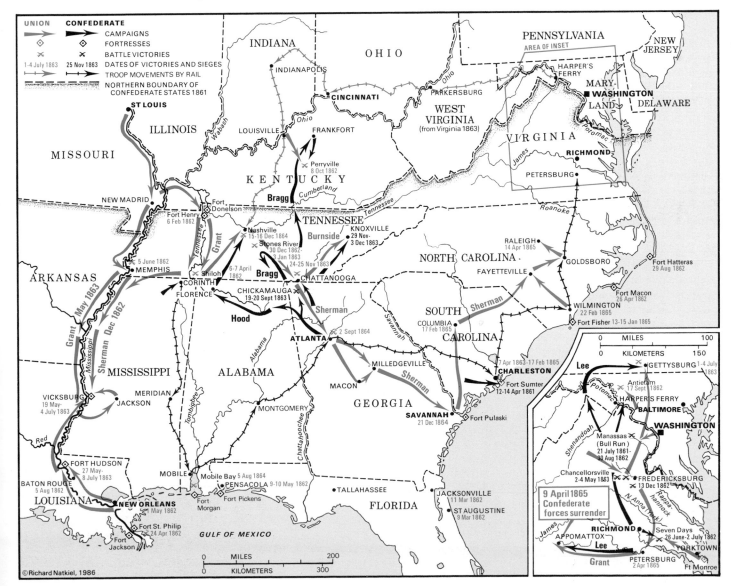

**Right: the indecisive First Battle of Bull Run.
Below: hard pressed by Confederate cavalry,
a Union brigade covers the retreat from Bull
Run.**

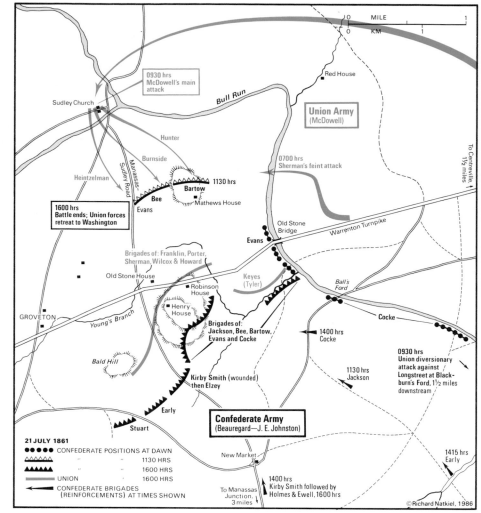

made this slaughter possible and, in the process, profoundly affected the tactics – and even the fundamental character – of war. In time these new technologies would also help the more industrialized North to win, but at the outset the preponderance of Northern strength was by no means so great as to give it a decisive advantage. This was perhaps even more true since the burden of the offensive lay entirely with the North.

The First Battle of Bull Run

The North quickly settled on a three-part strategy: a primary offensive intended to drive south from the vicinity of Washington and capture the Confederate capital of Richmond, Virginia; a second offensive designed to secure the entire length of the Mississippi River; and a total naval blockade of the Confederate coast.

The attack on Richmond began on 16 July 1861. An army of 35,000 Federal troops, under the command of Brigadier General Irwin McDowell, set out from Washington to engage a Confederate army of 20,000, commanded by Brigadier General P G T Beauregard, that had taken up station at Manassas Junction, just 30 miles away. McDowell arrived at Manassas on the 18th, to find Beauregard well positioned for defence behind Bull

Run Creek. But the Union commander did not launch his attack until three days had passed, long enough for Beauregard to be reinforced by 9000 additional men brought to him by Brigadier General Joseph E Johnston. When McDowell did attack, on the 21st, his effort to break the Confederate left flank failed. When he attempted to disengage his troops became disorganized, and the retreat turned into a rout that swept the Federals all the way back to the outskirts of Washington. Here the Union Army remained for the rest of the year.

The Battle of Shiloh

The campaign of 1862 began in the West. In February Brigadier General Ulysses S Grant's Union army moved from Kentucky into northwestern Tennessee, capturing Forts Henry and Donelson and some 15,000 Confederate prisoners. Major General Henry W Halleck, the western theater commander, then ordered Grant to proceed south to Shiloh, in southern Tennessee, there to join forces with another Union army that Major General Don Carlos Buell would bring down from Nashville. The opposing Confederate generals, Beauregard and Albert Sidney Johnston, made haste to strike before this juncture could take place. On 6 April they caught Grant completely by surprise at Shiloh when they attacked his men with a slightly larger force of 40,000. Their initial assault nearly carried the day, but Brigadier General William T Sherman's highly

Left: Grant leads the Union cavalry at the Battle of Shiloh.
Below: the Battle of Shiloh, one of the most costly battles of the conflict.

spirited defense of Grant's flank frustrated the Confederates' attempt to roll up the Union army from right to left and gave the Union commander time to consolidate his decimated forces for a last-ditch stand on the bank of the Tennessee River. Buell's reinforcements, which arrived only just in time to prevent a Union disaster, permitted Grant to make a successful counterattack the next day, but the Federal troops were by then too exhausted to pursue the withdrawing Confederates. The final butcher's bill for this inconclusive battle, about 24,000 dead or wounded, shocked both sides. Worse was to come.

The Battle of Hampton Roads

The outbreak of the Civil War in the United States in January 1861 had created an unusual situation. The North retained control over most of the country's ships and industrial assets, but the Confederacy kept the loyalty of many of the ablest officers. The result was a display of considerable ingenuity by the Confederate States' Navy.

In April 1861 Confederate troops captured Norfolk Navy Yard, and found the new steam frigate *Merrimack* lying burned out and scuttled. Salvage proved comparatively easy and when the frigate's machinery was found to be undamaged the new Confederate States' Navy administration decided to convert her into an ironclad, using railroad iron to give her an armored casemate on the cut-down hull. With nothing to fear from Federal artillery she

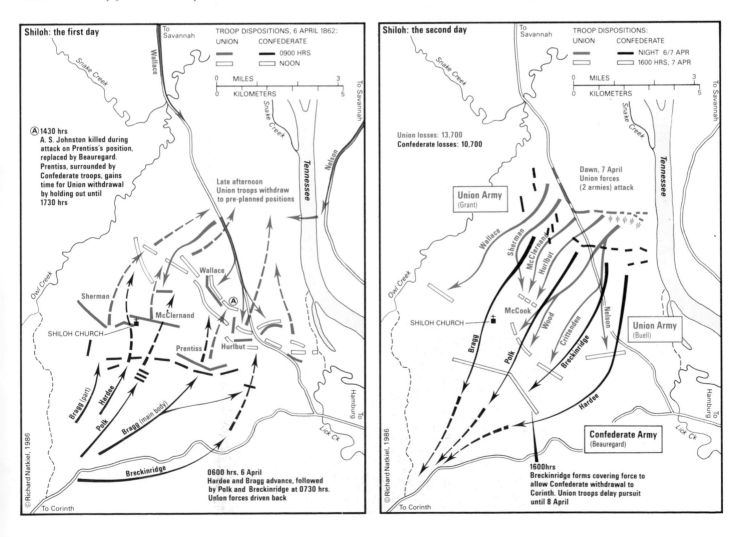

Right and below right: the Battle of Hampton Roads in early March 1862.
Below far right: the ironclads *Merrimack* (left) and *Monitor* exchange close-range shots.

would be able to run the gauntlet and defeat the blockading squadron.

By early spring 1862 she was ready, a cumbersomely slow ship but armed with ten heavy guns firing shells and armor-piercing shot. The Union Navy was well informed about the Confederate plans, and in August 1861 accepted a design for an even more remarkable ironclad, from the Swedish designer John Ericsson. Her name was the USS *Monitor*, 'that she might be a warning to others,' and although armed with only two heavy guns, the revolving turret permitted her to fire on any bearing.

Although built with utmost haste the *Monitor* was nearly too late. The day she was due off Hampton Roads, 8 March 1862, the *Merrimack* (now known as the CSS *Virginia*) put to sea. The ironclad destroyed the wooden Union frigates *Congress* and *Cumberland* with ease, showing just how helpless an unarmored sailing warship could be, especially when caught in restricted waters. The *Cumberland* lost nearly a third of her complement and the *Congress* more than half. Morale in the Union fleet was at a low ebb, and only the *Monitor* could avert a disaster.

Next day the *Merrimack* reappeared, making straight for the big frigate *Minnesota* which had been run aground the previous day. Her lookouts sighted what they first mistook for a water tank, but when the mysterious 'cheesebox on a raft' drew closer and opened fire with her 11-inch guns, the *Merrimack* turned on her smaller antagonist. The action continued for some three-and-a-half hours, with the *Monitor* firing every seven or eight minutes, and the *Merrimack* taking up to 15 minutes between each broadside. Neither ship could penetrate the other's armor, and eventually the baffled Confederate ship tried to ram, but the little *Monitor* could turn in one-sixth of the *Merrimack*'s length.

The Battle of Hampton Roads came to an end when the *Merrimack* withdrew to her anchorage. The two ships put to sea again on 11 April but the Union Admiral Goldsborough had strict orders not to allow the *Monitor* to be endangered, and they did not engage. History might have been different if on 9 March the *Monitor*'s gunners had been allowed to use full charges for the 11-inch guns, but as they had not been proof-fired they were restricted to a light powder charge, and so could not penetrate the *Merrimack*'s armor. Even so, Ericsson's revolving turret and the armored raft hull had proved themselves in battle, and many improved 'monitors' were immediately ordered for the Union Navy.

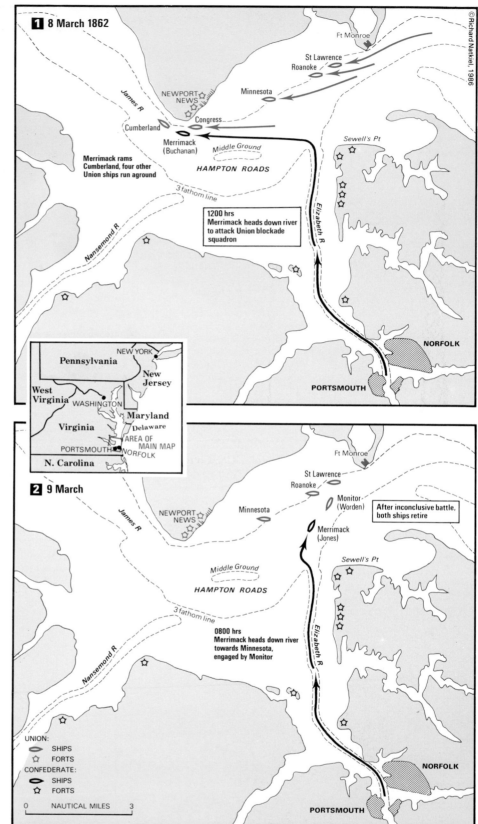

Although the monitor-style ships were not particularly seaworthy, they were adequate for the inshore and riverine operations which the Union Navy was prosecuting against the Confederacy. Other navies also favored the revolving turret principle but fitted in conventional higher-sided ships rather than with the minimal freeboard of the American monitors.

Proof of how limited the monitors' seakeeping qualities were was provided by the fate of the *Monitor* herself, which foundered under tow in a moderate sea later the same year. The *Merrimack* had to be burned by the Confederates in May 1862, after the abandonment of Norfolk to the Union land forces as she drew too much water to go up the James River.

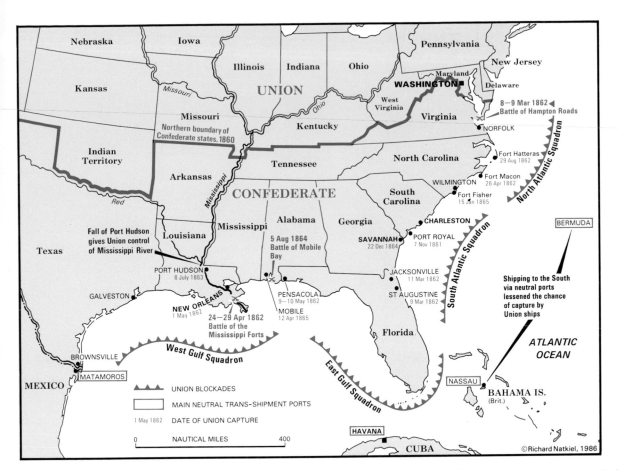

Strangling the Confederacy

Federal naval strategy against the Confederacy was clear-cut but not easy to implement. Although the pre-war US Navy was officered predominantly by Southerners who joined the Confederate forces, the bulk of merchant shipping and most of the navy was in Northern hands. Most shipyards were also in the North.

King Cotton was vital to the economy of the South, so it was essential to cut the Confederacy off from the sinews of war which could be bought in Europe. That meant a blockade of southern harbors.

The US Navy was in poor shape at the outbreak of war. It had been run down steadily since 1815; out of 90 ships on the Navy List only 41 were in commission, and only half of those were officially regarded as modern. However the US Navy's ordnance side was well served by officers like Captain Robert Parrott and Rear Admiral John A Dahlgren, whose gun designs were as good as anything available in Europe. More important was the fact that the bulk of heavy industry was in the North, whereas the South was largely agricultural. Although the bulk of the senior officers chose to join the Confederate States' Navy, a few officers of high caliber, such as Farragut, remained loyal to the Union and gave the Federal Navy the leadership it needed.

The crisis which led to the fall of Fort Sumter took the government in Washington by surprise and so the navy could do little to intervene, but when a few days later Confederate President Jefferson Davis urged would-be privateers to take out 'letters of marque' (licenses to attack Federal shipping on the high seas), President Lincoln retaliated by declaring a blockade of the entire Confederacy. The main, if not the only, hope of the Confederacy lay in broadening the conflict to embroil Great Britain. As the chief importer of cotton, it was hoped that Britain would side against the North, whose small navy would be powerless against the Royal Navy.

Of all the miscalculations made by the Confederacy this was the worst. Patient and assiduous diplomacy prevented Great Britain from being drawn into the war. The need for cotton was balanced by moral sympathy for the Northern anti-slavery movement, and in any case cotton became available from other sources, including Northern states.

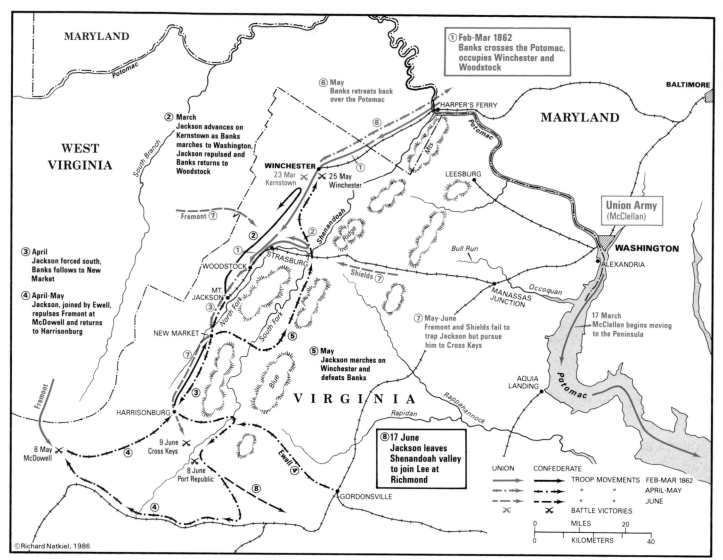

① Feb-Mar 1862
Banks crosses the Potomac,
occupies Winchester and
Woodstock

⑥ May
Banks retreats back
over the Potomac

② March
Jackson advances on
Kernstown as Banks
marches to Washington,
Jackson repulsed and
Banks returns to
Woodstock

③ April
Jackson forced south,
Banks follows to New
Market

④ April-May
Jackson, joined by Ewell,
repulses Fremont at
McDowell and returns
to Harrisonburg

⑤ May
Jackson marches on
Winchester and
defeats Banks

⑦ May-June
Fremont and Shields fail to
trap Jackson but pursue
him to Cross Keys

⑧ 17 June
Jackson leaves
Shenandoah valley
to join Lee at
Richmond

17 March
McClellan begins moving
to the Peninsula

Union Army
(McClellan)

UNION		CONFEDERATE		
→		→	TROOP MOVEMENTS	FEB-MAR 1862
→		→	" "	APRIL-MAY
→		→	" "	JUNE
✗		✗	BATTLE VICTORIES	

© Richard Natkiel, 1986

The effort to establish privateers had only a brief success. Despite panic the early successes of the privateers brought little profit to the Confederacy. The North quickly established four blockading squadrons, two in the Atlantic and two to close the Gulf of Mexico, and it became difficult for the privateers to carry their prizes back into Charleston and New Orleans. Nor could they sell their prizes abroad, as the State Department ensured that European ports were also closed to the privateers.

The use of 'auxiliary cruisers' was much more successful. Well armed ships like the *Sumter*, *Alabama* and *Shenandoah* preyed on Northern shipping on the high seas and disrupted trade with Europe. The success of these commerce-raiders lay not so much in the number of captures but the strain which their raiding put on the blockade. The presence of commerce-raiders meant that scarce warships had to be detached from blockade duty. At first only three warships had been available but the Federal Secretary of the Navy, Gideon Welles, took energetic steps to fill the gap by purchasing and arming hundreds of merchant ships. This motley collection of paddle- and screw-steamers were badly out-classed by the Confederate ships, but as the Royal Navy had

shown against Napoleon 60 years earlier, numbers rather than quality are essential for a successful blockade.

The success of the blockade did much to redress the balance after the Confederacy's string of brilliant early victories on land, and the shortage of vital commodities soon began to tell. In a desperate attempt to beat the blockade the Confederate Navy started building a series of ironclads but this effort was countered by the Federal Navy with its own armored ships. The industrial resources of the North made this an easy task and by the spring of 1862 the first of the new 'monitors,' ironclads and gunboats were beginning to take the offensive.

The hard-won benefits of the blockade were nearly thrown away when the Confederate Army under Lee and Jackson took the offensive in Virginia in June 1862. The failure of that offensive was crucial, for it convinced Great Britain that she should not support the Confederacy. In November that year Britain vetoed a suggestion by France for an armistice, under which the blockade would have been lifted for six months. A succession of bad harvests in Europe had allowed the United States to increase exports of beef and grain to Europe, and this, combined with serious

moral doubts about supporting slavery, prevented the Confederacy from achieving international recognition as an independent belligerent nation.

Although commerce-raiders continued to harry Northern shipping, the blockade was slowly strangling the South and Southern ports were gradually being captured. By the end its patrols had captured or sunk nearly 300 steamships, 44 large sailing ships and 683 schooners. The total value of their cargoes was $24,5 million and a further $7 million was lost when blockade-runners were wrecked. By the surrender all commodities, from uniforms down to necessities of life, were almost unobtainable. The blockade did not defeat the Confederacy single-handed, but without it the Union armies could not have succeeded.

Jackson's Valley Campaign
The land war in the east resumed in March with a two-pronged Union offensive designed to capture Richmond. The major attack was to be delivered by a 100,000-man army, under Major General George B McClellan, which was to be landed on the tip of the Virginia peninsula, thence to march on the Confederate capital, only 75 miles away. A secondary attack, to be launched overland, was to clear

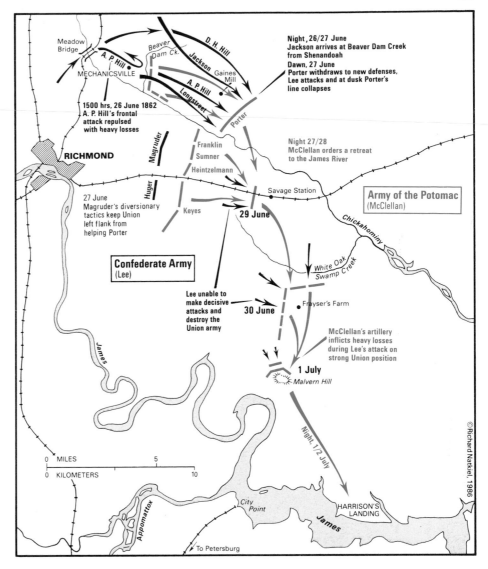

the Shenandoah Valley of Confederate forces and then converge on Richmond from the northwest. In the event it was the Valley campaign that was the more decisive, for here the brilliant defensive tactics of Confederate General Thomas J 'Stonewall' Jackson not only frustrated the Union advance but pinned down troops badly needed by McClellan to reinforce his army on the peninsula. Throughout March and April Jackson had fought a skillful delaying action against the southward advance of Major General Nathaniel Banks, and when, in May, Banks attempted to trap Jackson between his own forces and those of Major General John C Frémont, who had entered the southern end of the valley from West Virginia, Jackson defeated both in succession. In early June Union Generals Frémont and James Shields again attempted to trap Jackson between converging columns, and again he defeated his pursuers individually in the battles of Cross Keys and Port Republic, fought in 24 hours.

Having reduced the Union advance in the Shenandoah to near chaos, Jackson withdrew from the valley in mid-June to join with the new commander of the Army of Northern Virginia, General Robert E Lee, in defending Richmond against McClellan's slow-moving advance up the peninsula.

The Seven Days' Battles
McClellan had reached the peninsula in early April but had wasted a month besieging Major General John Magruder's forces at Yorktown. The Confederates abandoned the town early in May and withdrew toward Richmond, fighting a delaying action at Williamsburg on the 5th. By the end of the month McClellan's army was closing in on Richmond but had become badly dispersed en route. Confederate General J E Johnston mounted an unsuccessful attempt to take advantage of this and defeat McClellan in detail in the Battle of Fair Oaks on 31 May. Johnston's subordinate commanders let him down and he himself was wounded in the fighting and replaced in charge by General Lee.

On 25 June Lee began his counter-offensive with a series of relentless attacks (subsequently known as the Seven Days' Battle). In engagements at Mechanicsville (26 June) and Gaines Mill (27 June) he forced McClellan to retreat toward a new base at Harrison's Landing. The Federal rearguard held Lee off at Savage Station and Frayser's Farm and by 1 July the Union army was in a strong position at Malvern Hill. Although Lee's attacks on this

position were beaten off, the Union forces retired to Harrison's Landing and abandoned the peninsula campaign. McClellan's army was finally withdrawn from the peninsula in early August.

Above: the Seven Days' Battles around Richmond.
Below: Union defenses outside Yorktown.

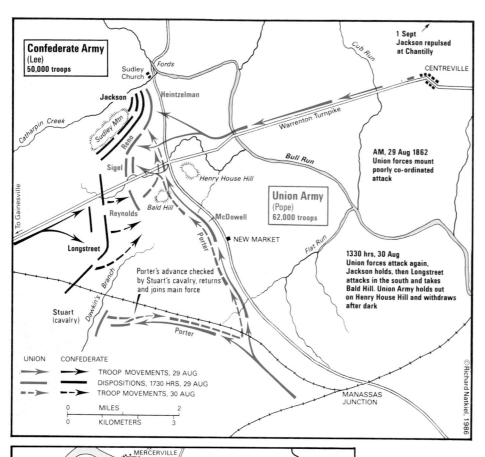

Manassas and Antietam

The North next attempted to repeat the strategy of the preceding year with direct overland offensives, originating from Washington and aimed at Richmond. Once again the contending armies clashed at Manassas, this time on 29 August 1862, and once again the Federal troops were routed, retreating in disorder back to Washington. Lee immediately seized the initiative and launched an offensive into Maryland. McClellan, at the head of 90,000 troops, caught up with Lee's 50,000 at Antietam Creek, near Sharpsburg, Maryland, in mid-September, and on the 17th McClellan attacked. None of his efforts to turn Lee's flanks was successful, and for the most part the battle was fought as a murderous confrontational slugging match, with neither side winning a clear decision. The Battle of Antietam was, however, the bloodiest battle of the war so far, producing 12,000 Union and 10,000 Confederate casualties. In the face of such devastating losses, Lee felt compelled to abandon his offensive and withdraw across the Potomac River into Virginia on the next day.

At the year's end the North made yet another attempt on Richmond. This offensive, involving about 100,000 troops led by Major General Ambrose E Burnside, was

conceived as a relatively straightforward advance south to Fredericksburg, on the Rappahannock River, and thence southeast to the Confederate capital. By the time (13 December) Burnside was ready to cross the Rappahannock and assail Fredericksburg, Lee's 70,000 troops were strongly entrenched in the hills around the town. Though the situation plainly called for some form of enveloping tactics, the unimaginative Burnside chose a frontal assault across the river and up the slopes before the town, always under heavy fire. The inevitable result: 15,000 Union casualties to a much smaller Confederate loss of about 5000, Fredericksburg still in Confederate hands and the Union offensive brought to a standstill.

Above: Union troops struggle to escape the Confederates at Second Bull Run, 29 August 1862.

Below: President Abraham Lincoln visits the battlefield of Antietam in October 1862.

168

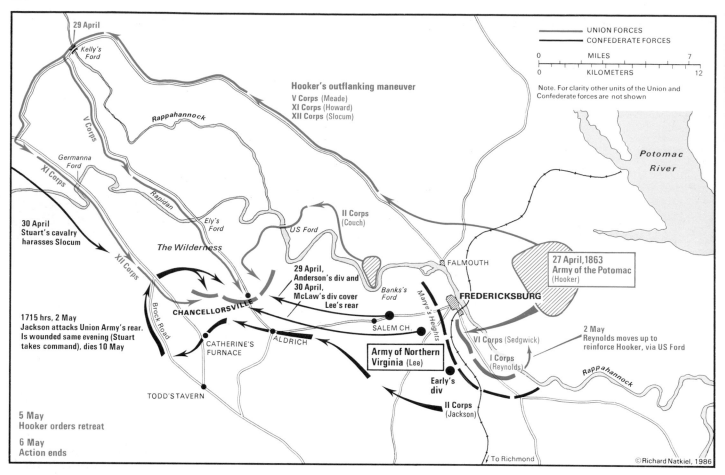

The Battle of Chancellorsville

The North sought to break the stalemate before Fredericksburg the following spring. Burnside's successor, Major General Joseph Hooker, now attempted a combined frontal assault and northern envelopment. Lee adroitly counterattacked Hooker's enveloping right wing and forced it to assume a defensive position at the town of Chancellorsville. Then Lee rapidly assembled a force of about 60,000 men, 42,000 of which he launched in a direct attack on Chancellorsville, while another 28,000, mostly cavalry, under the command of Lieutenant General Thomas J

Below: a typical cavalry encampment during the war.

Jackson, swung around the town on Hooker's right. The ferocity of this attack (begun on 2 May 1863) nearly undid Hooker's 90,000-man army. Though in the end it barely managed to hang together, Hooker ordered it to begin its retreat on 5 May. Again, casualties were enormous: 17,000 Union and 13,000 Confederate (of whom Jackson was one).

While the dismayed Union command was trying to think what to do next, Lee acted with characteristic boldness. Virtually ignoring the Federal forces still before Fredericksburg (he left only a single corps to defend the town), he abruptly hurled 75,000 troops northwest in an invasion of Pennsylvania. As panic spread in the North Hooker could only turn his army around and follow as best he might.

The Battle of Gettysburg

For the better part of the month of June 1863 Lee's forces fanned out over southern Pennsylvania, spreading chaos and destruction and capturing much-needed supplies. Only by the month's end had the fragmented elements of the Union army, now commanded by Hooker's replacement, Major General George G Meade, begun to coalesce sufficiently to prompt Lee to concentrate his own forces. He did so before the small crossroads town of Gettysburg, where Union troops were desperately trying to set up defensive positions. On 1 July 1863 the Confederates attacked Gettysburg from the northwest and drove the defenders south from the town into a chain of low hills. All through the following day of

savage fighting Lee's lieutenants tried in vain to dislodge the Union defenders from this high ground: Cemetery Hill and Culp's Hill on the north, Cemetery Ridge in the center, and Round Top and Little Round Top in the south. On 3 July the Confederates made a last all-out assault – 15,000 men led by Major General George Pickett – on Cemetery Ridge.

It was bloodily repulsed, costing the attackers an appalling 60 percent in casualties. Lee, who had thus far lost nearly 30,000 men in his Pennsylvania offensive, realized he could do no more and on 4 July ordered his army back to Virginia. This decisive Union victory broke forever the South's capacity to mount major offensive operations in the eastern theater.

Above: Union reserves rush to the front line at Gettysburg.

Below: General Robert E Lee (center). Below left: the Battle of Gettysburg, the end of Confederate hopes of outright victory in the civil war.

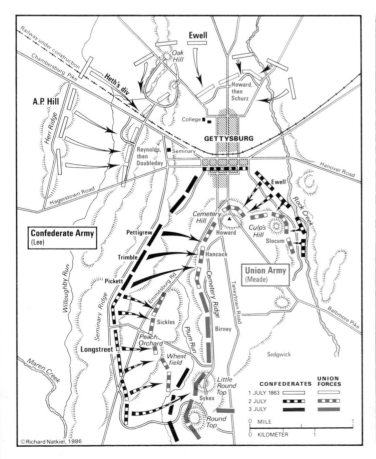

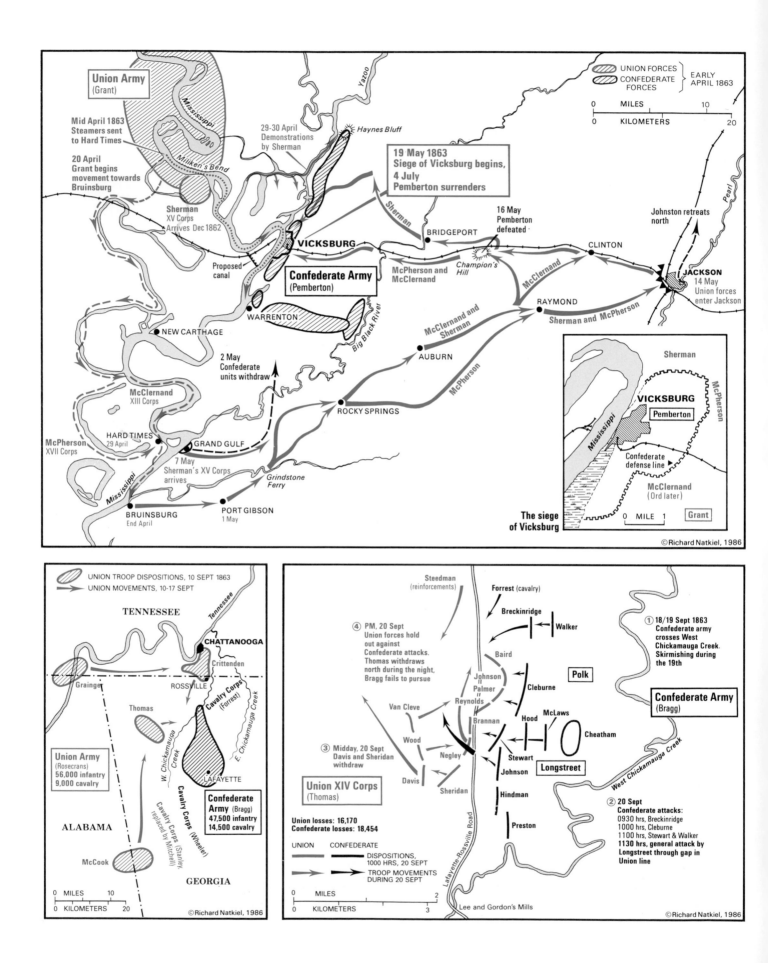

Top map: Vicksburg Campaign

UNION FORCES
CONFEDERATE FORCES
EARLY APRIL 1863

MILES 0 — 10
KILOMETERS 0 — 20

Union Army (Grant)

Mid April 1863 Steamers sent to Hard Times

20 April Grant begins movement towards Bruinsburg

Sherman XV Corps Arrives Dec 1862

29-30 April Demonstrations by Sherman

Haynes Bluff

Milliken's Bend

Yazoo

Proposed canal

19 May 1863 Siege of Vicksburg begins, 4 July Pemberton surrenders

16 May Pemberton defeated

Johnston retreats north

Peal

Sherman

BRIDGEPORT

CLINTON

VICKSBURG

Confederate Army (Pemberton)

McPherson and McClernand

Champion's Hill

McClernand

JACKSON 14 May Union forces enter Jackson

RAYMOND

WARRENTON

Big Black River

McClernand and Sherman

Sherman and McPherson

NEW CARTHAGE

2 May Confederate units withdraw

AUBURN

McPherson

McClernand XIII Corps

ROCKY SPRINGS

McPherson XVII Corps

HARD TIMES 29 April

GRAND GULF

7 May Sherman's XV Corps arrives

Grindstone Ferry

Mississippi

BRUINSBURG End April

PORT GIBSON 1 May

Inset: The siege of Vicksburg

Sherman

VICKSBURG

Pemberton

McPherson

Mississippi

Confederate defense line

McClernand (Ord later)

0 MILE 1

Grant

©Richard Natkiel, 1986

Bottom left map: Chickamauga area

UNION TROOP DISPOSITIONS, 10 SEPT 1863
UNION MOVEMENTS, 10-17 SEPT

TENNESSEE

Tennessee

CHATTANOOGA

Crittenden

Grainger

ROSSVILLE

Cavalry Corps (Forrest)

Thomas

W. Chickamauga Creek

E. Chickamauga Creek

Union Army (Rosecrans) 56,000 infantry 9,000 cavalry

LAFAYETTE

Cavalry Corps (Stanley, replaced by Mitchell)

Cavalry Corps (Wheeler)

Confederate Army (Bragg) 47,500 infantry 14,500 cavalry

ALABAMA

McCook

GEORGIA

0 MILES 10
0 KILOMETERS 20

©Richard Natkiel, 1986

Bottom right map: Battle of Chickamauga

Steedman (reinforcements)

Forrest (cavalry)

Breckinridge

Walker

① 18/19 Sept 1863 Confederate army crosses West Chickamauga Creek. Skirmishing during the 19th

④ PM, 20 Sept Union forces hold out against Confederate attacks. Thomas withdraws north during the night, Bragg fails to pursue

Baird

Johnson
Palmer
Reynolds
Brannan

Van Cleve

Cleburne

Polk

Confederate Army (Bragg)

Hood
McLaws

Cheatham

Wood

Negley

Stewart

Longstreet

West Chickamauga Creek

③ Midday, 20 Sept Davis and Sheridan withdraw

Davis

Johnson

Sheridan

Hindman

② 20 Sept Confederate attacks: 0930 hrs, Breckinridge 1000 hrs, Cleburne 1100 hrs, Stewart & Walker 1130 hrs, general attack by Longstreet through gap in Union line

Preston

Union XIV Corps (Thomas)

Union losses: 16,170
Confederate losses: 18,454

UNION	CONFEDERATE	
		DISPOSITIONS, 1000 HRS, 20 SEPT
		TROOP MOVEMENTS DURING 20 SEPT

0 MILES 2
0 KILOMETERS 3

Lafayette-Rossville Road

Lee and Gordon's Mills

©Richard Natkiel, 1986

Below: a romantic celebration of the civil war showing the Union, personified as 'Liberty,' encouraging troops to revenge Fort Sumter.

Below: a romantic celebration of the civil war showing the Union, personified as 'Liberty,' encouraging troops to revenge Fort Sumter.

Vicksburg and the Western Campaign

Meantime, equally dramatic developments had been unfolding in the west. At the beginning of 1863 the South had only one remaining important foothold on the Mississippi River, the fortress city of Vicksburg. But Grant was finding this 'Gibraltar of the West' a tough nut to crack. Natural and manmade defences made the city almost impregnable on its north, west and south sides, while the eastern approaches were guarded both by the city's strong garrison and by Joseph E Johnston's potentially formidable Confederate army headquartered just 40 miles due east in Jackson. None of the several attempts that Grant made on Vicksburg during the first quarter of the year met with any success. Then, in April, he moved a 45,000-man force down the west bank of the Mississippi, crossed the river at a point about 50 miles below the city and marched rapidly northeast toward Jackson. He took that city on 14 May, driving Johnston's troops off to the north, then wheeled west and struck at Vicksburg. The city gallantly withstood his grim siege for six weeks, surrendering only on 4 July, the same day Lee began his withdrawal from Gettysburg.

With the capture of Vicksburg the Union had achieved the preliminary goal of its western strategy: the Greater South was now bisected along a north-south axis. The next goal would be to split the Old South along an east-west axis, and the necessary first step in this enterprise would be the capture of Chattanooga, a key Confederate stronghold on Tennessee's southern border with Georgia. Defending Chattanooga was Major General Braxton Bragg, with an army of about 62,000. Marching all too slowly to the attack was Major General William S Rosecrans, with an army of about 65,000. By the time the dilatory Rosecrans arrived on the scene in early September Bragg had not only established himself in a superb defensive position south of the city but also was being reinforced by extra men from Lieutenant General James T Longstreet's corps, brought all the way from Virginia. When Bragg realized he had gained numerical superiority, he quickly went over to the attack, striking at the Union army on 19 September in a wooded area near Chickamauga Creek. The main phase of the battle was fought the following day, with Bragg unsuccessfully concentrating his main attack on Rosecrans' well-defended left. In the midst of the fighting, Longstreet noticed that a gap (the result of a misunderstood order) had opened in the Union center. Longstreet

immediately led a charge through the gap, collapsing the Union right flank and threatening to roll up the whole line. Only a dogged delaying action on the Union left, coupled with Bragg's pig-headed refusal to give Longstreet the support he needed, saved Rosecrans' disintegrating army from annihilation. The price of this victory to the Confederates was very high – 18,000 casualties that the South could ill-afford – but the beaten Union army had

been driven back into Chattanooga and had to remain there in a humiliating state of siege until relieved by Grant in October.

It took Grant a full month of campaigning to repair the damage done at Chickamauga. But he finally did so, the climax coming on 25 November 1863, when, in the freakish battle of Missionary Ridge, his troops stormed up the side of a small mountain to overwhelm strongly entrenched Confederate positions at the top (an almost unheard-of feat in this war of intense firepower). This success cracked the entire Confederate line, and the dispirited Bragg was forced to retreat to Dalton, Georgia, some 25 miles away. The Union offensive into the Deep South could now begin.

The North finds a Winning Strategy

Early in 1864 Lincoln appointed Grant General in Chief of the US Army and brought him back east to help plan what the president expected to be the closing phase of the war. This final Union strategy was again tripartite. First, the great offensive from the west into the Deep South would of course continue: directed by Sherman, it was intended to drive southeast from Chattanooga all the way through Georgia to the coast, capturing Atlanta along the way. Second, in the east, yet another attempt would be made on Richmond: several armies would be employed in this task, but the main thrust was to be made by Meade, now commander of the Army of the Potomac, starting from a point about 35 miles northwest of Fredericksburg. Last, far to the south, Major General Nathaniel Banks was to move east from New Orleans to capture Mobile, Alabama, and then, Montgomery.

It was as well that the third part of this plan was the least important, for Banks failed utterly. Yet thanks to the US Navy Mobile was, if not captured, effectively neutralized as a Confederate port. This occurred in the summer of 1864, well after the major offensives in the west and east had begun. On 5 August now-Admiral David Farragut led an 11-ship squadron, spearheaded by four ironclad monitors, in an attack on Mobile Bay. The narrow navigation channels leading into the bay, along with strategically placed Confederate minefields and underwater obstructions, forced the attackers to pass close under the guns of Fort Morgan, the most powerful of the forts that guarded the bay's entrance. In addition to suffering a punishing barrage from the forts, Farragut's ships had to endure severe enfilading fire from CSS *Tennessee*, a more heavily armed version of the ironclad *Virginia*, which had taken up station in the channel beyond the forts. Many of the Union ships were roughly handled in this passage, and one, the monitor *Tecumseh*, was sunk by a mine. At last the battered Union flotilla straggled past the forts to confront the formidable, virtually unsinkable *Tennessee*. Neither cannonades nor repeated rammings seemed to harm this armor-plated giant, and it was not until a lucky shot carried away her rudder chain, leaving her dead in the water and unable to bring her guns to bear, that the Union ships were finally able to pound her into surrender. Farragut then returned to the forts and succeeded in capturing them all (Morgan by assault from the land). Now in complete control of the waters of Mobile Bay, Farragut had

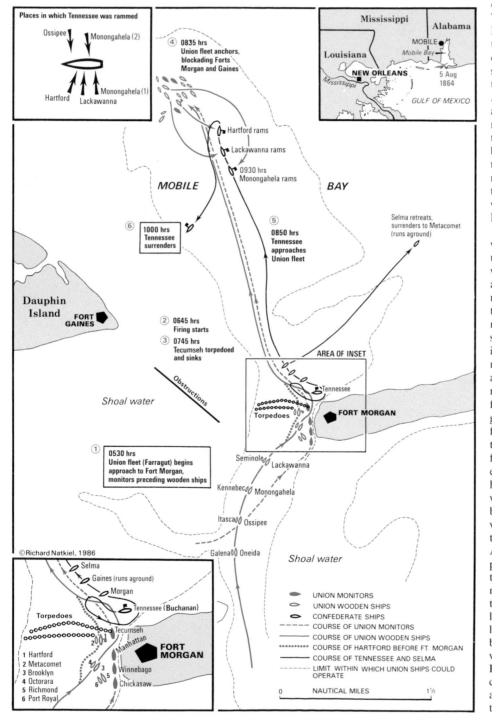

Places in which Tennessee was rammed

Ossipee Monongahela (2)

Monongahela (1)
Hartford Lackawanna

④ 0835 hrs
Union fleet anchors, blockading Forts Morgan and Gaines

Mississippi Alabama
MOBILE
Mobile Bay
Louisiana
NEW ORLEANS 5 Aug 1864
Mississippi
GULF OF MEXICO

Hartford rams

Lackawanna rams

0930 hrs
Monongahela rams

MOBILE   *BAY*

⑥ 1000 hrs
Tennessee surrenders

⑤ 0850 hrs
Tennessee approaches Union fleet

Selma retreats, surrenders to Metacomet (runs aground)

Dauphin Island   FORT GAINES

② 0645 hrs
Firing starts

③ 0745 hrs
Tecumseh torpedoed and sinks

AREA OF INSET

Obstructions

Tennessee

Shoal water

Torpedoes

FORT MORGAN

① 0530 hrs
Union fleet (Farragut) begins approach to Fort Morgan, monitors preceding wooden ships

Seminole
Lackawanna

Kennebec Monongahela

Itasca Ossipee

© Richard Natkiel, 1986

Galena Oneida

Shoal water

Selma
Gaines (runs aground)
Morgan
Tennessee (Buchanan)
Torpedoes
Tecumseh
Manhattan
FORT MORGAN
1 Hartford
2 Metacomet
3 Brooklyn
4 Octorara
5 Richmond
6 Port Royal
Winnebago
Chickasaw

UNION MONITORS
UNION WOODEN SHIPS
CONFEDERATE SHIPS
COURSE OF UNION MONITORS
COURSE OF UNION WOODEN SHIPS
COURSE OF HARTFORD BEFORE FT. MORGAN
COURSE OF TENNESSEE AND SELMA
LIMIT WITHIN WHICH UNION SHIPS COULD OPERATE

0   NAUTICAL MILES   1½

effectively sealed off the Confederacy's last major port in the Gulf of Mexico.

The two big offensives in the west and the east had begun on the same day: 4 May 1864. Sherman, with 100,000 men, had left Chattanooga, slowly making his way toward Atlanta in the teeth of stiff resistance from Joseph Johnston's 65,000-man Army of Tennessee. The fighting was incessant, several times flaring into major battles. Sherman's losses were staggering, and by July the Union army had advanced only 100 miles. It was not until 9 August (and after Johnston had been relieved, for political reasons, by the less successful General John B Hood) that Sherman reached Atlanta, and it was not until 1 September that he was finally able to force Hood to withdraw to Alabama and fight his way into the city. He would remain there in occupation for the next two months.

Far left: the Battle of Mobile Bay.
Above: General Grant and the staff of the Army of the Potomac.

Below: the siege of Atlanta, one of the South's main railroad junctions.

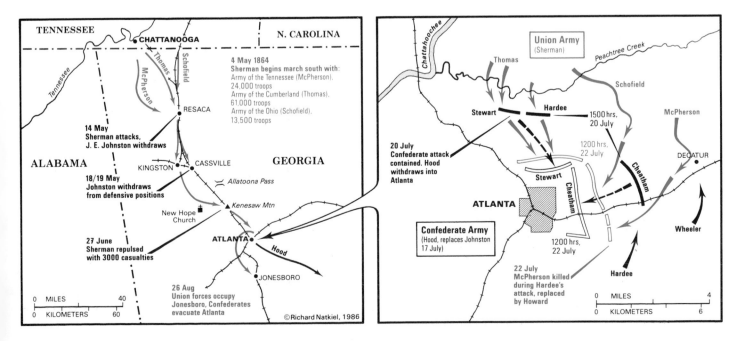

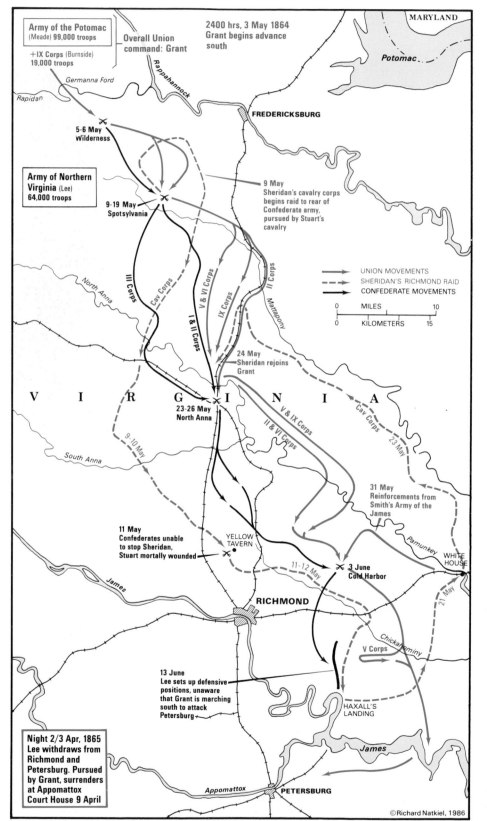

Army of the Potomac
(Meade) 99,000 troops

**Overall Union
command: Grant**

+IX Corps (Burnside)
19,000 troops

Germanna Ford

Rappahannock

Rapidan

2400 hrs, 3 May 1864
Grant begins advance
south

MARYLAND

Potomac

FREDERICKSBURG

5-6 May
Wilderness

**Army of Northern
Virginia** (Lee)
64,000 troops

9-19 May
Spotsylvania

9 May
Sheridan's cavalry corps
begins raid to rear of
Confederate army,
pursued by Stuart's
cavalry

North Anna

III Corps

Cav Corps

V & VI Corps

IX Corps

I & II Corps

II Corps

Mattapony

UNION MOVEMENTS
SHERIDAN'S RICHMOND RAID
CONFEDERATE MOVEMENTS

0 — MILES — 10
0 — KILOMETERS — 15

24 May
Sheridan rejoins
Grant

V I R G I N I A

23-26 May
North Anna

9-10 May

South Anna

II & VI Corps

V & IX Corps

Cav Corps

23 May

31 May
Reinforcements from
Smith's Army of the
James

Pamunkey

11 May
Confederates unable
to stop Sheridan,
Stuart mortally wounded

YELLOW
TAVERN

11-12 May

3 June
Cold Harbor

WHITE
HOUSE

21 May

James

RICHMOND

Chickahominy

V Corps

13 June
Lee sets up defensive
positions, unaware
that Grant is marching
south to attack
Petersburg

HAXALL'S
LANDING

James

Night 2/3 Apr, 1865
Lee withdraws from
Richmond and
Petersburg. Pursued
by Grant, surrenders
at Appomattox
Court House 9 April

Appomattox

PETERSBURG

©Richard Natkiel, 1986

Grant's Advance on Richmond

On the day that Sherman left Chattanooga (4 May 1864) Grant, with Meade's 99,000-man Army of the Potomac, began his long advance southeast toward Richmond. Lee and his 64,000-man Army of Northern Virginia counterattacked immediately. For two days the armies fought a series of savage battles near Chancellorsville in an area known as The Wilderness. By 6 May Grant's forces had suffered 17,000 casualties, and Lee's, 6000; but no decision had been reached, and Grant doggedly resumed his advance. Lee next tried to halt the momentum of the Union offensive by setting up an immense fortified roadblock about ten miles farther southwest at Spotsylvania. Here, and at a flank redoubt at North Anna Creek, the armies fought another bloody, inconclusive series of battles of attrition between 9 and 18 May. Again Grant disengaged and continued his advance. And again Lee raced south to intercept him, this time at Cold Harbor, where, between 3 and 12 June, the antagonists fought yet a third round of battles as sprawling, sanguinary and indecisive as their predecessors. By now Grant's casualties stood at an awesome 55,000 (to Lee's 32,000), yet still he persisted. For the last time he disengaged and, in a brilliantly executed maneuver, contrived to transfer his whole army across the James River in such secrecy that Lee did not realize he had been outflanked until six days after the operation had begun. By the time Lee caught up with him on the 18th, Grant was already south of Richmond and preparing to lay siege to Petersburg, an important rail junction on one of the capital's major supply routes.

Lee now sought to create a diversion dramatic enough to draw Grant away from Richmond. In early July he sent Major General Jubal A Early's cavalry corps up the Shenandoah Valley to threaten Washington. But Grant refused to be drawn, and Early's alarming attack was eventually beaten off by local forces. Grant then ordered Major General Philip H Sheridan to pursue the overextended Early back down the valley. This Sheridan did, and by the end of the year he had thrice defeated Early and driven him from the Valley, securing it once and for all for the Union.

Meantime, Grant's forces had settled in for a long siege of Petersburg. The Confederates had set up an arc of formidable earthwork fortifications before the town, and major Union efforts to breach these defenses in June and July (the second involving a spectacular – though ultimately unsuccessful – use of mines)

had been bloodily repulsed. For the remainder of the year the two armies remained
stalemated on the Petersburg front.

Victory for the Union

In Atlanta, however, Sherman was now preparing to launch the final phase of his great
offensive from the west. After sending 30,000
men north to reinforce Major General George
H Thomas in Nashville. Tennessee (Sherman
rightly guessed that Hood might make an
attempt on that key Union base), Sherman
burned Atlanta and, on 15 November, set out
with 62,000 men on his famous march through
Georgia to the sea. Virtually unopposed, he
left a trail of deliberate and highly demoraliz-
ing devastation in his wake. By 21 December
he had reached the coast, had captured Savannah and was ready to wheel north and join
forces with Grant. Simultaneously, Thomas

**Above: General Sheridan (center, standing)
and his senior cavalry commanders.
Right: a Union siege mortar – its crew pose
for the camera.**

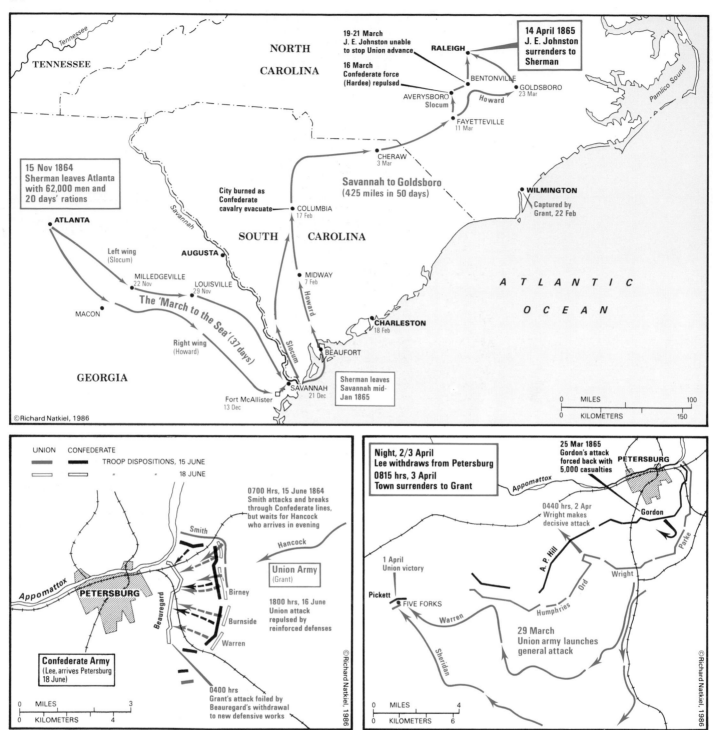

had repelled Hood's anticipated attack on Nashville and by 16 December, while Sherman was investing Savannah, had counterattacked so successfully as to destroy Hood's army.

Lee's army at Petersburg was now the only major military organization left to the Confederacy, and by early 1865 its position there was becoming untenable: Sheridan had completed his conquest of the Shenandoah Valley and was already beginning to rejoin Grant, while Sherman was rapidly approaching from the south. On 25 March Lee made a final, unsuccessful attempt to break out of the trap by trying to open a corridor through Grant's line at Fort Stedman. Four days later Grant sent She-

ridan off to the southwest to try to turn Lee's right flank, and on 1 April, at the Battle of Five Forks, Sheridan succeeded in doing so. The next day Grant mounted a frontal assault on the disintegrating Confederate line, and within another 24 hours he was at long last in Richmond. On 9 April Lee formally surrendered at Appomattox Court House, Virginia.

With Lee's capitulation Southern resistance collapsed. The remaining Southern military forces were still in the process of laying down their arms when, on 14 April, at Ford's Theater in Washington, Abraham Lincoln was assassinated.

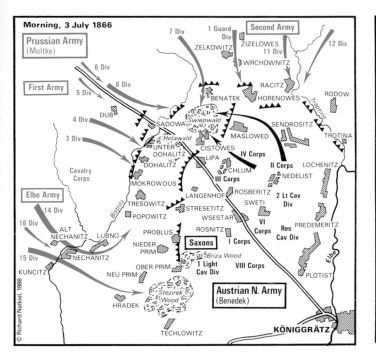

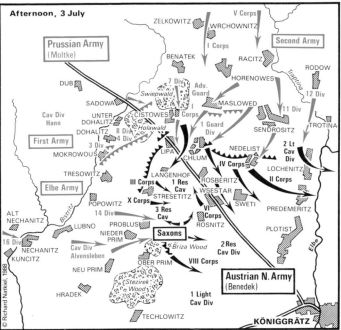

The Austro-Prussian War

Between 1862 and 1866 there was considerable rivalry between Austria and Prussia over the independent states of the German Confederation. Basically, it was a rivalry about which of these two great powers was to dominate Germany. Bismarck, the Prussian Chancellor, was determined to promote Prussia as the dominant power in Germany and to exclude Austria. Both Bismarck and Graf Helmut von Moltke, the Chief of the Prussian General Staff, were determined that Prussia should annex Schleswig-Holstein and believed that a war with Austria was inevitable. In 1865 Moltke worked on a plan for a limited war to force Austria to accept Prussia's political aims. Although Austria could count on the support of the majority of the German states, Moltke calculated that the Prussian Army could be mobilized faster and more decisively than Austria and her allies could concentrate their overwhelming numerical superiority. The smaller German states could be discounted because many of their officers were impressed by the Prussian Army and were reluctant to fight against it. Moltke planned to concentrate the main body of the Prussian Army, some 250,000 men, against the Austrians in Bohemia, leaving 50,000 troops to deal with Bavaria, Baden and Württemberg. Meanwhile, Bismarck used all his diplomatic skills to neutralize France and Russia, and encourage Italy to threaten Austria's southern flank.

On 7 June 1866 Prussian troops marched into Holstein, and on the 12th Austria broke off diplomatic relations with Prussia. The Prussians had already concentrated their armies against Austria. In Central Silesia was Crown Prince William's Second Army of 115,000 men; in eastern Saxony was Prince Frederick Charles' First Army of 93,000; and farther west marching on Dresden was the Army of the Elbe with 48,000 men. A Western Army of about 50,000 men was concentrated in Prussian Saxony. The three main Prussian armies were to advance into Bohemia and converge east of Prague, the expected concentration area of General Benedek's Austrian Army of 190,000 with its 25,000 Saxon allies.

The Austrians were neither bold enough nor concentrated enough to try to defeat the Prussians in detail. There were three sharp clashes in Bohemia on 27 June as the Austrians fell back north of Prague in the face of the First Army. Despite some local successes, Benedek faced disaster and pulled back his scattered corps to concentrate for a defensive battle west of the upper Elbe River, near the fortress of Königgrätz. Moltke ordered a concentration of his three armies, and on the 30th King William I, Bismarck and Moltke joined the First Army near Gitschin.

Moltke, learning that Benedek was concentrating in the vicinity of Königgrätz, saw an opportunity to encircle the Austrians. On 1 July he ordered the First Army to advance toward Königgrätz; the Second Army to advance on the Austrian right wing; and the Army of the Elbe River south of Königgrätz to attack the Austrian left flank and rear.

On the 2nd the First Army commander learnt that there were at least three Austrian corps deployed to his left, and so Prince Frederick Charles shifted direction to the east, issuing orders for an attack the next day against what appeared to be the main Austrian position between Sadowa and Königgrätz. Moltke confirmed the prince's decision to attack before the Second Army arrived, merely sending a message to Frederick William to advance with all speed to attack the Austrian right flank.

In driving rain, the First Army and the Army of the Elbe attacked at dawn on 3 July. Overeager, the Elbe Army did not extend its front sufficiently, and its advance crossed the path of the First Army. The confused Prussians were met by a strong Austrian counter-attack and massed artillery fire. By 1100 hours the Prussian advance had been checked and their reserves drawn into a costly frontal attack. The Prussians were very vulnerable to a cavalry charge, but Benedek held his cavalry back. The situation was only retrieved for the Prussians by the arrival of the Second Army which began to attack the Austrian's northern sector, and the deployment of more artillery which unleashed devastating fire on the Austrian center. By 1420 hours the Austrian right wing was on the point of breaking and Benedek began a gradual withdrawal, ably covered by his cavalry and artillery. The Austrians were able to withdraw across the Elbe almost unmolested as the Prussians, exhausted by marching and fighting in intense heat, were in no condition to pursue them. The Prussians had suffered about 10,000 casualties, the Austrians 40,000.

After a day to reorganize, the Prussians resumed the advance south toward Vienna. But although the Prussians had triumphed against Austria's German allies, the Italians had been soundly beaten at Custozza and the Austrian victor, Archduke Albert, had been ordered north to replace Benedek. On the 5th Napoleon III offered mediation, which the Prussians and Austrians accepted. By the Treaty of Prague signed on 23 August Austria was excluded from German affairs, and the German states north of the River Main formed a North German Confederation under Prussian leadership.

Above: the Battle of Königgrätz, July 1866.

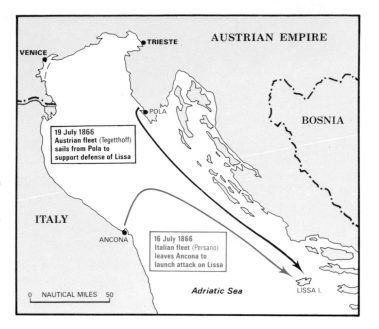

The Battle of Lissa

Following the Austrian defeat in 1866 at Königgrätz (Sadowa) at the hands of the Prussian Army, the Emperor Franz Josef ceded Venice to Italy, but fighting continued between Austria and Italy. The fighting shifted to the Adriatic, where the Austrian fleet challenged the Italians.

On paper the Italian fleet was more powerful, with 12 armored ships out of a total of 34, against only seven Austrian ironclads in a fleet of 27 ships. But Rear Admiral Wilhelm von Tegetthoff was a bold and imaginative leader whereas Count Carlo Pellion de Persano was irresolute. Tegetthoff knew that with only 74 modern rifled guns against 200 modern guns in the Italian fleet he must either avoid action or try to use superior seamanship and tactics. He chose the latter course, ordering his ships to fight at close range so that his older muzzle-loading guns could penetrate Italian armor. He also ordered his ironclads to ram at every opportunity to throw the Italian squadron into confusion.

The Italian fleet left Ancona on 16 July 1866 to attack the Austrian garrison holding the island of Lissa (now Vis), and four days later they were brought to action by the Austrians from Pola (now Pula). In arrowhead formation Tegetthoff's ships bore down on the Italian line and threw it into confusion. The action quickly degenerated into a melée, with Austrian ships trying ineffectually to ram amid dense clouds of powder-smoke. At first the Italians seemed to do well, and the flagship, the new turret ram *Affondatore*, inflicted severe damage on the Austrian wooden two-decker *Kaiser*.

Suddenly the tide of battle turned, as through the smoke Tegetthoff's flagship, the *Ferdinand Max*, sighted the big Italian frigate *Re d'Italia* lying disabled from a hit in the rudder. The Austrian ship bore down and struck her opponent full amidships, tearing an enormous hole with her projecting ram bow. The *Re d'Italia* capsized rapidly, taking over 600 men with her. The Italians had suffered another reverse when the small ironclad *Palestro* caught fire, but the loss of the *Re d'Italia* was too much for Persano. With a show of bravado he hoisted a signal for 'General Chase' but withdrew to Ancona leaving Tegetthoff's fleet the clear victors. Nearly three hours later the blazing *Palestro* blew up. It is generally argued by modern commentators that Count

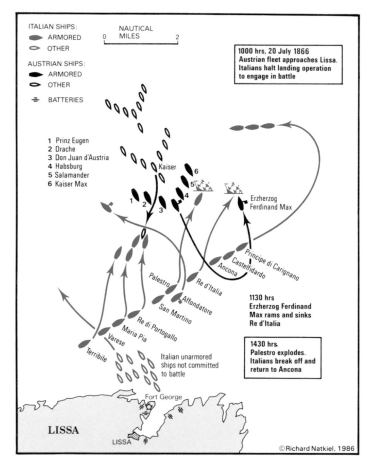

Persano's poor leadership and lack of drive were the main causes of the Italian defeat.

Although Lissa was a decisive victory and the fledgling Italian Navy was humiliated, Austria gained little. Weakened by the defeat at Königgrätz she could not pursue a prolonged war, and could not halt the complete reunification of Italy.

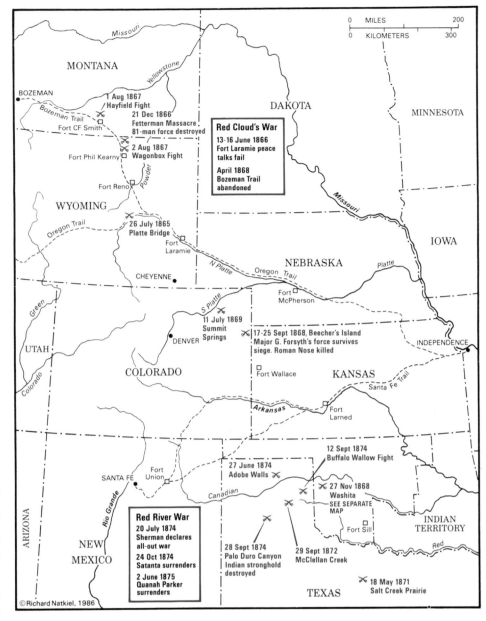

Indian Wars of the Great Plains

The first big eruption of violence on the Great Plains occurred in Minnesota during the Civil War. In August 1862 the normally peaceful Santee Sioux, annoyed both by the economic pressure created by settlers thronging into the state and by the neglect and dishonesty of the Federal Indian Agents, rose up in bloody revolt, attacking settlements and, for a time, besieging Fort Ridgely. It took the Volunteer Army and local militias over a month to put down this uprising, by which time some 700 whites had been killed. Many Santee fled to the Dakota Territory. Of those who surrendered or were captured, 38 were condemned to death.

Hardly had the regular army returned to the west after the end of the Civil War than it was engaged in a major campaign in the Wyoming and southern Montana Territories against Sioux, Cheyenne and Arapaho tribesmen who opposed the building of a chain of new army forts along the Bozeman Trail. This so-called Red Cloud's War, which lasted the better part of a year, began with the ambush and annihilation of an 81-man army detachment led by Captain William Fetterman (the Fetterman Massacre, 21 December 1866). It included a siege of the army's Fort Phil Kearny and several famous small battles (such as the Hayfield Fight and the Wagonbox Fight, both in August 1867) and only subsided in the autumn of 1867 after the signing of the Medicine Lodge Treaty.

In 1868 the army's campaigns against the Plains Indians shifted south. Custer's Battle of the Washita in Oklahoma (27 November) saw the bloody massacre of Black Kettle's Southern Cheyenne. That same autumn Major George Forsyth was fighting the Cheyenne in Colorado in a campaign that culminated in the desperate Battle of Beecher's Island (17-25 September), in which the Cheyenne war leader Roman Nose was killed.

The army was temporarily diverted from the Plains wars in the early 1870s by the Modoc War in California, but by the middle of the decade a major new confrontation developed in the Dakota Territory as the result of a white gold rush into the Black Hills, an area sacred to many Sioux and Cheyenne and reserved to them by treaty. By 1876 some 50,000 Indians were in rebellion, and the army's General

George Crook had been sent to put it down. Crook's strategy was to converge three columns on the Indians' main camp in the valley of the Little Bighorn River in the Montana Territory: he would approach from the south, Colonel John Gibbon from the west and General Alfred Terry from the east. But the great Sioux war leader Crazy Horse succeeded in halting Crook's advance at the Battle of the Rosebud on 17 June. Terry and Gibbon joined forces on 21 June and, afraid that the Indians might elude them before Crook's arrival, ordered Colonel George Custer's 7th Cavalry Regiment to go on ahead and try to bottle up the Indians in the valley. In the ensuing Battle of the Little Bighorn, fought on 25 June 1876, Custer's group (five troops) was surrounded and annihilated, and the other two were forced to retreat with heavy losses. It took the army another year and a half of vigorous campaigning to restore peace to the western Plains.

This peace was broken for the last time in 1890. The army became alarmed by what it considered the militant fervor induced in the tribes by a new religious movement, the Ghost Dance cult, and sent an expedition into the Dakotas to restore order. This inept effort produced, on 29 December, the last battle of the Indian Wars, that of Wounded Knee, in which 150 Sioux were killed.

Above: Indian wars of the Great Plains, 1865-75.

The Franco-Prussian War

If the Prussian victory at Königgrätz was a shock to the Austrians, it was no less a surprise to the French, who now found a powerful and threatening neighbor to the north. The French, like the Austrians, had believed in the principle of a small, professional army, and in 1868 Marshal Niel proposed a series of military reforms to change the comparatively weak French position. The reforms which were adopted fell far short of his expectations, and conscription was never universal or fair. It was relatively simple to buy one's way out of military service. But French foreign policy did not reflect this weak military position. On the contrary, French troops were placed in Mexico, Indo-China, Algeria and elsewhere, and under the leadership of Napoleon III, the nephew of the great emperor, dash and initiative proved poor substitutes for massive strength, economic power and a rail network geared for war – all of which the Prussians had. French artillery was poor and its organization weak compared to Prussian. Above all, in Marshals Bazaine and MacMahon, as well as the emperor himself, the French lacked the impressive political and military expertise of Bismarck and von Moltke.

In a clever move by Bismarck that forced the vain Napoleon III to declare war against Prussia despite his unreadiness – the Ems Dispatch – French mobilization went particularly badly. Food and munitions were scarce and indiscipline was rife. MacMahon, in Alsace, called for reinforcements and was forced to retreat by the Prussian Third Army. By mid-August Bazaine was encircled in the fortress

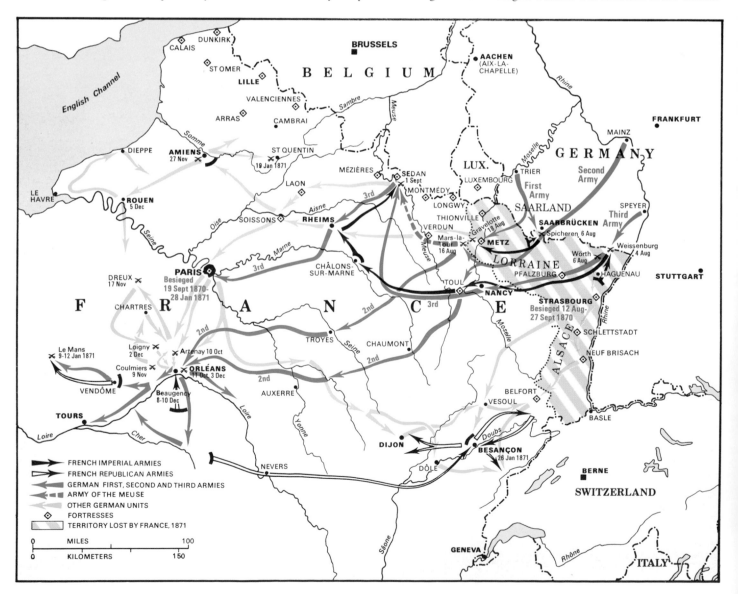

FRENCH IMPERIAL ARMIES
FRENCH REPUBLICAN ARMIES
GERMAN FIRST, SECOND AND THIRD ARMIES
ARMY OF THE MEUSE
OTHER GERMAN UNITS
FORTRESSES
TERRITORY LOST BY FRANCE, 1871

MILES 100
KILOMETERS 150

Below: an early photograph, showing the Battle of Sedan (August 1870). Note the dead and the skirmish line at right.

of Metz in Lorraine. On the 18th, the Prussians, although suffering heavy casualties, won a key victory at Gravelotte-St Privat. The Prussian Second Army then crossed the Meuse below Verdun. French forces were trapped in a pocket, and von Molkte ordered his armies to move northward to engage the remainder of the French troops, the Army of Châlons, under the command of MacMahon and the emperor himself. Moltke ordered the Army of the Meuse to advance on Sedan from the east, while the Third Army attacked from the south, cutting the French lines of retreat. By the evening of 31 August 1870, the French were surrounded. As one of their generals, Ducrot, remarked: '*Nous sommes dans un pot de chambre et nous y serons emmerdes*' (We are in a chamber pot and we are about to be covered in shit). In the early hours of 1 September the Prussians and Bavarians attacked. MacMahon was wounded and was replaced by Ducrot, and then General Wimpffen arrived to turn chaos into disaster. He ordered that no retreat was possible, saying, 'We need a victory, not a retreat!'

Unfortunately for him, a retreat was virtually impossible at this juncture, and a defeat unavoidable. German artillery fire caused heavy casualties among the French, and Wimpffen attempted a breakout, which was a dismal and bloody failure, due to the chaotic conditions within his defensive perimeter.

Napoleon himself spent the day riding about within the perimeter in a state of fatalistic resignation, looking for death. One of his staff was cut in half riding beside him, but death eluded the emperor. However, 17,000 casualties were suffered by the French, while 21,000 prisoners were taken. The white flag was raised later in the afternoon, and Napoleon tried to arrange a meeting with Wilhelm I of Prussia to discuss truce terms. The meeting never took place, and Napoleon's sword was placed in the hands of the King.

The capitulation took place the next day, 2 September 1870, when Wimpffen and Castelnau met with Moltke and Bismarck. Castelnau killed all hopes of a moderate peace by

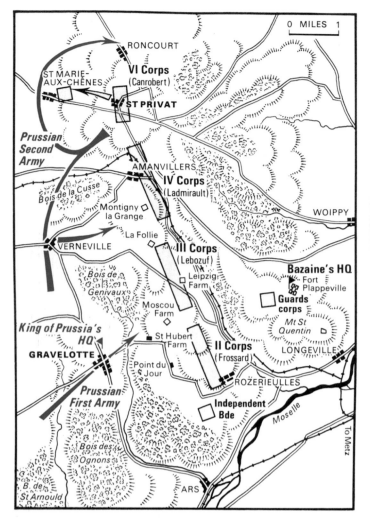

Left: One of the key battles of the early part of the war, Gravelotte saw the Prussians win a costly victory.
Right: the Battle of Sedan.
Below: Napoleon III surrenders after the disaster at Sedan.
Bottom: Communardes defend barricades in Paris.
Below right: Prussian troops pose for the camera in the ruins of Fort Issy, February 1871.

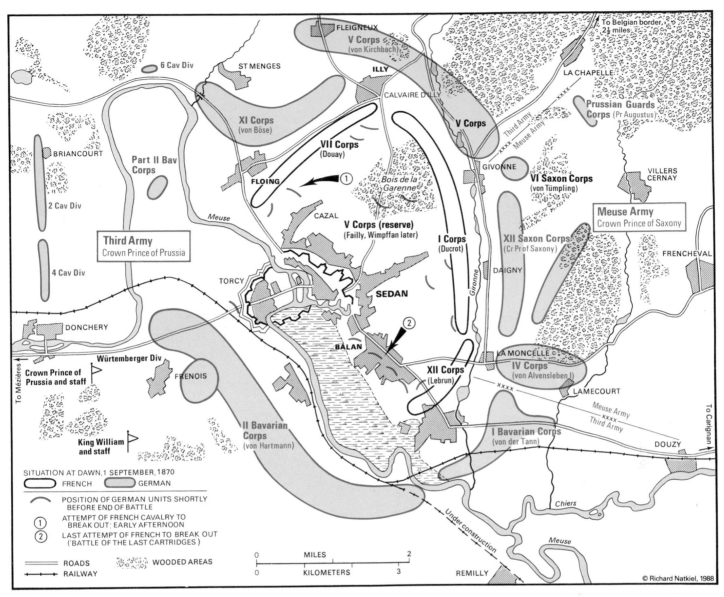

SITUATION AT DAWN, 1 SEPTEMBER, 1870
FRENCH   GERMAN

POSITION OF GERMAN UNITS SHORTLY
BEFORE END OF BATTLE

① ATTEMPT OF FRENCH CAVALRY TO
BREAK OUT: EARLY AFTERNOON

② LAST ATTEMPT OF FRENCH TO BREAK OUT
('BATTLE OF THE LAST CARTRIDGES')

ROADS   WOODED AREAS
RAILWAY

© Richard Natkiel, 1988

announcing that the loss of the battle, the armies and the emperor did not signify a surrender by France. The entire army became prisoners-of-war, giving the Germans 83,000 more men to look after. German casualties numbered only 9000, indicating the importance of Prussian artillery in the battle. As Napoleon was driven off into captivity in Bismarck's black carriage, a revolution took place in Paris, bringing a left-wing government into control. German armies surrounded Paris and besieged the city for months. The Paris Commune fell and was replaced by the Third Republic, eventually presided over by the unfortunate MacMahon. In the peace negotiations, which concluded in May 1871, France lost Alsace-Lorraine, the German Empire was proclaimed at the Palace of Versailles, and German unification was complete. France had fallen to the second rank among world powers and Germany was propelled into the first. The Battle of Sedan was the most significant and vainglorious battle to be fought in Europe between Waterloo and the first months of World War I. It also worsened the relations between France and Germany.

The World in 1900

© Richard Natkiel, 1986

RUSSIAN EMPIRE

OTTOMAN
EMPIRE

Cyprus
(Br.)

EXANDRIA

PT

Prot.)

IRAN

Tehran

Baghdad

KUWAIT
(Br.Prot.)

Bahrain
(Br.Prot.)

AFGHANISTAN

CHINA

Peking

Weihaiwei
(Br.)

Shanghai

KOREA

JAPAN

Tokyo

Pacific

Ocean

ANGLO-
EGYPTIAN

SUDAN

artoum

ABYSSINIA

ERITREA

FR. SOM.

OMAN
(Br. Prot.)

ADEN
BR.
SOM.

ITALIAN
SOMALILAND

Socotra
(Br.)

Kuria Muria Is
(Br.)

Delhi

Karachi

INDIA

NEPAL

SIKKIM

BHUTAN

Diu (Port.)

Daman (Port.)

Chandernagore
(Fr.)

Calcutta

BOMBAY

Goa (Port.)

Yanaon (Fr.)

Mahé (Fr.)

Pondicherry (Fr.)

Laccadive Is
(Br.)

Karikal (Fr.)

COLOMBO

CEYLON

Andaman Is
(Br.)

Nicobar Is
(Br.)

Macao
(Port.)

HONG KONG
(Br.)

Formosa
(Jap.)

THAI-
LAND

FRENCH
INDO-
CHINA

Manila

PHILIPPINE
ISLANDS
(US)

MARIANA
IS (Ger.)

GUAM (US)

MARSHALL
IS (Ger.)

CAROLINE
IS (Ger.)

UGANDA

BRITISH
EAST
AFRICA

GERMAN
EAST
AFRICA

MOMBASA

ZANZIBAR
(Br.Prot.)

Seychelles
(Br.)

Amirantes
(Br.)

Maldive Is
(Br.)

Chagos
(Br.)

MALAYA

SINGAPORE

BRITISH
NORTH BORNEO

BRUNEI

SARAWAK

DUTCH EAST INDIES

Batavia

KAISER
WILHELMS
LAND

PAPUA

SOLOMON
IS.

DESIA

NYASALAND
(Br.Prot.)

PORTUGUESE
EAST
AFRICA

Comoro Is
(Fr.)

MADAGASCAR

Mauritius (Br.)

Réunion
(Fr.)

Indian Ocean

Christmas I
(Br.)

Cocos Is
(Br.)

PORTUGUESE
TIMOR

AUSTRALIA

NEW
CALEDONIA
(Fr.)

SOUTH
FRICAN
REP.

Pretoria

F.S.

NATAL

BASUTOLAND
(Br.Prot.)

Perth

Melbourne

SYDNEY

AUCKLAND

NEW
ZEALAND

Wellington

Kurile Is

◉ IMPORTANT BRITISH BASES
AND COALING STATIONS

BRITISH POSSESSIONS

FRENCH "

PORTUGUESE "

SPANISH "

DUTCH "

ITALIAN "

GERMAN "

The First Boer War

Relations between the British and the Boer republics in South Africa had been uneasy before the financial disagreements of 1876, but when the British announced the annexation of the Transvaal in 1877, this unease slowly developed into outright anger. From the British perspective, they were saving the Boers·in the Transvaal from economic bankruptcy and the possibility of annihilation by the natives. To the Boers, annexation was totally incompatible with their desire for complete independence. Vice-President Paul Kruger of the Transvaal led the opposition to annexation, but failed to change government policy. Even the election of a Liberal government in Britain in 1880 failed to resolve the dispute; the Boers became determined to fight for independence.

Britain was unprepared for an armed struggle with the Boers. Sir George Colley, the High Commissioner in the Transvaal, only had three battalions available and these were spread out in penny packets throughout the territory. Colley underestimated both the Boers' dissatisfaction and their military capability. In November 1880 there was a revolt by local Boers against the authority of a local magistrate of Potchefstroom which soon spread into a general rebellion against British authority, the investment of British garrisons and the appointment of a Boer administration. Colley decided to reinforce his local garrisons, and Colonel Anstruther led a column consisting of 250 men and several wagons 190 miles from Lydenbury to reinforce Pretoria. In Christmas week 1880 Anstruther's column was ambushed by Boers and within a few minutes had suffered 120 casualties.

Colley then attempted to relieve the Transvaal garrisons by advancing from Natal, but 2000 Boers took up a defensive position at Laing's Nek across the line of the British advance. Colley with a mixed force of infantry, cavalry and artillery attacked Laing's Nek on 26 January 1881, but was repulsed with 150 casualties. The Boers lost 41 men. In February Colley was nearly surprised by the Boers at Ingogo but succeeded in extricating his troops from a trap.

Frustrated by his early repulse at Laing's Nek, Colley decided to occupy the flat-topped Majuba Hill which dominated the west end of the Boer position. At dawn on 26 February Colley led a mixed force of 365 infantry up the hill and established a position on its summit.

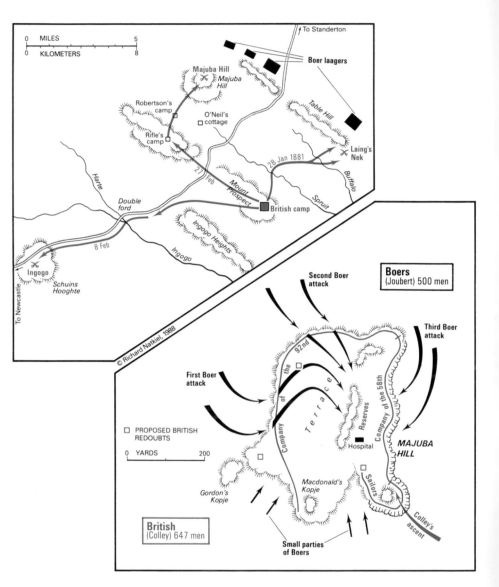

However, he was unable to bring up reinforcements and failed to establish proper defensive positions on the exposed hilltop. The initial Boer reaction to the news that the British were on top of Majuba was panic, but calmer councils prevailed. The Boers began to swarm up the sides and were able to pour a withering fire onto the British positions and then attack them. Although some British soldiers fought bravely, others ran away. In the ensuing fight Colley was killed. The Boers killed, wounded or captured 280 out of the original force. After this defeat peace talks took place at O'Neill's Farm and the Boers were effectively given their independence.

Top: the First Boer War was fought over a relatively small area, and once the British had failed to break the Boer line (the Battle of Laing's Nek), Colley and his men were forced on to the defensive for most of the remaining campaign.

Above: Majuba Hill was a disaster for the British. The preliminary night march to the summit was successful, but Colley's force was later cut to pieces by accurate Boer fire.

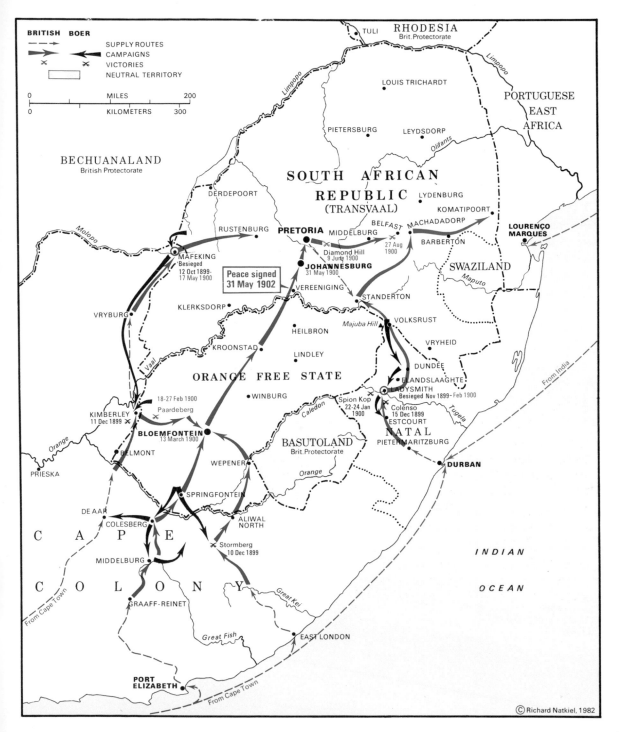

BRITISH BOER
- - - ➝ SUPPLY ROUTES
━━━━➤ CAMPAIGNS
✕   ✕ VICTORIES
▭   NEUTRAL TERRITORY

MILES 200
KILOMETERS 300

TULI
RHODESIA
Brit. Protectorate

Limpopo

LOUIS TRICHARDT

PORTUGUESE
EAST
AFRICA

PIETERSBURG   LEYDSDORP

Olifants

BECHUANALAND
British Protectorate

DERDEPOORT

SOUTH AFRICAN
REPUBLIC
(TRANSVAAL)

LYDENBURG

KOMATIPOORT

Molopo

RUSTENBURG   PRETORIA   MIDDELBURG   BELFAST MACHADADORP
                                                                        LOURENÇO
                                                                        MARQUES

MAFEKING
Besieged
12 Oct 1899-
17 May 1900

Peace signed
31 May 1902

JOHANNESBURG
31 May 1900

Diamond Hill
9 June 1900

27 Aug
1900

BARBERTON

SWAZILAND

Maputo

VEREENIGING

VRYBURG

KLERKSDORP

STANDERTON

VOLKSRUST

Majuba Hill

VRYHEID

From India

HEILBRON

Vaal

KROONSTAD   LINDLEY   DUNDEE

ORANGE FREE STATE   ELANDSLAAGTE

18-27 Feb 1900
Paardeberg

WINBURG

Caledon

Spion Kop
22-24 Jan
1900

LADYSMITH
Besieged Nov 1899- Feb 1900

Colenso
15 Dec 1899

KIMBERLEY
11 Dec 1899

BLOEMFONTEIN
13 March 1900

ESTCOURT

NATAL

BELMONT

Orange

WEPENER

BASUTOLAND
Brit. Protectorate

PIETERMARITZBURG

Tugela

PRIESKA

Orange

SPRINGFONTEIN

DURBAN

DE AAR

COLESBERG

ALIWAL
NORTH

Stormberg
10 Dec 1899

MIDDELBURG

CAPE

COLONY

INDIAN

OCEAN

GRAAFF-REINET

Great Kei

From Cape Town

Great Fish   EAST LONDON

PORT
ELIZABETH

From Cape Town

© Richard Natkiel, 1982

The Boer War

Although it was the Dutch-speaking settlers, the Boers or Afrikaners, who sent the ultimatum, the Boer War was really started by the British, whose provocations of the Boers amounted to a successful attempt at a preventive war. In South Africa the Afrikaners out-numbered the British settlers, and the republic which President Kruger led, far to the north in the Transvaal, threatened to gain the allegiance of those Boers who lived in the two British colonies of Cape Colony and Natal. Moreover the

Transvaal had been producing gold since the mid-1880s.

In the first phase of the war, from October 1899 to January 1900, the Boers moved into Natal and Cape Colony, encouraging the local Afrikaners to join them, or at least to revolt. Mafeking, Ladysmith and Kimberley were besieged. In one week in early December the British forces lost three battles, at Stormberg, Magersfontein and, worst of all, at Colenso. The British Commander in Chief, General Buller, had made the mistake of dividing his forces to relieve Ladysmith and Kimberley at the same time. He was soon replaced by Lord Roberts, who brought General Kitchener as his chief of staff.

Kitchener decided that the British must no longer be tied to the railroads in their advance, and this extra flexibility, together with the arrival of reinforcements, helped win the Battle of the Modder River, where a Boer army was encircled and forced to surrender. This was accompanied by the relief of Kimberley, and shortly afterward the siege of Ladysmith came to an end. The Battle of Spion Kop, which preceded the relief of Ladysmith, was the hardest-fought battle of the war for both sides. Their victories enabled the British to annex the Boer Orange Free State, Bloemfontein being captured and most of the Free State's army surrendering. After some weeks Johannesburg and Pretoria were taken, and in

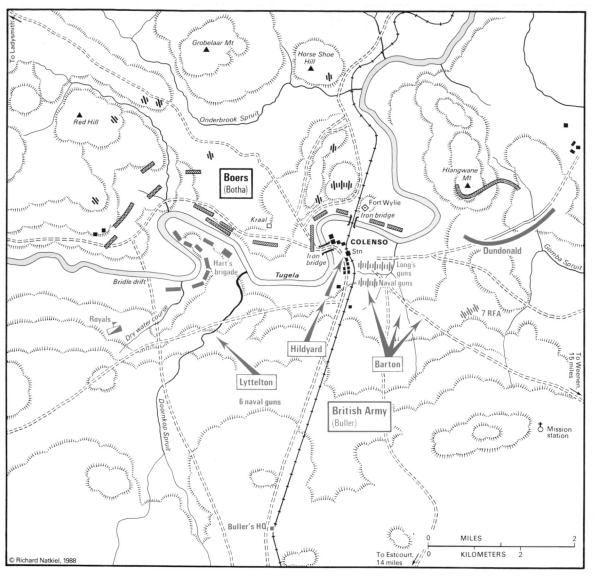

To Ladysmith

Grobelaar Mt

Horse Shoe Hill

Onderbrook Spruit

Red Hill

Boers (Botha)

Hlangwane Mt

Fort Wylie
Iron bridge

Kraal

COLENSO
Stn

Iron bridge

Hart's brigade

Tugela

Dundonald

Gomba Spruit

Bridle drift

Long's guns

Naval guns

Royals

Dry water course

7 RFA

To Weenen, 15 miles

Hildyard

Barton

Lyttelton

Doornkop Spruit

6 naval guns

British Army (Buller)

Mission station

Buller's HQ

MILES
0 — 2

KILOMETERS
0 — 2

To Estcourt, 14 miles

© Richard Natkiel, 1988

September 1900 the British were strong enough to annex the Transvaal formally.

This brought the second stage of the war to a close.

The final stage lasted longest of all. Beaten in the field, the Boers refused to surrender. Exploiting their advantages of mobility and marksmanship, they settled down into fast small-scale warfare. Their *commandos*, a kind of mounted infantry, ensured that the British could not settle down in their conquered territories but needed to maintain a large and expensive army to defend all possible targets. It was only in 1901, after Kitchener had taken over command and introduced ruthless measures which included concentration camps, burning of farmsteads, and execution of Boer irregulars, that the Boers agreed to negotiate. The Peace of Vereeniging promised the Boers self-government, from which natives would be excluded, and the preservation of their language, in exchange for which all the Boers became British subjects. In 1906 the British did grant responsible government to the Transvaal and Orange Free State, and in 1910 the Union of South Africa was formed to unite them with Cape Colony and Natal.

Above: the Battle of Colenso.
Left: Boer artillery in action.

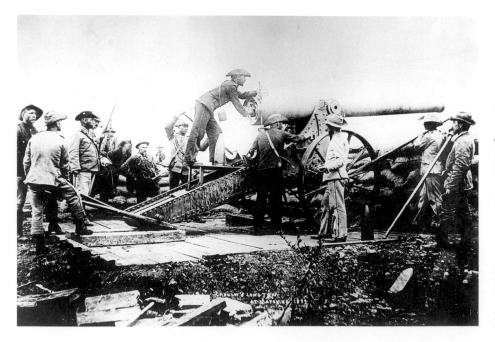

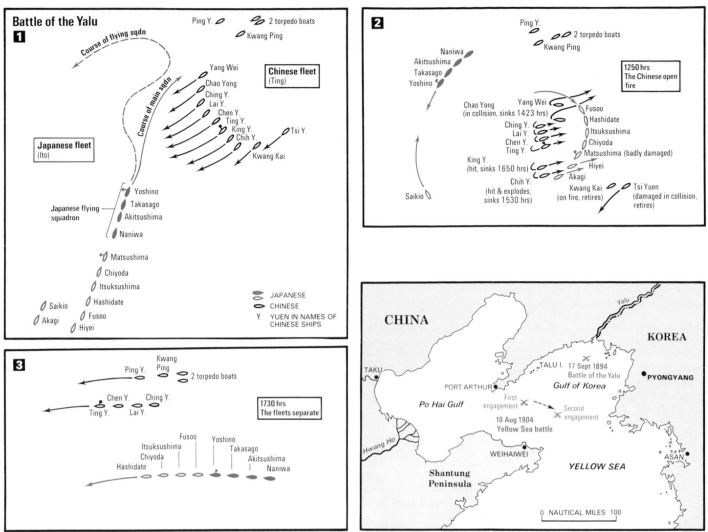

Battle of the Yalu River

The transition of Japan from a medieval society cut off from all foreign influence in the early 1850s to a modern industrial power by the end of the century is one of the most remarkable phenomena of modern times. As soon as Japan's civil war was over in 1868 students were sent to Europe to learn about engineering and shipbuilding and within 20 years the nucleus of a modern navy existed. By 1894 Japan's rulers felt able to use their new-found skills to foster commercial expansion, and inevitably began to copy the European colonial powers in acquiring possessions on the Asian mainland.

Korea, barely 100 miles from the southern Japanese islands and well-placed to command the Yellow Sea and China's northern ports, was chosen as the objective. A series of provocations followed, culminating in landing of troops in the northwest of the country. The Chinese replied by moving troops by sea, and it was this force, covered by a naval squadron, which encountered Japanese warships off the Yalu River on 17 September 1894.

Admiral Ting steamed out in line abreast at a speed of only six knots, having given his captains orders to fight in pairs wherever possible. Admiral Ito chose the more practical line ahead formation, with his fast ships in the first division. This enabled him to sweep across the Chinese front to attack the weakest ships at a range of 2-3000 yards.

As the two fleets approached across a glassy sea the Chinese opened an ineffectual fire at 5-6000 yards, but the Japanese held their fire for another 15 minutes. As the leading Japanese ships turned to port Admiral Ting in the *Ting Yuen* led her sister, the *Chen Yuen*, out ahead of the formation, trying to close with the Japanese. The Chinese force immediately lost cohesion, turning in pairs to port in a fruitless attempt to follow the Japanese movement and then losing formation as the Japanese fire intensified. The confusion was increased as Ito's flying squadron turned through 180 degrees and started to punish the ships at the rear of the Chinese line. By now the Japanese were circling around the Chinese ships, including Ting's hapless pair of battleships, firing accurately at a range of little more than a mile. Although the *Chen Yuen* succeeded in hitting the cruiser *Matsushima* with a 12-inch shell which decimated her gun crews it could only postpone the result. Four of the

Chinese ships had already been destroyed and a fifth had been sunk in collision. After four hours of intense firing, as sunset was approaching, Admiral Ting retired with his survivors to Port Arthur, where temporary repairs could be effected, and the squadron then retreated to Wei-hai-Wei.

After the battle the war was confined to troop movements by sea, bombardments in support of Japanese troops and attacks by torpedo boats on Ting's ships at Wei-hai-Wei. The Chinese defenses were inadequate, with no nets or medium-caliber guns to prevent the Japanese torpedo boats from torpedoing the flagship *Ting Yuen* and another ship.

After the fall of Port Arthur Japanese troops invested Wei-hai-Wei, and when that port fell into their hands they captured the *Chen Yuen*. The negotiated peace which followed gave Japan Korea, Formosa (Taiwan) and the Liaotung peninsula, as well as an indemnity covering half the cost of the war.

The Spanish-American War

Throughout the nineteenth century a succession of Latin American nations won their independence from Spanish rule, and by 1895 the only New World colonies left to Spain were Cuba and Puerto Rico. In that year the Cubans, as they had several times before, rebelled in an effort to throw off the Spanish yoke. The measures taken by the Spanish to put down the insurrection, harsh enough in fact, were wildly sensationalized in the American 'yellow' press and in the propaganda issued by the Cuban lobby. Popular sentiment for intervention in Cuba was already high in the US when, on 15 February 1898, the battleship USS *Maine* blew up in Havana harbor, an incident that most

Americans immediately attributed (though without compelling evidence) to Spanish sabotage. By 20 April an enraged Congress had authorized the president to use military force to secure Cuban independence and shortly thereafter Spain declared war. But since the small US Army was not immediately capable of fighting a foreign war, and a mobilization plan had yet to be drawn up, the initial burden of offensive operations perforce fell to the navy – in the form of a largely ineffective blockade of Cuba and an unexpectedly effective attack on the Spanish-held Philippines.

In the early morning hours of 1 May 1896 Commodore George Dewey of the navy's Asiatic Squadron led the cruisers *Olympia*, *Baltimore*, *Boston* and *Raleigh*, accompanied by two gunboats and a revenue cutter, into Manila Bay. Anchored at the southern end of the bay, off Cavite, was Admiral Patricio Montojo's Spanish squadron, consisting of the modern cruiser *Reina Cristina* and ten other

elderly light cruisers and gunboats. Braving fire from both the Spanish shore and naval batteries, Dewey approached to the limit of his guns' range and opened fire at 0548. The ensuing gunnery duel was interrupted at 0735 when, acting on mistaken information about a shortage of ammunition, Dewey withdrew to count casualties. There were none, so the Americans had a leisurely breakfast and then returned to the fray at 1116. By this time the dense smoke of battle had cleared sufficiently to reveal that the Spanish line was in a bad way, with the *Cristina* and the wooden-hulled *Castilla* sunk and most of the other ships heavily damaged. In little over an hour all the remaining ships had been put out of action. The only US casualties had been eight men injured when *Baltimore* was hit by a shell fired from the Cavite arsenal.

It was nearly three months before the army could take advantage of this decisive naval victory. In late July General Wesley Merritt's

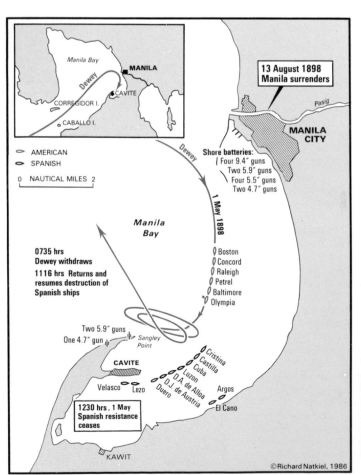

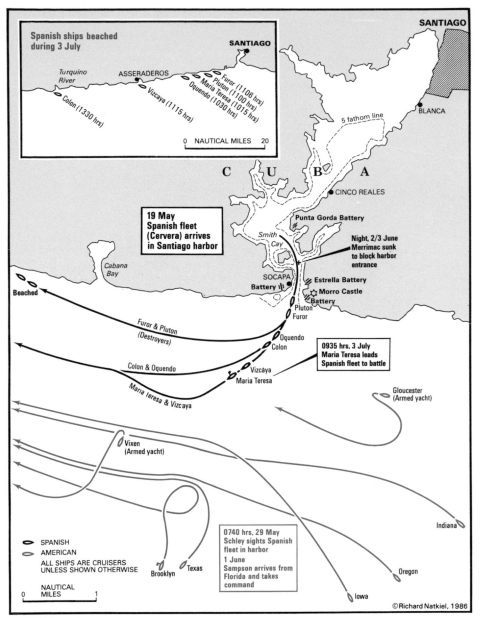

Spanish ships beached during 3 July

Turquino River

ASSERADEROS

SANTIAGO

Furor (1106 hrs)
Pluton (1100 hrs)
Maria Teresa (1015 hrs)
Oquendo (1030 hrs)

Vizcaya (1115 hrs)

Colon (1330 hrs)

0   NAUTICAL MILES   20

SANTIAGO

BLANCA

5 fathom line

C   U   B   A

CINCO REALES

19 May
Spanish fleet
(Cervera) arrives
in Santiago harbor

Punta Gorda Battery

Smith Cay

Night, 2/3 June
Merrimac sunk
to block harbor
entrance

Cabana Bay

SOCAPA
Battery

Estrella Battery

Morro Castle
Battery

Beached

Pluton
Furor

Furor & Pluton
(Destroyers)

Oquendo
Colon

0935 hrs, 3 July
Maria Teresa leads
Spanish fleet to battle

Colon & Oquendo

Vizcaya
Maria Teresa

Maria Teresa & Vizcaya

Gloucester
(Armed yacht)

Vixen
(Armed yacht)

Indiana

SPANISH
AMERICAN
ALL SHIPS ARE CRUISERS
UNLESS SHOWN OTHERWISE

0740 hrs, 29 May
Schley sights Spanish
fleet in harbor
1 June
Sampson arrives from
Florida and takes
command

Oregon

NAUTICAL
MILES
0   1

Brooklyn   Texas

Iowa

©Richard Natkiel, 1986

Left: the Battle of Santiago.
Below far left: Dewey's fleet defeats the
Spanish off Manila.
Below left: Commodore George Dewey
(seated), victor of Manila Bay.
Below: 'Teddy' Roosevelt, leader of the
Rough Riders at San Juan Hill.

ron. But Cervera avoided battle and by late May had brought his ships under the protection of the batteries dominating Santiago Bay, at the southeastern end of the island. Thus a new plan was hatched, whereby the army would first send an expedition against the forts around Santiago Bay and expose Cervera to naval attack. Accordingly, beginning on 22 June, 17,000 troops of General William R Shafter's V Corps landed at Siboney and Daiquiri, east of Santiago.

Although the landings were unopposed, Spanish General Arsenio Linares attempted to block the American advance on Santiago at Las Guasimas on 24 June. When he was worsted in this small battle he withdrew to his main defensive position on the San Juan Heights, which guarded Santiago from the east. Shafter's plan for the attack on these heights, scheduled for 1 July, included a frontal assault by General Joseph Wheeler's dismounted cavalry and a simultaneous assault on the left by General Jacob Kent's infantry division. In a co-ordinated operation General Henry Lawton's infantry was to seize the town

15,000-man VIII Corps landed in the Manila area, to find the Spanish garrison on Luzon eager to negotiate surrender terms. They were duly accepted on 13 August, two days after Spain and the US signed an armistice to end the fighting in all theaters.

Under the terms of the final peace treaty, ratified by Congress on 6 February 1899, Spain ceded the Philippines to the US, but while the Americans were still debating what to do with this unlooked-for acquisition, Emilio Aguinaldo's militant Filipino nationalists, impatient with the US military occupation, resorted to armed insurrection. By mid-summer some 35,000 US troops and 40,000 Filipino insurgents were embroiled in a comparatively formless, but nonetheless savage, guerrilla war. Though the US re-established control over Luzon in the autumn of 1899, fighting in other parts of the archipelago did not finally end until 1902, by which time 4000 Americans and perhaps 200,000 Filipinos had been killed. The pointlessness of all this was underscored by the fact that within little more

than a decade the US would grant the Philippines virtual domestic autonomy, and, after 30 more years of harmonious relations, complete sovereignty.

The Cuban Campaign

When war broke out between America and Spain in late April 1898 the US Army was subjected to intense public and political pressure to invade Cuba immediately. But the regular army numbered only 26,000, mobilization of volunteers was just beginning, training facilities and equipment were lacking and the army's high command had no strategic plan suitable for the occasion. That the army should have been able to send an expedition to Cuba as early as mid-June is remarkable; that this expedition was relatively small and ill-coordinated is less so.

The first American plan was to land troops somewhere on the northwest shore of Cuba, in the vicinity of Havana, as soon as possible after the US Navy had neutralized Spanish Admiral Pascual Cervera's Caribbean squad-

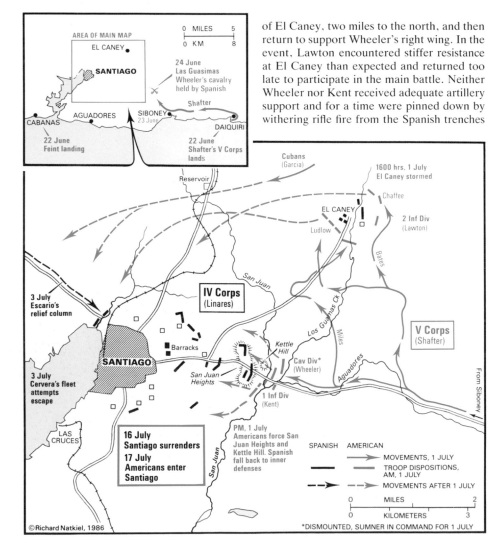

of El Caney, two miles to the north, and then return to support Wheeler's right wing. In the event, Lawton encountered stiffer resistance at El Caney than expected and returned too late to participate in the main battle. Neither Wheeler nor Kent received adequate artillery support and for a time were pinned down by withering rifle fire from the Spanish trenches atop the hills. But eventually troopers of the 10th and 19th Cavalry, assisted by Colonel Theodore Roosevelt's volunteer Rough Riders, succeeded in storming Kettle Hill, and a little later, after a Gatling gun battery had driven some of the defenders from their trenches, Kent's infantry took the main Spanish position on San Juan Hill.

While the army and the War Department were debating what to do next, Cervera, on 3 July, attempted to extricate his four cruisers and two destroyers from Santiago Bay. Even before they made their move they were intercepted by an American squadron of five cruisers (four of them of near battleship strength) and two armed yachts under the temporary command of Commodore Winfield Scott Schley. In short order five of the Spanish ships were disabled and driven aground. The sixth, the fast cruiser *Cristobel Colon*, almost escaped, but when bracketed by fire from the 13-inch guns of USS *Oregon* she too was forced ashore. In this decisive action, which lasted three hours and 40 minutes, only one US sailor was killed.

The 23,000 Spanish troops in the Santiago area now felt themselves to be in a hopeless position, and on 16 July they surrendered. On 25 July General Nelson Miles, with 3000 men, invaded Puerto Rico and encountered so little resistance that by 16 August he had secured the whole island. By this time Spain had already agreed to an armistice and preparations for peace negotiations were under way.

In all, the Cuban campaign had cost the US only 379 battle deaths, but the real cost was very much higher, since over 5000 troops succumbed to tropical diseases. In return for this, Cuban independence had been won.

The Russo-Japanese War

By 1900 conflicting colonial ambitions in Manchuria and Korea had convinced both the Japanese and Russian governments that a war was inevitable, but it was Japan which took the plunge at a carefully planned moment, in February 1904. The ice was melting in the Korean ports, modern reinforcements for the Russian Pacific Squadron were expected only in 1905, and the Trans-Siberian Railway, on which the Russians would rely to transport reinforcements, was not quite finished.

The war started with that has since been described as 'a rehearsal for Pearl Harbor.' Without any declaration of war, Japanese torpedo boats made a night attack on the Russian squadron anchored outside its base at Port Arthur. Losses were less than the Japanese had hoped, but the morale of the Russians was

shattered until, some weeks later, a new admiral, Makarov, arrived. He was a bold innovator and tactician, who could also inspire his officers and men, and under his leadership efficiency improved rapidly. Sadly he lost his life in April 1904, when his flagship, *Petropavlovsk*, struck a mine during a sortie out of Port Arthur. Offensive mine warfare, laying mines in enemy waters, was a feature of naval warfare for the first time, although mines had previously been used defensively. Subsequently the Japanese were caught in a similar trap, when the battleships *Hatsuse* and *Yashima* were also lured into a minefield and sunk.

Makarov's successor, Admiral Vitgeft, had none of his enterprise, and refused to take advantage of his 6:4 ratio of superiority in battleships. In August he was at last forced to attempt a breakout to Vladivostok but was brought to action by the Japanese Commander in Chief Admiral Togo. Both sides opened fire at maximum range without scoring any hits at first. Firing continued through the afternoon of 10 August, with neither side will-

ing to close to more decisive range. After a loss of contact Togo caught up with Vitgeft's force again, and the two lines steamed ahead in parallel, exchanging shots. The Russians were probably doing slightly better than the Japanese up to this point for their long-range gunnery proved remarkably accurate, and only chance prevented the Japanese from sustaining severe damage. Then the luck changed dramatically as the *Tsarevitch* was struck by a 12-inch shell which burst in the conning tower, killing Vitgeft and some of his staff, and wounding the captain and gunnery officer among others.

Worse was to follow, as a fault in the steering caused the *Tsarevitch* to turn circles. The next astern, the *Retvisan*, started to follow the flagship round, but when the mistake was discovered she turned in the opposite direction.

Far left: Spanish prisoners of the Americans at Santiago.
Below far left: the Battle of Santiago.
Below: Japanese artillery outside Port Arthur.

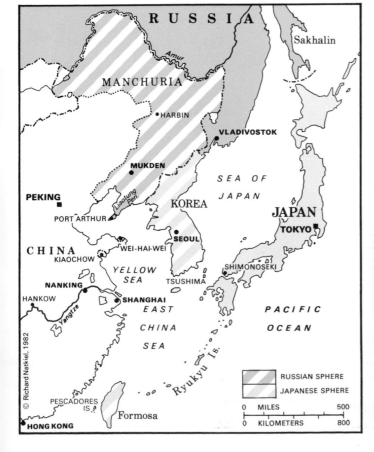

194

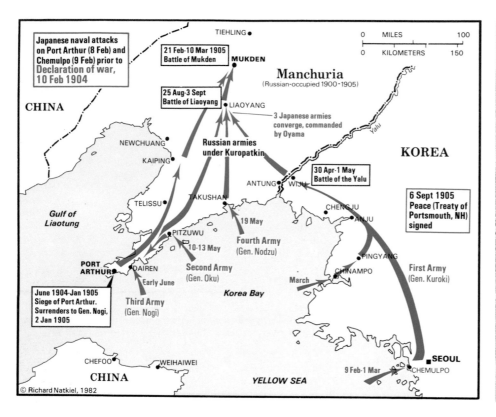

The ships astern turned in different ways, throwing the whole line into disorder, and Vitgeft's second-in-command seems to have lost his head, and signaled all ships to return to Port Arthur. The Japanese were unable to stop the Russians, despite bringing the range down to 4-5000 yards, but the *Tsarevitch* was cut off from her squadron and eventually escaped to Tsingtao, where the Germans interned her under International Law.

Japanese troops landed at Chemulpo (Inchon) on the first day of the war and advanced to the Yalu, where they won their first battle against the Russians. Further landings were made on the south Manchurian coast and soon the Japanese had cut off Port Arthur; their Third Army was left under General Nogi to besiege this strongpoint, while their main forces advanced northward against the Russian army under Kuropatkin. In the initial battles on the latter front, at Telissu, Tashihchiao and Liaoyang, the Japanese prevailed, but the Russians might have won had they been less preoccupied with their fear of defeat. In the final big battle, outside Mukden, the Russians were again beaten, but paradoxically the Japanese now faced defeat, for whereas they had reached the end of their

manpower resources the Russians were only just beginning to tap and send east their huge reserves. In the meantime, Port Arthur had surrendered, after a stubborn defense behind strong fortifications. The czarist regime then had to face the 1905 Revolution and the catastrophic naval defeat of Tsushima. Both sides were therefore ready for the Treaty of Portsmouth, which gave Japan much less than she had wanted, but opportunity enough to expand her activity in Korea and Manchuria.

The Battle of Tsushima
It had always been assumed that the Russians would send reinforcements as soon as Port Arthur was threatened but the Baltic Fleet did not sail from Kronstadt until late September 1904. It included four of the new Borodino-class battleships and a motley collection of colliers and auxiliaries, in addition to cruisers and destroyers. The reputation of the Baltic Fleet was not enhanced when on the night of 22 October lookouts mistook British fishing trawlers off the Dogger Bank in the North Sea for Japanese torpedo boats. In 12 minutes of confusion four trawlers were sunk and another was badly damaged, while the cruiser *Aurora* was hit by shells from the battleship *Orel*.

Below: General-Adjutant Kuropatkin of the
Russian Manchurian Army inspects his
officers.
Right: the attack on the Russian fleet at Port
Arthur by Japanese destroyers.

195

PORT ARTHUR

NEW CHINESE TOWN
OLD CHINESE TOWN

NOVGOROD

Retvisan aground

Six 11" howitzers
Five 10" guns

Golden Hill
Electric Cliff

Six 9" howitzers

Arsenal

Searchlights

Lutin Rock

Four 11" howitzers
TIGER'S TAIL
Four 9" howitzers

ROADS

Four 9" howitzers

Night, 23/24 Feb 1904
Cement-filled Japanese blockships
(hindered by searchlights)
attempt blockade of Port Arthur

0   NAUTICAL MILES   2

© Richard Natkiel, 1986

203m hill

NOVGOROD

PORT ARTHUR

Arsenal

Line of main land defenses

TIGER'S TAIL

KOREA BAY

LIAOTISHAN

0   NAUTICAL MILES   4

MUD DRY AT LOW WATER
PORT ARTHUR HARBOUR
DRY AT LOW WATER
MUD DRY AT LOW WATER
MANTOW HILL
SING-TSE-YUEN
CHINGTOW HILL
FORT
POND
FORT WITH QUICK FIRING GUNS
RUSSIAN DESTROYERS
LIGHTHOUSE
PINNACLE ROCK
RUSSIAN DESTROYER
AURORA
PETROPAVLOVSK
SAVASTOPOL
POLTAVA
RUSSIAN
ENCOUNTER WITH RUSSIAN DESTROYERS
COURSE OF JAPANESE DESTROYERS.
DRY DOCK
LAKE
EAST PORT BASIN
FORT
340 FEET
FORT
GUARD HOUSE
NORTH
FORT
ELECTRIC SEARCH LIGHT STATION
ELECTRIC CLIFF
DIANA
NOVIK
BAYAN
BOYARIN
POBIEDA
PALLADA
PERESVIET
RETVISAN
TSAREVITCH
COURSE OF JAPANESE DESTROYERS
ASKOLD GUARD SHIP
JAPANESE DESTROYERS HAILED TO ASKOLD

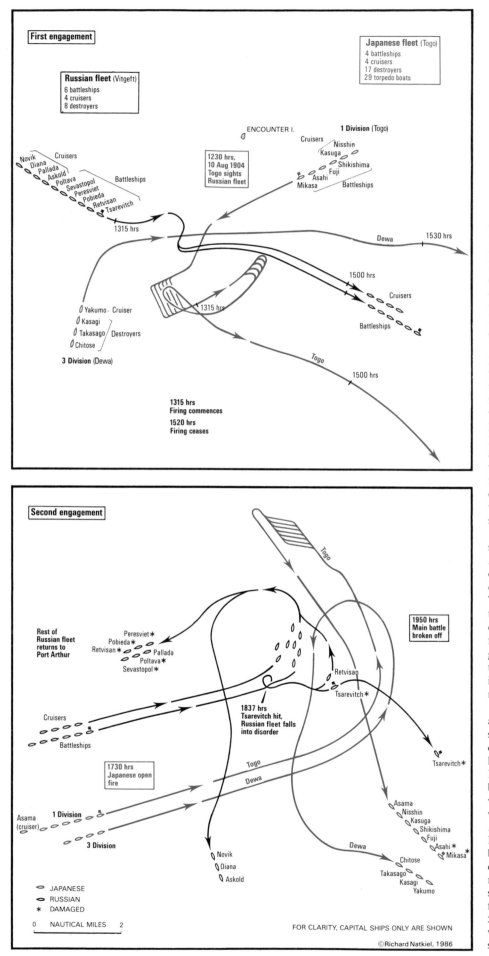

First engagement

Russian fleet (Vitgeft)
6 battleships
4 cruisers
8 destroyers

Japanese fleet (Togo)
4 battleships
4 cruisers
17 destroyers
29 torpedo boats

ENCOUNTER I.

1 Division (Togo)

Cruisers
Nisshin
Kasuga
Shikishima
Fuji
Asahi
Mikasa
Battleships

1230 hrs,
10 Aug 1904
Togo sights
Russian fleet

Novik
Diana
Pallada
Askold
Poltava
Sevastopol
Peresviet
Pobieda
Retvisan
Tsarevitch
Cruisers
Battleships

1315 hrs

Dewa   1530 hrs

1500 hrs

Cruisers

Battleships

1315 hrs

Yakumo - Cruiser
Kasagi
Takasago   Destroyers
Chitose

3 Division (Dewa)

Togo

1500 hrs

1315 hrs
Firing commences

1520 hrs
Firing ceases

Second engagement

Togo

1950 hrs
Main battle
broken off

Rest of
Russian fleet
returns to
Port Arthur

Peresviet *
Pobieda *
Retvisan *   Pallada
Poltava *
Sevastopol *

Retvisan

Tsarevitch *

1837 hrs
Tsarevitch hit,
Russian fleet falls
into disorder

Cruisers

Battleships

Togo

Tsarevitch *

1730 hrs
Japanese open
fire

Dewa

Asama
(cruiser)   **1 Division**

Asama
Nisshin
Kasuga
Shikishima
Fuji
Asahi *
Mikasa *

3 Division

Dewa

Novik
Diana
Askold

Chitose
Takasago
Kasagi
Yakumo

JAPANESE
RUSSIAN
* DAMAGED

0   NAUTICAL MILES   2

FOR CLARITY, CAPITAL SHIPS ONLY ARE SHOWN

©Richard Natkiel, 1986

Left and below left: the Russian attempt to break out of Port Arthur, thwarted by the Japanese under Togo.

The Dogger Bank incident infuriated the British, and to add to the troubles of the Russians, they were trailed by Royal Navy warships clearly spoiling for a fight. But the British held back and left the Russians to round the Cape of Good Hope and reach Nossi Bé in Madagascar, where they learned of the fall of Port Arthur. After making a rendezvous with reinforcements coming through the Suez Canal, the Russian commander Rozhdestvensky set sail for the East Indies early in March 1905.

With fine disregard for the Japanese, the Russian commander took the direct route through the China Sea, heading for Vladivostok. Anything more subtle would have been useless anyway, as the fast Japanese cruisers would have kept in touch whichever route he had followed. In fact they detected the Second Pacific Squadron early on 27 May as it approached Tsushima Strait. Little attempt was made to drive off the Japanese scouting forces and so they were able to send Togo a constant stream of radio reports on Rozhdestvensky's strength, formation, course and speed.

The Russian line was led by the new battleships *Kniaz Suvorov*, *Imperator Alexander III*, *Borodino* and *Orel*, followed by four more older battleships, then a scratch force of elderly coast defense ships and the cruisers. Togo's four battleships had been reinforced by two powerful armored cruisers to form a first division, and his remaining six large cruisers formed the second division, a more homogeneous force which had the enormous advantage of a margin of six knots speed. Even more important was the high state of training and morale in the Japanese ships.

At 1320 Togo saw the leading Russian ships ahead to port, heading on an opposite course, so he turned his ships across the Russian line of advance, then made another turn to bring his fleet on to a course parallel with the Russians, who were now on his starboard bow. As the courses of the two fleets converged slightly the flagship *Mikasa* came within 7000 yards of the Russian flagship *Kniaz Suvorov* and the Russians opened fire. Had they been able to score any hits Togo's bold tactics might have got his ships into a tight corner but, although the ships were surrounded by splashes and some secondary shells struck home, no major damage was suffered. By 1420 the distance had closed to about 5500 yards and the leading Japanese ships were concentrating their fire on Rozhdestvensky's flagship. She began to take severe

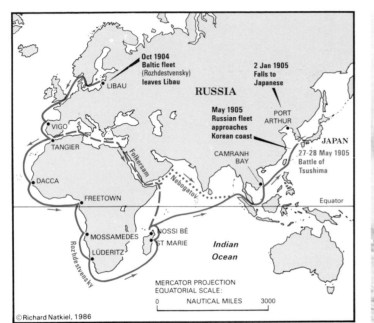

Above right: Japanese ships open fire.
Below right: the opening phase of Tsushima.

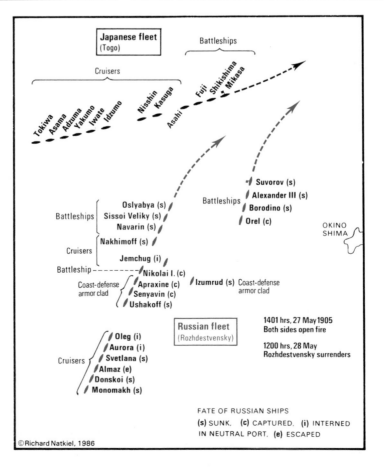

punishment from hits in her upperworks, and the admiral and several of his staff were wounded when splinters penetrated the conning tower.

Farther down the line the Japanese cruisers had inflicted severe damage on the battleship *Oslyabya* to the point where she was sinking. They drew ahead and started to engage the Russian leading division. By now the flagship *Kniaz Suvorov* had become detached from the main body and she received terrible punishment as she passed Togo's battleships at a distance of only 1000 yards. Later that day, still burning and steering erratically, she was torpedoed by a destroyer but failed to sink. She was finally sunk after sunset. Her dying commander had been taken off by a destroyer but still she fired with the few guns left undamaged. Her long agony was brought to an end with three torpedoes.

The remaining Russian ships had long since lost all formation and were circling aimlessly, trying to cope with fires and fending off attacks by the Japanese, who used their superior speed effortlessly. The battleship *Borodino* tried to shape course for Vladivostok but she and her consorts were soon under attack from Togo's battleships, which cut off their line of escape. The *Imperator Alexander III*

Below right: the destruction of the Russian fleet at Tsushima. The battle announced the arrival of Japan as a world power.

staggered out of line, heeled over and sank. Then the *Borodino* blew up when fires reached her magazines. Later the battered *Orel* surrendered to overwhelming force, while Japanese light forces rounded up other survivors.

Tsushima stunned the world by its very decisiveness. A century of inconclusive naval battles had led people to forget Nelson's concept of a battle of annihilation. Togo's tactics had kept the initiative firmly in his hands, leaving the Russians with nothing but dogged heroism to put against modern guns and training. Even more far-reaching were the consequences of the humiliation of a major European power. The first rumblings of the 1917 Bolshevik Revolution were heard in 1905 when Russia learned that its best ships and men had been destroyed by an upstart oriental nation. Suddenly Japan was a world power, and her statesmen and soldiers had taken the first steps which would lead to Pearl Harbor and Hiroshima.

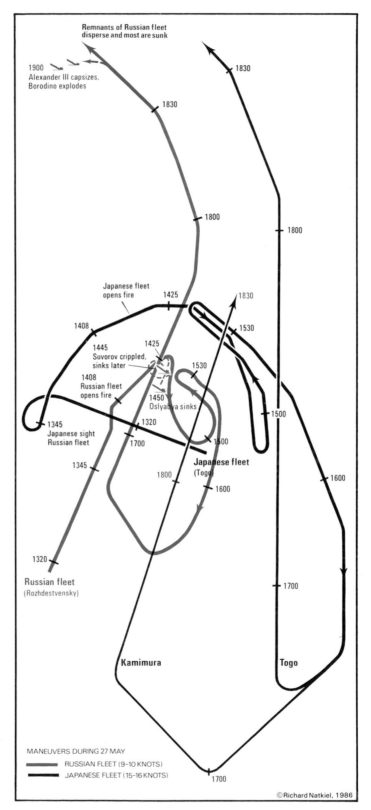

Remnants of Russian fleet disperse and most are sunk

1900 Alexander III capsizes, Borodino explodes

1830

1830

1800

1800

Japanese fleet opens fire

1425

1830

1530

1408

1445 Suvorov crippled, sinks later

1425

1530

1408 Russian fleet opens fire

1450 Oslyabya sinks

1500

1345 Japanese sight Russian fleet

1320

1700

Japanese fleet (Togo)

1345

1800

1600

1600

1320

1700

Russian fleet (Rozhdestvensky)

Kamimura

Togo

MANEUVERS DURING 27 MAY

RUSSIAN FLEET (9–10 KNOTS)

JAPANESE FLEET (15-16 KNOTS)

1700

©Richard Natkiel, 1986

The Italo-Turkish War, 1911–12

Despite being rebuffed in Abyssinia in 1889 and being treated as a poor relation at the Algeciras Conference of 1906, Italy was hungry for a place in the sun and a position like other European nations as a major colonial power. Being the weakest of the major European states, Italy had come late to the colonial supper and as a result was forced to devour the crumbs. Her positions in Eritrea and Italian Somaliland, both of questionable economic and strategic value, were insufficient to Italian pride. Successive Italian governments were determined to annex something, preferably defensible and nearby. Turkish control over Tripolitania and Cyrenaica was becoming increasingly weak in the early twentieth century, and Britain and France were not displeased to have a weak Italian buffer standing between French North Africa and British-controlled Egypt. Therefore in 1911 the Italians launched a two-pronged attack against Libya. Surprisingly they did not have an easy victory, but by early 1912, after a naval attack against the Dardanelles, the two parts of Libya were annexed, along with the Greek-speaking Dodecanese Islands off the coast of Turkey itself. An Italian empire in the Mediterranean was born chiefly because of two factors. First, Britain and France were not interested in the territory, and these two countries felt that Italy could be pushed around even more easily than the Ottoman Turks. Secondly, the Ottoman Empire was in a state of collapse and Italy could benefit from that collapse at little cost to herself while the Italian government could appear to the public as a virile colonial power with little danger of opposition. As it was the Italo-Turkish War nearly exhausted Italy's military, naval and financial resources. The seemingly cheap Italian victory proved to be more expensive than anyone in Rome bargained for.

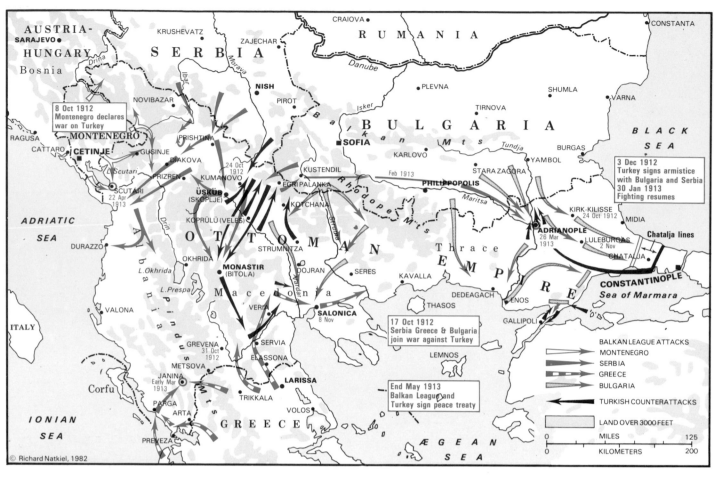

The Balkan Wars

For a hundred years before 1914 the decline of the Ottoman Empire had periodically resulted in tension and war in the Balkans as the various nationalities sought to involve rival big powers in their struggle for independence from the Turks. In 1908, for example, there had developed the Bosnia crisis, which so soured the atmosphere be-

tween Russia and Austria as to make it one of the factors in the outbreak of World War I. Bosnia had been occupied by Austria since 1878, with international agreement even though it was still formally part of the Turkish Empire. In 1908 Austria annexed it, fearing Turkish resurgence there. This was resented by the Russians, who demanded compensation for Austria's gain, but the latter called upon her ally Germany to persuade the Tsar, not very amicably, to accept the situation.

This crisis was followed by the two Balkan Wars of 1912 and 1913. Normally the Balkan nations, though united in hatred of the Turk, disliked or despised each other so much that cooperation between them was impossible. But in 1912 two Russian diplomats, who thought that all Slavs should work together under the benevolent supervision of Mother Russia, persuaded Bulgaria and Serbia to forget their differences and partition, rather than fight over, neighboring Macedonia, where the Turkish rule seemed in its final

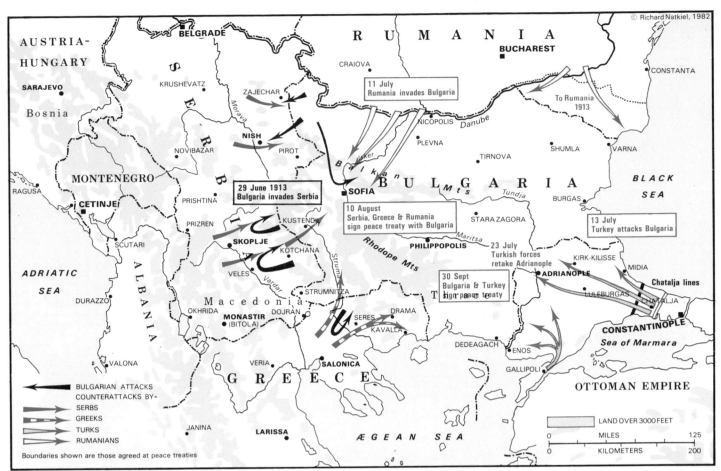

© Richard Natkiel, 1982

29 June 1913 Bulgaria invades Serbia	
11 July Rumania invades Bulgaria	
10 August Serbia, Greece & Rumania sign peace treaty with Bulgaria	
13 July Turkey attacks Bulgaria	
23 July Turkish forces retake Adrianople	
30 Sept Bulgaria & Turkey sign peace treaty	

BULGARIAN ATTACKS
COUNTERATTACKS BY—
SERBS
GREEKS
TURKS
RUMANIANS
Boundaries shown are those agreed at peace treaties

LAND OVER 3000 FEET

Below left: a Bulgarian supply column moves up to the front.
Below: guns cover the harbor at Durazzo in Albania.

stages. This diplomatic miracle was followed by another, achieved largely by *The Times* correspondent in Athens, when Bulgaria and Greece came to an agreement, despite the fact that both intended to take the port

of Salonica as soon as the Turks could be ousted. In October 1912 these three, with Montenegro, attacked Turkey and won several victories; the Bulgarian Army was only a few miles from Constantinople when disease and transport difficulties halted it. The race to Salonica was won by the Greek Army, which got there a day ahead of the Bulgarians. At a conference in London a settlement was attempted in which Turkey was required to abandon most of her European territory, and a new state of Albania was to be created on the Adriatic. The Albanian idea was bitterly resented by Serbia and by King Nikita of Montenegro. Moreover, the Bulgarians realized that Greece and Serbia were conspiring to split Macedonia between themselves, leaving out Bulgaria, which had suffered most of the casualties in the war. So, before the peace settlement was made, a new war started, with the Bulgarians attacking Greece and Serbia. The Turks and Rumanians joined in against Bulgaria, which was thoroughly defeated. The resulting Treaty of Bucharest maintained Albania, gave most of Macedonia to Greece and Serbia and part of Bulgaria's southern Dobruja to Rumania. Greece was now the dominant Balkan state, having acquired the key Aegean port of Salonica. Balkan politics remained unsettled with the competing ambitions of the Balkan states being supplemented by the influence of the great powers Austria-Hungary and Russia.

These pages: soldiers of the Czech Legion rest outside a battle-damaged building during the Russian Civil War.

OLD HUN LINE.

THE INTER-WAR YEARS

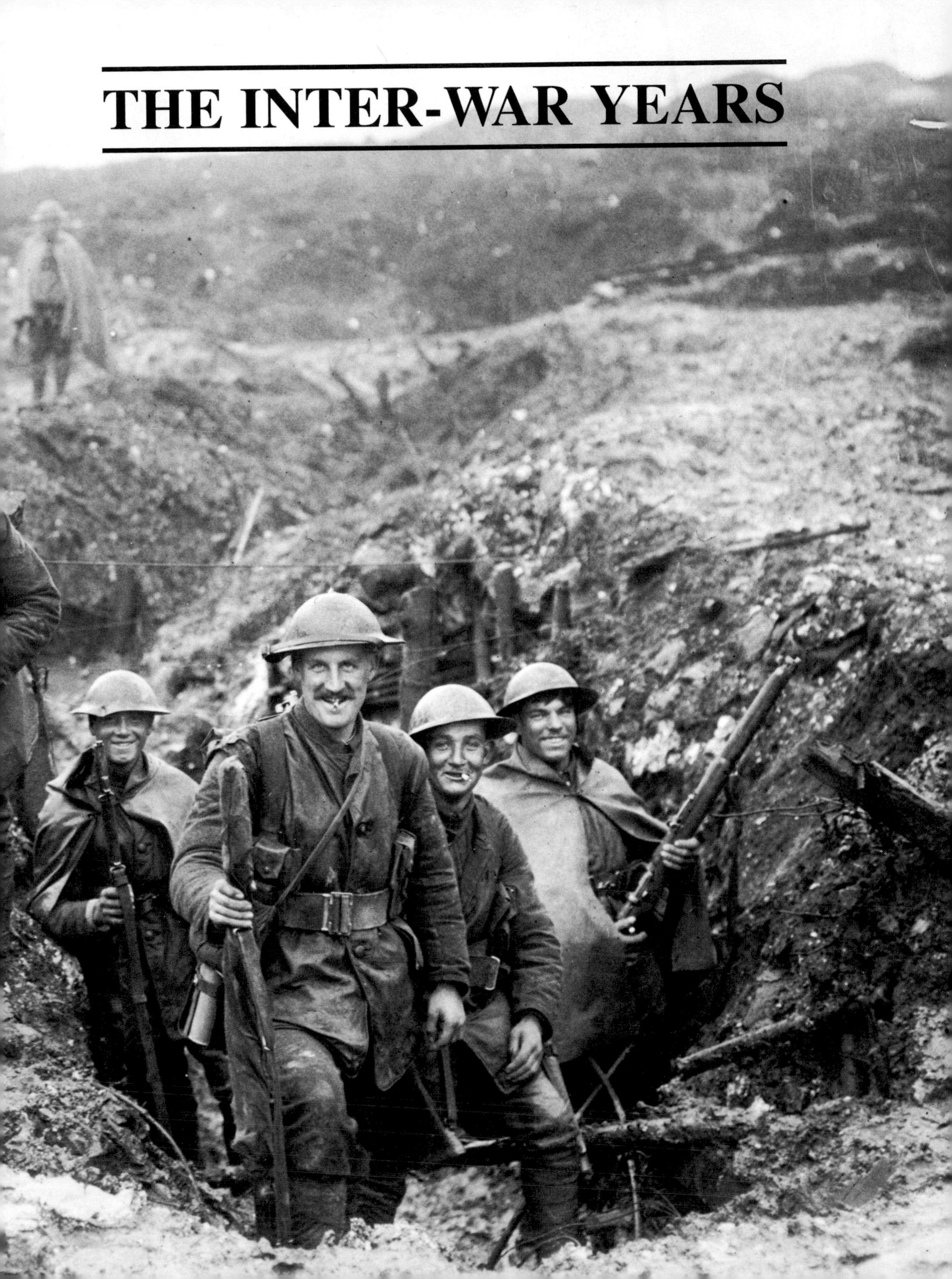

CENTRAL POWERS, 1914
NEUTRAL COUNTRIES LATER ALIGNED WITH CENTRAL POWERS
ALLIES, 1914
NEUTRAL COUNTRIES LATER ALIGNED WITH ALLIES
ALLIED WITH CENTRAL POWERS, DECLARED NEUTRALITY AT OUTBREAK OF WAR, THEN JOINED ALLIES
COUNTRIES REMAINING NEUTRAL

© Richard Natkiel, 1982

The European Alliance System, 1914

The two alliance systems of the European powers were insurance policies in case of conflict rather than a cause of war. But they did imply that once hostilities occurred between two powers, the conflict would spread.

Having defeated France in the war of 1870–71, the German chancellor, Bismarck, had sought protective alliances to isolate France and to prevent Germany having to fight a war on two fronts. His 1879 secret alliance with Austria, which had pledged the two powers to come to each other's aid in the event of attack by Russia, was supplemented in 1882 by the Triple Alliance, in which Germany, Austria, and Italy pledged mutual support in the event of an attack by

France. These alliances were still in force in 1914.

During the 1890s, to counter these agreements, France and Russia drew closer in an open alliance with secret provisions. Germany could only assume that France and Russia would come to each other's assistance in the event of either being attacked by Germany or Austria. In fact, secret conventions meant that military cooperation between France and Russia was well developed by 1914.

Britain had traditionally steered clear of continental entanglements in peacetime, but she no longer had the confidence to continue her policy of 'splendid isolation.' In 1902 came the Anglo-Japanese agreement, which offered some protection to British interests in the Far East. Then, in 1904, the *Entente Cordiale* between France and Britain settled longstanding disputes between the two countries. This was not a formal alliance and was not directed against

Germany, but in the following decade it provided the right atmosphere for Anglo-French collaboration. Such collaboration included secret military and naval understandings about which parliament knew little or nothing. One such understanding was Britain's agreement to send an expeditionary force to France in the event of a German attack. This meant that in the 1914 crisis Britain could no longer honorably follow her old and often advantageous strategy of holding back, in order to enter the conflict at a time and place and with a strength of her own choosing. It was an understanding, therefore, which was to cost Britain dear. Meanwhile, since Russia had an alliance with France, it was only natural that Britain and Russia should patch up their differences, which mainly centered around colonial rivalry in the east.

Russia had its own understanding with Serbia, so when the latter was threatened by

Below: in 1905 Count Alfred von Schlieffen devised a plan for Germany to fight a war on two fronts with France and Russia.

Austria in 1914, a conflict between Russia and Austria became imminent. Their alliances meant that Germany and France were drawn in. Britain and Italy were not, formally, required to step in. Italy decided that her partners Germany and Austria had not been attacked, and stayed out for the time being. Britain, because of her gentleman's agreements with France, and steeled by Germany's invasion of Belgium, did declare war.

And so, thanks to interlocking alliances, when in 1914 Austria made war on Serbia, Germany made war to help Austria and Russia made war to help Serbia. France made war for Russia, Britain made war for France, and Japan made war for Britain.

The Schlieffen Plan

For several decades before 1914, the possibility of a war on two fronts preoccupied the German military planners. The combined strength of Russia and France was far greater than that of Germany. A solution to this problem was proposed in 1905 by the Chief of the German General Staff, Count von Schlieffen. Germany would deploy her main strength to win a quick victory over France. Then the efficient German railroads would shift the victorious armies to the Eastern Front, where the Russians, thanks to their very sparse railroads, would only just be completing their mobilization. Against France, two armies to the south of Metz, the left wing, would initially advance against the bulk of the French Army to pin it down or to lure it eastward. Meanwhile five armies to the north of Metz would cross Belgium, turn southwest, envelop Paris, attack the rear of the main French forces and rout them.

In 1906 the younger von Moltke succeeded Schlieffen, and soon modified the plan. Notably, he strengthened the left wing at the expense of the wheeling attack through Belgium. Meanwhile, with French help the Russian railroad network was so improved that the Russians expected that they would be able to mobilize two thirds of their enormous army in eighteen days, just three days longer than the Germans planned to mobilize their own. These two circumstances alone meant that in 1914 the Schlieffen Plan would not work as anticipated.

The mechanics of the Schlieffen Plan exerted an enormous influence on the German political and diplomatic leaders. The pressure of the mobilization timetable gave every incentive for an early and perhaps hasty decision to go to war while the detailed arrangements of the plan meant that a desire to help Austria against Russia virtually compelled Germany to attack France. The violation of Belgian neutrality that the plan required was also a major motivation for Britain's decision to fight Germany. Thus the effects of the Schlieffen Plan complemented the alliance system and helped make a Balkan quarrel into a world war.

Below: the younger von Moltke succeeded von Schlieffen as Chief of the German General Staff and attempted to put the Schlieffen Plan into execution in August, 1914. He is pictured second from the right with the Kaiser during maneuvers in 1913.

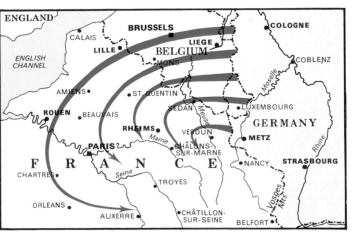

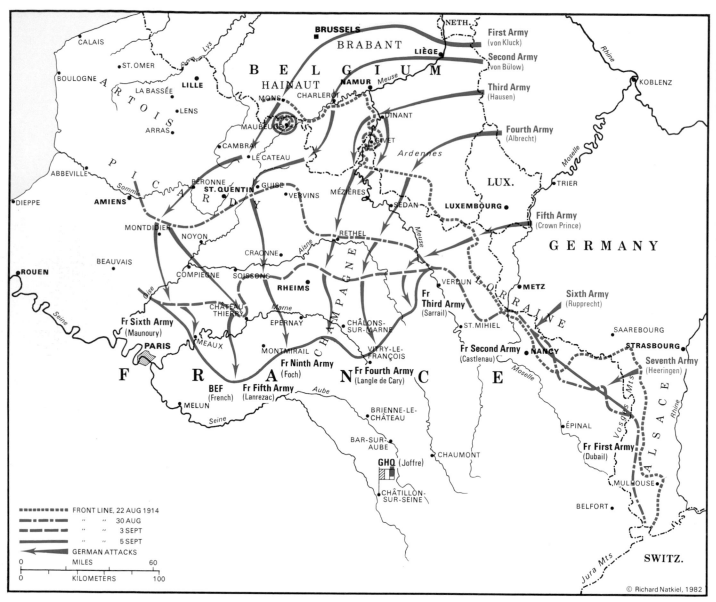

FRONT LINE, 22 AUG 1914
" " 30 AUG
" " 3 SEPT
" " 5 SEPT
GERMAN ATTACKS
MILES 0 60
KILOMETERS 0 100

© Richard Natkiel, 1982

The Battle of the Frontiers

On 3 August 1914 German cavalry led the German formations into Belgium whose territory was essential for the passage of the armies destined to wheel through northern France in accordance with the Schlieffen Plan. The Belgian defenders of the fortified city of Liège were finally subdued on 16 August. On 8 August the French Commander in Chief, Joffre, ordered his First and Second Armies to advance into Lorraine and, in accordance with the Schlieffen Plan, the German Sixth Army withdrew under this attack. In mid-August Joffre realized that the main German forces were in Belgium.

Meanwhile, although the original Schlieffen Plan had hoped to lure the main French forces into Lorraine so as to make it easier to take them in the rear from the north, personal ambitions persuaded the com-

mander of the German Sixth Army to take the offensive against the advancing French First and Second Armies. He pushed the French back out of the trap into which they had been lured, but both his Army and the supporting Seventh Army took heavy losses in this fighting. The French also suffered heavily. The Schlieffen Plan was further compromised when the German First, Second and Third Armies, advancing through Belgium, had to detach part of their strength to take care of Antwerp and Namur, and when Kluck's First Army was ordered to turn southwestward instead of taking the westward course laid down in the Plan. This latter change also meant that an opportunity to take the British Expeditionary Force (BEF) from the flank at Mons was lost. The BEF was able to make a fighting withdrawal from Mons.

As the German plan became clear, Joffre launched his Third and Fourth Armies, into the difficult Ardennes region to cut the three northern German armies from their bases. This advance was unsuccessful. More-over, it meant that the BEF and the French

Fifth Army alone had to bear the brunt of the German attack as it wheeled south-westward. On 22 August the Fifth Army was mauled at Charleroi by the German Second and Third Armies, and the French left wing began to retreat toward Paris.

Above right: a column from the 2nd Battalion Scots Guards marches through a Belgian village in 1914.
Right: Belgian troops man a barricade outside Louvain during the retreat to Antwerp, 1914.

The Battle of the Marne

As the German right wing wheeled toward Paris, the French created their Sixth Army to cover the capital. Back at his headquarters, still in Germany, Moltke urged a rapid advance so as to allow the French no time to recover. Kluck's First Army was to advance west of the Oise and pass to the west of Paris. Bülow's Second Army was to move directly toward Paris, while the Third and Fourth Armies were to march, respectively, on Château-Thierry and Epernay. Further to the east, the Sixth and Seventh Armies were to prevent the French advancing into Lorraine and Alsace, while the Fifth Army was to besiege the key French fortress at Verdun. Kluck and Bülow, with Moltke's approval, soon modified this plan; Kluck's army was to move to the east, so as to give better support to Bülow. For some reason, both commanders took little notice of reports that the French were bringing troops by rail to places such as Amiens and Montdidier.

On 1 September Joffre ordered Maunoury's Sixth Army to retire toward Paris, and hinted that this Army, with the Paris garrison, might be used in an offensive role. Meanwhile Kluck's and Bülow's armies moved more and more east of their intended line of advance. The German First Army, which was to have passed to the west of Paris, was now well to the east, crossing the Marne and paying little attention to the skirmishes on its right flank as Maunoury's patrols made contact. Joffre, meanwhile, strengthened his defenses by forming the Ninth Army, under Foch, to fill the gap between his Fourth and Fifth Armies, and then began to plan a counter-offensive.

This counter-offensive, known as the Battle of the Marne, consisted of numerous engagements all the way from the Parisian region to the frontier near Verdun. On 5 September fighting near the River Ourcq between the French Sixth Army and Kluck's right flank grew fiercer. When Kluck realized the seriousness of his situation, he transferred two corps from his left flank. This had the effect of widening the gap between his army and Bülow's Second Army. To help Maunoury cope with this German reaction the Governor of Paris, General

Galliéni, commandeered 1200 taxi-cabs to take reinforcements to him from the Paris garrison. However, Maunoury was saved when the French Fifth Army, which the Germans had thought to be in full retreat, fell upon Kluck's left wing. This French attack, in the direction of Montmirail, threatened the flank of Bülow's Second Army, forcing it to retire behind the River Petit Morin on 7 September. A further French success made Bülow retire another six or seven miles east, opening farther the gap between his army and Kluck's First Army. An attempt by the German Third Army to repair the situation by breaking through Foch's Ninth Army was hard-fought but unsuccessful.

The smaller BEF faced the gap between the German First and Second Armies. A personal appeal from Joffre to the British commander, Sir John French, had secured British cooperation in the intended French offensive. On 6 September the BEF crept forward, meeting no resistance. Its progress was slow, but it outflanked two German armies; as a French commentator later put it, 'Sir John French saved the situation even though he did not understand it.' Although it took the British three days to move forward 25 miles, both the German and French Commanders in Chief saw that the situation was now dramatically changed. Joffre ordered his Fifth Army to cover the British right flank. Moltke, whose headquarters were still outside France, sent a staff officer to assess the situation and he ordered a withdrawal. The Germans withdrew to the Aisne and dug themselves in. The Battle of the Marne had lasted seven days, and marked the failure of the Schlieffen Plan.

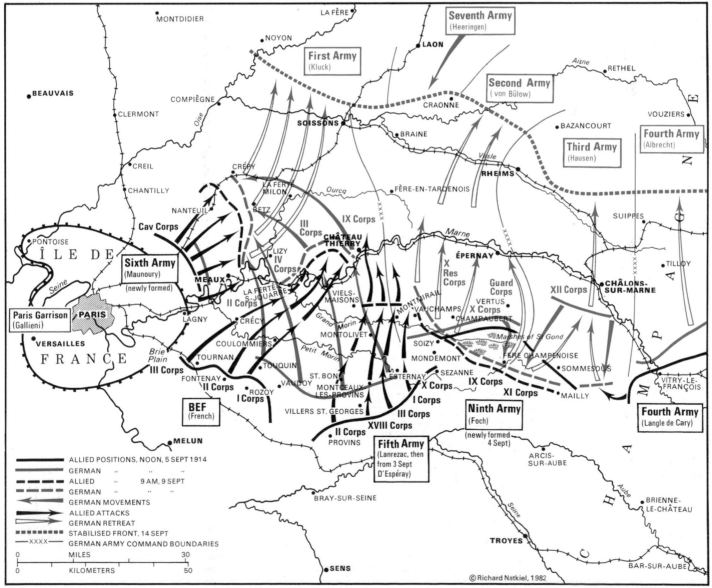

MONTDIDIER

LA FÈRE

Seventh Army
(Heeringen)

NOYON

LAON

First Army
(Kluck)

Aisne

RETHEL

BEAUVAIS

COMPIÈGNE

CRAONNE

Second Army
(von Bülow)

VOUZIERS

CLERMONT

Oise

BAZANCOURT

Fourth Army
(Albrecht)

SOISSONS

BRAINE

CREIL

Vesle

RHEIMS

Third Army
(Hausen)

CRÉPY

CHANTILLY

LA FERTÉ
MILON

Ourcq

FÈRE-EN-TARDENOIS

SUIPPES

NANTEUIL

BETZ

IX Corps XXXX

Marne

Cav Corps

III
Corps

CHÂTEAU
THIERRY

ÉPERNAY

TILLOY

PONTOISE

ÎLE DE

LIZY
IV
Corps

Sixth Army
(Maunoury)

MEAUX

X
Res
Corps

VERTUS

**Guard
Corps**

X Corps

XII Corps

CHÂLONS-
SUR-MARNE

Seine

(newly formed)

LA FERTÉ-
S-JOUARRE

II Corps

VIELS-
MAISONS

VAUCHAMPS

MONTMIRAIL

CHAMPAUBERT

Paris Garrison
(Gallieni)

PARIS

LAGNY

Grand Morin

MONTOLIVET

Marshes of St Gond

VERSAILLES

CRÉCY

SOIZY

MONDEMONT

FÈRE CHAMPENOISE

SOMMESOUS

*Brie
Plain*

Petit Morin

ST. BON

COULOMMIERS

FRANCE

III Corps

TOURNAN

TOUQUIN

VAUDOY

ESTERNAY

SÉZANNE

IX Corps

MAILLY

VITRY-LE-
FRANÇOIS

FONTENAY

II Corps

ROZOY

ST. BON

MONTCEAUX
LES-PROVINS

X Corps

XI Corps

I Corps

VILLERS ST. GEORGES

III Corps

Ninth Army
(Foch)

BEF
(French)

II Corps

XVIII Corps

(newly formed
4 Sept)

ARCIS-
SUR-AUBE

MELUN

PROVINS

Fifth Army
(Lanrezac, then
from 3 Sept
D'Espéray)

BRIENNE-
LE-CHÂTEAU

Seine

Aube

BRAY-SUR-SEINE

Fourth Army
(Langle de Cary)

	ALLIED POSITIONS, NOON, 5 SEPT 1914
	GERMAN " " "
	ALLIED " 9 AM, 9 SEPT
	GERMAN " "
	GERMAN MOVEMENTS
	ALLIED ATTACKS
	GERMAN RETREAT
	STABILISED FRONT, 14 SEPT
XXXX	GERMAN ARMY COMMAND BOUNDARIES

TROYES

BAR-SUR-AUBE

0   MILES   30

0   KILOMETERS   50

SENS

© Richard Natkiel, 1982

Bottom: Russian troops prepare to camp
on the German frontier in November 1914.

Map labels:
Königsberg Garrison
KÖNIGSBERG
LABIAU
Cav Corps
XX Corps
I Corps
TAPIAU
INSTERBURG
STALLUPÖNEN
III Corps
18 Aug
GUMBINNEN
21 Aug
1 Cav Div
Remained here
ALLENBURG
First Army
(Rennenkampf)
Crossed border
17 Aug
IV Corps
BRAUNSBERG
XVII Corps
I Res Corps
NORDENBURG
GOLDAP
I Corps
to Usdau
BARTENSTEIN
3 Res Div
ANGERBURG
1 Cav Div
G E R M A N Y
Alle
SUWALKI
Eighth Army
(Prittwitz,
then Hindenburg)
RASTENBURG
LÖTZEN
Masurian
Lakes
E A S T   P R U S S I A
WARTENBURG
SENS-
BURG
AUGUSTOW
ALLENSTEIN
BISCHOFSBURG
NIKOLAIKEN
LYCK
II Corps
21 Aug, transferred
from Second to
First Army
OSTERODE
3 Res Div
JOHANNISBURG
HOHENSTEIN
GRAJEWO
TANNENBERG
ORTELSBURG
R U S S I A
XX Corps
WILLENBERG
4 Cav Div
VI Corps
OSOWIEC
USDAU
NIEDENBURG
XIII Corps
SOLDAU
XV Corps
OSTROLENKA
XXIII Corps
Second Army
(Samsonov)
Crossed border
21/22 Aug
I Corps
MLAWA
P O L A N D
Narew

Legend:
FRONT LINE, EVENING 25 AUG 1914
RUSSIAN ATTACKS
GERMAN MOVEMENTS
GERMAN FORTIFIED POSITIONS
HELD DURING RUSSIAN ADVANCE
MAIN RAILROADS
OTHER RAILROADS
MILES 0 — 50
KILOMETERS 0 — 80

The Battle of Tannenberg

The German Schlieffen Plan had relied on a slow Russian mobilization, but in 1914 not only did the Russians mobilize faster than Schlieffen had envisioned, but in order to help the French they sent two armies into East Prussia even before mobilization was completed. Rennenkampf's First Army moved westward while Samsonov's Second Army moved northward from Poland. There was little liaison between these two armies, and there was personal antipathy between their commanders; Rennenkampf had let Samsonov down in the Russo-Japanese War, and had had his face publicly slapped by the latter on a Manchurian railway station. In addition, the Russian Army was poorly supplied and its communications were weak; as the Germans soon found, Russian radio messages were uncoded.

Nevertheless, so weak were the German forces in the east, and so unexpected the Russian assault, that the German Eighth Army was defeated at Gumbinnen and had to withdraw to a new defense line astride the Masurian Lakes, where it was in danger of being caught between the two Russian armies. Moltke became alarmed, dismissed its commander, Prittwitz, and sent out a retired General, Hindenburg, with Luden-

dorff as Chief of Staff. A few units were withdrawn from the Western Front and sent east.

In fact, these measures were unnecessary, because the German corps commanders on the scene, as well as the Eighth Army's director of operations, Hoffmann, were well in command of the situation. Hoffmann's plan was to hold Rennenkampf with just a single cavalry division, anticipating that the Russian general's characteristic caution would hold him back. The bulk of the forces could then be sent against Samsonov, whom it was intended to encircle. Making good use of rail transport, and benefiting from intercepted Russian radio messages, the plan succeeded. After capturing one or two towns, the Russians realized on 22 August that they were in danger of encirclement but the order to withdraw came too late. Samsonov's underfed and confused army was virtually destroyed near Tannenberg, most of its soliders being taken prisoner. Samsonov shot himself. Rennenkampf, meanwhile, had advanced toward the Masurian Lakes and, because the German forces were now tired, was able to resist their attack, withdrawing from Prussia slowly and without losing control.

Below: a German soldier escorts captured Russian infantry, who are towing their machine guns.

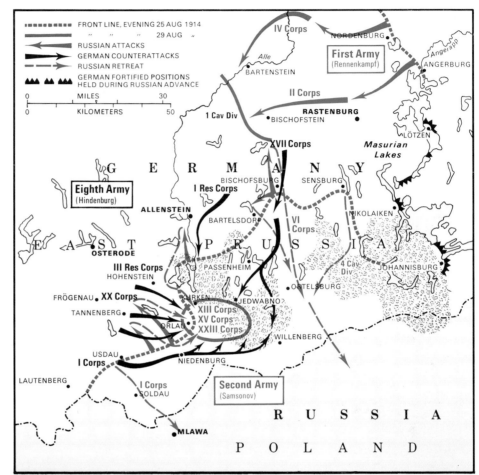

FRONT LINE, EVENING 25 AUG 1914
" " " 29 AUG "
RUSSIAN ATTACKS
GERMAN COUNTERATTACKS
RUSSIAN RETREAT
GERMAN FORTIFIED POSITIONS
HELD DURING RUSSIAN ADVANCE

MILES 30
KILOMETERS 50

IV Corps
NORDENBURG
First Army
(Rennenkampf)
ANGERBURG
Angerapp
Alle
BARTENSTEIN
II Corps
RASTENBURG
1 Cav Div
BISCHOFSTEIN
LÖTZEN
XVII Corps
Masurian Lakes
G E R M A N Y
Eighth Army
(Hindenburg)
BISCHOFSBURG
SENSBURG
I Res Corps
ALLENSTEIN
BARTELSDORF
NIKOLAIKEN
VI Corps
E A S T   P R U S S I A
OSTERODE
PASSENHEIM
4 Cav Div
JOHANNISBURG
III Res Corps
HOHENSTEIN
ORTELSBURG
FRÖGENAU **XX Corps**
KURKEN UEDWABNO
XIII Corps
TANNENBERG
XV Corps
ORLAU
XXIII Corps
WILLENBERG
USDAU
I Corps
NIEDENBURG
LAUTENBERG
I Corps
SOLDAU
Second Army
(Samsonov)
R U S S I A
MLAWA
P O L A N D

The Race to the Sea

Apart from defeating the Germans' Schlieffen Plan, the Battle of the Marne marked the beginning of the end for mobile warfare. As soon as the German retreat began, British and French generals talked of an end to the war within a month or so but the Allied offensive was not as rapid as the German advance had been. As soon as the Germans dug themselves into defensive positions it became clear that the machine gun and other products of modern war technology had given the defense a great advantage over the attack. However, before this realization dawned, both sides sought to gain positions from which they could launch outflanking attacks. Their battle-lines ended north of the Aisne, and each tried to extend northward so as to turn his opponent's flank. This meant that they moved northward until the open flanks were closed by the sea. This short phase of the war is often called the 'race to the sea' even though it was essentially a race to the flanks; both sides, however, realized the importance of the Channel ports through which British supplies and troops had to pass. The new German Commander in Chief, Falkenhayn (who had replaced Moltke, dismissed as soon as the Battle of the Marne was lost), was the first to realize the possibilities of an outflanking movement, but he had insufficient forces to carry out his intentions. Joffre was slow to abandon his strategy of a frontal assault, and missed his chance.

One reason the Germans were short of troops was that many of their forces were engaged in Belgium, where the Belgian Army continued to resist. The siege of the fortified city of Antwerp demanded many troops. The British and French were reluctant to send help to the Belgians, although Churchill did raise a small naval division to help defend Antwerp. Even after Antwerp fell the Belgians continued their fight, which had the effect of hampering the Germans in the 'race to the sea.'

Far right top: German gunners manhandle a field piece.
Far right: troops of the British Expeditionary Force rest in a Belgian village, October 1914.

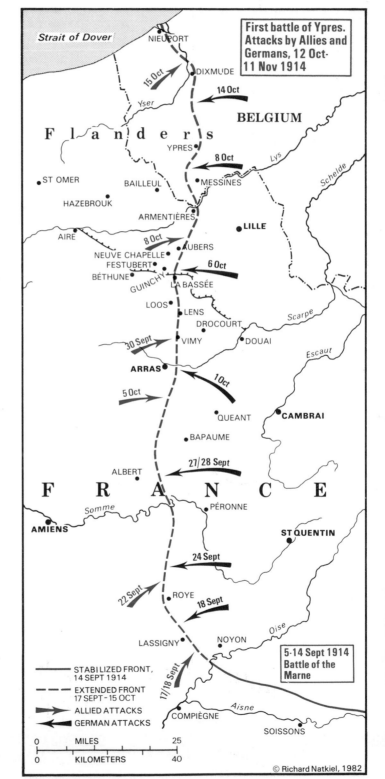

First battle of Ypres. Attacks by Allies and Germans, 12 Oct–11 Nov 1914

STABILIZED FRONT, 14 SEPT 1914
EXTENDED FRONT 17 SEPT–15 OCT
ALLIED ATTACKS
GERMAN ATTACKS

5-14 Sept 1914 Battle of the Marne

0   MILES   25
0   KILOMETERS   40

© Richard Natkiel, 1982

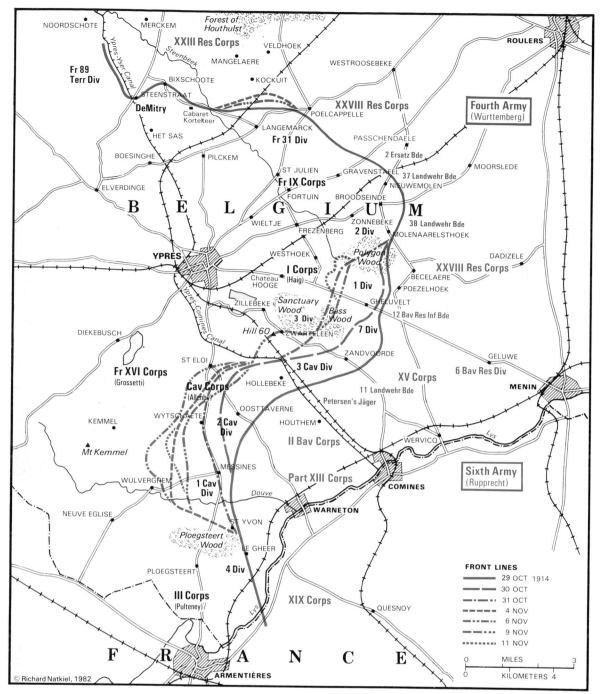

NOORDSCHOTE MERCKEM · *Forest of Houthulst* · ROULERS
XXIII Res Corps · VELDHOEK
Ypres-Yser Canal · MANGELAERE · WESTROOSEBEKE
Fr 89 Terr Div · BIXSCHOOTE · KOCKUIT
STEENSTRAAT
DeMitry · Cabaret KorteKeer · POELCAPPELLE · **XXVIII Res Corps** · Fourth Army (Württemberg)
HET SAS · LANGEMARCK
Fr 31 Div · PASSCHENDAELE
BOESINGHE · PILCKEM · 2 Ersatz Bde · MOORSLEDE
ELVERDINGE · ST JULIEN · GRAVENSTAFEL · 37 Landwehr Bde
Fr IX Corps · NIEUWEMOLEN
FORTUIN · BROODSEINDE
B E L G I U M
WIELTJE · ZONNEBEKE · 38 Landwehr Bde
FREZENBERG · **2 Div** · MOLENAARELSTHOEK
YPRES · WESTHOEK · *Polygon Wood* · DADIZELE
I Corps (Haig) · **1 Div** · BECELAERE · **XXVIII Res Corps**
Chateau HOOGE · POEZELHOEK
ZILLEBEKE · *Sanctuary Wood* · *Bass Wood* · GHELUVELT
3 Div · **7 Div** · 12 Bav Res Inf Bde
DIEKEBUSCH · Hill 60 · ZWARTELEEN
ZANDVOORDE · GELUWE
ST ELOI · **3 Cav Div** · 6 Bav Res Div
Fr XVI Corps (Grossetti) · **XV Corps** · MENIN
Cav Corps (Allenby) · HOLLEBEKE · 11 Landwehr Bde
WYTSCHAETE · OOSTTAVERNE · Petersen's Jäger
KEMMEL · **2 Cav Div** · HOUTHEM
Mt Kemmel · **II Bav Corps** · WERVICQ · *Lys*
MESSINES · Sixth Army (Rupprecht)
WULVERGHEM · **1 Cav Div** · **Part XIII Corps** · **COMINES**
Douve
NEUVE EGLISE · ST YVON · WARNETON
Ploegsteert Wood · LE GHEER
PLOEGSTEERT · **4 Div**
III Corps (Pulteney) · **XIX Corps** · QUESNOY
Lys
F R A N C E · **ARMENTIÈRES**
© Richard Natkiel, 1982

FRONT LINES
— 29 OCT 1914
— 30 OCT
— 31 OCT
— 4 NOV
— 6 NOV
— 9 NOV
— 11 NOV

0 MILES 3
0 KILOMETERS 4

The First Battle of Ypres

Toward the end of the 'race to the sea' both sides made a last and almost simultaneous effort to turn their opponent's flank. The BEF moved north by train from the Aisne to La Bassée, aiming to outflank the Germans near Ypres. The Germans were moving to the same town from the other direction, in the hope of outflanking the Allies. The two attacks collided. Although the British troops were fresh, not having been required to fight very hard in the Battle of the Marne, they were smaller in numbers, the Germans having brought up a new reserve corps, largely composed of student volunteers who had been given little military training.

On 20 October the Germans attacked with great spirit, in mass formations. The British infantry, whose rapid rifle fire had long been well rehearsed in training, took a fearsome toll. However, at one point the Germans did breach the British lines, but the defenders were able to bring up reinforcements sufficiently fast to hold the attackers. Outnumbered and dug in, the British continued to conduct a solid defense, though at the expense of heavy casualties. The fighting front was quite narrow, and with each side being reinforced daily it was possible to feed in thousands of men to replace the losses. After their lack of success on 20 October, the Germans attacked again on 31 October, but could not dislodge the British. Finally, just outside Ypres, at Nun's Wood, the Prussian Guard was committed to the battle on 11 November. Again there was much slaughter and little movement. In all, the Germans lost about 135,000 killed and wounded. The BEF losses were smaller, but meant that that force, which was the best part of Britain's professional army, was shattered.

Below: a German 5.9-inch howitzer battery in action on the Western Front, November 1914. This weapon was perhaps the most effective artillery piece employed during World War I.

The Western Front at the End of 1914

The 'race to the sea' came to a natural end when both armies extended their lines to Nieuport, on the North Sea just inside Belgium. The Western Front now stretched hundreds of miles from there down to the Swiss frontier. Only a small part of Belgium was unoccupied by the Germans, but the Belgian Army was still fighting. The German line also enclosed much of north-western France, which was the site of the French coal industry and much of her steel industry and engineering. The Channel ports, so important for the movement of British supplies and troops, seemed secure.

It was now realized that entrenchment rendered warfare static, yet no troops could survive against modern weapons without entrenchment. Later, the machine gun was singled out as the decisive instrument of mass slaughter. But in the early part of the war, at least, the magazine rifle was enough to dampen an assault. As the Germans had discovered at Mons and at Ypres, British infantry could manage fifteen rounds per minute; this was considerably less than a machine gun, but as the numbers of rifles was as large as the number of infantrymen and, as rifles were usually better-aimed than machine guns, the lethal effects were not dissimilar.

It was thought that heavy bombardment might enable attacks to break through. But at the end of 1914 the artillery was not yet sufficiently organized nor were the munitions industries ready to deliver shells at the rate needed. In this way, and in others, trench warfare meant that the war had become a conflict between industries as well as between soldiers. Britain and Germany were well placed to increase their output of munitions and weapons, but Austria and Russia were not so fortunate. France had much to do to recover from the loss of the industrial areas near the Belgian border.

The advantage given to the defender by trench warfare enabled the Germans to transfer troops to the east, where their Austrian allies were retreating before the Russians. The first such reinforcements were sent just as the Battle of Ypres was ending, and helped to turn the tide of war against the Russians.

© Richard Natkiel, 1982

The Battle of Heligoland Bight

Although the Royal Navy had given up any idea of maintaining a close blockade of Germany at the outbreak of war in August 1914, both sides still believed that a great sea battle would follow within weeks, if not days. As, however, neither side was prepared to risk its expensive capital ships, what fighting there was fell mainly to the light forces.

The first big operation was a British raid on the German outposts in the Heligoland Bight, to occupy the German High Seas Fleet's attention while the British Expeditionary Force was being transported to France. The plan was ambitious, involving an outer patrol line of submarines which was to decoy German torpedo boats and destroyers out to sea, where they could be attacked by light cruisers and destroyers.

The forces selected were the Harwich Force of cruisers and destroyers under Commodore Tyrwhitt and submarines under Commodore Keyes, but poor staffwork at the Admiralty re-

sulted in neither commander being told that reinforcements had been sent, in the form of a light cruiser squadron and five battlecruisers from the Grand Fleet, under the command of Vice Admiral Beatty. As well as this potential source of confusion another error, caused by inexperience, was the uninhibited use of radio signals, which ought to have warned the Germans of the British approach.

In spite of the errors, the Germans were still caught on the wrong foot early on the morning of 28 August, for their heavy units were still at anchor in the Jade River, without steam up and penned behind the bar until high tide.

28 Aug 1914 Battle of Heligoland Bight

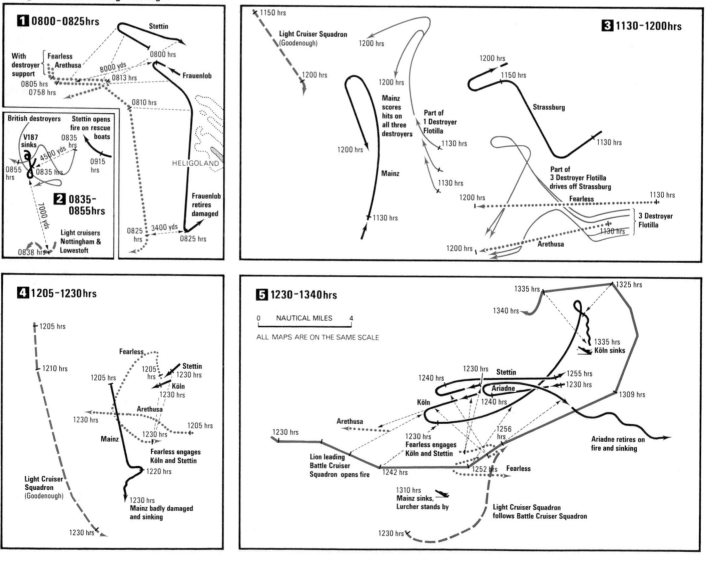

Above: the British light cruiser *Amphion* hits a mine on 7 August 1914.
Left: Sir Roger Keyes, seen here as a Vice-Admiral later in his career, devised the British battle plan at Heligoland Bight.

Their first hint of a major action came at 0700 when the destroyer *G.194* came under fire from HMS *Laurel*. During the next hour the light cruisers *Arethusa* and *Fearless* and 32 destroyers engaged the German inner patrol line, although the hazy conditions made accurate shooting almost impossible.

The Germans' luck changed dramatically when the light cruisers *Frauenlob* and *Stettin* arrived on the scene at 0800, for they managed to silence the *Arethusa* with 35 hits. Their intervention did little to save the torpedo boats, for the British destroyers continued to engage them fiercely, and eventually *V.187* sank. What was already a confused battle became worse when at 0838 two strange four-funneled cruisers were sighted approaching. Thinking they were German reinforcements, the battered *Arethusa* and the *Fearless* prepared for a desperate fight, but the arrivals soon identified themselves as HMS *Nottingham* and HMS *Lowestoft*, the first of Commodore Goodenough's four light cruisers, the reinforcements sent by the Admiralty. They had arrived in the nick of time, for the *Strassburg* had just appeared out of the mist and had opened fire at long range.

The British force was now intent on extricating itself, for the time allowed for the raid had long passed, and every minute spent in these dangerous waters increased the risk as German ships raised steam in the Jade. The next ship on the scene was the light cruiser *Mainz*, which scored several devastating hits on the British destroyers. For the second time the *Arethusa* prepared to go down fighting, but suddenly the *Mainz* was hit by a destroyer's torpedo. She began to sink slowly, and Goodenough's four light cruisers closed in for the kill.

Commodore Tyrwhitt had already sent a signal asking for reinforcements, and to Vice Admiral Beatty this was ample justification for a bold if risky counterstroke. Disregarding the risk of mines and torpedoes he took his flagship HMS *Lion* and the *Queen Mary*, *Princess Royal*, *Invincible* and *New Zealand* headlong into the fight.

The sight of these enormous ships, thrusting through the seas and firing their heavy guns, marked a disastrous turn for German fortunes. The *Strassburg* prudently fled into the mist, but a salvo of shells caught the *Köln* and inflicted grievous damage. Then the *Ariadne* blundered out of the mist, and it was her turn to be blasted. She took a rapid list to starboard, and with fires glowing lurched away, trying to get to safety.

While the *Arethusa* and her force withdrew under the guns of Goodenough's light cruisers the battlecruisers headed north and then west to find the crippled *Köln*. She was relocated at 1325, and survived this second battering for only ten minutes before sinking with all hands. The entire British force could now withdraw to the northwest, knowing that the German heavy forces were too late to intervene.

Against the backdrop of World War I the action of 28 August 1914 was no more than an ill-planned skirmish, in which luck had played a big part in saving the British from embarrassing losses. But fortune always favors the bold, and the British had sunk three light cruisers and a destroyer and inflicted heavy casualties. The moral effects, however, far outweighed the matériel losses. The Kaiser reiterated his warnings to his Naval Staff about risking losses in battle, and plans for an offensive policy in the North Sea were hurriedly shelved. The Royal Navy could overlook the slipshod planning of the operation and rejoice at its ability to operate in the enemy's 'back yard' for nearly six hours without suffering more than minor damage to a single light cruiser and some destroyers.

Bottom: Turkish artillery fire scores a near-miss on a pier at Gallipoli.
Right: a congested clutter of sandbagged shelters and dugouts huddle on Anzac Beach, 1915.
Far right: the steamer *River Clyde* aground on 'V' Beach during the Gallipoli operation, April 1915. The landings in this sector were the most costly of the initial attacks.

Gallipoli

When the Western Front became static British ministers began to seek ways of livening up the war to reach a quick victory. Turkey had entered the war on the German side in October 1914, and this had raised problems for Russia. Some British ministers, including Kitchener, the War Minister, and Churchill, the First Lord of the Admiralty, favored an attack on the Dardanelles. This, it was claimed, would obtain the capture of Constantinople, the surrender of Turkey, and a supply route by which munitions could be passed to the enormous but poorly-equipped Russian Army. Churchill initially proposed that ships alone could do the job; when this incentive had swung ministers in favor of the project, he decided that troops would, after all, be needed.

Nevertheless Churchill authorized the Royal Navy to bombard the Turkish guns defending the Dardanelles. After two bombardments, on 26 February sailors and marines were landed to inspect the damage and blow up some of the remaining gun emplacements. In March there were more bombardments, one of whose effects was that the Turks were warned that an attack was impending. Their precautions not only took the form of reinforcing the land defenses but also of more sophisticated methods of mining. In the last and most important bombardment on 18 March three old battleships were destroyed by mines, and this persuaded the commanding admiral not to risk any more close bombardments. In fact, if the naval bombardment had been pressed home in its initial stages, the navy might indeed have been able to force the Dardanelles.

About 75,000 troops were in the initial landings on 25 April 1915. Of these 30,000 were Australians and New Zealanders and 17,000 were French. The landings, at five points on the tip of the Gallipoli Peninsula, were well-planned. Except in one place, resistance was slight and casualties were few. However, there was delay and confusion once the men were ashore. A supplementary landing to the north, at a place later called Anzac Cove, was also successful, but was soon assailed by strong Turkish forces. In general, the advantage of the successful landings was dissipated by unadventurous leadership, and the troops settled down to a long hot summer of bloody attacks and counterattacks. Both sides dispatched more troops to the Peninsula. Rather than abandon the project, Churchill and Kitchener persuaded ministers to send even more troops. On 6 August new landings were made at Suvla Bay, five miles to the north of Anzac Cove. The intention was to advance inland to capture the vital high ground, thereby disorganizing the Turkish dispositions and enabling the Allies to capture the entire Peninsula and open the way to Constantinople. The landings were again very successful but, once ashore, officers made no effort to press on; they intended to 'consolidate' first. Thus, the advantage of surprise was lost once again. When the high ground was finally attacked, the Turks were ready. August was a month of costly battles which brought no great gains. It was clear that the project could no longer succeed, but it was not until the winter that the British Cabinet could steel itself to order a withdrawal. The evacuation was very successful, with no lives lost, and ended in January 1916.

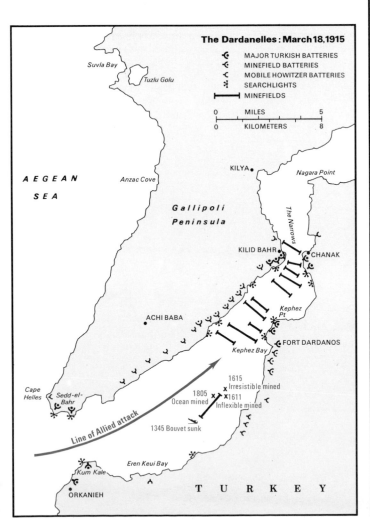

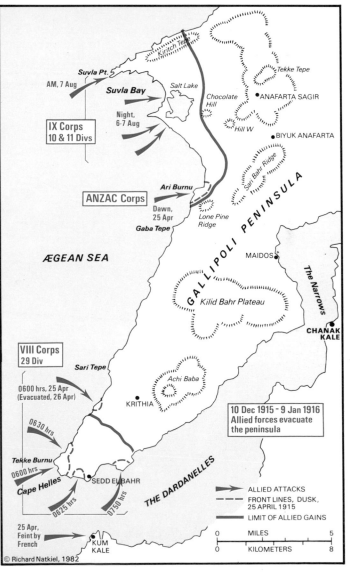

The Dardanelles: March 18, 1915

- ⚓ MAJOR TURKISH BATTERIES
- ⚓ MINEFIELD BATTERIES
- ⚓ MOBILE HOWITZER BATTERIES
- ⚓ SEARCHLIGHTS
- ▬▬ MINEFIELDS

0 — MILES — 5
0 — KILOMETERS — 8

Suvla Bay

Tuzlu Golu

KILYA

Nagara Point

AEGEAN SEA

Anzac Cove

Gallipoli Peninsula

The Narrows

KILID BAHR · CHANAK

ACHI BABA

Kephez Pt.

Kephez Bay

FORT DARDANOS

1615 Irresistible mined
1805 Ocean mined
1611 Inflexible mined
1345 Bouvet sunk

Cape Helles *Sedd-el-Bahr*

Line of Allied attack

Eren Keui Bay

Kum Kale

ORKANIEH

TURKEY

Kiritch Tepe

Tekke Tepe

AM, 7 Aug
Suvla Pt.
Suvla Bay
Salt Lake

Chocolate Hill
ANAFARTA SAGIR

IX Corps 10 & 11 Divs

Night, 6·7 Aug

Hill W
BIYUK ANAFARTA

ANZAC Corps
Ari Burnu
Dawn, 25 Apr
Gaba Tepe
Lone Pine Ridge

Sari Bahr Ridge

AEGEAN SEA

GALLIPOLI PENINSULA

MAIDOS

Kilid Bahr Plateau

The Narrows

CHANAK KALE

VIII Corps 29 Div
Sari Tepe

0600 hrs, 25 Apr (Evacuated, 26 Apr)

0630 hrs

Achi Baba

KRITHIA

10 Dec 1915 - 9 Jan 1916 Allied forces evacuate the peninsula

Tekke Burnu
0600 hrs
Cape Helles
0625 hrs
SEDD EL BAHR
0750 hrs

THE DARDANELLES

25 Apr, Feint by French

KUM KALE

➤ ALLIED ATTACKS
--- FRONT LINES, DUSK, 25 APRIL 1915
▬ LIMIT OF ALLIED GAINS

0 — MILES — 5
0 — KILOMETERS — 8

© Richard Natkiel, 1982

The Second Battle of Ypres

As the Western Front settled down into static positional warfare, with little prospect of either side making a really decisive breakthrough, commanders began to seek locations where a minor victory might be possible. In early 1915 the French and British on the Western Front undertook several offensives. In February there was a French offensive in Champagne which cost the attackers 50,000 casualties and gained only a few hundred yards of ground. In March the British attacked at Neuve Chapelle and because they were short of shells, did not make a preliminary bombardment. In this way, by accident, they achieved surprise and a breakthrough, but were unable to make use of the temporary gap in the German line. Further French and British offensives were similarly costly and unsuccessful. The Germans were content to stay on the defensive, inflicting heavy casualties on the attackers. But at Ypres they did launch an attack of their own. This began on 22 April with a poison gas emission which drifted over the French and British trenches. This was the first time poison gas was used on the Western Front, although the Germans had previously tried it out on the Russians. At Ypres it was spectacularly successful. The French and British defenders fled from their trenches, gasping. The Germans were able to capture the trenches with almost no loss, and by evening there was a gap of four miles in the Allied front. It was only by desperately combing the rear area for reserves that the British were able to plug the gap the following day.

Although the use of gas took the defenders by surprise and made a wide gap in their line, German forces had not been assembled in sufficient numbers to burst through the gap decisively. Not for the last time in this war, a technological surprise had been wasted. There were renewed Allied offensives later in 1915, at Festubert and Vimy Ridge in May-June and at Loos and in Champagne in September-October. Despite heavy casualties there were only minor gains.

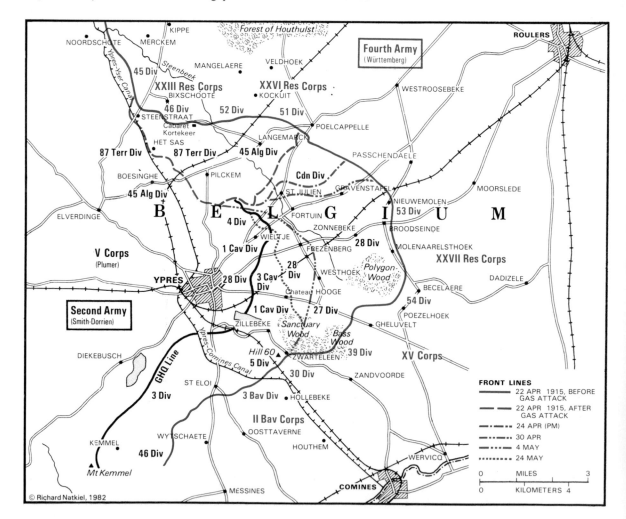

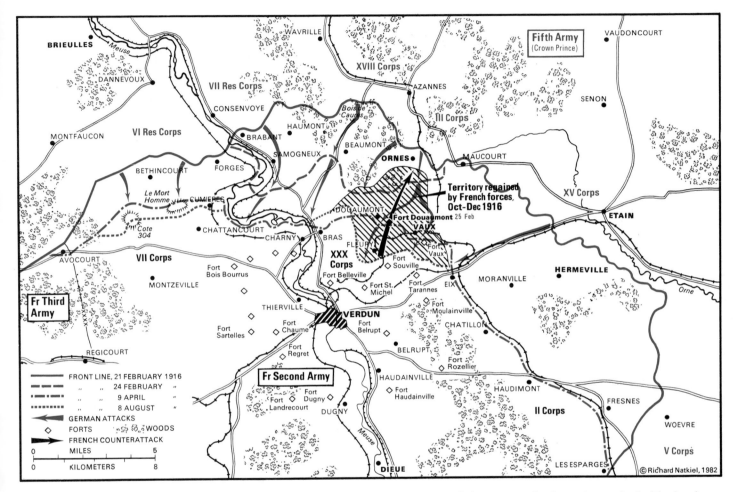

Verdun

By 1916 both sides saw that the war might be won by exhausting the enemy's manpower reserves and the German commander, Falkenhayn, decided that Verdun would be an advantageous site for a battle in which French infantry could be drawn under the destructive power of German artillery. Verdun was one of France's great fortresses, situated by the frontier on the River Meuse. There had been little fighting in this area, so the French defenses could be assumed to be slack. Moreover, the Germans had numerous railways leading toward Verdun, whereas the French had not.

The German attack opened on 21 February with a bombardment heavier than any hitherto seen. It was concentrated on a couple of French divisions holding an eight-mile front on the right bank of the Meuse. Resisting doggedly, the French began to withdraw from this first line of defense the next day. Meanwhile, as Falkenhayn had expected, the French began to send fresh infantry divisions to Verdun. On 24 February the second French line was broken and the Germans advanced to the third. This, four miles from Verdun, was a line of trenches joining two strong forts, Douaumont and Vaux. The former was not properly garrisoned, and the Germans captured it without any trouble. Pétain, who by this time had been appointed to command the French defense, called for more artillery, and insisted on full use being made of it. He also widened the highway leading to Verdun; this carried a dense traffic of supplies and reinforcements in, and thousands of wounded out, and soon became known as the *Voie Sacrée*. On 6 March a new German assault on both sides of the river captured new ground at heavy loss to both sides but it was not until 6 June, after a heroic defense, that the fort at Vaux was captured. There were further attacks and French counterattacks, but the German effort at Verdun was weakened by new Allied offensives elsewhere. It was not until December that the attack could be regarded as abandoned. Verdun did not fall, but the French army suffered about 360,000 casualties in defending it. Falkenhayn's intention had been to inflict totally disproportionate losses on the French but he had been drawn into a far longer and more costly battle than he originally envisioned.

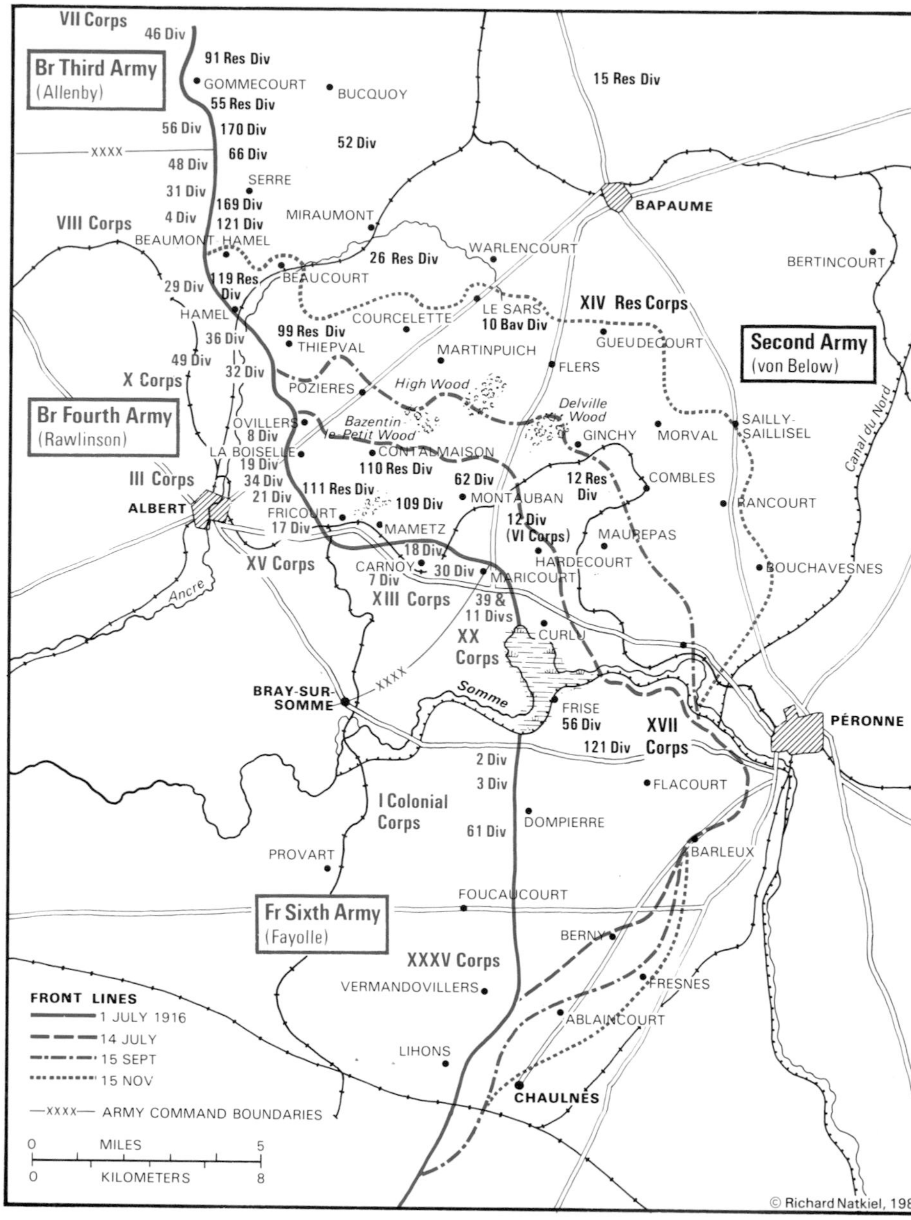
VII Corps
46 Div
Br Third Army
(Allenby)
91 Res Div
GOMMECOURT
BUCQUOY
55 Res Div
15 Res Div
56 Div
170 Div
66 Div
52 Div
XXXX
48 Div
31 Div
SERRE
169 Div
BAPAUME
VIII Corps
4 Div
121 Div
MIRAUMONT
BEAUMONT HAMEL
26 Res Div
WARLENCOURT
BERTINCOURT
119 Res Div
BEAUCOURT
29 Div
LE SARS
XIV Res Corps
HAMEL
COURCELETTE
10 Bav Div
36 Div
99 Res Div
THIEPVAL
GUEUDECOURT
Second Army
(von Below)
49 Div
MARTINPUICH
X Corps
32 Div
FLERS
POZIERES
High Wood
Br Fourth Army
(Rawlinson)
OVILLERS
8 Div
Bazentin-le-Petit Wood
Delville Wood
SAILLY-SAILLISEL
GINCHY
MORVAL
Canal du Nord
LA BOISELLE
CONTALMAISON
19 Div
110 Res Div
III Corps
34 Div
62 Div
12 Res Div
COMBLES
ALBERT
21 Div
111 Res Div
MONTAUBAN
RANCOURT
FRICOURT
109 Div
17 Div
MAMETZ
12 Div
(VI Corps)
MAUREPAS
18 Div
XV Corps
HARDECOURT
BOUCHAVESNES
CARNOY
30 Div
MARICOURT
7 Div
XIII Corps
Ancre
39 & 11 Divs
XX Corps
CURLU
BRAY-SUR-SOMME
Somme
FRISE
56 Div
XVII Corps
PÉRONNE
121 Div
2 Div
3 Div
FLACOURT
I Colonial Corps
DOMPIERRE
61 Div
PROVART
BARLEUX
FOUCAUCOURT
Fr Sixth Army
(Fayolle)
BERNY
XXXV Corps
FRONT LINES
1 JULY 1916
14 JULY
15 SEPT
15 NOV
VERMANDOVILLERS
FRESNES
ABLAINCOURT
LIHONS
CHAULNES
XXXX ARMY COMMAND BOUNDARIES
0 MILES 5
0 KILOMETERS 8
© Richard Natkiel, 1982

The Battle of the Somme

By mid-1916 the British share of the Western Front had been extended south to the River Somme, and it was here that the Anglo-French command planned a great offensive for the summer. In the final plan the French were to contribute eight divisions, attacking on an eight-mile front and the British were to attack along 18 miles with 14 divisions, with a further eight in reserve.

The preliminary artillery barrage lasted almost a week, with over a million shells being dispatched to the German trenches. At 0730 on 1 July it ceased. On the German side men began to pour upward from their deep dugouts bringing their machine guns, to take up station in the fresh shell holes and the ruins of their trenches. On the British side, men rapidly began to assemble in front of their own trenches, and then move off in dense extended lines across a No Man's Land which became progressively more impassable as they entered the shell-churned belt in front of the German lines. In the French sector of the line, comparative peace and quiet prevailed. The French, at the last minute, had postponed their advance for a couple of hours; when they did advance, therefore, they took the Germans by surprise and won considerable ground for few casualties. The British had expected the German resistance to be negligible, after so much bombardment. As it turned out, with No Man's Land being about a quarter of a mile wide, the Germans had time to install themselves before the British could reach their trenches. The first British line was laid low by rifle and machine-gun fire, and so then was the second. German artillery pounded the British side of No Man's Land. But still the lines of khaki-clad men came on. Not since the Japanese assaults of the Russo-Japanese War had so many men been sacrificed for so little gain of ground. By the end of the first day 20,000 British soldiers had been killed and 40,000 wounded. The attacks by the 32nd Division on Thiepval Wood were particularly bloody.

Here and there, part of the German first line was taken, and the French did well. A night advance then secured the German second line. But an attempt by three reserve cavalry divisions to exploit the gap was crushed by machine-gun fire, and the Allied command settled down to a battle of attrition which lasted until November, when a last big battle, on the Ancre, was called off when the battlefield mud became impassable. There had also been a renewed offensive in September, the Battle of Flers Courcelette, notable because for the first time a few tanks were used. They made a deep penetration, but were too few and too slow to exploit it. In all, the Battle of the Somme cost more than 600,000 Allied casualties. German casualties were also heavy. Although the British generals' conduct of the battle has been much criticized, with considerable justice, for its lack of imagination and sophistication, German accounts of the battle say that it wrecked the German Army because of the heavy losses in the senior NCO and junior officer grades.

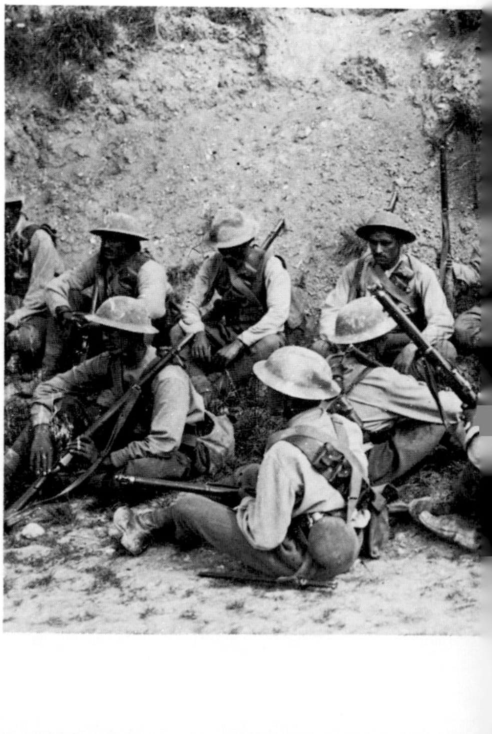

Below: men of the Border Regiment rest in a trench near Thiepval during the bitter fighting on the Somme.
Bottom: Indian cavalry fought as dismounted troops in July 1916.

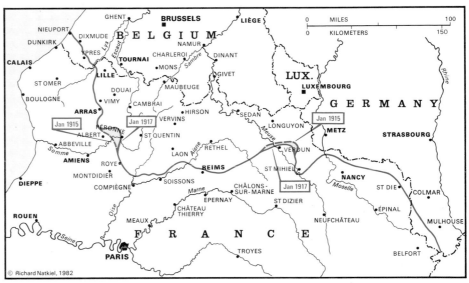

© Richard Natkiel, 1982

The Western Front at the End of 1916

Despite the heavy fighting and the enormous number of casualties, the most arresting feature of the front line of December 1916 was its similarity to that of a year previously. Only around the sites of the two great 1916 battles, the Somme and Verdun, was there perceptible change. Around the Somme, where British casualties had amounted to a number no less than one per cent of the entire British population, the Western Front had been pushed forward for just about six miles over an 18-mile length. At Verdun, which had shattered both the French and German Armies, the Germans had gained a mile or two, but had already begun to fall back under French counter-pressure.

The technical reasons for this lethal stalemate were by now accepted by both generals and politicians. Entrenchment, plus the new weapons of mass destruction, meant that troops either stayed in their trenches and lived, or advanced from their trenches and died. Of the new weapons, it was the machine gun which both then and thereafter struck the human imagination as the most dramatic and death-dealing weapon on the Western Front. This was only partly true, although the survivors of the Battle of the Somme, who had seen lines of advancing British infantry thrashed down by well-sited defen-

sive machine guns, would never have doubted it. In fact it was the artillery which claimed the most victims. The role of the artillery in this slaughter was perhaps under-rated because the number of shells which exploded harmlessly far outnumbered those doing any damage. At Verdun, for example, the opposing sides fired off 37 million shells, whereas the total French and German casualties were well under one million, and these were from all causes. But well-placed shrapnel shells could wreak mass destruction on troops in their forming-up areas, while intense bombardment of entrenchments could sometimes take a serious toll of troops lacking overhead cover.

On the Western Front, therefore, 1916 had presented a horrifying picture, and it was not only the front-line infantry who were asking how much longer this could be allowed to go on. But President Wilson's suggestion of a negotiated peace was politely ignored by the belligerent governments. In Britain, moreover, Lloyd George's ostentatious determination to fight the war to a finish brought him enough support to enable him to replace the less bloodthirsty Asquith as prime minister.

Below: a column of Russian prisoners-of-war march to the rear under escort. Although the Russians had overcome many of their equipment shortages by 1916 the casualty rate remained high.

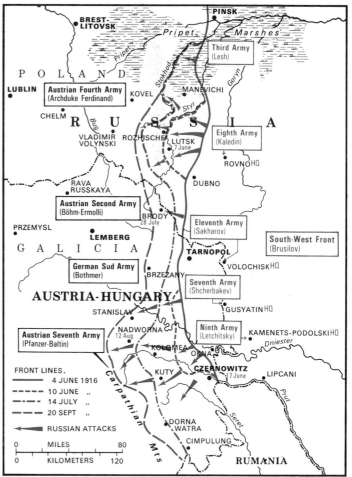

The Brusilov Offensive

On the Eastern Front the Russian Army had been forced back in a retreat during 1915, but in 1916 it began to attack. Early drives against the Germans around Lake Narosh were unsuccessful, but the Russians soon began to plan a great offensive. However, before this was ready an urgent appeal for a diversionary attack came from the Italians, whose army had been heavily attacked by the Austrians in the Trentino district. General Brusilov, the new commander of the Southern Front defending the Ukraine, was thereupon given unusual liberty of action to attack the Austrians at short notice. In fact, Brusilov was well prepared.

He had earlier instructed his commanders to dig their trenches closer to the Austrian lines; on the Eastern Front, No Man's Land was sometimes up to several miles wide, and Brusilov believed that 100 yards was more appropriate where an attack was envisioned. Secondly, Brusilov had abandoned the concept of massing reserves before an attack. Knowing his enemy had more railroad lines serving the front, he realized that for every Russian reserve division moved up, the enemy, alerted by the Russian movement, could bring up three.

The attack, soon called the Brusilov Offensive, began on 4 June. Opposing the Russians were the Austrian Fourth and Seventh Armies on the flanks, with the Second and Southern Armies in the center. Only the Southern Army included German divisions. A powerful artillery bombardment demoralized the Austrians, and their front, when assaulted, began to dissolve in headlong retreat. So fast was the Russian breakthrough that the commander of the Fourth Army, Archduke Joseph Ferdinand, had his birthday ruined by Russian fire.

Eventually, lack of reserves caused Brusilov's advance to falter. Meanwhile the Germans had collected forces around Kovel, threatening his salient from the north. When the Germans struck, he had to retreat, and by the time he had got back to his original line he had suffered about one million casualties. But his offensive had cheered the Allies at a difficult time, probably weakened the German attack at Verdun, and had shattered what morale the polyglot Austrian army had retained up to that time. Although it was the most successful Russian operation of the war to that time the continued high Russian casualties helped pave the way for revolution in 1917.

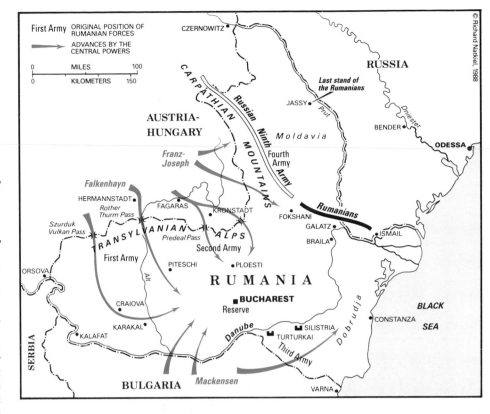

The Rumanian Campaign

At the outbreak of World War I, Rumania remained neutral, although she had a formal defense treaty with Austria-Hungary. But the Rumanian government was pro-Entente, enticed by promises of acquiring land from its neighbors and subsidized with financial credits. By the summer of 1916 the Rumanian government was prepared formally to enter the war on the side of the Allies. The moment appeared opportune and opportunistic as the Germans were heavily engaged at Verdun and on the Somme. The Austrians were tied down on the Italian Front and had suffered a major defeat in Russia. On 27 August 1916, Rumania declared war on the Central Powers and deployed an army of some 560,000 soldiers along her borders. Unfortunately, Rumania was vulnerable to attack from both the north and the south.

The Central Powers were not altogether unprepared for a war against Rumania. Field Marshal von Mackensen was placed in command of a mixed force of Austrian, Bulgarian and German divisions to the south, while General von Falkenhayn commanded a similar mixed force to the north. A Turkish fleet under the German Admiral Souchon was available to bombard the Rumanian Black Sea ports. The Allied powers advised the Rumanians to hold the mountain passes and defend the Dobrudja region, but the Rumanians preferred to prepare an offensive to take Transylvania. But their plans were upset by Mackensen striking first in the south. On 2 September Mackensen's force had crossed the Dobrudja frontier. By the 26th his troops had captured the Danube fortress of Tatrakan. Despite assistance from the Russians, the Rumanians were unable to drive the enemy back, and by the beginning of November Mackensen's troops were beyond the Rumanian port of Constanza, nearing the mouth of the River Danube.

In the north Falkenhayn's Austro-German army advanced into Transylvania and drove the Rumanians back into the Transylvanian passes by the middle of October. Falkenhayn was able to force the pass at Szurduk. After a three-day battle in the foothills the invaders emerged into the Rumanian plain. It was now mid-November and the weather had broken, with incessant rain and snow slowing move-

ment. By 26 November Falkenhayn and Mackensen's forces had met and pushed the Rumanians eastward.

The Rumanians stoutly defended the line of the Argesul River west of Bucharest, but on 5 December the Germans entered the capital and reached the oilfields at Ploesti. The German pursuit was continued on the 8th under the most appalling weather conditions. The Rumanians, assisted by Russian reinforcements, attempted to make a stand at Ramnicu Sarat near the Sereth River. They succeeded in holding the Germans. The belligerents

settled down to trench warfare for the winter and the front remained static until the Russian Kerensky Offensive in July 1917. The German losses in the campaign were some 60,000, with more than 66,000 sick. Rumanian casualties were estimated at 310,000.

Below: a German 21cm howitzer in action during the Rumanian campaign.

226

Below right: a German shell explodes amidships on the *Queen Mary* just before she blew up in the early stages of the battle. Bottom: a squadron of German pre-dreadnought battleships in line ahead. Second in the line is the *Pommern*, sunk at Jutland.

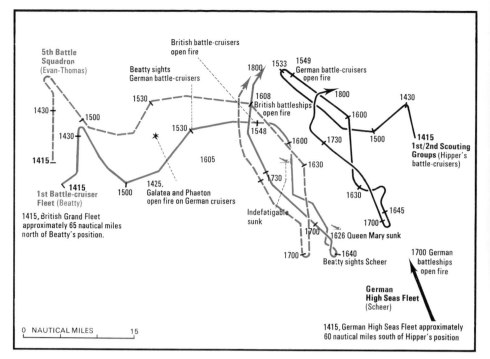

The Battle of Jutland

Up to 1916 the German High Seas Fleet had evaded a full-scale battle against the larger British Grand Fleet, hoping eventually to maneuver the latter into a battle with only part of its strength facing the whole German battlefleet.

On 30 May 1916 intercepted radio messages indicated that the German fleet was preparing to leave harbor. Admiral Jellicoe, the British Commander in Chief, took his Grand Fleet on an intercepting course, with Admiral Beatty's battlecruiser squadrons and four new fast battleships scouting ahead. Cruisers from Beatty's squadron made contact off Jutland with German cruisers and soon the British battlecruisers sighted the German battlecruisers, which were screening the advance of the German battleships. Battle was joined between these scouting groups in the afternoon. German gunnery and German armor protection proved superior to British and in this preliminary engagement two of Beatty's battlecruisers

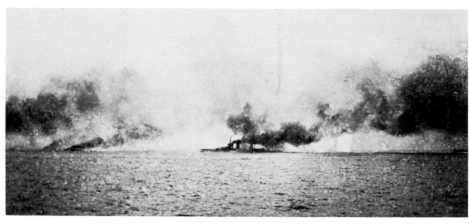

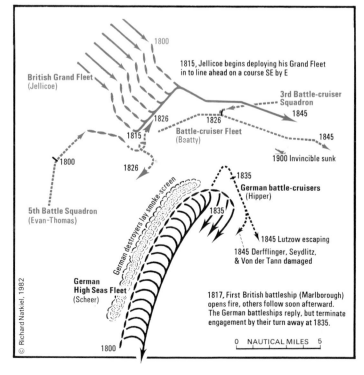

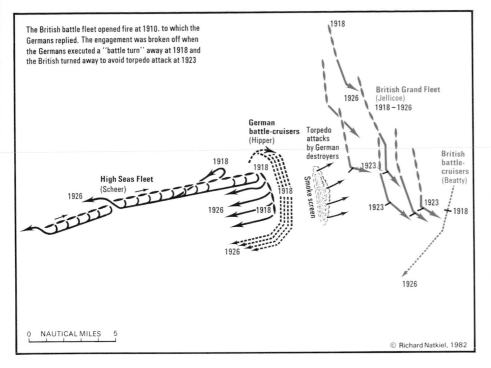

The British battle fleet opened fire at 1910, to which the Germans replied. The engagement was broken off when the Germans executed a "battle turn" away at 1918 and the British turned away to avoid torpedo attack at 1923

© Richard Natkiel, 1982

blew up. Beatty, who had caught sight of the German battleships approaching from the south, continued to maneuver so as to draw the Germans to the main British force.

Beatty, however, was not keeping Jellicoe well-informed of the enemy's position and course. Jellicoe's problem was to choose the best possible moment for deploying his battlefleet of 24 Dreadnoughts, which were moving in six parallel columns, a formation suitable for cruising in search of the enemy but less suitable for fighting a battle. In battle, line ahead gave all ships a chance to use their guns, and Jellicoe had to deploy into line ahead before the enemy was in

range but not before he knew the enemy's position and bearing. At 1815 the German battlecruisers encountered the three battlecruisers which had remained to screen Jellicoe. One more British battlecruiser blew up, but Jellicoe was now able to calculate the likely position of the main German forces. He started his deployment into line ahead and 20 minutes later the unsuspecting German admiral, Scheer, with his battleships in line ahead, was confronted by the British battlefleet passing ahead of him at right angles. With all the British battleships able to concentrate their fire on his leading ships, Scheer was in a perilous situation, and he

ordered his ships to do an 'all-together' reversal of course, a very difficult maneuver to perform. Half an hour later Scheer again found himself in this situation. Once more there was a brief exchange of fire while the Germans withdrew under cover of a smokescreen. This time, German destroyers made a torpedo attack on the British. Jellicoe turned away and thereby lost contact with the Germans. He was later criticized for this move, but Churchill was probably right, later, when he emphasized the enormous responsibility carried by Jellicoe.

During the night Jellicoe tried to interpose his ships between the fleeing Germans and their bases. Thanks to a muddle in the Admiralty, which failed to pass vital intercepted German radio messages and to negligent British commanders, who failed to report their ships' actions with the enemy during the night, the Germans were able to slip back to their ports. Thus the long-awaited encounter between the two fleets had ended unsatisfactorily for the British. They had lost three battlecruisers and three armored cruisers against a German loss of one battlecruiser, one old battleship, and three armored cruisers. But it was the Germans who had fled; Britain was still mistress of the seas.

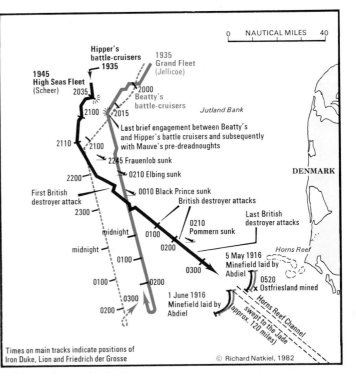

© Richard Natkiel, 1982

Below right: British and French warships in
Grand Harbour, Malta.
Below: the launch of the British battleship
Queen Elizabeth in 1918.

The Blockade of the Central Powers

As the world's principal naval power in 1914 Great Britain was able to impose her strategic concepts, as far as maritime affairs were concerned, on her French ally. Broadly it was hoped to repeat the success of the Napoleonic Wars, this time by blockading Germany and starving her into surrender.

Geography still favored Great Britain for she dominated the exits to the North Sea, and with France friendly for the first time in 600 years, the commitment was in fact smaller than it had been 100 years earlier. In practice, of course, things proved more difficult, and even with the addition of Italy as an ally in 1915 the French Navy was not strong enough to contain the Austro-Hungarian Navy in the Adriatic unaided. Nor could total control of the sea be guaranteed in the face of underwater mines and submarines.

German plans had counted on the Royal Navy trying to maintain a close blockade of their coasts, and it was hoped to use torpedo craft and submarines to inflict serious losses on the British. What was not known was that in 1913 the threat of attrition had been recognized by the Admiralty, and 'close' blockade with ships patrolling near enemy ports had been replaced by a new doctrine of 'distant' blockade to confine the Germans and their navy in the North Sea.

The result was that both fleets stayed in harbor much of the time and left their light craft and submarines to probe each other's defenses. The British public was denied a second Battle of Trafalgar, this time in the North Sea, but equally the German High Seas Fleet never achieved the position of parity which it had planned for. Although the Royal Navy suffered losses from attack, particularly by mines and torpedoes, its Grand Fleet patrolled regularly from its main base at Scapa Flow, ensuring that only a handful of German commerce-raiders escaped into the Atlantic.

To reduce the demands on major warships a number of liners were turned into Armed Merchant Cruisers (AMCs), and as the Northern Patrol they watched the area between Iceland and the Orkneys. A similar patrol line was established in the Western Approaches to the British Isles, and as a result British losses in 1914-15 from commerce raiding were a negligible two percent of the total mercantile marine. Conversely the patrols enforced the blockade effectively, preventing contraband (including foodstuffs as well as war materials) from reaching Germany.

The strain of the blockade forced Germany to desperate measures. The first 'unrestricted' U-Boat campaign of 1915 claimed that the harshness of the British blockade justified Germany abandoning the rules of International Law guaranteeing non-naval shipping from being sunk 'at sight.' Allied shipping losses soon rose to alarming levels but the effect on neutral opinion was disastrous and Germany was eventually forced to abandon the campaign under pressure from the United States and other influential neutrals.

Efforts to seal in the U-Boats with minefields were hampered by the lack of an efficient British mine until 1917, by which time the US Navy was able to help in laying the enormous North Sea Barrage. The Dover Barrage was finally made impenetrable to U-Boats in May 1918 but the Otranto Barrage never succeeded in blocking the Adriatic to the same extent. The disastrous losses in the land battles of 1916, and the ensuing stalemate in 1917 made the German High Command desperate. The German Navy was given authority to start a second unrestricted U-Boat campaign and this time it came close to knocking Great Britain out of the war. When the United States entered the war in April 1917 Admiral Sims (commander of the US naval forces in the European theater) was horrified to learn that the British were losing 25 percent of all ships sailing to UK ports, and food supplies had sunk to only six weeks' reserves.

At the darkest hour defeat was staved off by an apparent miracle. Convoy, the grouping of merchant ships in formations protected by warships, was an old remedy against commerce-raiding but it had been assumed that modern weapons and steam propulsion had made it redundant, or too expensive in escorts. In practice the enormous numbers of Auxiliary Patrol ships wasting their time on fruitless searches were better employed with convoys, and the large number of destroyers attached to the battlefleet could be thinned out with very little risk to the efficacy of the blockade.

Two other measures, less well-known but equally crucial, combined to defeat the U-Boats. A large replacement shipbuilding program was started in 1916, and at about the same time the Admiralty set up a large-scale salvage administration to recover as many damaged merchantmen as possible. It is hard to credit today, but for two years Britain had watched her large merchant fleet dwindle steadily without lifting a finger to reverse the downward trend. These measures amounted to a new drive to conserve shipping, and within a matter of weeks the worst of the crisis was over. Losses fell dramatically and U-Boat losses started to climb.

By 1918 the U-Boats were on the defensive. The had failed to stop the flood of American reinforcements from crossing the Atlantic, and by mid-1918 British offensive minelaying was causing losses even in home waters. Before the Armistice the first magnetic mines had been laid by the British, and although morale in the submarine service remained high, the mutiny of the German High Seas Fleet in November 1918 brought all resistance to an end. The fleet was later scuttled by its crews at Scapa Flow.

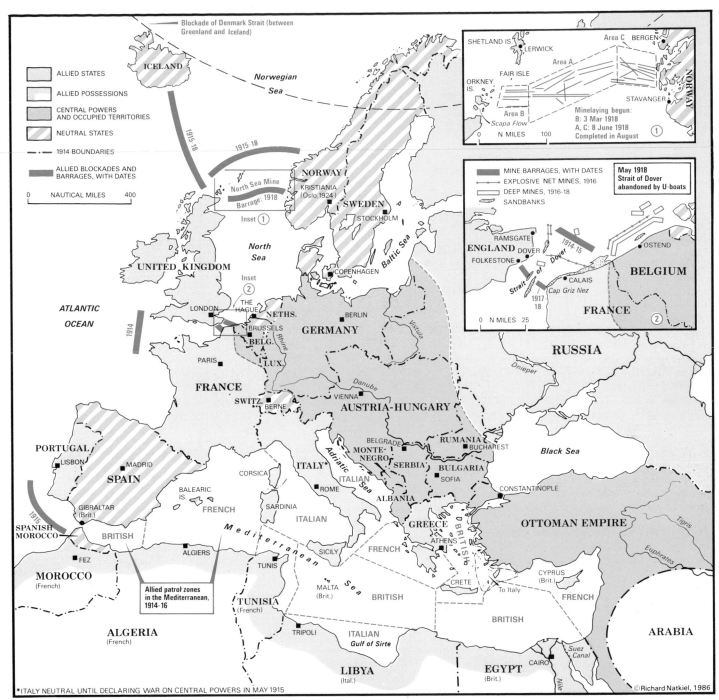

Inset 1

SHETLAND IS.
LERWICK
Area C — BERGEN
FAIR ISLE
Area A
ORKNEY IS.
Area B
Scapa Flow
STAVANGER
NORWAY

Minelaying begun:
B: 3 Mar 1918
A, C: 8 June 1918
Completed in August

0   N MILES   100

Inset 2

MINE BARRAGES, WITH DATES
EXPLOSIVE NET MINES, 1916
DEEP MINES, 1916-18
SANDBANKS

May 1918
Strait of Dover
abandoned by U-boats

RAMSGATE
ENGLAND
DOVER
FOLKESTONE
1914-15
Strait of Dover
CALAIS
Cap Griz Nez
1917 18
FRANCE
OSTEND
BELGIUM

0   N MILES   25

Legend

ALLIED STATES
ALLIED POSSESSIONS
CENTRAL POWERS AND OCCUPIED TERRITORIES
NEUTRAL STATES
1914 BOUNDARIES
ALLIED BLOCKADES AND BARRAGES, WITH DATES

0   NAUTICAL MILES   400

Blockade of Denmark Strait (between Greenland and Iceland)

Allied patrol zones in the Mediterranean, 1914-16

*ITALY NEUTRAL UNTIL DECLARING WAR ON CENTRAL POWERS IN MAY 1915

© Richard Natkiel, 1986

The Crisis of the U-Boat War

Despairing of victory on land, in September 1916 the German High Command authorized a 'restricted' campaign against British and Allied shipping. It ran for four months from 6 October 1916 to the end of January 1917, and in spite of the restrictions placed on the U-Boats they sank nearly 500 ships. In January 1917 the total tonnage sunk reached 368,500 tons in that month alone, and nearly 2000 British merchant ships had been sunk since August 1914. This slaughter had been achieved at a price of roughly 65 ships for each U-Boat sent to the bottom.

With such losses it was understandable that the German Naval Staff under Admiral Scheer wanted to switch to 'unrestricted' warfare as soon as possible, that is to adopt a 'sink at sight' policy. Only the fear of offending America held the Germans back. Finally in December 1916 approval was won from the emperor. The calculations were careful and cold-blooded: if 600,000 tons of Allied shipping could be sunk each month and if 1,200,000 tons of neutral shipping could be 'frightened off' from trading with Britain the Allies' supply system would be wrecked within

Below: British Auxiliary Patrol trawlers move in to assist the crew of a torpedoed merchant ship.

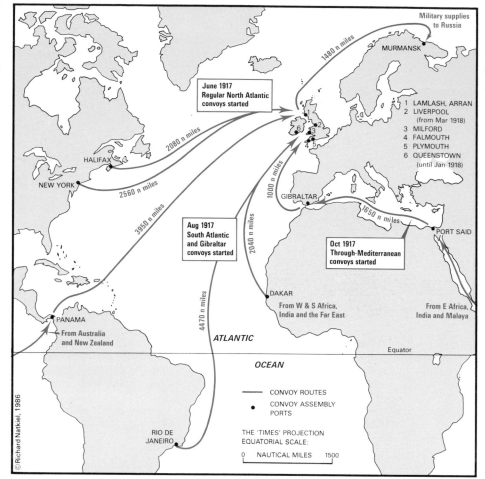

June 1917
Regular North Atlantic
convoys started

Military supplies
to Russia

MURMANSK

1480 n miles

1 LAMLASH, ARRAN
2 LIVERPOOL
(from Mar 1918)
3 MILFORD
4 FALMOUTH
5 PLYMOUTH
6 QUEENSTOWN
(until Jan 1918)

HALIFAX

2080 n miles

NEW YORK

2560 n miles

3950 n miles

1000 n miles

GIBRALTAR

1650 n miles

PORT SAID

Aug 1917
South Atlantic
and Gibraltar
convoys started

2040 n miles

Oct 1917
Through-Mediterranean
convoys started

4470 n miles

DAKAR

From W & S Africa,
India and the Far East

From E Africa,
India and Malaya

PANAMA

From Australia
and New Zealand

ATLANTIC

Equator

OCEAN

— CONVOY ROUTES
• CONVOY ASSEMBLY
PORTS

THE 'TIMES' PROJECTION
EQUATORIAL SCALE:

0   NAUTICAL MILES   1500

RIO DE
JANEIRO

© Richard Natkiel, 1986

Above: Otto von Weddigen, commander of the German submarine *U.9*, who sank three British armored cruisers, *Aboukir, Cressy* and the *Hogue*, in the North Sea on 22 September 1914, largely because of the poor precautions taken against submarine attack. Left: German submarines meet in the Mediterranean. The larger vessel is the *U.35*, the command of the most successful submarine captain ever, von Arnauld de la Perière.

five months. This in turn would starve Britain into submission and bring about the collapse of her effort on the Western Front where the British armies were now taking the leading role on the Allied side.

At first all went as planned. Losses rose from 360,000 tons in January to 540,000 tons in February, then to 594,000 tons in March, just short of the level required for victory. This was achieved by only 43 U-Boats operating from Germany, 23 each in Flanders and the Mediterranean, and 13 elsewhere.

A typical operating cycle required four U-Boats, one on station, one heading west to relieve her, one returning home and one under repair, but when the boats began to move further west into the Atlantic the cycle was increased to seven boats. This was, however, only a minor inconvenience, and the 'exchange rate' went from 53 merchantmen for each U-Boat sunk in February to 74 in March and then to 174 in April.

It was now a race between Britain's survival (with only six weeks' food supplies left) and American outrage at this slaughter of civilian sailors and passengers on the high seas. One in four ships approaching British waters was bound to be sunk and contemporary accounts describe seas strewn with corpses, mule carcasses and splintered boats.

The countermeasures were totally unavailing. Hundreds of small yachts and other craft had been impressed into the Auxiliary Patrol,

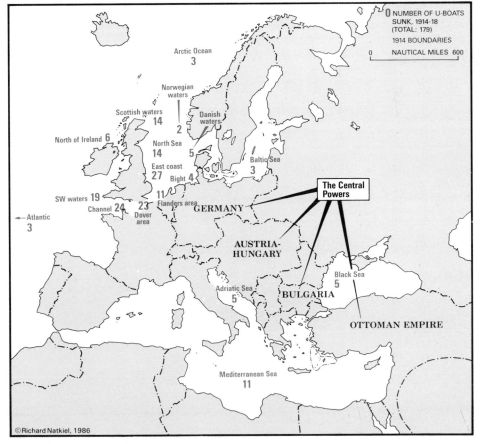

© Richard Natkiel, 1986

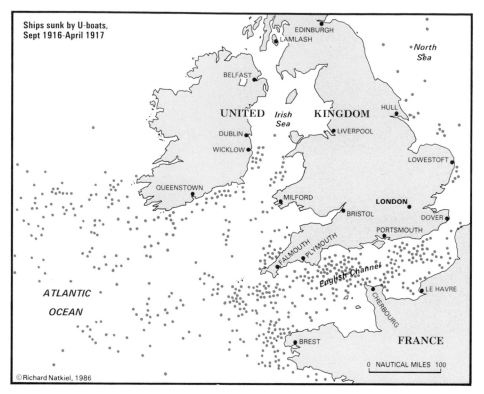

Ships sunk by U-boats, Sept 1916-April 1917

© Richard Natkiel, 1986

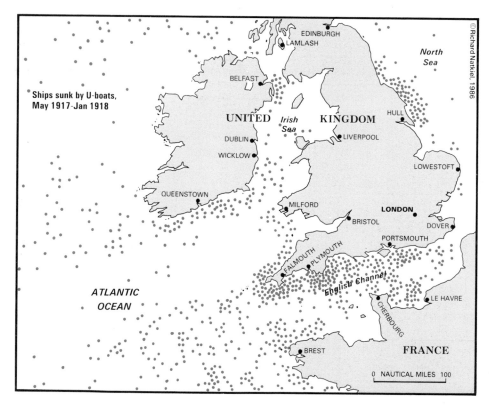

Ships sunk by U-boats, May 1917-Jan 1918

© Richard Natkiel, 1986

Above: a German submarine engages an armed merchantman.
Below left: a convoy late in the war is escorted by US destroyers.
Right: the typically cramped control room of a German U-Boat.

disguised 'Q-Ships' tried to trap U-Boats and even the British Army was to attempt the bloody Passchendaele offensive later in 1917 to capture the U-Boat bases in Flanders. Piecemeal improvements in weaponry had been made, the first depth-charges being introduced in 1916 and a directional hydrophone in 1917, but apart from minelaying across the exit-routes there seemed little else that could be done. To make matters worse there were no plans to replace shipping and until mid-1916 there was no salvage organization to recover damaged ships.

Only in May 1917 were the first fumbling attempts made to introduce a new countermeasure – convoy. This method of protecting merchant shipping had been in use since the fourteenth century but had become discredited during the peaceful years of the nineteenth century. Arguments that there were

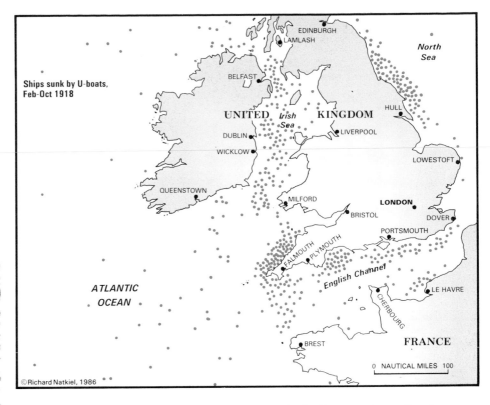

Ships sunk by U-boats,
Feb-Oct 1918

© Richard Natkiel, 1986

insufficient escorts were met by redeploying
the hundreds of vessels uselessly tied up in
patrolling, and the assurance that the intervention of the United States in the war (on 6
April) had made many more escorts available.

The Germans had calculated that America
would come into the war eventually, but not so
soon. Nor did they allow for the seizure of half
a million tons of their own ships, lying
interned in American ports, the equivalent of
a new building program. At last the Allies
tackled the problems of new building and salvage, so that the introduction of convoy was

more the final keystone in a policy of conserv-
ing shipping than a 'miracle cure.'

A miracle is what it must have seemed like
when the sinkings began to fall. On 20 May
1917 the first convoy from Gibraltar arrived in
Britain with no loss, followed by one from
Hampton Roads. Even when the U-Boats
switched to attacking weakly escorted out-
ward-bound ships they made little impression,
and by October only 24 ships out of 1500 had
been sunk. Part of the U-Boats' problem was
that convoy in effect scoured the sea of targets. Instead of waiting near a focal point

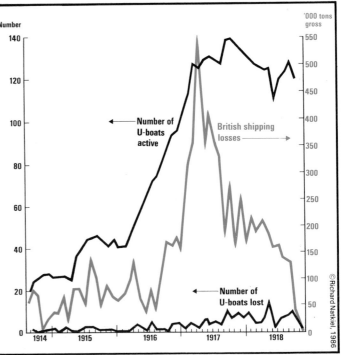

234

**Left: the cruiser *Vindictive* (right) and the destroyer *Warwick*, Admiral Keyes' flagship for the Zeebrugge raid.
Below: the attack on Zeebrugge, April 1918.**

One of the most important German submarine bases in Flanders was at Bruges and on the night of 22/23 April 1918 a dramatic attempt was made to block the entrance to the port at Zeebrugge. Three old British cruisers, *Thetis*, *Intrepid* and *Iphigenia* were to be sunk in the canal entrance while the defenses on the harbor mole were destroyed in a diversionary attack by landing parties from another old cruiser, the *Vindictive*. Despite the bravery with which the attack was carried out it proved a failure because the blockships were not correctly positioned and the port was quickly put back into use.

Despite this failure the Allied navies continued to hold the upper hand. When the Armistice came in November 1918 the U-Boat arm of the Imperial German Navy had lost some 5364 officers and men out of an estimated total of 13,000.

where shipping routes converged U-Boats now had to approach a dense mass of shipping surrounded by vigilant warships. At most one target could be fired on before breaking away to avoid counterattack, and even if that target was hit, 19 ships out of the 20 had escaped.

There were other countermeasures too: airships and flying boats flew over the convoys, and destroyers and submarines sowed a new type of mine in the routes from Heligoland and Flanders. Losses of U-Boats began to rise noticeably, putting further strain on the crews.

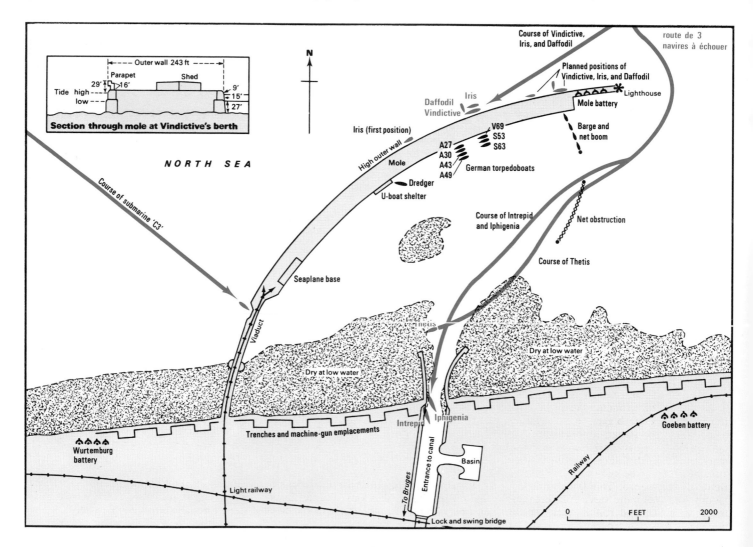

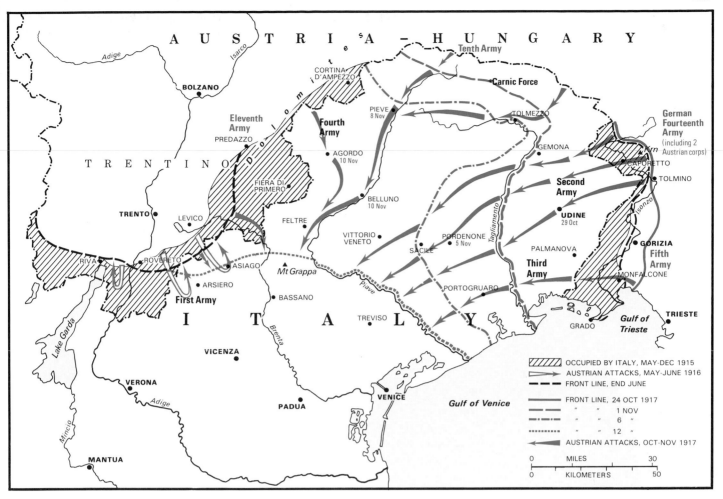

Map legend:

- OCCUPIED BY ITALY, MAY-DEC 1915
- AUSTRIAN ATTACKS, MAY-JUNE 1916
- FRONT LINE, END JUNE
- FRONT LINE, 24 OCT 1917
- " " 1 NOV
- " " 6 "
- " " 12 "
- AUSTRIAN ATTACKS, OCT-NOV 1917

0 MILES 30
0 KILOMETERS 50

Battles of the Isonzo

Italy declared war on the side of Britain and France on 23 May 1915, mainly in the hope of conquering the South Tyrol and Trieste, which were Austrian territory although largely Italian-speaking.

Still feeling the effects of the Libyan War of 1912, the Italian Army was ill-prepared. The expected drive northward into the Trentino was blocked by the Austrians in their strong mountain defenses and, so long as the Austrians held out here, they could threaten the rear of any Italian excursion eastward toward Trieste and Istria. In the Italian attempts to get within striking distance of Trieste the River Isonzo, backed by mountains, was the scene of eleven major battles and numerous skirmishes. In the first 10 of these battles the Italians suffered over half a million casualties but gained little significant ground. Meanwhile the Italian Army grew bigger, even including many returned Italian-Americans in its ranks. On 18 August 1917 the Italian commander, General Cadorna, launched an attack destined to be known as the Eleventh Battle of the Isonzo. This lasted almost a month, and was more successful, breaking the defense line and rolling back the demoralized Austrian troops. The Austrians

appealed for German assistance to be sent.

As Russia was already practically out of the war, the German command had seasoned troops available for transfer, and it decided to send to Austria six divisions, four of which were experienced in mountain warfare.

These six German divisions, with nine Austrian, began a massive attack on the Italian line near Caporetto on 24 October. Thanks partly to the unprecedented artillery bombardment, which included shells filled with a new type of poison gas, the Austro-German Fourteenth Army took the Italian positions with very few casualties. The capture of key positions at Caporetto and Tolmino gave the attackers the opportunity to sweep down on the disorganized Italians and cut off many of their columns. By the following day the Italians found that they were engaged in a military disaster, later known as the Battle of Caporetto. The attacking mountain troops, rapidly advancing over the high ground, were not only able to outflank the retiring Italian troops, but also the reserves moving up the valleys to restore the situation. That same day, therefore, the Italian General Cadorna ordered his shattered Second Army to retire as far as the Tagliamento.

The Italians finally established a defensive line on the Piave. This was 70 miles back, and only about 15 miles north of Venice at its closest point.

The Third Battle of Ypres (Passchendaele)

Following the dismissal of Joffre late in 1916 General Nivelle took command of the French armies. Nivelle promised that, using methods tried out on a small scale in French attacks during the Verdun battle, he would prepare a grand offensive which would destroy the German forces. The Germans had decided in any case to shorten their line on the Western Front by a withdrawal, completed in April 1917, to an elaborately prepared defensive position, the Hindenburg Line. Despite this withdrawal Nivelle began his attack on 16 April but it quickly ended in failure. After having suffered terrible casualties during the first years of the war, the spirit of the French Army was broken and units began to mutiny. Eventually soldiers of 54 divisions were involved. There was, therefore, no prospect of significant French attacks for the rest of the year and even after Pétain had taken over from Nivelle and done much to restore morale it was uncertain if the French would withstand a serious German offensive.

Field Marshal Haig, the British com-

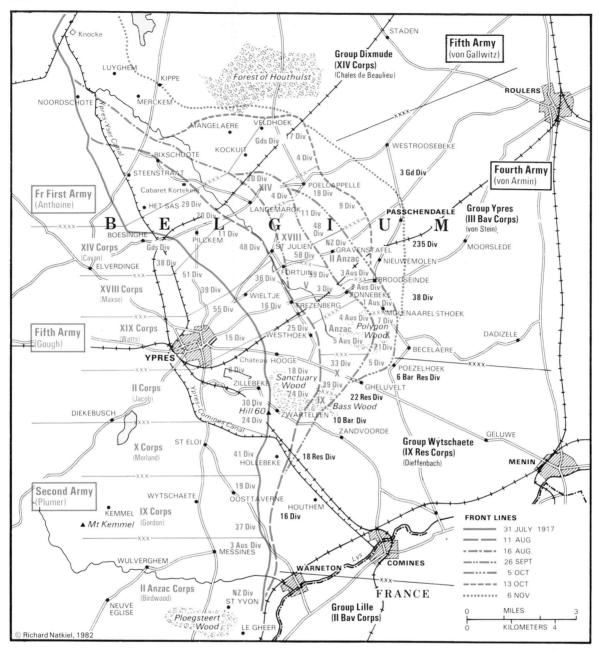

Knocke
LUYGHEM
KIPPE
NOORDSCHOTE
MERCKEM
Forest of Houthulst
STADEN

Group Dixmude (XIV Corps)
(Chales de Beaulieu)

Fifth Army
(von Gallwitz)

ROULERS

MANGELAERE
VELDHOEK
BIXSCHOOTE
Gds Div
17 Div
WESTROOSEBEKE
STEENSTRAAT
4 Div
3 Gd Div

Fourth Army
(von Armin)

Cabaret Kortekeer
20 Div
XIV
POELCAPPELLE
18 Div

Fr First Army
(Anthoine)

HET SAS 29 Div
LANGEMARCK
11 Div
9 Div
PASSCHENDAELE

Group Ypres (III Bav Corps)
(von Stein)

B E L G I U M

20 Div
11 Div
48 Div
XVIII
ST JULIEN
58 Div
NZ Div
GRAVENSTAFEL
II Anzac
235 Div

BOESINGHE
PILCKEM

MOORSLEDE

XIV Corps
(Cavan)
Gds Div
ELVERDINGE
38 Div
51 Div
36 Div
FORTUIN
9 Div
3 Aus Div
BROODSEINDE
NIEUWEMOLEN

XVIII Corps
(Maxse)
39 Div
V
3 Div
ZONNEBEKE
2 Aus Div
1 Aus Div
38 Div

WIELTJE
WESTROOSEBEKE

55 Div
16 Div
FREZENBERG
4 Aus Div
7 Div
MOLENAARELSTHOEK

Fifth Army
(Gough)

XIX Corps
(Watts)
YPRES
15 Div
25 Div
WESTHOEK
Anzac
5 Aus Div
Polygon Wood
DADIZELE

Chateau HOOGE
18 Div
33 Div
5 Div
POEZELHOEK

II Corps
(Jacob)
ZILLEBEKE
Sanctuary Wood
24 Div
39 Div
X
GHELUVELT
6 Bar Res Div

DIEKEBUSCH
30 Div
Hill 60
IX
Bass Wood
22 Res Div

24 Div
ZWARTELEEN
10 Bar Div
ZANDVOORDE

X Corps
(Morland)
ST ELOI
41 Div
HOLLEBEKE
18 Res Div
GELUWE

Group Wytschaete (IX Res Corps)
(Dieffenbach)

MENIN

Second Army
(Plumer)
WYTSCHAETE
19 Div
OOSTTAVERNE
HOUTHEM
16 Div

KEMMEL
IX Corps
(Gordon)
Mt Kemmel
37 Div

FRONT LINES
— 31 JULY 1917
— — 11 AUG
— · — 16 AUG
— · · — 26 SEPT
━━ 5 OCT
— — — 13 OCT
· · · · 6 NOV

WULVERGHEM
MESSINES
3 Aus Div
WARNETON
Lys
COMINES

II Anzac Corps
(Birdwood)
NEUVE EGLISE
NZ Div
ST YVON

Group Lille (II Bav Corps)
FRANCE

MILES 0—3
KILOMETERS 0—4

Ploegsteert Wood
LE GHEER

© Richard Natkiel, 1982

mander in France, had already planned attacks in the Ypres area which he hoped would turn the tide of the war. The Royal Navy supported this effort in the hope that German submarine bases in Belgium would be taken. The mutinies made the offensive seem even more necessary in order to distract the Germans from attempting to exploit French problems.

At Ypres the British salient was narrow, and its defenders were under fire from two sides. Haig intended to attack here, first to widen the salient and then to advance to Ostend and beyond. As a preliminary, at the beginning of June, mines beneath the German-held Messines Ridge (high ground dominating the Ypres salient) were detonated by British sappers, who had been burrowing beneath it for months. The ridge was then captured in a short sharp attack.

Then, on 31 July, after a week of bombardment, the main battle began. The first stage lasted until 4 August, by which time, under heavy rain, the British had won just two miles at the expense of 32,000 casualties. Two days later the struggle recommenced, but only a little ground near Langemarck was captured and the Germans remained unworried. In late September, a few days of sunshine helped meticulously prepared attacks by Plumer's Second Army to make gains in the Menin Road and Polygon Wood sectors on the right of the salient. The rain resumed early in October and the mud which had hampered the initial stages of the battle, was even thicker by November, often being at least waist deep. Nevertheless, although the army commanders wished to call a halt Haig ordered a final drive toward the village of Passchendaele. The final bloody and muddy attack came to an end on 10 November after nearly 250,000 casualties on each side and the offensive was then terminated.

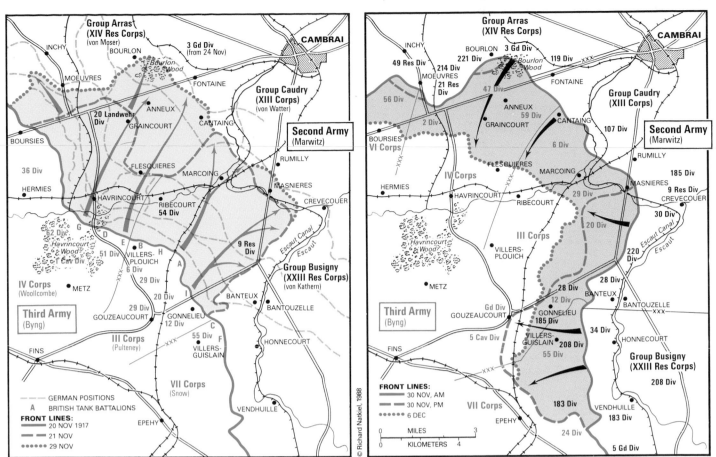

© Richard Natkiel, 1988

The Battle of Cambrai

During August 1917 British staff officers at General Headquarters began the planning of a large-scale raid against German positions around the French town of Cambrai, a major and novel feature being the massive use of tanks to spearhead the operation. The lack of success encountered by the British Army in their main offensive of 1917 – the Third Battle of Ypres (Passchendaele) – encouraged them to expand the raid into a limited offensive in its own right. The plan took the form of a surprise attack by General Sir Julian Byng's Third Army, comprising two infantry corps, each of three divisions, plus the Cavalry Corps acting in reserve. Rolling downland and uncratered ground offered a good opportunity for the employment of tanks – impossible in the low-lying terrain of Flanders – and surprise was to be ensured by 'predicted shooting' whereby the bombardment would commence without previous registration by the artillery. Predicted shooting was an innovation on the British front although the technique had been pioneered with considerable success by the Germans in the east. Despite careful preparations for the assault, the plan had a major weakness, however, namely a lack of reserves to exploit what was becoming an increasingly ambitious offensive.

At 0620 hours on 20 November 1917, 1000 guns opened fire with a single crash on the unsuspecting Germans and 378 fighting tanks lumbered toward the German lines. The combination of whirlwind bombardment and mass tank attack proved too much for the German frontline toops; already unnerved by the pounding inflicted upon them by the British guns, many Germans broke and fled at the sight of the tanks emerging from the autumn mist that cloaked the battlefield.

By midday the British had penetrated the German positions to a depth of four miles. But the cavalry which had been intended to move forward to exploit the breakthrough failed completely, and with many tanks now out of action (mostly through mechanical failure) the offensive began to slow down. Recovering from their initial surprise the Germans began to move up reserves to the front line and by the end of the day held strong positions on the flanks of the British advance. Once more the battle degenerated into the trench-to-trench fighting so characteristic of the Western Front and, short of reserves, the British made only limited territorial gains over the next few days.

On 30 November it was the turn of the Germans to spring a surprise: a counter-attack spearheaded by storm troops, soldiers specially trained in the tactics of 'infiltration,' which were designed to find and exploit the weak points in the British line and then dislocate it by deep penetration and encirclements. This was the debut of this tactic on the Western Front and, like the British combina-

tion of predicted shooting and tanks, it worked well. The German attack was preceded by a short 'hurricane' bombardment, with gas and smoke shells covering the first stage of the assault. Equally surprised, the British fell back in disorder and only the timely arrival of much-needed reinforcements stemmed the German advance. By 5 December, when the battle ended, the British had lost most of their gains of ground and both sides had suffered about 45,000 casualties. Although the tactical stalemate continued as before, the importance of Cambrai lay in the use of massed tank attacks and infiltration tactics – their success was a potent augury for the future.

238

Germany's 1918 Offensives

In early 1918 the German High Command would still accept peace only on its own terms. The Russian Revolution had enabled 70 German divisions to be transferred from the Eastern to the Western Front. With these, the generals believed, it would be possible to win a crushing victory over the demoralized French and exhausted British before American forces could be ready in France in large numbers.

General Ludendorff, effectively in command of the German armies, planned to attack the British Fifth and Third Armies, breaking through north and south of Peronne, and then advancing northward with the right wing so as to drive the British farther away from the French. New tactics and specially trained storm troops were prepared for the attack. The artillery was to bombard the British rear areas using a large proportion of gas shells to disrupt communications rather than destroy defenses while the storm troops infiltrated through the front line, avoiding the strongpoints.

On 21 March the so-called *Kaiserschlacht*

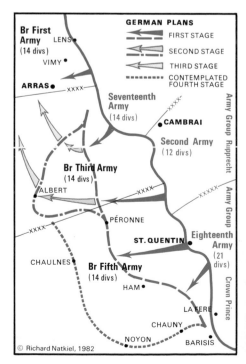

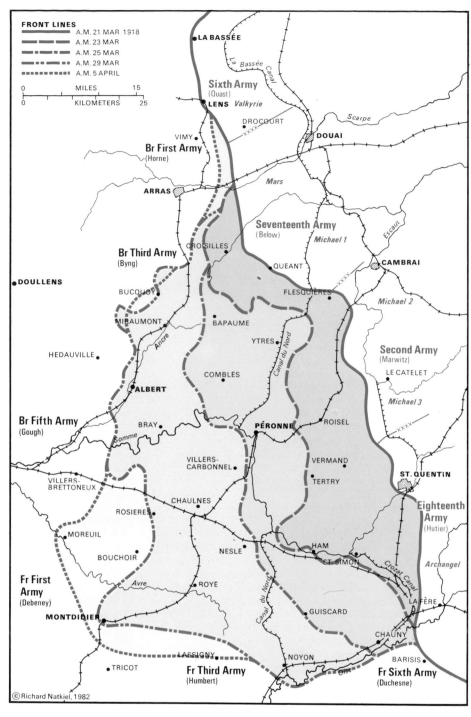

© Richard Natkiel, 1982

Bottom left: a British eighteen-pounder battery moves up to the front during the March 1918 German offensive.
Bottom: German troops bring a flamethrower into action.

(Emperor's Battle) began. The gas shell bombardment was very effective and fog helped the initial infantry attacks. By 24 March the Germans had broken through the British line on a wide front and advanced 14 miles. This, in terms of the Western Front, was an enormous success. The British and French generals, Haig and Pétain, could not reach agreement; Pétain was pessimistic and envisioned a retreat toward Paris, while Haig was more optimistic and felt Pétain was too reluctant to send French reserves to help the British. To settle this discord, General Foch was appointed as grand coordinator.

By 5 April the initial momentum of the attack was exhausted, leaving the Germans in possession of a wide salient reaching to nine miles east of Amiens. To maintain the initiative, the Germans then attacked the British First Army from 9–30 April. This advance was also brought to a halt after desperate defense had limited the German gains to another salient.

The Germans then decided to turn against the French. Just before dawn on 27 May the Chemins des Dames ridge was taken by assault and by 3 June Château Thierry was reached. But this drive, too, died out. There were two more offensives, but the German reserves were becoming exhausted and casualties among the best units were high. German morale was declining whereas the Allied forces were being augmented by more and more fresh American units. On 18 July Foch began his counter-offensive eastward from Villers Cotterêts. He pushed back the Germans until, in early August, a massive and decisive Anglo-French attack completely changed the situation.

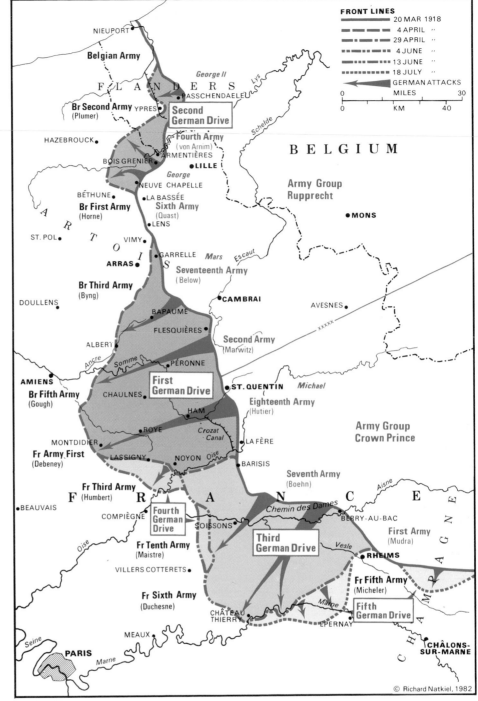

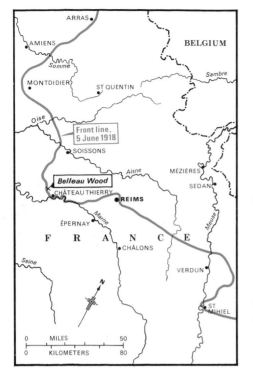

The Battle of Belleau Wood

Lundendorff had counted on defeating the Allies in his final 1918 offensive before American troops were ready to fight in large numbers in France. Five German divisions had defeated the French in fighting on the Aisne and by 3 June were approaching Château Thierry, which was almost un-defended by the French. The latter did scrape together some reserves, and these were joined by the US 2nd and 3rd Divisions, fresh infantrymen and marines. The 85,000 American troops made a counterattack near Belleau Wood, their riflemen advancing against the trenches through wheatfields. The battle, known also as the Battle of Château Thierry, lasted six days and prevented the Germans from gaining a foothold on the south bank of the River Marne.

That some units of the US Army were already in position and ready to fight was a triumph of organization which surprised the German High Command by its rapidity. Assembling the expeditionary forces, sending them across the Atlantic, keeping them supplied and giving them final training on arrival, was a huge task carried out very smoothly, thanks in part to the enormous resources devoted to the undertaking. In France the Americans had their own supply dumps, warehouses and recreation camps. Supplies and troops were carried by railroads manned by US railwaymen using US rolling stock. By these means the Americans were able to bring their forces into the final stage of the war, taking up a long sector of front on both sides of Verdun.

'The Black Day of the German Army'

The series of final Allied offensives was launched on 8 August 1918. Known by the British as the Battle of Amiens and by the French as the Battle of Montdidier, the first attack was to clear the Germans from the Paris-Amiens railroad. Tanks, which had proved themselves already in the Battle of Cambrai (November 1917) were used decisively in this battle. The British had no fewer than 554 of these weapons. Although easily knocked out by artillery, and having no great firepower themselves, their effect on morale was shattering. The German infantry was already demoralized by the apparent lack of success of the arduous offensives which it had been fighting. The soldiers' morale was further sapped by the knowledge that back home their families were starving.

The attack began at dawn in a dense fog. It had been well planned, and the assembly of 14 infantry divisions, more than 2000 guns, with cavalry and tanks, in a small area close to the Germans east of Amiens was a smooth operation conducted in effective secrecy. Much of the infantry force was Australian and Canadian. A creeping artillery barrage, tanks looming out of the fog, and a spirited infantry assault, were too much for the Germans, who fled or surrendered quite readily. By the end of the day six German divisions had been shattered, and the Allies had advanced seven miles on a wide front. The demoralization of the German Army had, after four years, finally set in. Ludendendorff called this the black day of the German Army.

However on 9 August only 145 of the British tanks were still in service, while German reinforcements were arriving. Progress was therefore slower; the French on the right wing were especially slow. On the 10th the French Third Army joined in. On the 11th the Australians and Canadians were ordered to advance to the Somme between Péronne and Ham, while the French First Army which had its own French-built tanks and had recaptured Montdidier, was to occupy Ham. However, stiffening resistance, and lack of tanks and guns, persuaded the commander of the British Fourth Army to postpone further attacks.

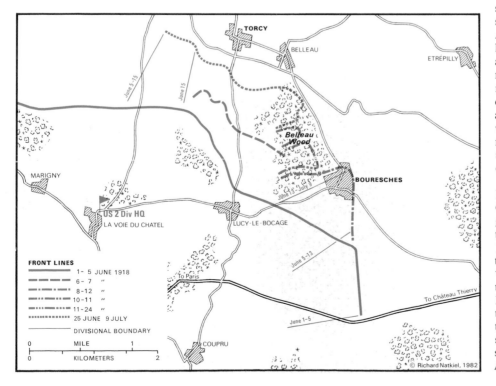

© Richard Natkiel, 1982

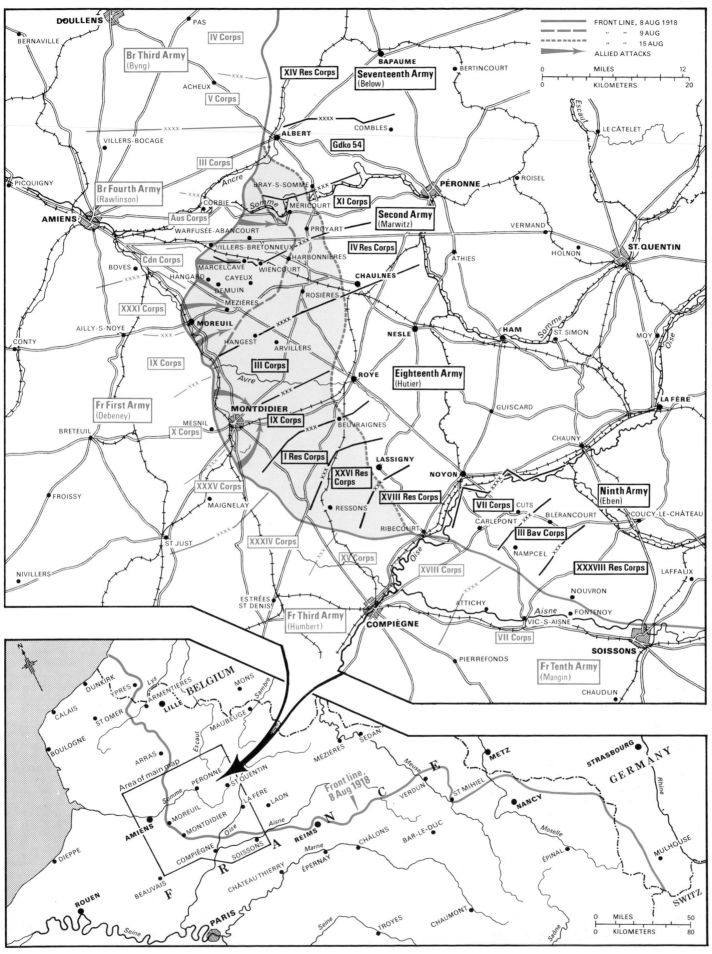

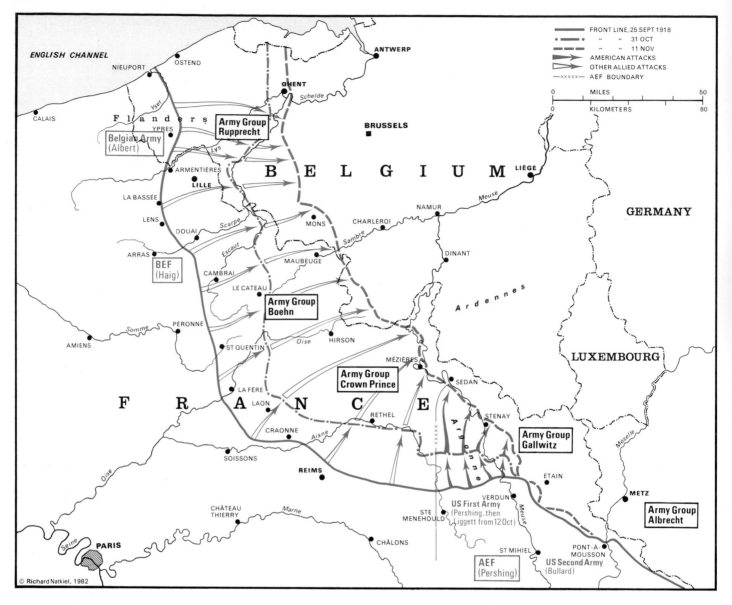

The Allied Victory on the Western Front

Only a few days after the Battle of Amiens the Allies were ready to resume their offensive against the demoralized Germans. By the end of August the whole line north of the Marne was moving. The British gained ground along the Somme, while south of the Oise the French advanced to recapture ground lost in the recent German offensive. On 12 September General Pershing's US First Army attacked the St Mihiel salient just as the Germans were evacuating it, thereby winning a victory which, because it entailed few casualties, was an ideal introduction to real warfare for fresh troops. The Germans retreated to what in effect was their final defense, the Hindenburg Line. While the French busied themselves with collecting reserves to exploit a breakthrough, the British won positions from which the line could be assaulted.

The big breakthrough was planned for 26 September. On that day the French Fourth Army and the US First Army attacked between Reims and the River Meuse. Next day, the British Third and First Armies attacked farther north, near Lens. On the 28th the British Second Army and the French Sixth joined with the surviving units of the Belgian Army in an offensive between Armentières and the sea. Finally, around Epéhy, the French First Army and the British Fourth began an offensive. The Allies had 160 full strength divisions to pit against about 100 under-strength German divisions. It was the advance of the British Fourth Army which was decisive; helped by tanks, it broke through the Hindenburg Line in the first day of its attack.

Ludendorff, additionally unnerved by the decision of Germany's ally Bulgaria to seek an armistice, and knowing that this would open Austria to Allied attack from Greece, advised the Kaiser to seek an armistice. This took some weeks to arrange, and the last weeks of the war were weeks of retreat for the German Army. Before the Armistice was

signed, Ludendorff resigned in protest at its terms. He thereby protected his reputation on two fronts: the armistice he had suggested saved him from total defeat, while his resignation proclaimed that he was a man who would have preferred to fight on.

Right: Austro-Hungarian troops in action on the Isonzo front.

Vittorio Veneto

The Italian stand on the Piave following their retreat from Caporetto had been bolstered by 11 British and French divisions sent from the Western Front. In their advance the German and Austrian forces had stretched their supply system and their consequently weakened attacks could not break through. These efforts came to an end in late December 1917. The new Italian commander, General Diaz, was more able than his predecessor Cadorna and under his direction the Italians spent the early months of 1918 re-forming and re-equipping their shattered forces. In this period also the German troops and six of the Anglo-French units were withdrawn to the Western Front.

With strong prompting from the Germans the Austrians renewed their attacks from 15–24 June 1918. The plan was for a two-pronged attack but neither General Boroević's group attacking over the Piave or Conrad's west of Monte Grappa was made sufficiently strong. Boroević gained some ground initially but air attacks and a rise in the river weakened the temporary bridges and the advance had to be abandoned. In the other sector the Austrians were quickly thrown back by British and French troops.

By 24 October the Italians themselves were ready to advance. Fourth Army made diversionary attacks in the Monte Grappa sector while crossings over the Piave were being won to the east. The most important initial gains were made by British and French troops which respectively formed part of the British and French led Tenth and Twelfth Armies. By 30 October the Austrian resistance was beginning to collapse and the Italian cavalry led a rapid pursuit. The battle is now known as the Battle of Vittorio Veneto. The armistice was agreed on 3 November.

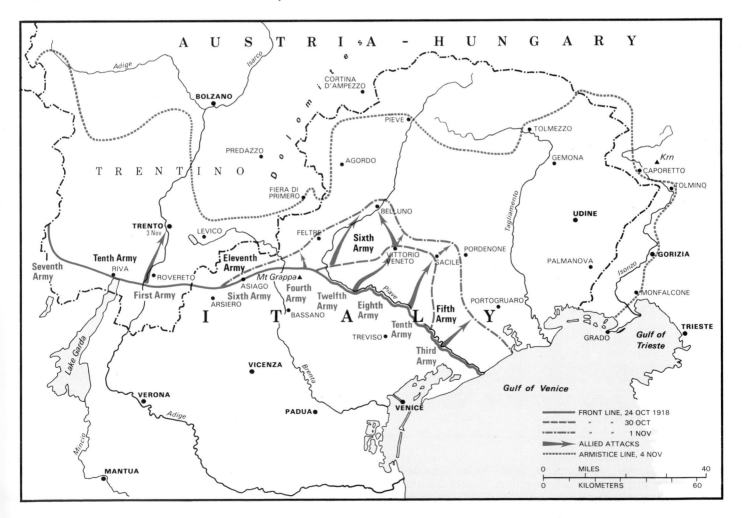

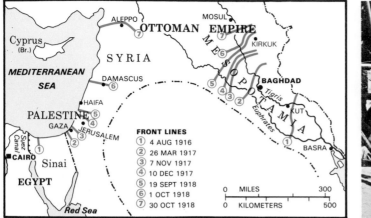

The Mesopotamia Campaign

In November 1914 an expeditionary force of Britain's Indian Army landed at the head of the Persian Gulf with the intention of marching up the valley of the Tigris and Euphrates rivers. In doing so, it was expected to divert Turkish forces from other fronts and possibly, it was hoped, encourage the Arabs of the Turkish Empire to revolt. The Anglo-Indian force was very successful and pushed on faster than had originally been hoped. After Basra had been captured, the possession of Qurnah was thought necessary to secure it. Then to secure Qurnah, Amarah and Nasiriyah were taken, and it was realized that the whole situation would be improved if Kut were taken. Having got as far as Kut, it seemed a pity not to go on to capture Baghdad, from where the British could threaten the Turkish homeland in Anatolia, or advance into Turkish Syria and Palestine. To some, the fact that Baghdad was the terminus of the Berlin-Baghdad Railway, the legendary instrument of German influence in the Middle East, made it a specially attractive target.

General Townshend, the British commander, had made a well-planned attack on Kut, which he captured despite strong resistance by German-trained Turks. But by this time his supply routes were extended, and his men, although used to the Indian climate, were tired after a long campaign in arid conditions. Moreover, whereas the Turks could easily call up reinforcements, Townshend had only 13,000 troops, of which two thirds were Indian. Nevertheless, a week after capturing Kut, Townshend was on his way, and by 12 November 1915 was within 24 miles of Baghdad, facing a Turkish defense line at Ctesiphon.

The Turks realized, just as well as the British, the strategic importance of Baghdad, and the defense they offered at Ctesiphon was strong, consisting of two lines of entrenchments on the eastern bank of the Tigris, with their right flank covered by a canal connecting the Tigris and Euphrates.

Townshend's plan of attack was similar to that of his attack on Kut, but this time he succeeded only in capturing the outer Turkish line, and that only after heavy fighting. The arrival of reinforcements enabled the Turks to make counterattacks which, though costly, persuaded Townshend to withdraw. This withdrawal degenerated into a near-rout and ended only when the reduced British force was safe behind the walls of Kut. Here it was besieged from the beginning of December by strong Turkish forces under German command. The Turks were now able to transfer troops from the Gallipoli front, from which the Allied forces were withdrawing and mounted a fierce assault on 23 December which, however, failed. A Russian relief attempt through Persia was held back at Kermanshah, while a British relief force from the south almost reached Kut, but was impeded at the final stage by floodwater. On 29 April 1916 Townshend surrendered; his surviving 2,000 British and 6,000 Indian troops had been starved into submission.

The capture of Kut was only a temporary cause for Turkish rejoicing. While their own and the world's attention had been gripped by Mesopotamia, the Russians had advanced into Turkey from the Caucasus and, in a brilliant campaign in bitter temperatures, captured the city of Erzerum, reputed to be the strongest fortress in the Turkish Empire. Later, Russian cavalry from Persia would move forward to meet Anglo-Indian forces in Mesopotamia.

The British forces were strengthened during 1916 and by the end of the year had begun to advance once again. Kut was taken in February 1917 and the able and popular General Maude led his force on to capture Baghdad. Some further advances were made before a halt was called for the duration of the summer heat. There were important British victories at Ramadi and in the Tigris valley later in the year.

Following the Russian Revolution the main British concern for 1918 was to send a contingent, led by General Dunsterville, to north Persia to try and protect the oilfields there from a Turkish advance. This effort was only partially successful. The campaign in Mesopotamia was resumed in earnest in

early October and the Turkish Sixth Army was quickly beaten. Mosul was occupied after the armistice.

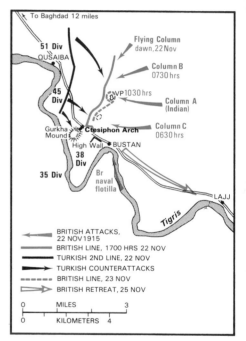

Palestine

After the British defeat in the Second Battle of Gaza General Allenby was appointed to command on this front, and was put under political pressure to capture Jerusalem 'in time for Christmas.' Making good use of his ample cavalry strength, he sent his artillery and infantry northward along the coastal plain, while his cavalry made sweeps inland to outflank the enemy. Von Falkenhayn, who had been replaced on the Western Front after he had failed to win dramatic victories, now commanded the Turkish forces, but although he was one of the most able generals of the war he was unable, with a force about one third in size of the British, to hold Allenby. In early November Allenby's men took Gaza; earlier frontal

Left: an Indian sentry mounts guard over a Maurice Farman biplane of the Royal Flying Corps in Mesopotamia.

attacks had failed, but Allenby then outflanked it by capturing Beersheba. The advance continued rapidly, and as early as 14 November the railroad junction for the branchline to Jerusalem was captured and the Turkish defenders of that city thereby deprived of their supply route. Two days later Jaffa was captured. Allenby then contrived a pincer movement against Jerusalem and that city surrendered on 9 December; Allenby had succeeded where King Richard the Lionheart had failed. He was unable to advance further at this stage, partly because of supply difficulties and partly because many of his infantry units were withdrawn early in 1918 and sent to France to help meet the German spring offensives. Allenby retained his strong cavalry force and was sent some largely inexperienced Indian infantry.

Allenby's campaign was considerably aided by Arab irregular and guerrilla forces. A revolt in the Hejaz had begun early in 1916 and had become a powerful force under the inspiring leadership of a British officer T E Lawrence (Lawrence of Arabia) who was sent to join it in December 1916. Considerable Turkish forces were held down in the Hejaz at first while in the later stages of Allenby's campaign the Turkish flank was threatened and harassed.

In the summer of 1918 the British line in Palestine ran about 10 miles north of Jericho, Jerusalem and Jaffa, and by mid-September Allenby felt strong enough to launch an offensive which was destined to force Turkey out of the war. His infantry first drove the Turks back to the key railroad junction of Tulkarm, while his cavalry made a long fast ride through the night to reach Beth Shean and Nazareth. Here they turned south-east and cut off the Turks' retreat. This series of moves resulted in the virtual destruction of two Turkish armies, while the third fled across the Jordan and gradually decomposed; by this time the Turkish soldier was usually ready to surrender or desert. After this, there was nothing to stop Allenby. Damascus was captured on 1 October, Beirut fell to French units on 7 October, and meanwhile Turkey was reeling back in Mesopotamia and surrendering her entire army on the Tigris. Aleppo was taken on 25 October and on 30 October Turkey was forced to sign an armistice. In doing so she provided one more incentive for the German High Command to call for an end of the war.

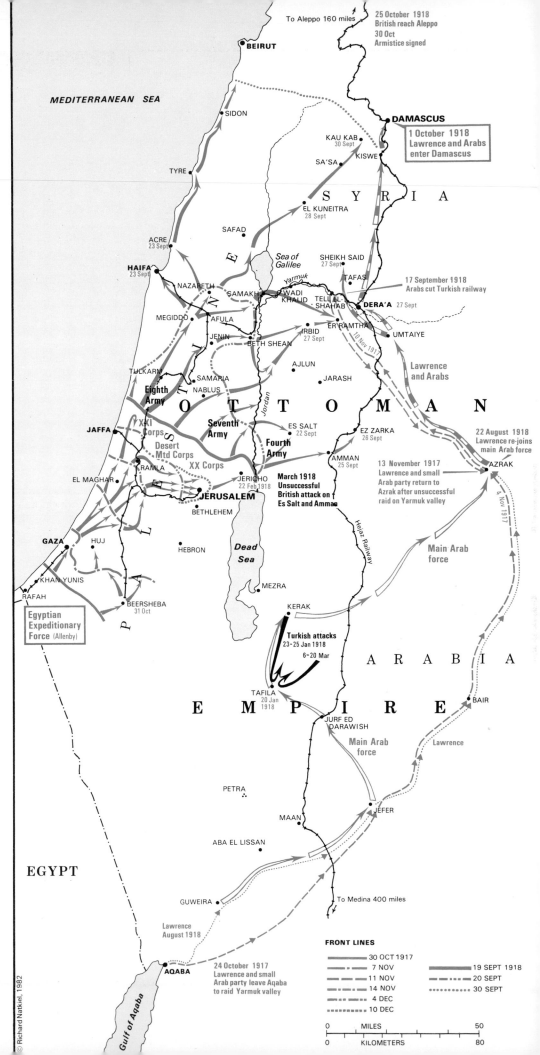

Africa in 1914

What became known as the 'scramble for Africa' began in the mid-1880s and continued to 1914. There was a series of agreements in which colonizing powers divided up Africa among themselves. They agreed, for example, that King Leopold of Belgium could hold the Congo as his personal property (he later bequeathed it, as the Belgian Congo, to Belgium). The French, apart from their hold on the island of Madagascar, concentrated on the vast areas of northwest Africa. To this extensive territory they joined the region to the north of the Congo (French Equatorial Africa). British expansion, mainly through chartered trading companies, meant that by 1914 Britain had important colonies in East Africa (Kenya and Uganda, Somaliland) and West Africa (Nigeria, the Gold Coast, Gambia,

and Sierra Leone). Cape Colony, Natal, the Orange Free State, and the Transvaal had united into the Union of South Africa under the British crown. Britain had also pushed northward into Bechuanaland, Rhodesia and Nyasaland, thereby interposing a wedge between German Southwest Africa and German East Africa.

The Germans, who had worked hard as latecomers to extend their colonies, possessed by 1914 the Kamerun, Togoland, Southwest Africa, and Tanganyika with Ruanda and Urundi. The Portuguese, asserting centuries-old rights of settlement, had the extensive territories of Angola and Mozambique, as well as Portuguese Guinea. The Italians, latecomers like the Germans, had managed to gain three barren territories, Libya, Eritrea and Italian Somaliland. There were a few small Spanish colonies, too, of which the most important was Spanish Morocco. By 1914 only Liberia and Abyssinia remained independent.

The East African Campaign

The campaign in East Africa was one of the most remarkable of the war. Despite being completely cut off from outside help the German forces, led by General Paul von Lettow-Vorbeck, remained in being to the end of the war and succeeded in tying down enormously greater Allied forces. Lettow-Vorbeck's strength was never greater than 4000 German and 12,000 native troops.

The Allied campaign began with landings by Indian troops in November 1914 but these were quickly repulsed with heavy losses. The events of 1915 were mostly indecisive cross-border raids by both sides but the Allies did manage to gain control of the great lakes and also to sink the German cruiser *Königsberg*. Following the conclusion of the campaign in

© Richard Natkiel, 1982

**Bottom: a bridge on the Dar-es-Salaam to Mikese railroad blown up by German forces in September 1916.
Bottom right: a company of German askaris forms a firing line.**

Southwest Africa in mid-1915 considerable South African forces were sent to East Africa. These units, under the command of General Smuts, led a major Allied offensive beginning in early 1916. Belgian forces from the Congo also began to advance. After much elaborate maneuvering but few major battles the German forces were gradually pushed southward. At the end of 1916 Smuts and most of the South African force left after suffering heavy losses to disease. They were replaced by British-trained East and West African troops.

When the fighting was resumed in July 1917 after the rainy season the Germans were forced even farther south and a large contingent was cut off at Mahenge and had to surrender. In November Lettow-Vorbeck led his remaining forces into Portugese East Africa. They were continually harried and occasionally small groups were captured but the Armistice in 1918 found the Germans in Rhodesia still ahead of their pursuers.

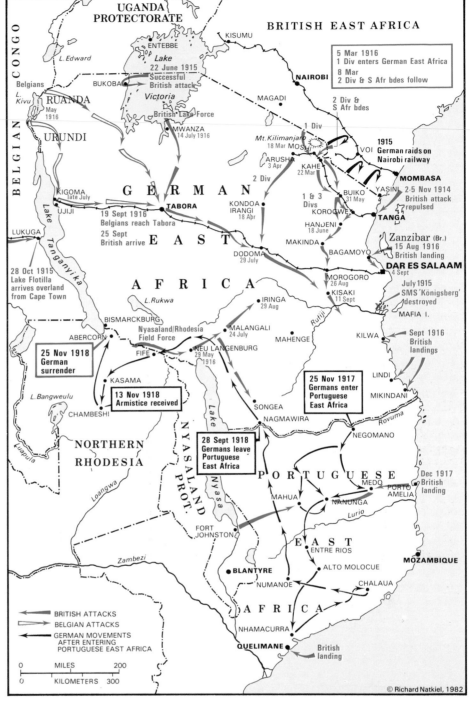

These pages: smiling British troops man a captured German trench near Serre, March 1917.

THE WORLD AT WAR,
1914-18

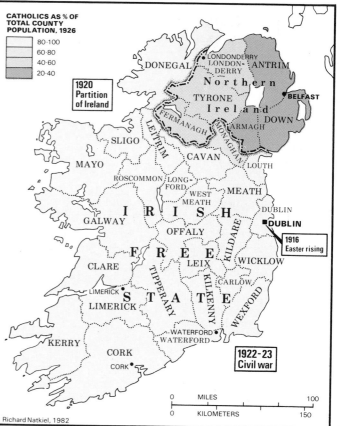

CATHOLICS AS % OF TOTAL COUNTY POPULATION, 1926

80-100
60-80
40-60
20-40

1920 Partition of Ireland

1916 Easter rising

1922-23 Civil war

© Richard Natkiel, 1982

The Partition of Ireland

The outbreak of war in 1914 meant that a Home Rule Bill for Ireland, which had finally passed through the British parliament, was shelved, and the war years gave its opponents time to prepare. In Ulster, largely Protestant and industrial, opposition to being ruled from Catholic Dublin had been so strong that para-military formations to fight the Bill had appeared in 1914. In the south, the Sinn Fein organization, mainly Catholic, which was opposed to the link with the British monarchy, staged a rebellion in Dublin at Easter 1916. This was quelled, but the movement went on to electoral successes in 1918. The Sinn Fein majority refused to take seats in the British parliament but set up its own *Dail* (national assembly) in Dublin. Guerrilla warfare against the British Army, and between Sinn Feiners and Ulstermen, became savage after the war, and in 1921 the British offered dominion status for southern Ireland, with the six counties of Ulster remaining British. An Irish delegation signed a treaty in London setting up the Irish Free State as a dominion, but it was then disowned by De Valera, the Irish President, and his allies, who denounced the partition of Ireland into Ulster and the Irish Free State. However, the treaty was ratified and De Valera resigned, a 1922 election giving the Free State government a strong majority. But political opposition turned to violent opposition, and a civil war broke out which the government won. The boundary with Northern Ireland was then confirmed. Theoretically, it was determined by the predominant religion of each county, but initially it included areas with Catholic majorities. Although the economic effect of the new frontier was smaller than had been feared, it could not really achieve the separation of Catholics from Protestants, due to the religious intermixing of each locality. Partition, as a temporary measure, seemed justified in view of the strong demand for independence on the one hand and the antipathy between Protestants and Catholics on the other, but it was far from being the final solution for which many Ulstermen had hoped; a divided Ireland was a contradiction of geography and a source of resentment for Catholics in the north and south.

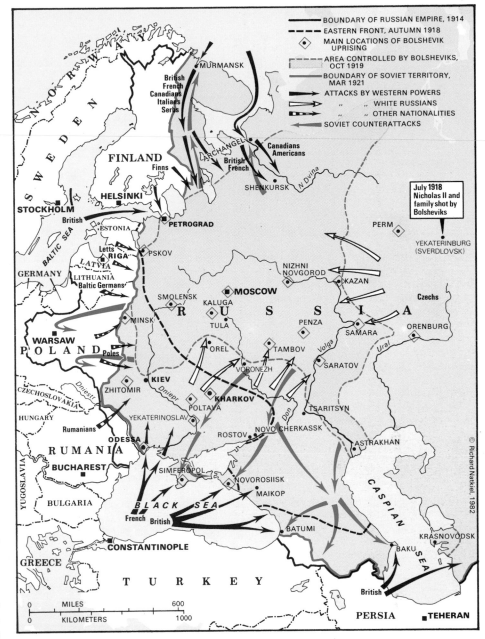

The Russian Civil War

The Bolshevik takeover of Petrograd (Leningrad) in November 1917 was followed by the withdrawal of Russia from World War I at the Treaty of Brest-Litovsk in the spring of 1918. This treaty guaranteed German domination of eastern Europe but it also guaranteed the enmity of Russia's former allies who, apart from being anti-Bolshevik in principle, felt they had been betrayed by the new regime as they were left to fight the German Empire alone without their strategically important but militarily inept eastern allies. The Germans set up states in Poland and the Ukraine which were amenable to her interests but when, in November 1918, the German government itself was overthrown and an armistice was signed with the allies, a power vacuum opened in eastern Europe and within the new Soviet Union. The Bolsheviks were effectively in control of little more than the corridor between Petrograd and Moscow. Finland and the Baltic states were created out of the western Russian provinces and an expanded Rumanian state rushed to claim Bessarabia. The newly formed state of Poland sought to expand in the east at Russian expense. For their part the Allies were hoping that the war between pro-Tsarist elements and the Bolsheviks would force Lenin's regime to collapse. The victorious western Allies helped the so-called White Armies by invading the northern ports of Murmansk and Archangel as well as the Black Sea ports.

Attacked from every direction, Leon Trotsky's newly formed Red Army struck back. Russian forces were at the gates of Warsaw before the French, led by General Maxime Weygand and Captain Charles de Gaulle, intervened. Although the French-backed Polish Army was able to capture large sections of White Russia, the Allied-supported Ukrainians were not so lucky. By the spring of 1920 the western allies and the White Russians whom they supported were thrown back and the armies dispersed. The Allies for their part were anxious to have their troops return home and the cohesiveness and power of the Red Army made it by far the most determined force in the field and it was ultimately victorious over all comers.

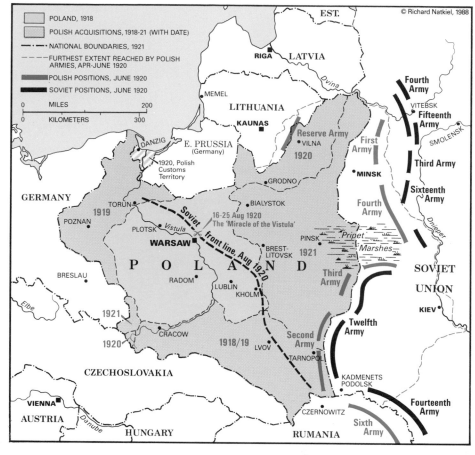

The Russo-Polish War

The Russo-Polish War (1919-20) was fought by Lenin's Bolshevik government for two main reasons: to re-establish Russian domination over areas of the former czarist empire and to spread the socialist revolution westward into Europe. The Polish government of Marshal Pilsudski fought to maintain the independence of these non-Russian territories. The catalyst for hostilities was the German withdrawal from the area in February 1919, an action that resulted in a clash between Polish and Soviet forces in Belorussia. Initially, the advantage lay with the Poles who recaptured Vilna in April and Minsk in August. Hostilities then broke out on a wide front stretching from Latvia in the north to Rumania in the south. By January 1920 the Red Army had concentrated some 700,000 men along the River Berezina, and a major offensive against Poland was launched under the command of General Tukhachevsky on 10 March.

The Poles were able to delay the advance of the Red Army by a series of daring moves including a march on Kiev in April and the bloody Battle of Berezina in May. But in the summer the Red Army regained the initiative when Budyonny's First Cavalry Army broke through the Polish positions in Galicia in June. On 4 July Tukhachevsky moved westward, and by the beginning of August five Soviet armies were approaching the suburbs of Warsaw, the Polish capital.

The situation was critical for the Poles. Allied diplomacy had failed to bring about an armistice, and the so-called 'Curzon Line' was rejected by both sides. Neither the British nor the French were prepared to give any real help to the Polish government. On 10 August Red Army cavalry crossed the Vistula west of Warsaw. There was a strange calm in the city as local Workers' Battalions and the militia marched out to meet the Red Army. While this took place and the Red Army was preparing to attack the capital, the Polish Army was reforming, with battered divisions being withdrawn from the line and then sent to the north and south. When Tukhachevsky did attack on 13 August, Warsaw's defenses held firm. The

Right: a Russian artillery crew prepare their howitzer before a battle with the Polish Army.

Above: senior officers of the Red Army confer at the Polish battle front in 1920.

main Red Army force was contained to the north by General Sikorski and on the 16th the Poles broke into the Red Army's rear areas, severing its lines of communication. Tukhachevsky found that his entire army was surrounded, 100,000 Russians were captured while 40,000 fled to East Prussia. The Poles had destroyed the Soviet armies in what became known as the 'Miracle of the Vistula.'

Pilsudski maintained the momentum of his success, nearly encircling Budyonny's Cavalry Army on 31 August in a massive cavalry battle. Budyonny was forced to retreat to the north on the River Niemen and the Red Army began to disintegrate, with mutinies in the garrison towns of Belorussia. It appeared that there was nothing to stop the Poles reaching Moscow. Lenin was forced to sue for peace, and the Poles were offered as much territory on the borderlands as they wanted as long as the fighting ceased within ten days. The armistice was signed on 12 October and, after much wrangling, the final terms were agreed at the Treaty of Riga on 18 March 1921. Everyone was aware of the significance of the outcome of this war. In Western Europe there was great relief at the victory of the Poles, whilst Lenin recognized the magnitude of the military defeat for communism.

The Emergence of Turkey

Following Turkey's surrender to the Allies in 1918 there were internal political troubles in Turkey while the Allies were squabbling among themselves over the division of the Ottoman Empire, still nominally ruled by the Sultan. The Middle Eastern lands were eventually allocated to Britain and France under League of Nations mandates. As for the Turkish heartland on Asia Minor, Italy, France and Greece all nursed claims and in pursuit of these Italy made landings in the Adalia area. With support from Britain and France, Greek troops were sent to Smyrna where there was a considerable Greek population, to ensure Italian gains remained limited. These incursions, Greek control of most of eastern Thrace and international control of the Straits Zone were all recognized by the Treaty of Sèvres.

However, as early as May 1919 nationalist moves to resist this partitioning were begun under the leadership of Mustapha Kemal. He soon had a considerable following and was proclaimed head of a provisional government in April 1920. The Allied response was to occupy Constantinople and to urge the Greeks to begin an advance inland from Smyrna which they did in June 1920. Adrianople and most of Thrace were also overrun and in Anatolia there were inconclusive battles near Eskishehr (the First and Second Battles of the Inönu) and at Afiun in early 1921. In July a Greek victory at Afiun allowed the Greek forces to make a general advance toward Ankara but Kemal's forces won a bitter battle in the bend of the Sakaria River and the Greeks retired to their July positions. By this time the Turks were receiving some Soviet help while diplomatic efforts had persuaded the Italians to leave the Adalia area and the French were ready to move out of southwest Turkey (not shown on map). Kemal's popularity was unquestioned and the Greek forces were exhausted. A Turkish offensive in August 1922 quickly took Afiun and in a lightning advance the Greeks were bundled out of Smyrna. In October the Allies allowed Turkey to reoccupy the Straits area and Thrace, and these gains and Turkish independence were confirmed by the Treaty of Lausanne in July 1923.

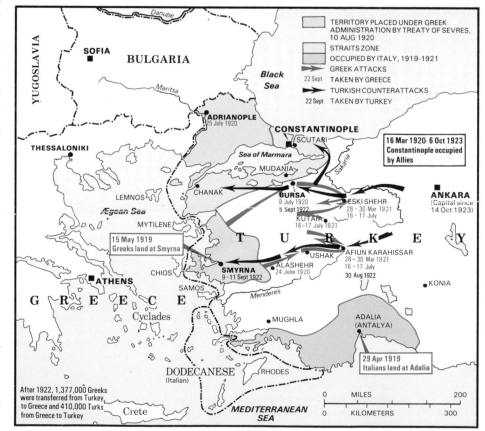

The Spanish Civil War

In 1931, following a period of civil disturbance, the Spanish monarchy was replaced by a republic, and a left-wing government introduced reforms: separation of the state from the church, state education, and the break-up of large estates. Having moved faster than most people wished, it was defeated in a 1933 election by right-wing parties, which began to reverse the reforms but were in turn defeated by a 'popular front' of the left-wing in a 1936 election. Reform then continued, despite violent resistance by Spanish fascists, known as the Falange. There were political assassinations, followed by a revolt against the government started by army officers in Spanish Morocco. In October 1936 the insurgent General Franco, who had flown to the mainland in a chartered British plane from the Canary Islands, was declared 'Chief of the Spanish State.' The cities of Cadiz, Seville and Zaragoza declared for the insurgents, as did Burgos, where Franco set up his headquarters. Soon Fascist Italy and Nazi Germany were sending forces to help the insurgents (the Nationalists) while Russia sent men and supplies to help the government (the Republicans). The latter were also reinforced, morally as much as militarily, by the International Brigade, made up of idealistic volunteers from various countries who saw this as the first great battle against European fascism.

By the end of 1936 the Nationalists held about half of Spain. They had benefited from their superior military strength and their supply routes through Portugal. The industrial areas as well as the Basque and Catalonian regions (which had been promised autonomy by the government) were strongly in support of the Republicans.

The Nationalist advance on Madrid had begun at the end of the first week of October 1936. The Army of Africa began a three-pronged attack; northward from Toledo; northeastward along the Navalcarnero road; and eastward from San Martin. The Nationalists believed that because of the retreat of the Republican forces the fall of Madrid was only a matter of maintaining a steady advance. The plan was for the Nationalist forces to enter the capital on 12 October, but a complicated command structure and unexpected Republican resistance slowed down the triumphant

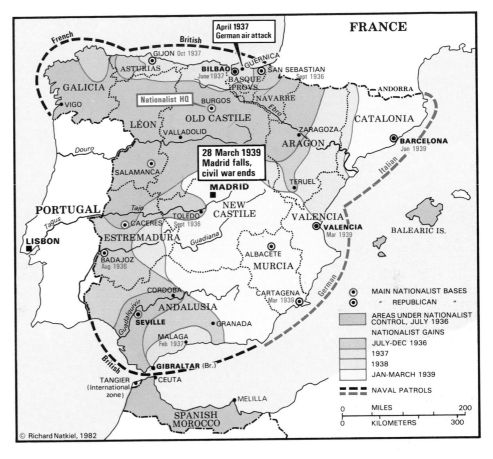

advance. However, the Republican government was paralyzed by conflict between the various political factions. The cabinet decided to withdraw from Madrid in the face of the Nationalist advance, and the capital was turned over to a junta under the command of General Miaja. On the night of 6 November the government left for Valencia.

The flight of the government actually provided the stimulus for the various political factions to work together, and the gut instinct of the population was to defend Madrid. On 8 November the Nationalists attacked with three assault forces against the western suburbs of Madrid. Although the Republicans outnumbered the attacking Nationalists two to one, few of them had any military experience and they were a heterogeneous mass of militia. In fact the Nationalists were unable to advance very far and this was an important psychological victory for the defenders of Madrid. The arrival of the XI International Brigade had a powerful moral effect on the population. On the 9th and again on the 19th

the Nationalists unsuccessfully attacked Madrid. Faced with these failures, Franco decided to bombard the city with artillery fire and air attacks. By the end of November the battle for Madrid had settled down into a cold, hungry siege, punctuated by bombardment, air raids and the occasional skirmishes.

On 8 February 1937, troops under General Llano, assisted by Italian troops, attempted unsuccessfully to cut the road from Madrid to Valencia. Soviet training and 'volunteer' reinforcements went far to steady the defenders of the capital. In March, two Italian divisions made a surprise penetration of Republican lines in an attempt to isolate Madrid. But Soviet bombers attacked their columns and scattered them across the countryside. In July the Republican forces in Madrid launched a counteroffensive, but after some success this was repulsed. There was no serious fighting on the Madrid front for another two years as Franco turned his attention elsewhere.

By August 1938, the Nationalists had captured most of Spain and began to move against

256

**Right: the Battle of Madrid.
Below: Republican troops wait for the order to advance.
Below right: Italian troops move forward during the Ethiopian campaign.**

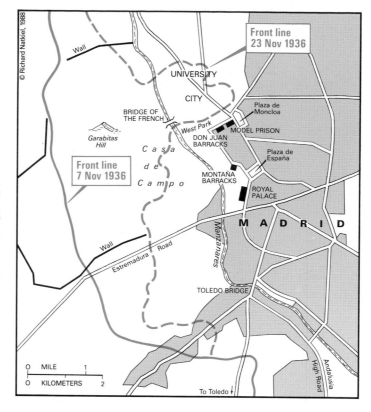

© Richard Natkiel, 1988

Front line
23 Nov 1936

UNIVERSITY
CITY

BRIDGE OF
THE FRENCH
West Park
Garabitas
Hill

Plaza de
Moncloa

MODEL PRISON

DON JUAN
BARRACKS

Plaza de
España

Front line
7 Nov 1936

*C a s a
d e
C a m p o*

MONTAÑA
BARRACKS

ROYAL
PALACE

M A D R I D

Wall

Wall

Estremadura   Road

Manzanares

TOLEDO BRIDGE

Andalusia

High Road

0   MILE   1
0   KILOMETERS   2

To Toledo

the scattered pockets of Republican resistance, including Madrid. On 26 March 1939 Franco launched a new offensive against the capital and on the following day members of the Republican Defence Council fled the city, which was then forced to surrender.

In early 1939, with the loss of Barcelona, Valencia, and Madrid, the government's military resistance ended. About 750,000 lives had been lost in the war, many by execution.

As well as its importance for Spain, the Civil War had significant influence on wider issues of international relations in several ways. It helped strengthen the relationship between Italy and Germany while weakening the possibility of anti-German agreements between France and the USSR because of the French refusal to help the Republicans. Both Britain and France appeared weak and unwilling to act decisively in support of their interests. Perhaps above all the war gave Hitler and Mussolini reason to believe that their aims could be achieved simply by ruthless military action. The fighting also gave the German and Italian armed forces useful experience. The German Luftwaffe gave several rather misleading demonstrations of its power, in particular the bombing of Guernica (April 1937). Belief in the might of the Luftwaffe contributed to the appeasement policy followed by Britain and France.

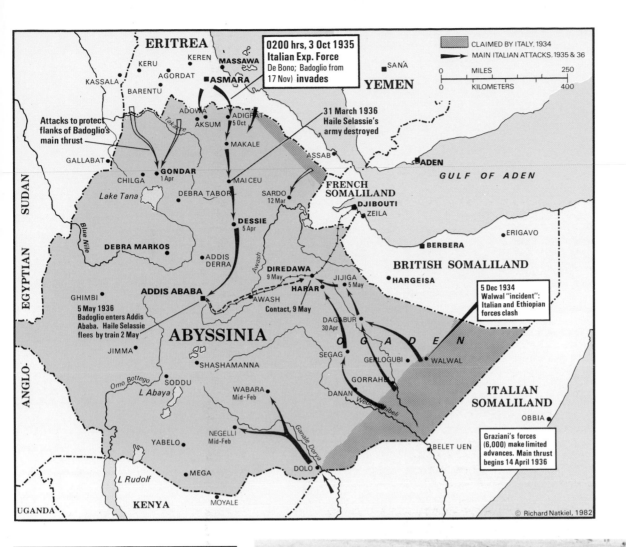

The Italian Invasion of Ethiopia

Ethiopia (Abyssinia), was a Christian kingdom which had retained its independence for centuries. As late as 1896 it had decisively defeated an Italian invading army at Adowa. In 1930 Haile Selassie became Emperor, introduced modernizing reforms, but took care not to invite Italian experts for technical assistance. In Italy, Mussolini was in power and seeking foreign conquest as well as revenge for Adowa.

There were frontier incidents on Ethiopia's frontiers with neighboring Italian colonies of Eritrea and Somaliland. At an oasis, Walwal, claimed as their territory by both Italians and Ethiopians, there was a serious clash in December 1934. Both disputants agreed to accept League of Nations arbitration, but Mussolini continued to send reinforcements to his east African colonies. The arbitrators, after some months, decided that neither side had been to blame, but by that time Mussolini, with the tacit acquiescence of France, was preparing to invade as soon as the rainy season ended. On 3 October 1935 Italian troops invaded from Eritrea and captured Adowa, while

forces from Somaliland made somewhat slower progress. The League of Nations introduced economic sanctions against Italy but these were ineffective because key states, including Switzerland and Austria, did not comply with them. Although the Italian advance was slowed by poor roads, modern weapons, including aircraft and poison gas, assured the defeat of the Ethiopians and on 5 May 1936 the capital, Addis Ababa, was captured. Haile Selassie fled, to return when the British drove out the Italians in 1941.

These pages: US troops wait aboard their assault craft before beginning the liberation of Europe, June 1944.

THE WORLD AT WAR, 1939-45

The Treaty of Versailles

Map legend:
- PRE–1914 BOUNDARIES
- BOUNDARIES AFTER TREATY OF VERSAILLES. 1919
- TERRITORIES LOST BY GERMANY
- UNDER LEAGUE OF NATIONS CONTROL
- DEMILITARISED ZONE

© Richard Natkiel, 1982

Germany, became an object of deep resentment in Germany. Germany also lost the city of Memel, which eventually went to Lithuania, and about 122 square miles which went to Czechoslovakia. In all, Germany lost 13 percent of her pre-war area. By another treaty, new states (Yugoslavia, Hungary, Poland, Czechoslovakia) had been established, largely at the expense of the old Austro-Hungarian Empire. But the Versailles Treaty expressly forbade a union of Germany with Austria, even though such a union was a possible solution to their problem of survival in the post-war world.

Unlike previous peace treaties, the Treaty of Versailles, signed by Germany in June 1919, was not negotiated, but imposed. It was also unfair and vengeful and therefore likely to lead to further conflict.

Under its provisions Germany lost all her colonies, mainly in Africa and the Pacific. Her army and navy were reduced to strengths characteristic of a third-rate power. The reparations clauses of the Treaty did not specify the payments in kind and in money which Germany was to pay to the victors, but left the door open for almost any demands which might be made. The moral basis for reparations were the so-called 'Honor' clauses of the Treaty, in which Germany admitted the entire blame for the outbreak of the war. This forced admission, which even in that emotional period must have been seen by most responsible statesmen as a lie, for long rankled with the German public and does much to explain the popularity of Hitler a dozen years later.

Territorially, Germany was required to return to France Alsace and Lorraine, taken by conquest in 1871. The mining area around Saarbrücken remained under German sovereignty but with commercial concessions for France. The west bank of the Rhine, which France unsuccessfully demanded in perpetuity, was to be occupied by France for 15 years. Belgium acquired 400 square miles, including the towns of Eupen and Malmédy. It was proposed that Schleswig and Holstein, conquered in 1864, should be returned to Denmark. With a maturity lacking in other, greater, powers, Denmark refused this gift, contenting itself with the Danish-speaking parts, and that only after a plebiscite in 1920. In the east, Poland was newly independent, and seeking to expand at German expense and with French support. But it was stipulated that Upper Silesia should not go to Poland unless its population wished it to. A plebiscite was held in 1921, but satisfied nobody, and the problem of the German-Polish frontier was handed over to a League of Nations committee whose recommendation was adopted despite its absurdities (in places it passed not only through the middle of towns and villages, but also through factories). The German province of Posen became the Polish territory of Poznan. Elsewhere, in order that Poland might have access to the sea, Danzig (declared a free city) was connected to Poland proper by a wide strip of former Prussian territory henceforth known as the 'Polish Corridor.' This Polish strip, cutting off East Prussia from the rest of

German Gains 1939-40

After the outbreak of war Germany's military triumphs continued where Hitler's political successes had left off. Poland, Norway, Denmark and France were all quickly defeated. Although Britain temporarily staved off invasion her army had been shattered by the campaign in France and, despite Churchill's inspirational leadership, it was hard to see how a comeback could be made. Encouraged by German successes Mussolini had joined the war but by the end of 1940 the Italian armies in Greece and North Africa were struggling. The United States was increasing its supplies sent to Britain but the German U-Boats were taking an ever greater toll on the convoy routes despite the increasing strength of the escort forces.

Ceded Rumanian territories:
1. Bessarabia & N. Bukovina to Russia, June 1940
2. S. Dobruja to Bulgaria, August 1940
3. Transylvania to Hungary, September 1940

© Richard Natkiel, 1982

The High Tide of German Expansion

Following his repulse in the Battle of Britain Hitler's thoughts turned to the Balkans and the USSR. By force or diplomacy the Balkans were brought under German influence by the early summer of 1941 while the Italian position in North Africa was propped up. Despite German confidence and enormous Soviet losses Operation Barbarossa was far from the expected easy victory. The Soviet Moscow counterattack demonstrated their resilience which was confirmed when the Germans were halted at Stalingrad despite their renewed victories in the summer of 1942. Although America had given Britain steadily increasing support only a foolish German declaration of war in the aftermath of Pearl Harbor confirmed that America would fight in Europe.

© Richard Natkiel 1982

Right: German infantry equipped with a
37mm antitank gun prepare to neutralize a
pocket of resistance in a Russian town.
Below: the opening phase of Operation
Barbarossa – German troops cross into
western Russia.

Germany's Long Retreat

Although the counteroffensive at Kharkov for a time revived German hopes for victory in the east the defeat at Kursk ended this false optimism and the long retreat was resumed. Although the western allies were only able to invade France in June 1944 they had already knocked Italy out of the war and taken much of her territory. The threat to the Atlantic supply routes had been defeated in 1943 and after a long struggle throughout that year the British and American heavy bombers were beginning to achieve important results in their attacks on centers of population and industrial targets in Germany.

© Richard Natkiel, 1982

The Fall of Hitler's Germany

By mid-1944 Germany's decline was completely irreversible. Her manpower losses had been immense; her industry was being pounded by Allied bombers; even her much-feared secret weapons were proving a disappointment. Although British resources were heavily strained by 1945 there was no doubt that the Allies were now far better organized and equipped. In the end despite the last German flurry in the Battle of the Bulge, there was no answer to the military and industrial might of the USA and USSR.

Long before the war ended it was becoming clear, however, that the Allies did not see eye-to-eye on the political future of the liberated European nations.

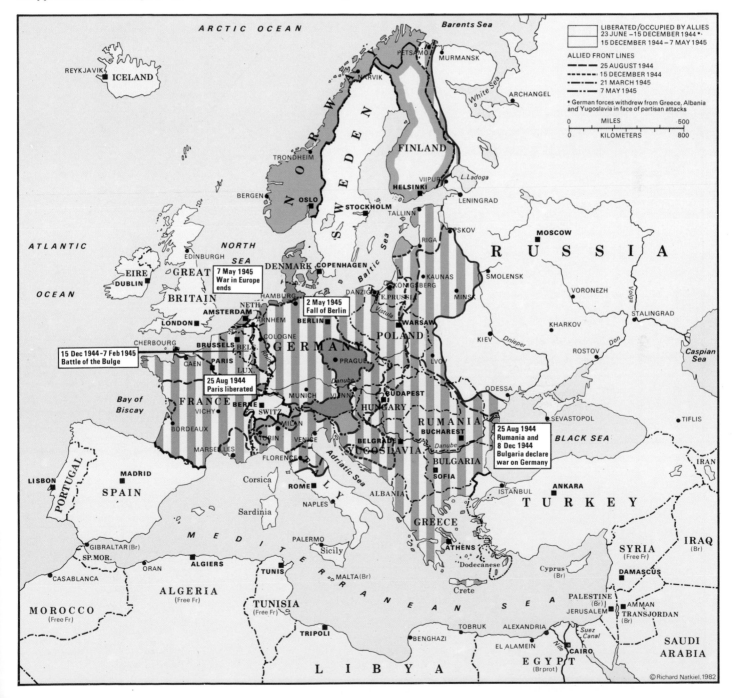

LIBERATED/OCCUPIED BY ALLIES
23 JUNE – 15 DECEMBER 1944 *·
15 DECEMBER 1944 – 7 MAY 1945

ALLIED FRONT LINES
25 AUGUST 1944
15 DECEMBER 1944
21 MARCH 1945
7 MAY 1945

* German forces withdrew from Greece, Albania and Yugoslavia in face of partisan attacks

0 MILES 500
0 KILOMETERS 800

7 May 1945
War in Europe ends

2 May 1945
Fall of Berlin

15 Dec 1944-7 Feb 1945
Battle of the Bulge

25 Aug 1944
Paris liberated

25 Aug 1944
Rumania and 8 Dec 1944 Bulgaria declare war on Germany

© Richard Natkiel. 1982

Japan's Months of Triumph

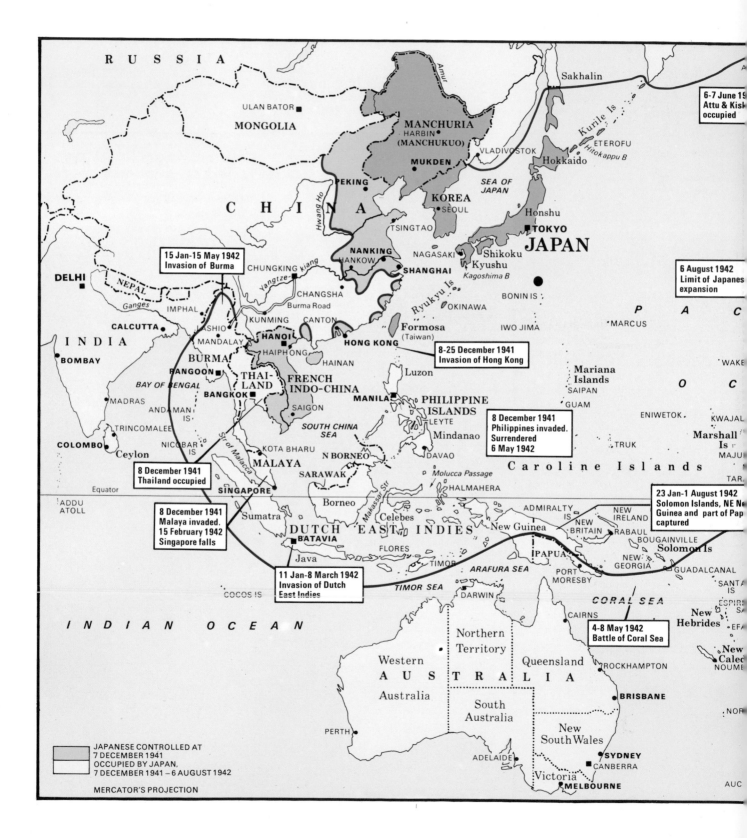

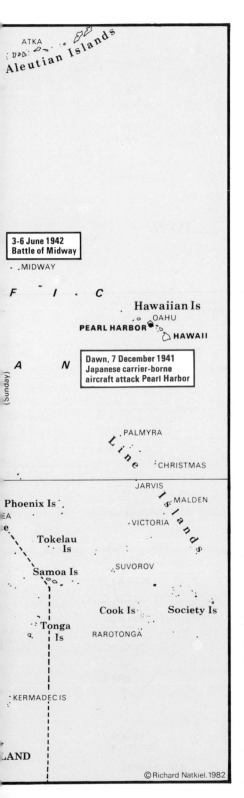

The Japanese recognized that in a long war American strength would become dauntingly great. They therefore planned to seize the resource-producing areas that they lacked and perimeter bases to defend them. These would be taken in the first rapid campaigns and the decadent Europeans and Americans would, it was expected, make peace rather than mobilize their power against a much-strengthened Japan. The first stages of the fighting went almost according to plan but the Battle of the Coral Sea offered a slight check and the defeat at Midway was a serious setback.

Below: although aircraft carriers played the most important role in the war at sea in the Pacific, battleships provided important softening-up bombardment prior to US landings.

The Allied Counteroffensive

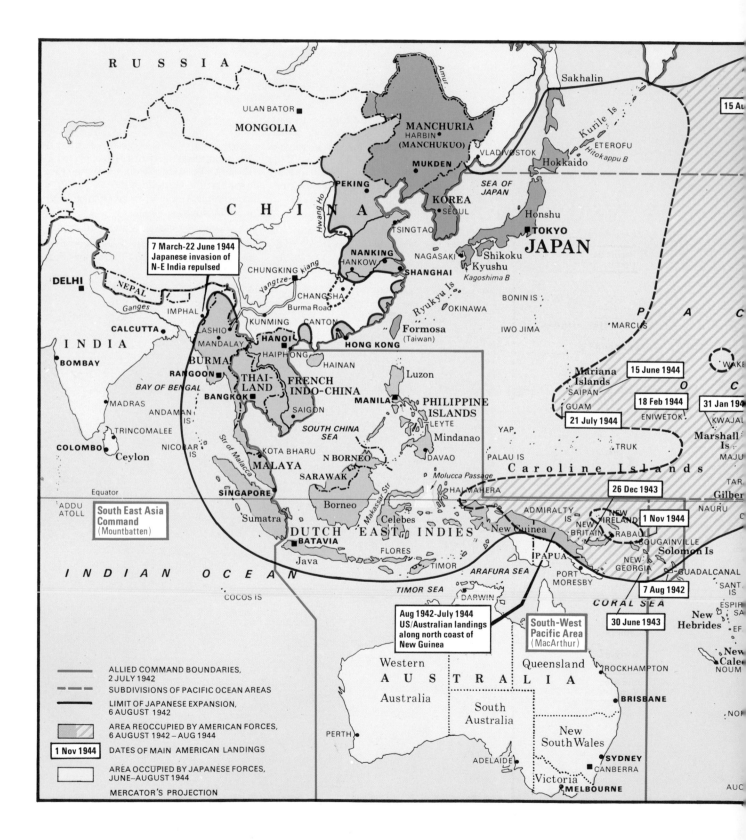

RUSSIA

Sakhalin

15 Au

ULAN BATOR •

MONGOLIA

MANCHURIA
HARBIN •
(MANCHUKUO)

VLADIVOSTOK •

Kurile Is

ETEROFU

Hitokappu B

Hokkaido

MUKDEN •

PEKING •

CHINA

KOREA
SEOUL •

*SEA OF
JAPAN*

TSINGTAO •

Honshu

TOKYO

7 March-22 June 1944
Japanese invasion of
N-E India repulsed

Hwang Ho

NANKING •
HANKOW •

JAPAN

CHUNGKING • kiang

SHANGHAI

NAGASAKI •

Shikoku

Kyushu

Kagoshima B

DELHI ■

NEPAL

Yangtze

CHANGSHA •

Burma Road

Ganges

IMPHAL •

KUNMING •

CANTON •

Ryukyu Is
• OKINAWA

BONIN IS

P

• MARCUS

CALCUTTA •

LASHIO •
MANDALAY •

HANOI ■

HAIPHONG •

HONG KONG

Formosa
(Taiwan)

IWO JIMA

A

INDIA

BURMA

HAINAN

O

C

BOMBAY •

RANGOON ■

THAI-
LAND

FRENCH
INDO-CHINA

Luzon

Mariana
Islands
SAIPAN

15 June 1944

• WAKE

BAY OF BENGAL

BANGKOK ■

SAIGON •

MANILA ■

PHILIPPINE
ISLANDS

YAP •

GUAM •

18 Feb 1944

31 Jan 194

KWAJAL

MADRAS •

ANDAMAN
IS

SOUTH CHINA
SEA

LEYTE

Mindanao

ENIWETOK •

21 July 1944

TRINCOMALEE •

NICOBAR
IS

KOTA BHARU •

N BORNEO

DAVAO •

PALAU IS •

TRUK •

Marshall
Is

MAJU

COLOMBO •

Ceylon

Str of Malacca

MALAYA

SARAWAK

Molucca Passage

Caroline Islands

TAR.

Equator

ADDU
ATOLL

South East Asia
Command
(Mountbatten)

SINGAPORE ■

Sumatra

Borneo

Celebes

Makassar Str

HALMAHERA •

26 Dec 1943

Gilber

NAURU •

C

BATAVIA ■

DUTCH EAST INDIES

New Guinea

ADMIRALTY
IS •

NEW
IRELAND

NEW
BRITAIN
RABAUL

1 Nov 1944

Java

FLORES

PAPUA

BOUGAINVILLE •

Solomon Is

TIMOR

PORT
MORESBY •

NEW
GEORGIA •

GUADALCANAL

INDIAN OCEAN

ARAFURA SEA

7 Aug 1942

SANT.
IS

COCOS IS

TIMOR SEA

DARWIN •

CORAL SEA

30 June 1943

ESPIR
SA

New
Hebrides

Aug 1942-July 1944
US/Australian landings
along north coast of
New Guinea

South-West
Pacific Area
(MacArthur)

EF

New
Cale
NOUM

Western

Queensland

ROCKHAMPTON •

AUSTRALIA

Australia

South
Australia

BRISBANE

NO

PERTH •

New
South Wales

SYDNEY

ADELAIDE •

■ CANBERRA

Victoria

■ **MELBOURNE**

AU

── ALLIED COMMAND BOUNDARIES,
2 JULY 1942

── ─ ─ SUBDIVISIONS OF PACIFIC OCEAN AREAS

── LIMIT OF JAPANESE EXPANSION,
6 AUGUST 1942

▨ AREA REOCCUPIED BY AMERICAN FORCES,
6 AUGUST 1942 – AUG 1944

1 Nov 1944 DATES OF MAIN AMERICAN LANDINGS

☐ AREA OCCUPIED BY JAPANESE FORCES,
JUNE–AUGUST 1944

MERCATOR'S PROJECTION

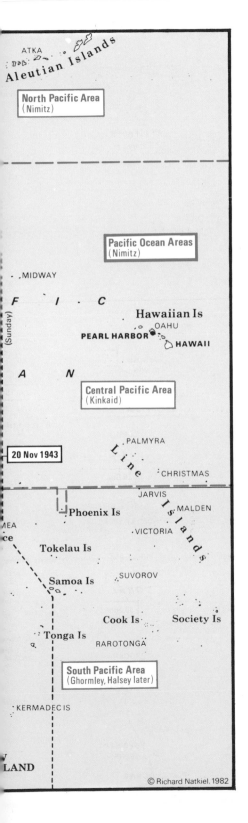

ATKA · Aleutian Islands

North Pacific Area
(Nimitz)

Pacific Ocean Areas
(Nimitz)

· MIDWAY

F · I · C

(Sunday)

Hawaiian Is
· OAHU
PEARL HARBOR · ♢ **HAWAII**

A · N

Central Pacific Area
(Kinkaid)

PALMYRA

20 Nov 1943

Line Islands

· CHRISTMAS

JARVIS

·MALDEN

· Phoenix Is

·VICTORIA

Tokelau Is

· SUVOROV

· Samoa Is

Cook Is·

Society Is

· Tonga Is

RAROTONGA

South Pacific Area
(Ghormley, Halsey later)

· KERMADEC IS

LAND

© Richard Natkiel. 1982

America proved strong enough to mount two major lines of advance against the Japanese. The US Navy built up its carrier forces and its amphibious assault capability and backed them by the ability of the newly-created fleet train to keep the fighting ships in action at great distances from their bases. These units advanced by the islands of the central Pacific in a series of bloody battles of which the assault on Tarawa at the start of the campaign is perhaps the most notorious. The other wing of the Allied offensive was in the South-West Pacific where MacArthur's Australian and American forces advanced doggedly with enormous support from land-based air power.

Below: the Mitsubishi Zero was the Japanese navy's main fighter aircraft throughout the Pacific War. This one was downed during the Solomons campaign.

The Japanese Defeat

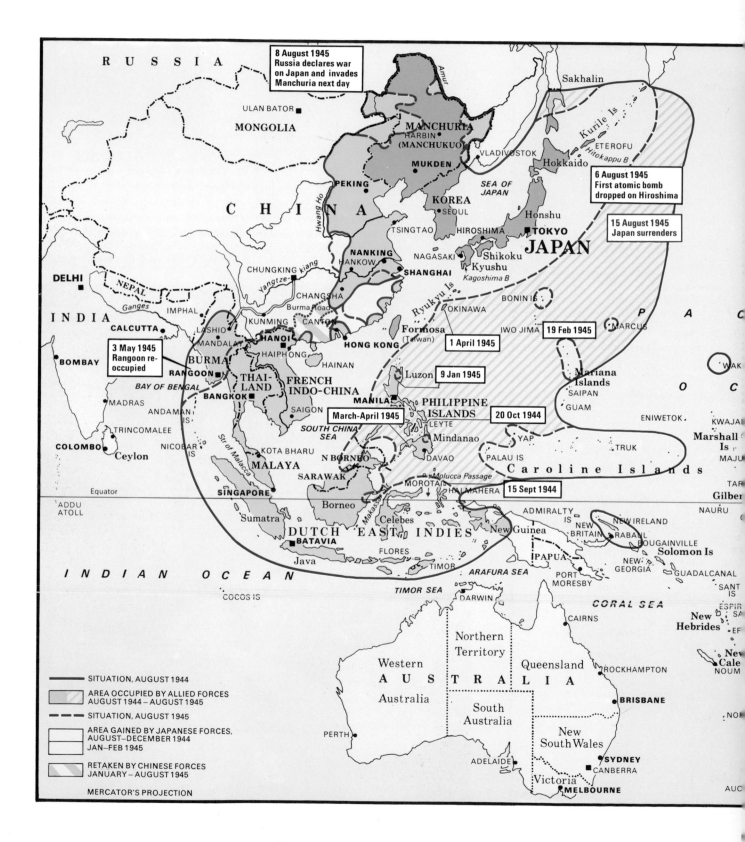

8 August 1945 Russia declares war on Japan and invades Manchuria next day

6 August 1945 First atomic bomb dropped on Hiroshima

15 August 1945 Japan surrenders

3 May 1945 Rangoon re-occupied

19 Feb 1945

1 April 1945

9 Jan 1945

March-April 1945

20 Oct 1944

15 Sept 1944

RUSSIA

ULAN BATOR

MONGOLIA

MANCHURIA (MANCHUKUO)
HARBIN
VLADIVOSTOK
MUKDEN
PEKING
KOREA
SEOUL

Sakhalin

Kurile Is
ETEROFU
Hitokappu B
Hokkaido

SEA OF JAPAN

Honshu

TOKYO
JAPAN

CHINA

Hwang Ho

TSINGTAO
HIROSHIMA
NAGASAKI
Shikoku
Kyushu
Kagoshima B

NANKING
HANKOW
SHANGHAI

CHUNGKING
Yangtze-kiang
CHANGSHA
Burma Road
KUNMING
CANTON

DELHI

NEPAL

Ganges
IMPHAL

INDIA

CALCUTTA

LASHIO
MANDALAY
HANOI
HAIPHONG
HONG KONG
HAINAN

Ryukyu Is
OKINAWA

Formosa (Taiwan)

BONIN IS

IWO JIMA
MARCUS

PACIFIC OCEAN

BOMBAY

BURMA
RANGOON
THAI-LAND
FRENCH INDO-CHINA
BANGKOK
SAIGON

Luzon
MANILA
PHILIPPINE ISLANDS
LEYTE
Mindanao
DAVAO

Mariana Islands
SAIPAN
GUAM

WAK

MADRAS
ANDAMAN IS
TRINCOMALEE

BAY OF BENGAL

SOUTH CHINA SEA

YAP
PALAU IS

ENIWETOK

KWAJA

Marshall Is

MAJU

COLOMBO
Ceylon
NICOBAR IS

Str of Malacca

MALAYA
KOTA BHARU
N BORNEO
SARAWAK

Caroline Islands

TRUK

TAR
Gilber

Equator

SINGAPORE

Borneo

Molucca Passage
MOROTAI
HALMAHERA

ADDU ATOLL

Sumatra

Makass

Celebes

DUTCH EAST INDIES

BATAVIA

Java

FLORES

TIMOR

New Guinea

ADMIRALTY IS
NEW BRITAIN
RABAUL
BOUGAINVILLE

NEW IRELAND

Solomon Is

NAURU

NEW GEORGIA
GUADALCANAL

SANT IS

INDIAN OCEAN

COCOS IS

ARAFURA SEA

PAPUA
PORT MORESBY

TIMOR SEA

DARWIN

CORAL SEA

CAIRNS

ESPIR SA

New Hebrides

EF

Northern Territory

Western Australia
Australia

Queensland

ROCKHAMPTON

New Cale
NOUM

NO

AUSTRALIA

South Australia

BRISBANE

PERTH

New South Wales

ADELAIDE

SYDNEY
CANBERRA

Victoria

MELBOURNE

AUC

—— SITUATION, AUGUST 1944

▨ AREA OCCUPIED BY ALLIED FORCES AUGUST 1944 – AUGUST 1945

--- SITUATION, AUGUST 1945

▢ AREA GAINED BY JAPANESE FORCES, AUGUST–DECEMBER 1944 JAN–FEB 1945

▨ RETAKEN BY CHINESE FORCES JANUARY – AUGUST 1945

MERCATOR'S PROJECTION

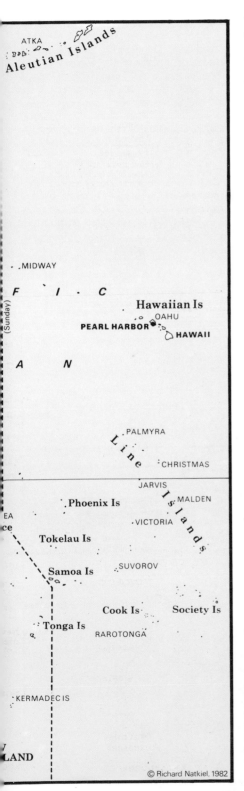

The final year of the war saw the Japanese defeated on all fronts, being thrown out of Burma, Iwo Jima and Okinawa and confined to unimportant pockets in the Philippines. At the same time US bomber forces were built up in the Marianas and, after a change in tactics in March 1945, they devastated city after city on the Japanese Home Islands. The first atomic bomb was dropped on 6 August. Faced by this new threat and the Soviet invasion of Manchuria, Japan capitulated.

Below: MacArthur led the land forces which retook the Philippines in an 'island-hopping' campaign.

The Invasion and Partition of Poland

No sooner had Hitler finished dismembering Czechoslovakia and seizing the Memel district from Lithuania in March 1939 than it became obvious that Poland would be considered next. Britain and France quickly issued a joint guarantee to Poland and hoped that with this lever they could persuade the Poles to make concessions like the Czechs at Munich, while still convincing Hitler of the need to be reasonable. However, throughout the spring and summer Hitler's aggressive attitude became more obvious especially after April when he revoked the 1934 German-Polish Non-Aggression Pact and the 1935 Anglo-German Naval Agreement. During this period both the western Allies and the Germans were courting Soviet assistance. The British and French efforts were poorly managed and, in any case, it soon became clear that Stalin wanted virtually a free hand in Eastern Europe in return for his help. The talks came to nothing. Instead, in August, the German diplomacy bore fruit and Foreign Minister Ribbentrop concluded first an economic agreement and then a Non-Aggression Pact with the USSR.

Despite some last minute uncertainty on Hitler's part, the German attack on Poland was free to begin on 1 September 1939. France and Britain each responded with an ultimatum to Germany demanding a withdrawal and when no satisfactory reply was received both countries declared war on Germany on 3 September 1939. Australia and New Zealand immediately followed suit and after some debate South Africa joined the war on 6 September. The Germans claimed that Polish provocation had caused the war and, to prove this, evidence of a Polish attack on a German radio station near the border at Gliewitz was shown to foreign pressmen. In fact the 'attack' was staged by the SS and the bodies in Polish uniforms left at the scene were those of concentration camp inmates.

The Germans deployed 53 divisions for the campaign against Poland leaving, by their own estimate, 10 divisions fit for action on the Western Front. Their six tank and their few motorized divisions were in the attack and together were used to form the various panzer corps. The German Army Commander in Chief, Field Marshal Brauchitsch controlled the campaign, largely without interference from Hitler. In their preplanning and their retrospective appreciations the German Army described the campaign in terms of traditional infantry and artillery battles, allocating the tanks subordinate supporting roles. Only a few enthusiasts supported theories emphasizing the part played by the armored forces. To support their armies the Germans had an enormous superiority in the air with about 1600 modern planes facing the 500 largely obsolescent machines possessed by the Poles. The Polish mobilization was not begun until 30 August so the German attack found the Poles with 23 infantry divisions deployed and another seven assembling. All units were short of artillery, there was one weak armored division and a mass of ineffective cavalry. The Polish forces had been foolishly placed by Marshal Rydz-Smigly, their Commander in Chief, in forward positions near the frontier and, although they fought bravely, the campaign was decided within a few days. There was a Polish counterattack along the Bzura River from 9–15 September but this only caused the Germans brief worries. Warsaw fell after a vicious air bombardment on 27 September and by 3 October the last significant resistance had been wiped out.

On 17 September Soviet forces invaded Poland from the east and on 19 September a German-Soviet Treaty of Friendship was announced. This confirmed the arrangements for the partition of Poland that had been secretly agreed in August. This partition had now been achieved.

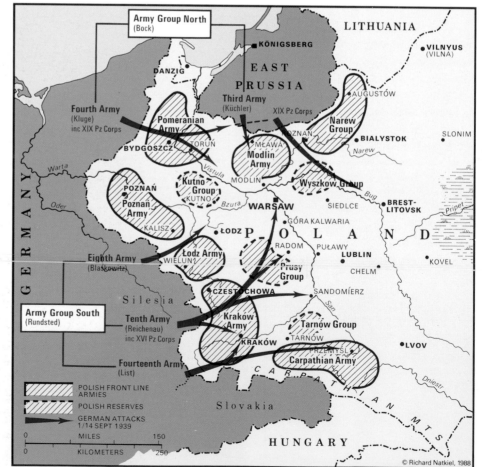

© Richard Natkiel, 1988

The Fall of France, 1940

The period from the end of the Polish campaign until the invasion of Norway and Denmark was known as the 'Phony War' because of the apparent inactivity along the Western Front. In fact many preparations were made.

Hitler initially wanted to attack in November 1939 but after several postponements a decision was made in January 1940 to wait until May. One reason for this hesitancy was difficulty in finding a satisfactory plan. Limited advances into Belgium and Holland were considered, as were variations on the 1914 Schlieffen Plan. None of these seemed adequate because, although they avoided the difficulties of a frontal attack on the French Maginot Line fortifications, they seemed too predictable and easy to counter. The plan finally adopted under the code name Sickle-stroke was largely developed by General von Manstein. He proposed that attacks into Belgium and Holland should be made (by Army Group B) to draw British and French forces forward from their prepared positions on the Franco-Belgian border. At the same time the main German advance (Army Group A), led by powerful tank forces, would move as quickly and secretly as possible through Luxembourg and the wooded and hilly Ardennes area to the Meuse River, cross it and drive to the Channel, cutting off the Belgians and Dutch and all the Allied forces which had advanced to help them.

The British and French took no account of any such possibility in their plans largely because they believed that the terrain in the Ardennes was not suitable for a large-scale advance. Instead they expected a variation on the Schlieffen Plan. The Maginot Line was garrisoned and the remaining forces deployed along the Franco-Belgian border ready for an advance to the line of the River Dyle if the Belgians should ask for help. The best French units and the British were earmarked for this advance. The weakest part of the Allied line was the sector opposite the Ardennes.

Clearly the Allied plan depended a great deal on co-operation from the Belgians and Dutch but this was never really established before 10 May because the Belgians and Dutch feared to compromise their neutrality and provoke the Germans into attacking. As well as this problem there were other basic weaknesses in the Allied position. General Gamelin, the Commander in Chief, was 68 years old and far from vigorous. His headquarters were badly sited with poor communications and chain of command.

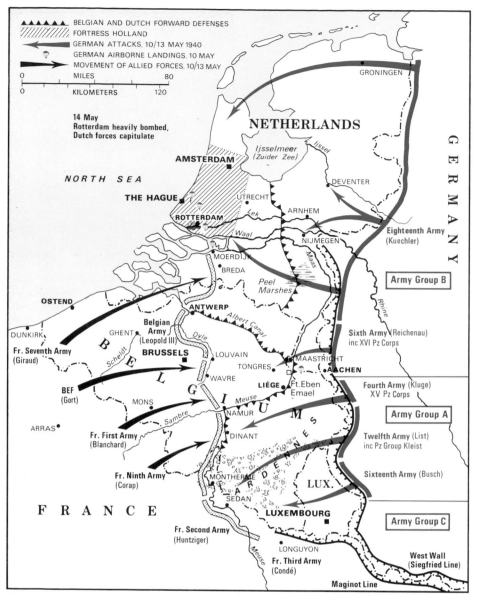

Map legend:

▲▲▲▲▲ BELGIAN AND DUTCH FORWARD DEFENSES
///// FORTRESS HOLLAND
◄━━━ GERMAN ATTACKS, 10/13 MAY 1940
⚐ GERMAN AIRBORNE LANDINGS, 10 MAY
━━━► MOVEMENT OF ALLIED FORCES, 10/13 MAY

0 ———————— MILES ———————— 80
0 ———————— KILOMETERS ———————— 120

14 May
Rotterdam heavily bombed,
Dutch forces capitulate

NETHERLANDS

GRONINGEN

Ijsselmeer
(Zuider Zee)

IJssel

AMSTERDAM

NORTH SEA

DEVENTER

THE HAGUE

UTRECHT

ARNHEM

ROTTERDAM

Lek

Waal

NIJMEGEN

Eighteenth Army
(Kuechler)

MOERDIJK

Maas

BREDA

Peel
Marshes

Army Group B

OSTEND

ANTWERP

Albert Canal

Belgian
Army
(Leopold III)

Rhine

Sixth Army (Reichenau)
inc XVI Pz Corps

DUNKIRK

GHENT

Dyle

Scheldt

Fr. Seventh Army
(Giraud)

BRUSSELS

LOUVAIN

MAASTRICHT

AACHEN

B E L G I U M

TONGRES

BEF
(Gort)

WAVRE

LIÈGE

Ft. Eben
Emael

Fourth Army (Kluge)
XV Pz Corps

MONS

Meuse

NAMUR

Sambre

Army Group A

ARRAS

Fr. First Army
(Blanchard)

DINANT

Twelfth Army (List)
inc Pz Group Kleist

A R D E N N E S

Fr. Ninth Army
(Corap)

MONTHERMÉ

LUX.

Sixteenth Army (Busch)

F R A N C E

SEDAN

LUXEMBOURG

Army Group C

Fr. Second Army
(Huntziger)

LONGUYON

West Wall
(Siegfried Line)

Meuse

Fr. Third Army
(Condé)

Maginot Line

Bottom: a French truck-mounted antitank gun moves forward to engage a German armored unit.

The French tank force was wastefully dispersed in small infantry support units and on the day the battle began there was no British armored division in position in France. (One such unit was sent, not fully prepared, immediately fighting began.) Perhaps the most telling German advantage, however, was in the air where the Luftwaffe had over 3000 modern aircraft with well trained pilots and crews to face a mixed bag of less than 2000 Allied machines. (The Allied forces could expect some help and reinforcement from UK-based RAF units.)

The combination of tanks and air power was central to the German success. The aircraft, and particularly the dive-bombing Stukas, acted almost as artillery support to the army both when it was necessary for the tanks to break through solid defenses and also when, in the advance to exploit success, armored columns ran into pockets of resistance after having left their own artillery behind. Few even in the German Army understood the potential of such a system but their leadership was so dynamic that the *Blitzkrieg* or lightning war which they advocated became a byword for military skill and success.

The German attack began on 10 May and for the first few days attention was held, as the Germans had hoped, by events in the

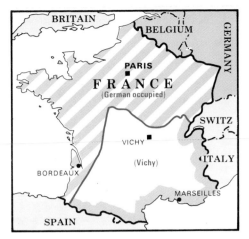

Low Countries. The Germans began with a number of daring paratroop and ground force attacks on important border defenses in both Belgium and Holland. These made important gains particularly the capture of Fort Eben Emael. The Dutch forces were left totally disorganized by a combination of paratroop drops and air attacks. Their defenses were never properly put into operation and after a particularly vicious air raid on Rotterdam on 14 May the Dutch surrendered. The French Seventh Army attempted to intervene but was thrown back.

Queen Wilhelmina and her government were evacuated to England from where they hoped to continue the fight.

In Belgium the German attacks were soon making good progress both in the north and in the tank advance to the Meuse. The British and French had advanced as planned to the Dyle but found that their positions there were weak and called in reinforcements from the reserve. Despite thus playing into the German hands, by 15 May it was necessary to order the evacuation of the Dyle Line in the face of the German attack. This was

even before the German tank advance became an obvious threat.

The German tank forces had quickly penetrated through the Ardennes and on 14 May they secured vital bridgeheads over the Meuse in what were probably the most decisive actions of the whole campaign. The local French forces failed to counterattack. The German armor then began rushing forward to the sea, hindered more by the caution of the higher German commanders than by the British or the French. General Weygand replaced Gamelin as French Commander in Chief and tried to organize a counteroffensive but the only significant response was a limited British attack near Arras.

After this effort there was little the Allied forces could do but retreat to the sea. They were helped in this by a strange order from Hitler and Rundstedt which largely halted the German armored advance from 23–26 May. Most of the Allied force was able to fall back to the Dunkirk perimeter and 338,000 men, including 120,000 French, were evacuated in the nine-day operation (26 May–4 June) at heavy cost in transport ships and covering aircraft.

While the Germans were concentrating on Dunkirk Weygand was trying to organize the remaining French forces for defense of the line of the Somme. The Germans began to attack south on 5 June and the line was soon broken despite brave resistance from many French units. The German advance continued apace and on 16 June Premier Reynaud and his government resigned. The new head of government was Marshal Pétain and on the 17th he announced that France was seeking an armistice. The armistice was signed on 22 June.

France was divided into an occupied and an unoccupied zone. The unoccupied zone was ruled by the Pétain government from Vichy and, although its independence was nominally preserved, on many issues there was complete co-operation with Germany. A comparatively junior army officer and politician, General de Gaulle, escaped to Britain with a small following and proclaimed himself leader of Free France, announcing that France had lost a battle but had not lost the war.

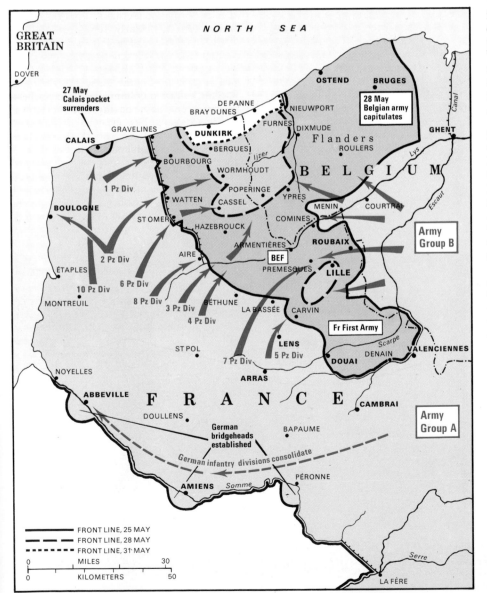

Bottom: the aftermath of the devastating Luftwaffe night raid on Coventry in November 1940. Civilian casualties were high in this unusually effective attack.

Battle of Britain

On 16 July 1940 Hitler issued his Directive 16 to the German Armed Forces. It began, 'I have decided to begin to prepare for, and, if necessary, to carry out, an invasion of England.' It went on to explain that the Luftwaffe must defeat the RAF so that the Royal Navy would be unprotected if it tried to interfere with an invasion force crossing the Channel.

If the British were to survive this threat the RAF had to gain time for the army to reequip after the losses of Dunkirk and if possible to hold the Germans off until bad weather in the fall made an invasion impossible.

The RAF was none too strong for its task but was well organized and led. Air Chief Marshal Dowding, who led Fighter Command, and his principal lieutenant, Air Vice-Marshal Park, were both particularly able and perceptive officers. The British

fighter direction system was well thought out with radar and other information being coordinated and instructions issued from operations rooms in each RAF sector. Although they understood its technical capabilities the Germans failed to appreciate the importance of radar within the British system and did little to attack the radar stations. In a sense this was part of the 'home advantage' which the British had throughout the battle. In order to plan, the Germans needed, and did not get, accurate information on damage done and losses inflicted while the RAF had a more clear-cut task and could husband its resources accordingly. The RAF's principal shortage was of trained fighter pilots and it was, therefore, of considerable importance that defending pilots who were shot down unwounded could immediately return to service. The Germans, of course, had no such second chance and their principal fighter aircraft, the short-range Messerschmitt Bf 109, could only fight over southern England for a very limited time.

All these British advantages would not have cancelled out the greater German strength and the experience of their pilots unless the German High Command had not been found wanting. Reichsmarshal Göring, the Commander in Chief of the Luftwaffe, controlled the German attack and made many wrong decisions. There was no real understanding of the urgency of the invasion timetable – the all-out Luftwaffe attacks only began on 13 August, more than two months after Dunkirk. There was, too, no clear understanding of the exact aim. For a few days in late August and early September the Germans came close to winning the battle, with attacks on No 11 Group airfields, but on 7 September the main German target became London and the RAF was allowed to recover. Although it was not obvious at the time, the last major German effort was on 15 September. There were many later daytime attacks, and the night 'Blitz' on Britain's cities continued well into 1941, but Hitler postponed the invasion on 17 September.

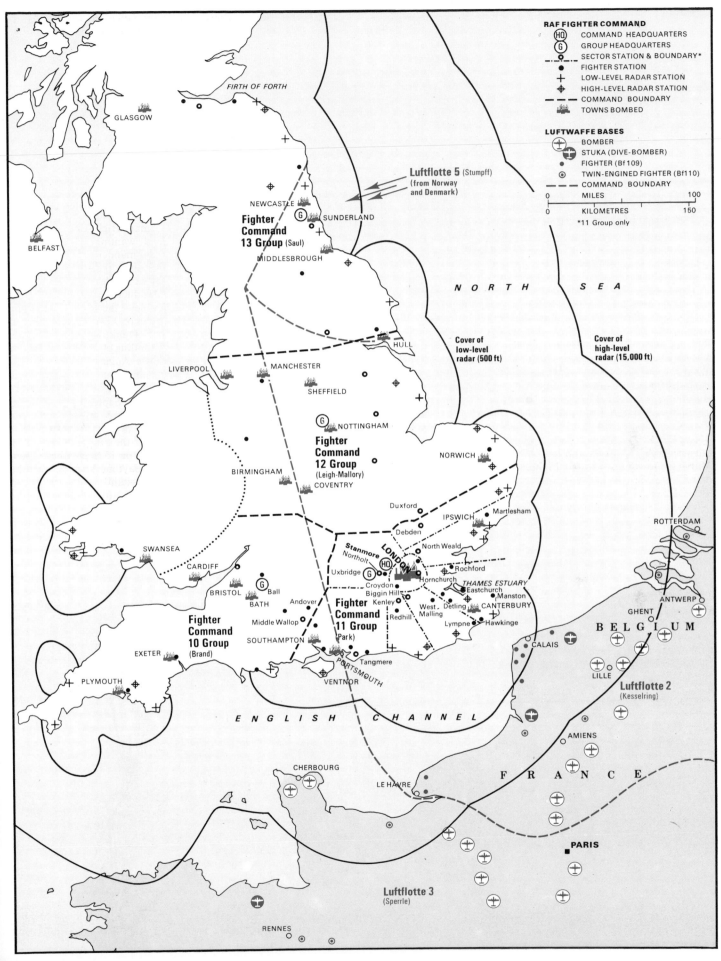

RAF FIGHTER COMMAND
- HQ COMMAND HEADQUARTERS
- G GROUP HEADQUARTERS
- SECTOR STATION & BOUNDARY*
- FIGHTER STATION
- LOW-LEVEL RADAR STATION
- HIGH-LEVEL RADAR STATION
- COMMAND BOUNDARY
- TOWNS BOMBED

LUFTWAFFE BASES
- BOMBER
- STUKA (DIVE-BOMBER)
- FIGHTER (Bf 109)
- TWIN-ENGINED FIGHTER (Bf 110)
- COMMAND BOUNDARY

MILES 0 — 100
KILOMETRES 0 — 150

*11 Group only

FIRTH OF FORTH

GLASGOW

BELFAST

NEWCASTLE

Luftflotte 5 (Stumpff)
(from Norway and Denmark)

SUNDERLAND

Fighter Command 13 Group (Saul)

MIDDLESBROUGH

NORTH SEA

HULL

Cover of low-level radar (500 ft)

Cover of high-level radar (15,000 ft)

LIVERPOOL

MANCHESTER

SHEFFIELD

NOTTINGHAM

Fighter Command 12 Group (Leigh-Mallory)

NORWICH

BIRMINGHAM

COVENTRY

Duxford

IPSWICH

Martlesham

ROTTERDAM

Debden

North Weald

SWANSEA

CARDIFF

BRISTOL
BATH
Ball

Andover

Stanmore
Northolt
Uxbridge
Croydon
Biggin Hill
Kenley
Redhill

LONDON

Rochford

Hornchurch

THAMES ESTUARY
Eastchurch

West. Detling
Malling

Manston

CANTERBURY

Lympne
Hawkinge

ANTWERP

GHENT

BELGIUM

CALAIS

LILLE

Luftflotte 2 (Kesselring)

Fighter Command 10 Group (Brand)

Middle Wallop

SOUTHAMPTON

Fighter Command 11 Group (Park)

Tangmere

PORTSMOUTH

VENTNOR

EXETER

PLYMOUTH

ENGLISH CHANNEL

AMIENS

CHERBOURG

LE HAVRE

FRANCE

PARIS

Luftflotte 3 (Sperrle)

RENNES

War in the Desert, 1940–41

Italy declared war on Britain on 10 June 1940 and in September the numerically strong Italian Tenth Army made a short tentative advance into Egypt. By December the much smaller British and Imperial force was ready to attack under the able leadership of Generals Wavell and O'Connor. The Italians were successively hustled out of defensive positions at Sidi Barrani, Bardia and Tobruk and thrown into abject retreat along the coast road. The Italian defeat was completed when a force sent across the Cyrenaica Plateau cut their retreat at Beda Fomm. In those two months the British forces never had more than two divisions in the fight. Ten Italian divisions were destroyed and 130,000 prisoners taken for the loss of 550 dead and 1400 wounded. Already, however, the British position was deteriorating. Troops had been withdrawn to East Africa and more were about to go to Greece. Even those forces remaining could not all be supplied at the front and so it was not solidly held, the more so because many of the tanks were worn out.

General Rommel arrived in Africa on 12 February 1941 with a small German force and instructions to block any further British advance. He quickly discerned the British weakness and by early April had begun an all-out attack which quickly overwhelmed the depleted British force. However, although the main front line was pushed back into Egypt, Rommel was unsuccessful in

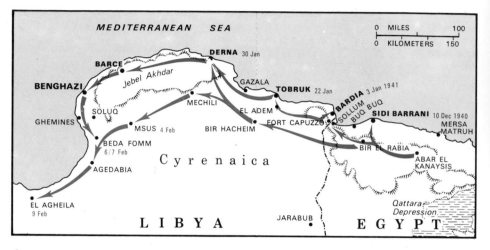

desperate attempts to capture Tobruk before his own acute supply problems forced a pause.

During the next phase of the campaign both sides tried to build up their forces and supply stocks for an offensive. A premature British attack in June, Operation Battleaxe, was soundly defeated but Tobruk remained a thorn in the German side. The British were again ready to attack in November 1941 under a new Commander in Chief, General Auchinleck and Operation Crusader accordingly began on the 18th. The British had far greater resources initially but the individual German units were better led and far more professional in their approach. The result, when combined with errors in generalship on both sides, was a prolonged and highly confused battle in the area between Tobruk and the Egyptian frontier. After very heavy losses on both sides Rommel was forced to retreat and because

of the lack of suitable defensive positions and the danger of being outflanked he had to go back as far as El Agheila. Once more, however, there were signs of a change: Malta was coming under heavier attack and the British naval forces had recently suffered serious losses; Rommel was receiving reinforcements even as he retreated and British and Australian troops were being withdrawn to reinforce the Far East against the threat from Japan.

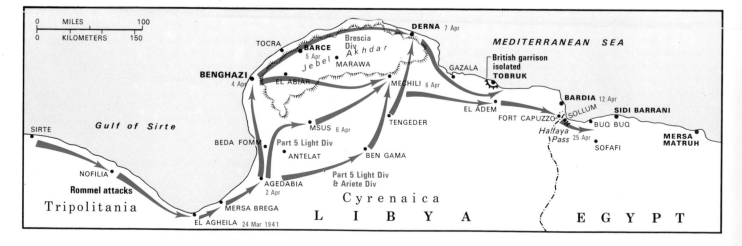

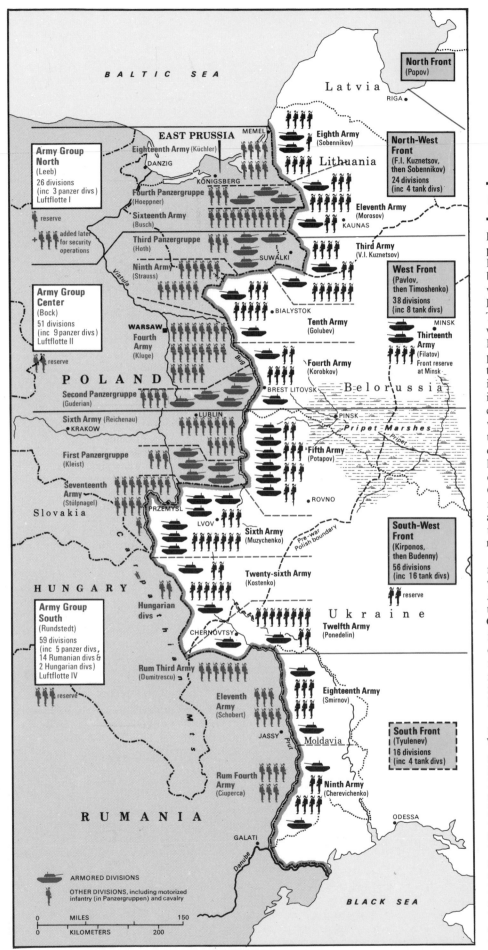

Army Group North (Leeb)
26 divisions (inc 3 panzer divs) Luftflotte I

reserve

added later for security operations

Army Group Center (Bock)
51 divisions (inc 9 panzer divs) Luftflotte II

reserve

Army Group South (Rundstedt)
59 divisions (inc 5 panzer divs, 14 Rumanian divs & 2 Hungarian divs) Luftflotte IV

reserve

BALTIC SEA

EAST PRUSSIA
MEMEL
Eighteenth Army (Küchler)
DANZIG
Fourth Panzergruppe (Hoeppner)
KÖNIGSBERG
Sixteenth Army (Busch)
Third Panzergruppe (Hoth)
SUWAŁKI
Ninth Army (Strauss)
Vistula
WARSAW
Fourth Army (Kluge)
Bug
POLAND
Second Panzergruppe (Guderian)
LUBLIN
Sixth Army (Reichenau)
KRAKOW
First Panzergruppe (Kleist)
Seventeenth Army (Stülpnagel)
Slovakia
PRZEMYSL
LVOV
HUNGARY
Hungarian divs
CHERNOVTSY
Rum Third Army (Dumitrescu)
Eleventh Army (Schobert)
JASSY
Moldavia
Prut
Rum Fourth Army (Ciuperca)
RUMANIA
GALATI
Danube

Latvia
RIGA
Eighth Army (Sobennikov)
Lithuania
Eleventh Army (Morosov)
KAUNAS
Third Army (V.I. Kuznetsov)
Tenth Army (Golubev)
BIALYSTOK
Fourth Army (Korobkov)
BREST LITOVSK
Belorussia
PINSK
Pripet Marshes
Pripet
Fifth Army (Potapov)
ROVNO
Sixth Army (Muzychenko)
Pre-war Polish boundary
Twenty-sixth Army (Kostenko)
Ukraine
Twelfth Army (Ponedelin)
Eighteenth Army (Smirnov)
Ninth Army (Cherevichenko)
ODESSA
BLACK SEA

North Front (Popov)

North-West Front (F.I. Kuznetsov, then Sobennikov)
24 divisions (inc 4 tank divs)

West Front (Pavlov, then Timoshenko)
38 divisions (inc 8 tank divs)
MINSK
Thirteenth Army (Filatov) Front reserve at Minsk

South-West Front (Kirponos, then Budenny)
56 divisions (inc 16 tank divs)
reserve

South Front (Tyulenev)
16 divisions (inc 4 tank divs)

ARMORED DIVISIONS

OTHER DIVISIONS, including motorized infantry (in Panzergruppen) and cavalry

| MILES | 150 |
| KILOMETERS | 200 |

Operation Barbarossa

In February 1941 a sympathetic German printer showed to Soviet diplomats in Berlin a new Russian phrasebook he had been ordered to print in large quantities, and which included phrases like 'Hands up or I'll shoot!' and 'Are you a communist?' This was just one of several signs that Hitler was preparing to turn against the USSR. He had in fact issued a general directive plan in December 1940 which, drawing on the experience and self-confidence gained in the French campaign, proposed that the initial aim should be nothing less than the complete destruction of the Red Army. This would be facilitated by the circumstance that the Russians, whose prevailing military doctrine was the doctrine of the offensive, had placed almost their entire active army close to the frontiers. Deep penetrations by German armor would be able to cut off the retreat of these Soviet formations. Having accomplished this, the German forces were to press eastward and establish a line running roughly from Archangel to Astrakhan.

After heavy German air attacks, directed mainly at airfields close to the frontier, and which had the effect of shattering the Red Air Force, German troops advanced across the frontier at dawn on 22 June. Army Group Center made a pincer movement from East Prussia and Poland toward Minsk, cutting off parts of two Soviet armies whose men, after a little confused resistance, surrendered en masse. Meanwhile Army Group South entered the Ukraine and forced large Soviet concentrations to surrender.

In September Budenny, a cavalryman and crony of Stalin since the Russian Civil War, allowed his South-West Front (that is – army group) to engage in catastrophic battles rather than retreat in good time. At Kiev alone half a million Red soldiers were taken prisoner, and by mid-November Rostov had been taken by the invaders, as well as the Perekop Isthmus commanding the Crimea. In the center there had been a big tank battle near Smolensk, and a second battle at Bryansk had allowed the Germans to take Orel, Tula and Vyazma. In the north the Baltic states had been occupied and some formations had penetrated east of Leningrad. The much-publicized 'Stalin Line,' had been shown to be virtually non-existent.

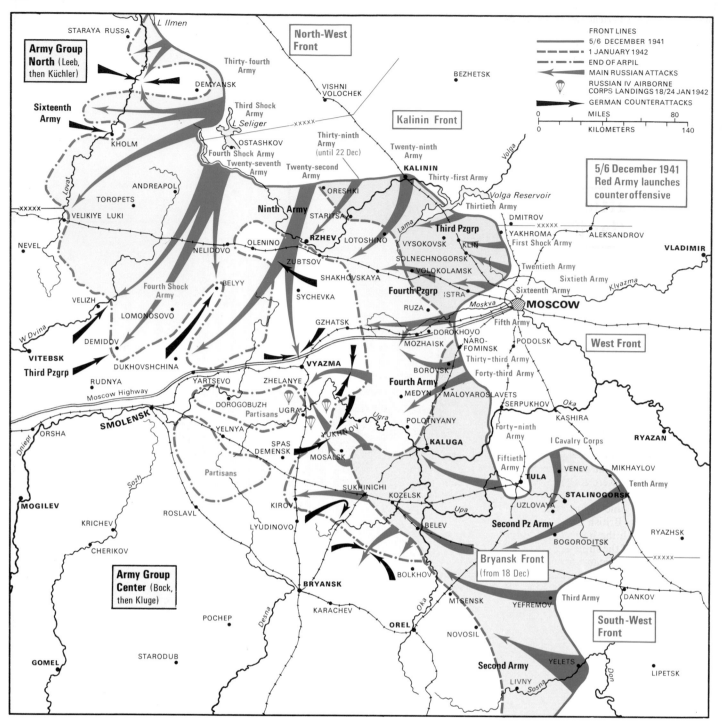

The Russian Counterattack, Moscow

On 8 December 1941 Hitler had announced a temporary suspension of operations outside Moscow, but the Soviet High Command soon showed that this was wishful thinking. It was, in fact, on the point of launching a counter-offensive for which it had been accumulating reserves over the previous weeks. Again, the situation of 1812 repeated itself, for the Soviet advance took the form of a mass infiltration which avoided the strongest German points. Passing over fields rather than following the roads, making great use of Cossacks, ski troops and guerilla forces, the Soviets forced the Germans to withdraw from one position after another by threatening them with attacks from the flank or rear. The Germans were handicapped by the effect of low temperatures on their internal-combustion engines, which effectively put the Luftwaffe out of action, and by their difficult supply position, which relied on thinly spread railroad links, hampered by a change of gauge, and the very poor Russian roads.

The Germans were pushed back most in the center. Kalinin and Tula were retaken, and the immediate threat to Moscow removed. The offensive continued to late February, by which time both sides were in need of rest and consolidation. This winter offensive had brought the Russians back as far as Velikiye Luki and Mozhaisk. At the same time, in the north the Germans had given ground around Leningrad, losing Tikhvin and control of Lake Ladoga, across which the Russians built a temporary ice road to the city. In the south the Kerch Isthmus was retaken and the Crimea re-entered, with Feodosia being reoccupied.

Below right: the American destroyer *Reuben James* was the first US Navy ship to be lost in World War II. She was sunk by a U-Boat in October 1941, before the USA joined the war.

The Battle of the Atlantic

Although the German submarine campaign of 1917 had nearly defeated Britain, Hitler's navy was not particularly well prepared to try to improve on this. Submarine building had not been given the highest priority and in the early months of the war Hitler imposed various restrictions on U-Boat operations to try to avoid offending neutral opinion. Drawing on the lessons of 1917 the British immediately introduced a convoy system but escorts could only be provided for part of some voyages and many ships sailed independently. Initially almost all U-Boat successes were from among these 'independents.' Nonetheless, in the first months of war U-Boat successes, although a serious problem, were certainly not out of control.

The events of June 1940 brought about a complete change. British naval responsibilities increased with the Italian entry into the war and the loss of the support of the French fleet, while the German strategic position was transformed by acquisition of bases in western France and Norway for the U-Boats and their supporting long-range reconnaissance aircraft. At this time also the U-Boats had many technical advantages. Their intelligence was good with the German Navy's B Dienst signals service having far more success with the British codes than the British were having with the German Enigma cipher machine. Although the British had Asdic equipment for detecting submerged submarines, radar was still comparatively primitive and escorts did not have sets capable of detecting U-Boats on the surface. A submarine on the surface could only be detected visually and at night a submarine was small and inconspicuous indeed. British patrol aircraft were few in number and, as well as lacking detection equipment, at this stage they were only armed with ineffective antisubmarine bombs. The Battle of the Atlantic became a struggle in all these fields; intelligence, technology, tactics, air support and others, as well as being in the obvious sense an industrial competition with graphs of merchant ship sinkings and cargoes delivered being compared with figures for new construction on both sides and for U-Boats lost. In each of these fields

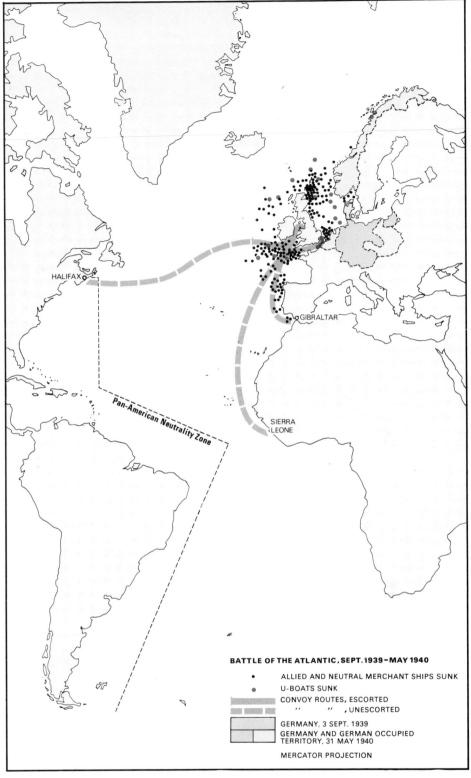

BATTLE OF THE ATLANTIC, SEPT. 1939 – MAY 1940

- ALLIED AND NEUTRAL MERCHANT SHIPS SUNK
- U-BOATS SUNK
- CONVOY ROUTES, ESCORTED
- " " , UNESCORTED
- GERMANY, 3 SEPT. 1939
- GERMANY AND GERMAN OCCUPIED TERRITORY, 31 MAY 1940

MERCATOR PROJECTION

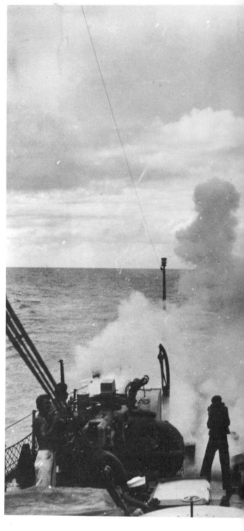

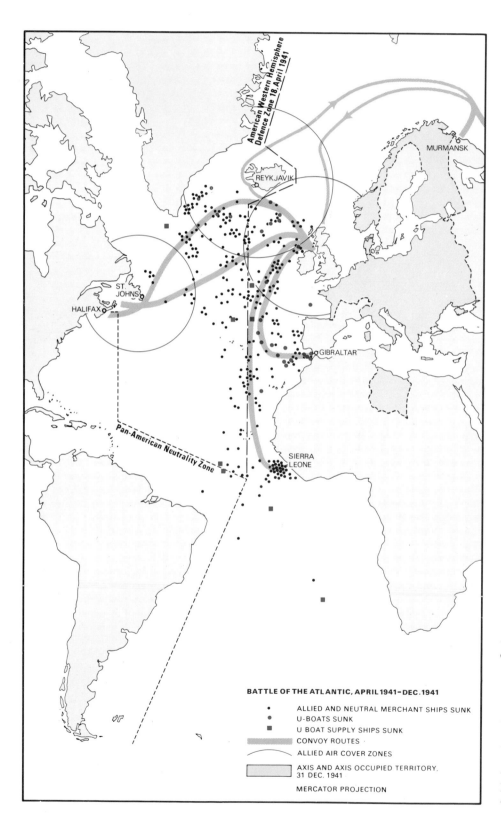

American Western Hemisphere Defence Zone 18. April 1941

MURMANSK

REYKJAVIK

ST. JOHNS

HALIFAX

GIBRALTAR

Pan-American Neutrality Zone

SIERRA LEONE

BATTLE OF THE ATLANTIC, APRIL 1941–DEC.1941

- ·   ALLIED AND NEUTRAL MERCHANT SHIPS SUNK
- ●   U-BOATS SUNK
- ■   U BOAT SUPPLY SHIPS SUNK
- ▬   CONVOY ROUTES
- ◠   ALLIED AIR COVER ZONES
- ▭   AXIS AND AXIS OCCUPIED TERRITORY, 31 DEC. 1941

MERCATOR PROJECTION

there were gradual developments and sudden breakthroughs.

For the second half of 1940 the U-Boats were on top and the period was known to the German submariners as the 'happy time.' A number of 'ace' commanders each achieved many successes. 'Wolf pack' tactics were developed in which a group of U-Boats made co-ordinated attacks on a convoy in order to swamp the escorts. However, by March 1941 the happy time was definitely over. The German U-Boat strength was virtually at its lowest point, the escort forces were becoming stronger, radar equipment was more widely available and in March three of the highest-scoring U-Boat aces were lost. Also in that month Churchill formed a high-level Battle of the Atlantic Committee (the first use of this title for the campaign) to oversee British efforts in all aspects of the struggle. The careful organization of military, industrial and scientific resources that this encouraged outmatched anything the Germans created and in time contributed greatly to Allied success.

The period from April to December 1941 was one of balance. The strength of the German operational U-Boat fleet was trebled but November 1941 showed the lowest shipping losses of the war to that date. There were various reasons for the

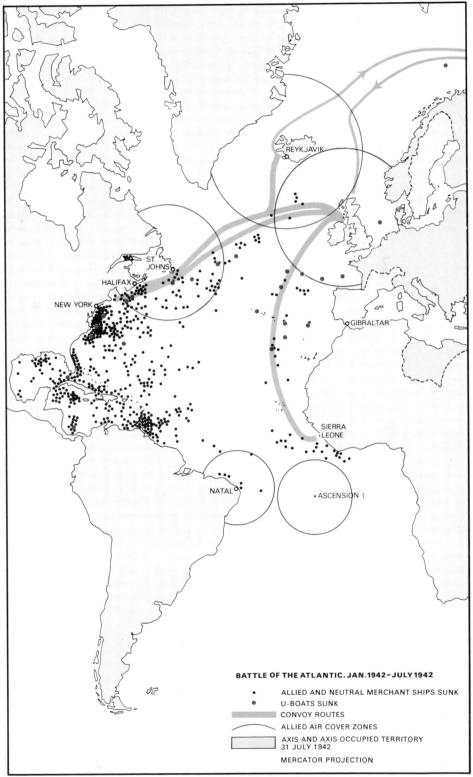

BATTLE OF THE ATLANTIC, JAN. 1942 – JULY 1942

- •   ALLIED AND NEUTRAL MERCHANT SHIPS SUNK
- •   U-BOATS SUNK
-   CONVOY ROUTES
-   ALLIED AIR COVER ZONES
-   AXIS AND AXIS OCCUPIED TERRITORY 31 JULY 1942

MERCATOR PROJECTION

better Allied performance. The United States was moving into a more belligerent position both as an industrial supplier and as a military partner providing escorts for convoys in some areas. Following a breakthrough in May 1941 British intelligence was able to read many German signals until changes in February 1942. Convoys were therefore diverted away from U-Boat packs and U-Boats and their supply ships were intercepted and sunk.

The situation was transformed once more with the US entry into the war. U-Boats quickly began operations off the US East Coast and to their delight found virtually peacetime conditions prevailing. Ships sailed unescorted, showed lights at night and even on occasion sent radio signals giving their positions in plain language. The US Navy was naturally distracted by the sudden demands of the Pacific war but the anti-submarine patrols mounted were easily avoided by the U-Boats and were no substitute for even the least effective convoy system. Gradually, however, a convoy system was introduced and in July 1942 was extended south from Florida to cover most of the Caribbean. By the end of July the U-Boats were beginning to resume the struggle for the main North Atlantic convoy routes and their second happy time was over.

Right: Pearl Harbor under attack by warplanes of the Imperial Japanese Navy on 7 December 1941.

Pearl Harbor

At 0755 local time on 7 December 1941 Japanese carrier aircraft attacked the main base of the US Pacific Fleet at Pearl Harbor. They gained complete strategic and tactical surprise. They sank or crippled five of the eight battleships in the port and destroyed 188 aircraft for the loss of 29 of the attacking planes.

The Japanese attack was planned by Admiral Yamamoto and the six aircraft carriers and two battleships of the strike force were led by Admiral Nagumo. The pilots were well trained and their equipment, some of it specially developed, was good. The fine Zero fighter in particular presented the Allies with many unforeseen problems in the months to come. There were, however, two omissions in the Japanese achievement. The US Pacific Fleet aircraft carriers were absent and escaped damage and the massive oil-storage facilities of the base were not struck as Nagumo's staff recommended. These factors combined to provide a solid foundation on which the industrial power of the United States could prepare a comeback. As the far-sighted Admiral Yamamoto had warned the other Japanese leaders, Japan could expect a few months of success but would then be swamped.

Nonetheless the American authorities had little reason for complacency. US code-breaking services had intercepted a mass of low-level Japanese radio traffic which suggested that an attack, perhaps on Pearl Harbor, was imminent. More importantly, the highest-level Japanese diplomatic cipher had been broken and the final message to the Japanese ambassador in Washington was intercepted. Partly because it was a Sunday, this intercept was passed slowly and there was a delay in sending a warning.

The warning did not reach Pearl Harbor until around midday.

Peacetime customs and inexperience had important detailed effects also. Aircraft on Oahu airfields were parked vulnerably close together; boxes for antiaircraft ammunition were kept locked; large portions of ships' crews were ashore for the day; a submarine sighting by a patrol ship was ignored and a radar warning was disregarded.

The 'day of infamy' (President Roosevelt's description) convinced the American people of the need for war and in the end Yamamoto's prediction was proved correct.

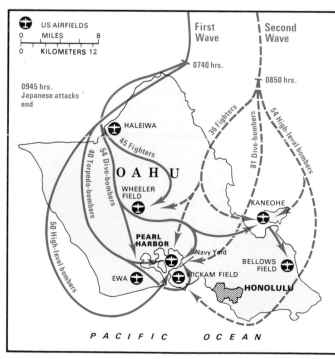

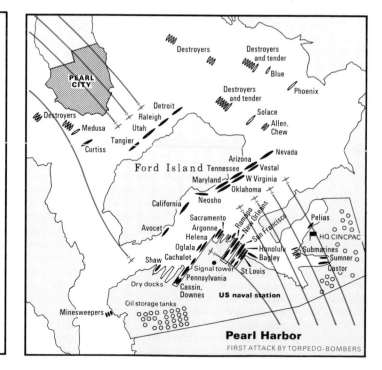

Pearl Harbor
FIRST ATTACK BY TORPEDO-BOMBERS

The Conquest of Malaya

The British withdrawal in Malaya and the fall of Singapore on 15 February 1942 were described by Churchill as the worst disaster in British military history. The British, Australian and Indian forces lost 138,000 men. Many of the prisoners later died of maltreatment or were murdered in the Japanese prison camps. The Japanese lost less than 10,000 casualties. By their own most optimistic assessments the campaign was expected to last 100 days. It took only 70.

The Japanese forces deployed for the attack were three divisions from General Yamashita's Twenty-fifth Army. They were supported by about 200 tanks and 500 aircraft. The Allied infantry force was at least as strong but had virtually no tanks and few antitank weapons. General Percival was in command. The RAF had about 150 aircraft in Malaya, most of them old and inferior types. As well as their crucial advantages in tanks and aircraft the Japanese forces were much better trained and led. By contrast the British military and civilian administration of Malaya was riddled with lethargy and inefficiency. Disruptive peacetime practices of all sorts were maintained up to the start of hostilities and beyond. There was a prevailing attitude of racial contempt for the Japanese who were held to be technologically backward and individually unsuited for military service. Such obtuse racist attitudes were even applied in part to Indian and Malayan soldiers and officers in British service with obvious effects on their morale and fighting efficiency. In a more purely military reckoning the British forces were organized and prepared logistically for a European style of campaign which, in Malayan conditions, made them totally dependent on the few main roads for supplies and tactical movement. The Japanese preferred to travel light, often by bicycle with a ration bag slung over the handlebars, making use of minor roads and tracks and, on the west coast, minor amphibious operations. Little movement was attempted by either side in the true jungle but the Japanese were nonetheless much more flexible and mobile despite, and in part because of, the more lavish scale on which the Allied forces were provided with motor transport. The Jap-

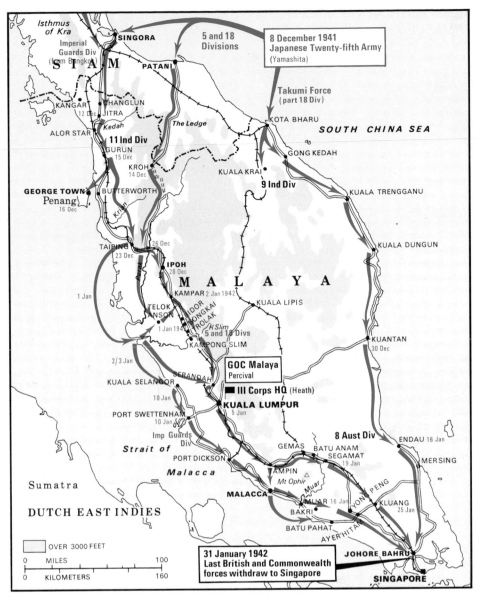

anese tactics were normally based on a combination of two simple techniques. Whenever possible minor roads or paths were used to outflank British forces who were consistently unable to tell whether they were being surrounded by a major force or being bluffed into retreat by a patrol. Alternatively when the Allied units held a strong position the Japanese tanks would break into the position along the main roads and force a retreat. In these ways the Allies were hustled from one defense line to another becoming more disorganized and dispirited as they went.

By the end of January only Singapore remained in British hands. The fleet which the great Singapore naval base had been built to nurture was already gone. The new battleship *Prince of Wales* and the older *Repulse* had been sent to Singapore specifically to deter the Japanese from attacking. They arrived only a few days before the outbreak of war, sailed to attack the Japanese landings on 8 December and were sunk with ease by Japanese aircraft on the 10th, leaving the Allies without a battleship in the Pacific.

The Singapore base did not long survive them. Japanese landings on Singapore Island began on the night of 8/9 February and the British forces surrendered on the 15th. The blow to British and European prestige was felt throughout southeast Asia.

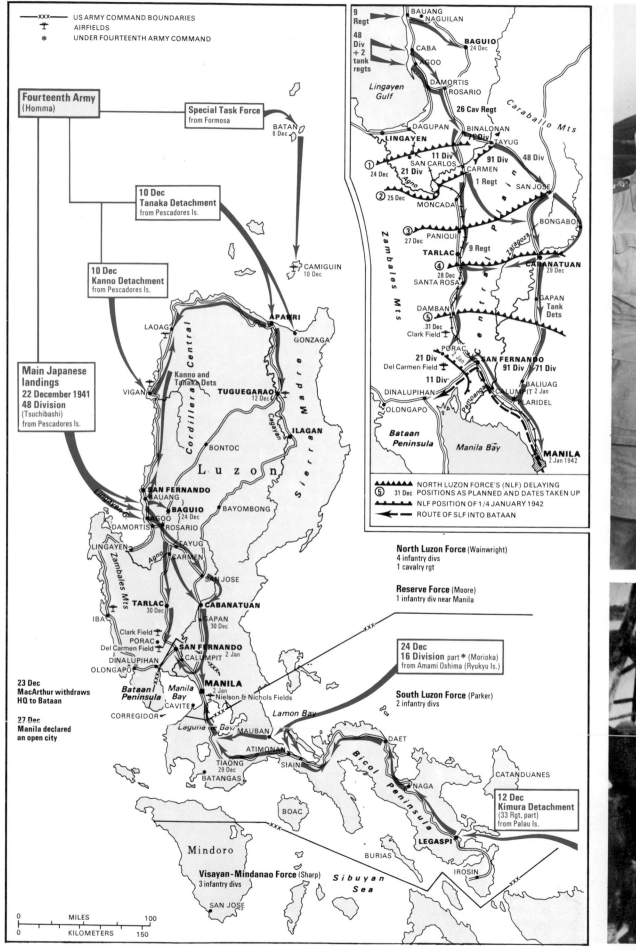

Left: General Douglas MacArthur commanded in the Philippines until President Roosevelt ordered him to leave. He is seen with General Blamey who led Australian troops in New Guinea under MacArthur's command later in the war. Bottom: Japanese Marines advance through Caba on Lingayen Gulf in December 1941.

The Fall of the Philippines

As was the case elsewhere in Asia and the Pacific the Allied forces in the Philippines were ill-armed and badly prepared for war. Although the US and Filipino forces had been joined under General MacArthur's command since late July 1941 their training and equipment remained inadequate. MacArthur had about 31,000 regular troops, 19,000 of them American, and something over 100,000 Filipino conscripts to defend the Philippine archipelago. Although the largest force was on Luzon many units were unavoidably dispersed to the other islands of the group. The units on Luzon were divided into the North and South Luzon Forces. The prewar US plan for defending the Philippines was for strong ground and air forces there to hold out until the US Pacific Fleet could bring help. Clearly this would not be forthcoming after the Pearl Harbor attack. Much therefore depended on MacArthur's air strength but at the outbreak of war his air commander General Brereton only had 150 aircraft. By a com-bination of mismanagement and ill-luck more than half of these were knocked out in Japanese raids on the first day of war. (7 December, Pearl Harbor = 8 December Philippines because of the International Date Line.)

After some early landings to seize air-fields for tactical support the main Japanese operation began on 22 December and by 24 December it was clear to MacArthur that he would have to order all his forces to retreat to the Bataan Peninsula. This retreat was successfully accomplished in the subsequent week. The Japanese believed that the campaign was then virtually over and withdrew their best infantry unit, the 48th Division, and a large part of their air support to be used in operations in the East Indies. Attacks by the less experienced Japanese units that remained had some success but by the end of January both they and the defenders were worn out and a long pause ensued. By April, however, the Japanese had built up their forces once more and their renewed attacks compelled an American surrender on the 9th. The final US positions on Corregidor were overrun on 5–6 May. General MacArthur had been evacuated from Bataan in March on orders from President Roosevelt, promising 'I shall return.'

The Japanese Invasion of Burma

With the invasion of Malaya going well the Japanese were ready to extend their offensive into Burma as they had planned. The attack began in mid-January when small units forced the British to abandon their airfields at Victoria Point and Mergui and was extended a few days later when the main body of Fifteenth Army, 33rd and 35th Divisions, moved on Moulmein. The defending forces were also about two divisions strong at this stage but the units had had little collective training and their equipment was poor.

The British plan was simply to defend as stubbornly as possible to prevent the Japanese from reaching Rangoon, the port through which all supplies and reinforcements had to flow. The Allied air forces initially had only one RAF squadron and one squadron of Chennault's American Volunteer Group (The Flying Tigers) to face over 200 Japanese aircraft, but they nonetheless had many successes both in defense of Rangoon and over the front line. On the ground too the battle was fairly well managed for the first three weeks of February, with the Allied forces gradually retreating to the Sittang River. Unfortunately on 23 February the one available bridge over the river was demolished prematurely when most of the 17th Indian Division was still on the wrong side.

After this disaster the pace of the Japanese advance increased and despite the appointment of General Alexander to take command of the British force and the arrival of the veteran British 7th Armoured Brigade, Rangoon quickly fell. The Japanese were now able to draw ground and air reinforcements from Malaya and advance in strength up the great river valleys. Chinese armies (each equivalent in strength to a European division) had by this time arrived to join the Allied forces but the best efforts of their American commander, General Stilwell, could not always make them fight effectively. Both they and the British were soon forced into rapid and continuous retreat. The remnants of the Allied force reached India in mid-May just as the monsoon was beginning to break. They had lost virtually all their heavy equipment.

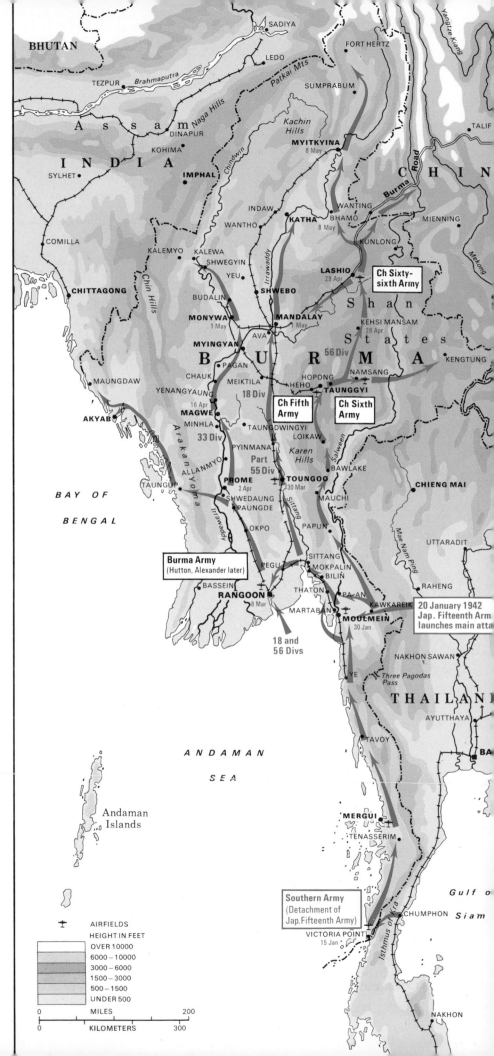

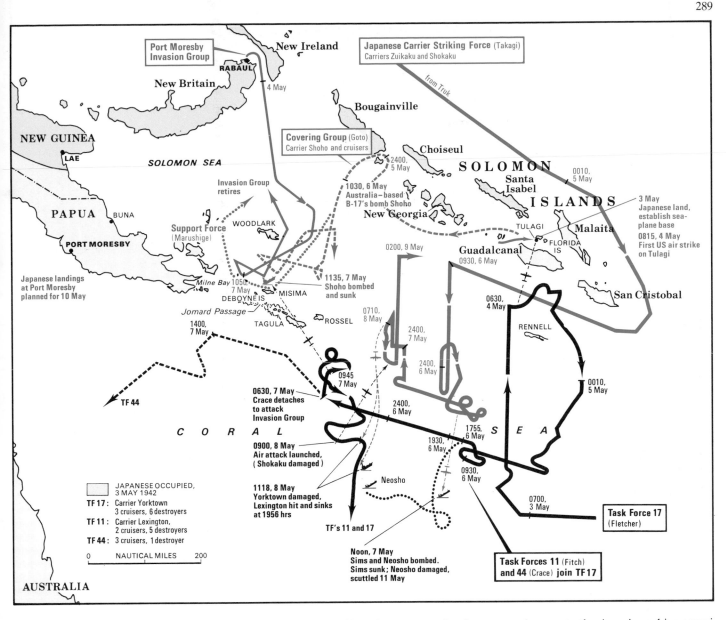

Japanese Carrier Striking Force (Takagi)
Carriers Zuikaku and Shokaku

from Truk

Port Moresby
Invasion Group

New Ireland

RABAUL
4 May

New Britain

Bougainville

Covering Group (Goto)
Carrier Shoho and cruisers

Choiseul

SOLOMON

NEW GUINEA

LAE

SOLOMON SEA

Invasion Group
retires

2400,
5 May

Santa
Isabel

0010,
5 May

ISLANDS

3 May
Japanese land,
establish sea-
plane base

1030, 6 May
Australia–based
B-17's bomb Shoho

PAPUA   BUNA

Support Force
(Marushige)

WOODLARK

New Georgia

TULAGI

Malaita

0815, 4 May
First US air strike
on Tulagi

FLORIDA
IS

PORT MORESBY

0200, 9 May

Guadalcanal
0930, 6 May

Japanese landings
at Port Moresby
planned for 10 May

Milne Bay 1050,
7 May

1135, 7 May
Shoho bombed
and sunk

0630,
4 May

San Cristobal

DEBOYNE IS

MISIMA

0710,
8 May

RENNELL

Jomard Passage

1400,
7 May

TAGULA

ROSSEL

2400,
7 May

2400,
6 May

0010,
5 May

0945
7 May

2400,
6 May

TF 44

0630, 7 May
Crace detaches
to attack
Invasion Group

2400,
6 May

1755,
6 May   S E A

C O R A L

1930,
6 May

0900, 8 May
Air attack launched,
(Shokaku damaged)

0930,
6 May

Neosho

JAPANESE OCCUPIED,
3 MAY 1942

1118, 8 May
Yorktown damaged,
Lexington hit and sinks
at 1956 hrs

0700,
3 May

TF 17: Carrier Yorktown
3 cruisers, 6 destroyers

TF 11: Carrier Lexington,
2 cruisers, 5 destroyers

Task Force 17
(Fletcher)

TF 44: 3 cruisers, 1 destroyer

0   NAUTICAL MILES   200

TF's 11 and 17

Noon, 7 May
Sims and Neosho bombed.
Sims sunk; Neosho damaged,
scuttled 11 May

Task Forces 11 (Fitch)
and 44 (Crace) join TF 17

AUSTRALIA

The Battle of the Coral Sea

Because of the ease with which they had achieved their many successes in the first months of 1942, the Japanese High Command began to consider extending the defensive perimeter which was being set up. This intention was confirmed by the Doolittle Raid on 18 April when bombers launched from an aircraft carrier attacked Tokyo to the shock and dismay of the Japanese leaders. Part of the plan for extending the perimeter was a decision to move into southern Papua by an amphibious attack on Port Moresby. This led to the Battle of the Coral Sea.

The Battle of the Coral Sea holds an important place in naval history as the first naval battle in which the opposing fleets were never in visual contact, leaving the action to be fought entirely by aircraft. Forewarned by codebreaking information the

Americans were able to have two carriers in position to face the Japanese as well as a force of cruisers and destroyers. In addition to the two carriers sent to cover the whole operation the Japanese had a third small carrier in closer support of the invasion group.

The first flurry of action was on 3–4 May when a Japanese seaplane base was established on Tulagi and then attacked the next day by aircraft from the USS *Yorktown*. The Americans then moved south to concentrate their forces and refuel just as the main Japanese operations were getting under way. The action was not renewed until 7 May when Japanese carrier aircraft successfully attacked an American tanker and a destroyer while heavy attacks by land-based aircraft failed to damage any ships of TF.44 which had been unwisely sent to cut off the Japanese Invasion Group. However, American carrier aircraft scored an important success by sinking the *Shoho*. By now the main carrier groups each knew the other's position and a full-scale battle was fought on the 8th. The Japanese lost more aircraft but did

more damage to the American ships especially after errors in damage control contributed to the loss of the *Lexington*. However, with their air strength dissipated the Japanese carriers had to withdraw and the invasion of Port Moresby was cancelled. Thus although the battle was perhaps a draw tactically it was a clear strategic victory for the Americans.

Above: Yamamoto, Japan's great naval strategist and the architect of the attack on Pearl Harbor.

Right: the Japanese heavy cruiser *Mikuma* **abandoned and sinking on 6 June 1942 during the Battle of Midway.**

The Battle of Midway

The Japanese High Command decision to extend their defensive perimeter had led firstly to the Battle of the Coral Sea but it was also the motive for the Japanese attack on Midway and the decisive battle which developed there. The Coral Sea battle had important effects on the Midway operation. The two Japanese carriers from the earlier battle were not repaired quickly enough to go to Midway nor were the survivors of their air groups used to bolster the Japanese strength on the other carriers. The Japanese also believed that the *Yorktown* was too seriously damaged to be made ready in time for Midway. In fact she returned to Pearl Harbor with damage that would certainly have taken months to repair in peacetime but she was patched up in 48 hours.

The false assessment of *Yorktown*'s status was only one of a number of intelligence and planning factors that contributed to the Japanese defeat. Admiral Yamamoto believed that, as well as the *Yorktown* being out of action, the other American carriers available, the *Enterprise* and *Hornet*, were likely to be in the South Pacific. Even if this was not the case diversionary attacks on the Aleutians were planned so that the Americans would be distracted from the landings on Midway. Once the capture of the island was complete, the Japanese, warned by their submarine patrols, would destroy the American forces in an all-out battle. Unfortunately for the Japanese the Americans were able to repeat their previous codebreaking successes and thus forewarned they were able to move their carriers into position before the Japanese patrols were established and equally able to disregard the Aleutians attacks so that these became in effect a wasteful dispersal of the Japanese resources (two powerful light carriers and many other ships were employed in the Aleutian operations). The various Midway forces were also widely dispersed leaving further small aircraft and seaplane carriers effectively out of the battle when their scout planes might well have been of decisive help and leaving Nagumo's carriers with only a few ships in company to provide supporting AA fire.

The Japanese were sighted approaching on 3 June and the action began in earnest on 4 June. The Japanese started by virtually wiping out the defending aircraft based on Midway at little cost to themselves. However it was not until the Japanese were ready to recover their aircraft from the first strike that their scouts found the American carriers. The American carrier aircraft were already on their way and made a series of attacks before the Japanese had reorganized to defend properly. Three of the four Japanese carriers were crippled and later sank. The fourth Japanese carrier, the *Hiryu*, fought back causing the *Yorktown* to be abandoned but the *Hiryu* herself was put out of action later in the day. The Japanese leaders made half-hearted attempts on 5 June to close in and fight a gun action with their vastly superior surface forces but the Americans refused to be drawn and the whole operation was abandoned.

Midway was one of the most decisive battles of the war for not only had the Japanese lost four of their best aircraft carriers but with them had gone the cream of their carrier pilots and crews. While they still had a useful supply of aircraft and aircraft carriers the veteran flyers could not be replaced. The next major naval battles in the Pacific, although close fought, would follow the American advance against Guadalcanal. The Japanese had irrevocably lost the initiative.

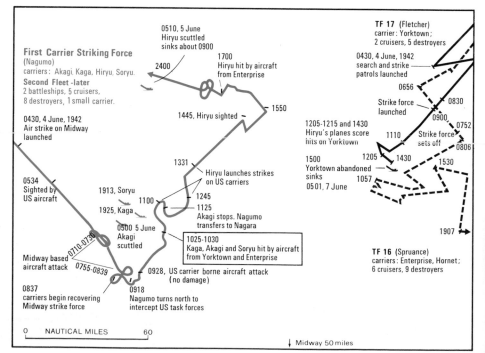

Below: a Soviet gun crew firing in Stalingrad's factory district during the bitter fighting in 1942.

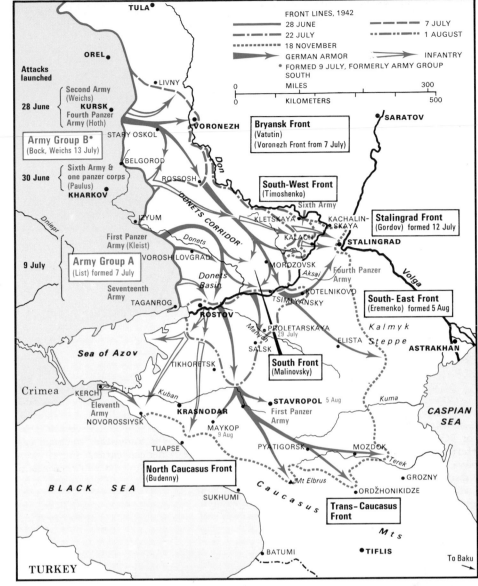

The German Advance to Stalingrad

In early April Hitler issued his instructions for the 1942 offensive. This time the central sector was to remain fairly quiet, while in the north the capture of Leningrad was envisioned. However, the main effort was to be in the south. Here the Red Army was to be engaged and beaten on the River Don, which would permit an advance to the prized Caucasian oilfields and the capture or neutralization of Stalingrad which, apart from being 'Stalin's City,' was an important rail and river center, and also the site of tank and armament factories. In preparation for this campaign General Manstein expelled the Red Army from the Kerch Peninsula and captured the Crimea, including the naval base of Sevastopol.

The main offensive by Army Group South was delayed for four weeks by a big Soviet attack at Kharkov, so it did not begin until the end of June. But it made good progress and reached the Don in mid-July. Here it was held by a Soviet counteroffensive at Voronezh, but in the south Rostov was again captured by the Germans. At this point

Below: Soviet Illyushin IL-2s were very successful ground-attack aircraft, but suffered heavy losses.

Hitler appears to have changed the emphasis of his attack; Stalingrad was to be the main target, although the Caucasian oilfields were to remain a priority. His staff officers realized that, with the Red Army still not decisively beaten, this division of effort was strategically risky, but they were overruled and some were dismissed by Hitler.

In the Caucasus the German Army Group A did make a rapid advance, capturing Novorossiysk. Paradoxically, shortly after occupying the outlying Maykop oilfield, the German advance ran out of fuel. The main Caucasian oilfields remained out of reach; the allocation of 300,000 troops to the capture of Stalingrad meant that the Caucasus thrust had not achieved its main object.

The German attack on Stalingrad was a simple frontal assault. To have encircled the city would have entailed crossing the Volga, which the Germans felt unable to undertake with the resources available. The Russians deliberately kept as few men as possible in the city itself, relying on high morale and determination to ensure that the Germans would need to fight bitterly for every street and building. This in fact is what happened. Soviet soldiers, joined by armed civilians, withdrew only inch by inch as shells and bombs destroyed the city about their ears. More and more German units were drawn into the brutal struggle while the Soviet commanders were able to husband their forces and prepare for a counteroffensive.

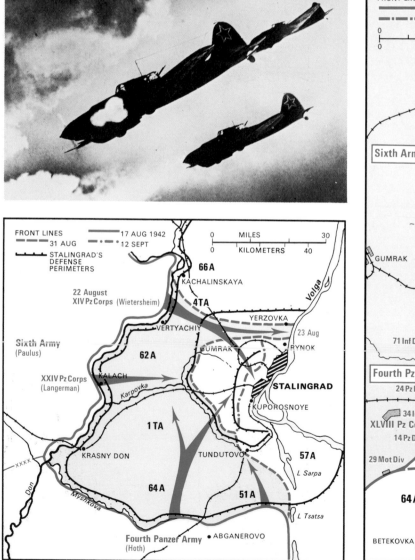

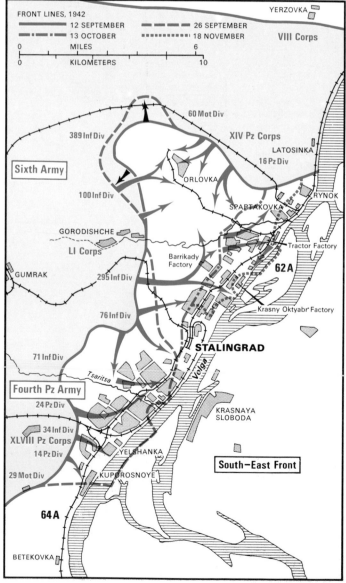

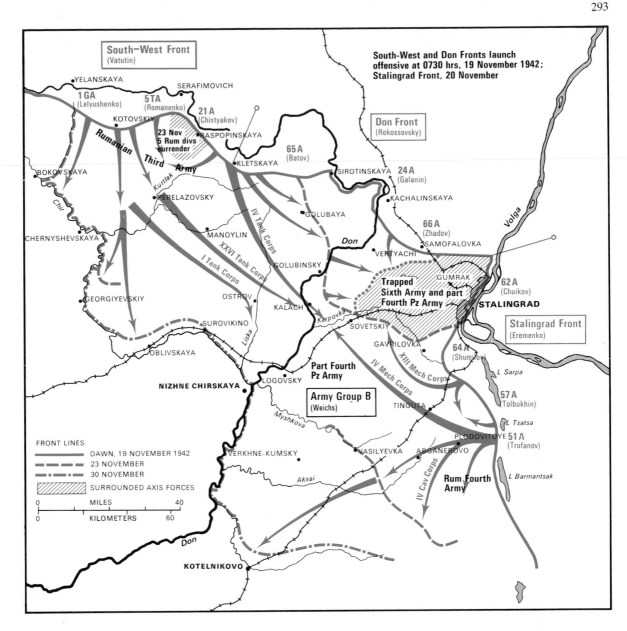

The following labels appear on the map:

South-West Front (Vatutin)

South-West and Don Fronts launch offensive at 0730 hrs, 19 November 1942; Stalingrad Front, 20 November

Don Front (Rokossovsky)

YELANSKAYA
SERAFIMOVICH
1 GA (Lelyushenko)
5 TA (Romanenko)
21 A (Chistyakov)
KOTOVSKIY
RASPOPINSKAYA
23 Nov 5 Rum divs surrender
Rumanian Third Army
BOKOVSKAYA
Kurtlak
KLETSKAYA
65 A (Batov)
SIROTINSKAYA
24 A (Galanin)
KACHALINSKAYA
CHERNYSHEVSKAYA
PERELAZOVSKY
Chir
GOLUBAYA
Don
66 A (Zhadov)
SAMOFALOVKA
Volga
MANOYLIN
XXVI Tank Corps
IV Tank Corps
VERTYACHI
GOLUBINSKY
GEORGIYEVSKIY
I Tank Corps
OSTROV
GOLUBINSKY
Trapped Sixth Army and part Fourth Pz Army
GUMRAK
62 A (Chuikov)
STALINGRAD
KALACH
Karpovka
Liska
SUROVIKINO
SOVETSKIY
Stalingrad Front (Eremenko)
GAVRILOVKA
64 A (Shumilov)
L Sarpa
OBLIVSKAYA
Part Fourth Pz Army
IV Mech Corps
XIII Mech Corps
57 A (Tolbukhin)
NIZHNE CHIRSKAYA
LOGOVSKY
Army Group B (Weichs)
TINGUTA
L Tsatsa
Myshkova
PLODOVITOYE
51 A (Trufanov)

FRONT LINES
——— DAWN, 19 NOVEMBER 1942
– – – 23 NOVEMBER
–·–·– 30 NOVEMBER
/// SURROUNDED AXIS FORCES
0 MILES 40
0 KILOMETERS 60

VERKHNE-KUMSKY
VASILYEVKA
ABGANEROVO
IV Cav Corps
L Barmantsak
Aksai
Rum Fourth Army
Don
KOTELNIKOVO

The Stalingrad Counteroffensive

While Soviet resistance inside Stalingrad prevented the Germans capturing that city in its entirety, the Soviet High Command was assembling forces north of the Don for a counteroffensive. The general situation was that the German general, Paulus, had about 300,000 men concentrated to the west of Stalingrad. His northwest flank was protected by Italian and Rumanian troops while on his southern flank he had more Rumanian units.

The Soviet offensive began on 19 November 1942. It consisted of some diversionary action on the central, Moscow, front with the aim of attracting German reinforcements which otherwise might be sent to Stalingrad, and the main thrust, which was to relieve Stalingrad. General Zhukov, disposing of the whole Soviet operational reserve, had three army groups ['fronts'] which were to attack from the north, south, and northwest, initially concentrating their blows on the Italians and Rumanians, whose morale was lower than the Germans'. In fact the Italian and Rumanian positions in the northwest soon crumbled, enabling the Soviet troops to penetrate into the German rear and then link up with the Stalingrad Front advancing westward from its concentration area in the south. Paulus was now surrounded but Hitler, assured by Göring that an airlift could keep the encircled troops supplied, insisted that the siege of Stalingrad should continue. In mid-December General Manstein led an attack which broke through the Russian lines, by then far to the west, in an attempt to relieve Paulus, but the Soviet high command, diverting troops from the battle with Paulus, blocked this move. With Hitler's agreement Paulus made no attempt to break out and join Manstein. The Red Army could then turn back to the steady destruction of Paulus's Sixth Army. On 2 February 1943 the German forces at Stalingrad surrendered, after being reduced to little more than a headquarters and isolated detachments. Although the Germans had been defeated earlier by the British at El Alamein, this was the first really major defeat suffered by the German Army and had an enormous psychological effect. Hitler had shown incompetent generalship; his refusal to allow Paulus to withdraw from Stalingrad while there was still time was directly responsible for this catastrophic defeat. Many thousands of the German troops taken prisoner died in Russian camps. Many were held for several years after the end of the war.

El Alamein

Following their defeat in the Battle of Alam Halfa and bearing in mind their continuing fuel supply problems which that battle highlighted, the German leaders prepared to conduct the next battle in the North African theater from strong defense lines rather than rely on the mobility which had been the Afrika Korps' trade mark in the past. Although the forward defenses were mainly manned by Italian troops, German units were intermingled with them to provide extra strength and reliability. The fuel shortage meant that the armored reserve had to be split up to ensure that at least part of it would have enough fuel to reach any threatened sector. For the month before the battle Rommel was in Germany on sick leave and General Stumme commanded in his place. Rommel returned to Africa on 25 October after the battle was under way.

Throughout his earlier career General Montgomery had shown himself to be deeply concerned with improving the morale and training of the troops, and planning the battle meticulously before beginning to fight. This concern was nowhere more evident than in the preparation for Alamein. Many of the faults which had affected Eighth Army in the past were ironed out and confidence was high. The plan, as shown below, was for infantry units of XXX Corps to win corridors through the Axis minefields through which the armor of X Corps would pass unhindered, ready to meet and destroy the German tanks in open ground.

Despite the careful preparations on which Montgomery insisted, the actual events were only broadly similar to this plan. The powerful preparatory artillery barrage helped the infantry attacks to make a good start

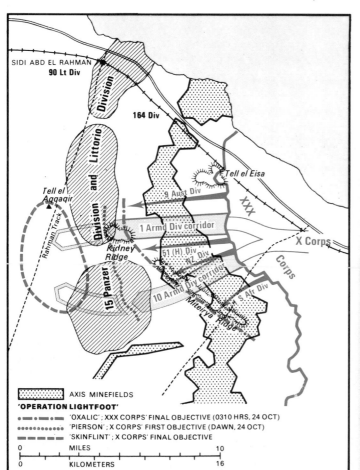

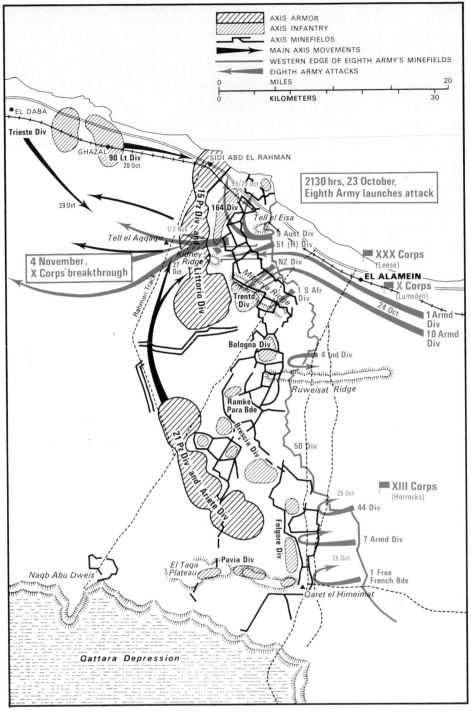

but it proved impossible to move the tanks forward in the way envisioned. The German defense was not helped by General Stumme's death from a heart attack on the afternoon of the 24th as heavy fighting continued. The German 21st Panzer Division was kept out of the main battle for the first days by diversionary efforts by XIII Corps. Although attempts to push the main British armored force forward continued, by the 26th it was clear that it had becomed bogged down and Montgomery largely halted his forces for regrouping. The chief events of the following five days were unsuccessful German counterattacks throughout the main sector and a powerful northward advance by 9th Australian Division which drew in the German reserves. Montgomery's revised breakthrough plan, Operation Supercharge, was put into action on the night of 1/2 November. Although Rommel's forces fought well, by the end of the 2nd he was left with only 35 tanks. He signalled to Hitler that he must retreat. Hitler immediately forbade this but by 4 November further German and Italian losses made the retreat inevitable. Although the Battle of El Alamein was undoubtedly a decisive success for the Allies, Montgomery was unable to follow up his victory quickly enough and the remainder of Rommel's forces was able to make good its retreat.

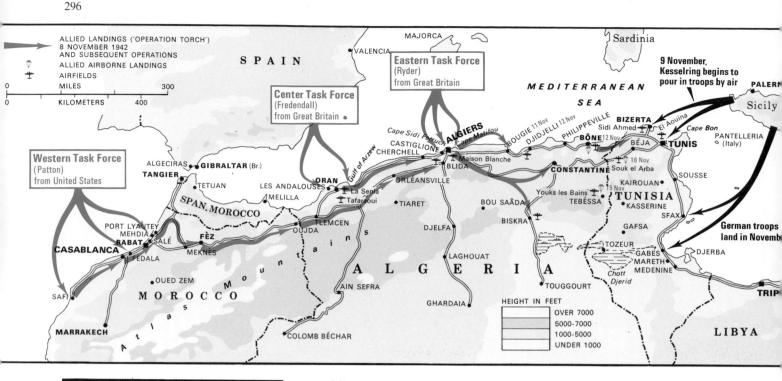

ALLIED LANDINGS ('OPERATION TORCH')
8 NOVEMBER 1942
AND SUBSEQUENT OPERATIONS
ALLIED AIRBORNE LANDINGS
AIRFIELDS

MILES 0 — 300
KILOMETERS 0 — 400

Western Task Force
(Patton)
from United States

Center Task Force
(Fredendall)
from Great Britain

Eastern Task Force
(Ryder)
from Great Britain

9 November,
Kesselring begins to
pour in troops by air

German troops
land in November

HEIGHT IN FEET
OVER 7000
5000-7000
1000-5000
UNDER 1000

Operation Torch

On 8 November 1942 as Rommel's forces were retreating from Egypt, American and British troops began a series of landings in French North Africa. The codename for the landings was Operation Torch. Although the operation gave US ground forces their first large-scale opportunity to fight in the European war, the plan had been strongly opposed by the US Chiefs of Staff who saw it as a diversion from their preferred strategy of preparing exclusively for a direct invasion of western Europe. This opposition had been overruled by President Roosevelt because he believed that if the US delayed becoming involved in Europe then pressure would grow in US political circles for the abandonment of the policy of putting the defeat of Germany first.

In preparation for the landings there had been secret talks with various local French leaders (the USA had maintained diplomatic links with Vichy France) in an effort to ensure that the landings would not be resisted by the strong Vichy forces in North Africa. The Americans had taken the lead in this as much Anglo-French hostility remained as a legacy of events of 1940. For this reason also the American presence in the initial phases of the operation was deliberately increased and publicly exaggerated when in fact the British contribution, particularly in warships and transport shipping, was rather larger. Nonetheless Torch was certainly the first truly combined Allied operation of the war. Whatever his other shortcomings as a general, the Commander in Chief, General Eisenhower, from the outset demonstrated the ability to create a genuinely integrated and efficient staff.

The map shows the three main landing areas and the early advances. Although there was sporadic resistance from the Vichy forces in most areas the landings generally went well with less than 2000 casualties all told. Admiral Darlan, one of the principal leaders of the Vichy government happened to be in Algiers on private business and was captured and persuaded to use his considerable influence in the Allied cause.

Despite the comparative success of the initial landings there were obviously logistic difficulties involved in pushing any large force quickly forward the 400 miles to Tunis. In retrospect it would probably have been better, as some of the planners of the operation had urged, for the initial landings to have been extended as far east as Bône. In the event the Germans reacted with very great speed and on instructions from Hitler and the Commander in Chief, Mediterranean, Field Marshal Kesselring, they poured in troops and aircraft. The Vichy forces in Tunisia made little attempt to resist this move and in a series of battles in late November and December the Germans were able to halt the Allied advance.

Left: a Panzer Mark IV fights to stem the Allied drive into Tunisia in the months after the Torch landings and the Battle of Alamein.

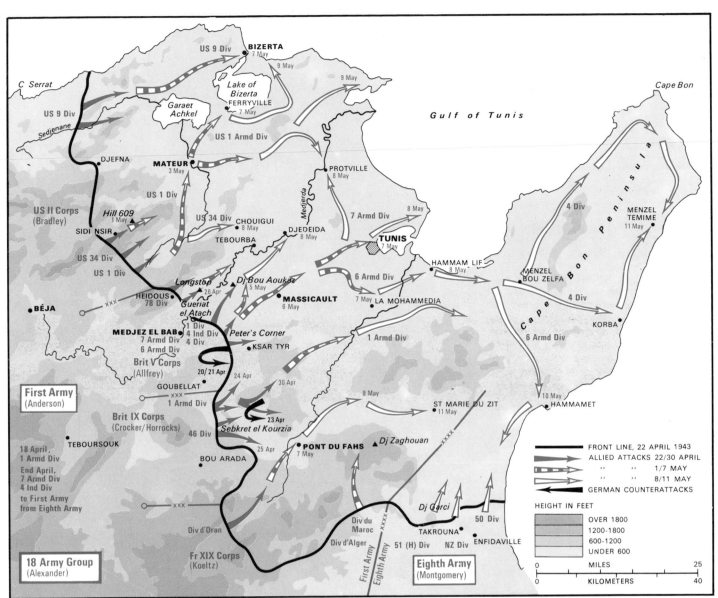

Map labels:

US 9 Div · BIZERTA 7 May · 9 May · 9 May · C Serrat · Lake of Bizerta · FERRYVILLE 7 May · Garaet Achkel · Gulf of Tunis · Cape Bon · US 9 Div · Sedjenane · US 1 Armd Div · DJEFNA · MATEUR 3 May · PROTVILLE 8 May · US 1 Div · US II Corps (Bradley) · Hill 609 1 May · SIDI NSIR · US 34 Div · CHOUIGUI 8 May · Medjerda · 7 Armd Div 8 May · TUNIS 7 May · US 34 Div · US 1 Div · TEBOURBA · DJEDEIDA 8 May · HAMMAM LIF 8 May · MENZEL TEMIME 11 May · Longstop 26 Apr · Dj Bou Aoukaz 5 May · 6 Armd Div · MENZEL BOU ZELFA · Cape Bon Peninsula · 4 Div · BÉJA · XXX · HEIDOUS 78 Div · Gueriat el Atach · MASSICAULT 6 May · 7 May LA MOHAMMEDIA · 4 Div · KORBA · MEDJEZ EL BAB 7 Armd Div 6 Armd Div · 1 Div 4 Ind Div 4 Div · Peter's Corner · KSAR TYR · 1 Armd Div · 6 Armd Div · Brit V Corps (Allfrey) · 20/21 Apr · GOUBELLAT · 24 Apr · 30 Apr · 9 May · ST MARIE DU ZIT 11 May · 10 May · HAMMAMET · First Army (Anderson) · XXX · 1 Armd Div · 23 Apr · Sebkret el Kourzia · Brit IX Corps (Crocker/Horrocks) · 46 Div · 25 Apr · PONT DU FAHS 7 May · Dj Zaghouan · XXXX · 18 April, 1 Armd Div · TEBOURSOUK · BOU ARADA · Dj Garci · 50 Div · End April, 7 Armd Div 4 Ind Div to First Army from Eighth Army · Div du Maroc · XXXX · TAKROUNA · ENFIDAVILLE · Div d'Alger · 51 (H) Div · NZ Div · 18 Army Group (Alexander) · Div d'Oran · Fr XIX Corps (Koeltz) · First Army Eighth Army · Eighth Army (Montgomery)

Legend:
FRONT LINE, 22 APRIL 1943
ALLIED ATTACKS 22/30 APRIL
" " 1/7 MAY
" " 8/11 MAY
GERMAN COUNTERATTACKS

HEIGHT IN FEET
OVER 1800
1200-1800
600-1200
UNDER 600

0 MILES 25
0 KILOMETERS 40

Tunisia

Although the German and Italian forces had fought a brave series of delaying actions during their retreat into Tunisia, particularly on the Mareth Line and at Wadi Akarit, by April 1943 Eighth Army had pushed well forward. Similarly, although the Allied units from the Torch landings had suffered heavily in mid-February when the Germans attacked at Kasserine, this setback had been overcome and the Axis forces driven back. By 14 April the Germans and Italians had taken up the positions shown on the map defending the last line of hills before the plain around Tunis and Bizerta.

Allied attacks on this line began on 22 April especially in the sectors between Hill 609 and Peter's Corner. Although some progress was made by American forces at Hill 609 and in the nearby Mousetrap Valley and by the British at Longstop Hill and toward Djebel Bou Aoukaz, no decisive gains were made at first. General Alexander

decided to switch experienced British units from Eighth Army to V Corps and with their help renewed British and US attacks from 5 May soon broke through. The German and Italian resistance collapsed and by 12 May Marshal Messe and General von Arnim had surrendered along with 250,000 troops.

Rommel had left Africa on 9 March and had urged that the German and Italian forces be evacuated. Hitler refused to countenance this and there can be little doubt that, despite the delaying actions they fought, the forces lost in Africa would have served the Axis better in defending Sicily and Italy against the seaborne assaults that would be the British and Americans' next move. The early stages of the battle for Tunisia also contributed to another German disaster by occupying large numbers of transport aircraft at a time when Göring was failing to fulfill his promise to supply Stalingrad by air.

Right: Italian troops on a desert reconnaissance mission.

The Battle of Kursk

For the summer of 1943 the German High Command planned no big offensive in Russia. It needed time to re-equip and, moreover, expected that its resources would be needed in other theaters. Nevertheless, to regain a psychological advantage, and to throw the expected Soviet offensive off balance, it was decided to stage a large but essentially limited attack toward Kursk. Here the Russians had ended the 1942–43 winter campaign holding a large salient which seemed very vulnerable to the kind of pincer movement which had won so many German successes in 1941.

Through various espionage channels, the Soviets were well informed of the German intentions, although they were probably not prepared for the repeated postponement of the operation; some German commanders were having second thoughts and were not in a hurry to get into position. All this enabled the Soviets to construct three lines of defense around the salient, each line consisting of elaborate trenches and antitank positions with appropriate artillery cover. The Germans began their advance on 5 July, in the belief that they were making a surprise attack, but immediately encountered resistance far stiffer than they had expected.

Thus the northern arm of the German pincer made only small penetrations into the Soviet salient, and at a very high cost. The southern arm, led by Manstein, fared somewhat better. His Fourth Panzer Army overcame the Russian Sixth Army but was then confronted with fresh Soviet tank units brought forward from reserve. Near Prokhorovka converging tank armies began what is regarded as the biggest tank battle of all time. It started on 12 July, and by the end of the next day the Germans seemed to be winning it, although both sides had already lost hundreds of tanks. However, at this point the German effort slackened, although the battle continued for five days longer. A Soviet offensive north of the salient toward Bryansk had altered the situation, and moreover the western Allies were landing in Sicily. Many of the German tanks were dispatched straight to Italy as soon as they were extricated from the Kursk battlefield. With this abandonment of the German offensive the Russians were free to begin their own advance all along the front south of Moscow.

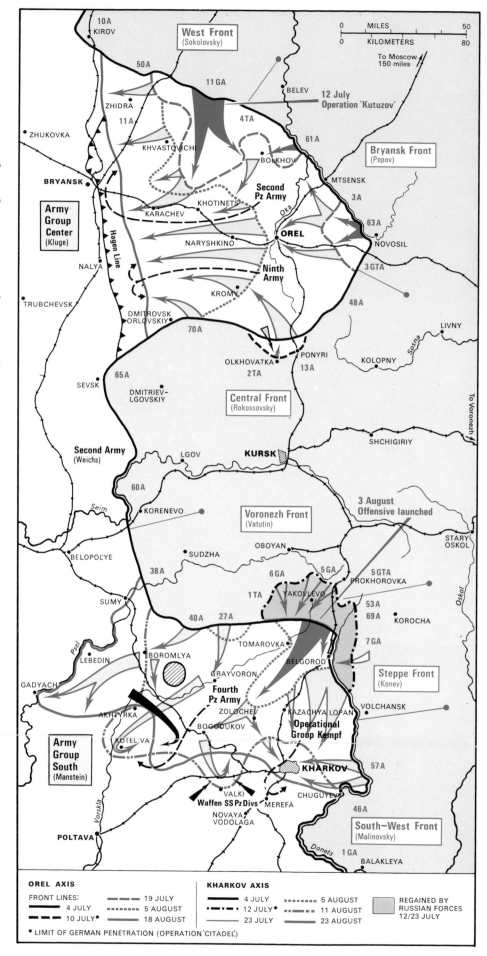

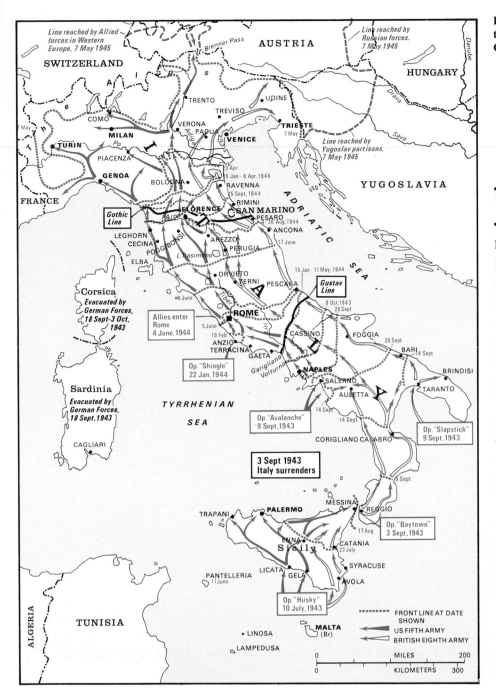

Below left: the ruins of Cassino town after the long battle to break through the German Gustav Line.

The Italian Campaign

By the time the Allied campaign in North Africa was coming to an end it was clear to the Allied leaders that there was no prospect of building up their forces in Britain sufficiently to allow the invasion of northwest Europe to take place in 1943. It had been agreed at the Casablanca conference in January that Sicily should be captured once the campaign in Africa was complete because this would largely free the Mediterranean sea lanes but this comparatively limited objective did not seem to be making full use of the very large Allied forces already in the theater or the massive base organization that had been built up there. The British were strongly in favor of moving on to attack mainland Italy and the Americans too came round to this opinion when Mussolini's government fell in July. Throughout the campaign in Italy the British remained far more ready to press for reinforcements to be sent and an aggressive policy to be followed. The American views prevailed, however, and thus in late 1943 experienced units and commanders were withdrawn to go to England to prepare for D-Day. Again in the summer of 1944, after Rome had been taken, a large proportion of the Allied force was withdrawn to take part in the invasion of southern France.

The campaign in Italy saw some of the fiercest battles of the war. The initial seaborne landings at Salerno and the Anzio attempt to outflank the German Gustav Line were both very vigorously opposed by the Germans because of Hitler's hope that this would deter the Allies from such operations in northwest Europe. Once ashore the Allied forces found themselves facing successive river crossings which were usually overlooked by rugged and dominating hills carefully fortified by the Germans. The most famous of these positions was that at Monte Cassino which defied repeated Allied attacks in the early months of 1944. Even when the Germans were retreating between defense lines demolitions, rear guard actions, booby traps and miserable weather often combined to reduce Allied progress on the few good roads. Only when the Allied attacks were resumed in April 1945, after a long pause, did the German resistance collapse. The German forces in Italy surrendered on 2 May 1945.

The Solomons Campaign

Although the Japanese plans to take full control of the Solomons and New Guinea had received a major setback in the Battle of the Coral Sea in May 1942, they made a further attempt to reach Port Moresby by an overland advance from Buna in July–September 1942. This was halted by the defending Australian formations. Australian and American forces had already begun to strike back by building and holding an airstrip at Milne Bay and despite the worst imaginable ground and weather conditions they then succeeded in advancing over the Owen Stanley Range to take Buna and Sanananda. (The later stages of the New

The advance in the Solomons, of course, began with the long drawn struggle for Guadalcanal. Once this initial base had been taken the operations took on the soon-to-be-familiar island hopping pattern. Naval and air superiority kept the Japanese guessing about the point of attack and once ashore the Construction Battalions or Seabees quickly built or repaired airstrips for local defense and as a base to provide cover for the next step. The technique is perhaps best

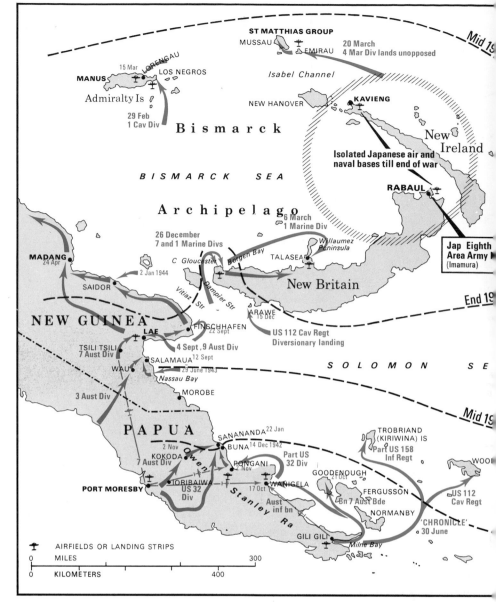

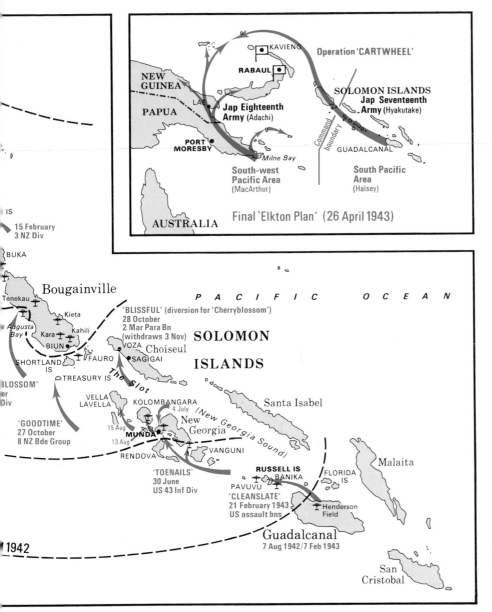

Final 'Elkton Plan' (26 April 1943)

Operation 'CARTWHEEL'

KAVIENG
RABAUL
NEW GUINEA
PAPUA
LAE
Jap Eighteenth Army (Adachi)
PORT MORESBY
Milne Bay
SOLOMON ISLANDS
Jap Seventeenth Army (Hyakutake)
GUADALCANAL
South-west Pacific Area (MacArthur)
South Pacific Area (Halsey)
AUSTRALIA

15 February
3 NZ Div
BUKA

Bougainville
Tenekau
Kieta
s Augusta Bay
Kara
Kahili
BIUN
SHORTLAND IS
FAURO
TREASURY IS
BLOSSOM'
er Div

PACIFIC OCEAN

'BLISSFUL' (diversion for 'Cherryblossom')
28 October
2 Mar Para Bn (withdraws 3 Nov)

VOZA
Choiseul
SAGIGAI

SOLOMON ISLANDS

The Slot

VELLA LAVELLA
KOLOMBANGARA
4 July
New Georgia
15 Aug
MUNDA
13 Aug
RENDOVA
VANGUNI

(New Georgia Sound)

Santa Isabel

'GOODTIME'
27 October
8 NZ Bde Group

'TOENAILS'
30 June
US 43 Inf Div

RUSSELL IS
BANIKA
PAVUVU
'CLEANSLATE'
21 February 1943
US assault bns

FLORIDA IS

Malaita

Henderson Field

1942

Guadalcanal
7 Aug 1942/7 Feb 1943

San Cristobal

shown in the landings on Bougainville. This island was defended by about 60,000 Japanese but only a few hundred of these were near Empress Augusta Bay and it was over four months before the Japanese could mount a full-scale attack against the beachhead, by then well defended.

When the plans for the Solomons were first made it seemed clear that it would be necessary to take both the main Japanese bases at Rabaul and Kavieng but in August 1943 it was agreed by bypass Rabaul and in March 1944 it was decided to leave Kavieng also. By that time the harbors and airfields at both bases were largely out of action. Landings in eastern New Britain and the Admiralty and St Matthias groups completed a very economical and effective campaign. The various isolated Japanese garrisons remained in being to the end of the war but could achieve little.

Below left: destroyer guns blaze during a confused night action which took place off Cape Esperance.
Below: an Aichi D3A is shot down directly over the carrier *Enterprise* in the Battle of the Eastern Solomons.

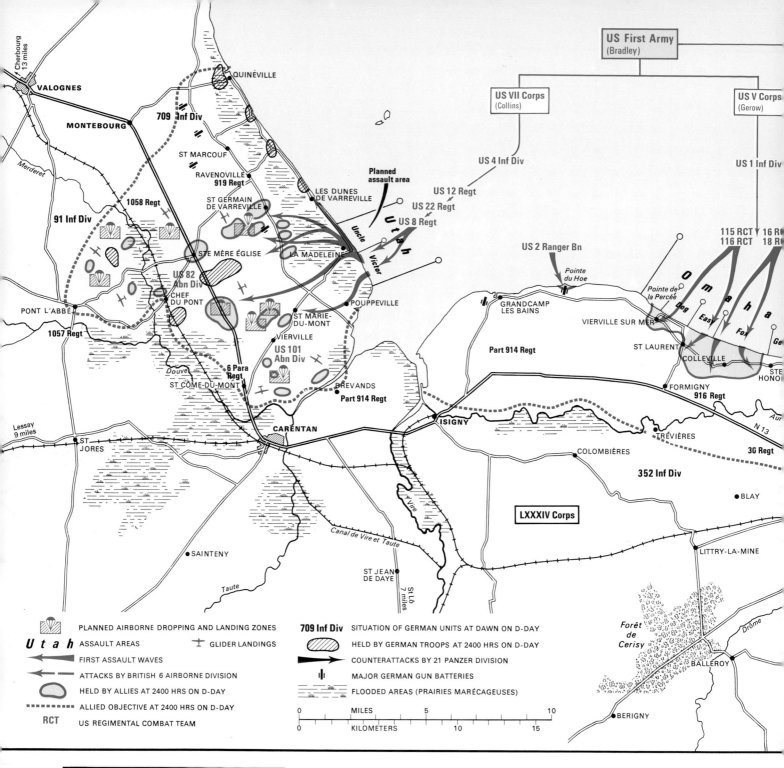

D-Day

The Allied invasion of France on 6 June 1944 was the largest combined land, sea and air operation ever undertaken in war. The planning process and the forces involved were on the largest and most elaborate scale. The Supreme Commander for Operation Overlord was General Eisenhower and he had nearly 3,000,000 men under his control. A massive quantity of equipment, much of it specially designed, had also been assembled. One of the most important aspects of the Allied plan was the preparation of parts for two artificial ports (Mulberry Harbors) which were to be towed across the Channel and sunk or anchored off the Omaha and Gold beaches to enable heavy supplies to be landed easily before a major port had been taken.

Although they had a crushing superiority in fighting aircraft and warships, because of shortages of paratroop-carrying aircraft and naval landing craft and the natural advantages of the defense, the Allied plan relied heavily on elaborate deception schemes and preparatory air attacks to prevent the Germans overwhelming the comparatively limited ground forces deployed initially. The main deception plan was to suggest – by way of reports from double agents, false radio traffic and other means – that a notional First US Army Group was being assembled in southeast England under the command of General Patton ready to invade across the narrowest part of the Channel. The many preparatory air attacks for the real operation were designed mainly to isolate the Normandy area from the rest of France but these were only a proportion of the attacks made and thus the true purpose was concealed and the deception reinforced.

The deception plan contributed greatly to uncertainties in the German command. The German Commander in Chief, West, Field Marshal von Rundstedt believed that beach defenses should come second to the assembly of a strong central reserve to

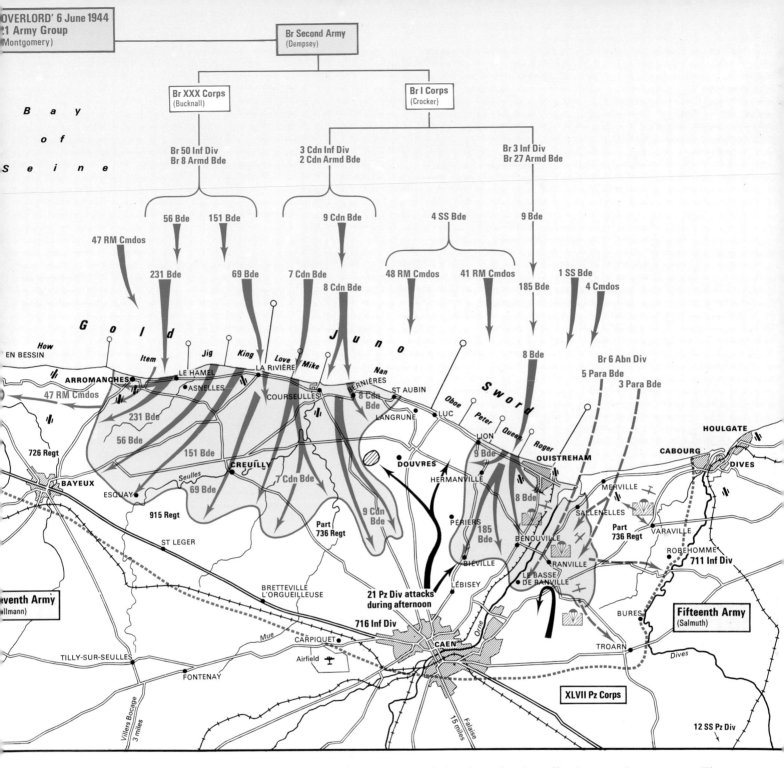

'OVERLORD' 6 June 1944
21 Army Group
(Montgomery)

Br Second Army
(Dempsey)

Br XXX Corps
(Bucknall)

Br I Corps
(Crocker)

Br 50 Inf Div
Br 8 Armd Bde

3 Cdn Inf Div
2 Cdn Armd Bde

Br 3 Inf Div
Br 27 Armd Bde

56 Bde   151 Bde

9 Cdn Bde

4 SS Bde

9 Bde

47 RM Cmdos

231 Bde   69 Bde

7 Cdn Bde
8 Cdn Bde

48 RM Cmdos   41 RM Cmdos

1 SS Bde
4 Cmdos

185 Bde

8 Bde

Bay

of

Seine

Gold   *Juno*   *Sword*

How
EN BESSIN

Item

Jig   *King*   *Love*   *Mike*   *Nan*

Br 6 Abn Div
5 Para Bde
3 Para Bde

ARROMANCHES   LE HAMEL   LA RIVIÈRE   BERNIÈRES   ST AUBIN

HOULGATE

47 RM Cmdos   ASNELLES   COURSEULLES   8 Cdn Bde   Oboe   Peter   Queen   Roger

CABOURG

231 Bde   LANGRUNE   LUC   LION   OUISTREHAM   DIVES

56 Bde   151 Bde   DOUVRES   9 Bde   MERVILLE

726 Regt   Seulles   CREUILLY   7 Cdn Bde   HERMANVILLE   8 Bde   SALLENELLES

BAYEUX   69 Bde   PÉRIERS   VARAVILLE

ESQUAY   915 Regt   9 Cdn Bde   185 Bde   BÉNOUVILLE   ROBEHOMME

Part 736 Regt   711 Inf Div

ST LEGER   BIÉVILLE   RANVILLE   Part 736 Regt

BRETTEVILLE L'ORGUEILLEUSE   LÉBISEY   LE BASSE DE RANVILLE   BURES

Seventh Army
(Dollmann)

21 Pz Div attacks during afternoon

716 Inf Div

Fifteenth Army
(Salmuth)

Mue   CARPIQUET   Orne   TROARN   Dives

TILLY-SUR-SEULLES   Airfield   CAEN   XLVII Pz Corps

Villers Bocage 3 miles   FONTENAY   Falaise 15 miles   12 SS Pz Div

throw the Allied forces back into the sea once they had clearly shown where their main attack was going to be. Rommel, who now commanded the German armies in northern France and the Low Countries, believed that Allied air power would prevent Rundstedt's reserve coming into action and that the Allies must instead be defeated on the beaches before they could develop their full strength. Hitler insisted on a compromise between these schemes, neither allowing Rommel to strengthen the forces defending the beaches as much as would have been possible, while hamstringing the action of the reserve forces by insisting that they remain under his personal control. On 6 June this arrangement meant among

other things that a counterattack by the powerful 21st Panzer Division from the Caen area was delayed for several hours until its effects could only be limited.

As the map shows, the Allies planned landings on five beach areas with paratroop units being dropped on either flank. There was hard fighting on each of the three beaches chosen for the British and Canadian forces but with the aid of specially designed armored vehicles the defenses were overcome and fairly good progress inland was made. The easiest progress of all was in the American area at Utah beach where navigational errors concentrated the landings in sectors that happened to be lightly defended. The other American beach,

Omaha, offered a complete contrast. The German defenses were strong and there were important errors in the planning and execution of the attack. As a result, casualties were high but a solid footing had been taken by the end of the day. Many of the airborne troops on either flank were not dropped in the correct areas but nevertheless they achieved most of their objectives.

By the end of 6 June the Allies had almost 150,000 men ashore and although the first day's objectives had not been reached a strong lodgment had been made. Rommel's plan to win on the beaches had failed and now it was a question of whether the Allied armies could be landed and supplied.

The Advance to the Rhine

The Allied advance in August and early September 1944 had been rapid and successful and in an ambitious effort to retain this momentum General Montgomery devised and had accepted a plan for paratroop landings to seize a series of important river and canal crossings which might otherwise provide serious checks to the advance. A further attraction of the scheme was that the route through Arnhem led into Germany round the north end of the supposedly formidable West Wall defenses. The whole operation had to be planned in a great hurry to fit in with the rapidly developing Allied advance. Although the two US airborne divisions achieved their objectives with the help of the advancing British XXX Corps, shortcomings in the preparation became more apparent with the third part of the operation. It was accepted that the British airborne division dropped at Arnhem would have a difficult task and so it was decided to drop it some way from its objectives to allow for some organization before the attack should go in. The consequent loss of surprise gave the German forces, which were in any case far stronger than Allied intelligence believed, time to recover and the paratroops were not able to reach their objectives in any strength. German resistance to the advance of XXX Corps also increased and after a bitter fight the operation was abandoned. Most of the British paratroops were taken prisoner.

Even as the Arnhem operation was coming to an end British and Canadian troops were beginning a long struggle to clear the Germans away from the Schelde Estuary and open the port of Antwerp. Arguably this operation should have been given higher priority and more of Montgomery's attention than the paratroop plan. The Allies were only able to begin minesweeping to open Antwerp on 4 November after elaborate amphibious attacks and much hard fighting in difficult conditions. The first cargoes were landed on 28 November and from then on the supply position for all the Allied armies improved dramatically.

Throughout this period the US forces were gradually pushing forward in a number of sectors but the German resistance was becoming better organized and their defense system more formidable. The battles fought by US First Army around Aachen and Patton's Third Army around Metz were particularly fierce. Hopes of finishing the war in 1944, however, had been abandoned.

FRONT LINE 15 SEPTEMBER 1944
FRONT LINE 8 NOVEMBER
FRONT LINE 15 DECEMBER
ALLIED ATTACKS
ALLIED AIRBORNE LANDINGS
ARMY GROUP BOUNDARY

MILES 0 — 80
KILOMETERS 0 — 120

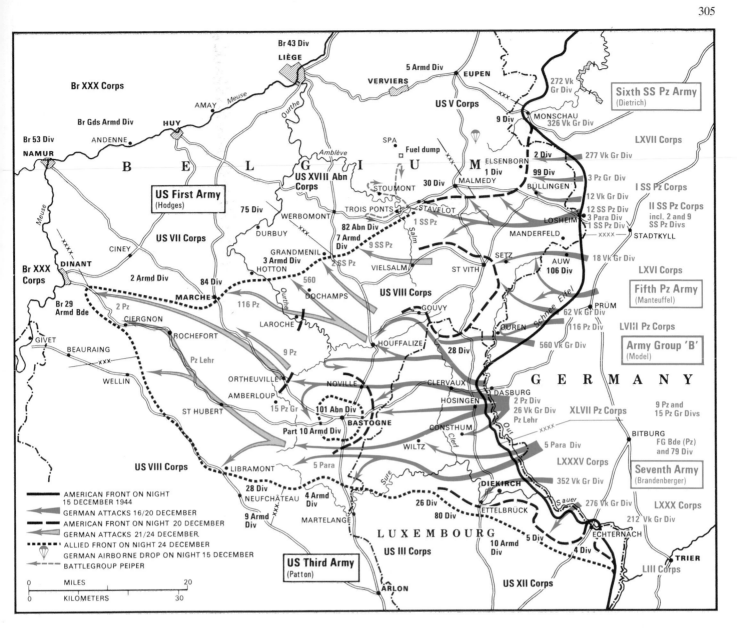

The following is a legend from the map:

- AMERICAN FRONT ON NIGHT 15 DECEMBER 1944
- GERMAN ATTACKS 16/20 DECEMBER
- AMERICAN FRONT ON NIGHT 20 DECEMBER
- GERMAN ATTACKS 21/24 DECEMBER
- ALLIED FRONT ON NIGHT 24 DECEMBER
- GERMAN AIRBORNE DROP ON NIGHT 15 DECEMBER
- BATTLEGROUP PEIPER

MILES 0 — 20
KILOMETERS 0 — 30

The Battle of the Bulge

When the German Ardennes offensive began on 16 December 1944 complete tactical and strategic surprise was achieved and the 24 German divisions in the attack were soon making gains at the expense of the six defending divisions of US V and VIII Corps. The Germans employed 10 armored divisions in the advance while most of their infantry was from newly-formed *Volksgrenadier* units. The German preparations had been conducted in extreme secrecy. The assembly of forces had been successfully concealed from Allied reconnaissance while radio traffic had been kept to a minimum, orders being distributed by land line or messenger. Although some information had reached the Allies they had become so accustomed to having clear and comprehensive proof of German intentions from their

codebreaking services that the scattered hints were ignored.

Several other factors contributed to the initial German success. The overwhelming Allied air support was largely grounded for the first few days of the battle because of bad weather. Special German units, composed of English-speaking troops wearing American uniforms, were sent through the front line on sabotage missions. Although their physical achievements were slight they did succeed in causing considerable confusion. The defending American troops were also an unfortunate mixture of inexperienced newcomers and tired veterans.

The Allied response to the German attack was, however, immediate. Patton's Third Army quickly pulled forces from its front line and rushed them north while the US 82nd and 101st Airborne Divisions were the first of many units to arrive from the main Allied reserve. On 19 December Eisenhower revised the Allied command arrangements giving Montgomery control of the British and American units north of the Bulge and

Bradley charge of the forces to the south. Despite Montgomery's unpopularity with many of the American generals this was an efficient and sensible arrangement.

The Ardennes terrain is dominated by steep wooded hillsides and this places great emphasis on road movement. The decisive points in the battle were, therefore, the junctions at St Vith and Bastogne. Bastogne was successfully defended in an epic struggle by 101st Airborne and 10th Armored Divisions under the command of General McAuliffe. St Vith held out until 22 December by which time so much delay had been inflicted on the advance that all the German commanders wanted the offensive to be abandoned. Hitler insisted that the attacks be continued but by Christmas Eve they had been halted for good. Bastogne was relieved on 26 December as Allied counterattacks got under way. There was hard fighting throughout January but by the end of the month all the German gains had been retaken. The overall result was a delay of a few weeks in the Allied operations

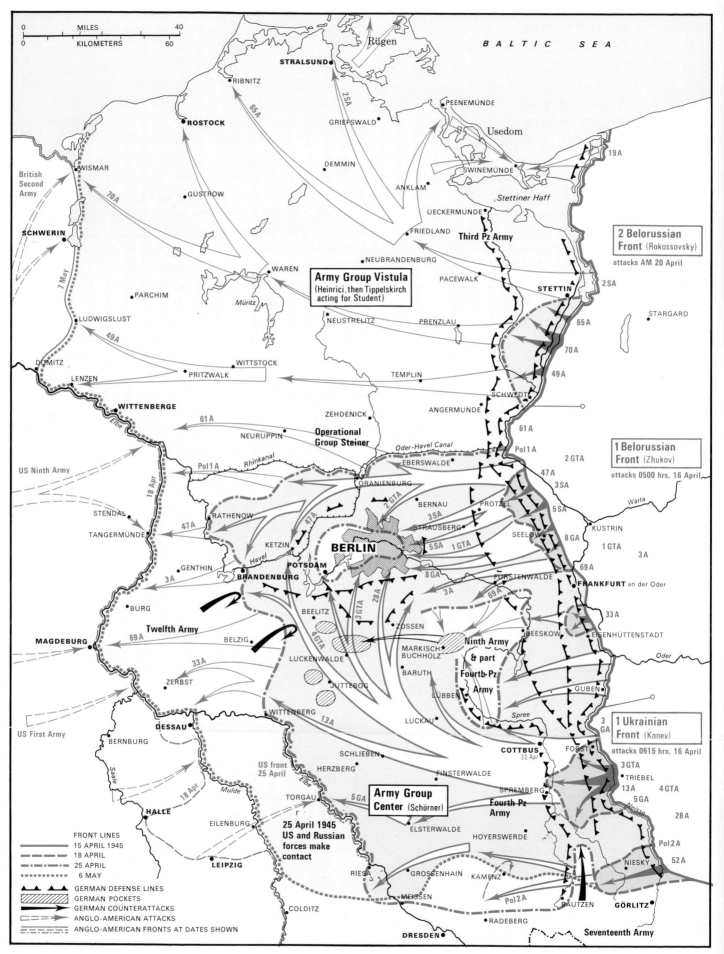

MILES
0   40
0   60
KILOMETERS

Rügen

BALTIC SEA

STRALSUND

RIBNITZ

2SA

PEENEMÜNDE

GRIEFSWALD

Usedom

ROSTOCK

DEMMIN

ANKLAM

SWINEMÜNDE

19A

British Second Army

WISMAR

65A

SCHWERIN

GÜSTROW

Stettiner Haff

UECKERMUNDE

FRIEDLAND

Third Pz Army

STETTIN

2 Belorussian Front (Rokossovsky)

attacks AM 20 April

70A

7 May

WAREN

PARCHIM

Müritz

NEUBRANDENBURG

PACEWALK

Army Group Vistula
(Heinrici, then Tippelskirch acting for Student)

2SA

STARGARD

LUDWIGSLUST

49A

NEUSTRELITZ

PRENZLAU

65A

DÖMITZ

LENZEN

PRITZWALK

WITTSTOCK

TEMPLIN

70A

49A

SCHWEDT

WITTENBERGE

Elbe

61A

NEURUPPIN

ZEHDENICK

ANGERMUNDE

61A

Operational Group Steiner

Oder-Havel Canal

EBERSWALDE

Pol1A

2 GTA

US Ninth Army

18 Apr

Pol 1A

Rhinkanal

ORANIENBURG

47A

3SA

1 Belorussian Front (Zhukov)

attacks 0500 hrs, 16 April

STENDAL

47A

RATHENOW

2 GTA

BERNAU

PROTZEL

5 SA

Warta

TANGERMÜNDE

KETZIN

BERLIN

3SA

STRAUSBERG

SEELOW

8 GA

KÜSTRIN

1 GTA

Havel

POTSDAM

5 SA

1 GTA

3A

GENTHIN

3A

BRANDENBURG

8 GA

FÜRSTENWALDE

69A

FRANKFURT an der Oder

BURG

BEELITZ

3 GTA

28 A

ZOSSEN

3A

69 A

33 A

Twelfth Army

BELZIG

4 GTA

LUCKENWALDE

MARKISCH-BUCHHOLZ

Ninth Army & part Fourth Pz Army

BEESKOW

EISENHÜTTENSTADT

MAGDEBURG

69 A

BARUTH

Oder

ZERBST

33 A

JÜTTEBOG

GUBEN

BERNBURG

DESSAU

WITTENBERG

13 A

LÜBBEN

Spree

US First Army

SCHLIEBEN

LUCKAU

COTTBUS
22 Apr

3 GA

1 Ukrainian Front (Konev)

attacks 0615 hrs, 16 April

Saale

18 Apr

HERZBERG

FINSTERWALDE

FORST

US front 25 April

Mulde

TORGAU

5 GA

Army Group Center (Schörner)

Fourth Pz Army

SPREMBERG

3 GTA

TRIEBEL

4 GTA

HALLE

EILENBURG

Elbe

25 April 1945 US and Russian forces make contact

ELSTERWALDE

13 A

5 GA

LEIPZIG

RIESA

GROSSENHAIN

HOYERSWERDE

28 A

Pol 2A

KAMENZ

NIESKY

Neisse

MEISSEN

Pol 2A

BAUTZEN

GÖRLITZ

52 A

COLDITZ

RADEBERG

Seventeenth Army

DRESDEN

FRONT LINES
15 APRIL 1945
18 APRIL
25 APRIL
6 MAY
GERMAN DEFENSE LINES
GERMAN POCKETS
GERMAN COUNTERATTACKS
ANGLO-AMERICAN ATTACKS
ANGLO-AMERICAN FRONTS AT DATES SHOWN

Bottom: Soviet tanks advance down a
street in Berlin during the closing weeks of
the war in Europe.

The Fall of Berlin

The Red Army's final advance began on 16 April 1945. From his two bridgeheads at Kustrin, Zhukov's troops broke through the German defenses and advanced toward Berlin. His ultimate objective was the River Elbe, beyond Berlin, which was the previously-agreed line where the Anglo-American and Russian occupation zones should meet. South of Zhukov, Konev used bridgeheads on the west bank of the Neisse to start an advance whose left flank was to take Dresden while its right turned north to help surround Berlin. It was Konev's men who, having bypassed Dresden, were the first Russian soldiers to link up with the Americans advancing from the west; this happened at Torgau, on the Elbe, on 25 April.

On 22 April, Zhukov's First Belorussian Front reached the autobahn ringing Berlin, and moved along it to Spandau. With Konev's troops, this effected the complete encirclement of the German capital. Inside Berlin were Hitler and his closest associates, about two million civilians, and 30,000 defenders. On the outskirts, however, were up to one million German troops destined for a last-ditch defense of the city. By this time the bottom of the German manpower barrel had been scraped, and many of these troops were only half-trained, or of doubtful health, or well below military age. Nevertheless, in the circumstances of a backs-to-the-wall struggle they could be expected to take a heavy toll of the attackers. The latter, with their supporting units, numbered about two and one-half million men, well-trained, well-equipped, experienced, and having the advantage of Soviet command of the air.

In the final assault, Zhukov's Front attacked from the north and Konev's First Ukrainian Front from the south. After two days of fierce fighting Zhukov's tanks reached the northern outskirts on 28 April, by which time Konev's infantry and tanks had fought their way as far as the Tiergarten, which lay close to the center of Berlin. The two Russian fronts were thus only a mile apart, but it took another four days of house-to-house fighting, a Stalingrad in reverse, before they linked up. By this time Hitler, whose bunker lay between these two Russian pincers, had killed himself. The senior surviving German officer, General Krebs, went to negotiate with the Russians and was confronted with a demand for unconditional surrender. By 2 May the red flag was flying from the chancellery and fighting had ceased.

Battle of the Philippine Sea

After the capture of Kwajalein and Eniwetok in the Marshall Islands the next targets for the US offensive were Saipan, Tinian and Guam in the Marianas. The main US carrier forces began preparatory attacks for the landings on 11 June 1944 and Admiral Toyoda, the Commander in Chief of the Japanese Combined Fleet, prepared for a full-scale battle. The Japanese naval forces came under the direct command of Admiral Ozawa and included five fleet carriers, two light and two seaplane carriers as well as five battleships and numerous supporting vessels. Altogether these ships carried about 470 aircraft and there were about 100 more on Guam which survived the preliminary American attacks to take part in the battle. The Americans had about 950 aircraft on their seven fleet and eight light carriers as well as superior numbers in other classes of ship. Most of the US ships were from Admiral Mitscher's TF.58 but Admiral Spruance, the overall commander of the Marianas invasion, was also present. The US forces were well warned of the

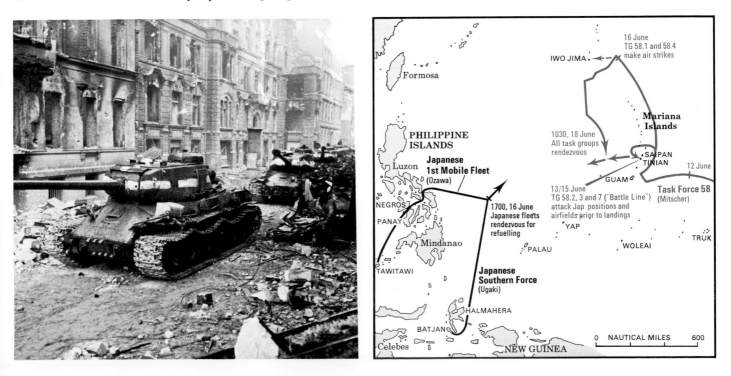

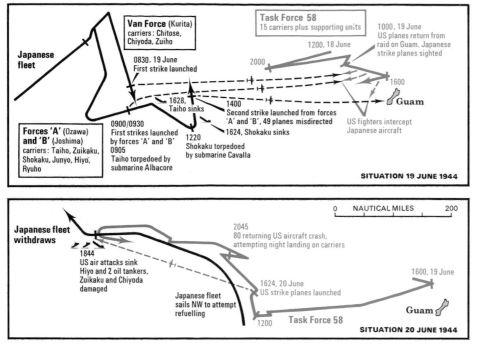

Van Force (Kurita)
carriers: Chitose, Chiyoda, Zuiho

Task Force 58
15 carriers plus supporting units

1000, 19 June
US planes return from
raid on Guam. Japanese
strike planes sighted

1200, 18 June

2000

**Japanese
fleet**

0830, 19 June
First strike launched

1628,
Taiho sinks

1400
Second strike launched from forces
'A' and 'B', 49 planes misdirected

1600

Guam

US fighters intercept
Japanese aircraft

Forces 'A' (Ozawa)
and 'B' (Joshima)
carriers: Taiho, Zuikaku,
Shokaku, Junyo, Hiyo,
Ryuho

0900/0930
First strikes launched
by forces 'A' and 'B'
0905
Taiho torpedoed by
submarine Albacore

1220
Shokaku torpedoed
by submarine Cavalla

1624, Shokaku sinks

SITUATION 19 JUNE 1944

0   NAUTICAL MILES   200

**Japanese fleet
withdraws**

2045
80 returning US aircraft crash,
attempting night landing on carriers

1844
US air attacks sink
Hiyo and 2 oil tankers,
Zuikaku and Chiyoda
damaged

1600, 19 June

1624, 20 June
US strike planes launched

Japanese fleet
sails NW to attempt
refuelling

1200   **Task Force 58**

Guam

SITUATION 20 JUNE 1944

The Battles for Leyte

After considerable discussion the Allied High Command decided that, on completion of the Marianas battles and the campaign in New Guinea, the American forces should next begin the reconquest of the Philippines with landings on Leyte Island. General MacArthur's forces from the Southwest Pacific command area combined with Admiral Nimitz's for this operation.

Japanese approach through submarine sightings and a further disadvantage for Ozawa was that the Marianas commanders had failed to inform him how badly hit their air forces had been by the early US attacks. Practically the sole Japanese advantage was that their aircraft generally had a longer range and so they could expect to get in their strikes first.

This in fact they did on 19 June, the first day of the battle. The Americans were content to defend and did so so successfully that their pilots and gunners dubbed the battle the 'Great Marianas Turkey Shoot.' The Americans lost 29 planes and the Japanese about 300 including a number destroyed over Guam. Only one bomb hit an American ship. Two Japanese carriers were sunk by American submarines. On the 20th the Americans pursued and managed to sink a third carrier but lost a number of aircraft.

The Battle of the Philippine Sea dealt a further serious blow to Japanese naval power. Far more than the ships lost, the trained carrier pilots and their aircraft could not be replaced and in the next major naval encounter, the Battle of Leyte Gulf, the Japanese carriers could only find token air groups to embark.

With the US naval forces dominant the ground battles for the Marianas Islands could only go one way despite the ferocious Japanese resistance. There were landings on Saipan on 15 June even before the Philippine Sea Battle, on Guam on 21 July and on Tinian on 24 July. The largest Japanese garrison, 27,000 men, was on Saipan but the last effective resistance there was wiped out on 9 July and the battles for Tinian (garrison 6000) and Guam (10,000) were both concluded by mid-August. Almost all the Japanese defenders on all three islands were killed while the Americans lost over 5000 dead and 20,000 wounded.

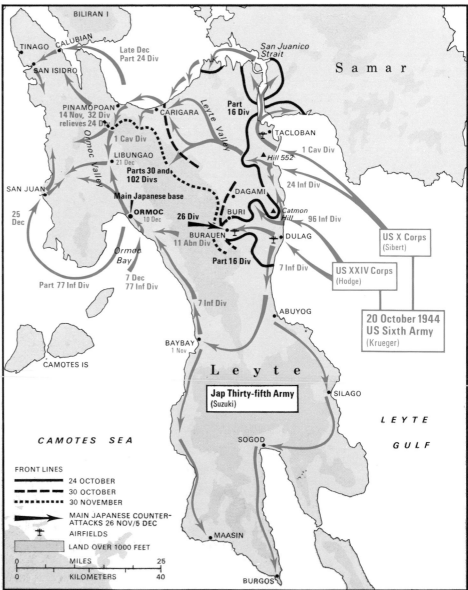

BILIRAN I

San Juanico
Strait

S a m a r

TINAGO   CALUBIAN

Late Dec
Part 24 Div

SAN ISIDRO

Part
16 Div

PINAMOPOAN
14 Nov, 32 Div
relieves 24 Div

CARIGARA

TACLOBAN

1 Cav Div

1 Cav Div

Hill 552

LIBUNGAO
21 Dec

24 Inf Div

**Parts 30 and
102 Divs**

SAN JUAN

DAGAMI

Catmon
Hill

96 Inf Div

25
Dec

Main Japanese base

ORMOC
10 Dec

26 Div

BURI

BURAUEN
11 Abn Div

DULAG

7 Inf Div

US X Corps
(Sibert)

Ormoc
Bay

Part 16 Div

7 Dec
77 Inf Div

7 Inf Div

US XXIV Corps
(Hodge)

Part 77 Inf Div

ABUYOG

**20 October 1944
US Sixth Army**
(Krueger)

BAYBAY
1 Nov

CAMOTES IS

L e y t e

SILAGO

Jap Thirty-fifth Army
(Suzuki)

L E Y T E

GULF

CAMOTES SEA

SOGOD

FRONT LINES

24 OCTOBER

30 OCTOBER

30 NOVEMBER

MAIN JAPANESE COUNTER-
ATTACKS 26 NOV/5 DEC

AIRFIELDS

LAND OVER 1000 FEET

MILES   25

0   KILOMETERS   40

MAASIN

BURGOS

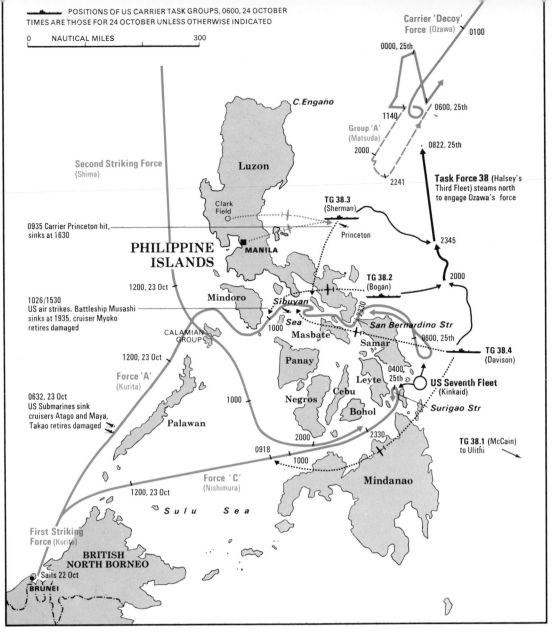

POSITIONS OF US CARRIER TASK GROUPS, 0600, 24 OCTOBER
TIMES ARE THOSE FOR 24 OCTOBER UNLESS OTHERWISE INDICATED

0   NAUTICAL MILES   300

309

Carrier 'Decoy'
Force (Ozawa)   0100

0000, 25th

Group 'A'
(Matsuda)
2000
1140
2241

0600, 25th

0822, 25th

Task Force 38 (Halsey's
Third Fleet) steams north
to engage Ozawa's force

2345

2000

Second Striking Force
(Shima)

Luzon

C. Engaño

TG 38.3
(Sherman)

Clark
Field

0935 Carrier Princeton hit,
sinks at 1630

Princeton

**PHILIPPINE
ISLANDS**

MANILA

1200, 23 Oct

Mindoro

Sibuyan

TG 38.2
(Bogan)

1026/1530
US air strikes. Battleship Musashi
sinks at 1935, cruiser Myoko
retires damaged

Sea

San Bernardino Str

2330

1000

Masbate

Samar

TG 38.4
(Davison)

0600, 25th

CALAMIAN
GROUP

1200, 23 Oct

Panay

0400,
25th

Leyte

US Seventh Fleet
(Kinkaid)

Force 'A'
(Kurita)

1000

Cebu

0632, 23 Oct
US Submarines sink
cruisers Atago and Maya,
Takao retires damaged

Negros

Bohol

Surigao Str

Palawan

2000

2330

TG 38.1 (McCain)
to Ulithi

0918

1000

Force 'C'
(Nishimura)

Mindanao

1200, 23 Oct

S u l u   S e a

First Striking
Force (Kurita)

**BRITISH
NORTH BORNEO**

Sails 22 Oct

BRUNEI

On land the familiar story of overwhelming American forces gradually wearing down a totally determined defense was repeated. General Krueger's Sixth Army could call on up to 200,000 troops of whom some 130,000 landed on the first day. Initially the Japanese had just over 20,000 men on Leyte and although substantial reinforcements were brought in, these usually took heavy casualties in transit from US air attacks. The Japanese 26th Division, for example, arrived practically bereft of rations and artillery. Although mopping up extended well into 1945 there were few important engagements after Christmas 1944. Japanese casualties have been estimated variously from 50–80,000. The Americans lost 3600 dead.

At sea the Japanese again tried to turn the tide of the war by bringing on a major fleet action. The three-part battle that resulted is known as the Battle of Leyte Gulf. The Japanese naval air arm had lost so many planes and pilots earlier in the war that the remaining aircraft carriers had very few aircraft to embark. It was decided, therefore,

to use the carriers as a decoy while the substantial battleship and cruiser force did the real damage. The strongest squadron, Force A, was to reach the American invasion area via the San Bernardino Strait while two smaller forces advanced by the Surigao Strait.

Force A was detected en route by American submarines and heavily attacked by them and aircraft summed from the main US carrier formation, TF.38. These attacks made Force A turn away. Mistaking this temporary move for a permament withdrawal, the American carriers then sped north to catch Ozawa's decoy force. Since Force C had also been detected the bombardment support ships of Seventh Fleet were moved to block its approach, in the belief that the San Bernardino Strait was still guarded by TF.38. Nishimura's ships were almost all destroyed in a night battle and Shima turned back after also suffering some losses. The American carriers sank many of Ozawa's ships including the last veteran of Pearl Harbor, the *Zuikaku*. However, Kurita had reversed course and on the morning of

25 October his battleships and cruisers came into gun range of some of the vulnerable and practically unsupported escort carriers of Seventh Fleet. If the Japanese ships had been well and resolutely commanded they might even have penetrated into the American transport fleet and caused untold destruction. Instead they withdrew tamely after only limited success. The Battle of Leyte Gulf was the last important effort of the Japanese Navy.

The task of the Allied naval forces was made more hazardous by the beginning of preplanned suicide attacks by Japanese aircraft. The first ship hit by a Kamikaze attack, on 21 October, was the cruiser *Australia*, one of several Australian ships serving with the American forces.

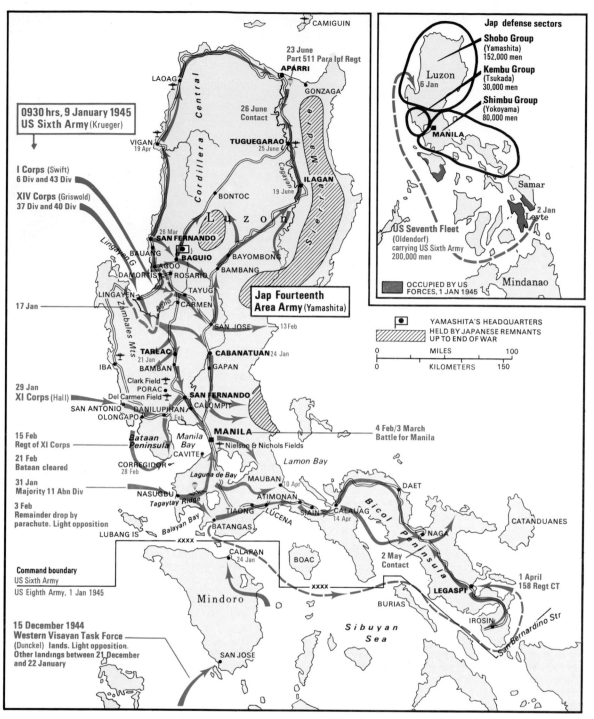

The Capture of Luzon

The Japanese commander responsible for the whole Philippines group, General Yamashita, had been ordered, against his better judgment, to do his utmost to hold Leyte in face of the American attacks. Thus when the Americans quickly moved to invade Luzon as the fighting on Leyte died down, the Japanese forces, though numerically strong, were neither well armed nor well prepared. Kamikaze attacks against the landing fleet were fairly successful in their way for the first few days of the operation but after this almost all the Japanese aircraft were with-

drawn from the Philippines to Formosa or had been destroyed.

After his losses on Leyte Yamashita did not believe that he could repel an American landing and accordingly the beach defenses were only lightly held. Instead Yamashita planned to make his stand in the inland mountain areas for as long as possible and so tie down large American forces. Particularly in north Luzon this was the pattern that the fighting took on. Baguio, where Yamashita had had his HQ, was not taken until 27 April and when he surrendered at the end of the war Yamashita still had some 50,000 fighting men under his command.

Undoubtedly the most bitterly contested part of the campaign was the recapture of

Manila. The city garrison died almost to a man in the defense and the fighting left Manila in ruins. By the end of the war landing operations in cooperation with Filipino guerrillas had taken control of most of the other islands of the Philippine group.

Top right: GIs take cover from sniper fire during the fighting to recapture Clark Field airbase in the Philippines.

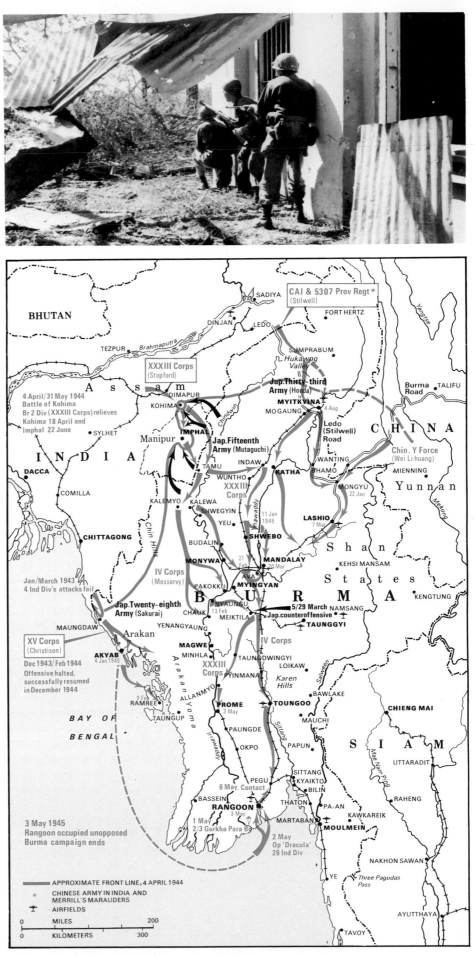

The Burma Campaign

To most of the Allied leaders the Burma theater came very low on the scale of priorities. Even when they agreed that resources could be sent there, the British and Americans rarely agreed on the strategy to be followed. The Americans thought that the main objective should be to reopen land communications with the Chinese Nationalists to help them against the large forces of the Japanese Army which were tied up in China. The British had far less respect for Chiang and the Nationalists (perhaps more realistically) and preferred to plan to recover the imperial territories lost to the Japanese in 1942.

Whatever strategy was to be followed it was first necessary to build a respectable fighting force from the shattered remnants that had retreated to the Indian border in April-May 1942. Much work had also to be done to improve communications between India and northern Burma. The first offensive move, an advance in the Arakan in early 1943, was decisively defeated by Japanese infiltration tactics. A new British commander, General Slim, took over at the end of this operation and developed new tactics. He laid down that, in future, encircled units should not retreat to restore their communications but hold out with the help of air supply while reserve units retook the rear areas. A further innovation based on the use of air supply was the establishment of independent units designed to operate behind the Japanese lines. The efforts of these Chindits or their American equivalent, the Maurauders, were not an unqualified military success but they made an important contribution to Allied morale by showing that it was possible to take on the Japanese in the jungle and win. The technique of supplying surrounded formations from the air helped stem a limited Japanese counteroffensive in the Arakan early in 1944 and played a vital part in defeating the major Japanese offensive that followed in the battles of Imphal and Kohima. This campaign was by far the heaviest defeat that the Japanese Army had suffered to that time. The Allied forces resumed their advance on all fronts in late 1944, after the monsoon, and the Japanese were again soundly beaten in the decisive battles around Meiktila and Mandalay.

Below: American Marines man forward positions on Iwo Jima facing Mount Suribachi. Casualties were very heavy on both sides in this operation.
Bottom: two Marines stand guard over a captured Japanese five-inch coastal gun on Iwo Jima.

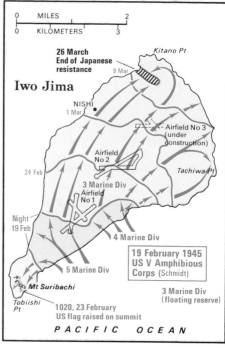

Iwo Jima

After Saipan and Tinian in the Marianas Islands were taken by the US forces in June and July 1944 huge air bases were constructed there from which B-29 Superfortress bombers could begin an all-out strategic bombing attack on Japan. Although the Japanese air defense system was never as efficient as the German effort to ward off the Allied bomber offensive in Europe, losses were uncomfortably high. A base on Iwo Jima could be used to provide needed fighter support and an emergency landing ground for damaged bombers unable to complete the long journey back to the Marianas. This was the principal reason for the US attack but since it was a part of metropolitan Japan the capture of Iwo Jima would be good for morale too.

From the outset it was clear that a stubborn defense of the island could be expected and a massive preliminary air and naval bombardment was ordered. However, the 21,000-strong Japanese garrison led by General Kuribayashi had constructed an astonishingly elaborate and resilient defense system much of which survived the early attacks. The Japanese plan was to wait until the landings had just begun before showing their hand and opening fire. In the event they held off a little too long and the Marines were able to fight their way off the beaches. By the end of the first day 30,000 US troops were ashore. Although the battle could now have only one result the complex of trenches, tunnels and strongpoints and the fanatical determination of the defenders meant that the US forces had to fight for virtually every yard of the island. Casualties were very high. The US forces lost 6800 dead and 20,000 wounded.

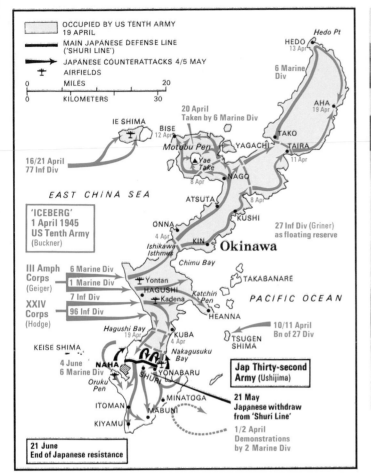

Okinawa

The attack on Okinawa was planned as the last major landing operation before the invasion of the Japanese home islands for which the capture of Okinawa was necessary to provide harbor and air base facilities. As was customary the campaign began with carrier and other air attacks to soften up the local defenses and the supporting air bases on Kyushu. The newly-active British Pacific Fleet joined in these operations. The carrier and bombardment groups continued to give support throughout the battle.

The Japanese Thirty-second Army defending Okinawa under General Ushijima's command was about 130,000 strong and had most of its forces concentrated at the southern end of the island behind a formidable position known as the Shuri Line. There was no intention of resisting the Americans on the beaches and the only heavily defended areas apart from the Shuri position were the Motobu Peninsula and the offshore island of Ie Shima.

The American landings began on 1 April and, as the map shows, most of the island was quickly overrun with little opposition. However, XXIV Corps made little progress once the Shuri Line defenses were met. Despite overwhelming air and bombardment support, gains were few until unsuccessful Japanese attacks in early May had

given away the locations of many of their defensive positions. From that time reinforced attacks by both US corps gradually pushed forward to finish the battle despite difficult ground and weather conditions.

The supporting naval forces had a fierce battle of their own to fight. The kamikaze attacks which had become a feature of Japanese tactics were here developed to their fullest extent. Several thousand Japanese aircraft were destroyed during the Okinawa operation, a great number of them kamikazes. The US and British naval forces had 36 ships sunk and 368 damaged, almost all of them by suicide attacks. Perhaps the most bizarre aspect of the campaign was the employment of the giant battleship *Yamato* which was sent off to Okinawa on what amounted to a suicide mission since too little fuel was carried to make a return journey possible. The *Yamato* was sunk by US carrier planes on 7 April long before she could reach the invasion area and without causing the hoped-for disruption to the American air defense system which would have allowed the simultaneous program of air attacks to achieve important successes.

The casualty lists on both sides were extensive. For the first time a significant number of Japanese troops, over 7000, was taken prisoner, but this still meant that over 120,000 died or committed suicide. In addition there were a great many civilian casualties. Okinawa was fairly densely populated and the local people had been in-

doctrinated with stories of American brutality. The US forces lost 12,500 dead, including the Army Commander General Buckner, and 35,000 wounded. As a rehearsal for the invasion of Japan these casualty totals were frightening to the Americans and could only support the case for bringing the war to an end by other means.

Above: Marines from the Sixth Division reach the outskirts of Naha on Okinawa, 6 June 1945.

These pages: men of the US 5th and 7th Marines fight their way through three Chinese divisions as they fall back on Hagaru-ri, Korea, in late November 1950.

CONFLICT IN
THE MODERN WORLD

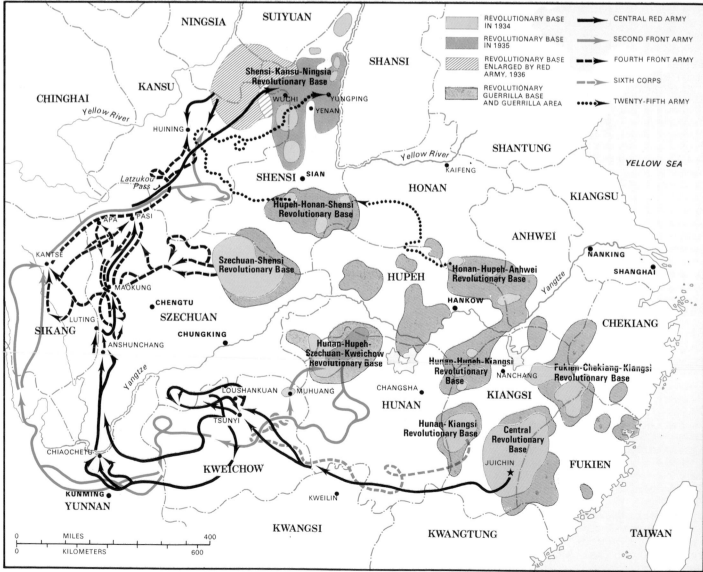

Left: smoke billows above Shanghai during the Japanese occupation of the city in 1937.

AREAS OCCUPIED BY COMMUNIST FORCES
1934–1945
1945–JUNE 1946
JULY 1946–JUNE 1947
JULY 1947–JUNE 1948
JULY 1948–JUNE 1949
JULY–SEPT 1949

Early-1946 Civil war begins

1 Oct 1949 People's Republic of China proclaimed

20 Apr 1949 "Amethyst" incident

Capital until 1949

End-1949 Nationalist Government flees to Taiwan

TIBET Invaded 1950

© Richard Natkiel, 1982

The Rise of Chinese Communism – The Long March

For a number of years following the overthrow of the Manchu dynasty in 1911 there had been little real government in China. Instead local war lords had competed for control with the nationalist party, the Kuomintang, and later with the Chinese Communist Party (founded 1921). In the 1920s the Kuomintang, under the increasingly dominant leadership of Chiang Kai-shek, improved its position and in 1927 they moved powerfully against the communists with whom relations had previously been fairly good.

After some attempts to establish communist enclaves in the cities had proved unsuccessful, the communists instead began to concentrate on winning over the rural peasantry. This change in technique was developed by the new communist leader Mao Tse-tung and in 1931 the communists proclaimed the establishment of a Chinese Soviet Republic from their main stronghold in Kiangsi province. Although faced by an increasing Japanese threat following their takeover of Manchuria in October 1931, Chiang decided that his priority ought to be to defeat the communists. Accordingly from 1930–34 the Kuomintang conducted a series of so-called Bandit Suppression Campaigns against the communist revolutionary bases.

The communists found it increasingly difficult to hold out against these attacks and therefore in 1934 they decided to move their whole operation to a less vulnerable area. In October 1934 the communist forces broke out of Kiangsi and began what is known as the Long March. The march lasted until November 1935 with some units covering as much as 6000 miles. There were very many casualties en route but a considerable force reached Yenan where Mao established a moderate socialist regime which was generally well-received by the inhabitants. The communists were also gaining support throughout China by their commitment to fighting the Japanese whereas Chiang seemed too concerned with fighting the communists. Chiang attempted to continue his bandit suppression operations but after a mutiny of some of his forces in Sian in late

1936 he was for a time personally in communist hands and was obliged to give undertakings to be more active against the Japanese. The Japanese attack in 1937 meant that these had to be fulfilled.

By April 1945 the Chinese communists had about one million men under arms, and looked forward to the post-war struggle for power against the Kuomintang with optimism, because although the latter was receiving American equipment its troops were believed to be of low morale. Stalin did not share this optimism and decided that Russian aid should be given to the communists. Despite the disappointment and resentment which this caused, the communists under Mao Tse-tung took the offensive and by mid-1946 a civil war was raging in Manchuria, where many of the Kuomintang troops deserted and others fought unenthusiastically. By late 1947 the Kuomintang's military superiority had declined from 4:1 to 2:1, and by the end of the civil war two million of the People's Liberation Army's troops were former Kuomintang soldiers. Having taken Manchuria in 1948, the communists drove southward and in 1949 the last remnants of the old regime took refuge in Formosa (Taiwan). There had been little foreign interference, although some British warships on the Yangtze were shelled and one of them,

Amethyst, was pinned down by artillery fire for a few days.

Having gained power, the communists set about the transformation of Chinese society. Mao Tse-tung, despite his mistrust of the Russians and the uneasy relations between Moscow and Peking, took a pro-Soviet line in foreign affairs; American policy-makers, who by this time included few who were willing or able to express an informed opinion, believed that China was simply a Soviet satellite, and behaved towards the new republic accordingly. Meanwhile the communist transformation was hampered by the dominance of Mao Tse-tung and his theories. There followed a series of mass campaigns like the Great Leap Forward (for rapid economic development in 1957–59) and the Cultural Revolution (for a replacement of old attitudes by new in 1965–67). These campaigns were accompanied by violence, bloodshed, and blind and exaggerated adherence to centrally laid-down theories; their results reflected the Chinese saying, 'They drained the pond to catch a fish.'

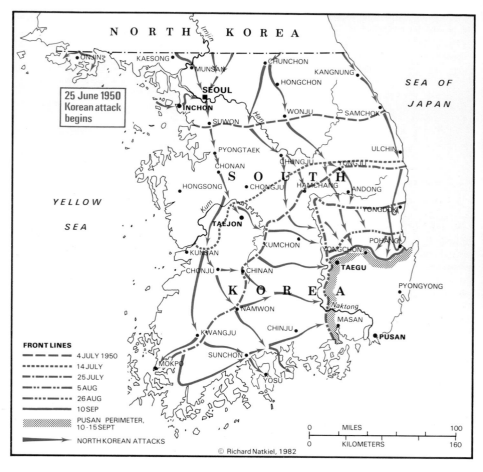

The Korean War

Although the Allies, including Russia, had agreed during World War II that Korea would become a free and independent state, the postwar tension between Moscow and the West meant that the country became divided into a northern, Communist, state and a southern, western-orientated, republic. The dividing line between North Korea (the Korean Peoples' Republic) and South Korea (the Republic of Korea or ROK) was the 38th Parallel of latitude. The intention, supported by votes in the United Nations, had been that the two halves should be reunited following free elections, but the USA and the USSR differed as to the definition of free elections, and it was this insuperable issue that led to the creation of the ROK and the Peoples' Republic in 1948. The tensions between the two Koreas was soon apparent.

It was not long before short outbursts of fighting occurred along the 38th Parallel, and

these continued up to the outbreak of the Korean War. In 1949 US troops were withdrawn from the ROK, on the assumption that

the new republic could look after itself. At this period US military planners believed that a future war would be global, and were not

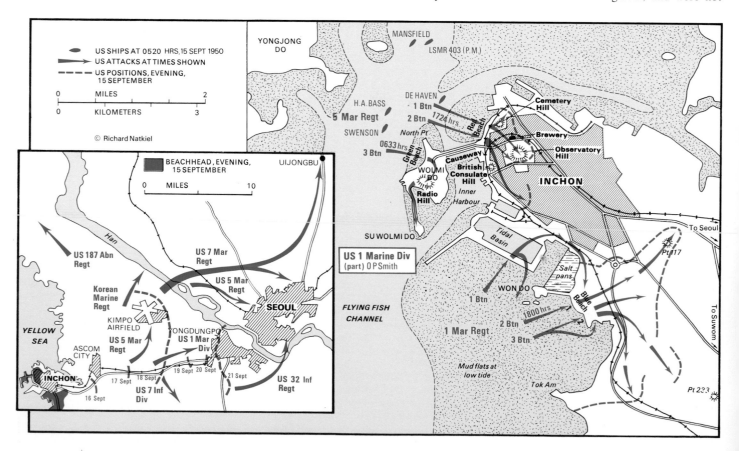

greatly interested in countries, like Korea, which they acknowledged to be outside the US defense perimeter.

When North Korea invaded the ROK in June 1950, the attack itself, its timing, and the scale of equipment of the attackers all came as a surprise to the US. Seven infantry divisions, supported by an armored division equipped with Russian-built T-34 tanks, swept over the 38th Parallel while diversionary amphibious landings were made along the east coast of the ROK. Within three days the ROK capital, Seoul, had been overrun, and by the end of the month North Korean armor was over the Han River, racing toward Taejon.

By that time the first US combat troops were in Korea, having been airlifted in from Japan. On 27 June, profiting from a walk-out on another issue by the Soviet delegate, the UN Security Council recommended UN members to help the ROK. General Douglas MacArthur became commander in chief of the UN Command. The war became a struggle between the Americans and the North Koreans for Pusan, the only remaining good harbor in South Korea.

The Inchon Landings

In mid-July North Korean tanks overwhelmed the US forces defending Taejon, and soon General Walton Walker's US Eighth Army was holding back the attackers only 40 miles from Pusan. However, Walker's men held fast long enough for reinforcements to arrive, and by September there was a stalemate, with neither side able to move forward. Against the advice of many of his subordinates, MacArthur decided to break this stalemate with a daring amphibious landing at Inchon, on the northwest coast of the ROK. The US X Corps, rather hurriedly organized, was put aboard ships and on 15 September the landings were made. Three Marine battalions went ashore over the mudflats to the south of Inchon, while three others landed on beaches to the north. Inchon was soon captured, infantry was landed to follow the Marines, and then the US forces moved on to Seoul.

This landing, over 200 miles in the rear of the North Korean advance units attacking Pusan, was a complete strategic surprise. It coincided with a counteroffensive by the US Eighth Army out of the Pusan pocket and by the end of September the North Korean Army, shattered, had been driven back behind the 38th Parallel.

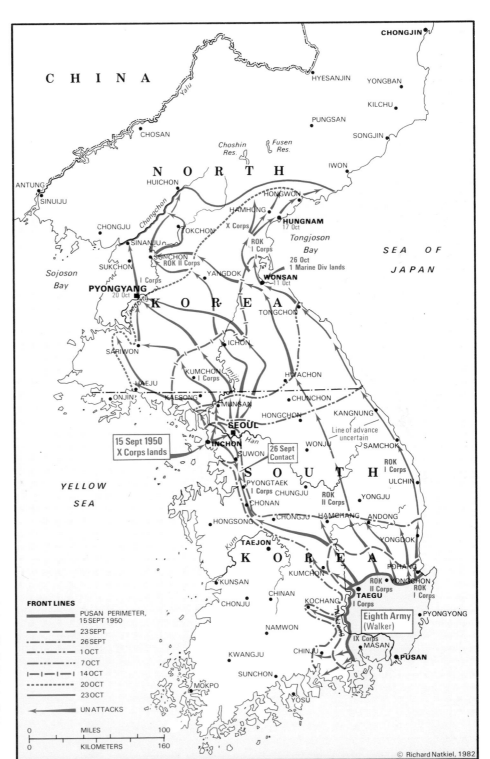

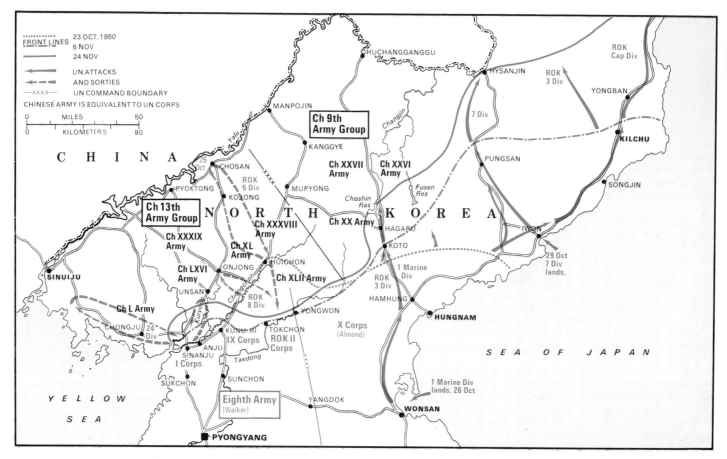

The Drive to the Yalu

The quick and overwhelming victory of the UN forces after the Inchon landings encouraged the American government, and its allies, to envisage setting up the unified, democratic, Korea that had always been the UN aim. MacArthur was therefore allowed to go beyond the 38th Parallel, on to the territory of North Korea. Meanwhile, in October, the General Assembly of the UN voted to arrange for all-Korea elections. Thus the original objective of the UN forces, a return to the 38th Parallel, had been replaced by something much more ambitious.

The UN forces, mainly American and South Korean but including contingents from Britain and several other countries, pushed northward on a broad front and on 20 October took Pyongyang, the capital of North Korea. On 26 October an ROK division reached Chosan on the Yalu, the river dividing Korea from China. However, MacArthur did not expect his main forces to reach the Yalu until about the end of December. In October MacArthur and Presi-

dent Truman met on Wake Island to discuss the future of the postwar Korea. The question of possible Chinese intervention was raised, and MacArthur seemed confident that there would be no such move by the Chinese Communists in support of their North Korean neighbors.

On 24 November what was intended to be the last, war-winning, offensive was launched, with the US Eighth Army crossing the Chongchon River and the X Marine Corps, in the northeast, moving up from the Choshin Reservoir. There had already been sporadic clashes with Chinese troops that had infiltrated over the border, and two days after the launch of MacArthur's offensive the UN troops found themselves engaged by massive Chinese concentrations.

Right: a British strike aircraft prepares to leave a Royal Navy carrier to attack Chinese positions in North Korea.

The Chinese Counteroffensive

By this time there were about 300,000 Chinese troops in Korea, infiltrated over the Yalu bridges in previous weeks. They were called 'Chinese Peoples' Volunteers,' even though they were regular soldiers, the aim being to avoid giving the impression that the Chinese Peoples' Republic itself had gone to war against the UN forces. The initial Chinese offensives quickly surrounded the US Marines at Choshin, while the US Eighth Army found itself in danger of being outflanked. MacArthur really had only one choice, a helter-skelter withdrawal, which included the evacuation by sea of units cut off by the rapidly advancing Chinese. At the end of the year, instead of standing on the Yalu as had been anticipated, the UN forces were back on the 38th Parallel. Moreover, the Chinese pushed on to capture Seoul in January. Only supply problems prevented them advancing much farther; they came to a halt about 60 miles south of Seoul.

This gave time for reinforcements to arrive for the Eighth Army which, commanded by General Matthew Ridgway, managed to fight its way back toward the 38th Parallel. Despite this recovery of lost ground, however, the UN situation was grim, for there was now the prospect of a long grinding war against the enormous manpower reserves of China.

Stabilizing the Front

In the spring of 1951, in an attempt to inflict such heavy losses on the Eighth Army as to weaken UN and US resolve, the Chinese began two great offensives. Advancing in masses against UN forces which were well-situated and well-equipped, they suffered enormous losses. The UN forces, taking advantage of this, then mounted their own offensive, with the demoralized Chinese surrendering in large numbers. This took the UN troops to a good defensive line just north of the 38th Parallel.

On Soviet initiative, armistice talks then began between the two sides. Soon the talks were moved to Panmunjon, where they continued until 1953. During this two-year period of protracted negotiations the war continued along the ceasefire line, but only on a local and sporadic scale, and naval and air strikes against North Korea were continued. Eventually, a demarcation line based on the existing front line was agreed, and a settlement reached about prisoners of war. This permitted a general ceasefire to be signed on 27 July 1953. US forces had suffered about 142,000 casualties, South Korean about 300,000, and

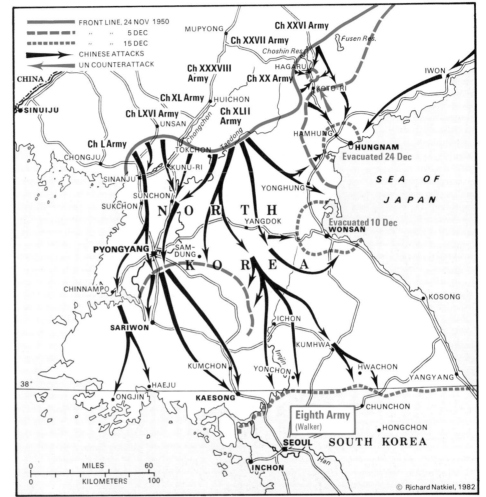

British Commonwealth about 7000. Chinese and North Korean casualties were estimated at two million, while civilian deaths may have exceeded one million.

The Partition of Palestine

After World War I Britain had received the League of Nations mandate to rule Palestine. During the 1930s Jewish immigration increased the Jewish population there from 11 per cent of the total in 1922 to 29 per cent in 1939. Local Arabs resented this, so shortly before the outbreak of war Britain restricted immigration.

After 1945 the Jews' wartime experience hardened their resolve to found their own state of Israel, while at the same time world opinion had come to sympathize with them. The British government, realizing that a Jewish state could be created in Palestine only at the cost of antagonizing Arabs all over the Middle East, continued to oppose the large-scale admission of Jewish refugees. Illegal Jewish immigration began, and Jewish terrorists began to prey on Britons in Palestine. In 1947 Britain asked the United Nations to take over the problem. The UN decided to divide Palestine into an Arab state, a Jewish state, and an internationalized city of Jerusalem. This was impossible to put into practice. In December 1947 war started between the Jews and the armed forces of the Arab League, continuing until the spring. In May 1948 the independent state of Israel was proclaimed by the Jews. Jewish troops fought better than the Arabs and won additional territory for Israel, but the Arabs refused to negotiate unless one million Palestinian refugees were returned to their homes.

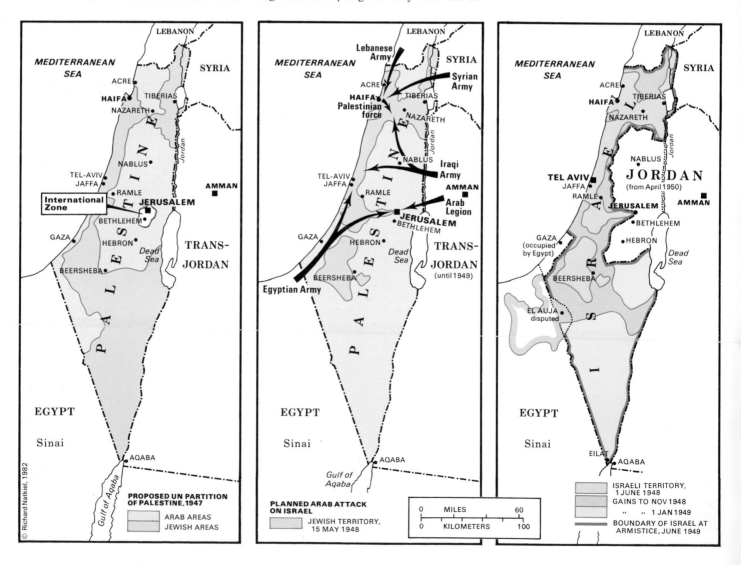

© Richard Natkiel, 1982

PROPOSED UN PARTITION OF PALESTINE, 1947
ARAB AREAS
JEWISH AREAS

PLANNED ARAB ATTACK ON ISRAEL
JEWISH TERRITORY, 15 MAY 1948

| 0 | MILES | 60 |
| 0 | KILOMETERS | 100 |

ISRAELI TERRITORY, 1 JUNE 1948
GAINS TO NOV 1948
" " 1 JAN 1949
BOUNDARY OF ISRAEL AT ARMISTICE, JUNE 1949

Below: British paratroopers land on Port Said's El Gamil airfield during the early stages of the 1956 war.

The Middle East, 1956

After the Arab-Israeli War of 1948–49 border battles, guerrilla activity, and terrorism continued. In 1955 President Nasser of Egypt, having earlier secured by agreement the evacuation of British troops from the Suez Canal Zone, announced that the Canal would be closed to Israeli commerce. Soon the Egyptian government also announced that ships using the Israeli port of Eilat might be shelled by guns commanding the Tiran Strait, and a British steamer was indeed hit by Egyptian shells. All this persuaded the Israeli government that some counterstroke was necessary.

Nasser, meantime, had projects both for a new Aswan dam on the Nile and for rearmament. Britain and the USA had expressed willingness to help with the dam but

Right: this Soviet-built tank of the Egyptian army was captured by Israeli forces in Sinai.

not with arms. Nasser therefore turned to the eastern block for arms, which so alarmed Washington and London that they announced that they would no longer help with the Aswan Dam. In retaliation, Nasser announced the nationlization of the Suez Canal. This action, while directly affecting France and Britain, the principal shareholders, was also a threat to international commerce, or so it was thought. Since international support for the Anglo-French rights over the Canal was more vocal than substantial, the US government being especially lukewarm, Britain, France and Israel evolved a plan for the invasion of Sinai and the Canal Zone. Israel commenced hostilities on 29 October 1956, and Britain and France then announced that they were going to occupy, forcibly, the Canal Zone in order to protect it from the damage it might suffer in the course of Israeli-Egyptian hostilities.

The Anglo-French invading forces had little difficulty in getting ashore near Port Said and advancing down the Canal; Egyptian forces had already been demoralized by defeats inflicted by Israel in the Sinai Desert. However, pressure exerted by the USA, and in the United Nations, persuaded Britain and France to halt their advance and soon, in December, to begin a withdrawal. The situation returned to normal, except that the Canal, blocked by Nasser, took several months to clear. British and French prestige had been irreparably damaged in the Middle East.

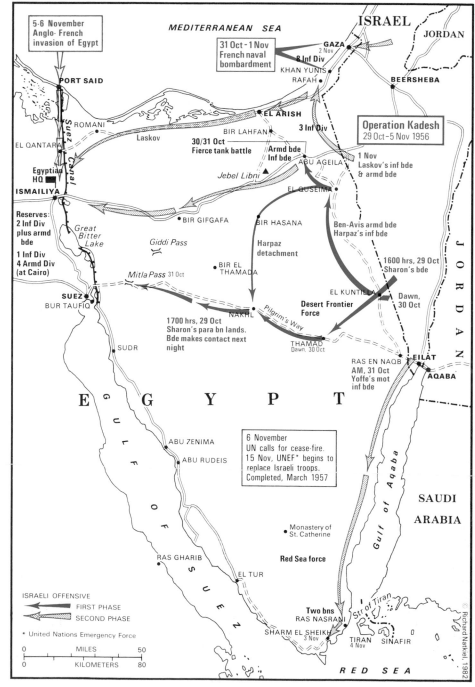

Right: the crews of an Israeli tank battalion line up in review order in front of their Centurion tanks.

The Six-Day War, 1967

The Suez War of 1956 had seen Israeli military successes in Sinai but her strategic position did not improve, despite the presence of a United Nations peacekeeping force in the buffer zone of the Sinai Desert. A new Iraqi regime quit the Western-sponsored Baghdad Pact in 1959 and allied itself with Egypt, while Egypt and other Arab countries began to receive armaments from the Soviet Union, as well as more diplomatic support. The Suez Canal was still blocked to Israeli commerce, and the Gulf of Aqaba was covered by Egyptian artillery, while the Palestinian refugees remained unsettled and presented a threat to Israel's security. Israel's frontier with Syria was especially troubled. Here, the Syrians' possession of the Golan Heights facilitated frequent bombardment of Israeli settlements close to the border.

In May 1967 Egypt, claiming that Israel was about to launch a reprisal attack against Syria, deployed its army on the frontier with Israel and at Sharm el Sheikh, meanwhile requesting the United Nations to remove its 3,000-strong peacekeeping force from Sinai. The UN, because it had no authority to station troops on Egyptian soil without Egyptian consent, complied with this demand. Statements by Egyptian and other Arab leaders seemed to indicate that another attack on Israel was imminent. Israel appealed to the United Nations and to various powers but did not obtain the reassurances which she requested. Moreover, on 25 May, Iraq, Jordan, Syria and Saudi Arabia deployed their forces along Israel's frontiers. The Strait of Tiran was declared by Egypt to be closed to Israeli shipping on 22 May.

By the beginning of June Israeli leaders calculated that they were outnumbered on the frontiers by about three to one and that they could be invaded any moment. Rather than wait for this to happen, they had planned a pre-emptive attack, and this was launched on the morning of 5 June, when Egyptian air bases, some as far distant as Cairo and even Luxor, were the victims of destructive surprise attacks by the Israeli air force. These attacks were well-planned and well-executed and resulted in the virtual removal of the Egyptian air force from the

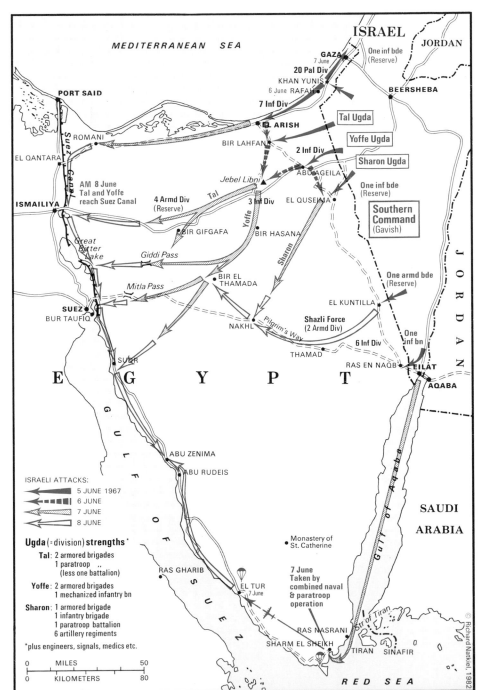

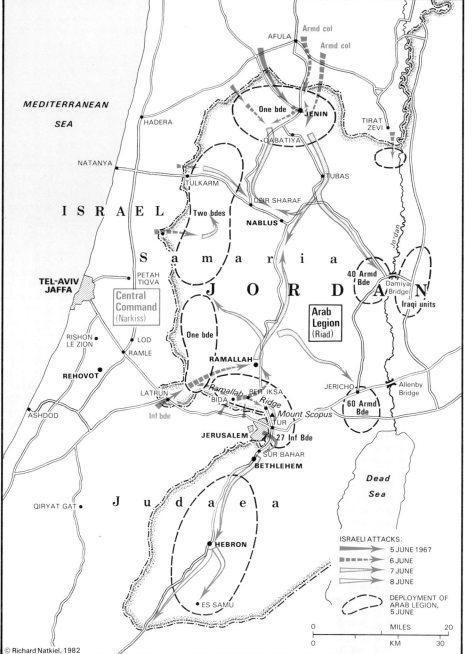

© Richard Natkiel, 1982

Map labels:

MEDITERRANEAN SEA

AFULA — Armd col — Armd col

ISRAEL

HADERA

One bde — JENIN — TIRAT ZEVI

QABATIYA

NATANYA

TULKARM — TUBAS

DEIR SHARAF

Two bdes — NABLUS

Samaria

PETAH TIQVA

TEL-AVIV JAFFA — Central Command (Narkiss)

JORDAN

40 Armd Bde — Damiya Bridge — Iraqi units

Arab Legion (Riad)

RISHON LE ZION — LOD

RAMLE

One bde — RAMALLAH

REHOVOT

LATRUN — Ramallah Ridge — BEIT IKSA — JERICHO — Allenby Bridge

BIDA — Mount Scopus — 60 Armd Bde

ASHDOD — Inf bde — TUR

JERUSALEM — 27 Inf Bde

SUR BAHAR

BETHLEHEM — Dead Sea

QIRYAT GAT — Judaea

HEBRON

ES SAMU

ISRAELI ATTACKS:
5 JUNE 1967
6 JUNE
7 JUNE
8 JUNE

DEPLOYMENT OF ARAB LEGION, 5 JUNE

0 — MILES — 20
0 — KM — 30

Below: Egyptian prisoners under guard at El Arish on the second day of the 1967 Arab-Israeli War.
Bottom: the Israeli army advances to the outskirts of Suez.
Right: an Israeli armored column advances into the Sinai Desert.
Bottom right: an Arab soldier surrenders to Israeli forces in Sinai.

following days' hostilities. Having won command of the air, the rout of the Egyptian army in Sinai followed almost automatically. On 9 June the Syrian Golan Heights were assaulted by Israeli forces, and after a day's fighting were captured. Israeli troops entered Kuneitra. Meanwhile, Israeli forces were also throwing back the Jordanians from west of the Jordan and in Jerusalem.

In these victorious circumstances, Israel was able to obtain ceasefire agreements within a week of the commencement of hostilities. As a result of this 'Six-Day War,' the whole of Sinai remained in Israeli hands, as well as the 'West Bank' (Jordan's territory west of the River Jordan) and the Golan Heights. Thus Israel had gained new frontiers which were more easily defensible than the old but the basic causes of hostility remained.

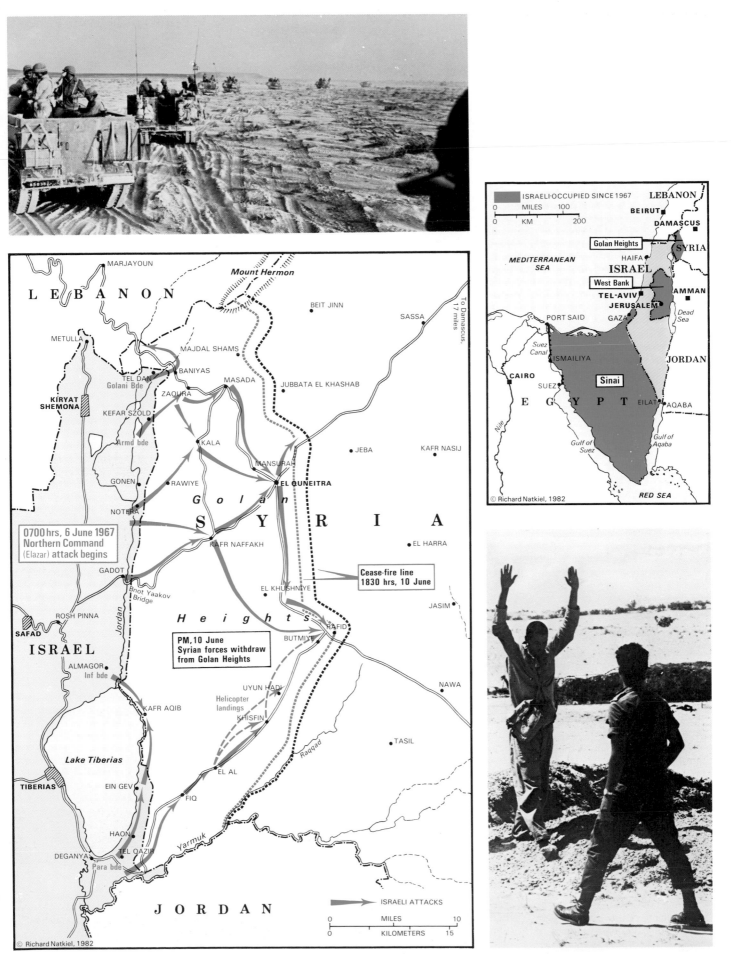

MARJAYOUN
Mount Hermon
To Damascus, 17 miles

L E B A N O N
METULLA
BEIT JINN
SASSA
MAJDAL SHAMS
TEL DAN
Golani Bde
BANIYAS
MASADA
ZAOURA
JUBBATA EL KHASHAB
KIRYAT SHEMONA
KEFAR SZOLD
Armd bde
KALA
MANSURA
JEBA
KAFR NASIJ
GONEN
RAWIYE
EL QUNEITRA
Golan
NOTERA
S Y R I A
EL HARRA
KAFR NAFFAKH

0700 hrs, 6 June 1967
Northern Command
(Elazar) attack begins

GADOT
H e i g h t s
EL KHUSHNIYE

Cease-fire line 1830 hrs, 10 June

Bnot Yaakov Bridge
JASIM
ROSH PINNA
RAFID
SAFAD
BUTMIYE

PM, 10 June Syrian forces withdraw from Golan Heights

ISRAEL
ALMAGOR
Inf bde
NAWA
UYUN HADI
Helicopter landings
KAFR AQIB
KHISFIN
Raqqad
TASIL
Lake Tiberias
EIN GEV
FIQ
EL AL
TIBERIAS
HAON
TEL QAZIR
Yarmuk
DEGANYA
Para bde

J O R D A N

➤ ISRAELI ATTACKS
0 MILES 10
0 KILOMETERS 15

© Richard Natkiel, 1982

ISRAELI-OCCUPIED SINCE 1967
LEBANON
0 MILES 100
0 KM 200
BEIRUT
DAMASCUS
Golan Heights
MEDITERRANEAN SEA
HAIFA
SYRIA
ISRAEL
West Bank
AMMAN
TEL-AVIV
JERUSALEM
Dead Sea
PORT SAID
GAZA
Suez Canal
CAIRO
ISMAILIYA
JORDAN
SUEZ
Sinai
EILAT
AQABA
E G Y P T
Nile
Gulf of Suez
Gulf of Aqaba
RED SEA

© Richard Natkiel, 1982

The October War, 1973

The ceasefire after the Six-Day War of 1967 was followed by six years of tension in the Middle East. Arabs and Israelis resorted to terrorism and counter-terrorism, with the occasional air battle punctuating the situation, as the Arab states bordering Israel continued to demand a restoration of the pre-1967 frontiers. By 1973 President Sadat of Egypt had enhanced, with Soviet help, the battleworthiness of his army, but he had then invited the Soviet military specialists to leave, thereby freeing himself from a possible restraining Soviet influence over his military ambitions.

On the Jewish Day of Atonement (*Yom Kippur*), 6 October 1973, Egyptian and Syrian forces launched a coordinated surprise attack on Israel, with the stated intention of regaining the 1967 frontiers. The Egyptian crossing of the Suez Canal, thanks to the surprise achieved, was successful, and the Israeli forces defending Sinai were put into disarray. In the north, too, the Israelis were thrown back, losing much of the Golan Heights. Help for both sides soon began to arrive. Iraq sent tanks to help the Syrians, and so did Jordan, while Kuwait and Saudi Arabia sent token forces to the same front. Egypt received some aircraft from Iraq, while Moroccan and Algerian troops arrived to release more Egyptian troops for the front. Meanwhile, the USA airlifted military supplies to Israel, while Soviet aid was sent by air and by sea to

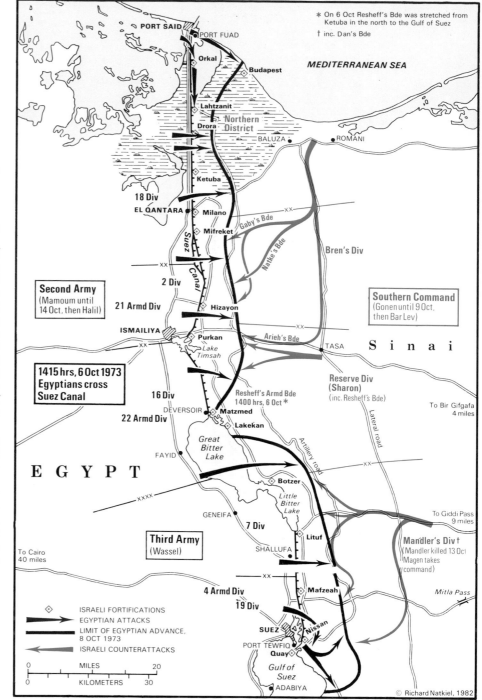

Left: the ceasefire line in the town of Suez at the end of the Yom Kippur War, October 1973.

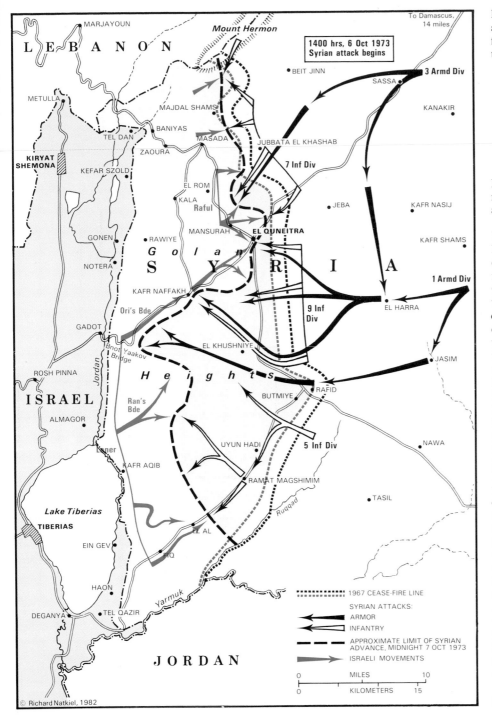

Map legend:

1400 hrs, 6 Oct 1973
Syrian attack begins

1967 CEASE-FIRE LINE

SYRIAN ATTACKS:
ARMOR
INFANTRY

APPROXIMATE LIMIT OF SYRIAN
ADVANCE, MIDNIGHT 7 OCT 1973
ISRAELI MOVEMENTS

MILES 10
KILOMETERS 15

© Richard Natkiel, 1982

Map labels: LEBANON, MARJAYOUN, Mount Hermon, To Damascus, 14 miles, BEIT JINN, SASSA, 3 Armd Div, KANAKIR, METULLA, MAJDAL SHAMS, BANIYAS, TEL DAN, MASADA, JUBBATA EL KHASHAB, 7 Inf Div, ZAOURA, KIRYAT SHEMONA, KEFAR SZOLD, EL ROM, KALA, Raful, JEBA, KAFR NASIJ, KAFR SHAMS, GONEN, RAWIYE, MANSURAH, EL QUNEITRA, Golan, SYRIA, NOTERA, KAFR NAFFAKH, 1 Armd Div, Ori's Bde, 9 Inf Div, EL HARRA, GADOT, Bnot Yaakov Bridge, EL KHUSHNIYE, JASIM, ROSH PINNA, Heights, Jordan, ISRAEL, Ran's Bde, BUTMIYE, RAFID, ALMAGOR, UYUN HADI, NAWA, KAFR AQIB, 5 Inf Div, RAMAT MAGSHIMIM, Lake Tiberias, TIBERIAS, TASIL, EIN GEV, Ruqqad, HAON, EL AL, FIQ, Yarmuk, DEGANYA, TEL QAZIR, JORDAN

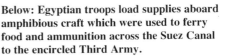

Below: Egyptian troops load supplies aboard amphibious craft which were used to ferry food and ammunition across the Suez Canal to the encircled Third Army.

Egypt and Syria. Israel was again out-numbered, having about 300,000 troops against Egypt's 650,000 and Syria's 150,000.

By 10 October the Israelis had beaten back the Syrians in the north, and were just holding the Egyptians in Sinai. Israeli aircraft, which had been vulnerable to Soviet-made missiles while attacking the Suez Canal bridges and the Syrian and Egyptian troops, were now free to deal with their opponents' own air forces. A strong counter-offensive was launched against the Syrians, whose defense line was pushed back. A threat to Damascus was avoided as this, it was feared, might have brought the USSR into the war in support of her protégé Syria. Having weakened the Syrian position, the Israelis concentrated their next effort on the Suez Front. Egyptian tanks, attempting to push eastward and especially toward the vital Mitla Pass, were routed in an enormous tank battle by Israeli armor and aircraft. This victory encouraged the Israeli generals, who were rarely in agreement with each other, to launch a decisive counterblow. The aim was to cross the Suez Canal in the area of the Great Bitter Lake, and thereby transform the situation. Despite some difficulty, when unexpectedly strong Egyptian action was encountered east of the Canal, a bridgehead was established and this was progressively enlarged until the Egyptian Third Army found itself almost cut off. A USSR delegation to Cairo realized that Egypt was facing total defeat, and with US and Soviet help the United Nations Security Council arranged a ceasefire, effective from 24 October.

Although Israel had emerged triumphant from this new ordeal, the war had shown

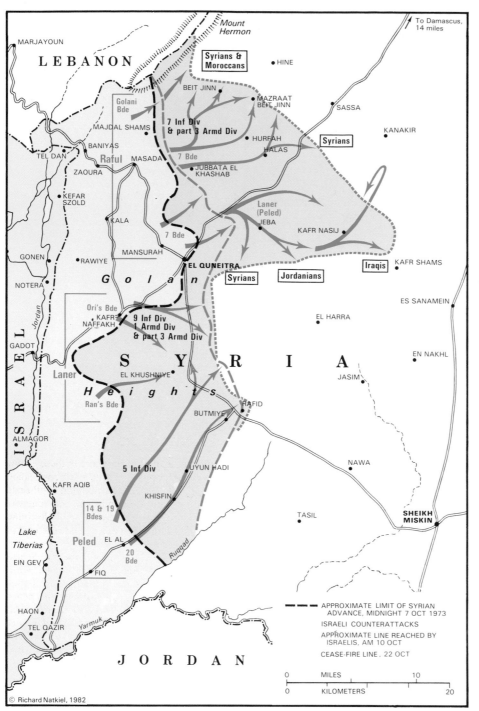

Below: these Palestinian terrorists were killed when the explosives they were carrying into Israel across the Golan Heights accidentally detonated.

that the Egyptian Army was more battle-worthy than had been believed, and that Israel was more vulnerable to surprise attack than had been thought. UN forces were sent to Sinai, while Israeli forces were withdrawn east of the passes. Egyptian forces remained on the right bank of the Canal, but the UN force separating the two armies was equipped to issue early warning of troop movements to both sides.

The Lebanon

Once part of the Ottoman Empire, and under French administration between the wars, the Lebanon emerged as an independent state after World War II. Socially it was finely balanced, for its population was divided between Moslems and Christians of various denominations, the delicacy of this situation being reflected in the practice of appointing a Maronite (Christian) president to balance the Moslem prime minister. Friction, however, was exacerbated by the presence of camps for Palestine refugees from Israel. These refugee camps provided both recruits and sanctuary for anti-Israeli guerrillas.

It became almost an Israeli custom to stage air attacks, military incursions, and assassinations in the Lebanon as reprisals for terrorist attacks on Israelis anywhere in the world. Against its will, therefore, the Lebanon became a battlefield in the Israeli-Arab struggle, and the resulting stress soon brought

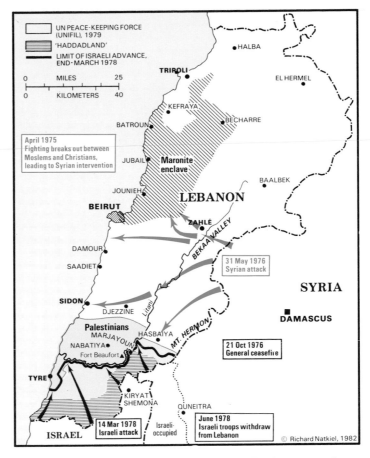

inter-communal violence; right-wing Christians began by attacking Palestinians but soon found themselves fighting their Moslem fellow-citizens. Syria intervened, at first quietly but finally, in May 1976, with a full-scale invasion. Even after this officially ended in October, Syrian troops remained in a peacekeeping role which, by and large, was sincerely if clumsily executed.

In March 1978, in reprisal for continuing Palestinian guerrilla attacks, Israeli troops occupied the south part of the Lebanon. A United Nations force was sent as part of a peace settlement, but when the Israelis withdrew they handed over their positions to a friendly right-wing Christian Lebanese militia. In April 1979 this militia, under Major Haddad, declared the area to be 'Independent Free Lebanon.' Meanwhile, farther north, the Syrian peacekeeping troops were fighting Christian militia forces around Beirut, and besieging Zahlé. The alliances and alignments of the Syrians seemed highly flexible, but one constant factor were the Israeli raids. In summer 1981 a general war on Lebanese soil between Syria and Israel seemed imminent, but US mediation postponed the crisis. It was sometimes difficult to discern whether the activities of Palestinian guerrillas were a justification or merely a pretext for these incursions. Israeli pressure in the south intensified early in 1982. The Israelis mounted a full-scale invasion in June 1982 and there was renewed fierce fighting involving Syrian and Palestinian forces. The Israeli forces again had the best of the fighting.

An agreement negotiated under US auspices in August provided for an Israeli withdrawal while the USA and a few other countries supplied troops to keep the peace for 30 days. The US Marines who were sent as part of this force were duly withdrawn in September but returned before the end of the month to help stabilize the very disturbed situation which had developed in Beirut following the assassination of the Christian Lebanese president.

The Marines were assigned to protect Beirut Airport, and lived in their own compound. On October 23 a suicide terrorist attack, consisting of a truck laden with explosives being driven into the compound entry, resulted in the death or injury of hundreds of Marines. Although locations beyond Beirut sheltering anti-government militias were attacked by US aircraft and shelled by US warships, American public opinion was unwilling to risk further lives in an intractable sectarian quarrel, and it was not long before US forces were withdrawn. The last elements of the international force left in April 1984. Although Israeli forces later staged a phased withdrawal from southern Lebanon against a background of rising casualties and war weariness at home, sporadic fighting and cross-border raids continued in the late 1980s.

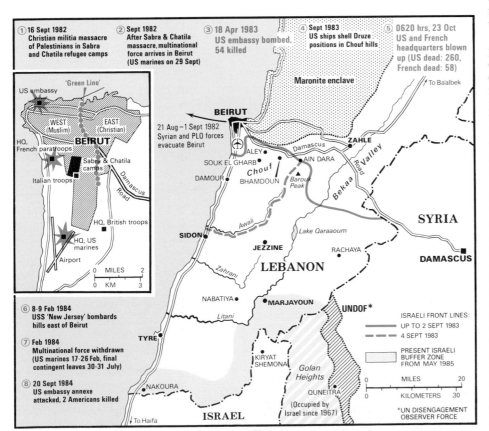

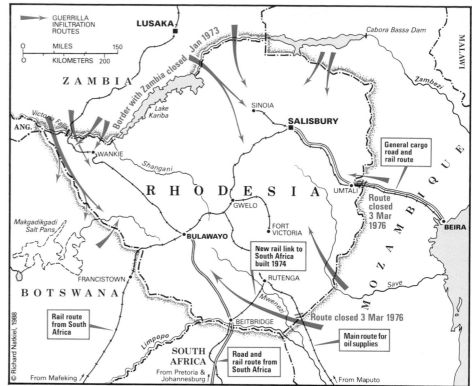

The Zimbabwean War of Independence

In January 1966 the British government initiated international economic sanctions against Rhodesia to promote majority black rule, but the rival black nationalist organizations, ZAPU and ZANU, were determined to embark on a guerrilla campaign. Their activities during the late 1960s and the early 1970s never posed a really serious threat to the survival of the established regime because the Rhodesian regular and reserve security forces had been reorganized to operate in a counterinsurgency role. Until 1971-72 Rhodesian security forces had only to contend with nationalist guerrillas infiltrating across the border with Zambia, an area that was far from ideal for the guerrillas. Main targets were far from the border, and the security forces had greater mobility and firepower. However, with the gradual disintegration of Portuguese authority in Mozambique's Tete province, ZANU guerrillas were able to re-open the more favorable northeastern front.

Then, with Portugal's withdrawal from Africa and Mozambique's independence in June 1975, Rhodesia's longest and most vulnerable border was exposed. From the beginning of 1976 guerrillas penetrated deep into southern and central Rhodesia from bases both in Zambia and Mozambique. The presence and activity of guerrillas in urban and semi-urban areas also increased markedly. By 1979 the security situation in Rhodesia was deteriorating. By the middle of the year over 90 percent of the country was under martial law. In March 1976 it was estimated that there were 700 guerrillas inside Rhodesia; by early 1979 this number had risen to 10,000 and by the end of November it was 15,000.

Apart from the geographical spread of the fighting, the intensity increased to such an extent that it was estimated that if the war had continued beyond 1979 then the casualties for the next 12 months would have exceeded the combined total for all the years since the early guerrilla operations. The deteriorating security situation meant that substantial increases in defense and defense-related expenditure had to be met by the government with increases in taxation. The lack of white manpower meant that more and more blacks were recruited by the security forces, with an eight-fold increase between 1972 and 1979.

Normal administration and services in the Tribal Trust Lands were severely disrupted or broke down. The most important barometer of white morale was the emigration rate. Over the period 1966-79 180,881 people entered the country while 202,950 departed.

A combination of internal and external pressures generated by sanctions and the guerrilla war moved a reluctant Rhodesia Front regime away from the policy of white supremacy toward black political participattion, and ultimately to an independent Zimbabwe in April 1980.

Above: Robert Mugabe (left) and Joshua Nkomo, leaders of the Patriotic Front, discuss the independence of Rhodesia/Zimbabwe at Lancaster Gate in 1978.

Above right: Vietnamese peasants during road building operations near Dien Bien Phu.

Right: the Hwachon Dam is attacked by US Navy Skyraider aircraft with torpedoes. The aim of the attack was to release floodwater which would disrupt enemy positions downstream.

Revolution in Indo-China

In 1945 the first Allied troops to arrive in French Indo-China were British. In Saigon they encountered confusion, as nationalist groups tried to take advantage of the situation to assert their own control, and Free French detachments arrived to support the French settlers. At one point the British were using, to maintain order, the same Japanese troops whose surrender they had come to accept.

By the end of 1946 the French seemed to have re-established themselves although, realizing the strength of national feeling, they had agreed in principle to the establishment of an independent Vietnam in a proposed Indo-Chinese Federation within the French Union. The leader of the most powerful nationalist organization, the Viet Minh, was the communist Ho Chi Minh, whose status had risen during the war, partly because of US support; the Americans had no love for French colonialism. But by the end of 1946 Ho Chi Minh, with his military commander, the former schoolmaster Giap, had realized that the French were determined to hold on to what they had, and retired to the mountains to develop guerrilla activities. In the following two years the French sent more troops to Vietnam, and

instituted a native but highly-supervised government under the titular Emperor, Bao Dai.

The victory of the Chinese communists in 1949 changed the situation, because Viet Minh forces could now obtain supplies over a friendly frontier. Giap began a campaign of attacks, usually successful, on isolated French garrisons and on the relief columns sent to help them. The French responded with the use of mobile columns and parachute troops. In 1950 Ho Chi Minh claimed to be the head of the true Vietnam government, and was recognized by China and the USSR. The USA, deciding that communism was worse than colonialism, granted Bao Dai military aid to fight the Viet Minh. Nevertheless, Giap was in sufficient strength to force the French to abandon most of the Red River Delta in October 1950. By this stage Giap had progressed beyond guerrilla warfare and possessed full-scale and properly equipped regular divisions. Overconfident, he made attacks on French strongholds at Vinh Yen, Mao Khe, and Phat Diem which were unsuccessful and costly. Guerrilla warfare continued throughout 1951–53.

The war between the French and the communist-led Viet Minh in French Indo China took a new turn in April 1953 when Giap's forces, instead of pursuing the war in Vietnam, invaded another French territory, Laos. French reinforcements poured in and Giap withdrew, having demonstrated that

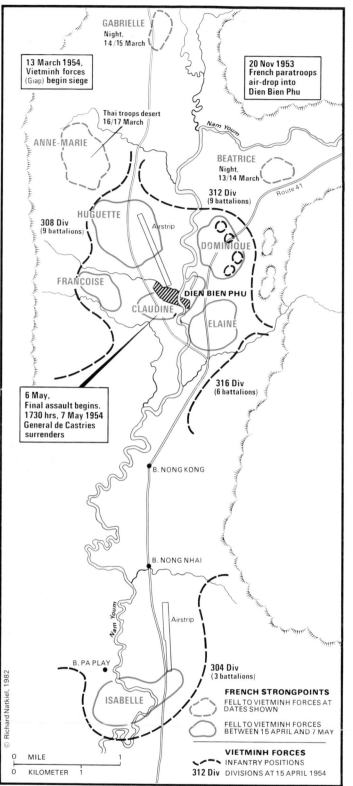

GABRIELLE
Night,
14/15 March

13 March 1954,
Vietminh forces
(Giap) begin siege

20 Nov 1953
French paratroops
air-drop into
Dien Bien Phu

Thai troops desert
16/17 March

ANNE-MARIE

Nam Youm

BEATRICE
Night,
13/14 March

312 Div
(9 battalions)

Route 41

HUGUETTE

Airstrip

308 Div
(9 battalions)

DOMINIQUE

FRANÇOISE

DIEN BIEN PHU

CLAUDINE

ELAINE

6 May,
Final assault begins.
1730 hrs, 7 May 1954
General de Castries
surrenders

316 Div
(6 battalions)

B. NONG KONG

B. NONG NHAI

Nam Youm

Airstrip

B. PA PLAY

304 Div
(3 battalions)

ISABELLE

FRENCH STRONGPOINTS
FELL TO VIETMINH FORCES AT
DATES SHOWN

FELL TO VIETMINH FORCES
BETWEEN 15 APRIL AND 7 MAY

VIETMINH FORCES
INFANTRY POSITIONS
312 Div DIVISIONS AT 15 APRIL 1954

© Richard Natkiel, 1982

0 MILE 1
0 KILOMETER 1

Below: Vietnamese porters carry supplies to the front by bicycle during the build-up to Dien Bien Phu.

he had the French on the run. Later in the year the French decided to block Giap's expected renewal of the attack in Laos. The settlement of Dien Bien Phu was selected as a French defensive strongpoint, rudimentary fortifications were built there, and fresh troops flown in. When the Viet Minh did attack, in March 1954, it had about 18,000 defenders, of whom about 3,000 were French and the rest colonial troops. But Giap had an overwhelming numerical superiority, and

was well-supplied with artillery, including anti-aircraft guns supplied by China. When the encirclement closed in, the airstrip could no longer be used: supplies could be parachuted in, at some risk, but wounded could not be moved out. The defense was genuinely heroic, and ended only when the Viet Minh divisions broke into the center of the position.

When Dien Bien Phu fell the conference to end this war was already in progress at

Geneva. Here the French agreed to the provisional formation of a Viet Minh North Vietnam and a French-orientated South Vietnam, with internationally supervised elections in both within two years. The independence of Cambodia and Laos, formerly parts of French Indo-China, was also recognized.

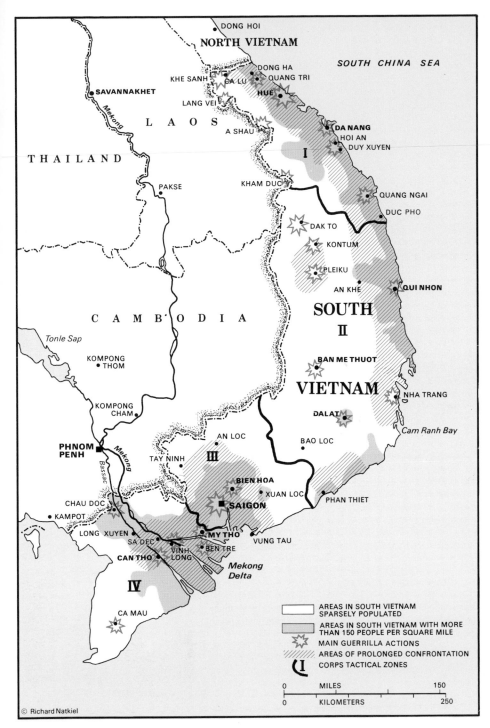

AREAS IN SOUTH VIETNAM
SPARSELY POPULATED

AREAS IN SOUTH VIETNAM WITH MORE
THAN 150 PEOPLE PER SQUARE MILE

MAIN GUERRILLA ACTIONS

AREAS OF PROLONGED CONFRONTATION

CORPS TACTICAL ZONES

© Richard Natkiel

attack on an outpost of the Army of the Republic of Vietnam (ARVN), during which an American adviser to the latter was killed. In 1960 the Viet Cong formed the National Liberation Front (NLF) with its regular army, supported by regional and village militias. Much of its strength in men and supplies came from North Vietnam, although this fact was concealed. The Ho Chi Minh Trail, a primitive but resilient line of communication along the Vietnam-Cambodia and Vietnam-Laos frontiers, became the lifeline of the NLF. In 1960 the continuing successes of the NLF against the ARVN prompted the US government to send further military advisers, backed up by financial and military aid. The advisers, who often led ARVN units into action, multiplied as the situation worsened, and eventually President Kennedy sanctioned the despatch of US combat troops. There were 16,000 of these in South Vietnam by 1963, and under President Johnson this figure rose dramatically to about 500,000 men by 1968.

Below: a member of the 173rd Airborne Brigade holds a position around the perimeter of Bien Hoa airfield, May 1965.

The Vietnam War

In 1954 the Geneva Conference brought to an end the first stage of the Vietnam War. This had been fought between the colonial power, France, and the Communist-led guerrillas of the Viet Minh independence movement. The later was headed by the French-educated Communist Ho Chi Minh, and its forces, which toward the end had become regular armies well-equipped with Russian arms by neighboring China, were commanded by General Vo Nguyen Giap. After 1954 the French, finally defeated at Dien Bien Phu, left

Indochina, which was divided into four states, Laos, Cambodia, the Democratic Republic of Vietnam, and South Vietnam. The frontier between Ho Chi Minh's North Vietnam and American-supported South Vietnam was the 17th Parallel.

It had been agreed that the two halves of Vietnam would be unified after elections, but South Vietnam refused to hold these on the grounds that they would not be freely conducted in North Vietnam. By the late 1950s, anti-government South Vietnamese, trained in North Vietnam, returned to the south and set up the guerrilla group, the Viet Cong. At first it concentrated on murdering government officials, but in 1958 it made a large-scale

Search and Destroy

By the end of 1966 four regular North Vietnamese infantry divisions, thinly disguised, with about 70,000 NLF troops were operating in South Vietnam, helped by the local and temporary forces supplied by the NLF militias. General William C Westmoreland, directing US and ARVN operations, favored a war of attrition at this stage. While US bombers pounded the Ho Chi Minh Trail, his ground forces tried to destroy Viet Cong base areas. In both lines of attack successes were won, but the enemy, who most often disappeared into the jungle at the first signs of attack, was usually back in action within a few days. In the summer of 1966, in South Vietnam's northernmost province, the build-up of North Vietnamese regular forces reached a point where large-scale engagements between them and US Marines took place, usually causing heavy casualties to both sides. US search-and-destroy operations also occurred farther south. In the jungles of Tay Ninh Province, near the southern end of the Ho Chi Minh Trail and not far from the South Vietnam capital of Saigon, Operation Attleboro took over 20,000 US troops, of whom nearly 1000 became casualties. In the same area, in

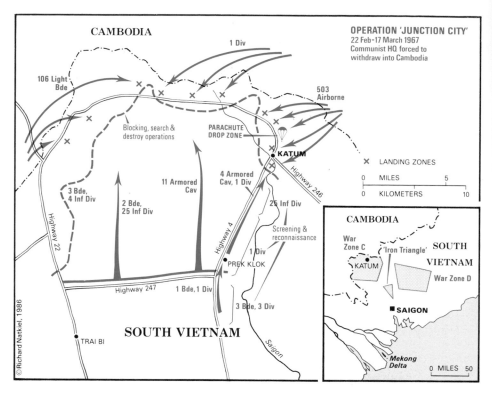

February-May 1967, Operation Junction City caused about 1800 casualties to US and ARVN forces. Viet Cong and North Vietnamese losses were considerably heavier, although inflated at the time by highly optimistic 'body counts' sent in by the US units. The NLF and North Vietnamese command was quite satisfied with the casualty ratio, believing (rightly as it turned out) the Americans would soon reach the limit of acceptable losses.

Left: a member of a US riverine patrol vessel provides cover during a routine search of a South Vietnamese boat.

**OPERATION
'ROLLING THUNDER'**
2 Mar 1965 – 1 Nov 1968
Main targets: airfields, SAM sites,
Thanh Hoa Bridge and supply routes
Bombing restricted in Hanoi-
Haiphong area (see separate map)

OPERATIONS:

'LINEBACKER I'
8 May-23 Oct 1972
Fewer target restrictions
than 'Rolling Thunder'

'LINEBACKER II'
19-30 Dec 1972
Unrestricted bombing.
All targets of importance
in Hanoi-Haiphong area hit

◇ NORTH VIETNAMESE AIR BASES
▲ US AIR BASES (JET-SERVICEABLE)
✦ US AIR BASES (NOT JET-SERVICEABLE)
⊕ US B-52 BASE
⊙ US AIR TANKER BASES
▭ AERIAL REFUELLING TRACKS
AND ANCHOR POINTS (AP)
--- AIR COMBAT ZONES

MILES 0 ——— 200
KILOMETERS 0 ——— 300

The Air War 1965-72

At first it was aircraft from US aircraft carriers which flew sorties over Vietnam. Then airbases were built and it was to protect one of these, Da Nang, that the US Marines were first put into Vietnam in 1965. Over the main zone of conflict, South Vietnam, the Americans had total command of the air, which they exploited with savage ground-attack sorties. However, because the Viet Cong presented few large targets, the damage inflicted was not at all equal to the effort expended.

As the involvement of North Vietnamese regular units became more obvious, the idea of bombing North Vietnam itself became attractive, the aim being to show that the Communist effort in South Vietnam might prove very costly in North Vietnam. In February 1965 Operation Flaming Dart, undertaken jointly with ARVN aircraft, resulted in strikes against army barracks at Dong Hoi. A year later, faced with a worsening military situation, President Johnson approved a longer bombing operation, Rolling Thunder: attacks began with the bombing of the naval base at Quang Khe in March 1965, and the raids continued into 1968, with Washington exercising a strict and sometimes resented control over the local air commanders with the

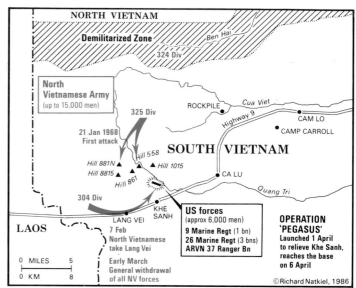

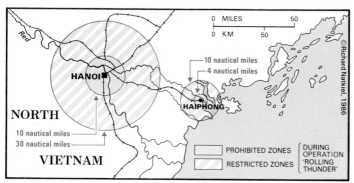

aim of avoiding undue damage to civilian targets. By mid-1965, 900 sorties a week were being flown. However, North Vietnamese morale showed no signs of cracking. In spring 1966 the ban on bombing in the heavily-populated Hanoi/Haiphong area was partially lifted so that oil and railroad installations could be hit. But despite the destruction inflicted (by end-1967 864,000 tons of bombs had been dropped, compared to the 503,000 tons dropped in the Pacific war of 1941-45), the North Vietnamese always seemed able to make good the damage.

In 1972 ground-attack strikes did much to turn back the Easter invasion of South Vietnam, and at the same time renewed bombing of North Vietnam was authorized. Then, later in the year, with a US-China rapprochement on the way and new pressure being needed to improve the US negotiating position in Vietnam, President Nixon authorized Operation Linebacker 1. This involved the destruction of airbases, power stations, oil installations and railroad facilities, some of them quite close to Hanoi. Thanks to more accurate 'smart' bombs, this seven-month campaign inflicted considerable damage and reduced supply movements. Finally, just as an American withdrawal was being negotiated, Nixon inaugurated Linebacker 2, 12 days of heavy bombing including Hanoi and Haiphong. The aim was to strengthen the US negotiating position at a critical point, and very heavy damage was caused, although civilian casualties were much lower than was reported at the time. Twenty-six US aircraft were lost, but most of the ground-to-air missiles launched against them failed, many of them exploding in urban areas and adding to the death toll of civilians.

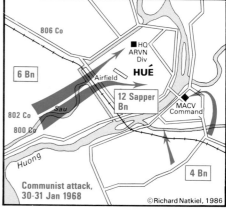

The Tet Offensive

The year 1968 marked a turning point in the Vietnam War, and also saw some of the bitterest fighting of the whole conflict. For the Americans, the year was crowned by several military successes but also by growing disillusionment with the war, both at home and in South Vietnam. Defeat in the field forced the North Vietnamese to accept a much longer war strategy.

The year began with the US Marine base at Khe Sanh still under close siege, though the NVA, harrassed by massive bombing raids, were unable to overrun the compound. Khe Sanh, however, was only the beginning of a much greater North Vietnamese effort to win the war outright. A major, widespread offensive, timed to coincide with Tet (the Buddhist New Year) was launched on 30 January.

The plan called for both Viet Cong and regular NVA forces to attack cities throughout South Vietnam, in particular the capital, Saigon, and the old imperial city of Hué. Some 50,000 men were earmarked for the offensive, many infiltrated their targets in the days before the Tet holiday.

The opening attacks did achieve some surprise. In Saigon, a sapper unit broke into the US Embassy and held security forces at bay for some time – the action was caught on camera and was to have a profound effect on public opinion in the US. However, US and South Vietnamese forces responded with

vigor and were able to deal with many of the North Vietnamese attacks, although vicious house-to-house fighting led to the destruction of large areas of some cities.

Only in Hué did the battle rage for more than a week. Here NVA units took the walled citadel and it took three weeks of close-quarters combat before US Marines, aided by close air support, were able to oust the NVA forces from their positions.

Tet was a military setback for the North: there was no popular uprising in the South and NVA casualties ran into tens of thousands. However, US commitment to South Vietnam was undeniably weakened by the offensive. The strategy of attrition had failed – the North, despite its losses, would continue the war until final victory.

Below: a Marine patrol moves along the dike of a rice paddy during operations against the Viet Cong in 1965.

Vietnam: the Fall of Saigon

The Tet Offensive was victory concealed in a failure. Although beaten militarily, the Vietcong had made a great impression in the USA. Americans asked themselves how it was that, after so much American blood and money had been spent, the enemy could install himself for a few hours or days in almost all the towns and cities. The key town of Hué had been held by the Vietcong for 25 days, and they had even penetrated into the US Embassy in Saigon. Also, as a preliminary to the Tet Offensive, North Vietnamese divisions had heavily attacked Khe Sanh, defended by American Marines. Although it had held out, it was a reminder

of the great fear in Washington that the USA, too, could suffer a Dien Bien Phu. It was from this time, January 1968, that the American government, and perhaps most Americans, came to believe that this was a war they could not win and the best thing to do was to get out in as dignified a manner as possible. The request by the American commander in Vietnam, Westmoreland, for reinforcements to exploit what he rightly saw as the enemy's failure during the Tet Offensive, was unsuccessful. Only a few thousand troops were sent, while at the same time American bombing was limited to the enemy's supply routes through Laos and a small part of North Vietnam close to the border.

The morale of American troops was deteriorating, and they began to be progressively withdrawn from 1969 as the US government sought to extricate itself from

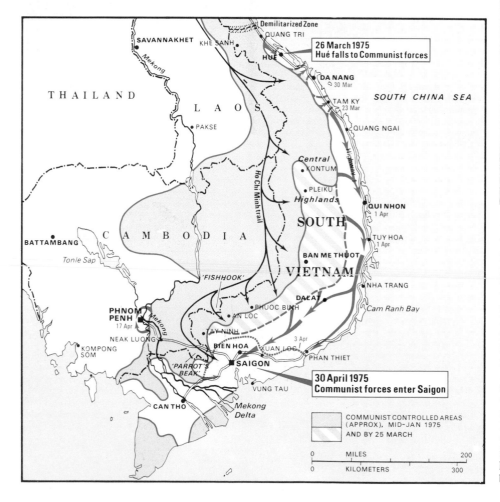

Vietnam by negotiation. But in the end the terms it wanted were unobtainable, despite periodic flurries of activity including a US invasion of Cambodia and a renewal of bombing attacks on Hanoi. In January 1973 the US signed an agreement by which its troops finally quit Vietnam, and in exchange North Vietnam merely agreed to release US prisoners of war. The ARVN was left to fight on alone. In late 1974 the North Vietnamese Army began an offensive in the Mekong Delta, followed in January 1975 by another in the Central Highlands. Meanwhile the ARVN had to deal with a successful revolt in Cambodia by the Khmer Rouge revolutionaries. It could not cope with so many crises, and was soon making its last stand before Saigon. This did not last long. At the end of April Saigon fell, bringing the 30-year struggle to a close.

Below: a guerrilla of the Mukti Bahini guards a bridge partly burned by retreating Pakistani forces in November 1971.

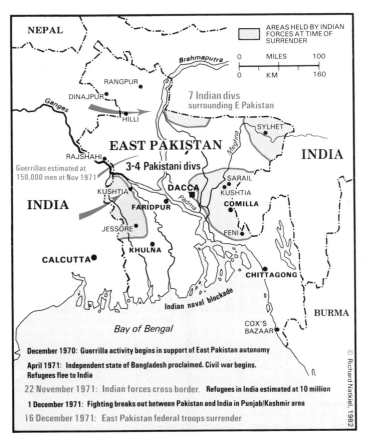

AREAS HELD BY INDIAN FORCES AT TIME OF SURRENDER

NEPAL

Brahmaputra

7 Indian divs surrounding E Pakistan

RANGPUR

DINAJPUR

Ganges

HILLI

SYLHET

EAST PAKISTAN

Meghna

INDIA

RAJSHAHI

3-4 Pakistani divs

Guerrillas estimated at 150,000 men at Nov 1971

KUSHTIA

DACCA

SARAIL

KUSHTIA

INDIA

FARIDPUR

Padma

COMILLA

JESSORE

FENI

KHULNA

CALCUTTA

CHITTAGONG

Indian naval blockade

BURMA

Bay of Bengal

COX'S BAZAAR

© Richard Natkiel, 1982

December 1970: Guerrilla activity begins in support of East Pakistan autonomy

April 1971: Independent state of Bangladesh proclaimed. Civil war begins. Refugees flee to India

22 November 1971: Indian forces cross border. Refugees in India estimated at 10 million

1 December 1971: Fighting breaks out between Pakistan and India in Punjab/Kashmir area

16 December 1971: East Pakistan federal troops surrender

The Creation of Bangladesh

The Bengali population of East Pakistan had become steadily disenchanted with its political situation because, although nominally equal with the West as a constituent of the state of Pakistan, in reality the East was dominated by numerically inferior West Pakistan. In 1970 the East's Awami League, which demanded greater independence for the East, won an overwhelming election victory, giving it a considerable majority in the all-Pakistan Assembly. Faced with this, the leader of the next largest, and mainly West Pakistan, party, Bhutto, decided to boycott the Assembly. There were protest demonstrations in East Pakistan. Bit by bit, the army took up the role of an oppressive army of occupation while the Awami League strengthened its resistance movement, the Mukti Bahini.

The Mukti Bahini began conventional terrorist and guerrilla activity, concentrated near the frontier with India, which was becoming increasingly cooperative. Meanwhile the flow of refugees from East Pakistan to India grew to perhaps 15 million, or no fewer than one in five of the population. In November, in a further step toward open war, the Indian and Pakistan governments announced that their troops were authorized to cross the frontiers in case of need.

On 3 December an excuse to go to war was provided by Pakistan, which began to make attacks on Indian positions in the west and in Kashmir. These attacks were small, and presumably intended as warnings; Pakistan was ruled by a general, Yahia Khan, whose political understanding was unsophisticated. The Indian forces destined for East Pakistan were given extra complements of engineering troops in order to speed the crossing of the many rivers and streams of the region, the plan being to make quickly for the towns and railroad junctions, relying on the Mukti Bahini to

hold down the Pakistanis' defensive positions. One Indian corps attacked from the west, around Hilli, while another made three thrusts from the east to capture the capital Dacca and cut off Chittagong. The third corps attacked from the southwest to capture Jessore and reach the Padma River. On 6 December India recognized the independence of the new state of Bangladesh, and ten days later Indian troops reached Dacca, bringing the war to a close and guaranteeing independence. Internal political problems and recurrent famine continued to unsettle Bangladesh throughout the 1970s and beyond.

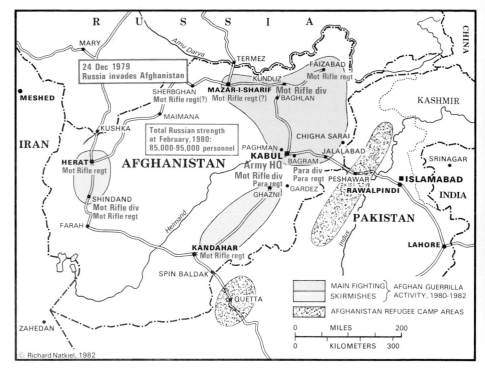

The Soviet Invasion of Afghanistan

In 1973 the King of Afghanistan was overthrown by Mohammed Daoud, who accepted Soviet military as well as economic assistance. Military help was required to back up Afghanistan's claim to territory on the Pakistan side of the frontier, provocatively called by the Afghans Paktoonistan. But in 1978, after attempting to limit Soviet influence, Daoud was overthrown in a Marxist coup and the new leaders were largely Soviet-trained army officers. The new government of Mohammed Taraki depended heavily on Soviet advisers, while the two wings (Parcham and Khalq) of the ruling communist party, the People's Democratic Party, remained in ideological and often violent conflict. In 1979 Taraki died in mysterious circumstances and the prime minister, Amin, became president and continued his hard-line policies. The latter aroused much resentment among the Afghans, many of whom had been arrested or had relatives arrested or executed. Amin pushed ahead with an attempt to transform social and economic life, but his attempt to end traditional feudal practices by land reforms, attacks on the priesthood and on landlords, abolition of the veil and dowries, intensified opposition. Rebels became bolder, and Amin called on Soviet-armed helicopters to bombard villages said to be harboring rebels. Armed conflict between rebels and government forces was marked by the ferocity employed by both sides.

Amin's presidency lasted only three months. His reliance on ever-increasing numbers of Soviet troops and advisers made it easy for the USSR to arrange a coup in which he was replaced by Babrak Karmal, a man regarded by the Soviets as a reliable communist who would tread more softly. This coup took place in December 1979, but did not bring peace. By the next summer former ministers who belonged to the Khalq faction had been executed, and the Red Army and Red Air Force were operating in Afghanistan in ever-larger numbers. Only the capital Kabul, and cities like Jalalabad, Herat, and Kandahar, could be considered safe by the government. The Afghan Army was demoralized, and large-scale desertion made it ineffective. In the countryside the rebels were dominant, becoming quiet only when a Soviet punitive expedition was sent to the particular locality. The Soviet forces, which numbered as many as 100,000, used helicopters and armored vehicles, but were handicapped by the lack of roads. Raids by helicopter gunships and ground-support aircraft on rebellious villages produced little effect even though the rebels had no way of opposing them. Meanwhile refugees poured over the frontiers; about a million crossed to Pakistan in 1980, settling around Peshawar. Another half-million went to Iran. By 1981 one in every seven Afghans had fled his country.

Since the 1979 invasion, the battle for control of Afghanistan had settled down into a stalemate. Although the guerrillas had received modern weapons, notably Stinger anti-aircraft missiles from the United States, they seemed unable to break the Soviet will to resist. However, public discussion of the war in the Soviet Union and a series of peace proposals suggested that the war would end through negotiation rather than outright military victory by either side.

Below: Afghan guerrillas pose for the camera, displaying a motley collection of weapons. They have, however, forced the Soviet Union to pull its forces out of Afghanistan.

The Gulf War

In April 1969, when the Shah of Iran enjoyed US backing and possessed powerful forces, he decided to abrogate a 1937 treaty defining the Iran-Iraq frontier in which the waterway known as the Shatt-al-Arab was entirely allocated to Iraq. Iran sent ships, flying the national flag, along this waterway, but this show of strength was followed by armed clashes in the area and in January 1970 the two countries severed diplomatic relations. However, relations were restored in 1973, and in 1975 the two countries declared themselves back on a brotherly footing, with an agreement that their frontier would pass along the center of the deepest main shipping channel of the waterway. Iran also agreed to stop helping the Kurds of Iraq, who had been fighting Iraqi government forces in the hope of establishing their own independent state. The Shah's annexation of the Persian Gulf islands of Abu Musa and the Greater and Lesser Tumbs, which had occurred in 1971, by threat in the first place and by invasion in the second, was, however, still resented by Iraq and other Gulf States. The Shah regarded these islands, commanding strategically important straits, as vital and had lost no time in taking them after Britain's withdrawal from this region.

To Iraq's wish to regain control of the entire Shatt-al-Arab and to secure the withdrawal of Iranian forces from the Musa and Tumb islands, was added fear of Shi'ite Moslem influence. After the fall of the Shah and his replacement in Iran by a priestly (Shi'ite) government in 1979 it seemed quite likely that the latter might encourage resistance by the Shi'ite majority in Iraq to the established Sunni leadership. In the meantime, Iraq had supported Arab demands that Iran should give autonomy to its territory in Khuzestan.

The Iranian revolution, its antagonizing of the USA by its detention of the US Embassy staff in Tehran, the murderous purge of the Iranian officer class, all suggested by mid-1980 that Iran was militarily weak. There were small frontier skirmishes, and on 22 September, following Iran's refusal to accept Iraq's demand that Iranian forces should be withdrawn from one disputed area, the Iraqi Army crossed the frontier on a 300-mile front. Iraq had announced its abrogation of the Shatt-al-Arab agreement on 16 September.

Iran's resistance proved stronger than expected. Its first response was to bomb not only

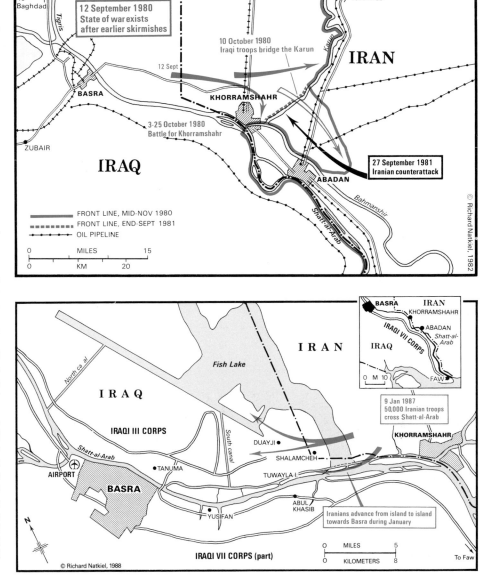

the advancing Iraqis, but also the port of Basra. The hostile capitals, Baghdad and Tehran, also came under air attack in September. By the end of that month the Iraqi Army was besieging the ports of Abadan and Khorramshahr and the town of Susangerd. But Iraq was unable to capture these objectives.

Mediation attempts failed during the winter and after the rains ceased in April 1981 full-scale warfare recommenced. In early June the Iranians fought some bloody battles to regain parts of their lost territory. But by the dry season in 1981 the campaign was still a stalemate.

In the years since 1981, the war has dragged on with neither side able to deliver a decisive blow, Iranian gains in the vicinity of Basra in 1986-87 have not significantly changed the stalemate. The most important development in the war has been its international repercussions: both Iraqi and Iranian attacks on shipping in the Gulf have led to the deployment of naval escort vessels from several leading powers, including the United States and the Soviet Union. While Iran and Iraq remain implacable foes, it seems unlikely that the war will end in the near future.

The Falklands Crisis

Although the Argentine invasion of the Falkland Islands on 2 April 1982 came as a complete surprise to the people of Britain and the rest of the world, the status of the islands had long been a source of dispute between Britain and Argentina. Despite the British military victory which ultimately ensued most Argentinians were and remain convinced that the islands, which they know as the Malvinas, ought rightfully to be part of Argentina. In negotiations over many years Britain had gone some way toward recognizing this claim. One suggestion had been to transfer sovereignty over the islands to Argentina but for Britain to continue to administer them on a 'lease-back' arrangement giving them a similar status as Hong Kong *vis-à-vis* China. However, Britain was unwilling to enforce such a deal against the wishes of the islanders who vehemently insisted that they wanted to remain British.

Negotiations in early 1982 made no new progress and, presumably after careful preparation, the invasion of the Falkland Islands and South Georgia followed. It has been suggested that a major motive for the Argentine military junta's decision was a desire to distract the Argentinian people from the country's appalling economic problems. The Argentinians were certainly surprised by the speed and anger of the British response. Britain was able to mobilize extensive diplomatic support in the UN and among her EEC partners who joined in imposing economic sanctions on Argentina. The USA at first remained neutral in the dispute and tried to mediate but after Secretary Haig's diplomatic efforts had failed America also condemned the Argentine aggression. The UN Secretary General also attempted to resolve the dispute but he too was unsuccessful.

While the diplomatic efforts were continuing the British task force was making its way to the South Atlantic. As well as sending warships the British government also requisitioned a number of merchant vessels, including luxury liners, to carry troops and supplies and act as hospital

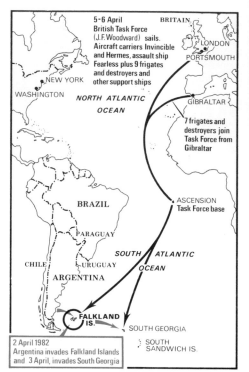

5-6 April
British Task Force
(J.F. Woodward) sails.
Aircraft carriers Invincible
and Hermes, assault ship
Fearless plus 9 frigates
and destroyers and
other support ships

BRITAIN
LONDON
PORTSMOUTH

NEW YORK
WASHINGTON

NORTH ATLANTIC
OCEAN

GIBRALTAR

7 frigates and
destroyers join
Task Force from
Gibraltar

BRAZIL

PARAGUAY

ASCENSION
Task Force base

CHILE
URUGUAY

SOUTH ATLANTIC
OCEAN

ARGENTINA

FALKLAND
IS.

SOUTH GEORGIA

SOUTH
SANDWICH IS.

2 April 1982
Argentina invades Falkland Islands
and 3 April, invades South Georgia

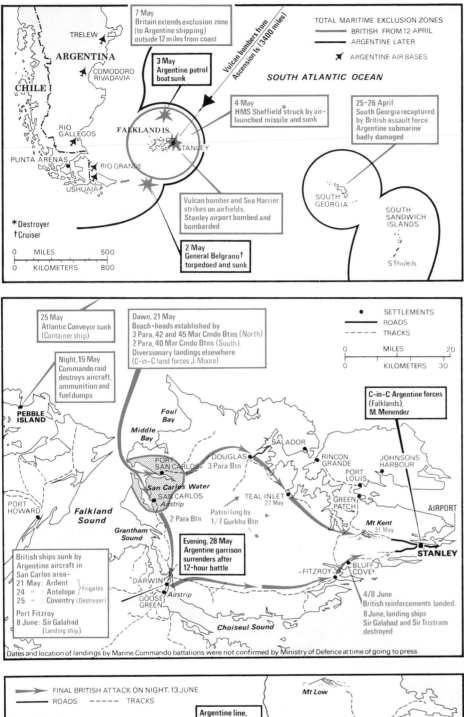

7 May
Britain extends exclusion zone (to Argentine shipping) outside 12 miles from coast

3 May
Argentine patrol boat sunk

Vulcan bombers from Ascension Is (3400 miles)

TOTAL MARITIME EXCLUSION ZONES
— BRITISH FROM 12 APRIL
— ARGENTINE LATER
✈ ARGENTINE AIR BASES

TRELEW

ARGENTINA

COMODORO RIVADAVIA

CHILE

RIO GALLEGOS

PUNTA ARENAS

RIO GRANDE

USHUAIA

FALKLAND IS.

STANLEY

SOUTH ATLANTIC OCEAN

4 May
HMS Sheffield * struck by air-launched missile and sunk

25-26 April
South Georgia recaptured by British assault force. Argentine submarine badly damaged

Vulcan bomber and Sea Harrier strikes on airfields. Stanley airport bombed and bombarded

SOUTH GEORGIA

SOUTH SANDWICH ISLANDS

S Thule Is

* Destroyer
† Cruiser

2 May
General Belgrano † torpedoed and sunk

0   MILES   500
0   KILOMETERS   800

---

25 May
Atlantic Conveyor sunk (Container ship)

Night, 15 May
Commando raid destroys aircraft, ammunition and fuel dumps

PEBBLE ISLAND

Dawn, 21 May
Beach-heads established by 3 Para, 42 and 45 Mar Cmdo Btns (North) 2 Para, 40 Mar Cmdo Btns (South). Diversionary landings elsewhere (C-in-C land forces J. Moore)

● SETTLEMENTS
— ROADS
--- TRACKS

0   MILES   20
0   KILOMETERS   30

Foul Bay

Middle Bay

SALADOR

DOUGLAS
3 Para Btn

RINCON GRANDE

JOHNSONS HARBOUR

C-in-C Argentine forces (Falklands), M. Menendez

PORT SAN CARLOS

PORT LOUIS

San Carlos Water

SAN CARLOS Airstrip

TEAL INLET 27 May

GREEN PATCH

AIRPORT

PORT HOWARD

Falkland Sound

2 Para Btn

Patrolling by 1/7 Gurkha Btn

Mt Kent 31 May

STANLEY

Grantham Sound

Evening, 28 May
Argentine garrison surrenders after 12-hour battle

British ships sunk by Argentine aircraft in San Carlos area —
21 May: Ardent ⎱ Frigates
24 " : Antelope ⎰
25 " : Coventry (Destroyer)
Port Fitzroy
8 June: Sir Galahad (Landing ship)

DARWIN

GOOSE GREEN Airstrip

FITZROY

BLUFF COVE

4/8 June
British reinforcements landed. 8 June, landing ships Sir Galahad and Sir Tristram destroyed

Choiseul Sound

Dates and location of landings by Marine Commando battalions were not confirmed by Ministry of Defence at time of going to press

---

→ FINAL BRITISH ATTACK ON NIGHT, 13 JUNE
— ROADS --- TRACKS

Mt Low

Murrell River

Argentine line, afternoon, 13 June

3 Para Btn
Mt Longdon

2 Para Btn

Port William

Cape Pembroke

2 Btn Scots Gds

Wireless Ridge

Two Sisters

Moody Brk

AIRPORT

45 Mar Cmdo

Tumbledown Mt

Government House

Stanley Harbour

Cath

STANLEY

42 Mar Cmdo
Mt Harriet

Mt William

1/7 Gurkha Btn

Sapper Hill

Rookery Bay

SOUTH ATLANTIC OCEAN

1 Welsh Gds

Mullet Creek

Phillips Point

14 June
Argentine forces surrender

Port Harriet

Seal Point

0   MILES   3
0   KILOMETERS   4

Below: loading a Tigerfish torpedo on the British nuclear submarine *Conqueror*. The *General Belgrano* was sunk by two of these weapons fired from *Conqueror*.
Below far left: British ships under attack from Argentinian aircraft, San Carlos Water, May 1982.

ships. The principal military problem for the British was in the air where the few Harrier aircraft carried by the two small aircraft carriers had, with help from missiles from the ships, to hold off the whole Argentine Air Force and support the troops in any landing. Although the Argentinian pilots fought very bravely and gained a number of successes as the maps show, they were unable, despite their own heavy losses, seriously to hinder the British operations. The Argentinian Navy had little chance to make any positive contribution and must have been deterred by the sinking of the cruiser *General Belgrano* by a British nuclear submarine.

South Georgia was quickly and easily recaptured by the British forces soon after they arrived but there then followed a delay, punctuated by air attacks by both sides before the main British landings at San Carlos. The first British formation to land was made up of elite Royal Marine and Parachute Regiment troops. Goose Green was captured after a hard fight and the British, reinforced by Ghurka and Guards units, pushed forward to surround, and eventually accept the surrender of Port Stanley. Although the Argentinian forces were numerically at least as strong as the British many of them were young conscripts, no match for the British regulars in morale or training.

In the aftermath of the surrender President Galtieri of Argentina was forced to resign but with the British seemingly more than ever determined to keep the islands any final settlement of the dispute remained unlikely.

The Superpowers

The present balance of strategic and conventional forces between the superpowers in Europe has to take into account a number of factors. The first is the need to bear in mind those forces held by both superpowers beyond the geographical region of Europe – in the event of a crisis these forces might be utilized either as long-distance weapons systems or as incoming reinforcements. Secondly, there is the question of definition in each of the major categories of weapons systems. The most difficult task in estimating the strategic nuclear balance is assigning nuclear warheads to the launchers of strategic systems. The impossibility of knowing or verifying the operational loadings of individual systems makes it necessary to assign warheads through elaborate

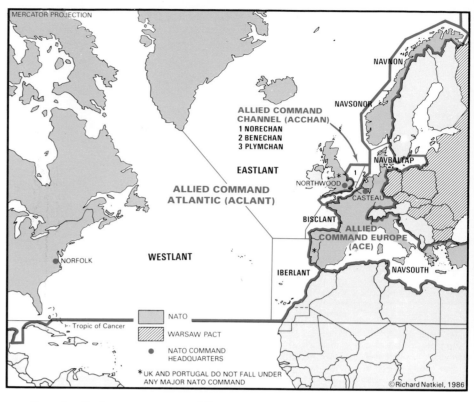

counting rules. Both superpowers can deliver strategic nuclear weapons from ICBMs, SLBMs and bombers. Thirdly, there is a distinction between strategic and intermediate

range nuclear weapons systems. By strategic, one infers that these are weapons which can reach the home territory of either the USA or the USSR. Intermediate range nuclear

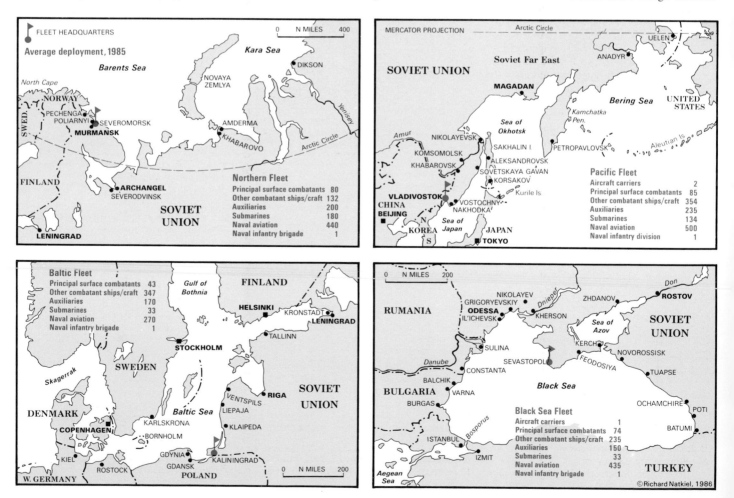

weapons systems have been deployed by both superpowers in Europe and are only capable of reaching European targets. To the Europeans, these weapon systems still appear very much strategic in their targetting and yield. The US-Soviet agreement to abolish intermediate range nuclear weapons will remove them from the arsenals of the superpowers.

Both superpowers, and in the case of the USA, certain of its allies, deploy a variety of short-range nuclear weapons which are directly related to conventional forces. It is this category of nuclear weapons which forms a gray area between the deployment of conventional forces and the ultimate use of strategic nuclear forces.

There is considerable difficulty in attempting to assess the superpower balance in conventional weapons in Europe. Both superpowers are members of an alliance – the US of NATO and the USSR of the Warsaw Pact. But there is one fundamental difference between these two alliances. NATO is an alliance of 16 independent sovereign nations, and while the US is the largest and most powerful member, it does not automatically control NATO or determine all alliance policy. This political independence has a military consequence that some regard as a weakness. NATO does not have a standard doctrine or set of weapons systems, and many decisions have to be reached by consensus. The Warsaw Pact is nominally an alliance of seven independent countries but in practice the alliance is controlled and led by the Soviet Union. This does mean that the Warsaw Pact has a common doctrine and weapons systems imposed by the Soviet Union.

Any objective assessment of the conventional forces of the two superpowers in Europe has to take into account differences in terms of military service, quantity and quality of weapons systems, reliability of allies, doctrinal differences, and the influence of geography and climate. In the Western Theaters the Soviet Union maintains 380,000 troops in East Germany, 40,000 in Poland, 80,000 in Czechoslovakia and 65,000 in Hungary, all with complementary air defense forces. There are, of course, substantial Soviet ground and air forces available within the Soviet Union to reinforce these units. Naval forces are available in the form of the Northern Fleet, the Baltic Fleet, the Black Sea Fleet and the Mediterranean Squadron.

The USA maintains the bulk of its ground forces committed to Europe in West Germany, some 204,000 troops with support from the US Air Force Europe. The US Navy maintains a presence in the Eastern Atlantic and the Mediterranean. Reinforcements for US conventional forces in Europe would have to come from the US mainland, and while some could be flown to Europe, the overwhelming majority would have to be moved by sea across the Atlantic. This reinforcement time compares unfavorably with the relatively easy reinforcement capability by land of the Soviet Union.

Both the USA and the USSR depend upon the conventional forces of their allies in Europe. These forces vary in size, quality, and effectiveness within each alliance. West Germany's conventional forces are larger and better equipped than those of Denmark, while those of East Germany are regarded as more reliable than those of Czechoslovakia. In the past it was always assumed that while the Warsaw Pact had numerical superiority over NATO, the latter maintained a qualitative superiority but, at least in term of certain items of equipment, NATO's qualitative lead may have narrowed. Apart from the conventional balance the capability for offensive and defensive use of chemical and biological weapons systems must be taken into account. The Soviet Union has maintained a massive stockpile of these weapons and has not responded to a NATO moratorium on their future production.

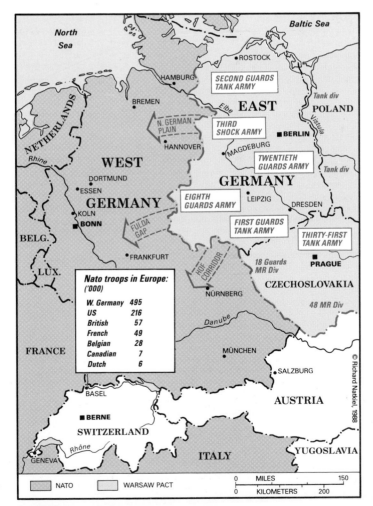

Nato troops in Europe: ('000)

W. Germany	495
US	216
British	57
French	49
Belgian	28
Canadian	7
Dutch	6

NATO   WARSAW PACT

© Richard Natkiel, 1988

INDEX

Page numbers in italics refer to illustrations and maps.

Credits

The authors and publisher would like to
thank David Burles for his extensive
work in the production of the maps and
Pat Coward for compiling the index.

**Aachen Cathedral Treasury/Anne
Munchow** page: 36(below).
Anne SK Brown page: 168
Archiv Gerstenberg pages: 1, 2-3,
6(both), 32, 36,(top), 71, 84, 110-111,
112, 122, 127, 131, 217(top), 231(right),
232-3, 233.
BBC Hulton Picture Library pages:
7(top), 13(right), 15(below), 34-35, 38,
40, 42, 43, 49, 51(both), 52, 53, 54, 55,
56, 58-59, 61, 64, 66, 70, 75, 101(both),
108(both), 137, 140-141, 143, 144, 145,
148(below), 149, 155, 156, 157, 158, 160,
161, 165, 167(both), 171, 173, 175(both),
181, 182(both), 183, 188, 193,
195(below), 217(below), 228, 229, 336.
Bison Picture Library pages: 74,
98(right), 100, 129, 132(below),
194(top), 248, 282-3, 297, 338.
Bundesarchiv pages: 205(top), 273, 296.
Collection Viollet page 256.
E.T. Archive page: 83(below).
Nicholas Fuentes page: 22.
Heersgeschichtlichen Museum, Vienna
page: 224.
Michael Holford pages: 18, 25, 29,
31(top 2), 39.
Imperial War Museum pages: 202-3,
208, 230, 231(left), 276, 304, 323, 325.
The Keystone Collection pages: 324,
326(below), 327(below), 328, 329, 330,
332, 341, 342.

The Mansell Collection pages: 10, 11, 12,
13(left), 15(top), 16, 28, 47, 57, 60, 62,
73, 85, 86, 95, 98(left), 244, 251, 254,
MARS pages: 197, 286-7(below).
IWM pages: 207(top), 209, 210, 211,
212-3(both), 215, 218, 219(both), 223,
226-7(both), 238, 239, 246-7(both),
294-5.
National Army Museum pages: 91,
132(top and center), 134.
National Gallery of Ireland page: 83(top
right).
National Maritime Museum pages: 65,
88, 234.
National Portrait Gallery page: 83(top
left).
**Newark Public Library Picture
Collection** page: 68.
Novosti Press Agency pages:
194(below), 252, 253, 291, 292, 307.
Peter Newark's Historical Pictures
pages: 67, 148(top), 152.
Photoresources pages: 17, 20, 21, 26,
31(below), 81, 114.
Popperphoto pages: 200, 201.
Robert Hunt Picture Library pages:
195(top), 222-3, 225, 236(top), 243, 250,
294, 295, 299, 316, 327(top), 333(both),
334.
**Royal Collection (Reproduced by
Gracious Permission of Her Majesty the
Queen)** page: 93.
Rolf Steinberg page: 24.
Ted Stone page: 281.
The Tate Gallery pages: 118-9.
Texas State Library page: 151
The Research House pages: 258-9, /**US
Marine Corps** pages: 314-5, /**US Navy**
page: 7(below).
Ullstein Bilderdienst page: 257.
US Air Force page: 311.
US Army pages: 286-7(top), 335,
339(top).
US Library of Congress pages 76-77,
190, 191.
US Marine Corps pages: 312(both), 313,
340.
US National Archives pages 4-5, 192,
263(both), 290, 300, 301.
US Naval Historical Center page: 232.
US Navy pages: 106, 267, 269, 271, 284,
289, 339(below).
Virginia Military Institute Museum
page: 160.
Virginia State Library page: 163
Weidenfeld Library pages: 23, 33, 46,
90, 104, 113, 169(both).